Wild Cats of the World

Wild
Cats

of the
World

Mel Sunquist *and*
Fiona Sunquist

With photographs by Terry Whittaker
and others

THE UNIVERSITY OF CHICAGO PRESS • CHICAGO AND LONDON

Mel Sunquist is associate professor in the Department of Wildlife
Ecology and Conservation at the University of Florida,
Gainesville. Fiona Sunquist is an editor for *International Wildlife
Magazine*. The Sunquists are co-authors of *Tiger Moon*, published
by the University of Chicago Press in 1988. The Sunquists can be
reached via electronic mail to wildcatsofworld@aol.com.

Frontispiece: Eurasian lynx (photo by Terry Whittaker)

The University of Chicago Press, Chicago 60637
The University of Chicago Press, Ltd., London
© 2002 by Fiona Sunquist and Mel Sunquist
All rights reserved. Published 2002
Printed in China

11 10 09 08 07 06 05 04 03 02   1 2 3 4 5

ISBN: 0-226-77999-8 (cloth)

Library of Congress Cataloging-in-Publication Data

Sunquist, Melvin E.
    Wild cats of the world / Mel Sunquist and Fiona Sunquist.
      p. cm.
    Includes bibliographical references (p.) and index.
    ISBN 0-226-77999-8 (cloth : alk. paper)
        1. Felidae.   I. Sunquist, Fiona.   II. Title.

QL737.C23 S863 2002
599.75—dc21
                                                    2001052771

This book is printed on acid-free paper.

Contents

Study and Conservation

CONTENTS

Color photographs follow pages 134 and 342

Preface

This book arose from our lifelong fascination with cats. Over the years we have collected thousands of publications on cats, on topics ranging from the structure of the domestic cat's middle ear to accounts of livestock depredation by tigers in Malaysia. When we first began assembling this informal cat library, the "bible" for people interested in finding information on cats was C. A. W. Guggisberg's *Wild Cats of the World*. Someone suggested that we write an updated version. The idea evolved into a book that would summarize what is known about the ecology and behavior of each of the thirty-six species of wild cats.

The purpose of this book is to bring together the literature on cats so that readers will have not only a current review of what is known about the ecology and behavior of each cat, but also a comprehensive source of reference material. It was very important to us that the book serve as a thorough guide to the literature for students and others who needed to dig further. We have deliberately included information from the "gray" literature: unpublished reports, theses, dissertations, newsletters, and personal communications. Where we have included such information, we have given the sources.

Both the taxonomy and the order of presentation of the species accounts follow Wozencraft's classification in *Mammal Species of the World* (edited by Wilson and Reeder). We have tried to follow the same format for each species account so that topics are easier to find and cross-reference between species. Summary tables and information on general topics such as scent marking, vocalizations, and reproduction are included as appendixes. Overall, our intent was to write a book that would be accessible to both scientists and the interested general public.

With our focus on ecology and behavior, there were many topics that we did not address. We did not have the expertise to include information on diseases and parasites, reproductive physiology, captive research and management, and the rapidly evolving field of molecular genetics. Information on status, recovery programs, and actions recommended for the conservation of felids are treated only briefly in this book. Readers are urged to consult Nowell and Jackson's *Wild Cats: A Status Survey and Conservation Action Plan* for a current review of this material. Portions of this valuable comprehensive review are available at the IUCN Cat Specialist Group website at http://lynx.uio.no/catfolk.

During this volume's extremely long gestation period we have had a great deal of help from hundreds of generous people. Jean McConville was an enormous help with all the editorial business that needed to be addressed. Librarians Kay Kenyon (National Zoological Park) and Nancy Matthews (Translation Publishing Program) at the Smithsonian Institution and Stephanie Haas and Vernon Kisling at the University of Florida helped track down obscure references from across the globe. Gustav Peters corrected our definitions and helped produce accurate tables of felid vocalizations that would never have been possible without his help. Warren Johnson kept us on the straight and narrow when it came to genetics and provided the diagram of felid lineages. Kerry Dressler patiently solved our frequent computer problems. Stimulating discussions with John Eisenberg inspired us to press on to the finish. Other biologists, zoo staff, and owners of private collections unselfishly shared information on every aspect of felid lives. Dale Johnson and Adam Freedman put together the figures. We would like to thank the following individuals for their valuable contributions to the book: Bill and Penny Andrews, Marcelo Aranda, Sean Austin, Ted Bailey, Sonny Bass, Robert Belden, Juan Beltrán, Ann Bennett, Liz Bennett, Bill Berg, Francisco Bisbal, Tomas and Cecila Blohm, Lief Blomqvist, J. du P. Bothma, Anatole Bragin, Urs Breitenmoser and Christine Breitenmoser-Würsten, Rainer Brocke, John Burton, Pat Callahan,

Tim Caro, Arturo Caso, Ravi Chellam, Sarah Christie, Peter Crawshaw, Tom Dahmer, Eric Dinerstein, Betsy Dresser, Siva Elagupillay, Louise Emmons, Laura Farrell, Dave Ferguson, Gail Foreman, Debra Forthman, Neil Franklin, William Franklin, Helen Freeman, Todd Fuller, Sam and Alicia Fulton, Rosa García-Perea, John Gittleman, Lon Grassman, Judith Hayter, Jeremy Holden, Rafael Hoogesteijn, Maurice Hornocker, David Houston, Don Hunter, Agustin Iriarte, Masako Izawa, Peter Jackson, Rodney Jackson, Martin Jalkotzy, David Jenny, A. J. T. Johnsingh, Ullas Karanth, Kae Kawanishi, Mohammed Khan, Andrew Kitchener, Devra Kleiman, Gary Koehler, Mike Konecny, Steven Laing, Paul Leyhausen, Fred Lindzey, Olof Liberg, Ken Logan, Mark Ludlow, Dave Maehr, Laurie Marker, Inés Maxit, Chuck McDougal, Jill Mellen, Heinrich Mendelssohn, Dennis Meritt, Dale Miguelle, Brian Miller, Sriyanie Miththapala, Fumi Mizutami, Edgardo Mondolfi, L.C. Moolman, Dieter Morsbach, Peter Norton, Andres Novaro, Kristin Nowell, Hideo Obara, Steve O'Brien, Gea Olbricht, Tadeu Oliveira, Junaidi Payne, Pablo Pereira, Kim Poole, Howard Quigley, Pat Quillen, Alan Rabinowitz, Rajan and Lynette Rajaratnam, Fateh Singh Rathore, Justina Ray, Kent Redford, Francisco Robles, Mark Rosenthal, Jim Sanderson, Charles Santiapillai, George Schaller, Krzyzstof Schmidt, Daniel Scognamillo, John Seidensticker, Alan Shoemaker, Alex Sliwa, Brian Slough, James L. D. Smith, Philippe Stahl, Philip Stander, Chris and Tilde Stuart, Claire Sunquist, Linda Sweanor, Andrew Taber, Michael Tewes, Valmik Thapar, Ron Tilson, Barbara Tonkin-Leyhausen, Blaire Van Valkenburgh, John Visser, Clive Walker, Susan Walker, Dave Webb, Chris Wemmer, Terry Whittaker, Vivian Wilson, Shigeki Yasuma, and Günter Ziesler.

And to Susan Abrams and all the wonderfully patient people at the University of Chicago Press, we thank you.

Introduction

God made the cat to give humankind the pleasure of caressing the tiger. —Anon.

For us, one of the most fascinating aspects of cat biology is that, from the two-pound black-footed cat to the five-hundred-pound tiger, cats are all variations on a common theme. When you have a cat in your home, you live with the essence of tiger. Indeed, the appeal of domestic cats may be that they are just a whisker away from their wild relatives. Just how close this relationship is, or how different the various species are from one another, can be discovered in what we have learned over the years about the intriguing world of wild cats.

Knowledge of the felids—the cat family—has increased significantly in the past quarter century. Twenty-five years ago, when C. A. W. Guggisberg wrote his classic *Wild Cats of the World,* the bay cat, the kodkod, and the Andean mountain cat were known only from a few museum skins and an occasional stuffed specimen. The biology of even easily recognizable species, such as the bobcat, puma, tiger, leopard, cheetah, and ocelot, was virtually unknown, and nothing was known about what they needed in terms of space and food. On the conservation front, hundreds of thousands of spotted cats were being trapped and their skins traded in the world's fur markets.

Today, we have basic information about the biology and behavior of most cat species. Our increased knowledge has given us greater cause for concern for some species and reasons to be optimistic about the survival of others. Information on reproduction and survival, much of it gleaned from captive animals, has shown us that trapping and hunting will have a heavy impact on many of the smaller spotted cats. Species such as the ocelot and margay have very small litters and may breed only once every two years. Other species, such as the tiger, have turned out to be surprisingly resilient. If their habitat and prey are protected, they will thrive even under low levels of poaching and hunting.

Though habitat loss, hunting, and illegal trapping of prey species threaten many of the world's cats, we have also made some major conservation advances in the past twenty-five years. One of the most significant has been CITES, the Convention on International Trade in Endangered Species of Wild Fauna and Flora. In effect since 1975, CITES is a global treaty designed to protect plant and animal species from unregulated trade.

In the 1970s and 1980s a powerful combination of public interest and effective legislation succeeded in shutting down the international trade in spotted cat skins. At the peak of the trade, nearly half a million cat skins were traded on world markets each year. Today, international trade in pelts of spotted cats has almost disappeared, and trade in the remaining species is decreasing.

This book is a compilation of what we know about the life histories, behavior, and ecology of the world's thirty-six species of wild cats. It is intended as a reference for all of those—cat lovers as well as professional scientists—who are fascinated by cats. In this book you will find information on each species, presented in sections on description, distribution, ecology and behavior (which includes habitat, feeding ecology, social organization, reproduction, and development) and status in the wild. For species such as the tiger, lion, jaguar, puma, bobcat, and the lynxes, the information is fairly extensive; for others, such as the Andean mountain cat, bay cat, and marbled cat, our knowledge remains limited.

We hope this volume will serve as a stimulus for further research. As cat lovers, we represent a powerful constituency. Collectively, we can influence policy, direct research funding, and help promote creative ways to solve human-cat conflicts. Conservation ultimately depends on political will, which comes, in the end, from public interest. The more we know about these alluring creatures, the more interested we become in their welfare and survival.

What Is a Cat?

The Essence of Cats

MORPHOLOGY

The cat's body is, in essence, a reflection of its diet. All cats are meat eaters, designed and specialized for capturing and killing live prey. They are sometimes called *hypercarnivores* because they need a much higher proportion of protein in the diet than almost any other mammal. For a domestic cat to remain healthy, its diet must contain 12 percent protein (by weight) for adult cats and 18 percent for kittens. Dogs can survive on much less; adult dogs can get by with only 4 percent protein. That is why dogs can survive and thrive on a vegetarian diet, while it is very difficult to create a vegetarian diet that contains sufficient protein for a cat.

Cats have relatively short but powerful forelimbs that can be rotated, forepaws with long claws, a lithe body, a flexible spine, and well-muscled hindlimbs, all of which combine to give them quickness, agility, and power. All cats are digitigrade; that is, they walk on their toes. The soft toe pads distribute the weight over the balls of the feet, giving cats their fluid walking motion. The cat's skull is highly domed, the zygomatic arches are wide, the face is foreshortened, and strong sagittal crests provide an anchor for powerful jaw muscles. The mechanical advantage provided by the foreshortened face and powerful jaw muscles increases the bite force on the canine teeth.

Excluding the short-tailed bobcat and lynx, most felids have tails that measure at least one-third to one-half of their head and body length (fig. 1). The margay, clouded leopard, and marbled cat have exception-

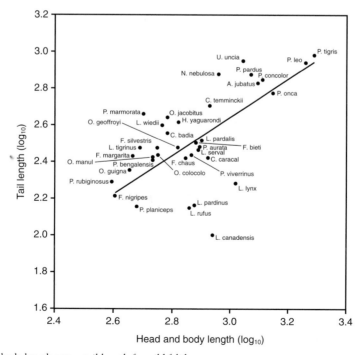

Figure 1. Plot of head and body length versus tail length for wild felids.

ally long tails, which are thought to function as balancing rods as they move about in the trees. A similar function has been attributed to the long tails of snow leopards, pumas, and cheetahs, but for these species the tail is presumably an aid to moving about in precipitous terrain or making rapid turns while pursuing prey.

Teeth

With a shortened face comes a shortened jaw with less space for teeth. Cats have fewer teeth than other carnivores—usually 28 or 30, compared with 42 for dogs and bears. The teeth are specialized for different tasks. Small incisors are used for holding and nibbling, and the rear molars (or carnassials) move against each other like scissor blades for slicing and cutting. The large, strong, somewhat flattened canines are used for stabbing and delivering the killing bite. Ethologist Paul Leyhausen suggests that the cat's canine teeth fit between the neck vertebrae of prey like a "key in a lock." Leyhausen also suggests that the many nerves at the base of the canine teeth allow cats to "feel" for the gap between the prey's vertebrae before biting down. As the cat bites, the tooth inserts itself between the vertebrae like a wedge, forcing them apart and breaking the spinal cord.

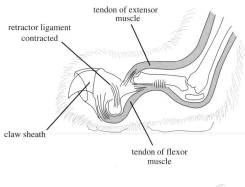

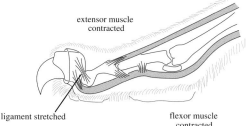

Figure 2. Diagram of protrusion mechanism of retractile felid claws.

Claws

While most cat species are terrestrial, many have retained the ability to climb, aided by the sharp, curved, retractile claws that also serve to hold prey. Among the Carnivora, only the cats use their forepaws to restrain prey with a clasping motion prior to the delivery of a killing bite. Cats are well known for their sharp claws, which remain fully retracted when they are resting or walking. Claw retraction is passive. Attached to the terminal bone of each toe, the claws are held back and off the ground by a retractor ligament. To extend its claws, the cat contracts the dorsal and ventral muscles of the toe; the ligament stretches, and the claw protrudes (fig. 2). Though the cheetah, serval, and flat-headed cat are sometimes described as having nonretractile claws, they actually have the same claw retraction mechanism as other cat species. The difference is that their claws protrude beyond the fur, and cheetah claws lack the sheaths that cover the claws of other cats.

Body Size

Felids vary enormously in size, sometimes even within the same species (figs. 3 and 4). The size disparity among leopards, for example, once led taxonomists to conclude that forest leopards and savanna leopards were different species. Similar size differences are also found among pumas, jaguars, and tigers, all species with broad geographic distributions. Male jaguars in Venezuela, which average 104 kilograms, are nearly twice as heavy as males in Belize, which average 56 kilograms. Which species is the smallest is still open to discussion, with the black-footed cat, kodkod, and rusty-spotted cat all candidates for the title.

An examination of the numbers and sizes of felid species that occur in large geographic regions shows that Southeast Asia has ten species, South America has ten species, and Africa has eight (figs. 5, 6, and 7). The greatest diversity occurs in the tropical zones, the least in the temperate zones.

Color Patterns

Most felids are blotched, spotted, or striped. Tigers are the only large cats marked with distinct transverse stripes; most of the other large cats are marked with rosettes. The cheetah's coat pattern of crisp, dark spots is quite distinctive. The unusual striped marking pattern of the king cheetah is reportedly due to a single recessive gene. In some smaller cat species the dark markings are fused to form bands, streaks, or stripes,

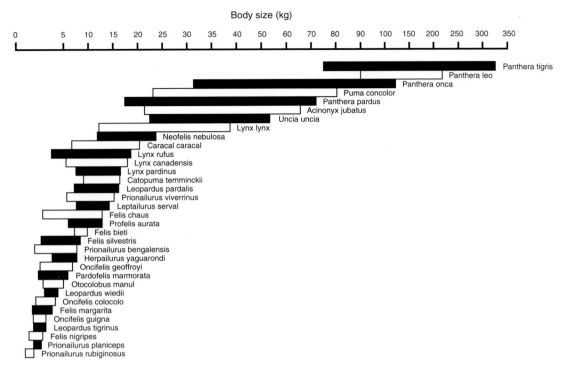

Figure 3. Range of variation in body sizes of felids.

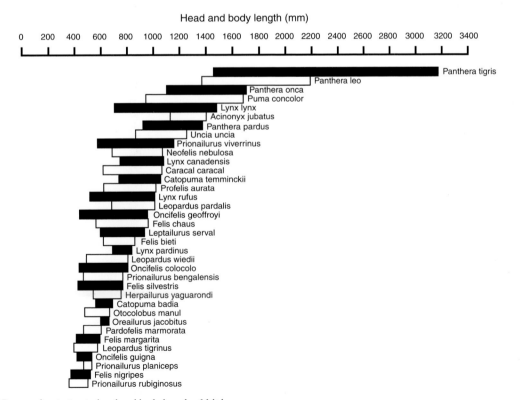

Figure 4. Range of variation in head and body length of felids.

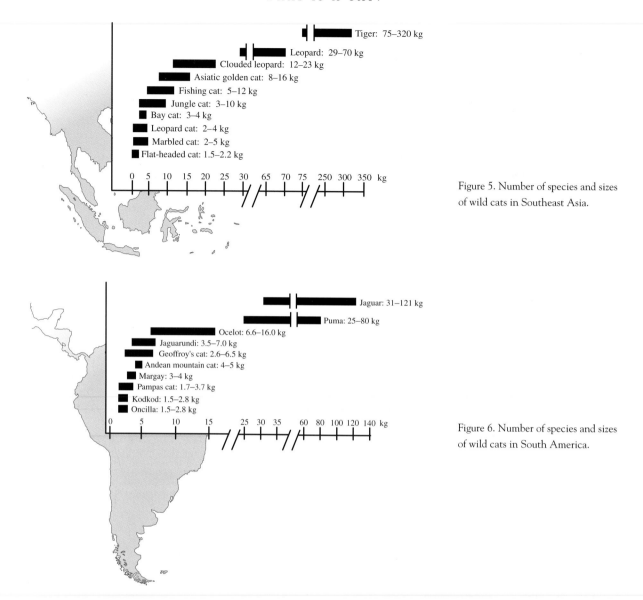

Figure 5. Number of species and sizes of wild cats in Southeast Asia.

Figure 6. Number of species and sizes of wild cats in South America.

especially along the back and across the limbs; in others, the pattern is small dark spots, and still other small cats are only faintly spotted. Clouded leopards and marbled cats have blotched coats. The lion and puma are more or less uniformly colored, although the manes of male lions may be quite distinctive. The young of both lion and puma are spotted. The caracal also has unpatterned fur except for dark spots above the eyes and shadowlike markings on the cheeks. The only other cat of uniform color is the jaguarundi, which has a reddish morph and a blackish morph. Melanism (black pigmentation) appears to be common in some species (e.g., serval, leopard, jaguar, kodkod, jungle cat, Geoffroy's cat, oncilla) and rare or extremely localized in several others (e.g., bobcat, clouded leopard, puma, cheetah).

White spots or bars are found on the back of the ears in many species, although in almost as many species the ear spots are poorly defined or absent (e.g., wildcat, jungle cat, Chinese desert cat, sand cat, black-footed cat, African golden cat, Asiatic golden cat, bay cat, caracal, jaguarundi, manul, puma, rusty-spotted cat, lion). Their function is unknown, although one suggestion is that the ear spots, along with

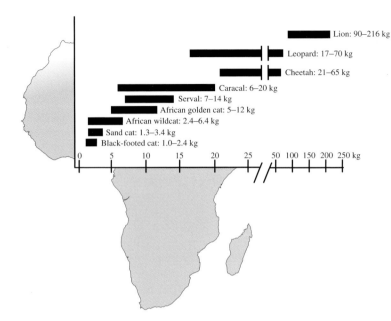

Figure 7. Number of species and sizes of wild cats in Africa.

the white on the underside of the tail tip of some species, serve as "follow me" signals to the young, which may be especially important in low-light conditions.

The primary function of coloration is concealment. Cats that live in the desert tend to be light and sandy-colored. Forest-living species are darker and marked with spots or streaks that disrupt the outline of their bodies, concealing them in dappled light. Cats living in mountainous terrain often have light-colored or grayish coats.

SENSES

Eyes

Of all their senses, cats probably depend most on vision to help them capture prey. Because cats hunt prey that is active both during the day and at night, their eyes must be able to function in a range of conditions from bright sunlight to almost complete darkness. Several adaptations allow a cat's eyes to function successfully in all light conditions.

Large eyes with large pupils generally have good light-gathering abilities. Cats' eyes are extremely large in relation to their body size; the eye of a domestic cat, for example, is only slightly smaller than the eye of a human. Like other animals, a cat can regulate the amount of light that enters its eye by dilating or contracting the pupil. On a sunny day, a cat's pupils contract to a vertical slit or pinprick, while in dim light the pupils dilate to a large circle or oval, sometimes appearing to take up the whole eye.

There are two types of light-sensitive cells in the retina of mammals: rods function in low levels of light and do not detect color; cones are used in color vision. Good light-gathering ability is associated with an abundance of rods, and not surprisingly, rods predominate in cats' eyes. However, cats also have a cone-rich patch in the center of the retina, so we know that they also have the ability to discern color, at least under daylight conditions. Experiments have shown that cats can see green, blue, and possibly red. Scientists speculate that not only do cats see fewer colors than humans, but the colors they do see are much less saturated than those we see.

The cat's sensitivity to light is also heightened by a structure known as the tapetum lucidum, a special reflective layer beneath the retina. Caught in the headlights of a car, a cat's eyes shine back with a yellowish green light. This eyeshine, as it is called, comes from the tapetum. The mirror-like tapetum reflects the light back through the retina to give the sensory cells a second chance to respond. It has been estimated that a cat's light sensitivity is nearly six times that of a human.

Cats have the most highly developed binocular vision of all the carnivores. Their eyes are set well forward and relatively high on the skull, allowing them to accurately judge distances while leaping from branch to branch or pouncing on prey. Cats also have an extensive field of peripheral vision, which, strangely enough, may be partially responsible for their reputation for aloofness. Because its peripheral vision is so good, a resting cat focuses its eyes infrequently. The result is the cat's typical wide-eyed, staring-into-space look that some people find so unsettling.

Whiskers

Cats have specialized touch-sensitive hairs, called vibrissae or whiskers, on either side of the muzzle, around the eyes, below the chin, and on the wrists. Whiskers provide a sort of vision by touch, a tactile third eye, that is critical to cats hunting at night. Sensitive enough to detect minor changes in air currents moving around objects, whiskers permit even blindfolded cats to avoid obstacles without touching them.

Stouter than other body hairs and embedded more deeply in the skin, whiskers are extremely sensitive to movement. They rest in tiny sacs of fluid, pivoting like a straw in a soda bottle. When anything brushes the hair, the information is passed down to a rich supply of nerve endings that line the sac.

A hunting cat holds its whiskers out on either side of its face like a fan. Just before pouncing on its prey, the cat shifts its whiskers forward, extending them like a net in front of its mouth. When the cat makes contact with its prey, the whiskers tell it exactly which way the animal is dodging in the final split second. A cat carrying a freshly caught mouse wraps its whiskers around the prey, sensitive to any twitch that would indicate that the mouthful might squirm free.

Hearing

Cats can hear in the 65–70 kHz range, well above the human limit of 15–20 kHz. Cats do not produce ultrasonic calls, so their ability to detect these high-frequency sounds is probably related to hunting. Rodent ultrasound communication occurs in the 20–50 kHz range, so small cats are well equipped to detect the sounds of their prey. Cats use their outer ears (pinnae) as directional amplifiers to increase their hearing sensitivity and pinpoint the location of sounds. The serval, renowned for using its huge dishlike ears to "sound hunt" for small mammals, is the extreme example of this ability.

The auditory bullae of cats also aid in detecting sounds. In mammals, the bullae are inflated, bony projections of the skull that protect the ossicles of the middle ear. Each bulla has two air-filled cavities, an outer chamber formed by the tympanic bone and an inner chamber formed by the entotympanic bone. The bullae are highly modified (inflated) in some species in connection with specialized modes of life, particularly the detection of low-frequency sounds.

Olfaction

The olfactory capabilities of cats are not well understood. Although there are occasional references to cats tracking prey by scent, they are generally considered to be less sensitive to smells than dogs. However, the complex structure of the cat's olfactory apparatus indicates that it has a highly sensitive sense of smell, and this view is corroborated by the fact that odors serve an important role in the social life of cats and other solitary species.

Felids produce odors from their anal sacs and their subcaudal, facial, and interdigital glands. They also deposit urine and feces at prominent locations. Cats use scents from these sources as a means of communication. Resident cats typically scent-mark more frequently in areas where their ranges abut or overlap with those of neighboring cats, especially when the neighbor is new to them. Females commonly increase their frequency of urine spraying prior to estrus, presumably to ensure that a male is present during the peak of sexual receptivity.

While few functions can be definitely assigned to odors, cat scent most likely contains information on identity, status, sex, reproductive condition, and the time when the mark was made. Because specific sites or objects are scent-marked repeatedly, especially along commonly traveled pathways or in zones of home range overlap, scent marks have been likened to traffic signals or signposts that cats can check to ascertain whether an area is being used, and by whom. Whether a cat proceeds or goes elsewhere may depend on the status, sex, and social relationships of the cats involved. A summary table and a more detailed explanation of scent marking can be found in appendix 3.

VOCALIZATIONS

Cats use sound to communicate at close range as well as at medium and long distances. They have a fairly standard vocal repertoire that consists of about twelve sounds and calls. The more familiar vocalizations include the "meow" call and the spit, hiss, and growl, which are common to all cat species. Purring, the most familiar close-range felid vocalization, is most common between mother cats and their kittens. A summary table and a more detailed explanation of felid vocalizations can be found in appendix 4.

LAND TENURE SYSTEM

While the availability of cover and water are important, the spacing patterns of female cats are essentially dictated by food supply. Females rear young by themselves, and their reproductive success is greatly influenced by access to food. Thus, the size of prey, how it is distributed in time and space, and how quickly it is renewed generally determine the distribution and density of female cats. Where prey is abundant, stable, and evenly distributed, females can meet their requirements in a small area, and they maintain small, exclusive ranges. Where prey is thin on the ground and migrates or fluctuates seasonally, female ranges are larger and often overlap.

Just as food determines the spacing patterns of females, the distribution of females drives male spacing patterns (fig. 8). Males compete for access to females, and where females live at high densities and are evenly distributed, a single male can monopolize several females. Under these conditions, male ranges are likely to be exclusive. Stronger, dominant males are likely to have ranges that include those of several fe-

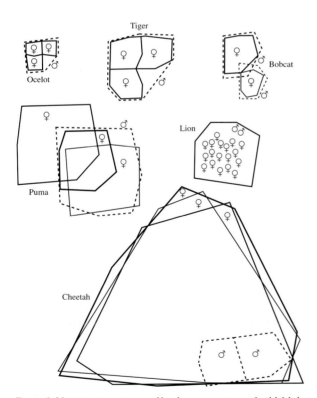

Figure 8. Variation in patterns of land tenure systems of wild felids. Dashed lines delineate male home ranges; solid lines delineate female home ranges.

males, whereas lesser males may be fortunate to monopolize a single female. Where females live at low densities and have large, overlapping ranges, male ranges may overlap one another, as it may not be possible for a male to maintain exclusive mating rights to a female. Under these circumstances, it is probably more profitable for a male to roam over a large area and compete for access to each female as she comes into estrus.

SOCIAL SYSTEMS

To help clarify how some common terms referring to felid social systems are used, some brief definitions of these terms and the context in which they are used are provided below.

Adults are animals that have bred or are capable of breeding, which distinguishes them from *subadults*, which physically look like adults but are not capable of breeding. A subadult cat is nutritionally independent of its mother but may continue to use its *natal* or *birth range*, which is the home range of its mother.

Small cubs or kittens are totally dependent on their mothers for food and protection. They are often hidden in a den for several weeks or months after birth. Weaning is a gradual process, and the transition from milk to solid food often coincides with an increase in mobility. The young begin to follow their mother about, or she may bring them meat or take them to kills. *Large cubs* are about one-half to two-thirds the size of an adult, have most of their permanent dentition, and frequently accompany their mother on hunts. While they are not yet accomplished hunters, some attempt to make kills of their own. They are nevertheless still dependent on their mother for food.

Home range, *home area*, and *range* are all used in the same general way to mean the space traversed by an animal in its daily activities. The equivalent in lions is the *pride area*. A home range contains the resources essential to survival and reproduction. If there are regular seasonal shifts in an individual's range, typically in response to migratory movements of prey or climatic conditions, the areas used are often called *seasonal ranges*, or they are combined and presented as an *annual home range*. Animals that live in such areas or ranges are called *residents*, since they reside predictably in certain areas.

When there is no spatial or temporal overlap in the home ranges of neighboring individuals of the same sex, these ranges are often labeled territories. A *territory* is sometimes defined as a defended area that is used exclusively by the occupant. Defensive or territorial behavior can be passive, such as leaving scent marks, or it may involve actual fighting. There is an assumption that occupancy confers some advantages in conflicts over resources, but there is little empirical evidence to support this notion. Other definitions of territoriality are not as restrictive, and suggest that territory holders have priority access to critical resources in an area, implying that territories are not exclusive.

Unfortunately, deciding whether a home range is a territory requires a level of information that is not easily obtained, especially for species that are secretive, live at low densities, and are often nocturnal. While radiotelemetry theoretically provides the means to monitor the movements of individuals at any time of the day or night, in many studies individuals are seldom located more than a few times per week. Rarely are the movements of neighbors monitored simultaneously, and even less is usually known about historical or recent events (e.g., length of territory ownership, mortality) that may be influencing the current social dynamics. Many studies are short-term—the equivalent of a single-frame snapshot in a long-running movie.

Dispersal is a phenomenon typically associated with subadults, many of which leave their natal ranges and travel through unfamiliar terrain in search of unoccupied areas where they can establish their own home ranges and reproduce. There is, however, little information for most species of cats on predispersal movements, the stimulus or timing of dispersal, distances and routes traveled, or the fate of dispersers. In mammals, males are the predominant dispersers, while females tend to establish home ranges that are close to or on their natal ranges. This tendency to stay close to home is called *philopatry*. A consequence of this behavior is the formation of clusters of related females or matrilineal groups living in close proximity.

Acquiring a home range and becoming a resident is associated with reproductive activity. Individuals without home ranges are unlikely to breed, even though they are sexually mature. These individuals are referred to by various terms, including *transients*, *floaters*, and *young adults*. They do not appear to have a permanent address. They characteristically live in marginal habitats, travel widely, and wait for vacancies or openings to occur in areas of suitable habitat. They periodically travel through these areas to assess the occupancy status of the home ranges therein. This assessment is presumably based on encounters with the occupant's scent marks and feces or with the occupant itself. The occupant's ownership may be challenged, or the transient may be discouraged from staying long in the area; alternatively, the transient may simply leave the area, preferring to take its chances elsewhere, or at a later date. It is well known, however, that residents are occasionally ousted, and competition is typically greater among males than females.

Subadults are sometimes mistaken for adults, and this has occasionally led to the assumption that two or more adults are occupying the same home range. Without information on the sex, age, and relatedness of the individuals in an area, some confusion is inevitable. Similarly, without detailed information on movement patterns, some confusion may arise in the interpretation of home range use patterns. The home range of an individual may overlap partially or almost completely with the ranges of neighbors of the same sex, but the cats may be using the area of overlap at different times. Alternatively, neighboring ranges may overlap extensively, but each individual may have a *central* or *core area* that it uses exclusively. These patterns may also be influenced by relatedness, as sharing resources with close relatives is preferable to sharing with unrelated individuals. An individual may have preferential use of the area of overlap based on a *dominance hierarchy* (pecking order), or it may be, as suggested for domestic cats, that use is regulated by checking a sign board. The sign is the scent mark of whoever is using the area, with fresh scent indicating current use. Individuals are thus able to avoid each other and any potential confrontations.

Most felids lead solitary lives. Except for lions and male cheetahs, adult cats live and hunt separately. However, females are not always alone; many of them spend a great deal of time caring for cubs or kittens. Long-term studies have shown that females may spend more than 80 percent of their lives either pregnant or accompanied by dependent young; however, this is likely to be true only in areas where prey is abundant. Where food is scarce, females may go for a year or more without successfully raising a litter.

Though the majority of felids are solitary, their lives are embedded in a social system that is maintained by scent marks, vocalizations, and occasional encounters. Although we have little direct evidence, it is more than likely that neighbors and animals sharing overlapping ranges know where they are relative to one another most of the time. Data from long-term studies of pumas, tigers, leopards, black-footed cats, and several other species also indicate that many female felids are philopatric and that neighboring females are likely to be related. In the Chitwan tiger study in Nepal, clusters of neighboring tigresses were as closely related as lionesses in a pride.

The only felids known to live in groups are lions, cheetah males, and domestic cats. Many hypotheses have been developed to explain why these species live in groups, but none is completely satisfactory. Almost everyone agrees that the answer involves food, but that group hunting is not likely to be the key to sociality. Craig Packer, who studied lions in the Serengeti, suggests that where females live at high densities in open habitats and hunt large prey, they should form groups. He argues that vultures and hyenas quickly find large kills in open habitats, and rather than sharing such kills with these competitors, it would behoove lions to share their kills with female relatives. Coming at the problem from another direction, Tim Caro, who studied cheetahs on the Serengeti plains, argues that most felids do not form groups because they typically live in areas where there is not enough large prey available to support a group.

Because domestic cats live in such a wide variety of habitats and under such a broad spectrum of circumstances, one might hope that they would provide some insights into the costs and benefits of sociality. Though there are no examples of groups of domestic cats living on natural prey, there are several well-known studies of groups of domestic cats living around dockyard garbage dumpsters, fish offal dumps, or farmyards. The artificial food sources at these sites were rich, predictable resource patches that supported several females. At the dockyard site, cats lived in family groups of 4–5 females. At the farmyard site, detailed behavioral observations showed that groups were highly structured in terms of individual relationships, and several social classes could be distinguished. Some females gave birth in communal dens, formed nursing coalitions, and jointly defended kittens against infanticidal males. Females formed matrilineal subgroups, which consisted of amicable, tightly knit associations of several generations of relatives descended from the same mother. As with lionesses in a pride, the matriline is the basic social unit of group-living domestic cats.

Related tigresses living in adjoining ranges on the prey-rich floodplain of Chitwan represent another expression of matrilineal organization, but one produced by different resource characteristics and dispersion. It is not too difficult to imagine the circumstances under which these neighboring sisters, mothers, and aunts might find it advantageous to get together to form a pride. If the habitat were open and supported abundant large prey, and if there were serious competition from vultures, hyenas, and other scavengers for kills, it might create conditions that would favor the formation of groups.

There are many different reasons why cats form groups. Male lions and male cheetahs form coalitions to gain access to females. Female lions and domestic cats form groups to enhance reproductive success and territorial defense. But we still do not completely understand all the complexities of the issue—to be able to tease apart the factors that promote group formation, we will need information on other cat species that measures up to the exquisitely detailed studies of lions and cheetahs in the Serengeti. Lions in India's Gir Forest illustrate just how complex the issue is. In the Gir, prey densities are low, large prey is scarce, and lions have no natural competitors for kills. Gir Forest lions eat many of the same species of ungulates that tigers eat in other parts of India. Prey density, prey size, lack of competitors, and habitat conditions would suggest that Gir lions ought to be solitary like tigers, but they are not. Like lions everywhere, Gir lions live in prides of two to eleven females. There seems to be no obvious reason for Gir lionesses to associate with one another, even in small groups. Why do Gir lions still behave like lions, even when they live in "tiger" habitat, feeding on "tiger" prey? Clearly, we are still missing a piece of the puzzle.

Taxonomy of the Cat Family

The systematics of felids has been the subject of long and bitter debate among taxonomists. Since 1858, when Severtozov divided the Felidae, or cat family, into five genera, there have been at least ten different classification schemes proposed, in which the numbers of genera have ranged from two to as many as twenty-three. There is less disagreement about the number of felid species, with numbers ranging from thirty-six to thirty-nine. These various classification schemes have been based on an array of morphological, behavioral, and genetic characteristics, including vocalizations, shape of the pupil, tooth number, tooth shape and size, cranial dimensions, foot and nose morphology, hybridization records, karyotype, and most recently DNA analysis.[1,2,3,4,5,6,7,8]

Much of the confusion stems from the fact that almost all the cats, with the exception of the cheetah, make their living in a similar fashion. They stalk, pounce, or rush and kill their prey using basically the same movements, teeth, and claws, and this means that their morphology is very similar. Despite the fact that felids have the greatest range in body size among the Carnivora, ranging from the seven-hundred-pound tiger to the two-pound rusty-spotted cat, they show little variation in morphology.

For practical reasons, this volume follows the taxonomy laid out by Wozencraft.[9] This taxonomic arrangement is also used by the Convention on International Trade in Endangered Species of Wild Fauna and Flora (CITES), the World Conservation Monitoring Center (WCMC), and the Wild Cats Status Survey and Conservation Plan.[10]

MOLECULAR GENETICS

The new and rapidly expanding field of molecular genetics promises to finally resolve the problem of felid phylogeny. Genetic material from different species can be analyzed with a variety of molecular tests to deter-mine how closely related species are to one another. Species that have been separated for a long time show greater divergence in their DNA. However, because the cat family evolved fairly recently, and because many species separated from one another within a short period of time, the differences are small and sometimes difficult to detect. The molecular genetic description of the felid phylogenetic tree is still evolving, and a few species remain a mystery, but the various methods converge on a "best guess" tree, which shows eight major lineages (fig. 9). The thirty-six species of modern wild cats evolved from these eight

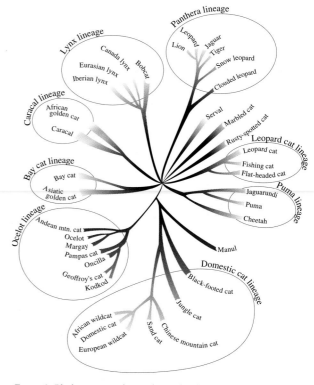

Figure 9. Phylogenetic relationships of eight cat lineages.

phylogenetic lineages within the past 10–15 million years.[11]

1. Ocelot lineage

According to morphological and molecular studies, the ocelot lineage diverged some 10–12 million years ago, leading to seven species of small spotted cats in Central and South America. Within the ocelot lineage, the species are thought to form two groups, one composed of the Andean mountain cat, ocelot, and margay, and another containing the pampas cat, oncilla, Geoffroy's cat, and kodkod.[12]

2. Domestic cat lineage

The domestic cat lineage has its origins in the Mediterranean region, about 8–10 million years ago. The black-footed cat of South Africa is believed to be the first of this group of six species to diverge, followed by the jungle cat and sand cat. The domestic cat, European wildcat, and African wildcat radiated very recently, and the molecular data support Wozencraft's classification of the African wildcat and European wildcat as a single species.[13]

3. Puma lineage

The puma lineage includes the puma, jaguarundi, and cheetah. The puma and jaguarundi are closely related, and have an older association with the cheetah, which diverged from the common ancestor some 8.25 million years ago.[13] Though the puma and jaguarundi are American cats and the cheetah African, fossil evidence shows that cheetahs were in North America some 2–3 million years ago.[14,15]

4. Leopard cat lineage

The leopard cat, fishing cat, and flat-headed cat are members of one of the most recent felid lineages, diverging from a common ancestor only 3.95 million years ago. All are closely related and live sympatrically throughout much of Southeast Asia.[13]

5. *Panthera* lineage

The *Panthera* lineage includes the jaguar, tiger, lion, leopard, snow leopard, and clouded leopard. The clouded leopard was the first to diverge from the ancestral line, followed by the snow leopard. The last group of four big cats diverged very recently, an estimated 2–3 million years ago,[16] and the internal branching of this group is still being investigated.

6. Lynx lineage

Among the lynxes, the Eurasian lynx and Canada lynx are closely related and share an older ancestor with the bobcat. The position of the Iberian lynx within this lineage has yet to be determined.

7. Caracal lineage

The phylogenetic association of the caracal and the African golden cat is supported by several genetic analyses. The two species are thought to have shared a common ancestor 4.85 million years ago.[13]

8. Bay cat lineage

Recent analyses[17] indicate that the bay cat diverged from a common ancestor with the Asiatic golden cat an estimated 4.9–5.3 million years ago, well before the geological separation of Borneo from other islands on the Sunda Shelf some 10,000–15,000 years ago.

REFERENCES

1. Hemmer, H. 1978. The evolutionary systematics of the living Felidae: Present status and current problems. *Carnivore* 1: 80–88.

2. Leyhausen, P. 1979. *Cat behavior: The predatory and social behavior of domestic and wild cats.* New York: Garland STPM Press.

3. Wurster-Hill, D. H., and W. R. Centerwall. 1982. The interrelationships of chromosome banding patterns in Procyonids, Viverrids and Felids. *Cytogenet. Cell Genet.* 34: 178–192.

4. Neff, N. A. 1982. *The big cats: The paintings of Guy Coheleach.* New York: Adams Press.

5. Collier, G. E., and S. J. O'Brien. 1985. A molecular phylogeny of the Felidae: Immunological distance. *Evolution* 39: 473–487.

6. Nowak, R. M. 1991. *Walker's mammals of the world.* Vol. 2. Baltimore: Johns Hopkins University Press.

7. Salles, L. O. 1992. Felid phylogenetics: Extant taxa and skull morphology (Felidae, Aeluroidea). *Am. Mus. Novitates* 3047: 1–67.

8. Peters, G., and B. A. Tonkin-Leyhausen. 1999. Evolution of acoustic communication signals of mammals: Friendly close-range vocalizations in Felidae (Carnivora). *J. Mammal. Evol.* 6: 129–159.

9. Wozencraft, W. C. 1993. Order Carnivora. In *Mammal species of the world,* ed. D. E. Wilson and D. M. Reeder, 279–348. Washington, DC: Smithsonian Institution Press.

10. Nowell, K., and P. Jackson. 1996. *Wild cats: A status survey and conservation action plan.* Gland, Switzerland: International Union for Conservation of Nature and Natural Resources (IUCN).

11. Pecon-Slattery, J., and S. J. O'Brien. 1998. Patterns of Y and X chromosome DNA sequence divergence during the Felidae radiation. *Genetics* 148: 1245–1255.

12. Johnson, W. E., M. Culver, J. A. Iriarte, E. Eizirik, K. L. Seymour, and S. J. O'Brien. 1998. Tracking the evolution of the elu-

sive Andean mountain cat (*Oreailurus jacobita*) from mitochondrial DNA. *J. Hered.* 89: 227–232.

13. Johnson, W. E., and S. J. O'Brien. 1997. Phylogenetic reconstruction of the Felidae using 16s rRNA and NADH-5 mitochondrial genes. *J. Mol. Evol.* 44 (suppl. 1): S98–S116.

14. Adams, D. B. 1979. The cheetah: Native American. *Science* 205: 1155–1158.

15. Van Valkenburgh, B., F. Grady, and B. Kurtén. 1990. The Plio-Pleistocene cheetah-like cat *Miracinonyx inexpectatus* of North America. *J. Vert. Paleontol.* 10: 434–454.

16. Turner, A. 1987. New fossil carnivore remains from the Sterkfontein hominid site (Mammalia: Carnivora). *Ann. Transvaal Mus.* 34: 319–347.

17. Johnson, W. E., F. Shinyashiki, M. Menotti Raymond, C. Driscoll, C. Leh, M. Sunquist, L. Johnston, M. Bush, D. Wildt, N. Yuhki, and S. J. O'Brien. 1999. Molecular genetic characterization of two insular Asian cat species, Bornean bay cat and Iriomote cat. In *Evolutionary theory and processes: Modern perspectives, papers in honour of Eviatar Nevo,* ed. S. P. Wasser, 223–248. Dordrecht: Kluwer Academic Publishers.

Species Accounts

Cheetah

Acinonyx jubatus (Schreber, 1776)

Cheetahs have had a long association with people, going back at least 4,000 years. A silver ornament found in a burial mound in the Caucasus that was dated between 700 and 300 B.C. shows cheetahs wearing collars, and Jonathan Kingdon speculates that even earlier cultures may have associated with the cat in that hunters were likely to have joined with other scavengers in robbing cheetahs of their kills.[1] A Mesopotamian seal dating from the third millennium B.C. depicts a cheetah-like cat on a leash, and tame cheetahs were enshrined on many Egyptian tombs and rock temples.[2] The pharaohs believed that the cheetah, as the fastest animal on land, would carry their spirits away after death.[1] Some of the earliest images of training and using cheetahs for hunting come from the seventeenth and eighteenth dynasties in Egypt. Later the cats were widely used in the Middle East, Afghanistan, southern Russia, Pakistan, India, and China.[2,3] Tame cheetahs were used to hunt goitered gazelles, foxes, and hares in Russia and Mongolia, and the sport flourished during the Middle Ages in Azerbaijan, Armenia, and Georgia. In 1474 one Armenian ruler owned 100 hunting cheetahs.[4]

In 1555 Akbar the Great was presented with a cheetah named Fatehbaz and thus was the first Indian potentate introduced to hunting with cheetahs. Akbar later devised a new method of capture and training for the cat, and at one time his menagerie held a thousand cheetahs. During his lifetime Akbar reportedly collected over nine thousand cheetahs, using them for hunting gazelles and blackbuck.[5]

In Europe the nobility have been hunting with tame cheetahs for nearly a thousand years. In November 1231, Frederick II went to Ravenna, Italy, with an entourage of bodyguards, astrologers, huntsmen, and falconers. Accounts of the time record that the court was accompanied by a menagerie that included elephants, dromedaries, camels, cheetahs, and falcons.[6] By the fourteenth and fifteenth centuries, the sport of coursing with cheetah had become extremely popular in Italy, France, and England. Wealthy landowners and royalty spent large sums of money to acquire and keep these elegant hunting cats, which were used to run down hares and roe deer. Paintings and tapestries of the time show that the cheetahs were carried to the hunt on horseback, perched on a pillow behind the handler.[2] In India, Jerdon reported that when taken out for hunting "the cheeta is carried on a cart, hooded, and when the game is raised the hood is taken off. The cheeta then leaps down, sometimes on the opposite side to its prey, and pursues the antelope. If the latter are near the cart, the cheeta springs forward with a surpassing velocity."[7]

If captured as adults, cheetahs were reputed to be easy to tame and train for hunting, presumably because they had been trained to hunt by their mother, but if they were taken as cubs and reared in captivity, their training was reported to be long and difficult. Various techniques were employed to capture cheetahs. While Akbar's techniques involved pitfalls with trapdoors, Pocock reports that cheetahs "were commonly caught in nooses set about trees which it was known they were in the habit of visiting to 'sharpen' their claws."[8]

Robert Sterndale quotes a letter written in 1880 that describes how cheetah were snared and tamed:

> The nooses were of the same kind as those used for snaring antelope, made from the dried sinews of the antelope. These were pegged down in all directions, and at all angles to a distance of twenty-five to thirty feet from the tree. . . . [The trappers then retreated to a blind made of bushes and waited; at sunset four cheetah appeared.] Two were large and the other two smaller; the larger had the best of the race, and were entangled by all four feet before they knew where they were. . . . Women and children are told to sit all day long close to the animals, and keep up a conversation so that they should get accustomed to the human voice. The female was snarling a good deal, the male being much quieter; they go through various gradations of education, and I was told they would be ready to be unhooded and worked in about six months time.[9]

The cheetah, sometimes called the hunting leopard, derives its name from the Hindi word *chita*, meaning spotted or sprinkled. There are several other animals whose names are also partially derived from the word, including the chital or spotted deer and the chita-bora, a snake. The cheetah's generic name *Acinonyx* was probably derived from the Greek words *akaina* (thorn) and *onyx* (claw), referring to the foot with its unsheathed claw. The species name *jubatus* is from the Latin, meaning having a crest or mane. In Europe the cheetah was variously known as *guepard* (France), *gepard* (Germany), and *onza* (Spain).[7,8,10,11]

While European nobility were familiar with it as a hunting animal, the cheetah was not native to Europe, but was imported from Africa. A cheetah-like cat did, however, live in Europe during the Villafranchian period, about 3.5 million years ago, but it was much larger than the present-day form. A large cheetah is also known from fossil deposits in India and China, suggesting that the distribution of a cheetah-like cat was extensive in prehistoric times.[3,12]

There are also records of cheetahs living in North America during the Pleistocene epoch. Excavations in late Pleistocene deposits in Wyoming have yielded remains of a cheetah-like cat that, except for size differences and some primitive features, is almost identical to the Old World cheetah. This ancient cheetah, called *Miracinonyx*, was found in Texas, Nevada, and Wyoming. Like the modern-day cheetah, it appeared to be highly specialized for a cursorial (running) lifestyle. The skull of *Miracinonyx* was very similar to that of the modern cheetah; both have a short face, small upper canines, and enlarged nasal passages. Unlike any other cat, both ancient and modern cheetahs lack a postcanine gap, and the upper and lower tooth rows act together as a pair of shears. *Miracinonyx* was considerably larger than today's cheetah and probably weighed more than 95 kilograms, compared with an average body weight of 57 kilograms for *Acinonyx*.[12]

Some paleontologists believe that cheetahs and pumas may have had a common ancestor that lived in Eurasia and North America during the Miocene and Pliocene epochs, and that the modern cheetah may have originated in North America.[12] Until quite recently the cheetah's many different morphological features and specialized characteristics led experts to believe that it had diverged early from the felid stem. However, recent analyses of molecular DNA revealed that the cheetah originated much more recently and in fact represents an early branch of the pantherine lineage, which began to radiate 4 to 6 million years ago and includes the Asian golden cat, caracal, serval, and puma.[13,14] Fossil remains of cheetahs from the late Pleistocene, some 700,000 years ago, are indistinguishable from the modern cheetah.[12]

DESCRIPTION

About the same general size as a leopard, but about 7.6 centimeters taller, cheetahs lack the heavily muscled, robust body of the other large cats, having instead the slim, lanky, deep-chested body of a sprinter. The slender, elongated body is supported on tall, thin legs, and the tail measures about half the head and body length. The general background coat color is yellow or tan, but may vary from tawny to grayish-white to bright rufous fawn. The pelt is covered with evenly spaced, solid black dots. Desmond Varaday found that the fur of his pet cheetah varied in texture. He writes, "I examined the texture of the spots and found them to be like soft, Persian-cat fur, while the golden parts were more like dog's hair." Varaday also counted the spots and came up with a total of 1,967 for his cheetah.[15]

Compared with the cheek whiskers of the leopard or tiger, cheetah whiskers are comparatively short, fine, and almost unobtrusive. Clearly, whiskers do not play an important role in the cheetah's prey-catching routine. The undersides of the belly and limbs are white, as are the throat, chin, and upper lip. There is also some white above the eyes and on the tip of the tail. The backs of the ears are black. A conspicuous black tear line runs from the inner corner of the eye to the mouth. The last third of the tail is marked with black stripes, while the first two-thirds is covered with black spots. Each individual has a unique pattern of spots on its face and chest; scientists have used these spot patterns to recognize their study animals.[16,17] The arrangement of black bands at the end of the tail also differs among individuals, and the tails of littermates resemble one another more closely than they resemble the tails of their mother and unrelated cheetahs.[2,3,18]

Cheetah fur is short and somewhat coarse, except for a mane of longer hair at the nape and shoulders, which may be 8 or more centimeters long. This mane in the adults is the remnant of a much more extensive capelike covering of long gray-blue hair possessed by cheetah cubs.

Melanistic and white cheetahs have been recorded, but they seem to be rare.[3] There is a record of a black cheetah from Kenya and another from Zambia. In India, the Emperor Jahangir described a white cheetah presented to him by Raja Bir Singh Deo in 1608 as having blue spots on a whitish-blue coat. In South Africa, two partially albino cheetahs were described by Sclater in 1877–1878. A third anomalous coat pattern is that of the rare king cheetah from South Africa. In 1926 a cheetah skin patterned with stripes and blotches, instead of the usual spots, was purchased by a farmer in southern Rhodesia. The farmer donated the skin to the museum in Salisbury; it was later examined by Major A. C. Cooper, who thought that it might be the result of a hybrid mating between leopard and cheetah. Cooper persuaded the museum authorities to send the skin to R. I. Pocock at the British Museum, and in 1927 Pocock published the official description of the king cheetah, *Acinonyx rex*. While it was originally described as a separate species, the king cheetah is in fact just an ordinary cheetah with abnormal markings. The king coat pattern is controlled by a single recessive gene; if both parents have the gene, about a quarter of their offspring will have the king coat pattern. Geneticists now believe that the king cheetah coat pattern results from a mutation of the "tabby" gene. Striped tabby domestic cats produce kittens with a blotched tabby coat pattern when a mutation of this gene occurs. In the wild, king cheetahs are found exclusively in Zimbabwe, Botswana, and the Transvaal, but they were virtually unknown in captivity until 1980. Between 1981 and 1984 nine king cheetahs were born to parents with normal coats at the De Wildt Cheetah Breeding and Research Centre near Pretoria.[3,19,20]

The cheetah has an unusually short-faced skull with a broad, highly domed forehead. Most cheetah skulls lack a prominent sagittal crest (central bony ridge), and the bones of the skull are thin and light, showing little evidence of muscular development. The highest part of the skull is above the eye, and from there the braincase slopes down sharply to the rear, so that in profile the skull appears almost triangular. Given this shape, the muscles between the skull and jaw are short, suggesting that the cheetah cannot open its jaws as widely as other large cats. It also implies that the bite force on the canines is reduced. Both upper and lower canines are small by felid standards and not very flattened, which is thought to be correlated with the fact that cheetahs use a throat bite to kill prey. This method kills by strangulation and does not require as specialized a dentition as one that severs the spinal cord. A reduction in the size of the canines also means that the nasal openings may be enlarged, thereby increasing air intake. As Ewer so perspicaciously suggests, "the cheetah has small canines because it runs so fast."[21]

The cheetah's teeth are also unusual in that the cheek teeth are narrow and that when the jaws close, the upper and lower cheek teeth overlap to such an extent that there is no gap behind the canines. This arrangement allows the top and bottom tooth rows to act together like a pair of shears, resulting in a set of teeth that is highly specialized for meat slicing. Other cats have a postcanine gap, a feature that is thought to be an integral part of being able to kill with a neck bite. Such a killing method requires that the canines gain maximum penetration, and the gap allows the teeth to be driven in to their full depth. The cheetah,

on the other hand, rarely uses a neck bite except on small animals such as hares.[10,21]

Cheetahs have many anatomical and physiological adaptations that represent specializations for speed.[21,22,23,24,25] They have large thigh muscles, and their limbs are longer than expected for their size. The tibia and fibula are tightly bound together so that there is little rotation in the lower leg, increasing stability while running but decreasing climbing ability. The cheetah's clavicle is greatly reduced and is joined to the scapula only by ligaments. Because the scapula and forelegs do not have a bony connection to the body, the body is suspended between the forelegs in a muscular sling. The obvious up-and-down motion of the shoulder blades when the cat walks reflects this anatomical arrangement. This arrangement frees the scapula to swing back and forth with each stride, increasing the effective length of the stride, and also acts as a spring or shock absorber. The cheetah's stride length is also increased by the flexion and extension of the spine. During the extended phase of the stride, the cat's back is hyperextended, allowing the hindlimbs to push against the ground longer and the forelimbs to reach out farther. In the flexed phase of the stride, the cat's back is so bowed that its hindlimbs land farther forward than where the forelimbs landed. Overall, this action adds another 76 centimeters to the cheetah's total stride length.[26,27] At 53 kilometers per hour, a cheetah's stride length is about 4.3 meters; at 90 kilometers per hour, it increases to 7 meters.[3]

Describing his tame cheetah in action, Desmond Varaday writes, "Her compressed body and narrow, fragile looking chest was built for speed; on her dainty feet she had hard pads like those of a dog and with her unsheathed claws she could take a firm hold on the ground to propel herself at lightning speed. She used her long stiffly stretched tail as a rudder which enabled her to achieve feints by turning quickly at amazing angles when speeding."[15]

All running carnivores include a suspension, or floating, phase in their gait, during which all the feet are off the ground. The distance the body moves forward during the floating phase also increases the stride length. Animals such as weasels have a short floating phase, whereas more than 50 percent of the cheetah's stride consists of the floating phase.[24]

A running cheetah covers about 7 meters with each stride, the same distance as a galloping horse. As a cheetah accelerates, it increases the number of strides per second, and at 93 kilometers per hour, it is taking an incredible three and a half strides per second. At this speed the cheetah is traveling about 25 meters per second, or nearly three times faster than the best human sprinter. There is some dispute over the cheetah's top speed, and estimates vary from 90 to 128 kilometers per hour. The most reliable measurement over a short distance is about 112 kilometers per hour.[21,25,26]

Cheetahs do not pursue prey for long distances. Instead, they are designed for a short, explosive sprint. Aided by enlarged lungs, heart, adrenal glands, and nasal passages, cheetahs accelerate rapidly, attaining a speed of 75 kilometers per hour in just two seconds. During sprints, their respiratory rate quickly climbs from 60 to 150 breaths per minute, and heat production increases more than fiftyfold. Cheetahs store about 90 percent of the heat they produce while sprinting; by comparison, African hunting dogs and domestic dogs store only about 20 percent of the heat they produce during a run. It seems likely that the length of the cheetah's sprint is determined by the amount of heat its body can store before its temperature reaches a dangerous level — probably 40–41°C. In an experimental trial, cheetahs refused to run when their body temperatures reached 40.5°C.[28]

Since the speeds attained by cheetahs exceed those recorded for all ungulates, the outcome of any chase would seem to be a foregone conclusion. However, antelope are adept at zigzagging, and to follow their prey, cheetahs have to make rapid turns at high speeds. During these high-speed maneuvers, cheetahs use their tails and feet to maintain balance and speed. The long tail is used as a balancing organ, and the claws are extended during a chase to increase traction. Cheetah claws are shorter and straighter than those of other felids, and there are no claw sheaths for the claws to retract into, so even when they are retracted, the claws are easy to see. This fact accounts for the common misperception that cheetahs have nonretractile claws like a dog's.[3] Varaday describes the claws of his pet cheetah as half-retractable, "but not so stiffly set as those of a dog."[15] The paws are small and compact, and the webbing between the digits is much less than in other felids, allowing the toes to be spread widely. Furthermore, the longitudinal ridges on the hard, pointed pads of the feet function like cleats on a running shoe, providing traction and grip during fast turns.[21,26,27]

DISTRIBUTION
The cheetah was once widely distributed throughout Europe, Asia, Africa, and North America. Four hun-

Figure 10. Distribution of the cheetah.

dred years ago it was common in western and central India south of the Ganges, where its range closely mirrored that of its major prey, the blackbuck.[29,30] In the Middle East it was found throughout Palestine, Syria, Iraq, Iran, Afghanistan, and the Sind.[31,32] In Africa, the species ranged through all suitable habitats except desert and tropical forest, from the Mediterranean to the Cape of Good Hope.[2]

Today, the cheetah has almost disappeared from Asia. It is extinct in India, but small populations may still exist in the former Soviet Union and in the region where the international boundaries of Iran, Afghanistan, and Pakistan meet.[4,30] Cheetahs were reported to occur in the Khosh Yeilagh Wildlife Refuge in northeastern Iran,[33] and there have been several recent sightings in that general area.[34,35]

In Africa, the cheetah's distribution has been fragmented and greatly reduced, and major reductions have occurred even since 1975. Though cheetahs inhabit a broad section of central, eastern, and southern Africa, their major strongholds are in eastern and southern Africa, principally Kenya, Tanzania, and South West Africa/Namibia. An estimated 300–500 survive in the Sahara, most of them in Mali, Niger, and Chad. In East Africa the cheetah's distribution overlaps that of Thomson's and Grant's gazelles and the gerenuk, and in southern Africa, that of the impala (fig. 10).[1,10,36,37,38,39,40]

ECOLOGY AND BEHAVIOR

The cheetah is an animal of open country, and in many parts of its geographic range, this cat is strongly associated with grassy plains, open woodlands, and semidesert. A few cheetahs still survive among the sandy plains and rocky hills of the Sahara, where they spend the day among the rocks and beneath bushes, avoiding the intense heat of the sun.[40] Cheetahs also thrive on the savannas and semiarid rangelands of Kenya. They can live equally well in areas with more cover; in the Masai Mara Reserve of East Africa they use moderate cover for both hunting and resting.[41]

Feeding Ecology

Cheetahs hunt mainly by day, but the hours vary slightly from area to area. In the Sahara, where daytime temperatures can reach 43°C, cheetahs do most of their hunting at night and in the relatively cool hours after daybreak.[40] In the Serengeti, cheetahs hunt slightly later in the morning and earlier in the afternoon than lions and hyenas, presumably as a strategy to avoid these other large carnivores.[42] In the Masai Mara region of southwestern Kenya, cheetahs are active mainly between 0730 and 1000 hours and again between 1630 and 1930 hours; they commonly rest during the midday period.[41]

Cheetahs have been seen hunting at night in the Serengeti and in Namibia,[43,44] but there is a general lack of information on their nighttime activities. Family groups generally spend the night resting in open grassy areas and are usually found in the same place in the morning where they were last seen in the evening,[45] whereas males and juvenile groups sometimes continue to move during the night.[41]

Lions, leopards, and hyenas all represent a threat to cheetahs. These larger and more aggressive carnivores kill adult cheetahs and cubs and steal cheetahs' kills, so the timid, retiring cheetah keeps its distance and maintains a careful lookout for these other predators. Even when resting, the cheetah is alert to danger, and "sentry" duty is shared among family members. If they are resting on top of a mound, cheetahs scan the surroundings simply by raising the head, but in tall vegetation they sit on their haunches. In the Mara, a total of twelve minutes of every daylight hour was devoted to looking out for danger. Not included in this estimate is time devoted to looking out for other carnivores while feeding, the situation in which most agonistic encounters occur.[41,45]

A hungry cheetah has two major ways of finding a meal. Watching from a rest site, the cat may see a potential hunting opportunity. When this happens, the cheetah usually waits for the animal to get close enough, then launches into a chase. Cheetahs also find prey by walking slowly through the grassland looking, or by scanning the area from a low branch or termite mound. To get close enough to attempt a chase, a cheetah may approach a herd of gazelles openly; if it can get within 60 to 70 meters before the gazelles flee, the cheetah may sprint at them. But wherever there is any cover at all, the cheetah makes full use of it to stalk as close as possible to its prey. Head lowered to shoulder level, body in a semi-crouch, it alternately creeps or runs forward, then freezes, maneuvering to within 30 meters or until it is close enough to the gazelles to launch a short, fast chase. Unlike wild dogs or hyenas, which tend to select their prey during the chase portion of the hunt, cheetahs seem to focus on one animal before the chase begins and rarely switch targets during the chase.[45,46,47,48]

In areas with less cover, cheetahs sometimes approach prey at a trot, then within 200 meters or so shift into high speed. A fast approach is also occasionally used in hunts of small Thomson's gazelles, impalas, or juvenile wildebeests. The flight response of prey appears to be an important component of the cheetah's hunting technique, as those prey that stand their ground or remain motionless are unlikely to be attacked.[17]

Cheetahs select gazelles based on proximity and level of vigilance; more vigilant gazelles are less vulnerable to cheetahs because they tend to react more rapidly when the cat begins its final rush. More vigilant gazelles probably also increase their survivorship by detecting cheetahs before the chase begins, because cheetahs abandoned nearly three-quarters of the hunts in which they were detected during the stalking phase.[46,47]

Wherever cheetahs are found, there are one or more species of gazelles or gazelle-like antelope in the 20–50 kilogram range. These cats feed mainly on medium-sized ungulates, and most of their prey weighs less than 40 kilograms. The list includes the impala, Thomson's and Grant's gazelles, springbok, reedbuck, waterbuck, kudu, steenbok, duiker, warthog, and wildebeest. Springbok are the dominant prey in the Kalahari of South Africa.[49] In the Serengeti, Thomson's gazelles are the primary prey, accounting for 91 percent of cheetah kills, although the frequency of hares in the diet increases when the migratory gazelles are scarce or absent.[43] In the bush and savanna woodlands of Kruger National Park, impalas are the dominant prey, constituting 68 percent of 2,532 kills, but cheetah show a preference for reedbuck.[50] Impalas figure prominently in the diet of cheetahs from the Transvaal, although in many areas of Botswana and South West Africa/Namibia, the bulk of the diet is springbok. In Nairobi National Park, impalas, Grant's gazelles, and Thomson's gazelles account for almost 75 percent of the cheetah's kills.[51] In almost all studies to date, fawns and half-grown gazelles make up more than 50 percent of cheetah kills, even though young and adolescent ungulates constitute only a small proportion of the prey population.[52]

In the Serengeti, prey preferences depend to a large extent on which and how many cheetahs are doing the hunting. Male coalitions hunt the 80-kilogram wildebeest, while single males usually hunt Thomson's gazelles. Subadult sibling groups, hunting together without their mother, choose Thomson's gazelles, but solitary subadults hunt more hares and infant Thomson's gazelles.[45]

In some hunts there appears to be a degree of cooperation, although whether it is deliberate or simply fortuitous is not clear. Burney describes five hunting episodes in which some degree of communal effort seemed apparent. In one case a young male cheetah chased a waterbuck calf toward his mother and a sibling waiting in ambush. Another time a family of cheetahs appeared to systematically search a patch of cover into which an impala fawn had run. A third form of cooperative hunting involved a type of relay, in which different family members took up the chase depending on how the prey turned.[41]

At the end of the chase, the cheetah trips or knocks the prey down and strangles it. While running slightly behind or beside it, the cheetah reaches out and hooks the prey with the large, strongly curved dewclaw, throwing the prey off balance. Alternatively, a strike or slap to the rump with the forepaw topples the quarry, and before the animal can recover, the cheetah has it by the throat. Cheetahs kill large prey by strangulation. Once a cheetah has its prey by the throat, it usually lies down and maintains the stranglehold for five minutes or so. The cat's grip closes off the trachea, and death is by suffocation. Small animals are grabbed by the muzzle or killed with a bite to the back of the neck; hares and very young impalas may be bitten through the skull. If shelter in the form of a bush or tree is available nearby, the cheetah often drags or carries its kill to the shade, then rests beside the carcass for five to fifty-five minutes, panting heavily.[45,51] If more than one cheetah is present, those not directly involved in the kill begin feeding immediately. Eating rapidly, they turn their heads sideways so that the scissorlike carnassial teeth can more effectively slice off chunks of meat, which are swallowed without chewing. Cheetahs are careful, tidy eaters, and they feed together quite peacefully, with only occasional growling and snapping. They usually begin to eat on the upper side of the hindquarters, then proceed to the abdominal muscles and back.[51] Cheetahs chew the ends of rib bones, but rarely tear limbs off a carcass. In South Africa, an articulated skeleton stripped of its flesh is considered to be a characteristic sign of a cheetah kill.[53]

While feeding, cheetahs pause frequently to look around. Mothers with young cubs are the most vigilant, spending more time observing their surroundings than lone females or mothers with their cubs hidden at a den.[54] As cubs grow older, mothers spend less and less time watching for predators and more time watching for potential prey.[55]

These slender cats are quite capable of eating large quantities of food. In Etosha National Park, Namibia, cheetahs consumed up to 10 kilograms of food in less than two hours and stayed with kills for as long as eleven hours. During a feeding experiment, two cheetahs abandoned a carcass after two to three hours of feeding, during which time they jointly consumed about 19 kilograms.[56] On another occasion, an adult male cheetah and two large cubs fed for five hours on a day-old carcass of a giraffe. However, lions and hyenas occur at fairly low densities in Etosha,[44] and the lack of competing predators may allow cheetahs to spend more time at kills.

Cheetahs were once thought to be one of the few carnivores that never scavenged, but it is now known that they occasionally feed from carcasses they have not killed themselves. In the Serengeti, a mother and her six nearly full-grown cubs fed on a wildebeest carcass for twenty minutes but were chased off by a spotted hyena.[57] And in Namibia, three cheetahs were seen feeding for five hours on a giraffe carcass.[44] That so few cheetahs are seen scavenging probably reflects the fact that they rarely encounter a dead animal that is not already being fed on by vultures or hyenas. Typically, in an area of moderate prey density, more than 20 vultures will be circling a carcass two minutes after it appears, and in less than forty minutes more than 100 vultures will have arrived.[58] On the Serengeti plains, the high density of vultures and spotted hyenas means that a 550-kilogram buffalo carcass is picked clean within forty-eight hours.[45]

Television documentaries often show cheetahs being robbed of their hard-won kills by hyenas or lions, and there seems to be a general notion that cheetahs lose at least half their kills to other predators.[59] Cheetahs do lose kills to other large carnivores, but studies show that the proportion is not nearly as high as was once believed; in the Serengeti, cheetahs lose 10–13 percent of their kills to other predators,[43,45,60] and an estimated 14 percent of cheetah kills are appropriated by spotted hyenas in Kruger National Park.[61] Cheetahs eat fast, however, and in the Serengeti, they had already fed from many of the carcasses that were stolen. Caro calculates that male cheetahs lost approximately 9.2 percent of the flesh they captured.[45]

In general, cheetahs seem to be more successful hunters than other large felids. Not unexpectedly, their success rates vary, depending on the type of prey being hunted and the sex and age class of the cheetah doing the hunting. Schaller found, for example, that adult cheetahs hunting small gazelle fawns were 100 percent successful, but only 53.5 percent of their hunts of older gazelles ended in a kill.[43] Similarly, McLaughlin reports that in Nairobi National Park, 37 percent of all chases were successful, but chases of juvenile animals were successful 76 percent of the time.[51] Caro also recorded high hunting success rates (81 to 100 percent) on Thomson's gazelle neonates for a variety of female cheetah age classes. Sibling groups of cheetahs had a much better success rate hunting subadult and adult Thomson's gazelles when they pursued the prey simultaneously (52 percent) than when hunting alone (15 percent). Adult cheetah males, on the other hand, were no more successful hunting as singletons, in pairs, or in trios, although larger coalitions tended to focus on larger prey (e.g., wildebeests) while singletons concentrated on Thomson's gazelles. Approximately 75 percent of hunts by solitary males or pairs were unsuccessful, while about 50 percent of hunts by trios were unsuccessful.[45]

Cheetah mothers spend more of their time hunting larger prey, hunt more often, and are more successsful than females without cubs. Lactating females were lighter and thinner than females without cubs, but met their increased energetic demands by spending more time hunting larger prey and eating almost twice as much. Mothers continued to hunt more large animals, such as adult Thomson's gazelles, until their cubs were about eight and a half months old.[45]

Social Organization

Cheetahs have a social organization that is unique among the felids. Females are solitary or accompanied by dependent young, and males are either solitary or live in stable coalitions of two or three. Some coalitions consist of brothers, but unrelated males may also be members of the group. Unlike the coalitions formed by male lions, which remain attached to and mate with the females in a single pride, cheetah male coalitions mate with as many females as possible.[45]

Cheetahs appear to have different land tenure systems in different parts of their geographic range. In the Serengeti, where Thomson's gazelles make up 90 percent of the cheetah's diet,[43] the ranging patterns of female cheetahs mirror the migration patterns of Thomson's gazelles.[62] Female cheetahs travel widely, covering areas of several hundred square kilometers as they follow the herds. The majority of males in the Serengeti live in coalitions and are more sedentary. They establish small territories of about 30 square kilometers in areas with good vegetative cover and a locally high abundance of antelope, but may temporarily abandon these territories when prey abundance is low. Females and nonterritorial males have home ranges that overlap extensively and cover about 800 square kilometers. Male territories are not continuous and may be separated by many kilometers of apparently unsuitable habitat. Mating opportunities arise as female cheetahs pass through a number of male territories during their travels.[17,45,63,64]

In South Africa's Kruger National Park, where prey are nonmigratory, male and female cheetahs have smaller, overlapping ranges that are similar in size.[65] In Nairobi National Park, two females and their offspring lived in overlapping ranges of about 80 square kilometers,[51] but female ranges in Namibia are extremely large, measuring 1,500 square kilometers.[37,53]

It is often observed that in comparison with other large African carnivores, such as lions and spotted hyenas, cheetahs live at low densities. This is certainly so on the Serengeti plains, where there are approximately 1.5 times as many leopards, 4 times as many lions, and 9 times as many spotted hyenas as there are cheetahs.[66] Overall, cheetah densities on the Serengeti plains were 0.8 to 1.0 per 100 square kilometers, but during some seasons densities can reach 40 cheetahs per 100 square kilometers.[45]

The spatial arrangements of cheetahs, like those of other felids, are largely mediated by indirect methods. Both male and female cheetahs scent-mark and leave their feces in prominent places. When scent-marking, a cheetah raises its tail, backs up to an object, and sprays a small amount of urine. Some observations suggest that males scent-mark more often than females,[41] and like other female cats, female cheetahs urine-mark with increasing frequency as they come into estrus. Both sexes show a great deal of interest in scent marks and frequently sniff stumps, tree trunks, termite mounds, and other elevated landmarks that have been sprayed. In Namibia and Botswana, certain easy-to-climb trees with sloping trunks and horizontal branches are focal scent-marking points in cheetah home ranges. Locally known as "playtrees," these scent-marking stations are used as bait by farmers who want to trap cheetahs. A farmer surrounds a playtree with thorn fencing, leaving an open trap as the only way to reach the tree. Once a cheetah is caught, it is held in a cage inside the fenced area, and its calls attract other cheetahs, which are caught in turn.[67]

Cheetahs have a rich vocal repertoire. They have a yelp, which is a brief, high-pitched "yow" sound with long-range capabilities; one researcher reported that it could be heard for 2 kilometers.[51] When uttering a yelp, the animal opens and closes its mouth rapidly, while its abdomen and head jerk with the effort. The yelp is used as a contact call, most commonly by mothers separated from their cubs or by young that have lost their mother or siblings.[1] Another contact call, the churr, is used by mothers to call or encourage their offspring, by males to relocate their siblings or coalition partners, and in a variety of other situations.[45] The churr or stutter can also indicate estrus when used by a female, while males use the same sound to indicate interest in a female.[68] The cat also gurgles, which is a friendly, close-range vocalization.[69] Cheetahs occasionally growl during agonistic encounters at kills, and they moan when they are attacked or threatened by lions, leopards, or other cheetahs.[43,45,51] After a meal, when resting, or during friendly encounters, these cats also purr.[70,71] The sound is like the purr of a domestic cat, but much louder.

Reproduction and Development

Cheetahs are seasonally polyestrous, and females come into estrus approximately every twelve days (the range is from ten to twenty-one days).[64] In a captive group, the males fought one another to stay close to the female, and one male eventually dominated the others. As the female came into estrus, males increased their urine spraying.[1]

In the wild, males cautiously move toward most unaccompanied females and sometimes approach mothers with cubs. When a male gets close enough, he sniffs the vegetation where the female has been lying and sometimes tries to sniff the female's vulva. When there is a coalition of two or three males they sometimes threaten one another during these encounters with females.[68] Cheetahs have rarely been seen mating, but during one mating at the Beekse Bergen Safari Park in the Netherlands, a male seized a female by the scruff of the neck and held her so that she could not move away. The copulation lasted for about one minute.[72] On another occasion, during a mating observed in the wild, a coalition of males struggled for the chance to mount a female by pushing each other off her with their heads.[73]

Cubs are born after a gestation period of ninety to ninety-five days.[74] Cheetahs have larger litters than most felids, and are unusual in that females have twelve teats, while other large cats have four or six. Litters as large as eight have been recorded, but the average number of cubs is between three and four. In 106 litters from East Africa, litter size varied from one to five, and the average was 3.7.[75] Pienaar reports that the usual litter size in South Africa is two to four, although as many as six cubs have been seen traveling with their mother.[50] Cubs weigh 150–300 grams at birth,[1] and zoo data suggest that captive young may be born slightly heavier than those in the wild. A study of twenty-one cubs born in the Columbus Zoo found a mean weight of 463 grams the morning after birth.[76]

Females give birth in a concealed den, often in long, dense grass or under a thornbush. Access to water may be an important factor in den choice because lactating cheetah mothers significantly increased the time they spent drinking.[77] In the Serengeti, one female was closely watched around the time she gave birth to four cubs. She left the den for less than an hour during the first two days after the birth, and on the third day she was away for only two hours. On the fourth and fifth days she attempted to hunt, but was unsuccessful, and did not eat for at least five days after her cubs were born.[77]

Newborn cubs are blind and helpless. The mother usually keeps them at the birth den for the first ten to fourteen days, then moves them to a new den every five or six days thereafter.[77] Joy Adamson's semi-tame female, Pippa, moved her cubs twenty-six times in six weeks; her longest stay at a single site was twelve days.[78] Similarly, George and Laurie Frame saw a female move her cubs ten times in fifteen days.[17]

Cheetah mothers carry small cubs by the scruff of the neck or sometimes by a leg or tail. Cubs more than a month old seem to be too heavy or awkward to carry, and the mother often puts them down after a short distance and lets them scramble along behind her.[77] After moving her litter, a mother will often revisit the previous den several times to make sure that no young were missed in the move. Mothers who lose litters to predators or in grass fires usually return to the den site to call and search for their cubs. On one occasion a female whose cubs died in a fire stayed near the den site for four days.[77] Females who lose a litter are capable of mating again two or three weeks after parturition.[64,79]

Compared with other cats, young cheetahs develop fairly rapidly. Captive cheetah cubs gain 40 to 50 grams a day.[76] Their eyes open at four to ten days, they are walking well by three weeks, and they can eat meat by five weeks.[80,81] Wild cheetah cubs can go for long periods of time without suckling. In the Serengeti, females with nonmobile cubs hidden at a den spent an average of 9.6 hours away from the den hunting, but this time varied considerably—3.8 to 27.8 hours—from day to day.[77]

Cubs begin to follow their mother at about eight weeks. Large litters seem to leave the den slightly earlier than small litters, probably because their mothers have to travel more widely to find food.[77] Young cubs spend a lot of time running, jumping, patting, biting, crouching, and chasing, playing with each other, their mother, or with objects. Two-month old cubs play most often—about 7.6 percent of the day. After four months of age, cubs play less and less frequently, until by ten months they play for less than 1 percent of the day. Running and dodging play peaks when cubs are two to four months old, the time when predators pose the greatest danger, and it may be that this type of play is useful in developing escape responses to lions and hyenas.[45]

Cubs are weaned at about three and a half months, and though they may continue to try to suckle until they are six months old, they probably do not receive any milk. At six months the cubs are half the size of an adult, and by eight months they have their permanent canines and full adult dentition.[1,45,50,51]

Young cheetahs have an unusual pelage, which consists of a long mantle of silver-gray fur that covers the crown of the head, the nape of the neck, and the back. By contrast, the fur on the flanks and undersides is dark. The mantle is unique to young cheetahs; no other young felid has such long dorsal hair. As the cubs get older, the underparts gradually lighten and the mantle is lost. It disappears first from the rear of the body, leaving a faint spot pattern in the shorter hair. By the time a cub is three to four months old, it has lost the posterior half of its mantle. The mantle continues to recede, and by four months, it is only a ruff of hair on the neck and shoulders. Young cheetahs retain the remnants of the mantle as a mane or crest through adolescence.[51]

Biologists who have spent a great deal of time observing cheetahs in the Serengeti have developed a set of guidelines for estimating the ages of older cubs. At two months, cubs had black manes and were less than one-quarter of their mother's height at the shoulder. By three months of age they still had black manes and were less than a third of their mother's height, while at four months they were more than a third of their mother's height and had fluffy shoulders. By five months they were just under half their mother's height, and at six months, just over half their mother's height.[45,51,82]

Various hypotheses have been advanced to explain the presence of the young cheetah's woolly mantle. It may provide camouflage when the cubs are immobile, or it may have a thermoregulatory function, protecting them from rain and sun. Kingdon has suggested that it may also serve an appeasement function, inhibiting male aggression by resembling the pale underbelly of adults.[1] Others have suggested that the markings and pattern of motion mimic that of the ratel or honey badger, a fierce and aggressive carnivore whose geographic distribution is remarkably similar to that of the cheetah.[2,83] However, the most likely function of this long, woolly coat is simple camouflage. Small cubs are so well disguised by their straw-colored cape of long hair that they are able to elude searching lions by scattering and hiding.[55]

Young cheetahs begin the process of learning to hunt when they are ten to fourteen weeks old. At this time, cheetah mothers begin to bring a few live prey back to the cubs to give them the opportunity to catch it. Young cubs chase the hapless animal, repeatedly knocking it down, but rarely manage to kill it. The mother normally intervenes after a few minutes and dispatches the prey. Later, when the cubs are four and a half to six and a half months old, cheetah mothers release almost a third of the prey they catch to their young, and the cubs continue to practice killing. At this time, the cubs are beginning to learn how to suffocate their prey, and by eight months of age, they are able to hold an animal down and kill it. However, Caro remarks that the hunting skills of young cheetahs remain poor up to and beyond the point at which they separate from their mother, and show surprisingly little improvement in the ten months after their introduction to live prey.[84,85]

Cheetah cubs sometimes alert prey and spoil their mother's hunting attempts by climbing on her or chasing each other while she is stalking. In a Serengeti study, cub play caused 9 percent of mothers' hunting attempts to fail, although the overall effects of play on hunting success were judged to be minimal.[82,86]

Cubs stay with their mother until they are fourteen to eighteen months old. Then, suddenly, over a few days or so, the cubs and mother separate. Siblings often stay together as a group for several months longer. Female siblings are the first to leave the group, but usually remain within their mother's home range. Male siblings often remain together for extended periods of time but, unlike their sisters, do not stay in their natal range.[45]

Several observers have reported that cheetah cubs suffer considerable mortality in the first few months of life,[17,43] but this is an extraordinarily difficult parameter to document because, like other carnivore species, cheetah mothers keep their cubs well hidden for the first six to eight weeks of life. In 1987 Karen Laurenson set out to document cheetah cub mortality, keeping tabs on twenty radio-collared females and following them to the birth den when they had cubs. Once a week, while the mother was away hunting, Laurenson carefully counted cubs and estimated their ages. During the study thirty-six litters were born to seventeen mothers, but of these only three or four litters survived to fourteen months of age.[54]

During the first eight weeks of life, when the cubs remained hidden at the den, 72.3 percent of the litters died. However, the highest mortality rate occurred in the first two weeks after they left the den. Only 51.4 percent of the eight-week-old cubs that emerged from the den were alive two weeks later, and by the time they were four months old, only 27.8 percent of the cubs that had emerged from the den were still alive. Though it was not always possible to determine how cubs died, two-thirds of the cubs in the twelve litters that died at the den of known causes were killed by predators, 16.7 percent died when they were aban-

doned by their mother, and 8.3 percent died in fires or of exposure. Lions were responsible for more than 80 percent of the predator-caused deaths at dens, and in all cases in which lions were the culprit, the entire litter perished. Lions discovered dens by noticing a cheetah mother sitting up when she was with her cubs or seeing a cheetah mother resting near a den. The larger cats actively searched for cubs after they had noticed a cheetah mother, and on finding the litter, killed the cubs by biting them through the skull or spine. Lions rarely ate the cubs they had killed, but the cheetah mother often ate her dead young after the lions had left.[54,87]

Laurenson found that newly mobile cubs were very vulnerable to predators. Spotted hyenas were seen killing all four cubs from one newly mobile litter and a single cub from another litter.[54] However, by the time cubs are four months old, they are able to outrun lions and spotted hyenas.[55] Ultimately, lion predation is by far the most important cause of death for cheetah cubs in the Serengeti. When all phases of the seventeen-month period between birth and independence are combined, predation accounted for 73 percent of cheetah cub deaths, environmental causes for 14 percent, and abandonment and starvation for 8 percent.[54] Cubs have also been lost to leopards, floods, cars, disease, male cheetahs, and village dogs.[41] Almost half of the young male cheetahs that survive to dispersal age die before reaching adulthood, probably in fights with other males.[67,73,88]

Twenty-five years of demographic data from cheetahs in the Serengeti show that cubs stayed with their mother until they were approximately 17.1 months of age. Females gave birth to their first litter at 2.4 years of age, and the interbirth interval was 20.1 months. The average litter size at independence was 2.1 cubs. Reproductive success of cheetahs was lower during years of high lion abundance. On average, females in the Serengeti managed to rear only 1.7 cubs to independence during their lifetimes.[89]

In the Serengeti, young females remained within their natal area after they became independent; their ranges overlapped their mothers' by 61 percent, and their sisters' by 30 to 90 percent.[45] Young males sometimes stayed in their natal area until they were 3 years old or left as a group with their brothers, probably chased away by older territorial males.[45] They dispersed 20 or more kilometers beyond their mother's home range.[90] Elsewhere dispersal distances of 25 to 40 kilometers have been recorded for both sexes.[41]

With very few exceptions, wild-caught cheetahs in zoos live for twelve to sixteen years of age,[91] and one survived to the age of 17,[90] but as with all the felids, longevity in the wild is likely to be much shorter, perhaps half the captive life span. Cheetahs are one of the few felid species for which there are good estimates of longevity for free-ranging animals. In the Serengeti the maximum life span of males was 9.3 years, but the average was 5.3 years. Territorial males did not live significantly longer than nonterritorial males or floaters.[89] During her study of cub mortality, Laurenson estimated that the mean life expectancy for females reaching three years of age was an additional 3.9 years.[88] This estimate has been revised to 6.2 years in the twenty-five-year data set, with the oldest female surviving to 13.5 years.[89]

Cheetahs have a high potential reproductive rate. They give birth to large litters, the young become independent at a relatively early age, and females have been known to breed at two years of age. In areas where cub survival is high, they can more than replace themselves. Indeed, in some South African reserves to which they have been introduced, where they are the only large predator, cheetah populations are expanding. Density estimates from the Suikerbosrand Nature Reserve exceed 22 cheetahs per 100 square kilometers.[92] In areas like the Serengeti, however, where litters suffer astoundingly high rates of predation from lions and hyenas, only 5 percent of cubs born survive to independence. In this case not enough cubs are surviving to replace the adult generation.[88]

While cub mortality rates are high in the Serengeti, the survival rates of cheetah cubs improve markedly where lions and hyenas are absent. In parts of Namibia where cheetahs still survive on farmland but lions and hyenas have been eradicated due to conflicts with livestock, cheetah litter sizes are large—the average size of ten-month-old litters in Namibia was 4.0,[93] nearly double the size of litters from the Serengeti.[52] In the Suikerbosrand Nature Reserve in South Africa, the average litter size was 4.13, and cub mortality was low, at 15 percent of thirty-three marked cubs. However, cubs were not marked until they were at least three months old.[92]

STATUS IN THE WILD

The cheetah is listed on appendix I of CITES and is fully protected over most of its range. However, in 1992, an appendix I annual quota system was estab-lished for Namibia (150), Zimbabwe (50), and Botswana (5).[94]

Cheetahs tend to live at low densities (0.25 to 5.0 per 100 square kilometers) compared with sympatric carnivores such as lions,[45] but their densities are similar to or higher than those of other felid predators such as pumas, tigers, or leopards. Reliable estimates of cheetah numbers exist for only a few portions of the cheetah's range. Burney estimated that there may be 100 cheetahs in the Mara region, representing a subpopulation of the larger Serengeti-Mara-Loita population of perhaps 700.[41] Namibia is believed to have some 2,500 animals.[53,95] A relict population of perhaps 200 Asiatic cheetahs is thought to survive in Iran,[33,34,96] with perhaps 300 to 500 in Africa north of the Sahara, in Mali, Niger, and Chad.[40] Surveys in 1989 in Malawi showed that some 15 to 30 cheetahs were resident in the Kasungu National Park, but there was little sign of reproduction.[97] Preliminary results indicate that cheetah populations once considered "relatively undisturbed" are now being affected by the settlement of previously nomadic people in remote dry areas in Kenya and Uganda.[98]

Threatened throughout its range by habitat loss and declining prey numbers, the cheetah presents an extraordinary challenge to conservationists. Free-ranging cheetahs living outside protected areas are often viewed as a threat by farmers, and inside protected areas these cats suffer high cub mortality due to larger predators. Throughout South Africa, prime cheetah habitat overlaps with privately owned land used for livestock grazing. Namibia has the largest cheetah population in all of Africa, with an estimated two to three thousand animals, but this represents less than half the number present a decade earlier. Ninety-five percent of these cheetahs live on farmland outside protected areas, in direct competition with farmers and game ranchers. Ranchers routinely shoot and trap cheetahs on their property because they believe the cats are a menace to their livestock. Cheetahs do kill livestock, particularly sheep and calves, and there are instances of cheetahs killing forty or fifty sheep in a week. Ranchers estimated that cheetahs were killing thirty to forty calves per cat per year, but Dieter Morsbach, who studied cheetahs on the private farmlands of southwestern Namibia, found that many calves were lost to other causes, such as accidents, miscarriages, and predation by jackals and caracals. Cheetahs were killing four to six calves per year, many fewer than estimated by ranchers.[53] In Namibia, cheetah numbers decreased by at least 6,782 animals between 1980 and 1991; 5,860 were killed and 922 were exported.[95]

Recent studies in the Serengeti show that juvenile mortality can be as high as 95 percent, much of it caused by lions and hyenas.[54,87] Cheetahs are able to persist in this environment by seeking out areas where lion and hyena densities are low, thus avoiding competition.[99] As lion and hyena populations are known to have increased in many protected areas, it may be that cheetahs will survive better outside national parks and reserves. Areas where prey species are not too heavily hunted and where pastoralists tolerate cheetahs may offer the best long-term hope for the species.[45,64]

STATUS IN CAPTIVITY

Cheetahs do not breed well in captivity, and captive populations are not self-sustaining.[91] Despite intensive management and extensive research into the reproductive genetics and physiology of captive animals, cheetahs still have problems conceiving in captivity. Early studies suggested that the problems lay with the cheetahs' genetics and physiology, as scientists found that the species had low testosterone levels, extremely low sperm counts, a high degree of sperm abnormalities, and ten to a hundred times less variation in its intrinsic genetic material than is normally found in other cat species.[100,101,102] But blood and semen samples showed that these problems were common to both wild and captive cheetahs, and wild cheetahs did not seem to have any problem conceiving: 95 percent of females in a study in the Serengeti reproduced.[64] In addition, captive cheetahs that bred and captive cheetahs that had never bred shared the low testosterone and low sperm count characteristics. In other words, wild cheetahs and some captive cheetahs seemed to have no problem conceiving despite their physiological and genetic problems, but most captive cheetahs do not reproduce. In 1991 less than 20 percent of captive cheetahs in North America had bred.[95] Biologists now believe that the answer to the cheetah's failure to breed in captivity will be found through behavioral research.[68] Ongoing studies are currently looking at captive conditions and husbandry practices at the few institutions where cheetahs have been bred successfully.[45,68]

Captive management and breeding success has improved since 1986, but most of the breeding has occurred at only a few institutions. Over 100 litters have been born at Whipsnade Zoological Park in England,[45] and at the De Wildt Breeding Center in South Africa, 102 cubs were born between 1987 and 1991. In North America, four institutions—the Columbus Zoo (Ohio), Fossil Rim Ranch (Texas), San Diego Wild Animal Park (California), and White Oak Plantation (Florida)—produced 71 percent of the cubs born from 1987 to 1991.[95] Despite these successes, the captive cheetah population is still not self-sustaining. Cub mortality remains high; 33.9 percent of 1,046 cubs born between 1978 and 1988 did not survive to six months of age.[95,103] However, unlike juvenile mortality in the wild, which stems largely from predation,[87] cub deaths in captivity were due to infections, stillbirths, cannibalism, congenital defects, hypothermia, maternal neglect, and unknown causes.[87,95]

CONSERVATION EFFORTS

The lack of success at breeding captive cheetahs has prompted intensive research into reproductive physiology, assisted reproduction, genetics, disease, and nutrition. This research is now beginning to pay dividends. September 1991 marked the first cheetah birth by artificial insemination,[104] and by the end of 1992, three litters consisting of seven cubs were born via the technique.[105] A North American and an international cheetah studbook have been in existence for some time, and captive breeding success is improving. In 1993 the Cheetah Species Survival Plan announced that the North American cheetah population was no longer in demographic crisis.[106]

In 1990 Laurie Marker-Kraus and Daniel Kraus established the Cheetah Conservation Fund in Namibia. Working with local government ministries, farm associations, conservation groups, and tribal councils, the Cheetah Conservation Fund runs an extensive public awareness campaign and conducts educational assembly programs at schools throughout Namibia.[107,108]

In Namibia, 95 percent of the country's 2,500 wild cheetahs live on farmland, and as wildlife belongs to the landowner, farming practices and the attitudes of private landowners are critical to the cheetahs' survival. Working with farmers and ranchers, the Cheetah Conservation Fund is compiling information on cheetah distribution, ranch owners' attitudes, and livestock predation problems.[109] The survey has found that farmers who have more wildlife prey species on their land lose fewer livestock to cheetah predation, and has highlighted the few ranchers who have come up with alternative solutions to the commonly used preventative eradication of predators. One farmer has reduced his losses to almost zero by keeping domestic donkeys with his calving herd. The more aggressive donkeys chase away jackals and drive off any cheetah that attempts to attack.[67] The Cheetah Conservation Fund is also investigating the use of guard dogs to protect livestock, and four Anatolian shepherd guard dogs were brought in from North America. Another six Anatolian shepherds were later donated by a private breeder in North America and placed with collaborating farmers.[110,111]

Though translocation or reintroduction of predators is a complicated and difficult exercise, cheetahs do appear to be one of the better felid candidates for these techniques. They are tolerant of a wide range of environmental conditions and do not pose a threat to humans.[112,113] With protection and sufficient prey they can survive well in arid marginal lands, even alongside nomadic pastoralists.[40] However, a reintroduction of two captive-bred and raised cheetahs into the Mthethomusha Game Reserve in South Africa was a disaster. Both animals were inexperienced at capturing prey. One was killed by hyenas two weeks post-release, and the other was recaptured in poor condition three weeks after release.[114]

Southern Africa has been the site of several cheetah translocation projects, as wildlife authorities are often called upon to trap and remove predators such as leopards and cheetahs from private ranches. In most of these cases the cheetahs have been translocated to habitats where lions or spotted hyenas are absent. Under these circumstances, cheetah cub survival has been high, and numbers have risen rapidly, sometimes causing a corresponding decline in prey species.[45,92,115]

In Zimbabwe, the Department of National Parks and Wildlife Management began a cheetah relocation program in response to ranchers who wanted cheetahs removed from their land. In 1993 four cheetahs were moved to an enclosure in Matusadona National Park, where they were held for six to eight weeks, then released. Eleven other cheetahs were later moved, held in the enclosure for a while, and released into the park. All appear to have adapted to their new surroundings, though one was later shot in a farming area adjoining the park.[116] The program is nevertheless promising.

TABLE 1 MEASUREMENTS AND WEIGHTS OF ADULT CHEETAHS

HB	n	T	n	WT	n	Location	Source
1,320	1m	660	1m	61 (58–65)	4m	East Africa	51
1,180	1f	730	1f	41, 63	2f	East Africa	51
1,228 (1,190–1,310)	7m	744 (600–840)	7m	55 (50–62)	4m	Southern Africa	51
				57	1f	Southern Africa	51
		717 (650–760)	7m	53.9 (39–59)	7m	South West Africa/Namibia	10
		667 (630–690)	6f	43.0 (36–48)	6f	South West Africa/Namibia	10
1,225 (1,130–1,360)	24m	681 (630–740)	24m	41.4 (28.5–51.0)	23m	Serengeti	45
1,245 (1,130–1,400)	16f	655 (595–730)	19f	35.9 (21–43)	19f	Serengeti	45

Note: HB = head and body length (mm), T = tail length (mm), WT = weight (kg). n = sample size. Sex: m = male, f = female, ? = unknown. Mean values are presented only for sample sizes of three or more. Range of values is in parentheses.

Prey item	Nairobi NP[51] Kills (n = 183)	Serengeti NP[45] Kills (n = 424)	Kalahari[49] Kills (n = 229)	Kruger NP[50] Kills (n = 2,532)
Gazella thomsoni Thomson's gazelle	21.9	65.8		
Gazella granti Grant's gazelle	24.6	4.0		
Aepyceros melampus Impala	27.4	32.3		68.0
Lepus capensis Cape hare	1.6	18.4		
Connochaetes taurinus Wildebeest		9.0	3.5	5.0
Alcelaphus buselaphus Hartebeest	12.0	0.2	1.7	
Equus burchelli Burchell's zebra	0.6	0.2		1.8
Antidorcas marsupialis Springbok			86.9	
Raphicerus campestris Steenbok	2.2		0.9	
Struthio camelus Ostrich			3.5	
Damaliscus korrigum Topi		0.2		
Kobus defassa Waterbuck	1.6			6.7
Phacochoerus aethiopicus Warthog	2.2	0.5		0.6
Tragelaphus strepsiceros Greater kudu				6.8
Tragelaphus scriptus Bushbuck	1.7			1.1
Hippotragus equinus Roan antelope				0.1
Cephalophus sp. Duiker				2.6
Ardeotis kori Kori bustard		0.2		
Cryptomys sp. Mole-rat		0.2		
Redunca redunca Reedbuck	3.8	0.5		5.3
Oryx gazella Gemsbok			2.6	
Syncerus caffer African buffalo				0.1
Giraffa camelopardalis Giraffe				0.2
Taurotragus oryx Eland		0.2		0.1

(continued)

TABLE 2 *(continued)*

Prey item	Nairobi NP[51] Kills (n = 183)	Serengeti NP[45] Kills (n = 424)	Kalahari[49] Kills (n = 229)	Kruger NP[50] Kills (n = 2,532)
Hippotragus niger Sable antelope				0.3
Damaliscus lunatus Tsessebe				0.7
Madoqua kirki Dik-dik	0.6	0.2		
Otocyon megalotis Bat-eared fox			0.9	

REFERENCES

1. Kingdon, J. 1977. *East African mammals.* Vol. 3, part A (Carnivores). Chicago: University of Chicago Press.

2. Guggisberg, C. A. W. 1975. *Wild cats of the world.* New York: Taplinger.

3. Wrogemann, N. 1975. *Cheetah under the sun.* New York: McGraw-Hill.

4. Heptner, V. G., and A. A. Sludskii. 1992. *Mammals of the Soviet Union.* Vol. 2, part 2, *Carnivora (Hyaenas and cats).* English translation, sci. ed. R. S. Hoffmann. Washington, DC: Smithsonian Institution Libraries and the National Science Foundation.

5. Divyabhanusinh. 1995. *The end of a trail.* Bombay: Banyan Books.

6. Klingender, F. 1971. *Animals in art and thought to the end of the Middle Ages.* Cambridge, MA: MIT Press.

7. Jerdon, T. C. 1867. *The mammals of India: A natural history of all the animals known to inhabit Continental India.* Roorkee, India: Thomason College Press.

8. Pocock, R. I. 1939. *The fauna of British India, including Ceylon and Burma.* Vol. 1, *Mammalia.* London: Taylor and Francis.

9. Sterndale, R. A. 1884. *Natural history of the Mammalia of India and Ceylon.* Calcutta: Thacker, Spink, and Co.

10. Smithers, R. H. N. 1983. *The mammals of the southern African subregion.* Pretoria: University of Pretoria.

11. Rosevear, D. R. 1974. *The carnivores of West Africa.* London: Trustees of the British Museum (Natural History).

12. Adams, D. B. 1979. The cheetah: Native American. *Science* 205: 1155–1158.

13. O'Brien, S. J., G. E. Collier, R. E. Benveniste, W. G. Nash, A. K. Newman, J. M. Simonson, M. A. Eichelberger, U. S. Seal, D. Janssen, M. Bush, and D. E. Wildt. 1987. Setting the molecular clock in Felidae: The great cats, *Panthera.* In *Tigers of the world: The biology, biopolitics, management, and conservation of an endangered species,* ed. R. L. Tilson and U. S. Seal, 10–27. Park Ridge, NJ: Noyes Publications.

14. Janczewski, D. N., W. S. Modi, J. C. Stephens, and S. J. O'Brien. 1995. Molecular evolution of mitochondrial 12s RNA and cytochrome *b* sequences in the pantherine lineage of Felidae. *Mol. Biol. Evol.* 12: 690–707.

15. Varaday, D. 1964. *Gara-Yaka: The story of a cheetah.* New York: E. P. Dutton.

16. Bertram, B. C. R. 1978. *Pride of lions.* London: Dent.

17. Frame, G. W., and L. Frame. 1981. *Swift and enduring: Cheetahs and wild dogs of the Serengeti.* New York: E. P. Dutton.

18. Caro, T. M., and S. M. Durant. 1991. Use of quantitative analyses of pelage characteristics to reveal family resemblances in genetically monomorphic cheetahs. *J. Hered.* 82: 8–14.

19. Bottriell, L. 1987. *King cheetah.* Leiden: E. J. Brill.

20. Lindburg, D. 1989. When cheetahs are kings. *Zoonooz* 62: 5–10.

21. Ewer, R. F. 1973. *The carnivores.* Ithaca, NY: Cornell University Press.

22. Gambaryan, P. P. 1974. *How mammals run: Anatomical adaptations.* New York: John Wiley and Sons.

23. Gonyea, W. J. 1878. Functional implications of felid forelimb anatomy. *Acta Anat.* 102: 111–121.

24. Taylor, M. E. 1989. Locomotor adaptations by carnivores. In *Carnivore behavior, ecology, and evolution,* ed. J. L. Gittleman, 382–408. Ithaca, NY: Cornell University Press.

25. Alexander, R. M. 1993. Legs and locomotion of Carnivora. *Symp. Zool. Soc. Lond.* 65: 1–13.

26. Hildebrand, M. 1959. Motions of the running cheetah and horse. *J. Mammal.* 40: 481–485.

27. Hildebrand, M. 1961. Further studies on locomotion of the cheetah. *J. Mammal.* 42: 84–91.

28. Taylor, R. C., and V. J. Rowntree. 1973. Temperature regulation and heat balance in running cheetahs: A strategy for sprinters? *Am. J. Physiol.* 224: 848–854.

29. Prater, S. H. 1971. *The book of Indian animals,* 3rd ed. Bombay: Bombay Natural History Society.

30. Roberts, T. J. 1977. *The mammals of Pakistan.* London: Ernest Benn Limited.

31. Gasperetti, J., D. L. Harrison, and W. Büttiker. 1985. The carnivora of Arabia. In *Fauna of Saudi Arabia,* vol. 7, ed. W. Büttiker and F. Krupp, 397–461. Basle: Pro Entomologia, c/o Natural History Museum.

32. Harrison, D. L., and P. J. J. Bates. 1991. *The mammals of Arabia,* 2nd ed. Sevenoaks, Kent, England: Harrison Zoological Museum.

33. Harrington, F. A. Jr., ed. 1977. *A guide to the mammals of Iran.* Tehran: Department of the Environment.

34. Mowlavi, M. 1985. Cheetah in Iran. *Cat News* 2: 7.

35. Karami, M. 1992. Cheetah distribution in Khorasan Province, Iran. *Cat News* 16: 4.

36. Myers, N. 1975. *The cheetah Acinonyx jubatus in Africa.* IUCN Monograph No. 4. Morges, Switzerland: International Union for Conservation of Nature and Natural Resources (IUCN).

37. Stuart, C. T., and V. J. Wilson. 1988. *The cats of southern Africa.* Bulawayo, Zimbabwe: The Chipangali Wildlife Trust.

38. Hufnagl, E. 1972. *Libyan mammals*. Stoughton, WI: Oleander Press.

39. Kowalski, K., and B. Rzebik-Kowalska. 1991. *Mammals of Algeria*. Warsaw: Polish Academy of Sciences.

40. Dragesco-Joffé, A. 1993. *La vie sauvage au Sahara*. Lausanne, Switzerland: Delachaux et Niestlé.

41. Burney, D. A. 1980. The effects of human activities on cheetahs (*Acinonyx jubatus* Schr.) in the Mara region of Kenya. Master's thesis, University of Nairobi.

42. Frame, G. W. 1986. Carnivore competition and resource use in the Serengeti ecosystem of Tanzania. Ph.D. dissertation, Utah State University, Logan.

43. Schaller, G. B. 1972. *The Serengeti lion*. Chicago: University of Chicago Press.

44. Stander, P. 1990. Notes on the foraging habits of cheetah. *S. Afr. J. Wildl. Res.* 20: 130–132.

45. Caro, T. M. 1994. *Cheetahs of the Serengeti plains*. Chicago: University of Chicago Press.

46. FitzGibbon, C. D. 1989. A cost to individuals with reduced vigilance in groups of Thomson's gazelles hunted by cheetahs. *Anim. Behav.* 37: 508–510.

47. FitzGibbon, C. D., and J. H. Fanshawe. 1988. Stotting in Thomson's gazelles: An honest signal of condition. *Behav. Ecol. Sociobiol.* 23: 69–74.

48. Estes, R. D. 1991. *The behavior guide to African mammals*. Berkeley: University of California Press.

49. Mills, M. G. L. 1984. Prey selection and feeding habits of large carnivores in the southern Kalahari. *Koedoe*, suppl. 27: 281–294.

50. Pienaar, U. de V. 1969. Predator-prey relationships amongst the larger mammals of the Kruger National Park. *Koedoe* 12: 108–176.

51. McLaughlin, R. 1970. Aspects of the biology of cheetahs *Acinonyx jubatus* (Schreber) in Nairobi National Park. Master's thesis, University of Nairobi, Nairobi.

52. FitzGibbon, C. D., and J. H. Fanshawe. 1989. The condition and age of Thomson's gazelles killed by cheetahs and wild dogs. *J. Zool.* 218: 99–107.

53. Morsback, D. 1987. Cheetah in Namibia. *Cat News* 6: 25–26.

54. Laurenson, M. K. 1994. High juvenile mortality in cheetahs (*Acinonyx jubatus*) and its consequences for maternal care. *J. Zool.* 234: 387–408.

55. Caro, T. M. 1987. Cheetah mothers' vigilance: Looking out for prey or predators? *Behav. Ecol. Sociobiol.* 20: 351–361.

56. Phillips, J. A. 1993. Bone consumption by cheetahs at undisturbed kills: Evidence for a lack of focal-palatine erosion. *J. Mammal.* 74: 487–492.

57. Caro, T. M. 1982. A record of cheetah scavenging in the Serengeti. *Afr. J. Ecol.* 20: 213–214.

58. Houston, D. C. 1974. Food searching behavior in griffon vultures. *E. Afr. Wildl. J.* 12: 63–77.

59. O'Brien, S. J., D. E. Wildt, and M. Bush. 1986. The cheetah in genetic peril. *Sci. Am.* 254: 84–92.

60. Frame, G. W., and L. H. Frame. 1977. Serengeti cheetah. *Wildlife News* 12: 2–6.

61. Mills, M. G. L., and H. C. Biggs. 1993. Prey apportionment and related ecological relationships between large carnivores in Kruger National Park. *Symp. Zool. Soc. Lond.* 65: 253–268.

62. Durant, S. M., T. M. Caro, D. A. Collins, R. M. Alawi, and C. D. FitzGibbon. 1988. Migration patterns of Thomson's gazelles and cheetahs on the Serengeti Plains. *Afr. J. Ecol.* 26: 257–268.

63. Caro, T. M., and D. A. Collins. 1986. Male cheetahs of the Serengeti. *Natl. Geogr. Res.* 2: 75–86.

64. Laurenson, M. K., T. Caro, and M. Borner. 1992. Female cheetah reproduction. *Natl. Geogr. Res.* 8: 64–75.

65. Mills, M. G. L. 1990. The lion (*Panthera leo*) and cheetah (*Acinonyx jubatus*) in Kruger National Park, South Africa. *Felid* 4(1): 13.

66. Borner, M., C. D. FitzGibbon, M. Borner, T. M. Caro, W. K. Lindsay, D. A. Collins, and M. E. Holt. 1987. The decline in the Serengeti Thomson's gazelle population. *Oecologia* 73: 32–40.

67. Marker-Kraus, L., and D. Kraus. 1993. The history of cheetah in Namibia. *Swara* 16(5): 8–12.

68. Caro, T. M. 1993. Behavioral solutions to breeding cheetahs in captivity: Insights from the wild. *Zoo Biol.* 12: 19–30.

69. Peters, G. 1984. On the structure of friendly close range vocalizations in terrestrial carnivores (Mammalia: Carnivora: Fissipedia). *Z. Säugetierk.* 49: 157–182.

70. Peters, G. 1981. Das schnurren der katzen (Felidae). *Säugetierk. Mitt.* 29: 30–37.

71. Peters, G., and M. H. Hast. 1994. Hyoid structure, laryngeal anatomy, and vocalizations in felids (Mammalia: Carnivora: Felidae). *Z. Säugetierk.* 59: 87–104.

72. Tong, J. R. 1974. Breeding cheetah at the Berkse Bergen Safari Park. *Int. Zoo Yrbk.* 14: 129–130.

73. Caro, T. M., and D. A. Collins. 1987. Ecological characteristics of territories of male cheetahs (*Acinonyx jubatus*). *J. Zool.* 211: 89–105.

74. Eaton, R. E. 1974. *The cheetah: Biology, ecology and behavior of an endangered species*. New York: Van Nostrand Reinhold.

75. Graham, A. D., and I. S. C. Parker. 1965. East African Wildlife Society Cheetah Survey. Report by Wildlife Services. East African Wildlife Society, Nairobi.

76. Wack, R. F., L. W. Kramer, W. Cupps, and P. Currie. 1991. Growth rate of 21 captive-born, mother-raised cheetah cubs. *Zoo Biol.* 10: 273–376.

77. Laurenson, M. K. 1993. Early maternal behavior of wild cheetahs: Implications for captive husbandry. *Zoo Biol.* 12: 31–43.

78. Adamson, J. 1966. Pippa returns to freedom in the bush. *Das Tier* 6(12): 4–7.

79. Thomas, W. D. 1965. Observations on a pair of cheetahs at Oklahoma Zoo. *Int. Zoo Yrbk.* 5: 114–116.

80. Florio, P. L., and L. Spinelli. 1968. Second successful breeding of cheetahs in a private zoo. *Int. Zoo Yrbk.* 8: 76–78.

81. Manton, V. J. A. 1971. A further report on breeding cheetahs at Whipsnade Park. *Int. Zoo Yrbk.* 11: 125–126.

82. Caro, T. M. 1995. Short-term costs and correlates of play in cheetahs. *Anim. Behav.* 49: 333–345.

83. Eaton, R. L. 1977. Mimicry in African carnivores. In *Proceedings of the 1975 predator symposium*, ed. R. L. Phillips and C. Jonkel, 183–190. Missoula: Montana Forest and Conservation Experiment Station, University of Montana.

84. Caro, T. M., and M. D. Hauser. 1992. Is there teaching in nonhuman animals? *Q. Rev. Biol.* 67: 151–174.

85. Kruuk, H., and M. Turner. 1967. Comparative notes on predation by lion, leopard, cheetah and wild dog in the Serengeti area, East Africa. *Mammalia* 31: 1–27.

86. Caro, T. M. 1987. Indirect costs of play: Cheetah cubs reduce maternal hunting success. *Anim. Behav.* 35: 295–297.

87. Laurenson, M. K., N. Wielebnowski, and T. M. Caro. 1995. Extrinsic factors and juvenile mortality in cheetahs. *Conserv. Biol.* 9: 1329–1331.

88. Laurenson, M. K. 1995. Implications of high offspring mortality for cheetah population dynamics. In *Serengeti II: Dynamics, management, and conservation of an ecosystem,* ed. A. R. E. Sinclair and P. Arcese, 385–399. Chicago: University of Chicago Press.

89. Kelly, M. J., M. K. Laurenson, C. D. FitzGibbon, D. A. Collins, S. M. Durant, G. W. Frame, B. C. R. Bertram, and T. M. Caro. 1998. Demography of the Serengeti cheetah (*Acinonyx jubatus*) population: The first 25 years. *J. Zool.* (Lond.) 244: 473–488.

90. Frame, G. W. 1984. Cheetah. In *The encyclopedia of mammals,* ed. D. W. Macdonald, 40–43. New York: Facts on File Publications.

91. Marker, L., and S. J. O'Brien. 1989. Captive breeding of the cheetah (*Acinonyx jubatus*) in North American zoos (1871–1986). *Zoo Biol.* 8: 3–16.

92. Pettifer, H. L. 1981. Aspects of the ecology of cheetahs (*Acinonyx jubatus*) on the Suikerbosrand Nature Reserve. In Worldwide furbearer conference proceedings: August 3–11, 1980, Frostburg, Maryland, ed. J. A. Chapman and D. Pursley, 1121–1142.

93. McVittie, R. 1979. Changes in the social behavior of South West African cheetah. *Madoqua* 11: 171–184.

94. Nowell, K., and P. Jackson. 1996. *Wild cats: A status survey and conservation action plan.* Gland, Switzerland: International Union for Conservation of Nature and Natural Resources (IUCN).

95. Marker, L., and J. Grisham. 1993. Captive breeding of cheetahs in North American zoos: 1987–1991. *Zoo Biol.* 12: 5–18.

96. Jackson, P. 1990. Cheetah surviving in Iran. *Cat News* 13: 13.

97. Gros, P. 1996. Status of the cheetah in Malawi. *Nyala* 19: 33–38.

98. Gros, P. 1991. Worldwide survey of the status of cheetahs living in the wild. *Cheetah News* 3(1): 7.

99. Durant, S. M. 1998. Competition refuges and coexistence: An example from Serengeti carnivores. *J. Anim. Ecol.* 67: 370–386.

100. O'Brien, S. J., M. E. Roelke, L. Marker, A. Newman, C. A. Winkler, D. Meltzer, L. Colly, J. F. Evermann, M. Bush, and D. E. Wildt. 1985. Genetic basis for species vulnerability in the cheetah. *Science* 227: 1428–1434.

101. Wildt, D. E., J. L. Brown, M. Bush, M. A. Barone, K. A. Cooper, J. Grisham, and J. G. Howard. 1993. Reproductive status of cheetahs (*Acinonyx jubatus*) in North American zoos: The benefits of physiological surveys for strategic planning. *Zoo Biol.* 12: 45–80.

102. Merola, M. 1994. A reassessment of homozygosity and the case for inbreeding depression in the cheetah, *Acinonyx jubatus:* Implications for conservation. *Conserv. Biol.* 8: 961–971.

103. Marker-Kraus, L. 1988. International cheetah (*Acinonyx jubatus*) studbook. Washington, DC: NOAHS Center, National Zoological Park, Smithsonian Institution.

104. Howard, J. G., A. M. Donoghue, M. A. Barone, K. L. Goodrowe, E. S. Blumer, K. Snodgrass, D. Starnes, M. Tucker, M. Bush, and D. E. Wildt. 1992. Successful induction of ovarian activity and laparoscopic intrauterine artificial insemination in the cheetah (*Acinonyx jubatus*). *J. Zoo Wildl. Med.* 23: 288–300.

105. Wells, S. 1992. National Zoo expands work with cheetahs at new facility. *Cheetah News* 4(2): 8–9.

106. Grisham, J. 1995. Cheetah master plan. *Cheetah News* 5(1): 2.

107. CCF Education Program. 1994. *Cheetah Conservation Fund Newsletter* 1: 4.

108. Marker-Kraus, L., and D. Kraus. 1995. Cheetah conservation fund. *Cheetah News* 5(1): 3.

109. Marker-Kraus, L., D. Kraus, D. Barnett, and S. Hurlbut. 1996. *Cheetah survival on Namibian farmlands.* Windhoek, Namibia: Cheetah Conservation Fund.

110. Sartini, B. 1994. Guard dog project. *Cheetah Conservation Fund Newsletter* 1(4): 1–2.

111. Marker-Kraus, L., and D. Kraus. 1994. A CCF note. *Cheetah Conservation Fund Newsletter* 1(4): 2.

112. Stanley-Price, M. R. 1989. *Animal re-introductions: The Arabian oryx in Oman.* Cambridge: Cambridge University Press.

113. Yalden, D. W. 1993. The problems of reintroducing carnivores. *Symp. Zool. Soc. Lond.* 65: 289–306.

114. Cat News. 1995. A disastrous cheetah re-introduction in South Africa. *Cat News* 23: 16–17.

115. Adamson, J. 1969. *The spotted sphinx.* London: Collins.

116. Atkinson, M. W., and P. Wood. 1995. The reintroduction of the cheetah into the Matusadona National Parks, Zimbabwe. *Reintroduction News* 10: 7–8.

Caracal

Caracal caracal (Schreber, 1776)

The caracal is known for its extraordinary ability to capture birds by leaping 2 meters or more into the air from a standing start. Until quite recently, Indian princes and potentates kept tame caracals for hunting hares and other small game. In 1923 Colonel A. E. Ward wrote, "Long ago a Punjab Zemindar had a small pack of caracals with which he used to hunt hares, and provided there were not too many bushes the results were good but the hares seemed to be quicker at turning and often got away in spite of the extreme agility of the Caracals."[1] During his travels in Kashmir, G. T. Vigne watched tame cheetahs and caracals hunting, and wrote, "The speed of the caracal, or Indian lynx, is, if possible, quicker in proportion than that of the chita. I saw one slipped at a grey fox, and he ran into him as a dog would at a rat. He often catches crows as they rise from the ground, by springing five or six feet into the air after them."[2] Tame caracals were also pitted against one another in pigeon-catching contests, in which the cats were released into a flock of feeding pigeons while bets were made as to which one would bring down the largest number of birds. A skillful caracal could knock down nearly a dozen birds before the remainder of the flock escaped. This contest was almost certainly where the expression "to put the cat among the pigeons" originated.[3]

The caracal is sometimes known as the lynx or caracal lynx, but the two species are quite different in many ways, the most obvious being fur coloration. The caracal has a plain, unmarked coat, while lynx are spotted, blotched, or barred. The geographic ranges of lynx and caracal overlap near the Caspian Sea, where the local Turkish name for the caracal is *garah gulak*, meaning "black ear," a reference to the caracal's characteristic black-backed ears. The English word *caracal* is thought to have been derived from the Turkish. In Africa the caracal is also called red cat, rooicat, red lynx, and African lynx.[4] In Ladakh it is called *Ech*,[1] and in Hindi and Persian, *siyeh gush*.[5] According to Dragesco-Joffé, the caracal is known as *ngam ouidenanga*, or "gazelle cat," in parts of Niger because of its reputation for hunting Dorcas gazelles.[6]

The historical range of the caracal mirrors that of the cheetah, and both coincide with the distribution of several small desert gazelles. In many parts of the caracal's present range, these 15- to 30-kilogram gazelles have either disappeared or are under intense pressure. Populations of blackbuck and chinkara in India and Pakistan, goitered gazelles in the former Soviet Union, and Dorcas gazelles in North Africa have all declined markedly over the past hundred years. In many regions these gazelles have been replaced by domestic sheep and goats, which to the caracal represent a perfect alternative food. Though caracals seem to be able to survive well on hare- and hyrax-sized prey, they are clearly "gazelle cats," as the nomads of North Africa have always called them.

DESCRIPTION

The caracal is a slender, long-legged cat of medium size (8–20 kg). When standing, a caracal appears taller at the rump than at the shoulders because its hind legs are somewhat longer than its forelegs. The powerfully built hindquarters enable this cat to make spectacular leaps, sprint short distances at high speed, and climb well when it needs to.[3,7,8,9] The tail is relatively short, about 36 percent of head and body length, and extends only to the animal's hocks.[9,10] The undersides of the caracal's feet look hairy because of the abundant stiff hairs growing from between the pads. These hairs are more obvious in caracals that live in sandy habitats and probably represent an adaptation for moving through soft sand.[9] Female caracals are lighter than males and smaller in most body dimensions. The broad, blunt face is topped with a pair of tall, triangular ears, each decorated with a long black tuft of hair. In older animals the tufts hang down like tassels.[11]

The black-backed, tufted ears are highly conspicuous against the caracal's otherwise plain coat. The back and sides are generally a uniform tawny gray or a reddish, frosted-sand color. The belly and the undersides of the legs and chest are whitish and spotted or blotched with pale red markings that vary from faint to distinct in different individuals. Black caracals have been recorded, and once again, the backs of the ears, which are covered with silver-gray hairs, provide the only contrast to a unicolored coat.[3,5,8,10,11,12] Though it is less strikingly marked than many other cats, the caracal does have distinctive facial markings. A dark line runs down the center of the forehead to near the nose, and another runs from the inner edges of the eyes to the nostrils. There are white patches above and below the eyes and on either side of the nose.

Cats are often said to have stern, aloof expressions or cruel, fierce eyes, and this description may fit the caracal better than most felids. In strong light the caracal's upper eyelid seems to cover the top half of its eye, giving it a narrow-eyed appearance that could be anthropomorphically described as cruel. However, the lowered upper eyelid is probably a protective adaptation against the sun's glare rather than a reflection of the caracal's fierce nature.[11]

The overall impression given by the caracal is of robust strength and power. Though not quite as tall as the serval, the caracal is much more sturdily built. The skull is high and rounded. The jaw is short, stoutly built, and equipped with large, powerful teeth. The second upper premolar is usually absent. In a study of 100 adult skulls, the second premolar was present in only eight.[9,13]

The caracal was originally thought to be closely related to the lynx group and was, at one time, known as the caracal lynx. Later studies separated the caracal from the lynxes, placing it closer to the domestic cat (*Felis*) lineage.[13,14] More recent molecular studies of DNA sequences and new multivariate analyses of skull and dental measurements have led to the conclusion that the caracal does not comfortably fall within either the *Felis* or the *Lynx* group. It is most closely related to the African golden cat.[15,16,17] Hence it is now classified as *Caracal caracal*, the only member of the genus.[18]

DISTRIBUTION

The caracal has a wide geographic range extending from North Africa and Turkey through the Arabian Peninsula and the Middle East to Turkmenistan and southeast to central India. It is found throughout Africa except the deserts of the Sahara and Namib and the dense forests of equatorial West Africa and the Democratic Republic of the Congo (formerly Zaire). The caracal is sparsely distributed over much of its range and is considered rare in many areas. In the Cape Province of South Africa, however, caracals are so numerous that they are regarded as problem animals and are hunted intensely (fig. 11).[7,12,19,20,21,22,23,24,25,26,27,28,29,30,31,32,33,34,35,36]

ECOLOGY AND BEHAVIOR

Unlike many other cats, caracals favor open country, and they can tolerate much drier conditions than the serval. In Niger caracals live in the semiarid regions around mountain massifs; in Israel they seem to prefer hilly terrain with acacia and grasses. In Pakistan they inhabit arid subtropical scrub forest and tropical thorn forest. East of the Caspian Sea, in a portion of the former Soviet Union known as Turkmenistan, these cats live in black saxul forest, desert foothills, and reed thickets associated with large rivers. While caracals have been seen in open grasslands at night, they seem to require some form of cover, such as trees, bushes, or

Figure 11. Distribution of the caracal.

rocks, and they do not live in true desert. They often seem to be associated with edge habitats, where forest and grassland meet.[6,8,9,10,11,37]

Two radio-tagged caracals in the Stellenbosch mountains of the Cape Province were most often located in scrub pine and riverine habitats at elevations below 600 meters; they were also radio-tracked to exotic pine plantations.[38] Radio-tagged caracals in Israel's Aravah Valley showed a preference for savanna habitats near human settlements and farming areas, especially where these areas were associated with streams, fishponds, or other water sources.[37]

Caracals share some of their habitats with, and occasionally fall prey to, larger predators such as lions, leopards, and hyenas. At a vulture feeding station in Israel, a caracal feeding on a donkey carcass was observed to chase off two subadult hyenas, one of which weighed twice as much as the cat.[39] Pienaar records an occasion in Kruger National Park when "the head of one of these spirited animals (caracal) was found near the Tsende picket, where it apparently disputed the carcass of a waterbuck calf with seven lions."[40] Caracals also share many habitats with jackals, and the latter appear to be superior competitors. Large-scale programs to reduce jackal populations have been carried out in parts of South Africa and Israel. In both areas, jackal control programs were followed by increases in prey populations and caracal numbers.[12,41,42]

Caracals hunt mainly at night and mainly on the ground, but they climb well and seem to be perfectly at home in the trees. They may be more active during the daytime in undisturbed areas.[10] In Israel, radio-tagged caracals were active from dusk to dawn, although there were seasonal changes in the amount of daytime activity, depending largely on temperature and the activity patterns of their prey.[36] These cats are adept at concealing themselves in meager cover. Even on bare ground, they can become almost invisible when they lie still. Reay Smithers remarked that the black markings on the ears of his pet caracal seemed to act as disruptive camouflage when the animal lay motionless with its head held low.[10]

Alain Dragesco-Joffé, who spent thirteen years in Niger photographing Saharan wildlife, describes the cat's behavior around humans, saying, "When an intruder approaches it climbs to a safe place and camouflages itself behind a rock or a tree. If it is surprised on open terrain, it immediately lies flat on the ground and remains absolutely motionless, relying on the blending of its color with the surroundings."[6]

Smithers's pet caracal also provided a few glimpses of this cat's behavior in the wild. As an adult she caught live doves "quicker than the eye could follow," and she killed hares by biting them on the back of the neck. Smithers also reports that "her reactions were very quick and she had extraordinary powers of leaping. When startled one night as she lay relaxed on the floor, she sprang up, hitting the wall with her front feet at a measured height of 3.4 meters."[10] Strong and agile, the caracal is an adaptable predator that can survive on a variety of birds, mammals, and reptiles. Smithers describes the cats succinctly when he writes, "They are fast in action and powerful, the heavily built limbs with the heavy curved claws on the front feet, especially the dew claws, capable of holding fast, once a grip is obtained. The skull is heavily built to support a strong set of jaw muscles, the canines well developed for delivering the killing bite."[10]

Feeding Ecology

Anecdotal reports mention caracals killing birds ranging in size from quail to guinea fowl, eagles, and ostriches, while their mammalian prey include almost anything from mice to hares and antelope. In general, though, the caracal lives mainly on prey that weigh less than 5 kilograms, including hares, hyraxes, small rodents, and birds. This cat will, however, take larger prey if the opportunity arises. Caracals can kill large antelope, sheep, and goats, and in some parts of its range

the caracal's appetite for domestic stock has resulted in its being regarded as a problem animal.[6,41,43]

In South Africa's Mountain Zebra National Park, mammals made up 94 percent of the prey species identified in caracal scats. Hyraxes, small (2 kg), colonial-living mammals of rocky scrub habitat, were the staple food, found in over 50 percent of the droppings. Twenty percent of the scats contained mountain reedbuck, a medium-sized (20 kg) antelope, which, because of its greater size, contributed more in terms of quantity of meat to the caracal's diet. Caracals also kill springbok, common duiker, steenbok, and springhares.[44]

A later study in Mountain Zebra National Park examined caracal scats collected from inside and outside the park. The results from inside the park paralleled those of the earlier study, with hyraxes being the most frequently occurring prey in scats and mountain reedbuck contributing the most in terms of weight. Hyraxes, rodents, and sheep were the most frequently occurring prey in scats from outside the park, with the latter contributing the most in terms of weight. These differences in food habits presumably reflect the relative abundance of various prey species available to the caracals.[43]

In Botswana, the stomach contents of nine caracals showed that gerbils and various species of mice were the most important food, but the cats also ate hares, springhares, quail, partridge, lizards, and impalas.[7]

In Israel, caracals feed mainly on hares, chukar, and desert partridge. Mammals constituted 62 percent and birds 24 percent of the caracal's diet in the Aravah Valley. Mole-rats, hedgehogs, and the Egyptian mongoose were also included as prey. Vegetable matter, insects, and reptiles were minor components in the diet.[37]

Not much is known about caracal food habits in Asia, but one study in the Karakum of Turkmenistan reported that small prey is an important part of the caracal's diet. Almost half of the 189 scats examined contained hares. Other prey identified in the scats included sand rats, jerboas, and ground squirrels (see table 4).

In some parts of South Africa, caracals have a reputation for killing livestock, and they are known to indulge in surplus killing. In one study in the Cape Province, there were seventy-nine incidents of domestic stock killed by caracals, and seventeen of these involved the killing of two or more animals. Twenty-one young goats were killed in a single incident.[45] Another account reported an incident of two caracals killing twenty-two sheep.[39] In the majority of cases, the incidents of surplus killing involved animals confined to pens or along fence lines. Caracals rarely fed on the carcasses of sheep and goats left after these killing sprees.

In another part of South Africa, a group of farmers used dogs to systematically hunt down caracals. Of 103 caracals killed, roughly half the stomachs contained the remains of sheep and goats, approximately a quarter were empty, and the remaining quarter contained hyraxes or unidentifiable prey. Though this report illustrates that caracals did kill domestic livestock, the numbers are not very meaningful, as the hunters selectively pursued caracals that were known to have killed livestock.[41]

An even larger collection of 394 caracal stomachs, most of which were from animals killed during control operations, showed a similar bias toward domestic stock. Thirty-seven percent of the stomachs were empty. Of the 246 stomachs that contained prey, nearly 28 percent held the remains of sheep and goats, a third contained remains of larger ungulates, and most of the remainder contained rodents (9.8 percent), hares and hyraxes (13.7 percent), and birds (8.1 percent). Like many of the felids, caracals also eat vegetation, and about 5 percent of the stomachs contained grass.[46]

Not many people have been fortunate enough to see a caracal hunting, but D. R. Rosevear recounts an incident that took place in Nigeria. "Traveling in a lorry in northern Nigeria in the early morning the driver sighted a flock of guinea-fowl in the road ahead and, as the custom is in such circumstances, accelerated rapidly in the hope of killing one or two. At that moment a fully grown caracal leapt from the grass at the roadside and seized a bird, with the consequence that both it and the guinea-fowl were immediately killed by impact with the vehicle."[3]

Caracals try to get as close to their prey as possible, usually stalking to within five meters or so. The cat may then wait for a long time before making the final dash and attack. It is an excellent sprinter, able to run faster than most similar-sized cats. Caracals use their agility and jumping skills to catch birds; one was filmed as it attacked a flock of birds, and the film shows the cat twisting and changing course in midair as it tries to hook the bird.

Fast and powerful, caracals are unusual among the small to medium-sized cats in that they regularly kill prey that is two to three times their size. A 1979–1980 study of scats in Mountain Zebra National Park found that about 72 percent of the meat consumed by caracals came from prey weighing two to two and a half times the average female caracal body weight (10 kg).[44] In 1981–1982 another study of scats in the same park found that nearly 62 percent of the meat consumed by caracals came from animals weighing two to three times as much as a female caracal. Outside the park, caracals killed domestic stock, and when these were included in the calculation, 91 percent of meat consumed came from prey two to three times female caracal body weight.[43]

When caracals catch mice and rats, they generally kill with a nape bite, sometimes snagging the rodent with a claw and then flinging it into the air. Caracals generally kill hares and similar-sized prey with a bite to the back of the neck.[3] Smithers says of his pet caracal, "In killing hares she would bite them on the nape of the neck and if they still showed signs of life she would throw herself on the ground and rake the prey with her back feet."[4]

Larger animals, such as antelope, duiker, sheep, and goats, are usually killed with a throat bite.[46,47] In Mountain Zebra National Park, J. H. Grobler examined twenty antelope of various species killed by caracals. He describes the killing bite and scene of the kill, saying, "The larger prey species (antelope) were killed with a bite in the throat at the junction of the lower jaw and neck. Cuts were present on the shoulders of the antelope killed and these were presumed to be claw marks. It was apparent that the prey was stalked to within 5 m and a short burst of speed appeared to culminate the stalk. The actual killing took place with little sign of a struggle." Grobler adds that a tame caracal of his often demonstrated the stalk, rush, and kill technique, "with the powerful hind legs playing an important part in the final thrust."[44]

Captive caracals pluck the feathers from birds before beginning to feed at the head, but in the wild small birds are consumed entirely except for a few feathers. With larger birds, the primary feathers, viscera, and portions of the skull are not eaten.[48] Antelope carcasses are opened at the anus, and the meat on the hindquarters is eaten first, followed by the forequarters.[10,46]

In sheep farming areas and places where caracals are persecuted, the cats readily abandon their kills, but in undisturbed areas they cover any remains with grass, and they continue to feed until the carcass is finished. There are also a few records of caracals carrying their prey into trees.[46]

Social Organization

Caracals are solitary hunters, but there are some records of two adults traveling together. Grobler recorded fifty-seven sightings in Mountain Zebra National Park, of which forty-one were of single adults, eleven were of pairs of adults, one was of a female with a single kitten, three were of a female with two kittens, and one was of a female with three kittens.[44]

The little information that is available on caracal home ranges suggests that they conform to the typical felid pattern. In Israel, the average range size of four radio-tagged female caracals was 57 square kilometers, with little overlap. Each female tended to occupy a small range, which she defended against other females. The average range size of five tagged males, at about 220 square kilometers, was much larger than that of females, and there was considerable overlap among male ranges. The ranges of tagged males in Israel changed little throughout the year, whereas that of a female varied when she was rearing young.[37]

Two young male caracals radio-tagged and released in the mountainous Stellenbosch area of the Cape Province traveled widely before one disappeared; it was killed a month later about 18 kilometers from where it was last located. The other male eventually settled in an area of 65 kilometers, where it remained for at least eleven months, suggesting that it had established a home range.[38]

Home range sizes of four females in the western sector of the Cape Province averaged 18.2 square kilometers, while that of a male was 65 square kilometers.[12] The range sizes of radio-tagged male caracals living on the farming areas outside Mountain Zebra National Park averaged 19.1 square kilometers, compared with 15.2 square kilometers for those living inside; range sizes of females inside the park averaged 5.5 square kilometers. For both sexes, there was considerable overlap in home ranges.[49]

Caracals do not cover their feces, which may serve to demarcate range boundaries. In captivity, both sexes have been seen to use urination sites, and males sometimes rake these sites with their hind feet. Males also spray urine on bushes, rocks, and logs.[47]

The caracal has the basic felid vocal repertoire, which includes meowing, gurgling, hissing, growling, spitting, purring, and another vocalization that Peters has labeled the wah-wah call. The lynxes, puma, jaguarundi, serval, and the Asiatic and African golden cats also have the wah-wah call.[50,51] Stuart heard caracals making a harsh, hissing "bark" when a strange animal was introduced into an enclosure, and an unreceptive female gave the same vocalization when a subadult male tried to mount her.[47] Peculiar barking sounds have also been heard between pairs occupying adjacent cages.[52]

Several cat species, including the lynx, bobcat, and jungle cat, have ear tufts, but the caracal's are by far the longest. Different authors have suggested various functions for these tufts, but basically their function remains unknown. They may accentuate facial expressions, or even facilitate the location of sounds. Kingdon believes that "the caracal's ears have evolved into a highly mobile and extraordinarily decorative signalling structure."[11]

Reproduction and Development

In a study of captive caracals, the onset of estrus was marked by an increase in the frequency of urine squirting by the female. When a male was introduced into a cage with an estrous female, he would inspect her urine marks before approaching her, indicating that information about her readiness to mate was contained in the urine. Those females who did not exhibit signs of estrus were not approached by males. The average length of the estrous cycle is two weeks, and females will continue to cycle for several months unless they become pregnant.[53]

In Israel, a study of radio-collared caracals found a somewhat unusual mating system, which in some ways resembles that of lions. Matings occurred over five to six days, during which time the female copulated with a number of males in a mating order that seemed to be determined by the age and weight of the males. During copulation, other males stayed nearby, awaiting their turn. Males copulated at intervals of forty-two to forty-eight hours.[37] In other areas males are not so passive and apparently fight regularly: every one of forty-six adult males killed as part of a predator control program in South Africa had scars on his head and ears.[41] Infanticide has also been observed; five adult male caracals had the remains of caracal kittens in their stomachs.[47]

Copulations have been seen to occur repeatedly over a period of one to three days, and the average length of each copulation is almost four minutes (range ninety seconds to eight minutes).[53] Copulations observed in most zoos fall within this time frame,[54] but one in the Mysore Zoo in India lasted almost ten minutes.[55] Following mating, the cats groom themselves, and sometimes the female is aggressive toward the male. Anecdotal observations from the wild confirm captive observations that estrus lasts for three to six days.[53,54] Expert trackers in Botswana say that tracks show that mating caracals move together for four days.[56]

Gestation lasts between sixty-eight and eighty-one days.[53,57,58,59] Litter size varies from one to six; the mean litter size is 2.19 ($n = 49$).[47,53,54] In South Africa, births have been recorded in every month of the year, although there is a pronounced peak in summer (October to February).[12] In Turkmenistan, caracal kittens are found in early April.[9]

Caracals use caves, tree cavities, or burrows dug by other animals as birthing dens. Newborn kittens weigh 198 to 250 grams.[12,59] The kittens open their eyes when they are between four and ten days old, but it is several more days before they can see clearly. By day eleven, a hand-raised kitten had begun to clean itself, and it was vocalizing by day twelve, making shrill birdlike twittering noises. The fur of kittens is light yellow or reddish brown at birth, with black markings on the face, and the backs of the ears are black.[10,51,60]

Chris and Tilde Stuart chronicled caracal development from birth to one year. They found that kittens have their full deciduous dentition when they are about fifty days old; permanent canines begin to emerge at about four to five months. At about five or six months the permanent canines displace the deciduous teeth, and by the tenth month all the deciduous teeth have been replaced.[61]

At birth, the kittens' ears are flattened against their heads, and their claws are nonretractable. The ears begin to stand up around the second week, and by the fourth week the ears are fully upright and the kittens can retract their claws. The kittens begin to venture outside their den when they are about a month old; this is also the time when they begin to eat solid food and show the first signs of play behavior. In Israel, kittens began moving with their mother to a new hiding place every day when they were a month old. Captive caracals were seen making their first kills when they were three months old, and were weaned at fifteen weeks.[37,61]

Young caracals are believed to disperse in search of their own ranges when they are nine or ten months old. In Israel, a young dispersing male traveled some 60 to 90 kilometers, whereas his sister remained in the general vicinity of their mother, sharing a partially overlapping range with her.[37]

Like domestic cats, caracals attain puberty and become sexually mature in their first year. Males can father litters when they are twelve to fourteen months old, and females have become pregnant at fourteen and fifteen months of age. However, microscopic examination of the ovaries and testes of younger animals showed that production of sperm and eggs begins between seven and ten months of age, well before the first successful copulation.[53]

Under favorable conditions females may have more than one litter a year, but this is unlikely to happen very often in the wild. In captivity, caracals have lived to be sixteen years old.[10,61]

STATUS IN THE WILD

Caracals are in the curious position of being classified as endangered in the Asian portion of their range and hunted as a problem animal in South Africa.[62] The caracal is quite common in Israel, considered to be rare but holding its own in Pakistan, and on the verge of extinction in India. The Turkmenistan subspecies *C. c. michaelis* is classified by the IUCN as rare.[63] In Arabia the caracal is rare and widespread, but it is easily trapped, and its continued existence is thought to be "precarious at best."[25]

The caracal is common over much of the southern African portion of its range. In 1976 John Visser remarked that "the caracal is classified as vermin in all provinces of South Africa, South West Africa, and Rhodesia," adding, "Outside of parks and reserves, enormous sums are being spent on extermination of the caracal. Yet it is remarkably resistant to persecution, partly as a result of the vast distances covered by individuals."[29] More recently, Chris Stuart of the IUCN/SSC Cat Specialist Group expressed the belief that caracals in South Africa and Namibia are quite common and increasing their range. Stuart says, "Present levels of control, although quite heavy, are not unduly influencing populations."[64] He believes that "the caracal is secure, for the foreseeable future, in South Africa, Namibia, Botswana, and much of eastern and southeastern Africa."[47]

In North Africa, caracals are rare. They are, however, not confined to desert regions and sometimes remain near the coast; they are found, for example, around Agadir, Rabat, and Oujda in Morocco and in some parts of the Libyan coastal plain.[6]

Habitat loss is one of the main threats to the caracal in the eastern part of its geographic range. It is often hunted; many accounts mention how easy this cat is to catch. In Pakistan, a Jogi animal trapper told Colonel Tom Roberts that the caracal was easy to catch with a bait of raw meat, and in his landmark book, *The Mammals of Pakistan*, Roberts adds that the Jogis capture caracal kittens by digging them out of underground burrows.[8] The caracal has suffered heavily from fur trappers in India, but caracal pelts have a very low value on the international market, and the world fur trade does not pose a threat to this cat. With genetic analysis is it possible to distinguish between the pelt of a caracal from the endangered population in India and one from the hunted population in South Africa.

STATUS IN CAPTIVITY

Caracals are commonly kept and bred in captivity. However, there is little information on the origins and relatedness of the zoo population, and as of 1990 there was no studbook for the caracal.

TABLE 3 MEASUREMENTS AND WEIGHTS OF ADULT CARACALS

HB	n	T	n	WT	n	Location	Source
881 (750–1,057)	65m	272 (210–340)	70m	12.7 (8.0–18.1)	61m	South Africa	47
834 (710–1,029)	40f	248 (198–305)	47f	10.1 (7.0–15.9)	40f	South Africa	47
778 (621–911)	4m	279 (229–315)	4m	13.5 (11.5–17.0)	3m	Botswana	7
728 (610–805)	5f	279 (195–340)	5f	9.7 (7.9–12.9)	5f	Botswana	7
				14.5 (8.6–20.0)	46m	South Africa	41
				10.9 (8.6–14.5)	32f	South Africa	41
630	1f	230	1f			Senegal	20
785	1m	285	1m			United Arab Emirates	25
777	6m			9.8	6m	Israel	37
692	5f			6.2	5f	Israel	37
737	1?	229	1?			Pakistan	8
783 (730–820)	5m	292 (274–320)	4m	11.8 (11.4–12.7)	4m	Russia/Turkmenistan	9
766 (690–810)	5f	285 (212–320)	4f	8.3 (8.0–8.7)	3f	Russia/Turkmenistan	9

Note: HB = head and body length (mm), T = tail length (mm), WT = weight (kg). *n* = sample size. Sex: m = male, f = female, ? = unknown. Mean values are presented only for sample sizes of three or more. Range of values is in parentheses.

TABLE 4 FREQUENCY OF OCCURRENCE OF PREY ITEMS IN THE DIETS OF CARACALS (PERCENTAGE OF SAMPLES)

Prey species	Mountain Zebra NP, South Africa (inside park)[44] Scats (n = 200)	Mountain Zebra NP, South Africa (outside park)[43] Scats (n = 85)	Eastern Cape Province[46] Stomach contents (n = 246)	SW Cape Province[46] Scats (n = 248)	Eastern Karakum, Turkmenistan[65] Scats (n = 189)
Procavia capensis Dassie or rock hyrax	60	34.1	8.9	11.3	
Redunca fulvorufula Mountain reedbuck	22	9.4	1.6		
Pronolagus rupestris Red rock rabbit	6	8.2			
Lepus saxatilis Scrub hare	6	2.4	9.3	6.4	
Lepus tolai Tolai hare					30.7
Rodents Unidentified rodents	5.5	27.1	13 / 3.7	62.5	17.5 / 26.5
Sylvicapra grimmia Common duiker	3	1.2	9.3	6.0	
Raphicerus campestris Steenbok	1	1.2	3.2	3.2	
Antidorcas marsupialis Springbok	0.5				
Pedetes capensis Springhare	0.5				
Tragelaphus scriptus Bushbuck			3.6		
Cephalophus monticola Blue duiker			2.4		
Raphicerus melanotis Cape grysbuck			13.8		
Pelea capreolus Rhebok			0.4	1.6	
Oreotragus oreotragus Klipspringer			0.4	2.8	
Unidentified antelope			8.9		
Carnivores	1		8.1	3.6	1.6
Insectivores			1.2		1.6
Birds	6	2.4	10.6	6.4	9.5
Reptiles	1				7.4
Domestic stock		25.9	27.8	21	
Minimum number of vertebrate prey items	225	96	327	310	179

REFERENCES

1. Ward, A. E. 1923. Game animals of Kashmir and adjacent hill provinces. *J. Bombay Nat. Hist. Soc.* 29: 23–35.

2. Vigne, G. T. 1842. *Travels in Kashmir, Ladak, Iskardo, the countries adjoining the mountain-course of the Indus and the Himalaya, north of the Punjab.* Vol. 1. New Delhi: Sagar Publications, 1981.

3. Rosevear, D. R. 1974. *The carnivores of West Africa.* London: Trustees of the British Museum of Natural History.

4. Smithers, R. H. N. 1966. *The mammals of Rhodesia, Zambia and Malawi.* London: Collins.

5. Prater, S. H. 1971. *The book of Indian animals,* 3rd ed. Bombay: Bombay Natural History Society.

6. Dragesco-Joffé, A. 1993. *La vie sauvage au Sahara*. Paris: Delachaux et Niestlé.

7. Smithers, R. H. N. 1971. *The mammals of Botswana*. Museum Memoir no. 4. Salisbury: The Trustees of the National Museums of Rhodesia.

8. Roberts, T. J. 1977. *The mammals of Pakistan*. London: Ernest Benn.

9. Heptner, V. G., and A. A. Sludskii. 1992. *Mammals of the Soviet Union*. Vol. 2, Part 2, *Carnivora (Hyaenas and cats)*. English translation, sci. ed., R. S. Hoffmann. Washington, DC: Smithsonian Institution Libraries and The National Science Foundation.

10. Smithers, R. H. N. 1983. *The mammals of the Southern African subregion*. Pretoria: University of Pretoria.

11. Kingdon, J. 1977. *East African mammals*. Vol. 3, part A (Carnivores). Chicago: University of Chicago Press.

12. Stuart, C. T., and V. J. Wilson. 1988. *The cats of Southern Africa*. Zimbabwe: Chipangali Wildlife Trust.

13. Werdelin, L. 1981. The evolution of lynxes. *Ann. Zool. Fennici* 18: 37–71.

14. Groves, C. 1982. Cranial and dental characteristics in the systematics of Old World Felidae. *Carnivore* 5: 28–39.

15. Werdelin, L. 1983. Morphological patterns in the skulls of cats. *Biol. J. Linn. Soc.* 19: 375–391.

16. Johnson, W. E., and S. J. O'Brien. 1997. Phylogenetic reconstruction of the Felidae using 16S rRNA and NADH-5 mitochondrial genes. *J. Mol. Evol.* 44 (suppl. 1): S98–S116.

17. Salles, L. O. 1992. Felid phylogenetics: Extant taxa and skull morphology (Felidae, Aeluroidea). *Am. Mus. Novitates* 3047: 1–67.

18. Wozencraft, W. C. 1993. Order Carnivora. In *Mammal species of the world*, 2nd ed., ed. D. E. Wilson and D. M. Reeder, 279–348. Washington, DC: Smithsonian Institution Press.

19. Corkhill, N. L. 1930. The caracal in Iraq. *J. Bombay Nat. Hist. Soc.* 34: 232–233.

20. Gaillard. 1969. Sur la présence du chat doré (*Felis aurata* Temminck) et du caracal (*Felis caracal* Schreber) dans le sud du Sénégal. *Mammalia* 33: 350–351.

21. Wilson, V. J. 1975. *Mammals of the Wankie National Park, Rhodesia*. Museum Memoir no. 5. Salisbury: Trustees of the National Museums and Monuments of Rhodesia.

22. Hufnagl, E. 1972. *Libyan mammals*. Stoughton, WI: Oleander Press.

23. Nader, I. A. 1984. A second record of the caracal lynx *Caracal caracal schmitzi* (Matschie, 1912) for Saudi Arabia (Mammalia: Carnivora). *Mammalia* 48: 148–150.

24. Lynch, C. D. 1983. *The mammals of the Orange Free State*. Memoirs van die Nasionale Museum Bloemfontein no. 18. 218 pp.

25. Gasperetti, J., D. L. Harrison, and W. Büttiker. 1985. The Carnivora of Arabia. In *Fauna of Saudi Arabia*, vol. 7, ed. W. Büttiker and F. Krupp, 397–461. Basle: Pro Entomologia, c/o Natural History Museum.

26. Stuart, C. T. 1984. The distribution and status of *Felis caracal* Schreber, 1776. *Säugetierk. Mitt.* 31: 197–203.

27. Meester, J. A. J., I. L. Rautenbach, N. J. Dippenaar, and C. M. Baker. 1986. *Classification of southern African mammals*. Transvaal Museum Monograph no. 5. Pretoria: Transvaal Museum.

28. Green, A. A. 1986. Status of large mammals of northern Saudi Arabia. *Mammalia* 50: 487–493.

29. Visser, J. 1976. Status and conservation of the smaller cats of southern Africa. In *The world's cats*, vol. 3, no. 1, ed. R. L. Eaton, 60–66. Seattle: Carnivore Research Institute.

30. Happold, D. C. D. 1987. *The mammals of Nigeria*. Oxford: Clarendon Press.

31. Chavan, S. A. 1987. Status of wild cats in Gujarat. *Tiger Paper* 14: 21–24.

32. De Smet, K. J. M. 1989. Studie van de verspreiding en biotoopkeuze van de grote mammalia in Algerije in het kader van het natuurbehoud. Ph.D. dissertation, Rijks University, Gent, Holland.

33. Crawford-Cabral, J. 1989. Distributional data and notes on Angolan carnivores (Mammalia: Carnivora). *Garcia de Orta, Sér. Zool.*, Lisboa, 14: 3–27.

34. Parihar, A. S. 1989. Caracal (*Felis caracal* Schreber) sighted in Panna forests. *J. Bombay Nat. Hist. Soc.* 86: 237.

35. Serez, M. 1992. Evolution of lynx population in Turkey. In *The situation, conservation needs and reintroduction of lynx in Europe*, 26–29 Environmental Encounters, no. 11. Strasbourg: Council of Europe.

36. Kowalski, K., and B. Rzebik-Kowalska. 1991. *Mammals of Algeria*. Warsaw: Polish Academy of Sciences.

37. Weisbein, Y., and H. Mendelssohn. 1990. The biology and ecology of the caracal *Felis caracal* in the northern Aravah Valley of Israel. *Cat News* 12: 20–22.

38. Norton, P. M., and A. B. Lawson. 1985. Radio tracking of leopards and caracals in the Stellenbosch area, Cape Province. *S. Afr. J. Wildl. Res.* 15: 17–24.

39. Skinner, J. D. 1979. Feeding behaviour in caracal *Felis caracal*. *J. Zool.* (Lond.) 189: 523–525.

40. Pienaar, U. De V. 1969. Predator-prey relationships amongst the large mammals of the Kruger National Park. *Koedoe* 12: 108–183.

41. Pringle, J. A., and V. L. Pringle. 1979. Observations on the lynx *Felis caracal* in the Bedford district. *S. Afr. J. Zool.* 14: 1–4.

42. Mendelssohn, H. 1989. Felids in Israel. *Cat News* 10: 2–4.

43. Moolman, L. C. 1984. 'n vergelyking van die voedingsgewoontes van die rooikat *Felis caracal* binne en buite die Bergkwagga Nasionale Park. *Koedoe* 27: 121–129.

44. Grobler, J. H. 1981. Feeding behaviour of the caracal *Felis caracal* Schreber 1776 in the Mountain Zebra National Park. *S. Afr. J. Zool.* 16: 259–262.

45. Stuart, C. T. 1986. The incidence of surplus killing by *Panthera pardus* and *Felis caracal* in Cape Province, South Africa. *Mammalia* 50: 556–558.

46. Stuart, C. T., and G. C. Hickman. 1991. Prey of caracal *Felis caracal* in two areas of Cape Province, South Africa. *J. Afr. Zool.* 105: 373–381.

47. Stuart, C. T. 1981. Notes on the mammalian carnivores of the Cape Province, South Africa. *Bontebok* 1: 1–58.

48. Leyhausen, P. 1979. *Cat behavior: The predatory and social behavior of domestic and wild cats*. New York: Garland STPM Press.

49. Moolman, L. C. 1986. Aspects of the ecology and behaviour of the caracal *Felis caracal* Schreber, 1776 in the Mountain Zebra National Park and on the surrounding farms. Master's thesis, University of Pretoria, Pretoria.

50. Peters, G. 1983. Beobachtungen zum Lautgebungsverhalten des Karakal, *Caracal caracal* (Schreber, 1776) (Mammalia, Carnivora, Felidae). *Bonn. Zool. Beitr.* 34: 107–127.

51. Peters, G. 1987. Acoustic communication in the genus

Lynx (Mammalia: Felidae)—comparative survey and phylogenetic interpretation. *Bonn. Zool. Beitr.* 38: 315–330.

52. Kralik, S. 1967. Breeding the caracal lynx at Brno Zoo. *Int. Zoo Yrbk.* 7: 132.

53. Bernard, R. T. F., and C. T. Stuart. 1987. Reproduction of the caracal *Felis caracal* from the Cape Province of South Africa. *S. Afr. J. Zool.* 22: 177–182.

54. Mellen, J. D. 1993. A comparative analysis of scent-marking, social and reproductive behavior in 20 species of small cats (*Felis*). *Am. Zool.* 33: 151–166.

55. Gowda, C. D. K. 1967. A note on the birth of caracal lynx at Mysore Zoo. *Int. Zoo Yrbk.* 7: 133.

56. Liebenberg, L. 1990. *The art of tracking.* Cape Town: David Philip.

57. Cade, C. E. 1968. A note on the breeding of the caracal lynx, *Felis caracal*, at the Nairobi Zoo. *Int. Zoo Yrbk.* 8: 45.

58. Seager, S. W. J., and C. N. Demorest. 1986. Reproduction of captive wild carnivores. In *Zoo and wild animal medicine*, 2nd ed., ed. M. E. Fowler, 667–706. Philadelphia: W. B. Saunders.

59. Andrews, P., Hexagon Farm Wild Feline Breeding Facility, 1187 Merrill Road, San Juan Bautista, CA. Personal communication.

60. Grobler, J. H. 1982. Growth of a male caracal kitten *Felis caracal* in the Mountain Zebra National Park. *Koedoe* 25: 117–119.

61. Stuart, C. T., and T. D. Stuart. 1985. Age determination and development of foetal and juvenile *Felis caracal* Schreber, 1776. *Säugetierk. Mitt.* 32: 217–229.

62. Cat News. 1995. CITES Conference of the Parties 1994. *Cat News* 22: 20–22.

63. Nowell, K., and P. Jackson. 1996. *Wild cats: A status survey and conservation action plan.* Gland, Switzerland: International Union for Conservation of Nature and Natural Resources (IUCN).

64. Stuart, C. T. 1986. Caracal in Africa. *Cat News* 4: 9–10.

65. Sapozhenkov, Y. F. 1962. The ecology of the caracal (*Felis caracal* Mull.) in the Karakum. *Zool. Zh.* 41: 1110–1112.

Bay cat

Catopuma badia (Gray, 1874)

The bay cat is the world's least known felid. Found solely on the island of Borneo, this elusive cat is known from only about twelve specimens. The first bay cat was collected by Alfred Russel Wallace in 1855 and acquired by the British Museum in 1856.[1] The place of collection is listed as Sarawak, with no other details. When Wallace first arrived in Sarawak in November 1854, he was based in the town of Sarawak, now known as Kuching. During the first four months he collected along the Sarawak River from Santubong at its mouth to Bow (Bau) and Bede inland, but "obtained very little." In 1855 he moved some 50 kilometers east of Kuching to an area of virgin forest where a coal mine had been established at the junction of the Simujan and Sadong rivers. He stayed there for nine months with the mining engineer, Mr. Coulson, and it was in this area that he obtained the major part of his collection.[2] Wallace does not state which of the two collecting sites his bay cat specimen came from, but it seems more likely it was the second.

When Wallace's type specimen arrived at the British Museum, it was in a poor state of preservation and was not immediately recognized as a new species. It was originally entered in the register as *Felis planiceps?*, a flat-headed cat. It was later assumed to be a young Temminck's cat, but that was ruled out when the skull was examined. After J. E. Gray decided that the specimen did indeed represent a new species, he delayed describing the animal for nearly twenty years in the hope of acquiring a more complete specimen, but finally gave up the wait and in 1874 described the bay cat from a badly preserved skin and an incomplete skull.[3]

It was not until 1888 that a second specimen turned up, this one collected by Alfred H. L. Everett. Everett was a naturalist who lived for many years in Borneo, where he collected extensively; more than 500 Bornean mammal specimens in the British Museum are attributed to him. This second specimen was first listed as being collected on the Baram River, Sarawak, but for no apparent reason the registry entry was later changed to read Suai River.[1]

The third bay cat was a gray specimen collected by Charles Hose, who was a contemporary and friend of Everett. It was collected in September 1894 on the Entoyut River, a tributary of the Baram, just south of Claudetown (now Marudi) and west of Mt. Mulu.[1] These three skins and partial skulls are now lodged in the British Museum. Over the next few years another

five skins trickled in and found their way to the Leiden Museum in Holland (one),[4] the Sarawak Museum in Kuching (two), the Smithsonian Institution's National Museum of Natural History (one), and the Chicago Field Museum (one). By 1928 there were eight skins, but scientists had still not seen a whole specimen.

It was not until November 1992 that a live bay cat surfaced. Caught by some trappers on the "Sarawak/Indonesia border," an adult female bay cat was brought into the Sarawak Museum in Kuching, emaciated and on the point of death. Knowing that the cat was rare and perhaps valuable, the trappers had apparently held the animal in captivity for some months while they tried to find an animal dealer willing to handle it.[5]

Since this was the first specimen to appear since 1928, it provided the opportunity to evaluate the cat's relationship with other Southeast Asian felids, especially the Asiatic golden cat. The bay cat was thought to be an island race of the Asiatic golden cat. Using molecular techniques, genetic material from the new specimen was compared with material extracted from the pelt of the original type specimen in the British Museum. Analyses confirmed that both specimens were the same species, that the bay cat was closely related to the Asiatic golden cat, and that the bay cat and the golden cat had been separated from a common ancestor for 4.9 to 5.3 million years, long before the geological separation of Borneo from mainland Asia. The bay cat is indeed a unique species.[6]

DESCRIPTION

About the size of a large domestic cat with an extra long tail, the bay cat looks like a miniature version of the Asiatic golden cat.[6,7,8] Like the Asiatic golden cat and the jaguarundi, the bay cat has two color phases. Of nine known skins, only two are of the gray phase, Everett's from the British Museum and the specimen in the National Museum of Natural History. The coat can be mahogany red or blackish gray on the back and flanks, but it is usually paler on the underparts, with some faint spots on the belly and limbs. A pale flash marks the inside of each eye, and there may be faint dark stripes on the top of the head and the cheeks. The hair on the nape, sides of the crown, cheek, and front of the throat grows forward. The last half of the tail is conspicuously white underneath. The ears are short and rounded, set well down on the sides of the head; there is no white spot on the back of the ears.[5,8,9,10]

The female bay cat brought into the Sarawak Mu-

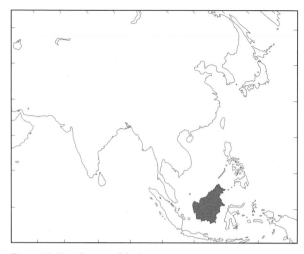

Figure 12. Distribution of the bay cat.

seum in 1992 weighed 1.95 kilograms, but was in a thoroughly emaciated condition, with wasted muscles and protruding bones. This cat's normal body weight was estimated to be 3 to 4 kilograms.[5]

DISTRIBUTION
The bay cat is restricted to the island of Borneo (fig. 12).

ECOLOGY AND BEHAVIOR
Naturalist Charles Hose, who traveled extensively in Sarawak, reported the bay cat to be rare.[11] The single specimen he obtained came from the Entoyut River. Indeed, three of the museum specimens were collected along rivers, but it is not known whether this reflects the cat's preferred habitat or the collector's preferred mode of transport in the rather difficult Bornean terrain. Beyond these observations, the only information on the bay cat is that the species is reported to live in dense forests.[12] In 1986, Biruté Galdikas reported seeing a bay cat in her orangutan study area in southern Kalimantan.[13]

STATUS IN THE WILD
The bay cat is clearly an extremely rare species. When villagers in Sabah and Sarawak were interviewed about local wildlife, most were familiar with clouded leopards, leopard cats, flat-headed cats, and marbled cats. None recognized pictures of the bay cat.[14] The bay cat is fully protected over most of its range, and hunting and trade are prohibited. However, the bay cat is listed on appendix II of CITES, which means that captive animals may be shipped out of the country with only an export permit. No import permit is required.

In 1998, a live bay cat was trapped in the wild and held at an undisclosed location, at which the first ever photograph of a living bay cat was obtained.[15] In 2000, two bay cats were caught in foot snares set by trappers near the villages of Nabawan and Soak in Sabah. They were sold to an animal dealer, who applied for a permit to export them to a North American captive breeding facility. Both cats died before they could be exported.[16]

Ironically, the high value placed on these rare cats is jeopardizing the survival of the species. Local trappers and animal dealers are well aware that foreign zoos and breeding facilities will pay U.S.$10,000 or more for a live animal, which has resulted in increased pressure on this already rare cat. Though it is illegal to trap bay cats, the practice continues. Unless demand decreases, which is unlikely, Western zoos and captive breeding facilities may ultimately be responsible for the extirpation of this species.

STATUS IN CAPTIVITY
There are no bay cats in captivity.

TABLE 5 MEASUREMENTS AND WEIGHTS OF ADULT BAY CATS

HB	n	T	n	WT	n	Location	Source
620 (skin)	1m	380	1m			Baram River	5
670 (skin)	1m	330	1m			Entoyut River	5
		320	1f			Mahakkan River	5
		385	1m			Sarawak	5
533	1f	391	1f			Sarawak	5

Note: HB = head and body (mm), T = tail length (mm), WT = weight (kg). n = sample size. Sex: m = male, f = female, ? = unknown.

REFERENCES

1. Hills, D. M., Curator, Mammal Section, The Natural History Museum, Kensington, London. Personal communication.

2. Wallace, A. R. 1905. *My life: A record of events and opinions*. London: Chapman and Hall.

3. Gray, J. E. 1874. Description of a new species of cat (*Felis badia*) from Sarawak. *Proc. Zool. Soc. Lond.* 1874: 322–323.

4. Jentink, F. A. 1901. On *Felis badia* Gray. *Notes Leyden Mus.* 23: 91–93.

5. Sunquist, M. E., C. Leh, F. Sunquist, D. M. Hills, and R. Rajaratnam. 1994. Rediscovery of the Bornean bay cat. *Oryx* 28: 67–70.

6. Johnson, W. E., F. Shinyashiki, M. Menotti Raymond, C. Driscoll, C. Leh, M. Sunquist, L. Johnston, M. Bush, D. Wildt, N. Yuhki, and S. J. O'Brien. 1999. Molecular genetic characterization of two insular Asian cat species, Bornean bay cat and Iriomote cat. In *Evolutionary theory and processes: Modern perspectives, Essays in honour of Eviator Nevo*, ed. S. P. Wasser, 223–248. Dordrecht: Kluwer Academic Publishing.

7. Blonk, H. L. 1963. *Wilde Katten*. Zutphen: N. V. W. J. Thieme.

8. Guggisberg, C. A. W. 1975. *Wild cats of the world*. New York: Taplinger.

9. Weigel, I. 1972. Small felids and clouded leopards. In *Grzimek's animal life encyclopedia*, vol. 12, *Mammals* III, ed. H. C. B. Grzimek, 281–332. New York: Van Nostrand Reinhold.

10. Pocock, R. I. 1932. The marbled cat (*Pardofelis marmorata*) and some other oriental species, with the definition of a new genus of the Felidae. *Proc. Zool. Soc. Lond.* 1932: 741–766.

11. Hose, C. 1893. *A descriptive account of the mammals of Borneo*. London: Edward Abbott.

12. Payne, J., C. M. Francis, and K. Phillips. 1985. *A field guide to the mammals of Borneo*. Kuala Lumpur: The Sabah Society.

13. Cat News. 1986. Some notes for the record. *Cat News* 5: 11.

14. Nowell, K., and P. Jackson. 1996. *Wild cats: A status survey and conservation action plan*. Gland, Switzerland: International Union for Conservation of Nature and Natural Resources (IUCN).

15. Taylor, K. 1998. Now you see it . . . *BBC Wildlife* 16(12): 42–43.

16. Yasuma, S., Sabah Wildlife Department, Kota Kinabalu, 88100, Sabah. Personal communication.

Asiatic golden cat

Catopuma temminckii (Vigors and Horsfield, 1827)

Over the last 150 years there has been a great deal of confusion over the classification of the Asiatic golden cat. The species resembles the African golden cat, and the two occasionally have been lumped together in the genus *Felis* or—more recently—split, with the African species assigned to *Profelis* and the Asian one to *Catopuma*, along with the bay cat.[1,2,3,4] Coincidentally, the African golden cat and the Asiatic golden cat were both described in the same year (1827), but by different authorities. Adding to the confusion, the African cat was described by C. J. Temminck (*Profelis aurata*—Temminck, 1827), while the Asian cat (*Catopuma temminckii*—Vigors and Horsfield, 1827) was named in honor of Temminck and is sometimes referred to as Temminck's cat.

More recently, immunological and chromosomal studies have suggested that the Asiatic golden cat is an early branch of the *Panthera* lineage, and indicate that the line to the African golden cat, cheetah, caracal, and puma split off roughly 6 to 8 million years ago.[5,6]

People in Southeast Asia associate the golden cat with tigers and leopards. In Thailand the name for this cat is *seua fai*, or "fire tiger," and the forest people believe that the golden cat is extremely fierce—the master of all other cats. The Karen, a local tribe, believe that carrying a single hair of the golden cat on your person will keep tigers away.[7] In China the golden cat is thought to be a kind of leopard and is known as the rock cat or yellow leopard. Different color phases have different names; those with black fur are called inky leopards, and those with spotted coats are called sesame leopards.[8]

DESCRIPTION

About the size of a large ocelot, the Asiatic golden cat looks quite similar to the closely related African golden cat, except that the Asian species is slightly heavier and the tail proportionately longer. The two species also share the trait of being cats of many colors. The Asiatic golden cat's coat may be golden brown to dark brown, pale cinnamon, bright red, or gray. The pelt is usually quite uniform in color, but it may also be marked with spots and stripes in a pattern similar to that of the leopard cat. In all forms, the backs of the short, rounded ears are black with a faint gray central area. The head is distinctly marked with white lines bordered with black running across each cheek and from the inner corner of each eye up to the crown. The underside of the distal third of the tail is white, while the dorsal surface is brown.[9,10,11]

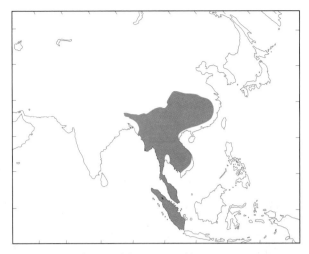

Figure 13. Distribution of the Asiatic golden cat.

DISTRIBUTION

The Asiatic golden cat is found from Tibet, Nepal, and Sikkim through southern China, Myanmar, Thailand, and peninuslar Malaysia and Sumatra (fig. 13).[3,7,9,10,11,12]

ECOLOGY AND BEHAVIOR

Like its African relative, the Asiatic golden cat is usually associated with forested habitats, including dry deciduous forest, evergreen forest, and tropical rainforest. The species ranges from the lowlands to altitudes of 3,000 meters and is sometimes found in more open, rocky areas.[13]

The Asiatic golden cat is primarily a terrestrial hunter, but it can climb when it needs to. A specimen captured by the naturalist Brian Hodgson was in a tree in the middle of a dense forest.[11] Pocock records one cat that was shot over a calf it had killed and another that was speared while feeding on a buffalo calf, indicating that the species is clearly able to kill large prey.[13] Nothing is known of this cat's biology and behavior in the wild, but it is thought to be active mainly at night, and its diet probably includes birds, lizards, rodents, and other mammals up to the size of small deer.[7] The cat will kill domestic poultry as well as sheep, goats, and buffalo calves.

T. C. Jerdon and Robert Sterndale referred to the golden cat in India as the bay cat,[14,15] and one of the few descriptions of this cat in the wild comes from Robert Sterndale's 1884 treatise, *The Natural History of the Mammalia of India and Ceylon*. Sterndale writes of a specimen that "was caught in a tree by some hunters in the midst of an extremely dense forest. Though only just taken it bore confinement very tranquilly, and gave evident signs of a tractable disposition, but manifested high courage, for the approach of a huge Bhotea dog to its cage excited in it symptoms of wrath only, none of fear."[15]

In captivity, golden cats kill small prey with a nape bite, as is typical of felids. They also pluck birds larger than pigeons before beginning to feed.[16]

Vocalizations of the Asiatic golden cat include the hiss, spit, purr, growl, meow, gurgle, and possibly others.[17,18] Other forms of communication include scent marking, and in captivity males have been observed to spray urine, to rub the head on objects, and to rake logs with the claws.[19,20]

Nothing is known about the reproductive behavior of Asian golden cats in the wild. Even the information from captive animals is extremely limited. A female Temminck's cat at the Washington Park Zoo, Oregon, showed a dramatic increase in the frequency of scent marking during estrus. At the same time, she often rubbed her neck and head on inanimate objects. She also repeatedly approached the male in the cage, rubbed on him, and adopted a receptive posture (lordosis) in front of him. The male's rate of scent marking increased during this time, as did his frequency of approaching and following the female. The male's mounting behavior included a nape bite, but in contrast to other small felids, the bite was not sustained.[20,21]

Only a single estrous cycle has been reported for Asian golden cats: it was thirty-nine days long, with estrus lasting six days.[20] The gestation period is thought to be seventy-eight to eighty days.[22] Litters are born throughout the year and typically consist of a single kitten, although there are records of litters of three.[11,23] A pair in the Washington Park Zoo produced ten litters, all consisting of one kitten;[21] two litters of a single kitten each were born at the Wassenaar Zoo in the Netherlands;[24] and a single kitten was reported for another litter.[25] Two litters of two kittens each were born at a private cat breeding facility in California, but neither litter survived.[22]

At birth kittens weigh approximately 220 to 250 grams, and their coats are marked exactly like those of the parents.[22,24] They open their eyes at six to twelve days. Their weight doubles by three weeks of age and triples by eight weeks.[24] Mating pairs are usually sepa-

rated when pregnancy is suspected because males will sometimes kill kittens,[21] although one male parent was observed licking a kitten when it was nine days old, and thereafter took an active role in rearing the young. The kitten was walking well at two weeks of age, at which time it weighed 650 grams, and by nine and a half weeks of age it weighed 1.3 kilograms.[24]

Asiatic golden cats attain sexual maturity by eighteen to twenty-four months,[22] and a captive-born female gave birth to her first litter at the age of twenty-five months.[26] Captive Asiatic golden cats have lived to be about seventeen years old.[27]

STATUS IN THE WILD

It is very difficult to determine reliably the status of the Asiatic golden cat in the wild because so little is known about the species and it is so rarely seen. Areas of good habitat still exist in Bhutan, parts of northeastern India, and China.[8,28,29] In China the golden cat is on the Protected Species List, but with tiger and leopard bones becoming ever rarer, local trade in golden cat bones has increased.[8] According to a survey conducted between 1977 and 1981 by Lu Houji and Sheng Helin, golden cats in Jiangxi Province had declined to 30 percent of their mid-1950 populations. An estimated 234 skins were purchased in Jiangxi in 1980–1981.[30] In 1986 George Schaller saw 17 golden cat skins for sale in the fur markets of Lingxia, Gansu Province.[31] In 1988 Chen Jun and Wang Taiansong of Lanzhou University, China, reported that "the authorities in most counties of the loess plateau in Gansu Province were collecting 30–100 pelts annually of golden cat *F. temminckii* and fox *Vulpes corsac*."[32]

Forests are being logged and transformed for agriculture in Bangladesh, Myanmar, India, and much of Southeast Asia, so, as a forest dweller, the Asiatic golden cat is threatened with habitat loss throughout much of its range.[29,33,34,35,36,37]

STATUS IN CAPTIVITY

There are very few Asiatic golden cats in zoos, and the species does not appear to breed well in captivity. In 1989 a total of twenty-four Asiatic golden cats were held in seven institutions participating in the ISIS species distribution report.[38] There is no studbook or Species Survival Plan for the Asiatic golden cat.

TABLE 6 MEASUREMENTS AND WEIGHTS OF ADULT ASIATIC GOLDEN CATS

HB	n	T	n	WT	n	Location	Source
(760–815)	?	(430–490)	?	(12–15)	?	Thailand	7
				14.5, 15.75	2m	China	8
				8.5	1f	China	8
840	1?	400	1?			China	10
(preserved skin)							
731, 940	2f	485, 490	2f			China	10
1,050	1m	560	1m			China	10
900, 950	2?	525, 575	2?			China	9
870	1?					Tibet	9
831	4m	476	4m	14.5	1m	Myanmar	9
(750–950)		(425–525)				Assam	
662, 750	2?	425, 425	2?			Sumatra	9

Note: HB = head and body length (mm), T = tail length (mm), WT = weight (kg). n = sample size. Sex: m = male, f = female, ? = unknown. Mean values are presented only for sample sizes of three or more. Range of values is in parentheses.

REFERENCES

1. Hemmer, H. 1978. The evolutionary systematics of living Felidae: Present status and current problems. *Carnivore* 1: 71–78.

2. Groves, C. 1982. Cranial and dental characteristics in the systematics of Old World Felidae. *Carnivore* 5: 28–39.

3. Corbet, G. B., and J. E. Hill. 1992. *The mammals of the Indomalayan region: A systematic review.* Oxford: Oxford University Press.

4. Wozencraft, W. C. 1993. Carnivora. In *Mammal species of the world*, 2nd ed., ed. D. E. Wilson and D. M. Reeder, 279–348. Washington, DC: Smithsonian Institution Press.

5. Collier, G. E., and S. J. O'Brien. 1985. A molecular phylogeny of the Felidae: Immunological distance. *Evolution* 39: 473–487.

6. Wayne, R. K., R. E. Benveniste, D. N. Janczewski, and S. J. O'Brien. 1989. Molecular and biochemical evolution of the Carnivora. In *Carnivore behavior, ecology, and evolution*, ed. J. L. Gittleman, 465–494. Ithaca, NY: Cornell University Press.

7. Lekagul, B., and J. A. McNeely. 1977. *Mammals of Thailand.* Bangkok: Association for the Conservation of Wildlife.

8. Tan, B. 1984. The status of felids in China. In The plight of the cats: Proceedings of the meeting and workshop of the IUCN/SSC Cat Specialist Group at Kanha National Park, Madhya Pradesh, India, 33–47. Unpublished report, IUCN/SSC Cat Specialist Group, Bougy-Villars, Switzerland.

9. Pocock, R. I. 1932. The marbled cat (*Pardofelis marmorata*) and some other Oriental species, with the definition of a new genus of the Felidae. *Proc. Zool. Soc. Lond.* 1932: 741–766.

10. Allen, G. M. 1938. *The mammals of China and Mongolia.* New York: American Museum of Natural History.

11. Guggisberg, C. A. W. 1975. *Wild cats of the world.* New York: Taplinger.

12. Ellerman, J. R., and T. C. S. Morrison-Scott. 1951. *Checklist of Palearctic and Indian mammals.* London: British Museum (Natural History).

13. Pocock, R. I. 1939. *The fauna of British India, including Ceylon and Burma.* Vol. 1, *Mammalia.* London: Taylor & Francis.

14. Jerdon, T. C. 1874. *The mammals of India; A natural history of all the animals known to inhabit continental India.* London: John Wheldon.

15. Sterndale, R. A. 1884. *Natural history of the Mammalia of Indian and Ceylon.* Calcutta: Thacker, Spink, and Co.

16. Leyhausen, P. 1979. *Cat behavior: The predatory and social behavior of domestic and wild cats.* New York: Garland STPM Press.

17. Peters, G. 1981. Das schnurren der katzen (Felidae). *Säugetierk. Mitt.* 29: 30–37.

18. Peters, G. 1984. On the structure of friendly close range vocalizations in terrestrial carnivores (Mammalia: Carnivora: Fissipedia). *Z. Säugetierk.* 49: 157–182.

19. Wemmer, C., and K. Snow. 1977. Communication in the Felidae with emphasis on scent marking and contact patterns. In *How animals communicate*, ed. T. A. Sebeok, 749–766. Bloomington: Indiana University Press.

20. Mellen, J. D. 1993. A comparative analysis of scent-marking, social and reproductive behavior in 20 species of small cats (*Felis*). *Am. Zool.* 33: 151–166.

21. Mellen, J. D. 1989. Reproductive behavior of small captive exotic cats (*Felis* spp.). Ph.D. dissertation, University of California, Davis.

22. Andrews, P., Hexagon Farm Wild Feline Breeding Facility, 1187 Merrill Road, San Juan Bautista, CA. Personal communication.

23. Seager, S. W., and C. N. Demorest. 1986. Reproduction in captive wild carnivores. In *Zoo and wild animal medicine*, 2nd ed., ed. M. Fowler. Philadelphia: W. B. Saunders.

24. Louwman, J. W. W., and W. G. Van Oyen. 1968. A note on breeding Temminck's golden cat at Wassenaar Zoo. *Int. Zoo Yrbk.* 8: 47–49.

25. Barnett, H. 1972. Asian golden cat born. *Int. Zoo News* 19–3: 93.

26. Acharjyo, L. N., and G. Mishra. 1980. Some notes on age of sexual maturity of seven species of Indian wild mammals in captivity. *J. Bombay Nat. Hist. Soc.* 77: 504–507.

27. Jones, M. L. 1977. Record keeping and longevity of felids in captivity. In *The world's cats*, vol. 3, no. 3, ed. R. L. Eaton, 132–138. Seattle: Carnivore Research Institute, Burke Museum, University of Washington.

28. Kharabanda, B. C. 1984. Bhutan cat notes. In The plight of the cats: Proceedings of the meeting and workshop of the IUCN/SSC Cat Specialist Group at Kanha National Park, Madhya Pradesh, India, 61. Unpublished report, IUCN/SSC Cat Specialist Group, Bougy-Villars, Switzerland.

29. Wright, A. 1984. A note on the wild cats of the north eastern region of India. In The plight of the cats: Proceedings of the meeting and workshop of the IUCN/SSC Cat Specialist Group at Kanha National Park, Madhya Pradesh, India, 81–84. Unpublished report, IUCN/SSC Cat Specialist Group, Bougy-Villars, Switzerland.

30. Lu, H., and H. Sheng. 1986. The status and population fluctuation of the leopard cat in China. In Cats of the world: Biology, conservation, and management, ed. S. D. Miller and D. D. Everett, 59–62. Washington, DC: National Wildlife Federation.

31. Schaller, G., Director for Science, Wildlife Conservation Society/NYZS, Bronx, NY. Personal communication.

32. Cat News. 1989. Symposium of Asian Pacific mammalogy. Cat News 10: 6–7.

33. Khan, M. A. R. 1986. The status and distribution of the cats in Bangladesh. In Cats of the world: Biology, conservation, and management, ed. S. D. Miller and D. D. Everett, 43–49. Washington, DC: National Wildlife Federation.

34. Panwar, H. S. 1984. Conservation of wild cats in India. In The plight of the cats: Proceedings of the meeting and workshop of the IUCN/SSC Cat Specialist Group at Kanha National Park, Madhya Pradesh, India, 63–80. Unpublished report, IUCN/SSC Cat Specialist Group, Bougy-Villars, Switzerland.

35. Biswas, B., and R. K. Ghose. 1984. Status survey of lesser cats in Eastern India. In The plight of the cats: Proceedings of the meeting and workshop of the IUCN/SSC Cat Specialist Group at Kanha National Park, Madhya Pradesh, India, 85–88. Unpublished report, IUCN/SSC Cat Specialist Group, Bougy-Villars, Switzerland.

36. Chatterjee, A. K., and A. K. Sen. 1984. Status of lesser cats in Arunachal Pradesh. In The plight of the cats: Proceedings of the meeting and workshop of the IUCN/SSC Cat Specialist Group at Kanha National Park, Madhya Pradesh, India, 89–93. Unpublished report, IUCN/SSC Cat Specialist Group, Bougy-Villars, Switzerland.

37. Humphrey, S. R., and J. R. Bain. 1990. Endangered animals of Thailand. Gainesville, FL: Sandhill Crane Press.

38. International Species Inventory System. 1989. Species distribution report: Mammals. Apple Valley: Minnesota Zoological Garden.

Chinese desert cat

Felis bieti (Milne-Edwards, 1892)

The Chinese desert cat was first recorded in 1889 by members of a scientific expedition headed by Prince Henry d'Orleans. Then, as now, the primary evidence for this cat's existence came from skins on sale in the fur markets of Szechwan Province. Prince Henry's expedition purchased two skins in a market in the Tatsienlu district of central Szechwan; these constitute the type specimen of the Chinese desert cat and are lodged at the Musée d'Histoire Naturelle in Paris.[1,2]

Only about twenty skins and a few skulls of the Chinese desert cat exist in the world's museums, so even morphological evidence is scanty, but the little there is suggests that the Chinese desert cat is probably related to the jungle cat, sand cat, and Eurasian wildcat.[3] However, some authorities maintain that when more specimens become available for study, the Chinese desert cat will eventually be declared a subspecies of the Eurasian wildcat.[4,5] Partly because of the rarity of living specimens, the Chinese desert cat remains one of only four cat species that have not yet been the subject of chromosomal studies.

DESCRIPTION

The Chinese desert cat is a fairly large animal, about twice the size of a domestic cat. Its coat is a nearly uniform pale yellow-gray, ticked with longer, dark brown or black guard hairs. The soft underfur is slaty gray near the skin and brownish at the tips. The belly fur is white with the yellowish brown underfur showing through. Faint dark stripes sometimes run across the outer sides of the hindlimbs and forelimbs. On the cheeks, two indistinct brownish stripes, one above and one below the eye, come together to form a horizontal Y-shaped marking. The lower lips and chin are white, and the throat is pale yellowish brown. The backs of the ears are yellow-gray, and the ear tips are adorned with a small tuft of dark hairs. The last part of the tail is encircled by three or four dark rings, and the tip of the tail is black. Long hair grows between the pads of the feet, but it does not cover or obscure the pads, as does the hair on the feet of the sand cat.[1,2,3] Like the black-footed cat and sand cat, which also live in dry areas, the Chinese desert cat has a broad skull and enlarged ear bullae.[3,6]

DISTRIBUTION

The Chinese desert cat has a limited geographic range. It is mainly distributed in Sichuan, Shanxi, Gansu, Inner Mongolia, Xingjiang, and Qjinghai (fig. 14).[1,7,8,9,10]

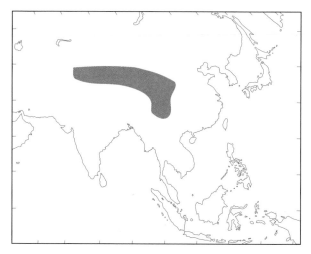

Figure 14. Distribution of the Chinese desert cat.

ECOLOGY AND BEHAVIOR

Little is known, but the few records there are suggest that it inhabits mountainous terrain, including montane forest, alpine meadows, semidesert, and loess hill steppe. It has been recorded at elevations of 2,800 to 4,100 meters.[7] Some authorities believe the name "desert cat" to be a misnomer; the limited information that is available suggests that the cat's habitat is probably steppe and mountainous terrain with bush and forest—the same sort of forest used by the giant panda and the golden monkey.[3] Localities and collector's information written on the labels of the few existing museum skins show that the specimens were taken on the steep slopes of the Tibetan Plateau from about 30 to 38 degrees north latitude at elevations up to 3,000 meters.[3]

In 1923, during the Stotznerschen China Expedition, Dr. Hugo Weigold found tracks of an animal he believed to be the Chinese desert cat in the snow in the wooded mountains of Wassuland. Later the expedition acquired two skins of Chinese desert cats, one of which came from an animal caught in a snare set for musk deer. On another occasion, early one evening at an altitude of about 3,000 meters in the mountains east of Sungpan, Weigold's foxhound discovered and chased a Chinese desert cat through low thickets. The dog fought with the cat and returned with two bites on its jaw. The cat was found in the same place the next day, but escaped.[1]

Feeding Ecology

An analysis of 32 scats showed that rodents are the major (90 percent) food items, but the Chinese desert cat also preys on pikas and birds, including pheasants. The cat is thought to be active primarily at dawn and dusk and at night; it rests in burrows during the day.[7]

Reproduction and Development

Mating occurs in January–March and most young are born in May. Birth dens are in burrows, usually situated on south-facing slopes.[7] Litter size is probably two to four.[11]

STATUS IN THE WILD

The cat's status is not well known and some authorities have suggested that the cat is not rare, while others believe it is rare. However, skins continue to find their way to city fur markets. The fur trade name for the species is "grass cat." However, there are no figures for the number of skins in trade except in Szechwan, where thirty pelts were taken in 1980.[11] In 1986 George Schaller saw sixteen skins for sale in the markets in Lingxia, Gansu Province, but reports that Chinese desert cat skins were less common than those of lynx.[12]

STATUS IN CAPTIVITY

There are few Chinese desert cats in captivity. The first of the species to be exhibited in captivity was an adult male that lived at the Beijing Zoo from 1974 until its death in 1978. In 1986 the world zoo population was believed to consist of four or five animals held in one zoo in China.[11,13]

TABLE 7 MEASUREMENTS AND WEIGHTS OF ADULT CHINESE DESERT CATS

HB	n	T	n	WT	n	Location	Source
				9.0	1m	China	14
				6.5	1f	China	14
816	4?	341	4?			China	1
(775–840)		(321–350)					
(preserved skins)							

Note: HB = head and body length (mm), T = tail length (mm), WT = weight (kg). n = sample size. Sex: m = male, f = female, ? = unknown. Mean values are presented only for sample sizes of three or more. Range of values is in parentheses.

REFERENCES

1. Allen, G. M. 1938. *The mammals of China and Mongolia.* New York: American Museum of Natural History.

2. Guggisberg, C. A. W. 1975. *Wild cats of the world.* New York: Taplinger.

3. Groves, C. P. 1980. The Chinese mountain cat. *Carnivore* 3: 35–41.

4. Haltenorth, T. 1953. *Die Wildkatzen der Alten Welt.* Leipzig: Academische Verlagsgesellschaft.

5. Corbet, G. B. 1978. *The mammals of the Palaearctic region: A taxonomic review.* Ithaca, NY: Cornell University Press.

6. Hemmer, H., P. Grubb, and C. P. Groves. 1976. Notes on the sand cat. *Z. Säugetierk.* 41: 286–303.

7. Liao, Y. 1988. Some biological informations on desert cat in Qinghai. *Acta Theriologica Sinica* 8: 128–131.

8. Gao, Y. T., S. Wang, M. L. Zhang, Z. Y. Ye, and J. D. Zhou, eds. 1987. *Fauna Sinica, Mammalia,* vol. 8: Carnivora. Beijing: Scientific Press.

9. Wang, Z.-Y., and S. Wang. 1986. Distribution and recent status of the Felidae in China. In *Cats of the world: Biology, conservation, and management,* ed. S. D. Miller and D. D. Everett, 201–208. Washington, DC: National Wildlife Federation.

10. Wang, S. 1990. The Chinese desert cat (*Felis bieti*). *Felid* 4(1).

11. Nowell, K., and P. Jackson. 1996. *Wild cats: A status survey and conservation action plan.* Gland, Switzerland: International Union for Conservation of Nature and Natural Resources (IUCN).

12. Schaller, G., Director for Science, Wildlife Conservation Society/NYZS, Bronx, NY. Personal communication.

13. Cat News. 1986. Some notes for the record. *Cat News* 5: 11.

14. Tan, B. 1984. The status of felids in China. In The plight of the cats: Proceedings of the meeting and workshop of the IUCN/SSC Cat Specialist Group at Kanha National Park, Madhya Pradesh, India, ed. P. Jackson, 33–47. Unpublished report, IUCN/SSC Cat Specialist Group, Bougy-Villars, Switzerland.

Jungle cat

Felis chaus (Schreber, 1777)

More than 2,000 years ago the Egyptians venerated, tamed, and even trained cats, depicting them in wall paintings and statues. Cats were worshipped as deities, kept as house pets, and entombed with their owners. Some cats were used to protect granaries against rats and mice, while others were trained for hunting. Among the mummified cat remains that have been examined, scientists have identified two species: the African wildcat and the larger jungle or reed cat. However, of 190 mummified remains examined, only three were those of jungle cats.[1] The African wildcat is generally considered to be the progenitor of the domestic cat.[2] While the Egyptians may have tamed the jungle cat and kept it for its rodent-catching ability, there is no evidence of true domestication of this species.[3]

DESCRIPTION

Jungle cats are somewhat larger and lankier than domestic cats. Adult males are larger and heavier than adult females. Like the caracal and the African wildcat, the jungle cat has a plain, unspotted coat, which varies from reddish or sandy brown to tawny gray. The fine black tips on the guard hairs give the cat a speckled appearance; the speckling is most intense along the back. Kittens may be both striped and spotted at birth but lose most of their markings as they reach sexual maturity.[4] Adult cats often retain some of their kitten markings as spots or dark stripes on the forelimbs and hindlimbs and two or three narrow black rings near the end of the tail. The black-tipped tail looks short compared with that of a domestic cat, measuring only about a third of the animal's head and body length.

The jungle cat has a long, slim face. Its muzzle is a bright white, and it has white lines above and below the eyes, with a dark spot in front of the eyes near the nose. Long, rounded ears are set close together and tipped with a small but distinct tuft of black hairs; the backs of the ears are reddish-brown. The throat is pale cream, and the belly is white or lighter colored than the rest of the body.[5,6,7] Black jungle cats occur regularly in southeastern Pakistan, and melanistic specimens have also been reported from India.[8,9,10]

Jungle cats were originally thought to be related to the lynxes because jungle cats also have tufted ears, a short tail, and long limbs,[4,11] but later they were included in the genus *Felis*.[6] More recent immunological and chromosomal studies indicate that the jungle cat is quite distinct from the lynx and place it in the domestic cat lineage.[12,13]

DISTRIBUTION

The jungle cat has a fairly wide geographic distribution, extending from Egypt through Israel, Jordan, northern Saudi Arabia, Syria, Iraq, and Iran to the northwestern shores of the Caspian Sea and the Volga River delta, and east through Turkmenistan, Uzbekistan, Tadzhikistan, and Kazakhstan to western Xinjiang, Afghanistan, Pakistan, Nepal, India, Sri Lanka, Myanmar, Laos, Thailand, Cambodia, Vietnam, and southwestern China (fig. 15).[7,8,14,15,16,17,18,19,20]

ECOLOGY AND BEHAVIOR

Judging by the habitat it frequents, a more appropriate name for the jungle cat might be "swamp cat" or "reed cat." It is not usually found in dense jungle, but prefers tall grass, thick brush, riverine swamps, and reed beds. It is most commonly found at elevations well below 1,000 meters (3,200 feet), but the species has been recorded in the Himalaya at 2,400 meters (7,800 feet).[21] Jungle cats have also been found well into mountainous areas in the Trans-Caucasus and Tadzhikistan, but they were invariably found along densely vegetated river valleys. Similarly, the presence of jungle cats in the mountainous and generally arid Seistan Basin of eastern Iran is associated with the valley's vast marshes and reed beds.[22] During systematic observations at Keoladeo Ghana National Park, India, jungle cats were seen in a variety of habitats, ranging from very wet marshy areas to dry grasslands, but twenty-one of twenty-eight sightings were in wetlands.[23] In contrast, radio-collared jungle cats living in the tall grass/riverine forest habitats on the floodplain in Chitwan National Park, Nepal, spent most of their time in the drier grasslands, the same habitat used by fishing cats.[24] The jungle cat's association with riparian habitats is well established, but there are also reports of them being found close to coasts, streams, reservoirs, lakes, and fishponds, and in some areas they even survive in flood- and sprinkler-irrigated landscapes.[7,15,19,25,26] Jungle cats are excellent swimmers and are clearly not averse to getting wet.[25,27]

Over much of peninsular India the jungle cat also lives in drier and more open forest and grassland habitats.[9] Surprisingly, jungle cats can survive in sandhill desert and steppe, where there is only sparse vegetative cover and limited water, and they sometimes settle in cultivated areas around villages.[7,8,9,14] The fact that this cat lives in such a broad range of habitats and under such a variety of conditions suggests that it is a very adaptable species.

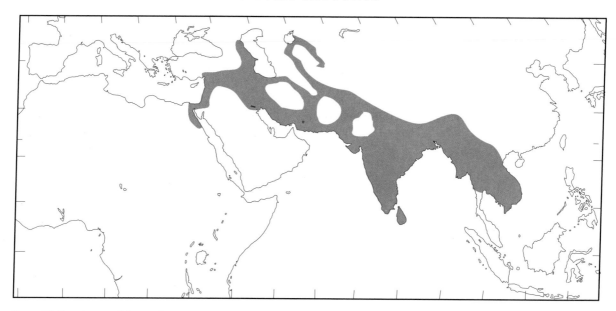

Figure 15. Distribution of the jungle cat.

Jungle cats have short, sparse, and coarse winter coats, offering little protection against severe cold and snow, and they do not appear to be tolerant of freezing temperatures and deep snow.[7] The northern limit of the cat's distribution is the far south of Russia; at this latitude the average January temperature is 2°C, which means brief periods of freezing weather and occasionally a light accumulation of snow. Many jungle cats in these areas perish from cold and hunger during winters of unusually harsh temperatures and deep snow.[7]

The jungle cat is not as strictly nocturnal in its habits as many cats. It is often seen hunting during daylight hours, most frequently in the early morning and late afternoon. At Keoladeo Ghana National Park, India, jungle cats were most active between 1830 and 2130 hours; they were not seen moving about in the daytime.[23] How far jungle cats travel during their daily activities is not known, but in one reportedly "good" area in Uzbekistan it was estimated that they cover 5 to 6 kilometers in a night.[27] In similar habitat in neighboring Tadzhikistan, the estimate was 3 to 5 kilometers per night.[7] On cold winter days these cats enjoy sunbathing; several naturalists have reported seeing jungle cats sunning themselves in the open.[8] During the daytime they rest in dense cover, out of sight among the reeds, canes, and thickets or inside rock crevices and tree cavities. In desert areas jungle cats enlarge or excavate underground burrows, but they are not as dependent on burrows as the wildcat,

and they often use grass thickets or scrub as daytime rest sites.[8]

Feeding Ecology

Hunting chiefly on the ground, the jungle cat captures most of its prey by stealth, using typical felid stalk and ambush techniques; prey are not often pursued if the cat misses in the first leap or two. However, this long-legged cat can run at great speed; in Iran one was clocked running at 32 kilometers per hour (20 mph).[19] Like the caracal, the jungle cat has been seen making high, nearly vertical leaps in attempts to capture birds.[11] It also uses high, arching leaps to spring onto small rodents and birds located in tall dense cover,[28] and a similar pounce, reminiscent of the hunting techniques of servals, is sometimes used to catch frogs in shallow water.[23] There are also observations of jungle cats digging into muskrat houses in pursuit of these rodents.[7]

Jungle cats feed mainly on prey that weighs less than a kilogram. Small mammals—principally rats, mice, and gerbils—are the prey most frequently found in feces and stomach contents. The stomach of one jungle cat contained the remains of ten ground squirrels,[7] and in Afghanistan the stomachs of three cats contained nineteen mice, three rats, and nine frogs.[29] Birds rank second in importance; various species, including pheasant, partridge, ducks, jungle fowl, peafowl, larks, and sparrows, are taken by the cats.[7,23,27,30,31,32,33] In southern Russia waterfowl are the mainstay of jungle cats in the winter — principally ducks and coots. With overwintering populations of waterfowl congregating in huge numbers on unfrozen rivers and marshes, the jungle cat hunts among reed beds and along edges of wetlands, searching for injured or weakened birds.[7]

Various other prey species, including hares, nutria, lizards, frogs, and insects, are taken more opportunistically.[7,8,25,29,31,34,35,36] Fish trapped in drying ponds are rapidly exploited,[7] and the jungle cat has been observed diving into the water and seizing fish in its mouth.[25] Jungle cats, albeit nervous ones, sometimes feed on the scraps at lion kills.[37]

Small snakes, such as racers, whip snakes, and sand snakes, are also killed by jungle cats,[38] but despite its strength and boldness, the cat itself may occasionally fall prey to larger snakes. In Pakistan a jungle cat was found entwined by a cobra; both animals were dead, and there were signs of a fierce fight.[8] In India the body of a jungle cat was recovered from the stomach of a python.[39]

Amazingly, in addition to this eclectic menu, jungle cats also eat fruit. In a study in southern Uzbekistan, the fruits of the Russian olive made up 17 percent of their diet in winter.[34] Where they live next to villages, the cats regularly prey on chickens, ducks, and geese.

While jungle cats appear to specialize on small prey, they are large and powerful enough to kill young swine, subadult gazelles, and chital fawns.[7,8,36,40] Adult chital obviously consider this cat to be a potential predator, as they react to its presence by giving alarm calls.[40,41]

In many parts of their geographic range jungle cats coexist with other carnivores of similar size, but it is not clear whether the larger fishing cat and the smaller jackal and wildcat compete with the jungle cat when resources are limited.[7,26,42] Jungle cats may also be killed by larger predators, and the rarity of jungle cats in some parks in Sri Lanka is thought to be due to predation by leopards.[43]

Social Organization

Despite being common, jungle cats are poorly studied, and many aspects of their social organization and lifestyle are unknown. They are solitary; outside of mating situations, the only enduring social contact is between mother and young. Spatial arrangements are likely to be maintained by indirect means, principally scent marking. Urine spraying has been observed in captivity[44] and in the wild;[40] in captivity males have also been seen to mark objects by rubbing with their cheeks. To what extent vocalizations play a role in the cat's social system is unknown since only limited data are available.[45,46] All observations of jungle cats at Keoladeo Ghana National Park were of singletons,[23] although not surprisingly, two adults have occasionally been seen together.[15,40] In Kanha National Park, India, Schaller observed that during the cool season (November–February), jungle cats congregated in an open meadow, apparently to mate.[35]

Reproduction and Development

Anecdotal accounts suggest that in the wild the mating season is marked by the shrieks and fighting of male cats.[7] In captivity, systematic observations of a pair of jungle cats revealed few behavioral indications of the onset of reproductive activity, especially for the female, although the male's rate of vocalizing increased prior to copulation, and at this time he was also very attentive to the female's movements.[47] The copulatory sequence is identical to that reported for the domestic cat,[47] and includes close following by the male, repeated vocalizations by both cats, sniffing of anogenital regions, and flehmen responses. When the female crouched in front of the male, he approached from behind, seized her by the nape, and straddled her raised hindquarters. At intromission the female gave a loud cry, and she immediately turned and growled at the rapidly dismounting male.

According to the records of births in the wild and in captivity, most young are born between December and June after a gestation period of sixty-three to sixty-six days.[47,48,49,50] However, mating and the subsequent timing of births varies latitudinally and also with seasonal temperature at the northern limits of the cat's range.[7] In Sri Lanka births are noted from December through March.[51,52,53] In Assam small kittens have been found at the end of January and in early February; in Pakistan three young kittens were found in a den in February.[8] In southern Russia mating takes place in January, February, and March; the young are born in April, May, and June, although in warm winters estrus may begin a month earlier. In some years a female may have two litters.[7,11,54]

Few den sites have been discovered in the wild, but animal trappers in the Sind Desert, Pakistan, report finding kittens in burrows.[8] In other areas kittens have been secreted in the roots deep beneath trees, inside hollow trees, and in paddy fields, thorny hedges, and dense reed beds; one of the latter nests was a raised platform lined with fur and soft grasses.[53,54] As many as six kittens have been recorded in a litter, but the usual number is three.[7,55] In one litter in the wild, the weights of four two-day-old young varied from 43 to 55 grams.[7] Newborn young in captivity are heavier; in one litter of four, kittens weighed 103 to 126 grams,[56] and in another litter of four, kittens weighed 150 to 161 grams.[55] Kittens open their eyes between 10 and 13 days of age; they continue to suckle until they are 90 days old, but begin to take solid food at day 49; and they are completely weaned by day 102.[7,55,57]

The kitten's predatory skills develop rapidly; two hand-reared females were seen to stalk, kill, and eat a crow when they were only six months old.[52] By eight to nine months of age the young are on their own, at which time they are about half the size of adults.[7] In captivity females become sexually mature at eleven months of age,[55] although there are other reports of females not attaining sexual maturity until eighteen, or even thirty to thirty-six, months of age.[58] One male was sexually mature at twenty-two months of age.[59]

Jungle cats are supposedly untamable,[4,7] although there are other reports that they tame easily and are not nearly as aggressive as young African wildcats.[52,53] Jungle cats breed readily in captivity, and captives have been known to live nine years and ten months.[60]

STATUS IN THE WILD
Today, in many part of Asia, the jungle cat is the small-cat equivalent of the jackal. Its rodent-catching abilities, wide habitat tolerance, and adaptability to living alongside villages and agricultural crops makes it the most common of the small felids.[6,8,9,14,61,62,63] However, its diurnal habits and ability to live near humans may result in overestimates of its abundance. In 1973 de Alwis reported that large-scale clearing of forests in Sri Lanka was having disastrous effects on the jungle cat, and that in the absence of natural prey, many jungle cats had begun killing poultry and goats. He reported that some goat farmers were killing as many as twelve jungle cats per month, and that females with kittens were being found in dry rice fields, a habitat not previously recorded.[64] A 1982 report from Bangladesh suggests that a viable population of jungle cats still survives in the forests, but the species is not abundant in villages due to the continuing loss of woodland groves.[61] In 1987 the conservator of forest in Gujarat, India, reported that the jungle cat enjoyed "good" status in that state.[63] However, in neighboring Rajasthan, there has been an alarming decline in jungle cats due to trade in cat skins.[65] The jungle cat has been heavily exploited in some countries, and in India, 306,343 jungle cat skins were declared as being held by traders when export was banned in 1979.[62] This ban was reflected in the international fur market, where in 1979 jungle cat skins accounted for 20 percent of the direct trade in felid species (17,280 jungle cat skins; 6,040 garments).[66] In 1980 the number of jungle cat skins and garments shipped was 14,242 and 5,422, respectively.

Although inevitable further losses of forest and wetlands will continue to reduce its numbers, the jungle cat appears to be more adaptable than many other small cats. Its generalist diet and ability to survive in a variety of habitats, including those altered by humans, will probably ensure its continued survival.

STATUS IN CAPTIVITY
Jungle cats are modestly well represented in zoos.

TABLE 8 MEASUREMENTS AND WEIGHTS OF ADULT JUNGLE CATS

HB	n	T	n	WT	n	Location	Source
763 (650–940)	13m	263 (200–310)	12m	8.1 (5–12)	11m	Russia	7
658 (560–850)	13f	263 (230–298)	12f	5.1 (2.6–7.5)	14f	Russia	7
689 (664–706)	4m	267 (226–286)	4m	6.7 (6.2–7.0)	3m	Nepal	24
				10.0 (7.4–12.2)	10m	Israel	26
				7.0 (5.9–9.0)	3f	Israel	26
745, 777	2m	272, 280	2m			Iraq	15,19

TABLE 8 *(continued)*

HB	n	T	n	WT	n	Location	Source
610, 661	2f	256, 270	2f			Iraq	15
803	1m	250	1m	9.0	1m	Pakistan	8
618	1f	256	1f			Pakistan	8
655	1m	260	1m	5.75	1m	China	17
595	1f	234	1f	4.5	1f	China	17
(550–650)	?	(240–310)	?	(4–6)	?	Thailand	14
(610–648)	?	(229–282)	?	(5–8)	?	Sri Lanka	51

Note: HB = head and body length (mm), T = tail length (mm), WT = weight (kg). n = sample size. Sex: m = male, f = female, ? = unknown. Mean values are presented only for sample sizes of three or more. Range of values is in parentheses.

REFERENCES

1. Morrison-Scott, T. C. S. 1952. The mummified cats of ancient Egypt. *Proc. Zool. Soc. Lond.* 121: 861–867.

2. Serpell, J. A. 1988. The domestication and history of the cat (*Felis s. chaus*). In *The domestic cat: The biology of its behaviour*, ed. D. C. Turner and P. Bateson, 151–158. Cambridge: Cambridge University Press.

3. Clutton-Brock, J. 1987. *A natural history of domesticated mammals*. Cambridge: Cambridge University Press.

4. Sterndale, R. A. 1884. *Natural history of the Mammalia of India and Ceylon*. Calcutta: Thacker, Spink.

5. Allen, G. M. 1938. *The mammals of China and Mongolia*. New York: American Museum of Natural History.

6. Guggisberg, C. A. W. 1975. *Wild cats of the world*. New York: Taplinger.

7. Heptner, V. G., and A. A. Sludskii. 1992. *Mammals of the Soviet Union*. Vol. 2, part 2, *Carnivora (Hyaenas and cats)*. English translation, sci. ed. R. S. Hoffmann. Washington, DC: Smithsonian Institution Libraries and the National Science Foundation.

8. Roberts, T. J. 1977. *The mammals of Pakistan*. London: Ernest Benn.

9. Prater, S. H. 1971. *The book of Indian animals*, 3rd ed. Bombay: Leaders Press.

10. Chakraborty, S., R. Chakraborty, and V. C. Agrawal. 1988. Melanism in jungle cat. *J. Bombay Nat. Hist. Soc.* 85: 184.

11. Novikov, G. A. 1962. *Carnivorous mammals of the fauna of the U.S.S.R.* Jerusalem: Israel Program for Scientific Translations.

12. Collier, G. E., and S. J. O'Brien. 1985. A molecular phylogeny of the Felidae: Immunological distance. *Evolution* 39: 473–487.

13. Wayne, R. K., R. E. Benveniste, D. N. Janczewski, and S. J. O'Brien. 1989. Molecular and biochemical evolution of the Carnivora. In *Carnivore behavior, ecology, and evolution*, ed. J. L. Gittleman, 465–494. Ithaca, NY: Cornell University Press.

14. Lekagul, B. M. D., and J. A. McNeely. 1977. *Mammals of Thailand*. Bangkok: Association for the Conservation of Wildlife.

15. Harrison, D. L. 1968. *The mammals of Arabia*. Vol. 2. London: Ernest Benn.

16. Van Peenen, P. F. D. 1969. *Preliminary identification manual for mammals of South Vietnam*. Washington, DC: Smithsonian Institution.

17. Shaw, T. H. 1962. *Economic fauna: Mammals*. Beijing: Scientific Press.

18. Corbet, G. B. 1978. *The mammals of the Palaearctic region: A taxonomic review*. Ithaca, NY: Cornell University Press.

19. Hatt, R. T. 1959. *The mammals of Iraq*. Miscellaneous Publications, Museum of Zoology, University of Michigan, no. 106.

20. Tan, B. 1984. The status of felids in China. In The plight of the cats: Proceedings of the meeting and workshop of the IUCN/SSC Cat Specialist Group at Kanha National Park, Madhya Pradesh, India, ed. P. Jackson, 33–47. Unpublished report, IUCN/SSC Cat Specialist Group, Bougy-Villars, Switzerland.

21. Blandford, W. T. 1888–1891. *The fauna of British India, including Ceylon and Burma*. Vol. 1, *Mammalia*. London: Taylor & Francis.

22. Harrington, F. A. Jr. 1977. *A guide to the mammals of Iran*. Tehran: Department of the Environment.

23. Mukherjee, S. 1989. Ecological separation of four sympatric carnivores in Keoladeo Ghana National Park, Bharatpur, Rajastan, India. Master's thesis, Wildlife Institute of India, Dehra Dun.

24. Smith, J. L. D., associate professor, Department of Fisheries and Wildlife, University of Minnesota, St. Paul. Personal communication.

25. Mendelssohn, H. 1989. Wild cats in Israel. *Cat News* 10: 2–4.

26. Dayan, T., D. Simberloff, E. Tchernov, and Y. Yom-Tov. 1990. Feline canines: Community-wide character displacement among the small cats of Israel. *Am. Nat.* 136: 39–60.

27. Allayarov, A. M. 1964. Data on the ecology and geographical distribution of the jungle cat in Uzbekistan. *Uzbekskii Biol. Zh.* 2: 46–50.

28. Tyabji, H. N. 1990. A hunting technique of the jungle cat *Felis chaus. J. Bombay Nat. Hist. Soc.* 87: 134.

29. Niethammer, J. 1966. Zur ernährung des sumpfluchses (*Felis chaus* Güldenstädt, 1776) in Afghanistan. *Z. Säugetierk.* 31: 393–394.

30. Jerdon, T. C. 1874. *The mammals of India: A natural history of all the animals known to inhabit continental India*. London: John Wheldon.

31. Nasibov, C. B. 1968. On the ecology of the jungle cat (*Felis chaus*) in Azerbaijan. *Bull. Azerbaijan Acad. Sci. USSR Biol. Ser.* 3: 51–56.

32. Dunbar Brander, A. A. 1931. *Wild animals in Central India*. London: Edward Arnold.

33. Tehsin, R., and F. Tehsin. 1990. Jungle cat *Felis chaus* and grey junglefowl *Gallus sonneratii. J. Bombay Nat. Hist. Soc.* 87: 144.

34. Ishunin, G. I. 1965. On the biology of *Felis chaus chaus* Güldenstädt in south Uzbekistan. *Zool. Zh.* 44: 630–632.

35. Schaller, G. B. 1967. *The deer and the tiger: A study of wildlife in India*. Chicago: University of Chicago Press.

36. Johnsingh, A. J. T. 1983. Large mammalian prey—predators in Bandipur. *J. Bombay Nat. Hist. Soc.* 80: 1–57.

37. Gee, E. P. 1964. *The wildlife of India.* London: Harper Collins.

38. Flower, S. S. 1932. Notes on the recent mammals of Egypt, with a list of the species recorded from that Kingdom. *Proc. Zool. Soc. Lond.* 1932: 369–450.

39. Karanth, U., zoologist, Centre for Wildlife Studies, Mysore, India. Personal communication.

40. Rathore, F. S., and V. Thapar. 1984. Behavioral observations of leopard and jungle cat in Ranthambhor National Park and Tiger Reserve, Rajasthan. In The plight of the cats: Proceedings of the meeting and workshop of the IUCN/SSC Cat Specialist Group at Kanha National Park, Madhya Pradesh, India, ed. P. Jackson, 136–139. Unpublished report, IUCN/SSC Cat Specialist Group, Bougy-Villars, Switzerland.

41. Bhatnagar, R. K. 1971. Reaction of chital [*Axis* (Erxleben)] to jungle cat *Felis chaus* Güldenstädt. *J. Bombay Nat. Hist. Soc.* 68: 444–445.

42. Akhtar, S. A., and J. K. Tiwari. 1991. Food piracy by jackal *Canis aureus* from a jungle cat *Felis chaus* in Chhari-Dhandh, Kutch. *J. Bombay Nat. Hist. Soc.* 88: 108.

43. Eisenberg, J. F., Ordway Professor of Ecosystem Conservation, Florida Museum of Natural History, Gainesville. Personal communication.

44. Mellen, J. D. 1993. A comparative analysis of scent-marking, social and reproductive behavior in 20 species of small cats (*Felis*). *Am. Zool.* 33: 151–166.

45. Peters, G. 1984. On the structure of friendly close range vocalizations in terrestrial carnivores (Mammalia: Carnivora: Fissipedia). *Z. Säugetierk.* 49: 157–182.

46. Peters, G., and M. H. Hast. 1994. Hyoid structure, laryngeal anatomy, and vocalization in felids (Mammalia: Carnivora: Felidae). *Z. Säugetierk.* 59: 87–104.

47. Mellen, J. D. 1989. Reproductive behavior of small captive exotic cats (*Felis* spp.). Ph.D. dissertation, University of California, Davis.

48. Colby, E. D. 1974. Artificially induced estrus in wild and domestic felids. In *The world's cats,* vol. 2, ed. R. L. Eaton, 126–142. Winston, OR: World Wildlife Safari.

49. Hemmer, H. 1979. Gestation period and postnatal development in felids. *Carnivore* 2(1): 90–100.

50. Seager, S. W. J., and C. N. Demorest. 1978. Reproduction of captive wild carnivores. In *Zoo and wild animal medicine,* ed. M. E. Fowler, 667–706. Philadelphia: W. B. Saunders.

51. Phillips, W. W. A. 1984. *Manual of the mammals of Sri Lanka,* 2nd ed. Colombo: Aitken Spence.

52. Zylva, T. S. U. de. 1968. The Ceylon jungle cat. *Loris* 11: 200–203.

53. Zylva, T. S. U. de. 1969. The Ceylon jungle cat. Part II. *Loris* 12: 288–292.

54. Ognev, S. I. 1962. *Mammals of the U.S.S.R. and adjacent countries.* Vol. 3: *Carnivora.* Jerusalem: Israel Program for Scientific Translations.

55. Schauenberg, P. 1979. La reproduction of chat des marais *Felis chaus* (Güldenstädt, 1776). *Mammalia* 43: 215–223.

56. Acharjyo, L. N., and R. Mishra. 1974. Weight and size at birth of two species of wild mammals in captivity. *J. Bombay Nat. Hist. Soc.* 71: 137–138.

57. Acharjyo, L. N., and S. Mohapatra. 1977. Some observations on the breeding habits and growth of jungle cat (*Felis chaus*) in captivity. *J. Bombay Nat. Hist. Soc.* 74: 158–159.

58. Eaton, R. L. 1984. Survey of smaller felid breeding. *Zool. Garten* (n.f.) 54: 101–120.

59. Acharjyo, L. N., and G. Mishra. 1980. Some notes on age of sexual maturity of seven species of Indian wild mammals in captivity. *J. Bombay Nat. Hist. Soc.* 77: 504–507.

60. Jones, M. L. 1977. Record keeping and longevity of felids in captivity. In *The world's cats,* vol. 3, no. 3, ed. R. L. Eaton, 132–138. Seattle: Carnivore Research Institute, Burke Museum, University of Washington.

61. Khan, M. A. R. 1986. The status and distribution of cats in Bangladesh. In *Cats of the world: Biology, conservation and management,* ed. S. D. Miller and D. D. Everett, 43–49. Washington, DC: National Wildlife Federation.

62. Panwar, H. S. 1984. Conservation of wild cats in India. In The plight of the Cats. Proceedings of the meeting and workshop of the IUCN/SSC Cat Specialist Group at Kanha National Park, Madhya Pradesh, India, ed. P. Jackson, 63–80. Unpublished report, IUCN/SSC Cat Specialist Group, Bougy-Villars, Switzerland.

63. Chavan, S. A. 1987. Status of wild cats in Gujarat. *Tigerpaper* 14: 21–24.

64. de Alwis, W. L. E. 1973. Status of Southeast Asia's small cats. In *The world's wild cats,* vol. 1, ed. R. L. Eaton, 198–208. Winston, OR: World Wildlife Safari.

65. Sharma, V., and K. Sankhala. 1984. Vanishing cats of Rajasthan. In The plight of the cats: Proceedings of the meeting and workshop of the IUCN/SSC Cat Specialist Group at Kanha National Park, Madhyra Pradesh, India, ed. P. Jackson, 117–135. Unpublished report, IUCN/SSC Cat Specialist Group, Bougy-Villars, Switzerland.

66. McMahan, L. R. 1986. The international cat trade. In *Cats of the world: Biology, conservation and management,* ed. S. D. Miller and D. D. Everett, 461–488. Washington, DC: National Wildlife Federation.

Sand cat

Felis margarita (Loche, 1858)

The sand cat was discovered in 1856 by Captain Victor Loche at Ngouca in the sand dunes of eastern Algeria, near the Libyan border. At the time Loche was the naturalist attached to a French expedition led by General Margueritte, and Loche named the new species after the expedition leader.[1] Over the next seventy years a few more sand cats were added to collections, but information on this cat was still so sparse that when S. I. Ognev studied the first specimens from Turkmenistan in 1926, he was convinced that he had discovered not only a new species, but a new genus.[2] Ognev named the Turkmenistan cat *Eremailurus thinobius*, but ten years later it was established that Ognev had simply rediscovered *F. margarita* in the northeasterly portion of its range.[2]

In the early 1970s there was some speculation that the sand cat was the ancestor of today's domestic breed of Persian cats. This view was based on the sand cat's geographic distribution and the fact that both the sand cat and the modern Persian have a mat of dense hair covering the pads of the feet.[3,4] However, this argument did not withstand scrutiny for long. Other scientists soon showed that cats with longer body hair simply tend to have longer hair on their feet as well, and that short-haired domestic Persians have no hair mats on their feet. Thus there is no reason to believe that the sand cat is the ancestor of today's domestic Persian breed.[5]

DESCRIPTION

Smaller than the African wildcat or the jungle cat, the sand cat is a stocky animal with a relatively long tail and short legs. It has large ears set low on the side of the head and a broad face with dense, well-developed cheek hair. The ears are more pointed than those of the manul; they are tawny brown at the base, with a black tip. The insides of the ears are covered with thick white hairs. The lower part of the face is whitish, and a faint reddish line runs from the outside corner of each eye, angling down across the cheek. The large greenish yellow eyes are surrounded by a white ring, and the naked tip of the nose is black. There are blackish bars on the limbs, and the tail has a black tip with two or three dark rings alternating with buff bands. The banding extends over only the final third of the tail.[2,6,7]

The coat is a pale sandy color, usually without spots or stripes except on the forelegs and tail, although some animals do have faint markings. The fur on the upper and lower lips, chin, throat, and belly is white. In northern regions the sand cat's winter coat can be long and thick; guard hairs have been measured at 55 millimeters, or more than 2 inches long. This rich, dense coat makes the 2- to 3-kilogram sand cat look considerably larger than it is.[2,6,7]

The sand cat is unique among Palearctic (Asian) cats in that it has long, dense hair growing between its toes. Locke, who first described the species, said that the feet were "clothed after the manner of hares," and Pocock writes that the feet of the sand cat "recall those of an Arctic fox in winter."[7] These hairs form a dense mat that covers the pads of the cat's feet, insulating them from the hot sand and acting as a sort of cushion on which the animal walks. The desert-dwelling black-footed cat of South Africa has similar but less well developed hairs on its feet; it is thought that the densely furred pads help these animals move across fine sand. The claws on the sand cat's hind feet are weakly curved and somewhat blunt, with a poorly developed retractile mechanism. Because the long hair on the feet also obscures the pads, the tracks of a sand cat are indistinct and difficult to follow. The partially protruding claws also make it easy to confuse its tracks with those of the fennec fox.[8,9]

The sand cat's skull is very different from that of the European wildcat or the jungle cat; the skull it most closely resembles is that of the manul. The sand cat's skull shows a high degree of specialization for desert life. Some of its more uncommon features include a shortened, bulging braincase, wide zygomatic arches, and very large, forward-directed eye sockets. The tympanic bullae are greatly enlarged, much more so than in other Old World cats. Skulls of males and females are similarly proportioned, but female skulls are smaller, about 85 percent of the size of male skulls.[2,6,7] Large tympanic bullae and ear pinnae are also found in other desert-living species, such as manuls, fennec foxes, springhares, and jerboas. This specialized hearing apparatus is thought to be used for amplifying sounds and detecting vibrations. Springhares, for instance, are known to rest with the top of the head pressed against the ground, probably so they can pick up the vibrations of an approaching predator.

Besides all these unusual physical characteristics, this extraordinary little cat also has a distinctive way of moving—belly to the ground, it moves at a fast run punctuated with occasional leaps. After seeing sand cats in the wild in Niger, Alain Dragesco-Joffé remarked that the animal has "a particularly clumsy air." "Its legs are unusually short and seem too wide apart. This oddity is even more accentuated by the fact that the animal tends to graze the ground as it walks." If pressed, the sand cat is capable of sudden bursts of speed; it can sprint at speeds of 30 to 40 kilometers per hour for short distances of perhaps 400 meters. It also uses crypticity to escape detection; when danger threatens, it crouches flat beside a small rock or tuft of grass, chin on the ground, ears down, becoming almost impossible to see.[8]

DISTRIBUTION

In Asia the sand cat has been reported from the deserts of central and northwestern Karakum in the former Soviet Union to the Iranian plateau and through the Nushki Desert in Pakistan.[6,10,11] It has also been recorded from Qatar, Yemen, and Oman on the Arabian Peninsula to the Sinai in Israel.[12,13] It is found in the western Sahara of northwestern Africa in Morocco, Algeria, Niger, Egypt, and possibly Tunisia and Libya (fig. 16).[8,14,15,16,17] However, because this species is so specialized in terms of its habitat requirements, being strictly confined to sandy deserts, it is very unevenly distributed within these areas. For this reason, distribution maps can be misleading and must be interpreted cautiously.

ECOLOGY AND BEHAVIOR

The sand cat is confined to areas of sandy desert, becoming less common where the substrate becomes compacted or turns to clay. In the former Soviet Union the sand cat seems to thrive in desert areas, especially among the sparsely vegetated ridges and sandy hillocks where gerbils are common.[6] These cats are rarely found in shifting sand dunes where there is no vegetation. In the Sahara, typical sand cat habitat is flat and open and covered with unstable sand, on which there grows little but a few tufts of grass and occasional small bushes.[8]

Throughout its range the sand cat must cope with extraordinary temperature variation. In summer in the Karakum Desert, air temperatures can exceed 40°C, while the temperature of the upper layer of sand rises to over 80°C. In winter the air temperature can fall as low as −25°C.[6] The sand cat handles these inhospitable conditions by retreating to a burrow during the worst of the heat or cold, and its thick coat offers some insulation from the cold. The mats of hair on its feet

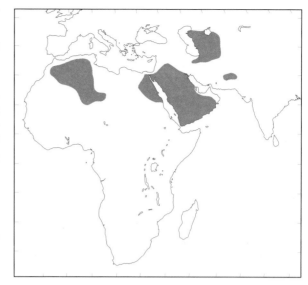

Figure 16. Distribution of the sand cat.

protect the pads from the baking heat and make it easier to move through the fine sand.

The sand cat's huge ears and enlarged tympanic bullae suggest that it relies on sound for detecting prey. Low-set ears enable it to take advantage of the scantiest cover, and the plain, pale sand-colored coat helps the cat conceal itself.

Given the nature of its desert habitat, it is not surprising that the sand cat can survive without free-standing water. Indeed, for most of the year, these cats do not drink, but obtain sufficient moisture from their prey. One captive fed on fresh rodents and birds refused all fresh water and did not drink for two months, but another drank freely.[6,11] Though they can live without water, wild sand cats will drink when water is available; in the eastern Karakum, their tracks have been found around pools of water.[6]

Sand cats begin to hunt a little before sunset or just as it becomes dark, continue through the night, and sometimes extend their activity into the early morning hours.[8,9,11] In cooler weather, before retiring for the day, they often spend time sunbathing at the entrance to the burrow.[8,10,11] During snowy weather the cat has been known to stay in its burrow for several days.[6]

Feeding Ecology

Though deserts such as the Sahara and Karakum seem to be unlikely places for a cat to live, these dry, inhospitable landscapes support a variety of potential cat food in the form of small mammals, reptiles, and birds. In the Karakum, midday gerbils, northern three-toed jerboas, mole-voles, and gray hamsters live and breed in the sparsely vegetated sand dunes. Some of these small mammals are active during the day and others feed at night, but all are part of the sand cat's catholic diet, which also includes sandgrouse, larks, and gray partridge. During the summer the sand cat hunts in the sand dunes, preying on midday gerbils, jerboas, and reptiles, but in the winter most of these prey species hibernate, so the cat shifts to more densely vegetated areas, where it feeds on Tolai hares and great gerbils.[6]

In other areas reptiles may play a more important role in the cat's diet. Sand cats in the Arava depression in southern Israel, for example, feed on the large, diurnal spiny-tailed lizard.[13] According to Alain Dragesco-Joffé, who spent thirteen years photographing Saharan wildlife, these cats have a reputation among the nomads for being snake hunters and regularly kill horned vipers and sand vipers.[8] Dragesco-Joffé photographed a sand cat attacking a sand viper 40 centimeters long. He recalls that the snake was forced to lower its head after being hit with several quick, light blows from the cat's paw. The cat then hit the snake's head with a swift blow, killed it by biting into the neck, then, beginning at the head, devoured it in ten minutes. In Arabia the sand cat's distribution coincides with that of sand skinks and Arabian toad-head lizards; both reptiles are thought be an important source of food for the cat.[18] Basically, sand cats are opportunistic hunters that will eat whatever they can catch. Almost anything from gerbils to geckos and birds to beetles is potential prey to be stalked, pounced on, or chased during the long night's hunt.

Like other felids, sand cats are capable of eating prodigious amounts of food when it is available, but under normal circumstances a sand cat probably consumes about 10 percent of its own body weight per day. A captive sand cat was satisfied with a 250-gram ground squirrel each day.[6] At Tel Aviv University, H. Mendelssohn once tried to find out how much an adult male sand cat would eat if it had continuous access to food. He fed the cat a succession of laboratory mice, each weighing about 25 grams, and the cat continued to eat until it had swallowed fifteen mice. At this point, Mendelssohn remarked, "I stopped, for I thought it might be too much, but he would have continued."[19] Sand cats are not known to scavenge,

but they do cover the remains of their prey if it is more than they can eat at a sitting.[8]

Social Organization

The sand cat rarely hunts by sitting and waiting. Instead, it searches for prey while walking and listening, and it often travels long distances while hunting. During a field study in Israel, a radio-collared male moved 8 kilometers in a single night, then returned to his burrow the following night. A male that was tracked for nine days moved an average of 5.4 kilometers per night.[9] Similarly, two observations from the Karakum record one cat traveling 7 kilometers in a night during the summer, and another moving 10 kilometers during a winter night's hunt.[6] The nature of the habitat in which they live and the great distances they travel during a night suggest that sand cats probably have extremely large home ranges. The study in Israel found that the home ranges of three radio-collared males overlapped and that one male used an area of 16 square kilometers.[9]

Saharan nomads call this species "the cat that digs holes," in contrast to the African wildcat, which does not dig.[8] Throughout its range the sand cat makes its home in burrows—either occupying abandoned burrows of the red fox, corsac fox, Ruppel's fox, or porcupine or enlarging gerbil and ground squirrel burrows. One such den, made by enlarging a giant gerbil burrow, was found to be home to a female sand cat, her three kittens, and five gerbils.[6] Sand cats often bask in front of their shallow burrows, which are dug into the compact soil at the base of a small mound, beneath a shrub or bush, or away from vegetation on a flat expanse of sand. Two sand cat burrows excavated in the eastern Karakum each had a single entrance and measured about 3 meters long.[6] Another burrow in Niger was about 15 centimeters in diameter and 1.5 meters long; it had been dug in a straight line and sloped gently to a point about 60 centimeters below the surface.[8]

One of the most striking aspects of the sand cat's behavior is its tameness and lack of fear of humans. In Pakistan, Anderson captured several animals alive in broad daylight by creeping up to the burrow out of the animal's line of sight, then grabbing the cat.[10] In 1984 Goodman and Helmy collected a specimen in Egypt. "We were struck by how unafraid the cat acted," they noted; "it allowed us to approach within 15 meters before fleeing into the cave."[15] Likewise, in Israel, two females did not move when caught in the headlights of a jeep and could be approached from behind and picked up by hand.[13] Sand cats reportedly continue to be quite tame even when they are taken into captivity, although young adults bred in captivity are more aggressive and shy than wild-caught animals.

There is a striking behavioral contrast between sand cats and black-footed cats. Both species are small and live under very similar desert conditions, feeding on an almost identical range of small mammals, birds, and reptiles. However, the sand cat is docile and unafraid almost to the point of absurdity, whereas the black-footed cat is famous for its ferocity and aggressive posturing. Zookeepers who work with both species describe the black-footed cat as "a sand cat with an attitude."[20] Part of the reason for their diametrically opposed characters may be the different kinds of predators and competitors that they face in their respective habitats. Black-footed cats live in areas where there is an array of larger predators, including hyenas, lions, leopards, jackals, and caracals. Under these circumstances, an exaggerated threat display and "an attitude" may be a life-saving adaptation. Sand cats, on the other hand, have far fewer large terrestrial predators to fear. Young sand cats are sometimes taken by eagle owls, and in some regions golden eagles, jackals, and wolves occasionally kill adult sand cats, but aside from these they have few enemies.[6,8,9]

Sand cats growl and spit much like domestic cats, but some of their other vocalizations are quite different from those of domestics. Sand cats have a loud barking call that has been likened to the noise made by a small dog.[21] The call has also been described as a rapidly repeated harsh cry, syllabified as "yea-yea-yea."[11] "Several times we observed a male on a hilltop, sounding sharp calls," Abbadi remarks.[9] The call is thought to be used by males seeking a mate, but in captivity both males and females have been observed to give the barking vocalization when they are introduced.[22] Male black-footed cats also have a very loud call, and it is not unreasonable to suppose that these calls allow males and females to find each other in an environment where individuals are normally widely spaced. The vocal repertoire of the sand cat also includes the gurgle, a friendly close-contact call.[23]

Scent marking is also likely to be an important mode of communication in the rather barren landscapes where these cats live, although no details are available. In captivity, feces are covered, but both sexes rub their cheeks and heads on objects, leave claw marks on logs and branches, and spray urine, all of which are thought to serve a communication function.[24,25]

Reproduction and Development

Because the sand cat has proved so difficult to keep in captivity, details of its reproductive behavior are sparse. The most comprehensive information comes from the work of Jill Mellen, who described the reproductive behavior of several small exotic felids in captivity.[22,25] Mellen found that male and female sand cats showed pronounced behavioral changes during the days surrounding copulation. A week before copulation the female showed a dramatic increase in scent marking and cheek rubbing. Her rate of scent marking rose from five per hour the week before, peaked at more than thirty per hour at the time of copulation, and dropped back to five in the week following mating. In contrast, the male's rate of scent marking decreased during times of copulation. When mating, the male performed the stereotyped neck bite, and on average, a mount lasted about nine minutes. Copulation occurs frequently during estrus.

Based on behavioral observations, Mellen estimated that estrus lasts five to six days, while gestation lasts sixty-six days — slightly longer than the fifty-nine to sixty-three days reported by Hemmer.[26] In a small sample, the mean litter size was three, but one litter of eight was recorded in captivity.[25] Though captive sand cats give birth throughout the year, the few records from the wild suggest that births are seasonal. In Turkmenistan young are born in April, and nursing kittens have been excavated from burrows in April and May.[6] In Pakistan sand cats may have two litters per year, as young have been found in March and April and a six-week-old litter was captured in October.[11]

The kittens are born blind and helpless, weighing 39 to 80 grams, and grow rapidly, gaining about 12 grams per day during the first three weeks of life.[21] Their fur is pale yellow or reddish gray, marked with small brown spots that join together to become transverse bands. By the time kittens are five months old they are three-quarters adult size; at ten to eleven months, a male weighs as much as or more than an adult female.[6] In captivity a female was sexually mature by fourteen months of age.[20] Apart from a single record of a male in the London Zoo living to be almost eight years old,[27] few details are known of dispersal or longevity. The limited birth and growth data that we do have from captive animals suggest that the sand cat will turn out to be a species with a fairly high reproductive potential and an effective colonizer. The young probably become independent when they are about one year old, and the long-distance nightly movements made by adults during the course of a normal night's hunting suggest that dispersing young would be capable of traveling great distances.

STATUS IN THE WILD

The overall status of the sand cat is unknown. J. Anderson, who discovered the sand cat in Pakistan in 1966, reported that the animal was not rare in the dune fields of Nushki. The fact that he managed to capture four males and five females near the Lora River northwest of Nushki lends credence to his report. However, following his discovery, there was a rush of trappers and collectors to the area, and several authorities believe that the sand cat's current status in Pakistan is due to commercial dealers who overexploited the population in the mid-1960s.[11] The cats were subsequently sold to zoos, where they usually died. By 1973 animal dealers maintained that it was nearly impossible to find sand cats in the Nushki area. The Pakistani government now prohibits the export of sand cats.

In Israel the sand cat is endangered through habitat loss as more and more of the desert is cultivated. Predators of the sand cat in Israel include domestic dogs, caracals, and wolves, which sometimes attain artificially high densities near human settlements. There are still quite large areas of suitable sand cat habitat on the Jordanian side of the Arava depression.[13] There are no recent status reports from the former Soviet Union, but in the 1960s sand cats were reported to be common in parts of the Karakum Desert. There is little commercial value in their fur, but they are sometimes caught in traps set for foxes or Tolai hares.[6] Like bobcats and lynx, sand cats sometimes go through major population crashes, but, like those other two felids, relatively large litter sizes and the potential of two litters per year allow sand cat numbers to recover quite fast. In Turkmenistan severe winters accompanied by heavy snows cause significant reductions in gerbil numbers, and deep snow makes hunting extremely difficult for the cats. During one such winter in Kyzyl Kum in 1953–1954, snow covered the ground from December to the end of March, causing mass mortality among sand cats and foxes. The following year fur trappers noted a reduction of two to ten times in their catch of sand cats.[6]

In the Sahara, nomads say that they have encountered sand cats inside their camps around dusk, just after milking time, drinking camel's milk from storage gourds. The nomads also say that these cats quite often kill and eat chickens and are sometimes caught in traps set in front of chicken enclosures. Despite these occasional conflicts, sand cats are generally not persecuted in this part of their range; rather, they are respected by the local people—Moslem tradition has it that, like the eagle owls and hoopoes, sand cats were the companions of the prophet Mohammed and his daughter Fatima.[8]

STATUS IN CAPTIVITY

Before 1967 sand cats were rarely seen in captivity. Only a handful of zoos in the Soviet Union and Europe had ever exhibited them, and little was known about their captive requirements. In 1966, when the species was discovered in Pakistan, a number of animals were captured and shipped to zoos in North America and Europe, resulting in a burst of captive breeding and a significant increase in the number of sand cats held in zoos.[28] Unfortunately, despite the fact that their unusual appearance makes them attractive exhibits, sand cats are very difficult to keep in captivity. Like the black-footed cat, the sand cat is sensitive to a combination of cold weather and high humidity. The species is also highly susceptible to respiratory tract infections and rhinitis. A few have survived in captivity for several years, but wild-caught animals often die within a year of being brought into captivity. Out of eighteen sand cats imported from the Nushki Desert, fifteen died of feline enteritis, despite having been vaccinated against the disease.[21]

TABLE 9 MEASUREMENTS AND WEIGHTS OF ADULT SAND CATS

HB	n	T	n	WT	n	Location	Source
(430–514)	12m	(278–290)	12m	(2.1–3.4)	12m	Russia	6
467	6f	277	6f	2.2	5f	Russia	6
(400–520)		(232–310)		(1.35–3.1)			
499	5m	273	5m	2.78	4m	Pakistan	11,14
(460–570)		(260–295)		(2.0–3.2)			
471	1m	261	1m	2.1, 2.7	2m	Egypt	15
453	3m	270	3m			Arabia	13,14,29
(440–470)		(250–300)					
420	1f	235	1f	2.06	1f	Algeria	14
455	1m	270	1m			Algeria	14
390	1f	245	1f			Niger	14
420	1m	270	1m			Niger	14

Note: HB = head and body length (mm), T = tail length (mm), WT = weight (kg). n = sample size. Sex: m = male, f = female, ? = unknown. Mean values are presented only for sample sizes of three or more. Range of values is in parentheses.

TABLE 10 FREQUENCY OF OCCURRENCE OF PREY ITEMS IN THE DIETS OF SAND CATS
(PERCENTAGE OF SAMPLES)

Prey items	Eastern Karakum, Turkmenistan[30] Stomachs and scats (n = 182)
Lepus tolai Tolai hare	1.6
Spermophilopsis leptodactylus Thin-toed ground squirrel	1.1
Rhombomys opimus Great gerbil	33.5
Meriones sp. Midday gerbil	18.7
Dipus sagitta Rough-legged jerboa	7.1
Paradipus ctenodactylus Comb-toed jerboa	3.8
Unidentified rodents	8.2
Birds	16.8
Reptiles	18.1
Insects	3.8
Other arthropods	7.1
Minimum number of vertebrate prey items	199.0

REFERENCES

1. Guggisberg, C. A. W. 1975. *Wild cats of the world*. New York: Taplinger.

2. Hemmer, H., P. Grubb, and C. P. Groves. 1976. Notes on the sand cat, *Felis margarita* Loche, 1858. *Z. Säugetierk.* 41: 286–303.

3. Petzsch, H. 1972. Barchan-wuestenwildkatze und "Perser" langhaarhauskatzen. *Das Pelzgewerbe* 21: 7–15.

4. Petzsch, H. 1973. Zur problematik der primar-domestikation der hauskatze (*Felis silvestris* "familiaris"). In *Domestikationsforchung und Geschichte der haustiere*, ed. J. Matolcsi, 109–113. Budapest: Akademie-Verlag.

5. Hemmer, H. 1978. Were the leopard cat and the sand cat among the ancestry of domestic cat races? *Carnivore* 1: 106–108.

6. Heptner, W. G., and A. A. Sludskii. 1992. *Mammals of the Soviet Union*. Vol. 2, part 2, *Carnivora (Hyaenas and cats)*. English translation, sci. ed. R. S. Hoffmann. Washington, DC: Smithsonian Institution Libraries and the National Science Foundation.

7. Pocock, R. I. 1938. The Algerian sand cat (*Felis margarita* Loche). *Proc. Zool. Soc. Lond.* 108 B: 41–46.

8. Dragesco-Joffé, A. 1993. *La vie sauvage du sahara*. Lausanne: Delachaux et Nestlé.

9. Abbadi, M. 1991. Israel's elusive feline: Sand cats. *Israel Land and Nature* 16(3): 111–115.

10. Lay, D. M., J. A. W. Anderson, and J. D. Hassinger. 1970. New records of small mammals from West Pakistan and Iran. *Mammalia* 34: 98–106.

11. Roberts, T. J. 1977. *The mammals of Pakistan.* London: Ernest Benn.

12. Harrison, D. L. 1968. *The mammals of Arabia.* Vol. 2. London: Ernest Benn.

13. Mendelssohn, H. 1989. Felids in Israel. *Cat News* 10: 2–4.

14. Schauenberg, P. 1974. Données nouvelles sur le chat des sables *Felis margarita* Loche, 1858. *Rev. Suisse Zool.* 81: 949–969.

15. Goodman, S. M., and I. Helmy. 1986. The sand cat *Felis margarita* Loche, 1858 in Egypt. *Mammalia* 50: 120–123.

16. Kowalski, K., and B. Rzebik-Kowalska. 1991. *Mammals of Algeria.* Warsaw: Polish Academy of Sciences.

17. Hufnagl, E. 1972. *Libyan mammals.* Cambridge: Oleander Press.

18. Gasperetti, J., D. L. Harrison, and W. Büettiker. 1985. The Carnivora of Arabia. In *The fauna of Saudi Arabia,* vol. 7, *Carnivora,* ed. W. Büettiker and F. Krupp, 397–461. Basel: Pro Entomologia, c/o Natural History Museum.

19. Mendelssohn, H., professor of zoology, Tel-Aviv University, Ramat Aviv, Tel Aviv, Israel. Letter dated 16 July, 1992.

20. Andrews, P., Hexagon Farm Wild Feline Breeding Facility, 1187 Merrill Road, San Juan Bautista, CA. Personal communication.

21. Hemmer, H. 1977. Biology and breeding of the sand cat. In *The world's cats,* vol. 3, no. 3, ed. R. L. Eaton, 13–21. Seattle: Carnivore Research Institute, Burke Museum, University of Washington.

22. Mellen, J. D. 1989. Reproductive behavior of small captive exotic cats (*Felis* spp.). Ph.D. dissertation, University of California, Davis.

23. Peters, G. 1984. On the structure of friendly close range vocalizations in terrestrial carnivores (Mammalia: Carnivora: Fissipedia). *Z. Säugetierk.* 49: 157–182.

24. Wemmer, C., and K. Scow. 1977. Communication in the Felidae with emphasis on scent marking and contact patterns. In *How animals communicate,* ed. T. A. Sebeok, 749–766. Bloomington: Indiana University Press.

25. Mellen, J. D. 1993. A comparative analysis of scent-marking, social and reproductive behavior in 20 species of small cats (*Felis*). *Am. Zool.* 33: 151–166.

26. Hemmer, H. 1976. Gestation period and postnatal development in felids. In *The world's cats,* vol. 3, no. 2, ed. R. L. Eaton, 143–165.

27. Jones, M. L. 1977. Record keeping and longevity of felids in captivity. In *The world's cats,* vol. 3, no. 3, ed. R. L. Eaton, 132–138.

28. Hemmer, H. 1976. Sand cats and zoos. *Int. Zoo Yrbk.* 16: 223–225.

29. Harrison, D. L. 1972. *The mammals of Arabia.* Vol. 3. London: Ernest Benn.

30. Sapozhenkov, Y. F. 1961. On the ecology of *Felis lybica* Forst, in eastern Kara-Kumy. *Zool. Zh.* 40: 1585–1586.

Black-footed cat

Felis nigripes (Burchell, 1824)

With such a descriptive name, one would expect the black-footed cat to have black feet, but this cat is somewhat confusingly named. Only the pads and the underparts of its feet are black; the upper parts are the same tawny buff as the general background coat color. To further complicate matters, the black-footed cat is not the only cat to have black-soled feet. The closely related African wildcat also has black pads and dark fur on the soles of its feet. Despite the fact that these two cats look quite different, the issue of black-footedness has led to some confusion between the species, and in 1980 the name "small spotted cat" was proposed for *Felis nigripes*. The new name was adopted by some, but many found it even more confusing, as a similar-sized "small-spotted genet" shares most of the black-footed cat's range, and there is a South American felid known as the "little spotted cat." Today, *Felis nigripes* goes by both common names, with different authorities having different preferences. It is also known locally as Sebala cat, Bont-kat, or by the Afrikaans name of *miershooptier* (anthill tiger), from its habit of sleeping in hollowed-out termite mounds.

DESCRIPTION

Smallest of the African felids, an adult black-footed cat weighs about 2 kilograms, roughly the same as the smallest cat species in Asia and South America. If the black-footed cat were measured against the diminutive kodkod of South America and the tiny rusty-spotted cat of India and Sri Lanka, the result would probably be a three-way tie. The black-footed cat has rounded ears, very large eyes, and a short black-tipped tail less than half the length of its head and body. The background color of its coat varies from cinnamon-buff to tawny, and the fur is patterned with conspicuous black or brown spots that merge to form bands or rings on the legs, neck, and tail. The backs of the ears are the same color as the background coat color. There are six mammae. Unlike that of other spotted cats, the black-footed cat's skin is unpigmented pink.[1,2,3,4]

DISTRIBUTION

The black-footed cat is endemic to Africa, where it is found in only three countries: Botswana, Namibia, and South Africa. The species is restricted to the more arid southern and central parts of southern Africa, from the west and southern coasts of the Cape Province to the Orange Free State, Transvaal, and across Botswana south of the Okavango Delta to eastern Namibia (fig. 17).[4,5,6]

Figure 17. Distribution of the black-footed cat.

ECOLOGY AND BEHAVIOR

The black-footed cat is typically found in dry, open habitats with some degree of vegetative cover. These cats apparently get all the moisture they need from their prey, as they live in essentially waterless areas. However, they will drink water when it is available.[1]

These tiny predators are extremely secretive and are rarely seen, even by the most knowledgeable observers. Reay Smithers, an eminent South African mammalogist, saw only a few solitary individuals during six hundred hours of spotlight surveys, and those he did see took cover immediately when picked up in the light.[5] Evasive, cryptic, and small, black-footed cats are also strictly nocturnal. They spend the day resting in dense cover or in unoccupied springhare, porcupine, or aardvark burrows or abandoned termite mounds, and emerge to hunt only after sunset.[7]

Strictly terrestrial hunters, black-footed cats in zoos characteristically spend hours walking or trotting around their enclosures, a behavior suggesting that they move over relatively large distances in the wild.[8] Two kittens raised at the National Zoo in Washington, D.C., first showed this trotting behavior when they were about five months old.[9] As might be expected, the black-footed cat is not an adept climber. Captive kittens show much less interest in climbing and jumping than other felids and ignore tree branches in their enclosure.[10] However, these cats are unusually diligent and skillful diggers. Unlike domestic cats, which scratch at the ground with one paw, black-footed cats dig vigorously using both front paws, almost like a dog.[8] When provided with an artificial burrow in which to rear her young, a female at the Wuppertal Zoo, Germany, pushed at the sand with her forepaws, creating a mound that reduced the size of the entrance. Later, as her kittens repeatedly flattened the ridge of sand during their comings and goings, the female rebuilt it again and again.[11]

Living in arid habitats, where vegetation and stalking cover is at a premium, the black-footed cat relies on camouflage and the cover of darkness to conceal its own approach to prey and to avoid becoming a meal for a larger carnivore. When it spots a potential meal, the black-footed cat flattens itself hard against the ground, then tries to creep toward the prey using every vestige of cover. Zoologist Jill Mellen described the stalk after watching a captive black-footed cat try to sneak up on a bird sitting just outside its enclosure: "When cautiously moving closer to the bird, the female moved from behind one small boulder to another in an almost 'serpentine' manner, appearing to almost 'flow' from rock to rock."[12]

Feeding Ecology

Despite the difficulties of stalking prey in an open landscape, black-footed cats are remarkably successful hunters. In the only field study to date, Alex Sliwa has captured and radio-collared nine male and ten female black-footed cats in the Northern Cape Province of South Africa.[13] He was able to habituate many of the radio-collared cats and follow them at distances of 10 to 30 meters at night while they hunted. Sliwa's detailed observations provide us with almost everything that is known about this tiny cat's hunting style and diet.[7,14,15,16]

Sliwa identified three different hunting styles. In the "fast hunt," the cat moves swiftly (2–3 kilometers per hour) through and over the vegetation, flushing prey from cover. A second style, "slow hunting," involves a slow (0.5–0.8 kilometers per hour) stalking movement, with the cat winding snakelike between grass tufts, turning its head from side to side, alert to movements and sounds. In the "sit and wait" hunt, the cat sits motionless beside a rodent den, waiting for signs of activity. This third style is difficult to distinguish from resting, as the cat sometimes sits with its eyes closed, but the cat's ears move constantly and its eyes open at the slightest sound.[7] When hunting small birds, the cat stalks as close as possible, then makes a quick run and launches itself at the bird with a great jump, up to 2 meters long in some cases and 1.4 meters high. The cat either pins the bird to the ground with its forepaws or grabs it in midair and pulls it down, then finishes it off with a quick bite. Small birds are not plucked, but eaten whole in two to four minutes.[14]

Sliwa has followed his radio-collared cats for over 2,800 hours, recording more than 2,000 kills.[13,17] He found that the cats hunt throughout the night, in all weather conditions, and in temperatures ranging from −10°C to 30°C.[7,16]

Three-quarters of the prey captured by black-footed cats were gerbils, mice, and shrews, but these little mammals represented only 39 percent of the total weight of prey consumed. Twenty-one percent of prey captured consisted of small birds such as larks, pipits, chats, and wheatears.[14]

Sliwa was also able to watch his habituated black-footed cats hunt and kill adult black bustards, which, at about 670 grams, were probably a third to a half of the cat's body weight. "The female cat stalked one for 20 minutes over a distance of 20 meters, then after a quick rush over the last three meters, grabbed it directly at the neck and killed it with a neck bite, holding it for two minutes until it stopped flapping. After the bird was dead the cat rested for a couple of minutes monitoring its surroundings and then started to feed."[15] She fed on the dead bustard for six hours, then cached parts of it, covering the remains with sand. A male cat captured a bustard with a rush from 3 meters away, grabbed the bird by the wing, then worked his grip up to the neck and killed it with a neck bite. He ate for an hour, consuming 200 to 250 grams of bone and meat, but with approaching dawn he retreated to cover, carrying the bird 50 meters to a termite mound.[15]

Black-footed cats also ate insects, but despite the large number consumed, insects made up only 2 percent of the weight of the prey eaten. Sliwa watched the cats catch and eat lacewings, locusts, grasshoppers, and moths, and twice saw one of the cats feeding on emerging alates of the harvester termite.[14]

Measured by weight, small birds, rodents, and insects were the staple food: 53 percent of the total weight of prey consumed consisted of creatures weighing less than 30 to 40 grams. However, the occasional large meal was obviously important. The cats sometimes managed to kill Cape hares as well as black bustards, and they also scavenged springbok lambs. These large carcasses weigh half to twice the cat's body weight—an unusual situation among small felids, which typically sustain themselves on prey weighing less than a tenth of their own weight. Large prey such as bustards and hares contributed 32 percent and carrion 15 percent to the total weight of prey eaten.[14]

Black-footed cats are astoundingly active and successful hunters, making roughly one hunting attempt every thirty minutes, with a 60 percent success rate. One male was seen to catch twelve rodents in three and a half hours. During a typical night's hunting, a cat would kill a bird or a mammal every fifty minutes on average, killing between ten and fourteen small birds and rodents a night. This represents approximately 250 to 300 grams of food, or about 20 percent of the cat's body weight. This is an enormous amount of food for a cat to eat on a daily basis. Large felids such as tigers typically eat 20 percent of their body weight in one night when feeding on a large kill, but then go for several days between kills without eating. Black-footed cats in zoos are less active than their wild relatives, but even captive animals require about 200 grams of food per day, a large amount compared with other small felids. It is not yet clear why black-footed cats have such high energy requirements, but they may have high metabolic rates.[7]

When feeding on bustard or young springbok, a black-footed cat gorges itself like a tiger, consuming as much as 20 to 30 percent of its own body weight in a night. On one occasion a male cat fed intermittently on a 3-kilogram springbok lamb, consuming about 1,100 grams of meat in two and a half days. One night he returned to the carcass four times, eating about 120 grams at each sitting. Amazingly, he continued to hunt and kill small birds and rodents between these scavenged meals.[15]

While kills of large birds and mammals play a surprisingly important part in the black-footed cat's diet, opportunities for scavenging may vary across the cat's range. Sliwa's study took place on a game farm where there were no large mammalian predators other than jackals and the occasional caracal, and vultures and jackals were unable to keep up with the abundance of carrion during the biannual springbok lambing season.[14]

On several occasions Sliwa saw black-footed cats cache small prey and cover the remains of larger carcasses,[14] behaviors that have not been reported for other small felids. More common to the dog family, caching prey clearly has its advantages in a harsh environment where prey may be hard to come by. However, if the habitat is open and there are many other predators and scavengers, it would seem prudent for the predator to eat as much of the surplus as possible, rather than risk storing it and then losing it to other predators.

Prior to Sliwa's study the only information on the black-footed cat's diet came from specimens that had either been shot or run over on the road. In Botswana, an examination of the stomach contents of seven black-footed cats found that mice, gerbils, spiders, and insects formed the bulk of the cat's prey, but small reptiles and birds were also eaten.[1] Grass and leaves are reported from stomach contents, and captives are known to consume large quantities of grass and reportedly go off their feed if denied access to it.[8] Sliwa has not, however, observed black-footed cats eating grass.[15]

Historical accounts mention the black-footed cat killing sheep and goats by fastening onto the neck and hanging on until the jugular vein is pierced. Indeed, Bushman legend suggests that this cat can even kill a giraffe. While this is an obvious exaggeration, black-footed cats have a well-established reputation for being fierce and intractable, even as tiny kittens. Penny Andrews, who runs a wild cat breeding facility in California, describes black-footed cats as "sand cats with an attitude."[18] Sliwa watched a female defend herself against a black-backed jackal, an animal eight times her weight. This 1.5-kilogram female also spent half an hour carefully stalking an 80-kilogram male ostrich sitting on a nest. As she was about to pounce, the bird stood up, briefly revealing feet that were longer than the cat's body, then bolted in a cloud of dust.[19]

In captivity, black-footed cats use a nape bite to dispatch prey. In comparison with other cats, they show little plucking behavior when dealing with birds.[20] In the wild these cats do not pluck small birds such as larks, but pull a few wing and body feathers from slightly larger button quail.[15] Like the fishing cat, black-footed cats have a particularly effective technique for overpowering wriggling prey. They slide themselves over the prey from the rear, lay the forepaws on either side of the animal, and using the dewclaws, hold the prey firmly against the ground. While the wriggling animal is held tightly in this position, the cat pulls its head back and waits for the right moment to deliver the killing neck bite.[20]

Social Organization

The social organization of black-footed cats follows the typical felid pattern. Male ranges overlap several smaller female ranges, with little range overlap between adults of the same sex. Though small in size, black-footed cats roam large areas, and on winter nights a cat may travel up to 16 kilometers (mean = 8 kilometers).[7] During the warm summer nights, they do not move as far or eat as much. Female home ranges measure 3.1 to 11.9 square kilometers, whereas male ranges are 10.4 to 16.8 square kilometers.[17] Sliwa estimates that in the northern portion of his study area there are eight adult black-footed cats in 6,000 hectares (13 cats per 100 square kilometers).[13]

Like other felids, adult black-footed cats maintain their home ranges by scent marking, including urine spraying, scent rubbing on objects, claw raking, and leaving their feces uncovered. Animals without territories were not seen to scent-mark. One of Sliwa's radio-collared adult females spray-marked throughout her home range, but the frequency of marking varied according to her reproductive state. She was not seen to scent-mark while her kittens were small, but when they were older, she was again observed spray-marking, and her marking rate increased dramatically about one month prior to mating.[7] Resident adult males scent-mark frequently (an estimated ten to twelve times per hour) as they move through their ranges, and marking rates of males also increase prior to mating. On the night before he mated, one male was seen to spray-mark 585 times[13]—an extraordinary feat for an animal that lives in an arid environment with little or no freestanding water.

Paul Leyhausen, who kept several black-footed cats in captivity, was the first person to comment on their loud vocalizations. He remarked that their "meow" was comparable to the roar of the tiger, only an octave higher, and suggested that this loud call was used to communicate over long distances.[20] Black-footed cats exist at low densities in their semidesert environment, and the female's period of sexual receptivity is extremely short, which means that males and females must have an effective means of locating one another when the female comes into estrus. Long-range vocalizations are likely to be an effective means of communication under these circumstances.

Black-footed cats also purr and have a friendly close-range "gurgle" used by males, females, and young.[10,21] During an aggressive encounter they spit, hiss, and growl, and they assume a characteristic "airplane" ear posture, in which the ears are extended laterally.[12] Though other cat species have a similar flattened-ear aggressive posture, the black-footed cat's display is particularly striking and is frequently photographed.

Reproduction and Development

Limited data from captivity suggest that female black-footed cats have a shorter period of estrus than most small cats.[8] Observations of mating in the wild also indicate a short period of sexual receptivity.[13] Estrus lasts one to two days, and the female will accept a male for only five to ten hours during this time. Copulation occurs approximately every twenty to fifty minutes during the period of acceptance. In comparison, in domestic cats and some of the other smaller wild cats, estrus lasts at least six days, and copulation occurs frequently over a three- to four-day period.[20]

Gestation lasts between sixty-three and sixty-eight days,[8,11,22,23,24] nearly a week longer than in the domestic cat. There are one to four kittens in a litter; the average size of 164 captive-born litters was 1.78.[25]

Captive-born kittens weigh 60 to 93 grams at birth.[8,10,24] They develop slightly faster than domestic kittens, and are able to crawl and hold their heads up on the day of birth. Four-day-old black-footed kittens have been observed crawling out of the maternity den.[11] The kittens' eyes open when they are two to ten days old. They can walk unsteadily but quite fast at two weeks and begin to climb a week later. Grooming was seen as early as thirteen days of age, compared with three weeks in domestic cats.[26] By the time they are a month old the kittens spend much of their time playing and start to show an interest in solid food. The first teeth erupt between 14 and 21 days of age, and the permanent teeth appear at 145 to 158 days of age.[24] At about five weeks the mother starts to bring live prey to the den. The kittens can run well by the time they are six weeks old and no longer regard the nest as a refuge.

According to Paul Leyhausen, females with kittens "demand" a new nest box every six to ten days. The mother begins carrying the kittens around and does not settle until a new nest box is provided. Nest hygiene is the usual explanation given for changing dens, but other small cats do not change dens with this frequency, Leyhausen suggests that the behavior may have arisen because in the wild black-footed kittens are particularly vulnerable to predators.[20]

In the wild, black-footed cats are reported to rear their young in burrows,[27,28] and Sliwa has found young kittens in termite mounds and hollows. One mother left her kittens for four hours on the first night after their birth, and by the fourth night she was away from the den for ten hours, suggesting that young kittens are adapted to going long periods without nursing. After the kittens were a week old, the female moved them frequently to new dens.[7] A radio-collared female was seen bringing mice and birds back to a den where she had a five-week-old kitten. One day the female brought a live mouse, which the kitten managed to kill and eat. Kittens are weaned by two months of age.[24]

As a small carnivore living in a treeless, arid environment, the black-footed cat is undoubtedly vulnerable to larger predators, including hyenas, jackals, and birds of prey. This tiny cat's reproductive biology and behavior are clearly adapted to life under these pressures. A short estrus and an extremely brief period of receptivity reduces vulnerability during mating, and a long gestation period, small litter size, and rapid development of young combine to shorten the time when the kittens are vulnerable to predation.

Recent reports from captivity on the age of first estrus for female black-footed cats vary from eight to twelve months.[7,10,23,29] This seems more likely than the twenty-one months of age previously reported.[20] A young male black-footed cat at the National Zoo in Washington, D.C., began spraying urine at seven and a half months of age.[10] A pair of black-footed cats, both caught in the wild as adults, lived for nearly ten years in captivity.[30]

STATUS IN THE WILD

There seems to be no doubt that the secretive and retiring black-footed cat is the rarest of the African cat species, but there the consensus ends. Experts differ in their opinions on its status. Some believe that the black-footed cat should be considered endangered, threatened, or rare. Others suggest that this cat's small size and shy, retiring nature results in its numbers being greatly underestimated. Because of its small size, the black-footed cat is not persecuted as a threat to livestock, and it is not easily trapped, although the use

of coyote-getters and poisons poses a threat to the species in the Eastern Cape.[31] Others believe it to be uncommon to rare, but widespread, throughout its restricted range, and think that the scarcity of sightings truly reflects the rarity of the species. They point out that the species is seldom killed in the large-scale nonselective predator control operations carried out by farmers and does not often show up among the animals caught by Botswana hunters who kill small predators for their pelts.[32] A skin buyer in South African reported that among the thousands of small-animal skins he had purchased in a year, only nineteen were those of black-footed cats.[33] Some South African game reserves and national parks list black-footed cats as present, although no estimates of numbers are available. Sliwa suggests that managed game farms, especially those with extensive grass areas and some reduction in larger carnivores, may be the most important habitat for black-footed cats.[16]

STATUS IN CAPTIVITY

Black-footed cats can be difficult to keep in captivity outside of their native range because they have very specific climatic requirements and must be kept under dry conditions. Studbook records show a high mortality rate for both adults and kittens, and the species is susceptible to respiratory infections and kidney disease. Indeed, kidney disease is the primary cause of death among captive animals; 54 percent of postmortem reports list nephritis as the cause of death.[7] Wuppertal Zoo in Germany has had excellent success breeding these cats, and the core of the captive population is held there. In July 1996, there were sixty-eight black-footed cats in twenty-one facilities in North America, Europe, and Africa. Dr. Ulrich Schürer at the Wuppertal Zoo is the studbook keeper for the black-footed cat.

TABLE 11 MEASUREMENTS AND WEIGHTS OF ADULT BLACK-FOOTED CATS

HB	n	T	n	WT	n	Location	Source
392 (367–433)	5m	177 (164–198)	5m	1.6 (1.5–1.7)	5m	Botswana	1
360 (353–369)	3f	153 (126–170)	3f	1.1 (1.0–1.4)	3f	Botswana	1
435, 440	2m	165, 195	2m	1.9, 2.1	2m	Transvaal	4
401 (387–415)	3f	165 (145–180)	3f	1.35 (1.2–1.6)	3f	Transvaal	4
447 (414–490)	3m	143 (80–200)	3m	2.0 (1.7–2.4)	3m	South Africa	34

Note: HB = head and body length (mm); T = tail length (mm); WT = weight (kg). n = sample size. Sex: m = male, f = female, ? = unknown. Mean values are presented only for sample sizes of three or more. Range of values is in parentheses.

TABLE 12 OCCURRENCE OF PREY ITEMS IN THE DIETS OF BLACK-FOOTED CATS (PERCENTAGE OF KILLS)

Prey items	Kimberley Region, South Africa[14] Prey killed (n = 575)
Crocidura cyanea Reddish-grey musk shrew	2.8
Dendromus melanotis Grey climbing mouse	1.6
Gerbillurus paeba Hairy-footed gerbil	4.0
Lepus capensis Cape hare	0.3
Malacothrix typica Large-eared mouse	5.9
Saccostomus campestris Pouched mouse	0.2
Tatera leucogaster Bushveld gerbil	3.0
Unidentified rodents	4.9
Anthus novaeseelandiae Richard's pipit	0.2
Chersomanes albofasciata Spike-heeled lark	0.9
Cisticola aridula Desert cisticola	0.5
Eupodotis afra Black bustard	0.3
Mirafra apiata Clapper lark	2.4
Mirafra sabota Sabota lark	0.2
Mirafra africanoides Fawn-colored lark	0.2
Oenanthe pileata Capped wheatear	0.2
Turnix sylvatica Kurrichane button quail	0.9
Unidentified small birds	0.7
Insects	70.8
Minimum number of vertebrate prey items	168

REFERENCES

1. Smithers, R. H. N. 1983. *The mammals of the southern African subregion.* Pretoria: University of Pretoria.

2. Guggisberg, C. A. W. 1975. *Wild cats of the world.* New York: Taplinger.

3. Rautenbach, I. L. 1982. Mammals of the Transvaal. Ecoplan, Monograph 1. 211 pp.

4. Lynch, C. D. 1983. The mammals of the Orange Free State. *Memoirs Nasionale Museum, Bloemfontein* 18: 1–218.

5. Smithers, R. H. N. 1971. *The mammals of Botswana.* Museum Memoir no. 4. Salisbury: The Trustees of the National Museums of Rhodesia.

6. Stuart, C. 1981. Notes on the mammalian carnivores of the Cape Province, South Africa. *Bontebok* 1: 1–58.

7. Olbricht, G., and A. Sliwa. 1997. In situ and ex situ observations and management of black-footed cats. *Int. Zoo Yrbk.* 35: 81–89.

8. Leyhausen, P., and B. A. Tonkin. 1966. Breeding the black-footed cat (*Felis nigripes*) in captivity. *Int. Zoo Yrbk.* 6: 178–182.

9. Armstrong, J. 1975. Hand-rearing black-footed cats at the National Zoological Park, Washington. *Int. Zoo Yrbk.* 15: 245–249.

10. Armstrong, J. 1977. The development and hand-rearing of black-footed cats. In *The world's cats*, vol. 3, no. 3, ed. R. L. Eaton, 71–80. Winston, OR: Winston Wildlife Safari.

11. Schürer, U. 1978. Breeding black-footed cats in captivity. *Carnivore* 1: 109–111.

12. Mellen, J. D. 1989. Reproductive behavior of small captive exotic cats (*Felis* spp.). Ph.D. dissertation, University of California, Davis.

13. Sliwa, A. 1997. Black-footed cat field research. *Cat News* 27: 20–21.

14. Sliwa, A. 1994. Diet and feeding behaviour of the black-footed cat (*Felis nigripes* Burchell, 1824) in the Kimberley Region, South Africa. *Zool. Garten* (n.f.) 64: 83–96.

15. Sliwa, A. 1994. Black-footed cat studies in South Africa. *Cat News* 20: 15–19.

16. Sliwa, A. 1996. Black-footed cat in situ, Benfontein Game Farm, Kimberley, South Africa. Report on four years of field research in Kimberley, South Africa. (Mimeographed, 15 pages.)

17. Sliwa, A. 1999. Field research on black-footed cats. Project Survival, Quarterly Newsletter of the Cat Conservation Group, vol. 1(4): 1, 3.

18. Andrews, P., Hexagon Farm Wild Feline Breeding Facility, San Juan Bautista, CA. Personal communication.

19. Sliwa, A. 1999. Stalking the black-footed cat. *Int. Wildl.* 29(3): 38–43.

20. Leyhausen, P. 1979. *Cat behavior: The predatory and social behavior of domestic and wild cats.* New York: Garland STPM Press.

21. Peters, G. 1984. On the structure of friendly close range vocalizations in terrestrial carnivores (Mammalia: Carnivora: Fissipedia). *Z. Säugetierk.* 49: 157–182.

22. Hemmer, H. 1976. Gestation period and postnatal development in felids. In *The world's cats,* vol. 2, ed. R. L. Eaton, 90–100. Seattle: Carnivore Research Institute, Burke Museum, University of Washington.

23. Schürer, U. 1988. Breeding black-footed cats (*Felis nigripes*) at Wuppertal Zoo, with notes on their reproductive biology. Paper presented at the 5th Conference on Breeding Endangered Species in Captivity, Cincinnati, Ohio.

24. Olbricht, G., and A. Sliwa. 1995. Comparative development of juvenile black-footed cats at Wuppertal Zoo and elsewhere. In *International studbook for the black-footed cat* (Felis nigripes), ed. U. Schürer and G. Olbricht, 8–20. Zoological Garden, Wuppertal.

25. Olbricht, G., Curator, Zoologischer garten der Stadt, Wuppertal, Hubertusalle 30, Wuppertal. Personal communication.

26. Morris, D. 1994. *Catwatching.* London: Ebury Press.

27. Shortridge, G. C. 1934. *The mammals of South Western Africa.* Vol. 1. London: Heinemann.

28. Grobler, H., A. Hall-Martin, and C. Walker. 1984. *Predators of Southern Africa: A guide to the carnivores.* Johannesburg: Macmillan South Africa.

29. Mellen, J. D. 1993. A comparative analysis of scent-marking, social and reproductive behavior in 20 species of small cats (*Felis*). *Am. Zool.* 33: 151–166.

30. Tonkin, B. A. 1972. Notes on longevity in three species of felids. *Int. Zoo Yrbk.* 12: 181–182.

31. Visser, J. 1978. Status and conservation of the smaller cats of Southern Africa. In *The world's cats,* vol. 3, no. 1, ed. R. L. Eaton, 60–66. Seattle: Carnivore Research Institute, Burke Museum, University of Washington.

32. Stuart, C., and T. Stuart. 1991. Survey of the small spotted cat in southern Africa. Unpublished report to the Fauna and Flora Preservation Society.

33. Visser, J. 1967. The cat with black feet. *Zoonooz* (May).

34. Sliwa, A., Department of Zoology and Entomology, University of Pretoria, Pretoria, South Africa. Personal communication.

Wildcat

Felis silvestris (Schreber, 1775)

The wildcats of Eurasia and Africa have been the subject of an intense and evolving taxonomic debate. In 1775, the German naturalist Schreber named the European wildcat *Felis silvestris*. A few years later the African wildcat was designated *Felis lybica;* then followed *Felis ornata* from India, *Felis caudatus* from Russia, *Felis ocreata* from Abyssinia, and dozens of others. This number of different wildcat species was clearly excessive, and in 1951 the well-known taxonomist R. I. Pocock declared that *Felis silvestris* was the species and that *lybica, ocreata,* and the others were simply subspecies. Pocock's list of forty subspecies was later reduced to twenty-one.

Until recently, *Felis silvestris* was most commonly divided into four groups. The thickset, heavily furred forest cats of Europe were known as the *silvestris* group, and the light-bodied steppe cats of Asia were the *ornata* group. The slim, long-legged *lybica* group lived in Africa, and *catus,* the domestic cat, was found throughout the world. Based largely on physical appearance and distribution, these convenient subdivisions have been popularly accepted as "species."

People generally believe that the European wildcat and the domestic cat are separate species; likewise, the African wildcat and domestic cat are also viewed as distinct species. But these views are incorrect. Genetic analysis confirms that the differences between these groups are very small, suggesting a recent common ancestor, and where they coexist, wildcats interbreed with domestic cats. In Britain, the indigenous wildcat and the introduced domestic cat have been sympatric,

and most likely interbreeding, for 2,000 years. Over the years, different authors have used pelage patterns, body sizes, cranial indices, and genetic analysis to discriminate between the various wildcats, domestic cats, and their hybrids. However, the search continues for a useful method of distinguishing wildcats from wild cats.

The same features that led early naturalists to subdivide *silvestris* into so many different species make it difficult to describe the appearance and biology of the animal as a single form. This cat's fur can be long and thick or short and sleek, depending on whether it lives in South Africa or Mongolia. In some places it lives on rabbits that weigh half as much as it does, while in others it survives perfectly well on invertebrates, fruit, and birds. But confusing as this variation may be, it should not obscure the fact that the wildcat's life history parameters are really keyed to feeding on small rodents. Over much of the species' geographic range small rodents make up more than three-quarters of the diet, and in many areas these small rodents undergo regular "boom and bust" cycles. To do well under these circumstances, a predator needs to be able to have large litters with a short interbirth interval during boom years.

While *Felis silvestris* stands as the species, the differences between the subspecies are such that it becomes cumbersome to combine them in a single account. Thus, we have arbitrarily divided our account into three sections: European wildcat, African and Asian wildcat, and domestic cat.

European wildcat

Felis silvestris silvestris

In Europe, wildcats are occasionally found during the daytime lying in a sunny clearing or sunning themselves on top of a secluded boulder. This habit is thought to lend credence to the theory that the European wildcat's ancestors came from the south; while they adapted to the cold, harsh climate and forests of the north, they are still "children of the sun."[1,2]

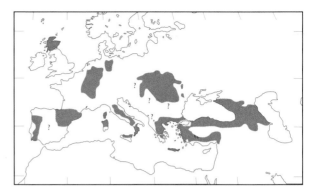

Figure 18. Distribution of the European wildcat.

DESCRIPTION

The European wildcat looks very much like a large domestic tabby cat. A long, thick coat (especially in winter), broad head, and comparatively flat face give it the appearance of a large, powerful cat, much more robust than the domestic cat or the African wildcat. Looks are deceiving, however, as European wildcats typically weigh 3 to 6 kilograms,[3,4] about the same as African wildcats. Females are somewhat lighter than males. A record male wildcat from Scotland weighed 7.1 kilograms,[5] and an 8-kilogram male is truly exceptional.[6] The European wildcat is a compact animal with comparatively short legs and a tail that usually exceeds half of its head and body length. The ears are set wide apart and have no hair tufts at their tips. The tip of the nose is flesh-colored.

The coat of the European wildcat is gray-brown with dark stripes on the head, neck, limbs, and along the back. Black spots sometimes dot the otherwise light gray undersides. The tail of adults is thick, blunt-ended, and marked with dark rings and a black tip; the tail of young is tapered. European wildcats are darker in color than wildcats from Africa or Asia, and black cats are reported from the Caucasus[7,8] and Scotland, although these are probably hybrids.[9]

DISTRIBUTION

The wildcat has often been designated as vermin and has been hunted heavily over much of its range. Despite this persecution, wildcats still occur throughout parts of Europe and adjoining Russia. Wildcats were formerly distributed throughout the British Isles except Ireland and the Outer Hebrides, but they had disappeared from England, Wales, and southern Scotland by the mid-nineteenth century.[10] The cat is still found in northern Scotland, Spain, Portugal, France, Belgium, Luxembourg, Germany, Poland, Switzerland, Italy, and on the islands of Sicily and Sardinia. Wildcats are also known from Hungary, the Czech Republic, Slovakia, Yugoslavia, Romania, Bulgaria, Greece, and Turkey. In the former Soviet Union, wildcats are found in a small area of Moldova, on the Romanian border, and in the Carpathian forests on the border with Slovakia. Wildcats are also thought to be present in Georgia, Azerbaijan, and Armenia (fig. 18).[4,6,11]

ECOLOGY AND BEHAVIOR

As might be expected from their wide geographic distribution, wildcats are able to live in a wide variety of habitats. They require some sort of cover for hunting and rest sites, but this can be almost anything from rocks to scrubby undergrowth or agricultural fields. In Scotland, radio-tagged wildcats preferred pine forest and scrub habitat.[12] A 1983–1987 survey in Scotland found wildcats in forested areas with scrub, woodlands, bogs, open heather moorlands, and marginal habitats between high mountains and moorlands.[13] Information on habitat use by wildcats in other parts of Europe is sketchy, but in general the cats appear to be associated with forests.[11]

In the Carpathian Mountains wildcats live in hornbeam-oak, beech, and mixed forests. In the Caucasus they are found in swamps, reed beds, and broadleaved forests. Here as elsewhere they are generally absent from the subalpine belt, coniferous forests, and spruce taiga. In the montane forests of eastern Europe wildcats prefer cliffs, rocky areas, and dense thickets. Because they are relatively short-legged, these cats are not well suited to moving through deep, loose snow. In general, wildcats live only in areas where the mean winter snow depth does not exceed 10 to 20 centimeters.[6]

Although they are excellent climbers, wildcats hunt almost exclusively on the ground. Most hunting occurs at night.[6,12,14] The wildcat hunts by moving slowly and quietly through its territory, watching and listening for signs of prey activity. Like other cats, it will also sit and wait in ambush. When the cat sees or hears something, it crouches and approaches with a low stalking run. The cat uses every available piece of cover to creep forward within striking range, then darts forward and strikes with a paw. Prey are typically killed with a bite to the nape of the neck. Those prey not caught within a few meters usually escape, since the cat does not usually pursue over long distances.

In Scotland, "snow tracking in dense forests indicated that they [wildcats] constantly zigzagged when hunting, occasionally backtracked and frequently investigated scrub and heather clumps and looked under the lowest branches of pine trees by pushing their heads through the snow 'walls.'" During bouts of heavy snowfall the cats remained inactive in their dens for as long as twenty-eight hours.[12] Wildcats in Scotland and Italy have also been observed to move to lower elevations in winter as snow depths increased at high elevations.[12,15]

Feeding Ecology
Though wildcats eat a variety of small prey, there are numerous reports indicating that these cats are primarily rodent catchers. They do, however, also feed on larger animals, such as hares, rabbits, and young deer.[15,16,17,18,19,20,21,22,23,24,25,26]

In the Carpathian Mountains wildcats feed mainly on the yellow-necked mouse, red-backed vole, and bank vole. All three rodents occur in large numbers in beech forests. Among the floating islands of the Prut swamp, wildcats feed mainly on water voles, Norway rats, and muskrats, but also eat birds such as warblers, white-eyed potchards, and coots.[6]

Wildcats in Scotland prey extensively on rabbits, with shrews and birds being minor prey items in the diet. Lagomorph remains were found in 92 percent of 546 scat samples. The cats preyed heavily on young rabbits when they were available in the spring and summer. In the winter, 22 percent of rabbits killed were infected with myxomatosis, which presumably increased their vulnerability.[12]

Despite the fact that wildcats live mainly on rodents, they are adaptable predators and can survive on other foods. Scats and stomach samples show that wildcats occasionally eat grasses, insects, frogs, fruit, roe deer fawns, young chamois, fish, martens, polecats, and weasels. The cats themselves may occasionally be killed by lynx or other large carnivores. Wildcats are capable of living close to humans and can become significant poultry predators.

Social Organization
Little is known of the wildcat's social habits. It is solitary with some home range overlap, more so between the ranges of males and females than between animals of the same sex. Even cats with partially overlapping ranges tend not to use the zone of overlap at the same time.[12] Males and females associate for mating, but otherwise the cats are seldom found together.

Monthly home range sizes of radio-collared female wildcats in Scotland averaged about 175 hectares, and male ranges were similar in size to those of females. There was considerable variation in the size of monthly ranges, but females showed a stronger fidelity to a site than did males. Both sexes made one- to six-day forays outside their normal ranges during the breeding season, apparently in search of mates, before returning to their former ranges.[12]

Radio-tagged wildcats in Hungary had home ranges measuring 1.5 to 8.7 square kilometers, and while they did not normally venture onto farms, during the breeding season male wildcats expanded their ranges to include areas occupied by female farm cats, with which they interbred.[27]

In France six radio-collared female wildcats occupied stable ranges that averaged 184 hectares. The ranges of six radio-collared males in the same area varied by a factor of five, being as small as 220 hectares and as large as 1,270 hectares; the average was 573 hectares. The largest male ranges were occupied by residents, while the smallest were those of an old transient male and a young male.[28] Young wildcats in Scotland also had much smaller ranges than adult cats.[12]

Radio-tagged female wildcats in France regularly patrolled all portions of their ranges, traveling an average of 5.2 kilometers per day. Resident males traveled an average of 8.2 kilometers per day, but since their ranges were much larger, it took them several days to visit all portions of their ranges. Each resident male's range overlapped the ranges of three to six females.[28]

The principal mode of communication among wildcats, as in other felids, is via scent and visual marks. Wildcats in Scotland frequently left their feces uncovered on conspicuous landmarks such as grass tussocks, rocks, and stumps and at the forks and intersections of trails. Feces were not randomly distributed; they were located in areas where the cats rested and hunted rather than along range boundaries. Wildcats also left urine and scratch marks at conspicuous places throughout their ranges.[12] Both sexes spray urine and mark inanimate objects with cheek and head rubbing as well.[29,30]

By injecting four adult and seven young wildcats with a radioisotope, Corbett was able to search the trails and roads within the home range of each "labeled" cat for feces containing the isotope. He found significantly more isotope-marked scats from adults than from young, suggesting a difference in marking behavior between adult and young wildcats. He also found that the marking rate of an adult male appeared to increase after a transient cat passed through his range.[12] Such changes in marking behavior have been noted in similar circumstances for other felid species. Based on the ratio of marked to unmarked feces found in his study area, Corbett estimated there was approximately one wildcat per 3.3 square kilometers.[12] Densities of three to five wildcats per 10 square kilometers are reported from optimal forest habitat in western Europe.[31]

Wildcats also communicate by vocalizations, but the majority of calls appear to function in close-range situations, in which they occur simultaneously with visual signals. The vocal repertoire of the wildcat is similar to that of the domestic cat. Wildcats purr, meow, hiss, spit, gurgle, and growl. A gentle 'mrrr' sound is used as a friendly greeting, reassurance, or appeasement. Both sexes have a loud call that begins with a loud meow and ends with a regular, deep, two-note "orrr-ow."[32,33] Loud calls occur most frequently during the mating season.[34]

Reproduction and Development

Studies of captive wildcats show that females come into heat several times a year, and that estrus lasts two to eight days. Females may have two litters in a single year. Litter sizes in captivity range from 1 to 8, with means varying from 3 to 5.5. Kittens are born after a gestation period of sixty-three to sixty-nine days.[35,36,37,38,39] Litter sizes in the wild average 2 to 5, with an overall mean of about 4, and one litter per year appears typical.[6,12,34,40,41] Reports of wildcats having two or even three litters a year seem unlikely, although females may occasionally be able to raise a second litter during times of peak rodent abundance. Most late litters probably represent replacements for an earlier lost litter or females that failed to conceive during previous estrous cycles.

Wildcats appear to be seasonal breeders. Most mating activity occurs between mid-February and late March, which means that young are born in April or May. Kittens are usually born in an underground den, but litters have been discovered in rock crevices, under brush piles, and even among agricultural crops. In Russia one den was found near the bank of the Kishi River in a thicket of trees. The kittens were inside the hollow trunk of a large fallen elm. Another litter of six kittens was found in a nest made of dry grass and reeds in the center of a large firewood pile.[6]

The kittens are born blind and helpless, with birth weights of 75 to 150 grams (mean 114 grams).[35,36,38,42] Kittens are covered with a fuzzy coat; dark brown spots fuse on the back into broad dark bands. Their eyes open at seven to twelve days of age, and incisor teeth appear at fourteen to thirty days. They are mobile at four weeks, when they begin to play outside the den, jumping off logs and boulders and climbing nearby trees. Kittens start to eat mice and birds when they are about six weeks old and begin to accompany their mother on hunting trips when they are ten to twelve weeks old. They are weaned by two to three months. A captive mother introduced her kittens to live prey when they were about sixty days old; a few days later the kittens were able to kill and eat mice. In captivity, deciduous dentition is complete by 42 to 49 days and permanent dentition by 175 to 195 days.[2,16,35,43]

The young begin to move independently as early as four and a half to five months of age. Young born in March or April in central Europe are said to begin to live independently by the middle of August, but littermates may continue to travel together for some time.[6] Young are nearly adult size by ten months of age, which is the earliest reported age of sexual activity.[35,36]

At present there is no information on the timing of dispersal, but the young probably remain in their natal area until they are about a year old. Their departure is likely to coincide with the birth of a new litter, which occurs annually. Captive wildcats have lived to be sixteen years old.[31]

STATUS IN THE WILD

Throughout much of the European wildcat's range, the species has long been thought of as vermin. Wildcats have been trapped as predators, hunted for their fur, and displaced by agriculture and land clearance schemes. Historically gamekeepers throughout Europe have put a great deal of effort into exterminating these cats because they are thought to be major predators of pheasant, grouse, and rabbits. Wildcats are also caught in traps set to catch wolves and foxes. A further threat to this species is the fact that it interbreeds freely with domestic cats, and as trapping and hunting have declined, hybridization has become the most important threat to the maintenance of the subspecies.[11,44] Others believe that disease transmission from domestic cats is just as serious a threat.

Efforts to reintroduce the wildcat at several sites in Europe have not been very successful.[11] At one site in Germany 237 captive-born wildcats were released between 1984 and 1993. While there are signs that the cats have settled in the area and are reproducing, mor-

tality rates have been high; the survival rate was estimated at 30 percent.[31] Because of hybridization concerns, conservation efforts are thought to be best directed toward protecting and augmenting existing populations rather than trying to establish new ones.[45]

The wildcat is listed on appendix II of CITES, which means that the species is strictly protected in countries that are signatories to CITES. To date, those countries are France, Germany, the United Kingdom, Switzerland, Greece, Italy, Luxembourg, Turkey, Spain, Austria, Belgium, the Netherlands, Portugal, and Hungary.

TABLE 13 MEASUREMENTS AND WEIGHTS OF ADULT EUROPEAN WILDCATS

HB	n	T	n	WT	n	Location	Source
564 (515–650)	26m	307 (235–356)	26m	4.7 (3.5–7.1)	26m	Scotland	46
543 (507–595)	16f	293 (240–360)	16f	3.9 (2.5–5.6)	16f	Scotland	46
574 (547–632)	9m	293 (267–315)	9m	4.4 (3.8–5.0)	9m	Scotland	12
563 (521–580)	7f	289 (258–300)	7f	4.0 (3.5–4.6)	7f	Scotland	12
440–650	114m	215–345	114m	5.0–7.7	114m	France	22
430–570	72f	215–340	72f	3.5	72f	France	22
595 (520–670)	36m	314 (275–348)	35m	5.36 (4.2–6.5)	8m	Germany	4
537 (445–640)	25f	291 (255–316)	27f	3.5 (3.0–4.2)	5f	Germany	4
686 (630–750)	m	305 (300–340)	m	6	m	Caucasus	4
610 (580–630)	f	305 (270–330)	f	4.5	f	Caucasus	47
				5.25 (3.3–7.7)	20m	Slovenia	36
				4.23 (2.6–5.84)	16f	Slovenia	36

Note: HB = head and body length (mm); T = tail length (mm); WT = weight (kg). n = sample size. Sex: m = male, f = female, ? = unknown. Mean values are presented only for sample sizes of three or more. Range of values is in parentheses.

TABLE 14 FREQUENCY OF OCCURRENCE OF PREY ITEMS IN THE DIETS OF EUROPEAN WILDCATS (PERCENTAGE OF SAMPLES)

Prey item	NE France[23] Scats (n = 373)	Glen Tanar, Scotland[12] Scats (n = 546)	Slovakia[24] Stomachs (n = 26)
Microtus sp. Meadow mouse/vole	60.9		61.5
Clethrionomys glareolus Red-backed mouse/vole	47.5	7.3	11.5

(continued)

TABLE 14 *(continued)*

Prey item	NE France[23] Scats (n = 373)	Glen Tanar, Scotland[12] Scats (n = 546)	Slovakia[24] Stomachs (n = 26)
Arvicola terrestris Water/bank vole	21.4	0.2	
Apodemus sp. Field mouse	48.3	0.7	19.2
Myoxus glis Fat dormouse	9.4		3.8
Muscardinus avellanarius Common dormouse	0.5		
Dryomys nitedula Forest dormouse			3.8
Mus musculus House mouse			3.8
Rattus norvegicus Norway rat		8.1	26.9
Unidentified small rodents			
Ondatra zibethicus Muskrat	0.3		
Lepus capensis/L. europaeus Cape/brown hare	1.6	4.2	7.7
Oryctolagus cuniculus European rabbit		76.4	
Unidentified lagomorphs		11.0	
Capreolus capreolus Roe deer		1.3	11.5
Birds	2.7	14.0	3.8
Insectivores	0.3	2.2	30.8
Carnivores	0.5		
Insects	0.5		
Plant material		9.0	53.8
Minimum number of vertebrate prey items	721	685	50

REFERENCES

1. Weigel, I. 1972. Small felids and clouded leopards. In *Grzimek's animal life encyclopedia*, ed. H. C. B. Grzimek, 281–332. New York: Van Nostrand Reinhold.

2. Guggisberg, C. A. W. 1975. *Wild cats of the world*. New York: Taplinger.

3. Condé, B., and P. Schauenberg. 1971. Weight of the European forest wildcat. *Rev. Suisse Zool.* 78: 295–315.

4. Piechocki, R. 1990. *Die wildkatze*. Wittenberg-Lutherstadt: A. Ziemsen Verlag.

5. Pocock, R. I. 1934. A record Scotch wild cat. *Scottish Naturalist*, March–April, 33–39.

6. Heptner, V. G., and A. A. Sludskii. 1992. *Mammals of the Soviet Union*. Vol. 2, part 2, *Carnivora (Hyaenas and cats)*. English translation, sci. ed. R. S. Hoffmann. Washington, DC: Smithsonian Institution Libraries and the National Science Foundation.

7. Satunin, C. 1904. The black wild cat of Transcauscasia. *Proc. Zool. Soc. Lond.* 1904: 162–163.

8. Aliev, F. 1974. The Caucasian black cat, *Felis silvestris caucasica* Satunin, 1905. *Säugetierk. Mitt.* 22: 142–145.

9. Kitchener, A. C., and N. Easterbee. 1992. The taxonomic status of black wild felids in Scotland. *J. Zool.* (Lond.) 227: 342–346.

10. Lagley, P. J. W., and D. W. Yalden. 1977. The decline of the rarer carnivores in Great Britain during the nineteenth century. *Mammal Rev.* 7: 95–116.

11. Stahl, P., and M. Artois. 1991. *Status and conservation of the wild cat (Felis silvestris) in Europe and around the Mediterranean rim*. Strasbourg: Council of Europe.

12. Corbett, L. K. 1979. Feeding ecology and social organization of wildcats (*Felis silvestris*) and domestic cats (*Felis catus*) in Scotland. Ph.D. dissertation, University of Aberdeen.

13. Easterbee, N., L. V. Hepburn, and D. J. Jefferies. 1991. *Survey of the status and distribution of the wildcat in Scotland, 1983–1987*. Edinburgh: Nature Conservancy Council for Scotland.

14. Scott, R., N. Easterbee, and D. Jefferies. 1993. A radio-tracking study of wildcats in western Scotland. In *Proceedings of a seminar on the biology and conservation of the wildcat* (Felis silvestris), *Nancy, France*, 94–97. Strasbourg: Council of Europe.

15. Ragni, B. 1978. Observations on the ecology and behaviour

of the wild cat (*Felis silvestris* Schreber, 1777) in Italy. *Carniv. Genet. Newsl.* 3: 270–274.

16. Lindemann, W. 1953. Einiges über die wildkatze der Ostkarpaten (*Felis s. silvestris* Schreber, 1777). *Säugetierk. Mitt.* 1: 73–74.

17. Allayarov, A. M. 1963. Information on the ecology and geographical distribution of the spotted cat in Uzbekistan. *Voprosy Biologii i Kraevoi Meditsiny* 4: 315–321.

18. Sládek, von J. 1970. Werden spitzmäuse von der wildkatze gefrressen? *Säugetierk. Mitt.* 18: 224–226.

19. Heidemann, G. von, and G. Vauk. 1970. Zur Nahrugsökologie "wildernder" hauskatzen (*Felis silvestris f. catus* Linné, 1758). *Z. Säugetierk.* 35: 185–190.

20. Nasilov, S. B. 1972. Feeding of the wild cat in Azerbaijan. *Ekologiya* 2: 101–102.

21. Condé, B., Nguyen-Thi-Thu-Cuc, F. Vaillant, and P. Schauenberg. 1972. Le régime alimentaire du chat forestier (*F. silvestris* Schr.) en France. *Mammalia* 36: 112–119.

22. Schauenberg, P. 1981. Eléments d'écologie du chat forestier d'Europe *Felis silvestris* Schreber 1777. *Terre et Vie* 35: 3–36.

23. Stahl, P. 1986. Le chat forestier d'Europe (*Felis silvestris*, Schreber 1777): Exploitation des ressources et organisation spatiale. Ph.D. dissertation, Université Nancy, France.

24. Kozená, I. 1990. Contribution to the food of wild cats (*Felis silvestris*). *Folia Zool.* 39: 207–212.

25. Kitchener, A. C. 1991. *The natural history of the wild cats.* New York: Cornell University Press.

26. Ionescu, O. 1993. Wildcat in Romania. In *Proceedings of a seminar on the biology and conservation of the wildcat* (Felis silvestris), *Nancy, France,* 57–58. Strasbourg: Council of Europe.

27. Szemethy, L. 1993. The actual status of wildcat (*Felis silvestris*) in Hungary. In *Proceedings of a seminar on the biology and conservation of the wildcat* (Felis silvestris), *Nancy, France,* 52. Strasbourg: Council of Europe.

28. Stahl, P., M. Artois, and M. F. A. Aubert. 1988. Organisation spatiale et déplacements des chats forestiers adultes (*Felis silvestris,* Schreber, 1777) en Lorraine. *Rev. Ecol. (Terre Vie)* 43: 113–132.

29. Mellen, J. D. 1993. A comparative analysis of scent-marking, social and reproductive behavior in 20 species of small cats (*Felis*). *Am. Zool.* 33: 151–166.

30. Wemmer, C., and K. Scow. 1977. Communication in the Felidae with emphasis on scent marking and contact patterns. In *How animals communicate,* ed. T. A. Sebeok, 749–766. Bloomington: Indiana University Press.

31. Nowell, K., and P. Jackson. 1996. *Wild cats: A status survey and conservation action plan.* Gland: International Union for Conservation of Nature and Natural Resources (IUCN).

32. Peters, G. 1984. On the structure of friendly close range vocalizations in terrestrial carnivores (Mammalia: Carnivora: Fissipedia). *Z. Säugetierk.* 49: 157–182.

33. Peters, G. 1991. Vocal communication in cats. In *Great cats,* ed. J. Seidensticker and S. Lumpkin, 76–77. Emmaus, PA: Rodale Press.

34. Haltennorth, T. 1957. *Die wildkatze.* Wittenberg-Lutherstadt: A. Ziemsen Verlag.

35. Meyer-Holzapfel, M. 1968. Breeding the European wild cat at Berne Zoo. *Int. Zoo Yrbk.* 8: 31–38.

36. Volf, J. 1968. Breeding the European wild cat at Prague Zoo. *Int. Zoo Yrbk.* 8: 38–42.

37. Condé, B., and P. Schauenberg. 1969. Reproduction du chat forestier d'Europe (*Felis silvestris* Schreber) en captivité. *Rev. Suisse Zool.* 76: 183–210.

38. Andrews, P., Hexagon Farm Wild Feline Breeding Facility, 1187 Merrill Road, San Juan Bautista, CA. Personal communication.

39. Condé, B., and P. Schauenberg. 1974. Reproduction du chat forestier (*F. silvestris* Schr.) dans le nord-est de la France. *Rev. Suisse Zool.* 81: 45–52.

40. Raimer, F., and E. Schneider. 1983. Vorkomen und status der wildkatze *Felis silvestris silvestris* Schreber, 1777 im Harz. *Säugetierk. Mitt.* 31: 61–68.

41. Eisenberg, J. F. 1986. Life history strategies of the Felidae: Variations on a common theme. In *Cats of the world: Biology, conservation, and management,* ed. S. D. Miller and D. D. Everett, 293–303. Washington, DC: National Wildlife Federation.

42. Caro, T. M. 1994. *Cheetahs of the Serengeti plains.* Chicago: University of Chicago Press.

43. Condé, B., and P. Schauenberg. 1978. Remplacement des canines chez le chat forestier *Felis silvestris* Schreb. *Rev. Suisse Zool.* 85: 241–245.

44. Hubbard, A. L., S. McOrist, T. W. Jones, R. Boid, R. Scott, and N. Easterbee. 1992. Is survival of European wildcats *Felis silvestris* in Britain threatened by interbreeding with domestic cats? *Biol. Conserv.* 61: 302–208.

45. Stahl, P. 1993. Status of the wildcat (*Felis silvestris*) in western Europe. In *Proceedings of a seminar on the biology and conservation of the wildcat* (Felis silvestris), *Nancy, France,* 16–25. Strasbourg: Council of Europe.

46. Kolb, H. H. 1977. Wild cat. In *The handbook of British mammals,* ed. G. B. Corbet and H. H. Southern, 375–382. Oxford: Blackwell Scientific.

47. Novikov, G. A. 1962. *Carnivorous mammals of the fauna of the USSR.* Jerusalem: Israel Program for Scientific Translations.

African-Asian wildcat

Felis silvestris lybica and *Felis silvestris ornata*

Archaeological evidence suggests that wildcats have been living around villages for a long time. Wildcat remains dating from about 7000 B.C. were found in excavations of Jericho.[1] However, these animals were almost certainly not domesticated in the true sense of the word, but more likely represent isolated individuals that had been found in the wild and kept for amusement, much in the same way as South American Indians catch and keep parrots and monkeys today.

Some 4,000 years ago the sculptors of ancient Egypt began to portray African wildcats in their art. By then, people obviously valued the wildcat for its rodent-catching abilities, and 3,400 years ago in the tomb of Nakhte, Thebes, an artist painted a picture of a cat catching a mouse under a chair.[2,3]

Today, African wildcats often live close to human settlements and frequently interbreed with domestic cats. The African wildcat seems to adjust quite well to living close to people. The South African biologist Reay Smithers, who raised two female kittens, wrote of them "rubbing themselves repeatedly against one's legs or, if one was reading, [they] would insinuate themselves between the book and one's face, purring loudly and rubbing themselves on the face." Both of Smithers's cats would take to the wild for varying periods, but always returned of their own volition.[3]

DESCRIPTION

There are two main features that distinguish wildcats from domestic cats and hybrids. In the African wildcat, the backs of the ears are characteristically a rich red-brown. Domestic-wild crosses usually have dark gray or black-backed ears, but sometimes retain a little red at the base of the ears. In Pakistan and India the backs of the Asian wildcat's ears are yellowish buff or khaki. A second striking characteristic is the wildcat's long legs. When the wildcat is sitting upright, its long front legs raise its body into an almost vertical position. This characteristic pose, which is almost impossible for domestic cats or crosses, can be seen in the ancient Egyptian bronze mummy cases and tomb paintings. Even when walking, the wildcat's long legs and high shoulder blades give it a distinctive action; it moves more like a cheetah than a domestic cat. The African wildcat is slender, weighing 4 to 6 kilograms, and has a long, thin tail that is 50 to 60 percent of the cat's head and body length. Combined with its short hair and long legs, these features make it look very different from its heavily built, long-haired relative, the European wildcat.[4,5,6,7]

Though its coat is usually depicted as looking exactly like that of a modern domestic tabby cat, the African wildcat's fur color and markings are extremely variable, ranging from grayish to reddish, with or without small spots. The spots sometimes form transverse stripes or bars, especially on the legs and tail. Generally, the paler forms of the African wildcat live in dryer areas and the darker, more heavily spotted and striped forms occur in more humid areas.[8]

In Pakistan and India the Asian wildcat is called the desert cat, although it does not inhabit true desert. In this part of its range the wildcat's coat is usually pale sandy yellow, marked with small spots that tend to lie in vertical lines down the trunk and flanks. Throughout its range the wildcat's coat is usually short, but the length of the fur can vary depending on the age of the animal and the season of the year.

The tail always has a short black tip, and the underparts of the paws are black. A small but pronounced tuft of hair up to 1 centimeter long grows from the tip of each ear. Males are usually larger and heavier than females.

DISTRIBUTION

The wildcat is widely distributed in Africa, being absent only in true desert and tropical forest. Outside Africa it is found along the eastern border of the Mediterranean Sea, in parts of the Arabian Peninsula, Iran, Iraq, Pakistan, eastern Afghanistan, and Ladakh and on the western plains of India (fig. 19). In some parts of its range this cat is considered to be the most common small carnivore.[4,5,6,8,9,10,11,12,13]

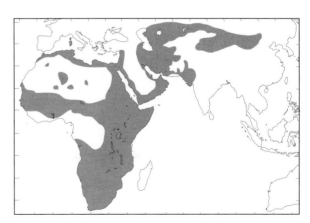

Figure 19. Distribution of the African-Asian wildcat.

ECOLOGY AND BEHAVIOR

In keeping with its wide geographic distribution, the wildcat lives in a wide variety of habitats. In Africa it is found at altitudes ranging from sea level to 3,000 meters. In Africa and elsewhere, wildcats do not normally live in areas that get less than 100 millimeters of mean annual rainfall, except where watercourses flow through drier country. They require some sort of cover for hunting and rest sites, but this can be almost anything from rocks to scrubby underbrush or agricultural crops. Wildcats even live on the treeless open grasslands in Ngorongoro Crater, but depend on holes dug by other animals to escape from larger carnivores.[14] In Botswana wildcats are commonly seen at night in open woodlands and grasslands, especially in the vicinity of rivers and wetlands.[15] However, wildcats in Zimbabwe's Wankie National Park are more often seen in drier woodland and scrub habitats than in areas close to water.[16] A radio-tagged wildcat in Kenya was located primarily in open woodlands and grasslands used for cattle grazing; it used riverine forest and agricultural lands infrequently.[17] Open Mediterranean forests in hilly areas are the preferred habitat of wildcats in Israel, where densities of one cat per square kilometer may be reached.[12]

The wildcat lives sympatrically with many other carnivore species, but the extent to which they compete with other small carnivores, or are themselves taken as prey by larger species, is not known. A study of canine diameters of small felids in Israel suggested that the four different cat species there took different-sized prey.[18]

Like its domesticated relatives, the African wildcat does most of its hunting on the ground, though it can climb well if pursued. The wildcat is reported to be strictly nocturnal and usually does not begin to move until well after sunset.[4,15,16] A radio-tagged wildcat in Kenya was found to be primarily nocturnal.[17] The wildcat hunts by moving silently through its territory, watching and listening for signs of prey activity. When the cat sees or hears something, it crouches and approaches with a low stalking run. The cat then uses every piece of available cover to creep forward within striking range, then darts forward and strikes with a paw and bites. Kingdon reports that African wildcats sometimes hunt in pairs or family groups, with cats advancing through an area separated by 3 to 30 meters.[5] However, most observations of wildcats are of solitary individuals.

Feeding Ecology

Though they thrive on a variety of small prey and eat a fair number of arthropods, wildcats are primarily rodent catchers. They also occasionally take larger animals such as hares, rabbits, and young antelope, which at 3 to 4 kilograms are thought to be at the upper limit of prey size.[3,5] However, there are also records of wildcats killing domestic lambs.[19] The stomach contents of wildcats from Zimbabwe and Botswana contained murid rodents in almost three-quarters of the samples. Birds such as domestic poultry, doves, quail, and weavers were next in importance, followed by insects and reptiles such as lizards, skinks, and snakes. Fruit was found in one stomach. The remains of hunting spiders were common in stomachs collected from semidesert areas in Botswana.[15,16,20] Studies of feces confirm the wildcat's preference for rodents. In the Namib Desert small mammal remains were found in over 90 percent of scats, while insect remains were found in 70 percent.[21] Similar percentages of small rodents and insects were found in wildcat feces from Karoo National Park.[22]

In the scrub habitat of western Rajasthan, India, the Asian wildcat lives largely on desert gerbils, but also hunts hares, doves, gray partridge, sandgrouse, peafowl, bulbuls, sparrows, and rats. It has also been observed killing cobras, saw-scale vipers, sand boas, geckos, scorpions, and beetles.[23]

Despite the fact that rodents dominate the wildcat's diet, these cats are adaptable predators and can survive on other foods. At the end of a four-year drought in Botswana, when murid rodent populations were at an all-time low, wildcats were found to be thriving on a diet of invertebrates, fruit, and birds. All the cats examined were in good condition with normal body weights.[4]

Social Organization

Little is known of the wildcat's social habits, but it is believed to be highly territorial. Two wild female kittens hand-reared by Smithers became very aggressive toward each other after reaching sexual maturity. Both cats scent-marked vigorously, and the dominant female actively pursued the subordinate well beyond the boundaries of her marked territory. Both males and females urine-mark, and in captivity both sexes bury their feces.[3]

The only information on range size comes from a radio-tagged adult male wildcat in Kenya, whose range measured 1.6 square kilometers over the short time he was followed.[17] In a study of radio-tagged European wildcats, adult female ranges measured about 2 square kilometers, whereas those of adult males were larger, up to 12.7 square kilometers.[24]

The vocal repertoire of the wildcat is similar to that of the domestic cat. Wildcats purr, meow, hiss, spit, and growl. A gentle "mrrr" sound is used as a friendly greeting, reassurance, or appeasement. Both sexes have a loud call that begins with a loud meow and ends with a regular, deep, two-note "orrr-ow." [25,26,27]

Reproduction and Development

African wildcats produce litters of one to five kittens, usually three, after a gestation period of about fifty-six to sixty-five days.[4,20,23,27,28,29] Estrus lasts two to eight days, and females may be followed by several males. Females may come into heat several times a year, and captive wildcats have produced two litters in one year.

The kittens are usually born in an underground den, but litters have been discovered in rock crevices, under brush, in hollows in haystacks, and even in fields of agricultural crops. Kittens are born at all times of the year, but in southern and eastern Africa there seems to be a birth peak during the wet season, when both rodents and vegetative cover are most abundant.[4,5] Wildcats in western India breed in the winter.[23]

The kittens are blind at birth and weigh 80 to 120 grams. Their eyes are open at nine to eleven days. They nurse for about thirty days, and are mobile at four weeks. In captivity, a mother introduced her kittens to live prey when they were about sixty days old; a few days later the kittens were able to kill and eat mice.[27] In India a wild female brought beetles and the eggs of ground-nesting birds to her kittens; she also brought in half-killed gerbils for the young to try to kill.[23] In the wild the young begin to accompany their mother on hunting trips when they are three months old. They acquire their permanent canine teeth by the time they are five months old, and are independent at six months.[5]

Given the short period of dependence, it would be possible for females to raise two litters in a single year in areas where ecological conditions are right. At present there is no information on the timing of dispersal, but the young probably remain in their natal area until they are about a year old, which is the age when sexual activity was observed in captives.[27] Captive wildcats have lived to be fifteen years old.

STATUS IN THE WILD

There are no density estimates available for the African wildcat, but given its flexible food habits, tolerance of a wide range of ecological conditions, and ability to survive near humans, the species is probably in no immediate danger in Africa. Wildcats may, in fact, be one of the few species of cats to have benefited from human activities in Africa, since agricultural development has increased rodent densities. In many parts of South Africa these cats are frequently encountered near cornfields, where rodents abound. They are also common in the fringes of urban areas. Widely distributed in southern Africa, this species is regarded as the most common cat in that region.

The status of the Asian wildcat in Pakistan and India is not nearly as good. In Pakistan the wildcat is comparatively rare and restricted in distribution. In this part of its range it often kills poultry and is frequently shot or trapped as a pest. Its soft, luxuriant fur is in great demand by the fur trade, and large numbers of skins are bought by traders in northern Pakistan. Village dogs have also been seen killing adult wildcats and kittens.

There is no recent information on the status of the wildcat in Iran, Iraq, or other countries in the Middle East, except for Israel, where wildcats are becoming increasingly rare.[30]

A major threat to the wildcat is the fact that it interbreeds freely with domestic cats. In his 1983 account of the African wildcat, South African biologist Reay Smithers stated that "it is becoming increasingly difficult to find pure-bred African wildcats anywhere near settled areas or even in the remoter areas near isolated trading stores where domestic cats have been kept."[4]

TABLE 15 MEASUREMENTS AND WEIGHTS OF ADULT AFRICAN-ASIAN WILDCATS

HB	n	T	n	WT	n	Location	Source
601 (545–665)	21m	305 (275–360)	21m	4.9 (4.0–6.2)	10m	Cape Province	19
550 (460–620)	15f	295 (250–355)	16f	3.7 (2.4–5.0)	10f	Cape Province	19
				5.1 (3.8–6.4)	32m	Botswana	4
				4.2 (3.2–5.5)	26f	Botswana	4
520	1m	280	1m			Algeria	9
520 (460–570)	4m	290 (250–320)	4m	3.2–4.5	6m	Yemen	31
500, 510	2f	250, 280	2f	3.2–4.5	6f	Yemen	31
507 (470–597)	5m	320 (267–368)	5m			Northern Africa	8
456 (406–558)	4f	300 (241–337)	4f			Northern Africa	8
497 (470–542)	4?	241 (219–290)	4?	4.0	1m	Pakistan	6
575 (490–740)	27m	311 (250–360)	26m	3.9 (2.0–6.0)	18m	Turkmenistan	32
520 (440–610)	18f	282 (240–340)	18f	2.7 (2.0–4.1)	11f	Turkmenistan	32

Note: HB = head and body length (mm); T = tail length (mm); WT = weight (kg). *n* = sample size. Sex: m = male, f = female, ? = unknown. Mean values are presented only for sample sizes of three or more. Range of values is in parentheses.

TABLE 16 FREQUENCY OF OCCURRENCE OF PREY ITEMS IN THE DIETS OF WILDCATS IN SOUTHERN AFRICA (PERCENTAGE OF SAMPLES)

Prey items	Zimbabwe[15] Stomachs (n = 58)	Botswana[20] Stomachs (n = 80)
Mastomys natalensis Multimammate mouse	31	8
Otomys angoniensis Angoni vlei rat	14	
Tatera sp. Gerbils	12	40
Saccostomus campestris Pouched mouse	3	8
Steatomys pratensis Fat mouse	3	5
Mus minutoides Pygmy mouse	3	15
Rattus rattus Black rat	2	
Pelomys fallax Creek or groove-toothed rat	2	
Aethomys sp. Rock mouse	2	3
Gerbillurus paeba Hairy-footed gerbil		6
Dendromus melanotis Pygmy climbing mouse		1
Other mammals	9	6

TABLE 16 (*continued*)

Prey items	Zimbabwe[15] Stomachs ($n = 58$)	Botswana[20] Stomachs ($n = 80$)
Birds	21	10
Reptiles	10	13
Amphibians	2	1
Insects	19	19
Fruit	2	1
Minimum number of vertebrate prey items	66	92

TABLE 17 FREQUENCY OF OCCURRENCE OF PREY ITEMS IN THE DIETS OF WILDCATS IN ASIA (PERCENTAGE OF SAMPLES)

Prey items	SE Kazakhstan, lower Ili[32] Scats ($n = 571$)	Eastern Karakum, Turkmenistan[33] Stomachs and scats ($n = 94$)
Capreolus capreolus Roe deer	1.0	
Sus scrofa Wild pig	0.2	
Lepus tolai Tolai hare	5.2	9.6
Spermophilopsis leptodactylus Thin-toed ground squirrel		4.2
Dipus sp. Jerboas		5.2
Rhombomys opinus Great gerbil	0.2	38.2
Meriones tamariscinus Crested or tamarisk gerbil	11.9	
Meriones meridianus Midday gerbil	7.8	19.1
Ondatra zibethicus Muskrat	22.3	
Arvicola sp. Water vole	0.2	
Unidentified voles	2.8	
Mus musculus House mouse	42.9	
Apodemus sp. Field mouse.	0.5	
Unidentified small rodents	4.7	1.0
Pheasants	11.7	
Other birds	6.7	7.3
Reptiles	0.7	14.8
Fish	2.1	
Insects	0.5	12.8
Nuts	1.5	
Plant material	1.9	
Minimum number of vertebrate prey items	677	97

REFERENCES

1. Zeuner, F. E. 1958. Dog and cat in the Neolithic of Jericho. *Pal. Expl. Q. Lond.* 52–55.

2. Clutton-Brock, J. 1987. *A natural history of domesticated animals.* London: Cambridge University Press.

3. Smithers, R. H. N. 1968. Cat of the Pharaohs. *Animal Kingdom* 71: 16–23.

4. Smithers, R. H. N. 1983. *The mammals of the southern African subregion.* Pretoria: University of Pretoria.

5. Kingdon, J. 1977. *East African mammals.* Vol. 3A, *Carnivores.* Chicago: University of Chicago Press.

6. Roberts, T. J. 1977. *The mammals of Pakistan.* London: Ernest Benn.

7. Dragesco-Joffé, A. 1993. *La vie sauvage au Sahara.* Lausanne: Delachaux et Niestlé,

8. Pocock, R. I. 1944. The races of the North African wild cat (*Felis lybica*). *Proc. Zool. Soc. Lond.* 114: 65–73.

9. Kowalski, K., and B. Rzebik-Kowalska. 1991. *Mammals of Algeria.* Warsaw: Polish Academy of Sciences.

10. Hufnagl, E. 1972. *Libyan mammals.* Cambridge: Oleander Press.

11. Gasperetti, J., D. L. Harrison, and W. Büttiker. 1986. The Carnivora of Arabia. In *Fauna of Saudi Arabia,* vol. 7, ed. W. Büttiker and F. Krupp, 397–461. Basel: Pro Entomologia, c/o Natural History Museum.

12. Mendelssohn, H. 1989. Felids in Israel. *Cat News* 10: 2–4.

13. Harrington, F. A. Jr. 1977. *A guide to the mammals of Iran.* Tehran: Department of the Environment.

14. Estes, R. D. 1991. *The behavior guide to African mammals.* Berkeley: University of California Press.

15. Smithers, R. H. N. 1971. *The mammals of Botswana.* Museum Memoir no. 4. Salisbury: The Trustees of the National Museums of Rhodesia.

16. Wilson, V. J. 1975. *Mammals of the Wankie National Park, Rhodesia.* Museum Memoir no. 5. Salisbury: Trustees of the National Museums and Monuments of Rhodesia.

17. Fuller, T. K., A. R. Biknevicius, and P. W. Kat. 1988. Home range of an African wildcat, *Felis silvestris* (Schreber), near Elmenteita, Kenya. *Z. Säugetierk.* 53: 380–381.

18. Dayan, T., D. Simberloff, E. Tchernov, and Y. Yom-Tov. 1990. Feline canines: Community-wide character displacement among the small cats of Israel. *Am. Nat.* 136: 39–60.

19. Stuart, C. T. 1981. Notes on the mammalian carnivores of the Cape Province, South Africa. *Bontebok* 1: 1–58.

20. Smithers, R. H. N., and V. J. Wilson. 1979. *Check list and atlas of the mammals of Zimbabwe Rhodesia.* Museum Memoir no. 9. Salisbury: Trustees of the National Museums and Monuments.

21. Stuart, C. T. 1977. Analysis of *Felis lybica* and *Genetta genetta* scats from the Central Namib Desert, South West Africa. *Zool. Afr.* 12: 239–241.

22. Palmer, R., and N. Fairall. 1988. Caracal and African wild cat diet in the Karoo National Park and the implications thereof for hyrax. *S. Afr. J. Wildl. Res.* 18: 30–34.

23. Sharma, I. K. 1979. Habitats, feeding, breeding and reaction to man of the desert cat *Felis libyca* (Gray) in the Indian desert. *J. Bombay Nat. Hist. Soc.* 76: 498–499.

24. Stahl, P., M. Artois, and M. F. A. Aubert. 1988. Organisation spatiale et déplacements des chats forestiers adults (*Felis silvestris,* Schreber, 1777) en Lorraine. *Rev. Ecol. (Terre Vie)* 43: 113–132.

25. Peters, G. 1981. Das schnurren der katzen (Felidae). *Säugetierk. Mitt.* 29: 30–37.

26. Peters, G. 1984. On the structure of friendly close range vocalizations in terrestrial carnivores (Mammalia: Carnivora: Fissipedia). *Z. Säugetierk.* 49: 157–182.

27. Tonkin, B. A., and E. Kohler. 1981. Observations on the Indian desert cat in captivity. *Int. Zoo Yrbk.* 21: 151–154.

28. Hemmer, H. 1979. Gestation period and postnatal development in felids. *Carnivore* 2: 90–100.

29. Mellen, J. D. 1993. A comparative analysis of scent-marking, social and reproductive behavior in 20 species of small cats (*Felis*). *Am. Zool.* 33: 151–166.

30. Nowell, K., and P. Jackson. 1996. *Wild cats: A status survey and conservation action plan.* Gland, Switzerland: International Union for Conservation of Nature and Natural Resources (IUCN).

31. Al-Safadi, M. M., and I. A. Nader. 1990. First record of the wild cat, *Felis silvestris* Schreber, 1777 from the Yemen Arab Republic (Carnivora: Felidae). *Mammalia* 54: 621–626.

32. Heptner, V. G., and A. A. Sludskii. 1992. *Mammals of the Soviet Union.* Vol. 2, part 2, *Carnivora (Hyaenas and cats).* English translation, sci. ed. R. S. Hoffmann. Washington, DC: Smithsonian Institution Libraries and the National Science Foundation.

33. Sapozhenkov, Y. F. 1961. On the ecology of *Felis lybica* Forst in eastern Kara-Kumy. *Zool. Zh.* 41: 1110–1112.

Domestic cat

Felis silvestris catus

Over the course of recent history, humans have tamed and domesticated many different animal species, the first of which was probably the dog some 12,000 years ago. *Felis silvestris* was almost the last species to be tamed, being added to the list of domesticated animals after goats, sheep, cattle, pigs, chickens, horses, and even water buffalo. However, from these modest and comparatively recent beginnings, the cat is now on the verge of becoming the Western world's most popular pet; current predictions are that cats will soon overtake dogs as the most commonly kept pet. According to the Pet Food Institute in Washington, D.C., cats already outnumber dogs in the United States. In 1997 there were an estimated 70.2 million pet cats in the United States, compared with 55.9 million dogs.[1]

Though many millions of cats are well-fed, well-loved family pets, millions more are feral, scavenging human leftovers. Many others live with and are fed by humans but supplement their diets with birds, rodents, and lizards.

Cats are believed to have been first domesticated in Egypt, some four thousand years ago, but the problem of identifying the exact period when domestication occurred is complicated by the fact that domestic cats are only recently descended from the African wildcat (*Felis silvestris lybica*). For this reason, the skeletons of domestic cats and wildcats are difficult to differentiate. When cat bones are excavated from archaeological sites, it is difficult to establish whether they belong to wildcats that were scavenging and hunting around human dwellings or to domesticated wildcats living with people.[2]

Though most of the evidence points to Egypt as the birthplace of the domestic cat, bones of small felids have been found at older archaeological sites in other areas. The remains of African wildcats have been excavated from Jericho and dated at 6000 to 7000 B.C., but there is no evidence that these were from domesticated animals; rather, they may have been the bones of cats killed for fur.[3,4,5]

Recent excavations of a six-thousand-year-old settlement on the Mediterranean island of Cyprus have unearthed a cat's jawbone, suggesting that cats may have been associated with people for longer than was previously thought. Wildcats do not occur naturally on Cyprus, so the animal on the island must have been brought there in a boat, either as an accidental stowaway or as a pet.[6]

Archaeological evidence shows that African wildcats were certainly spending time around Egyptian towns and villages some four to five thousand years ago, but their exact status and the process of domestication remain unclear. One theory is that wildcats simply began to hang around farms, granaries, and town middens, drawn by the abundant rodents that were attracted by the grain and garbage. Historical and biblical accounts record plagues of rats and mice decimating grain stores and spreading disease, and almost any predator that reduced the numbers of these rodents would undoubtedly have been encouraged.

Others argue that the most likely route to domestication was through people taming captured kittens, just as many South American and Asian people tame monkeys and birds today. It is known that the Egyptian people of that time had an extraordinary passion for taming wild animals, and it was common for wealthy families to have large menageries containing baboons, lions, mongooses, hyenas, and gazelles. Given that cats were objects of worship and thought to be the earthly representatives of various deities, it is highly likely that the Egyptians attempted to tame them in order to add them to their animal collections.[7]

For the Egyptians, the process of domestication was aided by the fact that the local subspecies of wildcat, *Felis s. lybica*, was a much less aggressive animal than the virtually untamable European wildcat, *F. s. silvestris*. Even so, pure *F. s. lybica* kittens are reported to be quite difficult to handle. The veteran South African zoologist Reay Smithers kept several purebred *F. s. lybica*, along with some *lybica*-domestic crosses. Smithers wrote that "the progeny of Komani and a pure male from Botswana, Igola [both *F. s. lybica*], were long-legged with red ears and from the earliest stages, unhandleable, spitting and scratching or diving for cover when approached." However, Smithers adds that crosses between domestic cats and wildcats are easy to handle and tame easily. When Smithers's wild-caught female mated with a domestic cat, the offspring "turned out to be splendid house cats, great hunters and reached an adult weight of 12 to 14 pounds, some two pounds heavier than their mother."[8]

Beginning about two thousand years B.C., the domestic cat's history becomes easier to follow, as this marks the time when Egyptian artists began to depict the cat in mosaics and paintings. Statues, amulets, and pictures show cats in a variety of contexts, sitting under chairs, riding in boats, and being worshipped as deities. In Thebes, in the tomb of Nakhte, dating to 1415 B.C., there is a painting of a cat killing a mouse under its owner's chair. In another tomb dated about 1900 B.C., the bones of seventeen cats were discovered, along with several small pots believed to be for offerings of milk.[2,8]

At that time in Egypt, the cat was associated with a confusing array of gods and religious beliefs. One papyrus depicts the sun god Ra as a cat with spots and barred markings, holding a knife in its paws. In the drawing the cat is cutting off the head of the serpent of darkness, who was believed to swallow the sun every evening. This association with the sun apparently gave rise to the string game "cat's cradle," versions of which are played all over the world. Though the meanings of the various patterns have been obscured by time, the string cradles were used as a means to control the movements of the sun.[9]

Lions were also associated with the sun god, and cats were seen as closely related to lions. The lion-headed goddess Sekhmet represented the destructive aspects of the sun and was associated with wrath and vengeance. According to one version of the myth, Bastet was the sister of Sekhmet, the daughter of Isis and Osiris the sun god.[9] Though Bastet was originally lion-headed, she became more and more frequently depicted with a cat's head and came to represent the good and benevolent aspects of the sun. Bastet eventually became the great cat goddess who was in charge of all growing things; she was a symbol of fertility for both crops and women, and eventually came to be known as the goddess of joy and love.

Around 1000 B.C. Bastet emerged as a major deity and the focus of the famous cat cult. The center of the cult was the great temple of Bastet in the city of Bubastis, which is east of the Nile delta and is today marked by a mound called Tel Basta. Herodotus, who visited the city in 450 B.C., describes the shrine of the goddess Bastet as "standing on an island completely surrounded by water except at the entrance passage." According to Herodotus's detailed description, the shrine itself was built of fine red granite and encompassed a sacred enclosure about 600 feet square, beyond which was a larger enclosure containing a canal, a grove of trees, and a lake. In addition to a huge statue of the goddess Bastet, the shrine contained thousands of cats, which were fed and cared for by innumerable priests and attendants.[9]

As the goddess of joy and love, Bastet was an extremely popular deity, and each year thousands of people celebrated the festival of the cat goddess with a pilgrimage to Bubastis. The event was one of the principal festivals in Egypt and seems to have been somewhat akin to a weeklong party; the mood was festive, and there was much drinking, singing, and dancing.

During the cat cult of Bastet, images of cats were carved and sculpted in every material from gold to mud. Paintings depicted cats of various colors, including ginger, orange-brown, and gray tabby. Cats were shown eating fish, springing at waterfowl, and catching mice. Bronze cat statues were used as votive offerings at shrines, and cat amulets made of gold, glass, jasper, and stone were worn around the neck and buried in cat graves. The penalty for killing a cat was death, and people would flee if they saw a sick or injured cat in the street for fear of being held responsible for the creature's demise. Cats were also highly esteemed as pets; many people owned cats, and the death of one of these pets sent the entire family into mourning. Behaving almost as if a human family member had died, people shaved their eyebrows as a sign of respect and had the dead animal embalmed and buried in a special cat cemetery. The embalming procedure and funeral trappings varied depending on how wealthy the family was. A poor man's cat was rolled in a piece of plain linen, whereas a rich man might commission an elaborately embalmed cat mummy with a decorated papier-mâché mask. Thus embalmed, the body was placed in a mummy case, or if it was a kitten, in a small bronze coffin. Food for the afterworld, in the form of mummified mice and small pots of milk, was buried with the cat.[9,10,11]

It was during this period that the great cat cemeteries were laid out along the banks of the Nile, where huge underground vaults and repositories held the mummified remains of several hundred thousand cats. One such burial ground was discovered at Beni Hasan in 1888 when a farmer accidentally dug into a vault containing thousands of mummified cats. The contents of this particular vault were so numerous that a businessman hired people to strip cloth and dried fur from the bones so that the bodies could be turned into fertilizer. Nineteen tons of mummified cat bones, or the remains of some eighty thousand cats, were shipped to Manchester in England to be ground up for use as fertilizer.[12]

Fortunately, a few of these cat skeletons survived to be examined and described by scientists. Eighty-nine skulls from Beni Hasan have been dated from 1000 to 2000 B.C., and of these, four or five are thought to belong to *Felis chaus*, the jungle cat, while the rest are *Felis s. lybica*. Another collection of skulls and mummified animal remains from Egypt, dating from 600 to 200 B.C., was presented to the British Museum in the early 1900s, but the box containing the specimens was put into storage, misplaced, and only rediscovered some fifty years later. When examined, the collection was found to contain one hundred and ninety-two cats, seven mongooses, three dogs, and a fox. Three of the skulls were from *Felis chaus*, the jungle cat, but the remainder were those of the African wildcat.[13]

The Egyptians kept their cats under close guard, and by making their export illegal, essentially prevented the spread of domestic cats to other countries. The earliest record of a domestic cat in Greece is a 500 B.C. marble bas-relief scene of a cat on a leash confronting a dog. This must have been an unusual event, because at that time cats were almost unknown in Greece and Rome; ferrets were the animals of choice for rodent control. Cats remained rare until the fourth century A.D., when the Roman writer Palladius recommended cats as an alternative to ferrets for getting rid of moles in artichoke beds.[12]

F. E. Zeuner, in his classic work *A History of Domesticated Animals*, suggests that cats began to spread from Egypt to the rest of the world soon after Christianity arrived in Egypt because this change released the restrictions on the movements of cats and eventually led to cats being imported to Rome.[14] Others believe that the cat's spread through Europe was linked to the spread of the brown rat and the house mouse.[15] Once the cat had arrived in Rome, it was almost inevitable that it would spread throughout Europe, quite likely as a camp follower and companion to the constantly traveling Roman armies. The domestic cat was introduced to Britain by the Romans, and the remains of cats have been found in many Roman settlements in England.

By the tenth century the cat was becoming more common throughout much of Europe. In Wales in the tenth century, a hamlet was defined as a place that contained "nine buildings, one herdsman, one plow, one kiln, one churn, one bull, one cock and one cat." According to the laws of Hywel Dda, a Welsh king who lived about A.D. 945, a cat was worth four pence. Thus it had the same value as a dog, but was worth more than a small pig, a lamb, or a goose, each of which were said to be worth one penny.[15] In Germany in the twelfth century the punishment for killing another person's cat was a fine of sixty bushels of corn.

Cats most likely spread through Europe and around the world by way of barges and sailing ships, and there are many nautical terms and weather descriptions that make reference to cats. A light breeze that ripples the surface of the water is known as a cat's paw, and a cat scratching the leg of a table or chair was thought to foretell a storm. Many other words with nautical associations began with the word cat, such as cat-o'-nine-tails, catboat, catwalk, and cat rig. Carried across oceans or walking from village to village, cats gradually spread across the globe, and by the tenth century they had reached Japan, by way of China.

Cats seemed to attract more than their fair share of myths and superstitions. In Scotland and Japan, tortoiseshell cats were believed to be able to foretell storms. People in eastern Europe thought that evil spirits took possession of cats during thunderstorms and that lightning was produced by angels in an attempt to exorcise the spirits. In that part of the world, cats were pushed outside as soon as a storm began so that the lightning need not strike the house to reach the cat. In other places, such as Indonesia, cats were used as rainmakers. They were carried three times around a dry field, then dunked into a container of water.

The Middle Ages marked the beginning of three centuries of persecution of the cat, and by the fourteenth century cats were in serious trouble in Europe. Long associated with the moon, cats were now considered to be the familiars of witches and disciples of Satan. Witches were believed to have an unnatural nipple with which they suckled their cats, and several witches are said to have confessed to feeding their cats milk and blood. At the trial of one woman in Essex, evidence was given of a cat who would "suckle bloud of her upon her armes and other places of her body." Women, especially the old and ugly, became special targets of investigation, and many were tortured and persecuted for being witches; their ability to transform themselves into cats was accepted as fact, and taken as evidence that they were witches.

Witches were thought to be able to bring all kinds of misfortune upon people, and as the servant of the witch, the cat-familiar took an active role in spreading the havoc. Therefore, an unknown cat on the doorstep often precipitated a crisis of confidence as the household wondered whether the creature was a cat or a witch come to cast a spell on someone. Witches were thought to be able to transform themselves into cats to disguise their activities, and some believed that witches rode to their midnight meetings on the backs of giant cats. The first official trial for witchcraft took place in 1566, and as a result Agnes Waterhouse and her daughter Joan were executed as witches. It was said at the trial that the women had "a whyte spotted catte" and that they "feed the sayde cat with breade and milkye . . . and call it by the name of Sathan." Hundreds of years later cats were still associated with the devil and bad luck, and were often viewed as the witch's familiar or companion who carried out her evil plans. Even the well-known saying that a cat has nine lives has its origins in witchcraft. According to a book titled *Beware of the Cat*, which was written in 1584, "It was permitted to a witch to take on her catte's body nine times."[15] Also connected with witchcraft is the old superstition that a black cat crossing a person's path brings bad luck; this originated with the belief that the black cat was marking a path to Satan.

It is astonishing that any cats managed to survive this period of European history. People killed cats whenever they encountered them, and one of the most common events of a feast day was the torture and death of any cat that allowed itself to be captured. The act was considered a symbolic way to drive out the devil. During this time cats were burned, beaten, drowned, and generally tortured and abused. For nearly three centuries the cruel treatment of cats was encouraged, as it was thought to be amusing and entertaining. One popular instrument of public torture, known as the cat organ, was said to have been invented in Brussels in 1549 for a festival in honor of Philip II. The device consisted of twenty cats confined in narrow cases with cords attached to their tails. The cords were attached to the keyboard of an organ so that when a trained bear pounded on the keys, the cords jerked the tails of the cats and made them howl.[12] Another unpleasant piñata-like contest survived in Scotland until as recently as the end of the eighteenth century. During this game a cat was placed in a hanging barrel of soot, and men on horseback took turns riding under the barrel, striking at it until a hole appeared and the cat leaped out and ran away.

Cats did not return to public favor until the seventeenth century, when the French Cardinal Richelieu took to keeping dozens of them at court. Other people followed suit, and the cat soon regained some of its former popularity in Europe. However, despite the fact that today cats are on the verge of surpassing dogs as the world's most popular pet, many people still dislike them. Surveys of attitudes in the United States show that there are nearly seven times as many cat haters as there are dog haters, and many people associate cats with allergies.[16]

One of the earliest descriptions of human allergy to cat hair comes from *The history of four-footed beasts*, written by Edward Topsell in 1607. Topsell writes that "the breath and favour of Cats consume the radical humour and destroy the lungs, and therefore they which keep their Cats with them in their beds have the air corrupted, and fall into several Hecticks and Consumptions."[7]

Both the Egyptian and Chinese words for "cat" seem to have been derived from the animal's vocalization; in Egypt the cat was called *mau*, and in China it was *mao*. Other names for the cat have been derived from the Nubian word *kadiz*, from which we get the English word *cat*, the French *chat*, the Greek *kata*, the German *katze*, Spanish *gato*, Italian *gatto*, Russian *koshka*, and Arabic *qutta*. Other words and names for the cat derive from Pasht, which comes from Bastet; these include the English *puss* and the Romanian *pisicca*.[12]

DESCRIPTION

Today's domestic cats have a much greater variety of coat colors, textures, and patterns than they did two hundred years ago, but the majority of the world's cats still have some variation of the tabby coat pattern. The tabby pattern is closest to the wild, or agouti, pattern, and on close inspection each hair can be seen to be made up of several different colors, including brown, black, gray, or white. The coat color of the domestic cat is thought to have originated by mutation from the original striped tabby coat of the African wildcat.[17]

The selective breeding of cats began comparatively recently, in the late nineteenth century. The move to breed new types of cats began in Britain and coincided with a surge of public interest in the newly introduced theory of evolution and a widespread fascination with the idea of improving and enhancing different breeds of animals.

Modern cat breeds originated from two main types: the European, or cold-weather, type, which has a large head, stocky body, and thick coat and resembles the European wildcat, and the Foreign, a warm-climate type with a slender body, long limbs, large ears, and short coat that resembles the African wildcat.[18] There is no exact definition of what constitutes a "breed," but in general, body conformation, geographic origin, color, and hair type are the major criteria used to define the characteristics of a breed. Many of today's breeds are just varieties of existing breeds that have been given fancy names: the Balinese is really a long-haired Siamese, and the Somali is a long-haired

Abyssinian. There are many other unusual-looking breeds of domestic cats, including the tailless Manx and the Japanese bobtail, both of which have existed for many centuries. More recent breeds with characteristic physical features include the Scottish Fold, with lop ears, the Cornish Rex, distinguished by its short, curly coat, and the Sphinx, a hairless cat. With only about a hundred years of selective breeding behind them, domestic cat breeds are just beginning their evolution, and it will be some time before they acquire the variety and dramatic differences that today's domestic dogs have.[7]

Folklore has long maintained that cats always land on their feet, and a study by the Animal Medicine Center in New York has now confirmed that cats do indeed manage to right themselves during a fall from a building or ledge. Doctors in the New York veterinary hospital looked at 132 cats that fell from tall buildings, from the second to the thirty-second floor. Astonishingly, 90 percent of the cats that fell from these heights survived, and almost two-thirds of them required no medical treatment. By comparison, people falling more than six stories are almost invariably killed. Cats survive these incredible falls because they turn their legs downward and extend their limbs outward, essentially assuming a flying squirrel or gliding position. This prevents them from tumbling head over heels through the air while falling and saves them from hitting the ground headfirst. The legs-out position also changes the aerodynamic drag on the cat's body and slows it down so that it hits the ground with the least possible force. One of the record falls involved a cat from New York named Sabrina, who fell from the thirty-second floor of an apartment building and landed on a concrete sidewalk. Sabrina walked away from the incident with a chipped tooth and a minor chest injury—an achievement not many other animals could match.[19]

DISTRIBUTION

From their beginnings in Egypt, the Middle East, and Europe, domestic cats have accompanied people to almost every corner of the globe. Wherever people have traveled, they have taken their cats with them. Geographic features such as major rivers and oceans that are barriers to most animals have the opposite effect on cats. Almost as soon as people began to move goods around on ships, cats joined ships' crews.[20] These cats traveled the globe, joining and leaving ships at ports along the way. Because the coat colors of cats do not occur with equal frequency all over the world, geneticists were able to create distribution maps for the most common color morphs.[21] The European distribution of the blotched tabby coat pattern—a relatively new mutation that has not yet spread worldwide—shows that this type has its central focus in Britain and exists at high frequencies across central France and Germany. This pattern seems superficially at odds with the dispersal by water theory, until the routes of the rivers Seine and Rhone and their barge canal systems are overlaid on the distribution.[21] There is also a suggestion that the distribution of the blotched tabby in New Zealand, Canada, Australia, and Tasmania reflects British migration. As settlers left to take up residence in their new countries, they took their placid-natured blotched tabbies with them. In addition to going along as traveling companions with colonists, cats also accompanied sailors on their voyages, with serious consequences for the native fauna wherever they disembarked. Time and time again the scientific literature tells the sad story of domestic cats let loose on remote islands, where they became serious predators on native wildlife. There are now major cat eradication programs in the Galápagos, New Zealand, Australia, and other places.[22]

ECOLOGY AND BEHAVIOR

Domestic cats are opportunistic predators, the ultimate generalists. They can live indoors year-round in a small apartment or outdoors, supplementing their diet of domestic cat food with birds and rodents. Though cats have been domesticated for some time, they quickly and easily revert to the wild or feral state. In the last hundred years cats have spread to virtually every corner of the globe, and today, feral cats live on remote subantarctic islands, in forests and farmlands, in suburbs, and in industrialized cities.

Feeding Ecology

Domestic cats hunt mainly on the ground, but they can also climb well. Cats are famous for their stealthy approach to prey. In mythology cats are often associated with thieves because of their ability to creep around unnoticed; in Sanskrit, the same word is used for both cats and thieves. A cat setting out for a hunt often appears to know where it is going. When it arrives, it begins to search, moving more slowly, looking around or crisscrossing the hunting area. If it is hunting rodents, the cat will sit and stare at a hole; when a mouse appears, the cat will usually wait until the prey has moved some distance from its burrow before pouncing.

Hunting birds requires different tactics. The cat stalks as near as possible, slinking silently toward the victim, belly to the ground, then stopping. All the time the cat is a picture of concentration, ears pricked, body tensed, eyes fixed on the intended prey. As the cat gets closer, it gets more and more excited; the tip of its tail twitches, its bottom wiggles, and its hind feet tread the ground as if seeking firm purchase. With eyes still fixed on the prey, the cat sometimes moves its head from side to side. Folktales have it that the cat is trying to mesmerize its intended victim, but in reality it is only trying to gauge the distance as accurately as possible.[23] The final rush is fast and determined, an all-or-nothing gambit. The hind legs provide the power for the leap, and the front legs are thrust out to grab the prey. If the pounce connects, the cat slams the prey to the ground with its forelegs and delivers a swift bite to the neck. Unless they are chasing grasshoppers or butterflies, cats rarely leap into the air to catch something; even when they are hunting birds, cats prefer to keep their hind legs planted firmly on the ground. This gives the cat a stable footing; if the prey starts to fight or is difficult to hold down, the cat can grapple without losing its balance.

Domestic cats are specialized predators, but they are versatile generalists in terms of what they eat. Where they are not subsisting on human-provided foods or refuse, cats take a wide variety of prey and readily switch prey with changes in availability. Excluding those on islands, the vast majority of cat studies show that small mammals, principally rodents, and rabbits or hares are the dominant prey.[22] Adult rabbits are occasionally taken, but they appear to be near the upper limit of prey size; thus predation on lagomorphs is heavier on young of these species. Similarly, adult Norway rats are sometimes killed by cats, but laboratory studies show that few cats will attack an aggressive adult Norway rat.[24] Despite frequent accusations, birds do not figure prominently in cat diets except on islands. Surprisingly, predation on reptiles, primarily lizards, appears to be important both on equatorial islands and on islands at much lower latitudes.

The effects of predation by domestic and feral cats on populations of small mammals are not well documented, but several studies suggest that it can be an important factor.[22,25,26] Where Norway rat numbers had been reduced severely by human efforts, cat predation was able to hold the population at these low levels, but

at high rat densities cat predation was ineffective as a means of control.[27,28] Similarly, experiments with enclosures have shown that predation, especially by cats, can hold rabbit numbers below those set by the food supply.[29] Predation by cats is also thought to be largely responsible for the 3- to 4-year cycle of vole numbers in California.[30]

Predation by cats can have a serious impact on wildlife, especially on islands where the native fauna has evolved in isolation from predators or where seabirds nest on the ground. Today in the Galápagos Islands, native rodents exist only on those islands where there are no cats.[31] Similarly, cats have eliminated several island species of birds, and others, such as the saddleback and New Zealand's kakapo, a large flightless parrot, are teetering on the brink of extinction largely due to predation by feral cats.[22]

There are several well-documented cases of local extinction caused by cat predation on seabirds, especially on islands.[22] At one time Ascension Island in the Atlantic Ocean was home to vast breeding colonies of several different species of seabirds, but once feral cats were introduced, the birds ceased to nest there. Remnant populations of ten other species of seabirds breed on isolated rocks around Ascension, but today only sooty terns breed on the island. In New Zealand feral cats eliminated large breeding populations of diving petrels and broad-billed prions from Herekopare Island. In 1949 five cats were introduced to Marion Island as pets of the members of a meteorological expedition; by 1975 an estimated 2,139 cats were thought to be killing about 450,000 burrowing petrels a year. Three of twelve species of petrels that breed on Marion Island were eliminated by cats in less than fifteen years.

Cats have also caused extinctions among island reptile populations. An estimated 15,000 Turks and Caicos Island iguanas were wiped out between 1974 and 1976 when a large hotel was built and domestic cats and dogs were introduced.[32] On the Galápagos Islands the endemic marine iguana is endangered on several islands because of the combined effects of predation by introduced cats, dogs, rats, and pigs.[33]

Cats can also be major predators of birds and small mammals in urban areas. In an amazingly detailed study of domestic cats in the small English village of Felversham, two scientists managed to persuade the owners of seventy cats to record and save all the prey items their pets brought home.[34] These cats brought in a total of 1,090 prey items during the year-long study.

There was great variation in individual hunting success: six cats never brought anything home; one cat brought in ninety-five items. Wood mice were the most frequent prey (17 percent), followed by house sparrows (16 percent), field voles (14 percent), and common shrews (12 percent). Five species made up 66 percent of the animals caught. The cats caught fewer prey in winter and on wet, windy days. At least 30 percent of sparrow deaths in the village were due to cats.

Though the idea is not popular with cat owners, there are indications that domestic cats can push small mammal populations to unnaturally low levels, which in turn may affect hawks and other birds of prey. Buffered by cat food and handouts from humans, cats can continue to hunt sparse rodent populations for longer than a wild predator could. Therefore cats fed by people could potentially reduce small mammal populations to a point where they would be unable to support wintering birds of prey.[35]

Social Organization

Feral domestic cats are common and fairly accessible compared with other species of wildcats, and there have been several long-term studies of their social systems and population dynamics. Information on many aspects of the biology of domestic cats, including their social life, predatory behavior, reproduction, and the development of young, is discussed in the excellent volume edited by Turner and Bateson.[36] Some of the best studies are those by Dards in a dockyard in southern England,[37] Liberg in rural Sweden,[38] Macdonald on English farms,[39] Natoli in a city park in Rome,[40] Izawa in a Japanese fishing village,[41] Jones and Coman in the Australian bush,[42] and Corbett on a remote island off the coast of Scotland.[43] The types of prey available to cats in these studies varied from rabbits and small mammals to fish offal, garbage, and cat food left by visiting cat lovers.

Though their social organization is sometimes dismissed as a product of domestication, domestic cat society provides us with an excellent model of the way in which ecological factors shape social systems. Domestic cats live in habitats as varied as city apartments, oceanic islands, and barnyards. Their social systems must accommodate densities that may vary from one cat per square kilometer to more than 2,350 cats per square kilometer.[41,44,45] Domestic cats may live solitary lives within a dispersed population of cats or in groups around a dumpster or other clumped food resource. As with other felids, females compete for food and safe den sites to rear young, while males compete for access to females. The result is a social system that is driven largely by the abundance and predictability of the food supply and, to some extent, the timing of female estrus.

Most studies have not measured food availability, but it is clear that the land tenure system of domestic cats varies with the distribution of food. Indeed, cat populations can be divided into those in which females form groups and those in which females live alone.[46] Where the food supply is sparse but evenly distributed, females live in nonoverlapping territories. Males occupy larger ranges that overlap the ranges of several females.[43] Where food is plentiful and clumped, such as at the offal dumps in a Japanese fishing village,[45] females live in groups and males are solitary.[37,47] Cats feeding solely on natural prey have not been found living in groups, presumably because natural prey is never clumped or abundant enough.

Home range sizes of domestic cats mirror food availability. Female range sizes may be as small as 0.1 hectare at a fish offal dump in Japan[41,45] or as large as 270 hectares in the dry grassland of Australia.[42] At these same sites, male ranges varied from 0.31 hectare in Japan to more than 900 hectares in Australia. In some regions female domestic cats are seasonal breeders, and in these populations breeding males expand their ranges during the mating season to gain access to as many females as possible.[38,43] Breeding male home ranges are usually three to four times larger than female ranges, while subordinate male cats generally have smaller, female-sized ranges.

One of the most intriguing characteristics of domestic cat social organization is the fact that, like lions, these diminutive felids are able to live in social groups when conditions are right.[39] Food seems to be the key factor favoring group living, and it is notable that all the documented incidences of domestic cats living in groups occur at clumped, abundant, artificial food sources such as dairy farms or garbage dumps.

In the early 1980s Olof Liberg conducted a now classic field study of the domestic cat's social behavior.[38,48,49] In a rural area of southern Sweden, Liberg radio-tracked thirty-seven cats, which he classified as either feral, if they hunted for themselves and were not fed by humans, or domestic, if they were attached to and provisioned by households. Only three female cats were feral, and they had home ranges of about 200 hectares, about four times the size of the ranges of their domestic female counterparts. Feral females also spent about twice as much time hunting as domestic females.

Domestic females lived alone or in groups of up to eight related adults. These females shared a small communal home range of about 50 hectares, and there was little overlap between females of different kin groups. Females of different kin groups behaved aggressively toward one another and excluded nonkin from "their" household. The household represented a clumped and defensible resource that provided the kin group with essential resources, food, and shelter.

Among males, young pre-dispersal males had the smallest ranges and were the least active, while breeders had the largest. Domestic male breeders had ranges averaging 380 hectares, whereas a feral breeding male covered an area of 990 hectares. Most domestic males were subordinate to the local feral males. Male ranges overlapped considerably.

At almost the same time that Liberg was following his cats in southern Sweden, Macdonald and Apps were beginning a study of a colony of farm cats in England. Macdonald and his co-workers focused more on quantitative observations of social behavior, using scan sampling to record the activities of the cats. The three females in this group had ranges averaging 13.1 hectares, while the adult male's home range was 83 hectares. The females gave birth to kittens in communal dens, and all tended, groomed, and nursed one another's young. In this colony the most obvious benefit of group living seemed to be alloparenting behavior. However, the costs of this behavior were also high, as at least two litters succumbed to feline panleucopaenia, an infectious viral disease, which is well suited for transmission at communal dens.[39]

As with lion prides, communal denning helps female domestic cats defend their young against infanticidal males, which is strongly suspected to be an important factor in group formation.[39,50] Though female domestic cats may sometimes live like lionesses, tomcats do not form male coalitions and associate like male lions, probably because they do not need to. A single barnyard tomcat can roam over two or three colonies of females, and unlike the male lion, which often relies on the lionesses of the pride to capture prey, he can catch his own food.

Male lions and male domestic cats do share one behavior that is rare in the felid family. In both species, several males may take turns mating with a female in heat.[51,52,53] Contrary to what one might expect, fights are rare, but an older dominant male probably gets most of the matings.[54] With the lion, this male tolerance can be explained by the fact that male coalitions are almost always relatives, but this is not so for male domestic cats. It is still unclear why domestic cats and lions should behave similarly in this regard. Though the techniques are now available to investigate paternity, we do not yet know which male sires the most kittens, or whether the number and order of matings affects conception.

Where female groups exist and the relationships between group members are known, the social system is similar to that of a lion pride in that the group is made up of related females and is stable over the long term.[55] Females in the group are unanimously hostile to outside females, but within the group they show distinct "friendships" or preferences for the company of other females. These affiliations appear to be governed by age, status, and blood relationships. Males usually leave or are driven out when they become sexually mature, and adult males are loosely attached to the female group. Several adult male ranges may overlap the range of the group of females, and in places where the food resource is superabundant, several groups of females with overlapping males may form a colony.

When it comes to breeding and raising kittens, females in a group may choose one of two strategies. Most rear their kittens alone, but there are cases of as many as four mothers pooling their litters and raising them together.[52,55] Like lions, females in a group sometimes show a high degree of synchrony of estrus, which makes communal care more feasible, but in one recorded case, litters were seven weeks apart, meaning that the first litter was highly mobile and almost weaned when the last was born. Females who raised their young together were closely related.

Just as with lions, when female domestic cats cooperate to care for several litters, the behavior is thought to be an adaptation for defense against infanticidal males.[50,52] Indeed, on the few occasions when it has been observed, infanticide in domestic cats has most often involved kittens from litters being raised by a solitary mother.

The social organization of domestic cats, like that of other felids, appears to rely on a system of visual, vocal, and olfactory signals. Each is used alone or in concert with others depending on the circumstances. Some studies suggest that cats avoid using common areas at the same time based on scent marks,[31,43] but among cats living in the same colony, there was little evidence that scent functioned to keep animals apart.[56,57] Adult male cats spray urine frequently while traveling, leaving their marks at locations where other cats are likely to encounter the signals. In Sweden, dominant males sprayed at rates of 22 marks per hour, compared with 12.9 urinations per hour for subdominant males. Feces deposited within the core areas of male ranges were always covered, but outside of those areas they were frequently left uncovered.[48] Similarly, female farm cats were more likely to cover their feces within the core of their ranges.[57] Females also spray urine while traveling, but not at the high rates recorded for males. Females spray at higher rates just prior to estrus, thus ensuring a male's presence at the appropriate time.[58]

Scent marking in cats also includes rubbing the cheeks, chin, and flanks on objects, on urine marks, and on other cats, a behavior that facilitates leaving one's scent and being marked with the odor of other cats as well.

Cats also communicate by vocalizations, and their vocal repertoire includes about a dozen calls.[59] Most calls function in close-range situations, including the purr, hiss, spit, growl, meow, and gurgle. The yowl or "caterwaul" is most often heard in the context of sexual activity. Body and tail postures, as well as facial expressions, are also used as signals in close-range encounters. Leyhausen has described many of the postures and expressions associated with agonistic behaviors in cats.[24]

Reproduction and Development

Female domestic cats are seasonally polyestrous, and the onset of sexual activity appears to be controlled by photoperiod.[60] The main breeding season is in early spring at northern latitudes, in mid-January in Italy[52] and in February–March in Sweden.[61] During this period females typically have a series of estrous cycles at fifteen-day intervals unless conception occurs. Estrus, or the period of receptivity, lasts one to four days, during which a female may attract as many as twenty males.[52] Females may be inseminated by as many as ten different males, and some litters have more than one father.[53] In most areas domestic cats commonly have two litters a year. In Sweden, for example, 60 percent of older females bred twice a year, and 7 percent bred three times.[61]

Toward the end of the sixty-three-day gestation period, the female begins to search for a safe place to deliver her kittens. Cats are highly individual in their choice of birth dens. A cat owner may provide the expectant mother with a secluded box, only to have the cat choose the back of a closet or the center of the bed. Feral cats make their dens in thickets, rockpiles, or almost any safe, out-of-the-way site. As labor begins, the cat becomes restless, licking her vulva and changing positions. Delivery times are highly variable; it may take as long as fifty minutes or as little as one minute for a kitten to be born, and the interval between successive births in a litter can be similarly variable.[12,17]

Kittens are born wrapped in a transparent membrane, which the mother removes and eats. She licks the kitten's nose and mouth to clear any mucus that might impede breathing, then licks the kitten dry. Because it is likely that a mother cat may be attending to a littermate and not attend to a kitten immediately after it is delivered, newborn kittens have the ability to survive without oxygen within the birth sac for a short while after birth. Some scientists have suggested that the newborn kitten's tolerance for lack of oxygen is the reason why kittens are reputed to be difficult to drown. After the whole litter is born, the female usually eats the placenta, thus cleaning the nest of anything that might attract predators.

A female cat can give birth to anywhere from one to ten kittens,[62] but an average litter consists of four or five.[63] The largest litter ever recorded consisted of thirteen kittens.[12] The young weigh about 90 to 110 grams at birth, or roughly 3 percent of the mother's body weight. In general, individual weight declines as litter size increases.[64]

Kittens are born with closed eyes, small, flattened ears, and a poorly developed sense of hearing. For the first two weeks, life is dominated by the senses of smell, touch, and temperature.[65] Within an hour of birth each kitten finds a nipple and begins to nurse. By the second or third day members of the litter have established teat ownership, and each kitten suckles exclusively from its own nipple. This saves time, avoids fighting, and ensures there is a functioning nipple for each kitten.[66] Suckling keeps the milk flowing, and within a few days the kittens have developed the characteristic "milk tread" in which they knead their mother's belly with their front feet. This motion stimulates milk flow and remains a part of the cat's behavior for life. Some older cats retain this kneading behavior to such an extent that anything soft and warm will set them off, and they seem unable to settle down to sleep without a few minutes of kneading. Others cats rarely seem to tread.

For the first few days of life kittens may spend as much as eight hours a day suckling; nursing bouts last as long as forty-five minutes, and the mother does not usually leave the nest for the first forty-eight hours. She keeps the kittens warm and licks them to clean them and stimulate defecation.[63] For the first three weeks after birth the mother initiates suckling by purring and lying down in a characteristic nursing position in which her nipples are easy to reach. Later, when the kittens become more mobile and the weaning process begins, the kittens initiate suckling as they run to their mother when she returns to the nest. The first kitten to begin nursing also begins to purr loudly, and the rest of the litter comes running to join in. Griff Ewer called this the "dinner gong" function of purring.

Most kittens open their eyes sometime during their second week of life, and vision begins to play a major role in their lives when they are about three weeks old. A kitten's eyesight gradually improves until the fluids in the eye clear at about five weeks, and visual acuity continues to improve until the cat is three or four months old. There does seem to be considerable natural variation in the time when kittens first open their eyes, and the range is two to sixteen days after birth. Experiments in the laboratory have shown that several factors influence this timing, including paternity, exposure to light, the kitten's sex, and the age of the mother. Kittens reared in the dark opened their eyes earlier, as did kittens of younger mothers and female kittens; however, paternity was the most important factor, suggesting that the timing of eye opening is strongly influenced by genetics.[65]

The milk of domestic cats contains eight times more protein than human milk and three times as much fat. Kittens grow rapidly as their mother uses her body reserves to produce milk. One study showed that mothers lost an average of 5.7 grams per day when lactating. As might be expected, kittens from larger litters are smaller and put on weight more slowly than kittens from smaller litters. Kittens in litters of seven or eight had a mean growth rate of 7.3 grams per day, whereas the mean growth rate nearly doubled to 13.7 grams per day for kittens in litters of two. In general, kittens double their birth weight in a week, triple it in two weeks, and quadruple it in three weeks. Initially, males and females grow at the same rate, but males start to grow faster at about eight weeks of age.[67]

By the time they are three weeks old, most kittens are beginning to acquire the ability to regulate their body temperature, and this allows the mother to spend more time away from the birth den. At seven weeks of age the kittens are able to thermoregulate as well as an adult. Feral domestic cats begin to bring prey back to their kittens from the fourth week onward, and by the time they are five weeks old, the kittens start to kill mice. Most kittens are introduced to solid food at four to five weeks of age, and this event generally marks the beginning of the weaning period.[68] Most kittens are weaned by the time they are seven weeks old, but may continue to suckle for several more months, particularly if the litter is small. As with most other features of the cat's life, the timing of weaning is highly individual. Some kittens continue to initiate nursing bouts long after they are physically weaned.[24]

Kittens are fairly inactive for the first two weeks of life and usually begin to walk during the third week. Teeth begin to emerge shortly before two weeks of age and continue until the fifth week. A kitten's adult teeth begin to appear when it is about three and a half months old.[69] By week five the kittens can run, and at eleven weeks they can complete complex tasks such as walking down a narrow branch and turning around when they get to the end. Kittens begin to play when they are about four weeks old. At first they play with littermates; later, when eye-paw coordination improves at about seven weeks, they begin to play with objects. The increase in object play coincides with the end of the weaning period, and if kittens are weaned early, the frequencies of certain types of play are increased.

It is commonly believed that play is an essential part of developing and honing future predatory skills, but experiments have shown that this is not necessarily true. Cats become competent predators through a variety of different experiences, and many different factors contribute to the development of predatory skills. Some kittens take a long time to become good at catching prey, and others are skilled predators from an early age, but these individual differences do not generally continue throughout life, and kittens that are poor predators have generally caught up by the time they become adults.[65] Experiments have shown that predatory skills can be improved by early experience, and for a kitten to learn to kill prey, the experience does not necessarily have to be "hands on." It seems that simply watching the mother or another cat kill a rat is enough to teach a kitten how to deal with live prey. This observational learning is facilitated if the cat performing the act is familiar to the observer cat.[70,71,72] When dealing with live prey, kittens tend to follow their mother's selection, and willingness to try new foods is also strongly influenced by the mother.[70,73] One scientist trained mother cats to eat bananas and found that when their kittens were offered a choice between a meal of familiar meat pellets and a meal of the unfamiliar banana, most of the kittens imitated their mother and ate the banana.[74]

Under natural circumstances kittens form strong social bonds with close kin and familiar individuals, usually their mother and littermates. Domestic cats have incorporated humans into the social group and react to familiar people with affection, but cats vary considerably in their friendliness. Some are adventurous and sociable with strangers; others are timid and shy, running from any loud noise. The difference can be apparent even in two kittens from the same litter.

While some of the differences among cats in friendliness can be accounted for by individual variation, several studies have examined the effect of early handling. These studies looked at variables such as the age of the kitten when first handled, the amount of time a kitten was handled each day, how many different people were involved, and whether the routine involved feeding. In general, kittens that were handled during the "sensitive period" (which is from two to seven weeks of age) approached people more readily and were willing to be held for longer.[65] The timing of this sensitive period for socialization would seem to pose a problem for cat owners, as most kittens are not adopted as pets until they are eight to ten weeks old, and indeed, many places have regulations that pro-

hibit the sale of kittens younger than eight weeks. Furthermore, all the evidence suggests that kittens should not be taken away from their mothers until they are naturally weaned, at about eight weeks. Separating a kitten from its mother earlier can cause stress and behavioral problems. Studies have found, however, that as long as kittens are handled during the sensitive period, they will relate well to the people who eventually adopt them. Cats that were never handled at all as kittens can be tamed, but it is a very time-consuming task. Individual idiosyncrasies aside, the best family pets are most likely to come from litters that have been handled gently and played with from an early age.[75]

While attempting to find out what makes one cat friendly and another timid, one study turned up an unexpected variable: Kittens fathered by some males were more friendly than others. Thus, friendliness in cats may be inherited.

Female cats become sexually mature between seven and twelve months of age.[69] Domestic cats have a high reproductive potential. According to the *Guinness Book of World Records*, the most prolific domestic cat produced 420 kittens in her lifetime.[76]

Domestic cats live longer if they stay indoors and are well looked after. One survey found a number of cats that were nineteen to twenty-seven years old.[12] The oldest recorded cat in the *Guinness Book of World Records* was a female tabby who lived to be thirty-four years old.[76]

REFERENCES

1. Pet Food Institute. 1997. Washington, DC.

2. Clutton-Brock, J. 1987. *A natural history of domesticated animals*. London: Cambridge University Press.

3. Zeuner, F. E. 1958. Dog and cat in the Neolithic of Jericho. *Pal. Expl. Q. Lond.* 52–55.

4. Clutton-Brock, J. 1979. The mammalian remains from the Jericho Tell. *Proc. Prehist. Soc.* 45: 135–158.

5. Clutton-Brock, J. 1981. *Domesticated animals from early times*. London: Heinemann/British Museum (Natural History).

6. Davis, S. J. M. 1987. *The archaeology of animals*. London: Batsford.

7. Serpell, J. A. 1988. The domestication and history of the cat. In *The domestic cat: The biology of its behaviour*, ed. D. C. Turner and P. Bateson, 151–158. Cambridge: Cambridge University Press.

8. Smithers, R. H. N. 1968. Cat of the Pharaohs. *Animal Kingdom* 71: 16–23.

9. Howey, M. O. 1930. *The cat in the mysteries of religion and magic*. London: Rider & Co.

10. Dale-Green, P. 1963. *The cult of the cat*. London: Heinemann.

11. Mery, F. 1968. *The life, history, and magic of the cat*. New York: Grosset & Dunlap.

12. Beadle, M. 1977. *The cat: History, biology and behaviour*. London: Collins & Harvill Press.

13. Morrison-Scott, T. C. S. 1952. The mummified cats of ancient Egypt. *Proc. Zool. Soc. Lond.* 121: 861–867.

14. Zeuner, F. E. 1963. *A history of domesticated animals*. London: Hutchinson.

15. Clutton-Brock, J., ed. 1988. *The walking larder: Patterns of domestication, pastoralism, and predation*. London: Allen and Unwin.

16. Kellert, S. R., and J. Berry. 1981. *Knowledge, affection and basic attitudes toward animals in American society*. Document no. 024–010–00–625–1. Washington, DC: U.S. Government Printing Office.

17. Bradshaw, J. S. 1992. *The behaviour of the domestic cat*. Wallingford, UK: C. A. B. International.

18. Kratochvíl, J., and Z. Kratochvíl. 1976. The origin of the domesticated forms of the genus *Felis* (Mammalia). *Zool. Listy* 25: 193–208.

19. Whitney, W. O., and C. J. Mehlhaff. 1987. High-rise syndrome in cats. *J. Am. Vet. Med. Assoc.* 191: 1399–1403.

20. Baldwin, J. A. 1979. Ships and the early diffusion of the domestic cat. *Carnivore Genet. Newsl.* 4: 32–33.

21. Todd, N. B. 1977. Cats and commerce. *Sci. Am.* 237: 100–107.

22. Fitzgerald, B. M. 1988. The diet of domestic cats and their impact on prey populations. In *The domestic cat: The biology of its behaviour*, ed. D. C. Turner and P. Bateson, 123–147. Cambridge: Cambridge University Press.

23. Turner, D. C., and O. Meister. 1988. Hunting behaviour of the domestic cat. In *The domestic cat: The biology of its behaviour*, ed. D. C. Turner and P. Bateson, 111–121. Cambridge: Cambridge University Press.

24. Leyhausen, P. 1979. *Cat behavior: The predatory and social behavior of domestic and wild cats*. New York: Garland STPM Press.

25. Potter, C., ed. 1991. *The impact of cats on native wildlife*. Canberra: Endangered Species Unit, Australian National Parks and Wildlife Service.

26. Liberg, O. 1982. Hunting efficiency and prey impact by a free-roaming house cat population. *Trans. Int. Congr. Game Biol.* 14: 269–275.

27. Elton, C. S. 1953. The use of cats in farm rat control. *Brit. J. Anim. Behav.* 1: 151–155.

28. Childs, J. E. 1986. Size-dependent predation on rats (*Rattus norvegicus*) by house cats (*Felis catus*) in an urban setting. *J. Mammal.* 67: 196–199.

29. Gibb, J. A., G. D. Ward, and C. P. Ward. 1969. An experiment in the control of a sparse population of wild rabbits (*Oryctolagus c. cuniculus* L.) in New Zealand. *N. Z. J. Sci.* 12: 509–534.

30. Pearson, O. P. 1966. The prey of carnivores during one cycle of mouse abundance. *J. Anim. Ecol.* 35: 217–233.

31. Konecny, M. J. 1983. Behavioral ecology of feral house cats in the Galapagos Islands. Ph.D. dissertation, University of Florida, Gainesville.

32. Iverson, J. B. 1978. The impact of feral cats and dogs on populations of the West Indian rock iguana, *Cyclura carinata*. *Biol. Conserv.* 14: 63–73.

33. Laurie, A. 1983. Marine iguanas in Galapagos. *Oryx* 17: 18–25.

34. Churcher, P. B., and J. H. Lawton. 1987. Predation by domestic cats in an English village. *J. Zool.* (Lond.) 212: 439–455.

35. George, W. G. 1974. Domestic cats as predators and factors in winter shortages of raptor prey. *Wilson Bull.* 86: 384–396.

36. Turner, D. C., and P. Bateson, eds. 1988. *The domestic cat: The biology of its behaviour*. Cambridge: Cambridge University Press.

37. Dards, J. L. 1978. Home ranges of feral cats in Portsmouth Dockyard. *Carnivore Genet. Newsl.* 3: 242–255.

38. Liberg, O. 1981. Predation and social behaviour in a population of domestic cat: An evolutionary perspective. Ph.D. dissertation, University of Lund, Sweden.

39. Macdonald, D. W., P. J. Apps, G. M. Carr, and G. Kerby. 1987. Social dynamics, nursing coalitions and infanticide among farm cats, *Felis catus*. *Advances in Ethology* (suppl. to *Ethology*) 28: 1–64.

40. Natoli, E. 1985. Spacing patterns in a colony of urban stray cats (*Felis catus* L.) in the historic centre of Rome. *Appl. Anim. Ethol.* 14: 289–304.

41. Izawa, M. 1984. Ecology and social systems of the feral cat (*Felis catus* Linn.). Ph.D. dissertation, Kuyshu University, Japan.

42. Jones, E., and B. J. Coman. 1981. Ecology of the feral cat, *Felis catus* (L.), in south-eastern Australia. I. Diet. *Aust. Wildl. Res.* 8: 537–547.

43. Corbett, L. K. 1979. Feeding ecology and social organization of wild cats (*Felis silvestris*) and domestic cats (*Felis catus*) in Scotland. Ph.D. dissertation, University of Aberdeen, Scotland.

44. Fitzgerald, B. M., and B. J. Karl. 1979. Food of feral house cats (*Felis catus* L.) in forest of the Orongorongo Valley, Wellington. *N. Z. J. Zool.* 6: 107–126.

45. Izawa, M., T. Doi, and Y. Ono. 1982. Grouping patterns of feral cats (*Felis catus*) living on a small island in Japan. *Jpn. J. Ecol.* 32: 373–382.

46. Liberg, O., and M. Sandell. 1988. Spatial organization and reproductive tactics in the domestic cat and other felids. In *The domestic cat: The biology of its behaviour*, ed. D. C. Turner and P. Bateson, 83–98. Cambridge: Cambridge University Press.

47. Dards, J. L. 1981. Habitat utilisation by feral cats in Portsmouth dockyard. In *The ecology and control of feral cats*, 30–36. Potters Bar, UK: Universities Federation for Animal Welfare.

48. Liberg, O. 1980. Spacing patterns in a population of rural free roaming domestic cats. *Oikos* 35: 336–349.

49. Liberg, O. 1984. Home range and territoriality in free ranging house cats. *Acta Zool. Fennica* 171: 283–285.

50. Natoli, E. 1990. Mating strategies in cats: A comparison of the role and importance of infanticide in domestic cats, *Felis catus*, L., and lions, *Panthera leo* L. *Anim. Behav.* 40: 183–186.

51. Packer, C., D. A. Gilbert, A. E. Pusey, and S. J. O'Brien. 1991. A molecular genetic analysis of kinship and cooperation in African lions. *Nature* 351: 562–565.

52. Natoli, E., and E. de Vito. 1988. The mating system of feral cats living in a group. In *The domestic cat: The biology of its behaviour*, ed. D. C. Turner and P. Bateson, 99–108. Cambridge: Cambridge University Press.

53. Passanisi, W. C., D. W. Macdonald, and G. Kerby. 1991. Wild cats and feral cats. In *Great cats*, ed. J. Seidensticker and S. Lumpkin, 162–169. Emmaus, PA: Rodale Press.

54. Natoli, E., and E. de Vito. 1991. Agonistic behaviour, dominance rank and copulatory success in a large multi-male feral cat, *Felis catus* L., colony in central Rome. *Anim. Behav.* 42: 227–241.

55. Kerby, G., and D. W. Macdonald. 1988. Cat society and the consequences of colony size. In *The domestic cat: The biology of its behaviour*, ed. D. C. Turner and P. Bateson, 67–81. Cambridge: Cambridge University Press.

56. Macdonald, D. W., and P. J. Apps. 1978. The social behaviour of a group of semi-dependent farm cats, *Felis catus*. *Carnivore Genet. Newsl.* 3: 256–268.

57. Panaman, R. 1981. Behaviour and ecology of free-ranging female farm cats (*Felis catus* L.). *Z. Tierpsychol.* 56: 59–73.

58. Mellen, J. D. 1993. A comparative analysis of scent-marking, social and reproductive behavior in 20 species of small cats (*Felis*). *Am. Zool.* 33: 151–166.

59. Peters, G. 1984. On the structure of friendly close range vocalizations in terrestrial carnivores (Mammalia: Carnivora: Fissipedia). *Z. Säugetierk.* 49: 157–182.

60. Kitchener, A. 1991. *The natural history of the wild cats*. Ithaca, NY: Cornell University Press.

61. Liberg, O. 1983. Courtship behaviour and sexual selection in the domestic cat. *Appl. Anim. Ethol.* 10: 117–132.

62. Robinson, R., and H. W. Cox. 1970. Reproductive performance in a cat colony over a ten-year period. *Lab. Anim.* 4: 99–112.

63. Deag, J. M., A. Manning, and C. E. Lawrence. 1988. Factors influencing the mother-kitten relationship. In *The domestic cat: The biology of its behaviour*, ed. D. C. Turner and P. Bateson, 23–39. Cambridge: Cambridge University Press.

64. Leitch, I., F. E. Hytten, and W. Z. Billewicz. 1959. The

maternal and neonatal weights of some mammalia. *Proc. Zool. Soc. Lond.* 133: 11–28.

65. Martin, P., and P. Bateson. 1988. Behavioural development in the cat. In *The domestic cat: The biology of its behaviour*, ed. D. C. Turner and P. Bateson, 9–22. Cambridge: Cambridge University Press.

66. Ewer, R. F. 1973. *The carnivores*. Ithaca, NY: Cornell University Press.

67. Deag, J. M., C. E. Lawrence, and A. Manning. 1987. The consequences of differences in litter size for the nursing cat and her kittens. *J. Zool.* (Lond.) 213: 153–179.

68. Baerends-van Roon, J. M., and G. Baerends. 1979. *The morphogenesis of the behaviour of the domestic cat: With a special emphasis on the development of prey-catching*. Amsterdam: North Holland.

69. Hemmer, H. 1979. Gestation period and postnatal development in felids. *Carnivore* 2: 90–100.

70. Caro, T. M. 1980. The effects of experience on the predatory patterns of cats. *Behav. Neural Biol.* 29: 1–28.

71. Caro, T. M. 1980. Effects of the mother, object play and adult experiences on predation in cats. *Behav. Neural Biol.* 29: 29–51.

72. Caro, T. M. 1980. Predatory behaviour in domestic cat mothers. *Behaviour* 74: 128–148.

73. Kuo, Z. Y. 1930. The genesis of the cat's response to the rat. *J. Comp. Psychol.* 11: 1–35.

74. Wyrwicka, W. 1978. Imitation of mother's inappropriate food preference in weanling kittens. *Pavlovian J. Biol. Sci.* 13: 55–72.

75. Karsh, E. B., and D. C. Turner. 1988. The human-cat relationship. In *The domestic cat: The biology of its behaviour*, ed. D. C. Turner and P. Bateson, 159–177. Cambridge: Cambridge University Press.

76. *The Guinness Book of World Records*. 1998. USA: Bantam Books.

Jaguarundi

Herpailurus yaguarondi (Lacépède, 1809)

J. R. Rengger, the Swiss naturalist who traveled extensively in Paraguay a hundred and fifty years ago, reported that captive jaguarundis quickly became tame and affectionate, but had a great proclivity for killing domestic ducks and chickens.[1] Although the jaguarundi is the most widely distributed and commonly seen cat in Central and South America, its biology and behavior are still largely a mystery. As Ernest Thompson Seton noted back in 1925, "A nearly clear view is offered to the young naturalist who first has a good chance to study this elegant creature."[2] To date, of the three projects that have managed to capture and radio-track jaguarundis in the wild, only one has followed more than three tagged animals. Thus, a "nearly clear view" of this cat remains.

DESCRIPTION

Taxonomically, the jaguarundi is an enigma. It differs from all the other small South American cats in many respects and shows some behavioral similarities with the puma. Various authorities have assigned the jaguarundi to its own genus (*Herpailurus*) or placed it in the genus *Felis* with most of the other small cats.[3] While all the other small South American cats have thirty-six chromosomes, the jaguarundi has thirty-eight—the same number as Old World cats. Furthermore, it is unique in that it not only has no F group chromosomes, but also has five pairs of E group chromosomes. One of these E group chromosomes is similar to that of the Old World leopard cat and fishing cat.[4] Recently developed molecular techniques place the jaguarundi in the *Panthera* lineage, confirming earlier suggestions that it originated in the same basic radiation as the puma. They also suggest that the jaguarundi is more closely related to the cheetah and puma than to the other South American cats.[5]

The taxonomic confusion over the jaguarundi's place in the cat family has been fueled not only by its unusual chromosome pattern, but also by its physical appearance. It hardly looks like a cat at all. Its elongated, low-slung body is slightly reminiscent of a marten, although others have compared it to a weasel or an otter.[6] A dark-colored jaguarundi superficially resembles a blackish-brown Neotropical mustelid called a tayra, but the tayra has a distinctive yellowish spot on its throat. The jaguarundi has comparatively short legs, a long, slender body, and a relatively long tail. Its small, slim head has short, rounded, widely separated ears, the backs of which lack the prominent white spots that are characteristic of many other felids.[7]

Figure 20. Distribution of the jaguarundi.

The jaguarundi is the least marked of all the small cats; apart from a few faint markings on the face and belly, its short, sleek fur is uniform in color. There are two main color phases, an iron gray morph and a red-brown morph. These phases were once thought to represent two distinct species; however, kittens of both colors can be born in the same litter.[8] The gray phase varies from ashy gray ticked with white through buff to brownish black, or occasionally all black. The red-brown phase varies from tawny to olive brown or bright chestnut red.

DISTRIBUTION

The jaguarundi's range extends from southern Texas through the coastal lowlands of Mexico, southward throughout Central America, and into South America east of the Andes to northern Argentina (fig. 20).[9] At one time its distribution reportedly extended into southeastern Arizona,[10] but there are no recent confirmed sightings from that state.[11] For some time the jaguarundi's presence in Texas was also in doubt, as no specimens had been seen since 1952, but a road-killed animal was found in 1986.[12] However, despite intensive searches and trapping efforts, no additional animals have been seen.[13]

ECOLOGY AND BEHAVIOR

Jaguarundis are found from sea level to elevations as high as 3,200 meters.[14] They frequent a wide variety of habitats, from semiarid thorn forest to wet grasslands. They generally seem to use more open areas than the sympatric ocelot, margay, and oncilla. But despite the fact that jaguarundis can live in pastures and brushlands, they are most often seen in areas of dense cover mixed with openings and edges. From Paraguay to Texas, this cat is a creature of thickets, scrub, dense brush, or chaparral, and it also hunts along the edges of open areas.[1,11,15,16,17,18,19,20] There are several recorded sightings of jaguarundis along streams and watercourses,[6,15,21,22] and a 1986 study confirmed these anecdotal observations. Radio-tagged jaguarundis in Belize used old fields and second-growth forest, preferring areas near streams.[23]

Jaguarundis have been seen moving about and hunting at all times of the day and night.[8,24,25] However, it would seem that this cat prefers to hunt by day, and its uniformly colored coat is thought to be indicative of a more diurnal lifestyle than that of the spotted cats.[6,22,26]

In one of the few studies that has followed radio-tagged individuals in the wild, Konecny found that the jaguarundi was active mainly during the daytime.[23] At his study site in the Cockscomb Basin, Belize, jaguarundis began moving before dawn, at about 0400 hours, and remained active throughout the day until sunset, at about 1800 hours. The peak hunting period was during the late morning, at about 1100 hours. In a recent study in Mexico with a large number of tagged cats, 85 percent of jaguarundi activity occurred during the daytime,[27] confirming earlier speculation that the cat is primarily diurnal.

The majority of observations indicate that jaguarundis hunt on the ground, but they are agile climbers, adept at moving along branches.[1,19,28] A jaguarundi may also spring 2 meters off the ground to swat at birds,[18] or investigate a noise in the bushes while standing in a tripod position, balanced on its haunches and tail like a kangaroo.

Feeding Ecology

Like most of our knowledge of the jaguarundi, what we know about its food habits is based largely on anecdotal evidence. This cat is thought to feed primarily on small prey (less than 1 kg), mainly rodents, birds, and reptiles, but there are records of jaguarundis killing larger animals such as rabbits, opossums, and armadillos. There is even a report of jaguarundis feeding on fish trapped in a temporary pond,[29] indicating that they are opportunistic predators. Jaguarundis probably take the most abundant and easily catchable prey available, which is why the proportions of each food item in scats or stomach contents vary throughout their geographic range.

In Belize small mammals were the most frequently consumed prey.[23] Small mammals occurred in over 90 percent of forty-six jaguarundi scats; most of these were cotton rats, a species associated with old-field habitats. Arthropod remains were found in 72 percent of the scats, but contributed little in terms of calories. Birds (21 percent) were the second most frequently occurring prey; opossums (13 percent), leaves (7 percent), and fruit (11 percent) made up the remainder of the diet.

An examination of the stomach contents of twenty road-killed jaguarundis in Venezuela revealed that birds and reptiles were as important to this cat as mammals; each occurred in 55 percent of the stomachs, and mammals occurred in half. By volume, however, mammals made the single greatest contribution to the cat's diet. Like many other cats, jaguarundis also eat grass. Small quantities of grass were present in the stomachs of almost half of the road-killed animals.[15,30]

The stomach contents of a female jaguarundi from Brazil included a small rodent and a lizard, whereas a male cat's stomach contained bird remains, including a tinamou and two doves.[29] Remains of a titi monkey—a small, diurnal, group-living marmoset—were found in the stomach of another cat from Brazil.[31]

The observations from Belize, Venezuela, and Brazil support the general consensus that this cat does much of its hunting during the daytime and that most of its prey are taken on the ground; even the birds in the jaguarundi's diet are species that spend time foraging on the ground.

Social Organization

According to Rengger, jaguarundis in Paraguay were "generally met with in couples which live within well-defined territories." He noted that his dogs once chased six adult jaguarundis out of a hedge.[1] In Belize, McCarthy saw a jaguarundi stalking an iguana at midday along a river; after the reptile escaped into the water, the cat was joined by another jaguarundi that had been hidden from view. He saw another pair stroll past some field workers at one o'clock in the afternoon. On another occasion a third pair was seen moving in the canopy.[28] It is uncertain whether pairs and groups of jaguarundis represent some permanent type of social unit, mating pairs, or females with large young. In captivity jaguarundis appear to be somewhat gregarious, at least among family members.[32] Most observations of jaguarundis in the wild are of solitary individuals, and adults are likely to be found in pairs only when the female is in estrus.

The jaguarundi's patterns of land use are not well known. In Belize the home ranges of two radio-tagged male jaguarundis were unusually large, measuring 88 and 100 square kilometers. Inexplicably, these ranges were several times larger than those of adult male jaguars living in the same area. An adult female jaguarundi in the Belize study area had a home range measuring 20 square kilometers. Both sexes traveled extensively about their ranges, averaging 6.6 kilometers a day, and each cat's daily movements were typically in one direction — that is, there was little backtracking or crisscrossing of travel paths.[23]

In an eighteen-day period, an adult female jaguarundi in the subtropical forest of southern Brazil used an area of 6.8 square kilometers before she was apparently killed by a puma.[33] In Mexico, the mean home range sizes of males and females were 8.9 and 8.3 square kilometers, respectively.[27]

Jaguarundis have an unusual and wide vocal repertoire: at least thirteen distinct calls have been recorded, including the wah-wah call.[32,34,35,36] They purr; they whistle; they scream; they chatter and yap. They also have an idiosyncratic vocalization that is appropriately termed a "chirp," for it sounds almost exactly like a bird call.

The marking behavior of jaguarundis is known only from captivity, where they frequently make scrapes with their hind feet; the scraping is sometimes accompanied by simultaneous urination. They also leave their feces uncovered, rub their heads on objects, and make claw marks on logs and branches; all these activities are thought to serve an olfactory or visual communication function.[32,37,38]

Reproduction and Development

Little is known of the reproductive biology of wild jaguarundis, and much of what has been reported is based on incidental observations. There are suggestions that jaguarundis have no breeding season in the tropics,[39] Mexico,[25] or Texas,[24] but contrary reports suggest they have two breeding seasons annually in Mexico,[18] or a single breeding season in the fall at the northern part of their range.[40] In captivity, births have occurred in January, June, and August through October.[37]

Observations of captive animals indicate that the length of estrus is short, about three to five days, and that the estrous cycle lasts for approximately fifty-three days.[37,41] During the period of sexual receptivity a female's behavior typically changes to include more rolling on the back and more scent marking. Females also vocalize faintly while depositing urine marks around the enclosure.[32,42] A male with reproductive experience will show a great deal of attention to a female in estrus, following her closely and tolerating a great deal of aggression from her, seldom exhibiting aggression in return.[42] Mating is accompanied by a loud scream at intromission and ends with the typical felid neck bite, in which the male grips the fur of the female's neck in his teeth.[32]

After a gestation period of seventy to seventy-five days, the female gives birth to one to four young.[32,41] In captivity, the average size for twelve litters was 1.83,[37] and for three other litters, 2.33.[32]

In the wild, kittens have been found in dens located in dense thickets, hollow trees, an overgrown ditch, and thick grassy clumps.[6,18,40] The kittens are born well-furred with spots on the belly.[41,43] When captive kittens are about three weeks old, the mother begins carrying food to the den; the kittens play with the food and chew on it before it is consumed by the mother.[32] These observations are supported by Rengger. "The mother never leaves her offspring alone for any length of time," he wrote, "and as they grow up she brings them birds and guinea pigs."[1] By the time they are six weeks old the young are capable of eating solid food.[32]

In captivity, jaguarundis have been recorded as reaching sexual maturity at different ages, ranging from about 1.4 years[37] through 22 and 26 months[41] to 2 and 3 years old.[32] Longevity in the wild is unknown, but in zoos jaguarundis have lived for more than ten years.[44]

STATUS IN THE WILD

Jaguarundi pelts have little commercial value, and the species is not subjected to the same intense hunting pressure as the small spotted cats. Globally, jaguarundis have the lowest conservation priority ranking, and they are considered to be relatively common in South American countries.[45] However, in Central America and North America, the jaguarundi is listed on appendix I of CITES.

Unlike some of the small spotted cats, the jaguarundi is not tied to primary forest. It can live in secondary forest, old fields, dense brush, and other human-modified habitats. As long as it is not persecuted, this flexibility may allow the jaguarundi to persist in areas where other small cats cannot.

STATUS IN CAPTIVITY
Jaguarundis are modestly well represented in zoos.[7]

TABLE 18 MEASUREMENTS AND WEIGHTS OF ADULT JAGUARUNDIS

HB	n	T	n	WT	n	Location	Source
590, 610	2m	430, 460	2m	5.1, 6.05	2m	Venezuela	46
610	1f	370	1f	4.2	1f	Venezuela	46
		406	5m			Venezuela	15
		(375–440)					
		402	5f			Venezuela	15
		(390–410)					
630, 680	2m	430, 515	2m	5.5, 6.25	2m	Belize	23
530, 630	2f	400, 475	2f	3.75, 5.0	2f	Belize	23
684	4m	386	4m	5.5	3m	Brazil	33
(665–735)		(310–430)		(5.0–6.0)			
595	3f	395	3f	4.1	3f	Brazil	33
(590–600)		(380–420)		(3.5–4.9)			
600	1?	410	1?			Argentina	9
605	1f	455	1f			Mexico	47
693	4m	451	4m	5.7	4m	Mexico	48
(650–755)		(420–475)		(5.0–6.5)			
596	3f	405	3f	4.1	3f	Mexico	48
(550–635)		(380–440)		(3.7–4.4)			
735	1f	515	1f	7.0	1f	Suriname	8

Note: HB = head and body length (mm), T = tail length (mm), WT = weight (kg). n = sample size. Sex: m = male, f = female, ? = unknown. Mean values are presented only for sample sizes of three or more. Range of values is in parentheses.

TABLE 19 FREQUENCY OF OCCURRENCE OF PREY ITEMS IN THE DIETS OF JAGUARUNDIS (PERCENTAGE OF SAMPLES)

Prey items	Cockscomb Basin, Belize[23] Scats (n = 47)	Venezuela[15,30] Stomach contents (n = 23)
Didelphis marsupialis Common opossum	13.0	
Oryzomys palustris Rice rat	15.2	
Oryzomys capito Rice rat		4.3
Ototylomys phyllotis Big-eared climbing rat	15.2	
Reithrodontomys gracilis Harvest mouse	8.6	
Zygodontomys brevicauda Cane mouse		4.3
Sigmodon alstoni Cotton rat		13.0

(continued)

TABLE 19 *(continued)*

Prey items	Cockscomb Basin, Belize[23] Scats (n = 47)	Venezuela[15,30] Stomach contents (n = 23)
Sigmodon hispidus Cotton rat	47.7	4.3
Rattus rattus Black rat	8.6	
Unidentified rodents		8.7
Sylvilagus floridanus Cottontail rabbit		13.0
Small birds	21.7	60.9
Domestic animals		8.7
Reptiles		65.2
Arthropods	71.7	
Fruit	10.8	
Grass		47.8
Minimum number of vertebrate prey items	60	42

REFERENCES

1. Rengger, J. R. 1830. *Naturgeschichte der säeugetheire von Paraguay*. Basel, Switzerland.

2. Seton, E. T. 1929. *Lives of game animals*. Vol. 1, part 1, *Cats, wolves, and foxes*. Garden City, NJ: Doubleday, Doran.

3. Wozencraft, W. C. 1993. Order Carnivora. In *Mammal species of the world*, ed. D. E. Wilson and D. M. Reeder, 279–348. Washington, DC: Smithsonian Institution Press.

4. Wurster-Hill, D. H., and W. R. Centerwall. 1982. The interrelationships of chromosome banding patterns in canids, mustelids, hyena, and felids. *Cytogenet. Cell Genet.* 34: 178–192.

5. Collier, G. E., and S. J. O'Brien. 1985. A molecular phylogeny of the Felidae: Immunological distance. *Evolution* 39: 473–487.

6. Guggisberg, C. A. W. 1975. *Wild cats of the world*. New York: Taplinger.

7. Oliveira, T. G. 1998. *Herpailurus yagouaroundi. Mammalian Species* 578: 1–6.

8. Husson, A. M. 1978. *The mammals of Suriname*. Leiden: E. J. Brill.

9. Cabrera, A. 1957. Catálogo de los mamíferos de América del Sur. *Revista del Museo Argentina de Ciencias Naturales "Bernardino Rivadavia," Ciencias Zoológicas* 4: 307–732.

10. Little, E. L. 1938. Record of the jaguarundi in Arizona. *J. Mammal.* 19: 500–501.

11. Tewes, M. E., and D. J. Schmidly. 1987. The Neotropical felids: Jaguar, ocelot, margay, and jaguarundi. In *Wild furbearer management and conservation in North America*, ed. M. Novak, J. A. Baker, M. E. Obbard, and B. Malloch, 697–711. Ontario: Ontario Trappers Association.

12. Endangered Species Technical Bulletin. 1986. Regional news. *Endangered Species Technical Bulletin* 11(8–9): 9. August–September.

13. Tewes, M., research scientist, Caesar Kleberg Wildlife Research Institute, Texas A&I University, Kingsville, Texas. Personal communication.

14. Cuervo, A., J. Hernández, and A. Cadena. 1986. Lista atualizada de los mamíferos de Colombia: Anotaciones sobre su distribución. *Caldasia* 15: 471–501.

15. Mondolfi, E. 1986. Notes on the biology and status of the small wild cats in Venezuela. In *Cats of the world: Biology, conservation, and management*, ed. S. D. Miller and D. D. Everett, 125–146. Washington, DC: National Wildlife Federation.

16. Bisbal, F. J. 1989. Distribution and habitat association of the carnivores in Venezuela. In *Advances in Neotropical mammalogy*, ed. K. H. Redford and J. F. Eisenberg, 339–362. Gainesville, FL: Sandhill Crane Press.

17. Vaughan, C. 1983. A report on dense forest habitat for endangered wildlife species in Costa Rica. United States Department of the Interior and the National University, Heredia, Costa Rica.

18. Davis, 1974. The mammals of Texas. *Texas Parks Wildl. Bull.* 41.

19. Hall, E. R., and W. W. Dalquest. 1963. *The mammals of Veracruz*. University of Kansas Publ. Mus. Nat. Hist. 14: 165–362.

20. Willig, M. R., and M. A. Mares. 1989. Mammals from the Caatinga: An updated list and summary of recent research. *Revista Brasileira de Biología* 49: 361–367.

21. Leyhausen, P. 1990. Cats. In *Grzimek's encyclopedia of mammals*, vol. 3, ed. S. P. Parker, 574–632. New York: McGraw-Hill.

22. Ricciuti, E. R. 1979. *The wild cats*. Weert, Netherlands: Ridge Press.

23. Konecny, M. J. 1990. Movement patterns and food habits of four sympatric carnivore species in Belize, Central America. In *Advances in Neotropical mammalogy*, ed. K. H. Redford and J. F. Eisenberg, 243–264. Gainesville, FL: Sandhill Crane Press.

24. Bailey, V. 1905. Biological survey of Texas. *N. Am. Fauna*, No. 25: 1–222.

25. Leopold, A. S. 1959. *Wildlife of Mexico*. Berkeley: University of California Press.

26. Kiltie, R. A. 1984. Size ratios among sympatric Neotropical felids. *Oecologia* 61: 411–416.

27. Caso, A., and M. E. Tewes. 1996. Home range and activity patterns of the ocelot, jaguarundi, and coatimundi in Tamaulipas, Mexico. Abstract, Southwestern Association of Naturalists 43rd Annual Meeting, McAllen, TX.

28. McCarthy, T. J. 1992. Notes concerning the jaguarundi cat

(*Herpailurus jagouaroundi*) in the Caribbean lowlands of Belize and Guatemala. *Mammalia* 56: 302–306.

29. Manzani, P. R., and E. L. A. Monteiro Filho. 1989. Notes on the food habits of the jaguarundi, *Felis yagouaroundi* (Mammalia: Carnivora). *Mammalia* 53: 659–660.

30. Bisbal, F. J. 1986. Food habits of some Neotropical carnivores in Venezuela (Mammalia, Carnivora). *Mammalia* 50(3): 329–339.

31. Ximénez, A. 1982. Notas sobre felidos neotropicales, VIII: Observaciones sobre el contenido estomacal y el comportamiento alimentar de diversas especies de felinos. *Rev. Nordest. Biol.* 5(1): 89–91.

32. Hulley, J. T. 1976. Maintenance and breeding of captive jaguarundis at Chester Zoo and Toronto. *Int. Zoo Yrbk.* 16: 120–122.

33. Crawshaw, P. G. 1995. Comparative ecology of ocelot (*Felis pardalis*) and jaguar (*Panthera onca*) in a protected subtropical forest in Brazil and Argentina. Ph.D. dissertation, University of Florida, Gainesville.

34. Peters, G. 1981. Das schnurren der katzen (Felidae). *Säugetierk. Mitt.* 40: 30–37.

35. Peters, G. 1984. On the structure of friendly close range vocalizations in terrestrial carnivores (Mammalia: Carnivora: Fissipedia). *Z. Säugetierk.* 49: 157–182.

36. Peters, G. 1987. Acoustic communication in the genus *Lynx* (Mammalia: Felidae)—comparative survey and phylogenetic interpretation. *Bonn. Zool. Beitr.* 38: 315–330.

37. Mellen, J. D. 1993. A comparative analysis of scent-marking, social and reproductive behavior in 20 species of small cats (*Felis*). *Am. Zool.* 33: 151–166.

38. Wemmer, C., and K. Scow. 1977. Communication in the Felidae with emphasis on scent marking and contact patterns. In *How animals communicate*, ed. T. Seboek, 749–766. Bloomington: Indiana University Press.

39. Ewer, R. F. 1973. *The carnivores*. Ithaca, NY: Cornell University Press.

40. Gaumer, G. F. 1917. *Mamíferos de Yucatán*. Departamento Talleres Gráficos, Secretaría de Fomento, Mexico. 331 pp.

41. Andrews, P., Hexagon Farm Wild Feline Breeding Facility, 1187 Merrill Road, San Juan Bautista, CA. Personal communication.

42. Mellen, J. D. 1989. Reproductive behavior of small captive exotic cats (*Felis* spp.). Ph.D. dissertation, University of California, Davis.

43. Weigel, I. 1972. Small felids and clouded leopards. In *Grzimek's animal life encyclopedia*, vol. 12, *Mammals* III, ed. H. C. B. Grzimek, 281–332. New York: Van Nostrand Reinhold.

44. Jones, M. L. 1977. Record keeping and longevity of felids in captivity. In *The world's cats*, vol. 3, ed. R. L. Eaton, 132–138. Seattle: Carnivore Research Institute, Burke Museum, University of Washington.

45. Nowell, K., and P. Jackson. 1996. *Wild cats: A status survey and conservation action plan*. Gland, Switzerland: International Union for Conservation of Nature and Natural Resources (IUCN).

46. Sunquist, M. Unpublished data.

47. Armstrong, D. M., J. K. Jones Jr., and E. C. Birney. 1972. Mammals from the Mexican state of Sinaloa. III. Carnivora and Artiodactyla. *J. Mammal.* 53: 48–61.

48. Caso, A., Zoology Department, Universidad Nacional Autónoma de Mexico, Mexico City. Personal communication.

Ocelot

Leopardus pardalis (Linnaeus, 1758)

The ocelot's name is derived from the Latin *cellatus*, which means "having little eyes" or "marked with eyelike spots." Unfortunately, the ocelot's beautiful dappled markings have created a huge demand for its pelt; as a result, it has been one of the most heavily exploited species of small cats.[1,2]

DESCRIPTION

The ocelot is a medium-sized cat, roughly the size of a bobcat. Most ocelots weigh 8 to 10 kilograms, but there is a single extraordinary record of an ocelot killed in Texas weighing about 45 pounds (20 kilograms).[3] The ocelot is a heavily spotted cat, with a relatively short tail and rounded ears, which are black on the back with a prominent white spot. The fur is short and sleek, lying close to the body. Females are slightly smaller than males. In some parts of South America this cat is locally known as the *manigordo*, meaning "fat hands," because its forepaws are much larger than its hindpaws.[4]

In 1929 Ernest T. Seton wrote that the ocelot's coat was "the most wonderful tangle of stripes, bars, chains, spots, dots and smudges . . . which look as though they were put on as the animal ran by."[5] This description perfectly portrays the animal that Richard Lydekker called "one of the most difficult members of the feline family to describe." Indeed, it seems that no single description can be made to fit the variety of markings or color patterns found on the ocelot's dappled coat. The background color can be anything from cream to tawny yellow, reddish gray, or gray. Ocelot fur is short and close, marked with solid or open-centered dark spots that sometimes run in lines across the body. Where the spots are open, their centers are often darker than the background coat color. The spots on the limbs and feet are smaller and solid. On the shoulders and back the spots may merge like links in a chain to form four or five dark stripes that run from the neck to the base of the tail. The neck and belly are white, and there are one or two transverse bars on the insides of the legs. The tail is ringed with black or has black bars on the upper surface. The hair at the nape of the neck forms a whorl.[6]

The ocelot and the margay (*Leopardus wiedii*) are very similar in appearance. As early as 1917 the problem of telling these two cats apart was summed up succinctly by the taxonomist R. I. Pocock: "As living animals, these two species are often very difficult to distinguish except by size and the length of the tail."[7] Although its coat pattern is very similar, the margay

Figure 21. Distribution of the ocelot.

has a relatively longer tail and generally weighs about half as much as the ocelot. The skull of a young ocelot can be mistaken for that of a margay, but skulls of the adult animals are easily distinguished. As they mature, ocelots develop marked crests on their skulls, whereas margays do not.[8]

DISTRIBUTION

There are fossil records of ocelots from Florida and Arizona in the United States and from the Yucatán in Mexico.[9] Historically, ocelots were found from as far north as Arkansas and Arizona in North America to northern Argentina in South America.[10] Currently, their distribution extends from southern Texas and the coastal lowlands of Mexico through Central America and into South America as far south as northern Argentina (fig. 21). The ocelot has also been recorded from the islands of Margarita and Trinidad in the Caribbean Sea.[11,12,13,14]

ECOLOGY AND BEHAVIOR

Prior to 1980, information on the ocelot's biology consisted largely of anecdotal accounts and natural history notes. Since then it has been studied using radiotelemetry techniques in Texas, Venezuela, Belize, Peru, and Brazil.[15,16,17,18,19,20,21,22,23] In less than fifteen years the ocelot has been elevated from the ranks of "little-known small cats" to one for which substantial field data exist.

Ocelots are found from sea level to elevations of about 1,200 meters in a broad range of tropical and subtropical habitats, including tropical evergreen forest, semideciduous forest, dry thorn forest, mangrove, and seasonally flooded savanna. They are also found in second-growth woodlands and abandoned cultivation that has reverted to brush.[13,24] Throughout a large part of its geographic range the ocelot is sympatric with the jaguar, puma, margay, jaguarundi, and oncilla.

Although ocelots can sometimes be found hunting at night in open areas, they are highly dependent on dense cover. Detailed radiotelemetry studies indicate that they occupy a narrower range of microhabitats than would have been predicted from their broad geographic distribution. Compared with the bobcat, which is a similar size, the ocelot is fairly specialized; it has become adapted to living in areas of dense cover with high rodent densities.[21,25]

Because ocelots are such agile climbers and leapers, and because they frequently escaped into trees when hunted, early naturalists thought that they were mainly arboreal. However, recent radio-tracking studies have revealed that ocelots do most of their hunting on the ground, although they do occasionally rest in trees during the day. Their daytime retreats also include a variety of shelters—in brush piles, in clumps of vines, in depressions on the ground at the base of large trees, and under fallen trees. Ocelots seem quite ready to take advantage of any cool, shady spot, and in Venezuela researchers found that ocelots regularly used concrete culverts as daytime rest sites. Their movements do not seem to be inhibited or impeded by water, and they are reported to be strong swimmers[26]—a not unexpected ability for a terrestrial cat that, in some areas, lives in a seasonally flooded environment. In Iguaçu National Park, Brazil, two dispersing male ocelots were radio-tracked as they crossed the Iguaçu River four and five times.[23] Although primarily nocturnal, ocelots also hunt during the daytime, especially on cloudy and rainy days; they may become completely nocturnal in areas where they are hunted.

During a night's hunting, ocelots cross and recross their ranges, using these areas intensively. They appear to have two basic foraging strategies: a slow hunting walk and a move-and-sit method. They may use these different strategies for hunting different types of prey. An ocelot using the slow hunting walk moves very slowly, at about 0.3 kilometers per hour. While walking this slowly, it is almost certainly watching and listening for prey, and probably kills whatever catchable prey it encounters. An ocelot using the move-and-sit method typically moves to an area, then sits and waits for thirty to sixty minutes or more, then moves to another area, where it sits and waits again. When moving between stops, it travels two to three times faster (0.8 to 1.4 kilometers per hour) than in the slow hunting walk.[21,27]

The amount of time ocelots spend moving and hunting each day is highly variable, but they are commonly active twelve to fourteen hours a day. They usually rest between dawn and late afternoon, then begin moving an hour or two before dark. Males travel farther than females in a night and rest less frequently. Emmons followed one unusually active male who walked for thirty-one out of thirty-four consecutive hours.[28]

Some form of vegetation seems to be important for hunting, and ocelots avoid open areas during the day and on nights when the moon is full. In Peru, Emmons found that bright moonlight probably hinders an ocelot's pursuit of rodents.[29] On full-moon nights ocelots avoided walking on trails and confined their hunting activities to brushy areas. It is probably difficult for an ocelot to approach prey in bright moonlight without being detected unless there is enough stalking cover.

Feeding Ecology
Ocelot food habits change with the seasons as the numbers of various prey species fluctuate. Most of their prey is terrestrial and nocturnal, and they generally feed on animals weighing less than a kilogram, or less than 10 percent of their own body weight. The diet consists mainly of mammals such as opossums, mice, rats, and rabbits, but they also eat birds, fish, snakes, lizards, insects, and land crabs. There are a few records of ocelots killing larger prey, such as agoutis, capybaras, deer, anteaters, peccaries, and armadillos, but these prey are far less abundant and do not figure prominently in ocelot diets.

To meet their normal energy requirements, ocelots need 600 to 800 grams of food each day, and they manage this by concentrating on the most common small prey.[19,30] In Belize, the largest part of the ocelot's diet consisted of opossums, with armadillos and birds ranking second and third in importance.[20] In Peru, over 92 percent of the ocelot's diet consisted of vertebrates weighing less than 1 kilogram—mostly rice rats and spiny rats.[30] In the seasonally flooded savannas of Venezuela, rodents and iguanas were the dominant prey in the dry season.[19] However, when land crabs became abundant during the wet season, ocelots fed intensively on them, and at this time of the year crabs and rodents were the most important foods. In Venezuela, as in Peru, about 94 percent of the ocelot's diet consisted of prey weighing less than 1 kilogram. Most prey is eaten on the spot, and captive ocelots will pluck the feathers from even the smallest bird before eating.[31]

Social Organization

Ocelots are solitary animals. Breeding females generally occupy nonoverlapping territories that vary in size from 0.8 to 15 square kilometers. Male territories are larger, varying from 3.5 to 46 square kilometers, and usually encompass the ranges of two to three breeding females.[16,17,18,19,20,21,22,23] Some females are known to have occupied the same home ranges for several years.[17]

The highest reported densities of ocelots are from Peru and Venezuela, where females have ranges of 2 to 4 square kilometers and males have ranges of 6 to 11 square kilometers. This translates to an approximate density of 40 to 80 adults per 100 square kilometers.[19,21] However, these figures may be misleading if extrapolated to other areas where suitable habitat is patchily distributed. In Iguaçu National Park, Brazil, the density of adult ocelots was estimated to be 13.7 per 100 square kilometers,[23] suggesting that prey density in Iguaçu is much lower than at other sites. Competition for space within the more productive areas of ocelot habitat is obviously high, and studies in Texas, Venezuela, and Peru have shown that vacant ranges are filled rapidly.[16,19,21]

Although ocelots hunt alone and females rear their young unaided by the resident male, they are not asocial. While traveling about their ranges, neighboring females probably encounter one another along common boundaries, and the territorial male undoubtedly crosses paths with the females in his range. Both males and females travel extensively within their relatively small ranges, about 3 to 7 kilometers per night,[17,19,20,21] and such movement patterns should produce high contact rates. Adult males and females obviously associate for mating, but there are also observations of an

adult male and female being together for several hours outside mating periods. Independent young are also known to associate with their parents.[18,21]

Ocelots leave scent marks throughout their territories. Both sexes spray urine onto bushes, trees, and other objects within their ranges; they also leave their feces uncovered and in prominent places. In some areas, repeated defecation at the same site results in the formation of latrines. At one location in Venezuela, researchers found a latrine containing at least 22 scats.[18] The ocelot also has a number of friendly close-range vocalizations, including a long, drawn-out yowling call given while mating.[32]

Reproduction and Development

In comparison with other cats of similar size, ocelots typically have longer interbirth intervals and smaller litters. In captivity, females can give birth to more than one litter a year if their kittens die or are removed, but in the wild there is more likely to be a two-year interval between litters. Captive females come into heat several times a year, and estrus lasts seven to ten days. Young may be born at any time of the year; gestation lasts seventy-nine to eighty-two days. Females sometime give birth to as many as three kittens, but the more usual number is one kitten per litter.[17,33,34,35]

In the wild, the well-protected birth den is usually in a dense thicket, a grass tussock, or an impenetrable tangle of fallen trees and vines. Following the birth of her young, the female alters her typical pattern of resting in a different spot every day, and returns each day to the young. In Texas, where two radio-collared females were closely followed from the time their young were born until they were independent, both females used two or three maternity dens for each litter, and young were kept at each den for anywhere from thirteen to sixty-four days.[17] One female used maternity dens for eighty-six days, at which time her kitten began to travel with her. Another female ceased to use her maternity den after sixty-five days, but this was only because her kitten died.[17] Disturbance may cause a female to move her young to another den, but she rarely moves them far.

Ocelot kittens weigh about 250 grams at birth, and have one of the slowest growth rates of all small cats. Kittens do not open their eyes until fifteen to eighteen days of age.[33] Suckling young places increased nutritional demands on the female, and she has to spend more time hunting. In Peru, a female with a month-old kitten doubled her normal activity and spent as much as seventeen out of every twenty-four hours foraging. Despite this effort, her kitten died.[21] Even when they are not nursing young, females spend almost half of every twenty-four hours hunting. It is likely that the ocelot's small litter size, long gestation period, and slow maturation are all adaptations for living under conditions in which food is difficult to find and animals have to spend much of the day hunting to meet their normal energy requirements.[21,25]

The young begin following their mother when they are about three months old, and remain dependent on her hunting skills for several more months. Young ocelots acquire their permanent canine teeth when they are about eight months old, but even when they can hunt for themselves they may continue to use their natal range until they are physically mature, at eighteen to twenty-four months. Data from captivity suggest that the young reach 70 percent of adult body weight when they are about a year old, 80 to 87 percent at eighteen months, and adult weight at twenty-four to thirty months. Females probably reach adult weight earlier than males.[33,35]

When they are about two to three years old, ocelots leave their natal areas and wander in search of an unoccupied territory. Little is known of this phase of their lives, but they are occasionally killed crossing roads or raiding poultry sheds, and many dispersers probably die before they have a chance to breed. In Venezuela two radio-tagged males dispersed when they were about two years old. Both dispersed through a narrow belt of gallery forest that paralleled a river; one traveled 10 kilometers and the other 12 kilometers from its natal range. One male was killed by a hunter three months after it dispersed, while the other was still alive when the study ended.[19] In Peru, three radio-tagged ocelots, two males and a female, dispersed. One male was able to establish a territory in an area that included the range of his presumed mother. The female appeared to have settled into an area, but then moved to another area 5 kilometers away. The skeleton of the other radio-tagged male was found 5 kilometers from his natal range; puncture marks in his skull exactly fit the pattern of male ocelot canine teeth, and it was surmised that he had died of injuries sustained in a fight with another male.[21] In southern Brazil, four males and two females were monitored during dispersal.[23] Both females were killed by poachers, one about 30 kilometers and the other about 7 kilometers from

their natal ranges. One subadult male was killed while raiding a chicken pen about 13 kilometers from his natal range. Another male disappeared suddenly and was presumably poached. The two remaining males traveled extensively between Iguaçu National Park, Brazil, and neighboring Iguazu National Park, Argentina. Both appeared to have survived and established ranges. Of thirteen (eight males, five females) radio-tagged dispersers in Texas, a male and two females were killed on roads within a month of leaving their natal ranges, while the others were still alive several months after dispersing.[15,16,17] Ocelots in Texas exhibited a protracted dispersal phase, spending from two to eight and a half months or longer in search of a place to settle, although most eventually established themselves on ranges that were less than 9 kilometers (mean = 6.4 kilometers, range 2.5–9.0 kilometers, $n = 6$) from their natal ranges.[17] In Texas and Venezuela, ocelots dispersed through narrow belts of forest cover along rivers.

In captivity ocelots are known to live for twenty years, but longevity in the wild is almost certainly less. If females produce their first litter at two and a half years of age, and thereafter rear one kitten every other year until they are twelve to thirteen years old,[34] the lifetime reproductive output is probably only five young. If the mortality rate of dispersing ocelots is as high as that recorded for the samples of radio-collared young, then the number of offspring that survive to reproduce may be only two. By contrast, the similar-sized bobcat breeds at one and a half years old, typically has two to four kittens per litter, and gives birth annually.[36] A female bobcat may have as many as thirty young in her lifetime. Clearly ocelots are much more specialized than previously thought. Any future conservation strategies that include plans to harvest ocelots on a sustained-yield basis must take the reproductive traits of this cat into consideration. It is doubtful that the species can tolerate the annual removal of more than 2 to 3 percent of the population, compared with the often recommended 20 percent for bobcats.[25]

STATUS IN THE WILD

The ocelot's current distribution in North America is restricted to a small population of 80 to 120 animals in southern Texas.[11,12,17] There are no population estimates available from other parts of its range, but the consensus is that populations have generally declined through hunting and habitat loss.[37] Currently, habitat loss is probably replacing hunting as the major threat. Ocelots require dense cover in the form of brush or forest and do not use pasture or cropland to any appreciable extent. Throughout this cat's range, clearing of forest areas for cattle ranching and agriculture is reducing the amount of suitable habitat. Studies show that the ocelot can live at high densities where conditions are suitable, but it does not survive well in human-altered habitats.

The ocelot was once the most frequently hunted cat in South America. In the early 1960s, when populations of the large spotted cats began to dwindle, the fur trade turned its attention to the smaller cats, particularly the ocelot, bobcat, and Canada lynx.[38,39] U.S. Customs figures from the 1960s show that ocelot dominated the U.S. fur market, reaching a high of about 140,000 skins in 1970. It takes an average of 12.9 ocelot skins to make a fur coat, and a coat may sell for as much as U.S.$40,000.[40] Between 1967 and 1973 a variety of different types of wildlife protection laws were enacted; many countries outlawed commercial export of wildlife, and the United States began to prohibit the import of most spotted cat skins.[40] A few years after this legislation was enacted, the number of ocelot skins in trade dropped significantly, and continues on a downward trend.

The high number of skins traded in 1983 includes a large number exported from France to the Federal Republic of Germany. These may have been in stock for some time. Apart from this, the figures show a steady decline. Most of the pelts traded were exported from Paraguay, which re-exports large numbers of wildlife pelts smuggled out of Brazil. Western European countries, mainly the Federal Republic of Germany, imported most of the skins. In 1986 the European Economic Community effected a ban on the import of all ocelot skins[41] and in 1989 the ocelot was moved to appendix I of CITES, which prohibits all international commerce in skins and live animals. However, implementation of these laws and regulations is patchy at best. Ocelots are still hunted for their skins, and furs appear regularly in local markets. As recently as April 1990 a shipment of over 1,000 cat skins—including ocelot, oncilla, margay, and jaguar—and 70,000 caiman skins was seized by Argentine Customs. The shipment was in transit through Argentina to Chile, from where it was to be sent by air to Germany. After months of discussion over whether the skins should be auctioned or destroyed, the Argentine authorities finally burned all the skins at a public bonfire.[42]

CONSERVATION EFFORTS

As part of a long-term study of ocelots in Texas, researchers at the Caesar Kelberg Wildlife Research Institute have been successful in establishing a new resident subpopulation of ocelots using translocation. An adult male and two females were translocated to an area on the western side of Laguna Atascosa in 1988, and in 1990 one of the females showed signs of having young.[43]

In Texas, the U.S. Fish and Wildlife Service and the local irrigation authorities have agreed to leave brush growing along 160 kilometers of irrigation ditches in Cameron County, the heart of the remaining ocelot range in the United States. The regrowth of brush along these ditches, while it will increase time and costs for ditch maintenance, will provide a vital dispersal corridor for ocelots.[44]

Results of recent molecular analyses indicate that ocelots are subdivided into four major phylogeographic groups: Central America, northern-northeastern South America (French Guyana, northern Brazil), northern-northwestern South America (Venezuela, Panama, Trinidad, northern Brazil), and southern South America. The partitioning of these groups is probably related to historic and natural barriers to movement, principally large rivers (e.g., Amazon, Orinoco, Negro, Branco). The degree of mitochondrial DNA (mtDNA) differentiation within each population indicates that there is little demographic connection (gene flow) to other regions. As such, ocelots in these groups should be conserved and managed as independent and evolutionarily significant units.[45]

TABLE 20 MEASUREMENTS AND WEIGHTS OF ADULT OCELOTS

HB	n	T	n	WT	n	Location	Source
810 (770–855)	7m	361 (350–390)	7m	13.6 (12.0–15.5)	7m	Brazil	23
770 (740–795)	7f	331 (300–370)	7f	9.8 (9.0–11.3)	7f	Brazil	23
821 (710–867)	4?	375 (345–410)	4?			Argentina	46
758 (675–830)	14m	351 (300–410)	14m	10.0 (7.0–14.5)	8m	Venezuela	13
739 (690–810)	7f	322 (300–380)	7f	9.1 (7.9–10.8)	7f	Venezuela	18
748 (726–1,000)	3m	335 (305–366)	3m			Ecuador	7
737, 782	2f	371, 427	2f			Ecuador	7
				11.0 (9.0–12.0)	4m	Peru	21
				8.7 (7.5–10.6)	3f	Peru	21
796 (782–823)	3f	318 (284–366)	3f			Panama	7
855 (775–911)	5m	298 (270–317)	5m	9.8 (8.7–10.9)	5m	Texas	16
788 (768–802)	4f	305 (286–324)	4f	7.5 (6.6–8.2)	4f	Texas	16
862 (782–905)	6m	307 (262–325)	6m	9.6 (8.3–10.3)	6m	Texas	17
822 (767–909)	7f	290 (255–307)	7f	7.7 (7.0–8.3)	7f	Texas	17

Note: HB = head and body length (mm), T = tail length (mm), WT = weight (kg). *n* = sample size. Sex: m = male, f = female, ? = unknown. Mean values are presented only for sample sizes of three or more. Range of values is in parentheses.

TABLE 21 FREQUENCY OF OCCURRENCE OF PREY ITEMS IN THE DIETS OF OCELOTS (PERCENTAGE OF SAMPLES)

Prey items	Manu NP, Peru[30] Scats (n = 62)	Iguaçu NP, Brazil[23] Scats (n = 56)	Guárico, Venezuela[19] Scats (n = 160)	Cockscomb Basin, Belize[20] Scats (n = 49)
Didelphis sp. Common opossum	1.1	12.5	3.8	38.8
Philander opossum Black four-eyed opossum				30.6
Metachirus nudicaudatus Brown four-eyed opossum	1.1			
Marmosa sp. Mouse opossum	3.4	5.4	7.5	12.2
Oryzomys sp. Rice rat	21.5		2.5	
Zygodontomys brevicauda Cane mouse			50.0	
Sigmodon alstoni Cotton rat			25.0	
Holochilus brasiliensis Marsh rat			19.4	

TABLE 21 (continued)

Prey items	Manu NP, Peru[30] Scats (n = 62)	Iguaçu NP, Brazil[23] Scats (n = 56)	Guárico, Venezuela[19] Scats (n = 160)	Cockscomb Basin, Belize[20] Scats (n = 49)
Heteromys anomalus Spiny pocket mouse			10.6	
Small rodents		55.4		
Unidentified small mice	4.5			
Echimys semivillosus Arboreal spiny rat			1.3	
Mesomys hispidus Spiny tree rat	0.6			
Proechimys sp. Spiny rat	31.6			
Rattus rattus Black rat				10.2
Sciurus sp. Tree squirrel	0.6	1.8		
Tamandua mexicanus Lesser anteater				2
Dasypus novemcinctus Nine-banded armadillo		12.5	1.3	20.4
Sylvilagus sp. Cottontail rabbit	1.1	5.4	8.1	
Cavia aperea Guinea pig		1.8		
Agouti paca Paca	0.6			12.2
Dasyprocta sp. Agouti	1.7	10.7	1.3	
Myoprocta pratti Acouchi	2.8			
Saguinus fuscicollis Tamarin monkey	0.6			
Saimiri sciureus Squirrel monkey	0.6			
Unidentified primate	0.6			
Carnivores	0.6	5.4		
Coendu prehensilis Porcupine	0.6	1.8	1.3	
Tayassu tajacu Collared peccary			0.6	
Odocoileus virginianus White-tailed deer			0.6	
Mazama sp. Brocket deer		1.8		6.1
Birds	11	5.4	5.6	
Reptiles	12	8.9	19.4	
Fish	1.1		0.6	
Bats	1.8			
Arthropods			16.9	
Plant material	11.3		18.8	8.2
Minimum number of vertebrate prey items	174	75	269	65

TABLE 22 OCELOT SKINS TRADED BETWEEN 1980 AND 1986

Year	Total skins in trade	Number from Paraguay
1980	30,563	25,390
1981	17,730	17,069
1982	9,676	9,370
1983	69,294	68,928
1984	2,741	2,741
1985	556	315
1986	513	—

REFERENCES

1. Koford, C. B. 1973. Spotted cats in Latin America: An interim report. *Oryx* 12: 37–39.

2. Caldwell, J. R. 1984. South American cats in trade: The German connection. *Traffic Bull.* 6: 31–32.

3. Davis, W. B. 1951. Unusual record of the ocelot in Texas. *J. Mammal.* 32: 363–364.

4. Enders, R. K. 1935. Mammalian life histories from Barro Colorado Island, Panama. *Bull. Mus. Comp. Zool. Harvard* 78: 383–502.

5. Seton, E. T. 1929. *Lives of game animals.* Vol. 1 (Part 1), *Cats, wolves, and foxes.* Garden City, NJ: Doubleday, Doran.

6. Goodwin, G. G. 1946. *Mammals of Costa Rica.* Bulletin of the American Museum of Natural History 87, article 5. New York: American Museum of Natural History.

7. Pocock, R. I. 1941. The races of the ocelot and the margay. *Pub. Field Mus. Nat. Hist., Zool. Ser.* 27: 319–369.

8. Allen, J. A. 1919. Notes on the synonymy and nomenclature of the smaller spotted cats of tropical America. *Bull. Am. Mus. Nat. Hist.* 41: 341–419.

9. Kurtén, B. 1965. The Pleistocene Felidae of Florida. *Bull. Fla. State Mus.* 9: 215–273.

10. Nowak, R. M. 1991. *Walker's mammals of the world.* Vol. 2. Baltimore: Johns Hopkins University Press.

11. Tewes, M. E., and D. D. Everett. 1986. Status and distribution of the endangered ocelot and jaguarundi in Texas. In *Cats of the world: Biology, conservation, and management,* ed. S. D. Miller and D. D. Everett, 147–158. Washington, DC: National Wildlife Federation.

12. Tewes, M. E., and D. J. Schmidly. 1987. The Neotropical felids: Jaguar, ocelot, margay, and jaguarundi. In *Wild furbearer management and conservation in North America,* ed. M. Novak, J. A. Baker, M. E. Obbard, and B. Malloch, 697–711. Ontario: Ontario Trappers Association.

13. Mondolfi, E. 1986. Notes on the biology and status of the small wild cats in Venezuela. In *Cats of the world: Biology, conservation, and management,* ed. S. D. Miller and D. D. Everett, 125–146. Washington, DC: National Wildlife Federation.

14. Bisbal, F. J. 1983. Dos nuevos mamíferos para la Isla de Margarita Venezuela. *Acta. Cient. Venezolana* 34: 366–367.

15. Navarro, L. D. 1985. Status and distribution of the ocelot (*Felis pardalis*) in south Texas. Master's thesis, Texas A&I University, Kingsville.

16. Tewes, M. E. 1986. Ecological and behavioral correlates of ocelot spatial patterns. Ph.D. dissertation, University of Idaho, Moscow.

17. Laack, L. L. 1991. Ecology of the ocelot (*Felis pardalis*) in south Texas. Master's thesis, Texas A & I University, Kingsville.

18. Ludlow, M. E. 1986. Home range, activity patterns, and food habits of the ocelot (*Felis pardalis*) in Venezuela. Master's thesis, University of Florida, Gainesville.

19. Ludlow, M. E., and M. E. Sunquist. 1987. Ecology and behavior of ocelots in Venezuela. *Natl. Geogr. Res.* 3(4): 447–461.

20. Konecny, M. J. 1990. Movement patterns and food habits of four sympatric carnivore species in Belize, Central America. In *Advances in Neotropical mammalogy,* ed. K. H. Redford and J. F. Eisenberg, 243–264. Gainesville, FL: Sandhill Crane Press.

21. Emmons, L. H. 1988. A field study of ocelots (*Felis pardalis*) in Peru. *Rev. Ecol. (Terre Vie)* 43: 133–157.

22. Crawshaw, P. G., and H. B. Quigley. 1989. Notes on ocelot movement and activity in the Pantanal region, Brazil. *Biotropica* 21: 377–379.

23. Crawshaw, P. G. 1995. Comparative ecology of ocelot (*Felis pardalis*) and jaguar (*Panthera onca*) in a protected subtropical forest in Brazil and Argentina. Ph.D. dissertation, University of Florida, Gainesville.

24. Koford, C. B. 1974. Jaguar and ocelot in Tropical American status survey. In *World Wildlife Yearbook 1973–74,* ed. P. Jackson. Morges, Switzerland: WWF.

25. Sunquist, M. E. 1992. The ecology of the ocelot: The importance of incorporating life history traits into conservation plans. In *Felinos de Venezuela: Biología, ecología y conservación,* 117–128. Caracas, Venezuela: Fundación para el Desarrollo de las Ciencias Físicas, Matemáticas y Naturales.

26. Guggisberg, C. A. W. 1975. *Wild cats of the world.* New York: Taplinger.

27. Sunquist, M. E., F. C. Sunquist, and D. E. Daneke. 1989. Ecological separation in a Venezuelan llanos carnivore community. In *Advances in Neotropical mammalogy,* ed. K. H. Redford and J. F. Eisenberg, 197–232. Gainesville, FL: Sandhill Crane Press.

28. Emmons, L. H. 1987. Jungle cruisers. *Animal Kingdom,* January/February, 22–30.

29. Emmons, L. H., P. Sherman, D. Bolster, A. Goldizen, and J. Terborgh. 1989. Ocelot behavior in moonlight. In *Advances in Neotropical mammalogy,* ed. K. H. Redford and J. F. Eisenberg, 233–242. Gainesville, FL: Sandhill Crane Press.

30. Emmons, L. H. 1987. Comparative feeding ecology of felids in a Neotropical rainforest. *Behav. Ecol. Sociobiol.* 20: 271–283.

31. Leyhausen, P. 1979. *Cat behavior: The predatory and social behavior of domestic and wild cats.* New York: Garland STPM Press.

32. Peters, G. 1984. On the structure of friendly close range vo-

calizations in terrestrial carnivores (Mammalia: Carnivora: Fissipedia). *Z. Säugetierk.* 49: 157–182.

33. Fagen, R. M., and K. S. Wiley. 1978. Felid paedomorphosis, with special reference to *Leopardus*. *Carnivore* 1: 72–81.

34. Eaton, R. 1977. Breeding biology and propagation of the ocelot (*Leopardus* [*Felis*] *pardalis*). *Zool. Garten* 47: 9–23.

35. Cisin, C. 1967. *Especially Ocelots*. New York: Harry G. Cisin.

36. McCord, C. M., and J. E. Cardoza. 1982. Bobcat and lynx (*Felis rufus* and *F. lynx*). In *Wild mammals of North America*, ed. J. A. Chapman and G. A. Feldhamer, 728–766. Baltimore: Johns Hopkins University Press.

37. Broad, S. 1987. The harvest of and trade in Latin American spotted cats (Felidae) and otters (Lutrinae). Cambridge: Wildlife Trade Monitoring Unit, IUCN Conservation Monitoring Centre.

38. McMahan, L. 1983. Cat skin trade shifts to smaller species. *Traffic* (USA) 5: 3–5.

39. Inskipp, T., and S. Wells. 1979. The international wildlife trade. Press Briefing Document 16, produced by Earthscan, a media information unit on global environment issues (10 Percy Street, London W1P 0DR, England).

40. McMahan, L. R. 1986. The international cat trade. In *Cats of the world: Biology, conservation and management*, ed. S. D. Miller and D. D. Everett, 461–488. Washington, DC: National Wildlife Federation.

41. EEC import restrictions. 1987. *Traffic Bull.* 8: 57–58.

42. Cat News. 1992. *Cat News* 16: 26.

43. Cat Conservation Newsletter. 1990. *Cat Conservation Newsletter* 1 (2): 1–2.

44. Saving room for ocelots. 1995. *Endangered Species Update* 12: 9.

45. Eizirik, E., S. L. Bonatto, W. E. Johnson, P. G. Crawshaw Jr., J. C. Vié, D. M. Brousset, S. J. O'Brien, and F. M. Salzano. 1998. Phylogeographic patterns and evolution of the mitochondrial DNA control region in two Neotropical cats (Mammalia, Felidae). *J. Mol. Ecol.* 47: 613–624.

46. Cabrera, A. 1961. Los félidos vivientes de la república Argentina. *Revista del Museo Argentina de Ciencias Naturales "Bernardino Rivadavia," Ciencias Zoológicas* 6: 161–247.

Oncilla

Leopardus tigrinus (Schreber, 1775)

The oncilla has the distinction of being known by more English common names than almost any other cat: little spotted cat, lesser spotted cat, tiger cat, and ocelot cat, to mention just a few. Some of these names have also been used for the margay and ocelot,[1] which presumably reflects the oncilla's resemblance to these two larger species. A multivariate analysis of cranial measurements showed that the oncilla, margay, and ocelot are closely related.[2] The geographic distributions of all three species overlap extensively, and all are members of the "ocelot lineage." There are, however, some differences in appearance among the subspecies of oncilla, and there is a suggestion that this classification may not be valid, since several of the subspecies do not interbreed.[3] Furthermore, recent genetic analysis supports the earlier suggestion that oncillas should be classified as two or possibly three distinct species.[4]

DESCRIPTION

The oncilla is one of the smallest of the South American cats; an adult weighs only 1.5 to 3 kilograms. The background color of the thick, soft fur varies from light to dark ochre, and the pelt is marked with black or dark brown spots and open rosettes. The centers of the open spots are darker than the background color of the fur. The paler belly fur is covered with dark spots, and large black spots form seven to thirteen irregular rings on the tail. The backs of the ears are black with a central white spot, while the limbs are marked with small black spots. Melanistic individuals are not uncommon among specimens from humid forests.[5,6,7,8]

The oncilla is often confused with the margay, but oncillas are smaller, more gracefully built, and have relatively larger ears and a narrower muzzle. Oncilla fur is firm, lies close to the skin, and does not turn forward in the nape region, as reported for the ocelot and margay. The oncilla's eyes are light honey brown, smaller than the margay's and located more laterally.[9] The oncilla's skull is very delicate compared with the margay's; the braincase is narrower, and the dorsal outline of the skull is much less convex. The zygomatic arches are weaker than those of the margay, and the bullae are less inflated.[10]

DISTRIBUTION

The oncilla has a broad geographic distribution in Central and South America, but within this general range its distribution is poorly known.[7,11] It is found from Costa Rica to the Andean zone of western Venezuela,

Figure 22. Distribution of the oncilla.

Colombia, and Ecuador, possibly in northern Peru, and through eastern Venezuela, the Guianas, and Brazil to Paraguay and northern Argentina (fig. 22).[11,12] However, it has not been recorded in Panama, and it may occur in Bolivia, though its presence there has yet to be confirmed.[13] The species has been collected from elevations ranging from sea level up to 3,200 meters.[7,8,12,14]

ECOLOGY AND BEHAVIOR

Oncillas were originally believed to be strictly forest animals, confined to humid, premontane lowland, and cloud forests at elevations from sea level to 3,200 meters[8,15] (and possibly up to 4,500 meters in Colombia).[16] Oncillas are, however, also reported to occur in subtropical forests, savannas (cerrado), wet savannas, and semiarid thorny scrub.[17,18,19] Oliveira reports that oncillas are thriving in the savannas and thorny scrub of Brazil, where they are the most common cat after jaguarundis in many areas.[20]

Feeding Ecology

Almost nothing is known of the oncilla's habits in the wild. Some information on the cat's food habits comes from five specimens that were collected in the wild. The stomach contents of a female oncilla collected in Costa Rica included two deer mice, a pocket mouse, and one shrew. Another female had eaten a finch.[14] The stomach of a female collected in Venezuela contained several small rodents of different sizes.[8] The stomachs of two oncillas taken in the Caatinga, a vast dry area of northeastern Brazil, contained lizards.[18] Similarly, lizards (Teiidae), centipedes, grasshoppers, beetles, and birds were identified in oncilla scats from another part of the Caatinga.[21] In this area rodents are a minor part of the oncilla's diet, probably because small mammal densities are low. The most abundant and available prey in the Caatinga are diurnal lizards, and thus it not surprising that oncillas are more diurnal here than elsewhere. The scats of five oncillas captured in secondary forest in southeastern Brazil contained feathers, hair of rats, and one mouse opossum.[22] The prey taken by oncillas are typically small (less than 100 grams) and terrestrial, suggesting that the cats hunt mainly on the ground, although they can climb with ease.

Social Organization

The vocal repertoire of the oncillas has not been studied in detail, but the young purr, and adults have a friendly close-range vocalization called a "gurgle," which is a soft, short, rhythmic call.[23,24]

Reproduction and Development

As with other small Neotropical felids, what is known of oncilla reproduction is derived largely from observations of captive animals. The estrous period lasts from three to nine days, with older females tending to have shorter cycles.[25] Following a gestation period of about seventy-five days—rather long for a cat of this size[3]—oncillas commonly give birth to a single kitten weighing 92 to 134 grams.[17,26] Despite the long gestation period and small litter size, the young appear to develop relatively slowly.[3,27] Kittens open their eyes at eight to seventeen days, show tooth eruption at fifteen to twenty-one days, and begin taking solid food at thirty-eight to fifty-six days.[3,26] At this age domestic kittens are already accomplished mousers. Weaning occurs at about three months of age,[28] and by eleven months the young are nearly adult size.[3]

One breeder noted that oncilla kittens seem to have exceptionally high caloric requirements. She also observed that this cat's pattern of tooth eruption was unusual. Instead of the more common pattern of incisors appearing first, followed by the gradual appearance of canines and molariform teeth, oncilla kittens showed no sign of tooth eruption until twenty-one days after birth, when all the teeth appeared together, within a matter of hours.[26]

There is little information on the age of sexual maturity, but two captive-born young showed no sign of sexual maturity by eleven months, and another captive female did not give birth until she was almost four years old.[26] Leyhausen reports that sexual maturity is not attained until two or two and a half years of age.[28] One female in captivity lived to be seventeen years old.

STATUS IN THE WILD

The oncilla appears to be rare in the wild, but there is very little information on its status and abundance. Deforestation has greatly reduced the area of suitable habitat available. In Brazil and Colombia, large areas of subtropical and cloud forest have been destroyed for coffee plantations,[29] and in Costa Rica over half of the oncilla's dense forest habitat was destroyed between 1940 and 1977.[30] Similarly, destruction of forest habitats in some parts of Venezuela is likely to have had a negative impact on oncilla populations.[31] However, these tiny felids may be somewhat tolerant of human activities. Oncillas are found in the metropolitan areas of São Paulo, the world's second largest city, and also in Pôrto Alegre, Brazil.[20]

The oncilla has been widely hunted for its fur.[32] Oncilla skins are easily confused with those of the margay, and thus the number of skins in trade in any given year may not be as accurate as for other species. However, there is little doubt that large numbers of oncillas were traded each year in the international fur market.[33,34] A report on South American cats in trade between 1976 and 1982 showed that the oncilla was one of the four most heavily exploited small cats.[35] By 1982, 69,163 oncilla skins were traded, and oncillas apparently supplied the great majority of spotted cat skins in trade, replacing Geoffroy's cat, which had been the most heavily hunted until then. In 1983 the number of oncilla skins in trade peaked at 84,493, but dropped to 35,007 in 1984 and to 2,052 in 1985.[36]

Until 1983 Paraguay was reported to be the main source of oncilla skins in trade; a large number of these were probably illegal re-exports from other countries. In 1984 Bolivia emerged as a major source of skins—which is curious, as the presence of oncillas has yet to be confirmed in that country. The switch in exporting countries probably represents changes in the effectiveness of controls.[36]

STATUS IN CAPTIVITY
There are very few oncillas in captivity. A private facility in California, which had fourteen animals, is the only breeder of this species in North America.

CONSERVATION EFFORTS
Oncillas have been legally protected from commercial hunting, internal trade, and commercial export in all countries where they are known to exist since at least 1981. On the basis of the declared countries of origin of the skins in trade, all exports of this species have been illegal since 1981.

In 1986 the European Economic Community banned all imports of oncilla skins, and in 1989 the Federal Republic of Germany sought to transfer the oncilla to appendix I of CITES. This proposal was approved.

TABLE 23 MEASUREMENTS AND WEIGHTS OF ADULT ONCILLAS

HB	n	T	n	WT	n	Location	Source
478 (452–514)	3f	256 (245–276)	3f			Costa Rica	14
466	1m	255	1m			Costa Rica	14
556	1m	345	1m	2.45	1m	Suriname	7
475, 493	2f	270, 305	2f	2.0	1f	Venezuela	8
		336 (317–360)	3m			Venezuela	8
480	1?	380	1?			Venezuela	37
380, 490	2m	330, 420	2m			Colombia	8,37
520	1?	290	1?			Ecuador	37
500	1m	225	1m			Brazil	37
517, 539	2m	248, 276	2m			Argentina	6
506 (430–591)	31m	283 (210–345)	31m	2.58 (1.8–3.47)	20m	Brazil	20
467 (400–514)	27f	256 (204–305)	27f	2.22 (1.75–3.2)	15f	Brazil	20

Note: HB = head and body length (mm), T = tail length (mm), WT = weight (kg). n = sample size. Sex: m = male, f = female, ? = unknown. Mean values are presented only for sample sizes of three or more. Range of values is in parentheses.

REFERENCES
1. Leyhausen, P. 1963. Über südamerikanische Pardelkatzen. *Z. Tierpsychol.* 20: 627–640.

2. Glass, G. E., and L. D. Martin. 1978. A multivariate comparison of some extant and fossil Felidae, Carnivora. *Carnivore* 1: 80–88.

3. Leyhausen, P., and M. Falkena. 1966. Breeding the Brazilian ocelot-cat *Leopardus tigrinus* in captivity. *Int. Zoo Yrbk.* 6: 176–182.

4. Johnson, W. E., and S. J. O'Brien. 1997. Phylogenetic reconstruction of the Felidae using 16S rRNA and NADH-5 mitochondrial genes. *J. Mol. Evol.* 44(Suppl. 1): S98–S116.

5. Guggisberg, C. A. W. 1975. *Wild cats of the world.* New York: Taplinger.

6. Cabrera, A. 1961. Los félidos vivientes de la República Argentina. *Revista del Museo Argentina de Ciencias Naturales "Bernardino Rivadavia," Ciencias Zoológicas* 6(5): 161–247.

7. Husson, A. M. 1978. *The mammals of Suriname.* Leiden: E. J. Brill.

8. Mondolfi, E. 1986. Notes on the biology and status of the small wild cats in Venezuela. In *Cats of the world: Biology, conservation, and management,* ed. S. D. Miller and D. D. Everett, 125–146. Washington, DC: National Wildlife Federation.

9. Weigel, I. 1972. Small felids and clouded leopards. In *Grzimek's animal life encyclopedia,* vol. 12, *Mammals III,* ed. H. C. B. Grzimek, 281–332. New York: Van Nostrand Reinhold.

10. Mondolfi, E., mammalogist, Caracas, Venezuela. Personal communication.

11. Emmons, L. H., and F. Feer. 1990. *Neotropical rainforest mammals: A field guide.* Chicago: University of Chicago Press.

12. Cabrera, A. 1957. Catálogo de los mamíferos de América del Sur. Vol 1. Metatheria, Unguiculata, Carnivora. *Revista del Museo Argentina de Ciencias Naturales "Bernardino Rivadavia," Ciencias Zoológicas* 4: 1–307.

13. Tello, J. L. 1986. The situation of wild cats (Felidae) in Bolivia. Including notes on other wildlife species and on general aspects of the conservation and utilization of natural resources. Lausanne, Switzerland: CITES Secretariat.

14. Gardner, A. L. 1971. Notes on the little spotted cat, *Felis tigrina oncilla* Thomas, in Costa Rica. *J. Mammal.* 52: 464–465.

15. Bisbal, F. J. 1989. Distribution and habitat association of the

carnivores in Venezuela. In *Advances in Neotropical mammalogy*, ed. K. H. Redford and J. F. Eisenberg, 339–362. Gainesville, FL: Sandhill Crane Press.

16. Melquist, W. E. 1984. Status survey of otters (Lutrinae) and spotted cats (Felidae) in Latin America. Report to IUCN, Gland, Switzerland.

17. Widholzer, F. L., M. Bergmann, and C. Zotz. 1981. Breeding the little spotted cat. *Int. Zoo News* 28(3): 17–23.

18. Ximénez, A. 1982. Notas sobre felidos neotropicales VIII. Observaciones sobre el contenido estomacal y el comportamiento alimentar de diversas especies de felinos. *Rev. Nordest. Biol.* 5(1): 89–91.

19. Oliveira, T. G. de. 1994. *Neotropical cats: Ecology and conservation*. São Luis: EDUFMA.

20. Oliveira, T. G. de, Department of Biology, Maranhão State University (UEMA), C.P. 09, São Luis, MA, Brazil. Personal communication

21. Olmos, F. 1993. Notes on the food habits of Brazilian "Caatinga" carnivores. *Mammalia* 57: 126–130.

22. Guix, J. C. 1997. Cat communities in six areas of the state of São Paulo, southeastern Brazil, with observations on their feeding habits. *Grupo de estudos ecológicos, Série documentos* 5: 16–38.

23. Peters, G. 1981. Das schnurren der katzen (Felidae). *Säugetierk. Mitt.* 40: 30–37.

24. Peters, G. 1984. On the structure of friendly close range vocalizations in terrestrial carnivores (Mammalia: Carnivora: Fissipedia). *Z. Säugetierk.* 49: 157–182.

25. Foreman, G. E. 1988. Behavioral and genetic analysis of Geoffroy's cat (*Felis geoffroyi*) in captivity. Ph.D. dissertation, Ohio State University, Columbus.

26. Quillen, P. 1981. Hand-rearing the little spotted cat or oncilla. *Int. Zoo Yrbk.* 21: 240–242.

27. Fagen, R. M., and K. S. Wiley. 1978. Felid paedomorphosis, with special reference to *Leopardus*. *Carnivore* 1: 72–81.

28. Leyhausen, P. 1990. Cats. In *Grzimek's encyclopedia of mammals*, vol. 3., 576–632. New York: McGraw-Hill.

29. Koford, C. B. 1973. Project 694. Status survey of jaguar and ocelot in tropical America. *World Wildl. Yrbk.* 1972–73: 215.

30. Vaughn, C. 1983. A report on dense forest habitat for endangered wildlife species in Costa Rica. United States Department of the Interior and the National University, Heredia, Costa Rica.

31. Bisbal, F. J. 1992. Estado de los pequeños felidos de Venezuela. In *Felinos de Venezuela: Biología, ecología y conservación*, 83–94. Caracas, Venezuela: Fundación para el Desarrollo de las Ciencias Físicas, Matemáticas y Naturales.

32. Koford, C. B. 1975. Felids of Latin America: Importance and future prospects. In *Symposium on wildlife and its environments in the Americas*, publication of Biologicas Instituto de Investigaciones Cientificas, O.A.N.L., Mexico, 1(7): 131–141.

33. McMahan, L. 1986. The international cat trade. In *Cats of the world: Biology, conservation and management*, ed. S. D. Miller and D. D. Everett, 461–488. Washington, DC: National Wildlife Federation.

34. Broad, S. 1987. The harvest of and trade in Latin American spotted cats (Felidae) and otters (Lutrinae). Cambridge, UK: Wildlife Trade Monitoring Unit, IUCN Conservation Monitoring Centre.

35. Caldwell, J. R. 1984. South American cats in trade: The German connection. *Traffic Bull.* 6: 31–32.

36. Broad, S., R. Luxmoore, and M. Jenkins. 1988. Significant trade in wildlife: A review of selected species in CITES Appendix II, Vol. 1: Mammals. Cambridge, UK: International Union for Conservation of Nature and Natural Resources Conservation Monitoring Centre.

37. Allen, J. A. 1919. Notes on the synonymy and nomenclature of the smaller spotted cats of tropical America. *Bull. Am. Mus. Nat. Hist.* 41(7): 341–419.

Plate 1. The cheetah's slim frame, narrow waist, and deep chest give it the look of a sprinter. The flexion and extension of the long back adds length to the cat's running stride.

Plate 2. Heaviest of the small African cats, caracals can weigh as much as 20 kg. The caracal's long black ear tufts are highly conspicuous against its otherwise plain-colored coat.

Plate 4. The bay cat is one of the world's least known felids. Since its discovery in 1855, only a handful of specimens have been collected; even fewer have been photographed.

Plate 3. These six-week-old caracal kittens will be dependent on their mother for food and protection for nearly nine months.

Plate 5. The powerful, stocky Asiatic golden cat roams the tropical forests of Southeast Asia, hunting prey up to the size of small deer.

Plate 6. The Chinese desert cat is found only in a small portion of the Tibetan plateau and Inner Mongolia. This rare species has never been studied.

Plate 7. The jungle cat's generalist diet and ability to survive in a wide variety of habitats make it one of Asia's most common small felids.

Plate 8. The sand cat inhabits the deserts of northern Africa, the Arabian Peninsula, and Turkmenistan. Mats of hair between its toes protect its feet from the hot sand.

Plate 9. The sand cat is one of the only felids known to dig its own burrows. Saharan nomads call the species "the cat that digs holes."

Plate 10. The tiny black-footed cat of southern Africa is one of the smallest cats in the world. Females weigh only 1.5 kilograms.

Plates 11 and 12. The European wildcat looks very much like a larger version of the domestic tabby cat. A long thick coat, broad head, and comparatively flat face give it the appearance of a large powerful cat.

Plate 13. Asian wildcats have large litters. The mother will soon begin to introduce these month-old kittens to solid food, bringing beetles, rodents, and lizards to the den.

Plate 14. The African wildcat is the likely progenitor of modern domestic cats. Short, close fur and long legs give it a very different appearance from the conspecific European wildcat.

Plate 15. Sometimes likened to a weasel or a marten, the unusual-looking jaguarundi has short ears, a long slender body, short legs, and an extremely long tail.

Plate 16. Ocelots are medium-sized cats, found from southern Texas through Mexico, Central and South America to northern Argentina. They prefer habitats with dense cover and high rodent densities.

Plate 17. One of the world's smallest cats, the daintily built oncilla has thick, soft fur marked with black and dark brown spots and rosettes.

Plate 18. The margay's markings are almost identical to those of the larger ocelot. Margays can be distinguished from ocelots by their larger eyes, more rounded heads, and longer tails.

Plate 19. The tall, long-legged serval has a small, slim head dominated by large oval-shaped ears. Servals use their large ears to locate rodent prey in tall grass.

Plate 20. Long legs and thick fur make the Canada lynx look larger than it really is. Large, densely furred feet help this cat "snowshoe" across deep, soft snow in pursuit of hares.

Plate 21. Largest of the bobtail cats, the Eurasian lynx is nearly twice the size of the Canada lynx. In most areas, the 20-kg roe deer is this cat's main prey.

Plate 22. Like other members of the Lynx genus, the Eurasian lynx has ear tufts and a ruff of long hair around its neck and under its chin.

Plate 23. The Iberian lynx has the most heavily spotted coat of all the lynxes. Critically endangered, the species survives only in a few scattered sites in Portugal and Spain.

Plate 24. The adaptable bobcat lives in a wide variety of habitats in North America, ranging from coniferous forests to deserts. However, deep snow limits its northern distribution.

Margay

Leopardus wiedii (Schinz, 1821)

The margay, also known as "tigrillo" or "gato monte," is often confused with the ocelot. In some parts of South America the natives refer to the margay as the little ocelot, or tree ocelot. The eighteenth-century naturalist Georges Buffon was the first person to use the name *margay*, which probably is derived from the Guarani *mbaracayá*, meaning "wild cat."[1] The margay has also proved to be a somewhat confusing animal for the taxonomists, and arguments over the number of subspecies and their supposed distribution have gone on for many years. At present there is still no agreement as to how subspecies should be determined, how many there are, or where they live.[2]

DESCRIPTION

The taxonomist R. I. Pocock described the margay as "a small, long-tailed, smooth-skulled representative of the Ocelot." He added, "The living examples of the two species, with which I was well acquainted at the London Zoological Gardens, were so strikingly alike that *wiedii* could only be distinguished by its smaller size and longer tail."[3]

The margay is intermediate in size between the ocelot and oncilla (*L. tigrinus*), and all three cats have very similar markings.[4] Margays and ocelots can generally be distinguished by size—even the largest margays are almost invariably smaller than the smallest ocelots. Of ninety margay specimens measured, only 2.2 percent overlapped with ocelots in terms of head and body length.[1] The margay is smaller and more slimly built than the ocelot and has a longer tail, but the pelts of ocelot and margay are easily confused. Fur trappers and traders have been known to take advantage of this similarity, and margay skins with the end of the tail cut off are sometimes traded as ocelot. Some experts maintain that the pelts can be distinguished by the number of whorls of reversed hair on the shoulders: the margay reportedly has a single whorl on each shoulder, whereas the ocelot has two. However, after examining many skins, Pocock concluded, "In both species the degree of reversal is individually variable and the feature may be altogether absent."[2] Oncillas are smaller than margays, have shorter legs and tails, and their spots are closed.

Margay fur is medium length, soft, and thick. The background color is yellowish brown to clay brown on the back and sides, white to buff on the belly and underparts. The fur is marked with dark brown or black, pale-centered, open spots and streaks arranged in longitudinal rows. The tail is long and bushy, about 70 percent

Figure 23. Distribution of the margay.

of the head and body length, and marked with about twelve dark rings and a blackish tip. The backs of the ears are black with central white spots. Compared with ocelots, margays have shorter, rounder heads and strikingly large eyes. The large orbits are a prominent feature of the margay's skull. Male and female margays are about the same size.

For a carnivore, the margay has an unusually low basal rate of metabolism, which may be related to the species' highly arboreal habits.[5]

DISTRIBUTION

The margay's range extends from the lowlands of northern Mexico south through Central America and into South America east of the Andes to northern Argentina and Uruguay (fig. 23).[1] It is apparently absent from the Caatinga of northeastern Brazil.[6] The margay's inclusion in the list of North American fauna rests on one specimen that was shot before 1852 on the Rio Grande in Texas.[7,8]

ECOLOGY AND BEHAVIOR

The margay is closely tied to primary forest, although it is sometimes found in shady coffee or cocoa plantations.[9] In Bolivia some margays still survive in areas of patchy forest, but these areas are rapidly being lost to the expanding human population.[10] In Costa Rica margays were once widely distributed in dense forest from the coastal lowlands to about 3,000 meters elevation in the interior mountains.[11] In Venezuela margays occur in the North Coast range, the Guyana highlands, and the Amazonas lowlands from 100 to 1,000 meters above sea level.[12,13] Within these areas, margays are found in several different forest types, including tropical dry forest, very humid tropical evergreen forest, very humid premontane forest, and montane cloud forest. In Belize, Konecny monitored the movements of a young adult male margay for six months using radiotelemetry. He found that the male used both primary and secondary forest, but spent significantly more time in late second-growth forest.[14]

Little is known of margay behavior in the wild. The single young adult male radio-tracked by Konecny in Belize was strictly nocturnal; it was most active between 0100 and 0500 hours. In contrast, a radio-collared male in southern Brazil was just as active during the daytime as at night.[15] Captive margays appear to be most active between 0100 and 0200 hours and again between 0400 and 0500 hours.[16] The radio-collared margay that Konecny tracked often traveled on the ground, but spent much of its time in the trees. During the daytime it rested in a tangle of lianas or in the bole of a palm tree, always at least 7 meters off the ground.

There are very few observations of the hunting behavior of wild margays, but Petersen has described the play behavior and acrobatic skills of a pair of captive animals.[16] Margays are amazingly agile climbers and leapers, and they are capable of ricocheting off objects while in mid-leap. They have been seen jumping 8 feet straight into the air and 12 feet horizontally. They can climb down a branch headfirst, and they can hang by their hind feet while manipulating an object with their front feet. Their reactions and agility are such that even during a fall, they can grab a branch or vine with one paw and climb up again.[16,17,18] These acrobatic abilities develop early. A four-month-old captive male was able to hang by his hind legs while manipulating objects with his front paws.[19] This young margay seemed to enjoy demonstrating his arboreal prowess: "He would start running across a slack clothesline no more than half an inch in diameter, lose his balance, swing under it, then move paw over paw the rest of the way up a slight incline. Coming down, he would hook his paws around the line and slide head first."

Margays have several anatomical adaptations that allow them to perform these aerial acrobatics.[17,18] Their hind feet can rotate inward through 180 degrees, allowing them to grip a branch equally well with the hindlimbs or forelimbs. Instead of the narrow, rather firm feet of domestic cats, margays have broad, soft feet with very mobile toes. These wide feet provide a good platform for precision balancing and jumping as well as an effective gripping surface for climbing and hanging onto branches. The cat's long tail is an important adaptation for arboreality, helping it to balance.

Petersen reported that his captive margays had excellent eyesight. They watched birds intently, and they could easily see small birds at a distance of 75 feet. They could also detect a fly at 30 feet. Leaping into the air, they would catch the fly with both paws simultaneously and draw it into the mouth before the hind feet touched the ground.[16]

In the wild, margays make full use of their long tails and acrobatic abilities. One night, while following his radio-collared margay, Konecny spotted the cat on a branch 5 meters off the ground, eating a rodent. Moments later the margay descended headfirst with the prey in its mouth, moved quickly onto a small lateral branch, leaped about 2 meters to an adjoining tree, and disappeared.[14] In Uruguay a margay was seen to capture a guan that was sitting on a branch 2 meters above the ground.[20]

Feeding Ecology

The limited information on margay food habits tends to support the notion that these cats do much of their hunting above the ground. In Guyana, Beebe reported that margays feed on large arboreal mammals such as porcupines and capuchin monkeys. However, the specimen he examined weighed 26 pounds and was probably an ocelot.[21] More recent analyses based on stomach contents and feces indicate that margays feed mainly on small rodents, birds, fruit, and insects. Most of the margay's prey are arboreal and nocturnal, but these cats also hunt on the ground. Konecny's radio-collared margay traveled from one hunting area to another on the ground, and margays probably kill whatever suitable terrestrial prey they encounter while moving between hunting areas.[14] In Brazil, Azevedo watched a margay spend twenty minutes trying to catch a bird that was 6 meters up in a bamboo clump. When the bird flew off, the cat came to the ground.

On another occasion he saw a margay eating an amphibian beneath a tree.[22]

In Venezuela the stomach contents of two margays contained the remains of a squirrel, a cane rat, and three spiny pocket mice. Of these, only the squirrel is arboreal.[9] Similarly, in Chiapas, Mexico, the margay is reported to take field mice, rabbits, and young pacas and agoutis, all of which are terrestrial.[23] The stomach of a margay in Panama contained only the remains of a common opossum.[7] In Brazil the stomach of a margay contained the remains of a guinea pig, tinamou feathers, and the fur and bones of a water rat.[20] In Belize, Konecny found that the climbing rat was the most common element in the margay's diet, occurring in almost half of the twenty-seven scats collected. Several other arboreal species were also found in scats, including mouse opossums, small birds, and squirrels. Insects were found in a third of the scats—and, surprisingly, fruit occurred in 14 percent of the samples. In captivity, margays readily eat figs, and they are also known to eat lettuce.[24]

Social Organization

Margays are solitary animals. They also appear to be rare, and all the evidence suggests that they live at much lower densities than ocelots. In Belize, a young adult male used an area of almost 11 square kilometers during the six months he was tracked. Within this area he traveled about 6 kilometers per day.[14] The home range of an adult male in southern Brazil measured 15.9 square kilometers.[15]

Like other felids, margays indicate occupancy of their home ranges by a variety of methods, including scent marking. Captive margays spray urine, make scrapes and scuff marks, rake their claws on logs and branches, and leave their feces uncovered.[25] However, in Belize, Konecny found that margay feces were usually covered with leaves or dirt.[14]

Margays have at least eight distinct vocalizations, all of which appear to be short-range calls.[18]

Reproduction and Development

All of the available information on margay reproduction is derived from a few studies of small numbers of captive animals. Females in estrus give a "long, moaning meow," while courting males have a barking meow or yelp and occasionally a trilling meow. Male vocalizations are accompanied by a rapid, ritualized shaking of the head, a mating behavior unique to the margay.[26] Females first come into heat when they are twelve to eighteen months old, but are usually two to three years old before they produce a first litter.[19,27,28] The estrous cycle varies from thirty-two to thirty-six days, and within this period females are receptive for four to ten days.[29,30] The margay's mating sequence is similar to that of other felids. A male approaches a receptive female from the rear, and uses a nape bite while holding and trying to position her. When she crouches and raises her posterior (lordosis), he straddles her and, while maintaining the neck bite, intromits and makes rapid copulatory thrusts. Copulation lasts from fifteen to sixty seconds. The sequence is repeated several times a day for three to four days. Courtship and copulation occur more frequently on elevated platforms than on the ground, which may reflect the cat's arboreal habits.[26]

Margay gestation is longer than that of most small cats, about eighty days.[19,31,32] Interestingly, margays have only one pair of teats,[32] and they follow the general rule that litter size is usually half the number of nipples. A recent survey reported one kitten in each of seventeen litters,[30] while other samples include seven litters of one kitten each born to the same female at Marlot Breeding Farm,[28] and two other litters of one kitten each.[19] One litter of two kittens was born at the New Orleans Zoo.[32]

At birth, kittens weigh between 85–125 grams[31] and 163–170 grams.[33] The young are relatively large at birth, as might be predicted from their long gestation period and small litter size. Kittens first open their eyes when they are about two weeks old. They begin to eat solid food at seven to eight weeks of age, and they acquire their permanent canine teeth when they are about five months old. By eight to ten months they are nearly adult size.[33]

Births are reported to occur from March to June in Chiapas, Mexico, and a female shot in neighboring Guatemala during April was carrying a single small fetus.[34]

Our understanding of the reproductive capabilities of the margay is limited by a lack of information. There are, for instance, no data on interbirth intervals. A "best guess" estimate might be obtained by looking at a closely related species for which such information does exist, such as the ocelot. The ocelot also has small litters, but the young mature slowly compared with those of margays, attaining adult size only at about two years of age. In the wild ocelots probably rear one young every two years.[35] Margays attain adult size by the time they are a year old, about a year earlier than ocelot, but they are similar to ocelots in that both first reproduce when they are two to three years old. The margay's relatively rapid early physical development may be related to the kitten's need to accompany the mother on arboreal hunting forays. Most arboreal mammals have young that are capable of clinging to the parent. The combination of phylogeny, relatively late age of first reproduction, small litter size, and low density suggests that the reproductive potential of margays is probably similar to that of ocelots, which rear one young every two years. Longevity in the wild is unknown, but a male in the Santa Fe Zoo in Gainesville, Florida, lived to be twenty-four years old.[36] Given this scant information, it is almost impossible to calculate lifetime reproductive output for margays, but it is likely to be low—similar to that of ocelots.

STATUS IN THE WILD

No population estimates exist for the margay, but it is reported to be rare throughout its range. Data from museum collecting expeditions suggest that margays live at much lower densities than ocelots—perhaps three to six times lower.[9,13] The margay's arboreal lifestyle makes it much more dependent on forested habitats, and thus it is likely to be particularly sensitive to deforestation.[37] These two characteristics, combined with the fact that females usually give birth to a single kitten, make the margay a potentially vulnerable species.

Habitat loss due to deforestation is now considered to be the major threat to the species.[1] As recently as 1980, hunting for the fur trade was the most serious threat, but international legislation appears to have been effective in reducing the number of margays killed for their pelts.[38,39]

The margay was once one of the four most heavily exploited spotted cats, and was subjected to intense hunting pressure throughout its range. Because margays are small, it takes at least fifteen skins to make a coat. In 1977 at least 30,000 margay skins were traded in the international fur market. Since then the number of skins in trade has declined: 19,981 skins were traded in 1980, and in 1981 and 1982 the number of skins reported in trade fell to 17,526 and 13,200, respectively. By 1985 the total reported trade by CITES parties had dropped to 138. The main source of the skins was reported to be Paraguay. Most of the skins were imported by Western European countries. Until 1982 the Federal Republic of Germany and Italy were the main importers, but in 1984 France was the major importing country.[40]

STATUS IN CAPTIVITY

Margays are fairly well represented in zoo collections.[1] However, margays do not breed well in captivity.

CONSERVATION EFFORTS

Most countries with margay populations have enacted legislation to prohibit hunting, internal trade, and commercial export. The effectiveness of these controls varies greatly from country to country, with some, like Paraguay, having an erratic enforcement policy. Several countries apparently still hold large stocks of skins, which are traded on the illegal market.

In 1989 the Federal Republic of Germany proposed that the margay (along with the ocelot and oncilla) be transferred to appendix I of CITES. The proposal was approved and resulted in the margay being given endangered species status. This listing should provide added protection for this very vulnerable spotted cat.

TABLE 24 MEASUREMENTS AND WEIGHTS OF ADULT MARGAYS

HB	n	T	n	WT	n	Location	Source
548, 568	2m	338, 374	2m			Mexico	3
477	1f	338	1f			Mexico	41
490, 540	2m	370, 400	2m	4.0, 4.0	2m	Belize	14
750, 762	2m	510, 518	2m			Nicaragua	3,42
580	1f	390	1f			Nicaragua	42
533	1f	447	1f			Panama	3
619	1m	426	1m			Colombia	3
619	1f	411	1f			Ecuador	3
558	1m	391	1m			Peru	3
562	4m	392	4m			Brazil	3
(508–589)		(350–441)					

(continued)

TABLE 24 *(continued)*

HB	n	T	n	WT	n	Location	Source
508, 508	2f	330, 396	2f			Brazil	2
792	1m	508	1m			Bolivia	3
525	1m	375	1m	3.9	1m	Uruguay	43
660	1f	368	1f			Bolivia	3
		400 (390–410)	3f	3.0, 2.6	2f	Venezuela	9
		393 (370–405)	4m	3.36	1m	Venezuela	9

Note: HB = head and body length (mm), T = tail length (mm), WT = weight (kg). *n* = sample size. Sex: m = male, f = female, ? = unknown. Mean values are presented only for sample sizes of three or more. Range of values is in parentheses.

TABLE 25 FREQUENCY OF OCCURRENCE OF PREY ITEMS IN THE DIETS OF MARGAYS (PERCENTAGE OF SAMPLES)

Prey items	Cockscomb Basin, Belize [14] Scats (n = 27)
Marmosa spp. Mouse opossum	18.5
Sciurus deppei Tree squirrel	22.2
Ototylomys phyllotis Big-eared climbing rat	48.1
Reithrodontomys gracilis Harvest mouse	18.5
Small birds	29.2
Arthropods	33.3
Fruit	14.4
Minimum number of vertebrate prey items	37

REFERENCES

1. Oliveira, T. G. 1998. *Leopardus wiedii. Mammalian Species* 579: 1–6.

2. Wayne, R. K., R. E. Benveniste, D. N. Janczewski, and S. J. O'Brien. 1989. Molecular and biochemical evolution of the Carnivora. In *Carnivore behavior, ecology, and evolution*, ed. J. L. Gittleman, 465–494. Ithaca, NY: Cornell University Press.

3. Pocock, R. I. 1941. The races of the ocelot and the margay. *Pub. Field Mus. Nat. Hist. (Zool. Ser.)* 27: 319–369.

4. Guggisberg, C. A. W. 1975. *Wild cats of the world.* New York: Taplinger.

5. McNab, B. K. 1989. Basal rate of metabolism, body size, and food habits in the Order Carnivora. In *Carnivore behavior, ecology, and evolution*, ed. J. L. Gittleman, 335–354. Ithaca, NY: Cornell University Press.

6. Emmons, L. H., and F. Feer. 1990. *Neotropical rainforest mammals: A field guide.* Chicago: University of Chicago Press.

7. Goldman, E. A. 1943. The races of the ocelot and margay in Middle America. *J. Mammal.* 24: 372–385.

8. Leopold, A. S. 1959. *Wildlife of Mexico.* Berkeley: University of California Press.

9. Mondolfi, E. 1986. Notes on the biology and status of the small wild cats in Venezuela. In *Cats of the world: Biology, conservation, and management*, ed. S. D. Miller and D. D. Everett, 125–146. Washington, DC: National Wildlife Federation.

10. Tello, J. L. 1986. The situation of the wild cats (Felidae) in Bolivia. Report to CITES, Lausanne, Switzerland.

11. Koford, C. B. 1983. *Felis wiedii.* In *Costa Rican natural history*, ed. D. H. Janzen, 471–472. Chicago: University of Chicago Press.

12. Bisbal, F. J. 1987. The carnivores of Venezuela: Their distribution and the ways they have been affected by human activities. Master's thesis, University of Florida, Gainesville.

13. Bisbal, F J. 1989. Distribution and habitat association of the carnivores in Venezuela. In *Advances in Neotropical mammalogy*, ed. K. H. Redford and J. F. Eisenberg, 339–362. Gainesville, FL: Sandhill Crane Press.

14. Konecny, M. J. 1990. Movement patterns and food habits of four sympatric carnivore species in Belize, Central America. In *Advances in Neotropical mammalogy*, ed. K. H. Redford and J. F. Eisenberg, 243–264. Gainesville, FL: Sandhill Crane Press.

15. Crawshaw, P. G. 1995. Comparative ecology of ocelot (*Felis pardalis*) and jaguar (*Panthera onca*) in a protected subtropical forest in Brazil and Argentina. Ph.D. dissertation, University of Florida, Gainesville.

16. Petersen, M. K. 1979. Behavior of the margay. *Carnivore* 2(1): 69–76.

17. Leyhausen, P. 1963. Über südamerikanische Pardelkatzen. *Z. Tierpsychol.* 20: 627–640.

18. Weigel, I. 1972. Small felids and clouded leopards. In *Grzimek's animal life encyclopedia*, vol. 12, *Mammals* III, ed. H. C. B. Grzimek, 281–332. New York: Van Nostrand Reinhold.

19. Wiley, K. S. 1978. Observations of margay behavior. *Carnivore* 1: 81.

20. Ximénez, A. 1982. Notas sobre felidos neotropicales, VIII. Observaciones sobre el contenido estomacal y el comportamiento alimentar de diversas especies de felinos. *Rev. Nordest. Biol.* 5: 89–91.

21. Beebe, W. 1925. Ecology of Kartabo. *Zoologica* 6: 1–193.

22. Azevedo, F. C. C. de. 1996. Notes on the behavior of the margay *Felis wiedii* (Schinz, 1821) (Carnivora, Felidae) in the Brazilian Atlantic Forest. *Mammalia* 60: 325–328.

23. Alvarez del Toro, M. 1977. *Los mamíferos de Chiapas.* Chiapas, Mexico: Universidad Autónoma de Chiapas.

24. Petersen, M. K. 1971. Lettuce prevents stomach irritation in margay. *Long Island Ocelot Club Newsletter* 15(6): 13.

25. Wemmer, C., and K. Scow. 1977. Communication in the Felidae with emphasis on scent marking and contact patterns. In *How animals communicate*, ed. T. A. Sebeok, 749–766. Bloomington: Indiana University Press.

26. Petersen, M. K. Courtship and mating patterns of margay. In *The world's cats*, vol. 3, ed. R. L. Eaton, 22–35. Seattle: Carnivore Research Institute, Burke Museum, University of Washington.

27. Leyhausen, P. 1990. Cats. In *Grzimek's encyclopedia of mammals*, vol. 3, ed. S. P. Parker, 576–632.

28. Eaton, R. L. 1984. Survey of smaller felid breeding. *Zool. Garten* (n.f.) 54: 101–120.

29. Seager, S. W., and C. N. Demorest. 1986. Reproduction in captive wild carnivores. In *Zoo and wild animal medicine*, 2nd ed., ed. M. Fowler, 667–706. Philadelphia: W. B. Saunders.

30. Mellen, J. D. 1993. A comparative analysis of scent-marking, social and reproductive behavior in 20 species of small cats (*Felis*). *Am. Zool.* 33: 151–166.

31. Fagen, R. M., and K. S. Wiley. 1978. Felid paedomorphosis, with special reference to *Leopardus. Carnivore* 1(2): 72–81.

32. Paintiff, J. A., and D. E. Anderson. 1980. Breeding the margay at the New Orleans Zoo. *Int. Zoo Yrbk.* 20: 223–224.

33. Petersen, M. K., and M. K. Petersen. 1978. Growth rates and other post-natal developmental changes in margays. *Carnivore* 1(1): 87–92.

34. Murie, A. 1935. Mammals from Guatemala and British Honduras. *Univ. Michigan Mus. Zool. Pub.* 26: 1–30.

35. Sunquist, M. E. 1992. The ecology of the ocelot: The importance of incorporating life history traits into conservation plans. In *Felinos de Venezuela: Biología, ecología y conservación*, 117–128. Caracas, Venezuela: Fundación para el Desarrollo de las Ciencias Físicas, Matemáticas y Naturales.

36. Brown, J., Director, Santa Fe Zoo, Gainesville, Florida. Personal communication.

37. Bisbal, J. 1992. Estado de los pequeños felidos de Venezuela. In *Felinos de Venezuela: Biología, ecología y conservación*, 83–94. Caracas, Venezuela: Fundación para el Desarrollo de las Ciencias Físicas, Matemáticas y Naturales.

38. Broad, S. 1987. The harvest and trade in Latin American spotted cats (Felidae) and otters (Lutrinae). Cambridge, UK: IUCN Wildlife Trade Monitoring Unit.

39. Broad, S., R. Luxmoore, and M. Jenkins, ed. 1988. Significant trade in wildlife: A review of selected species in CITES Appendix II, Vol. 1: Mammals. Cambridge, UK: International Union for Conservation of Nature and Natural Resources Conservation Monitoring Centre.

40. McMahan, L. R. 1986. The international cat trade. In *Cats of the world: Biology, conservation, and management*, ed. S. D. Miller and D. D. Everett, 461–488. Washington, DC: National Wildlife Federation.

41. Armstrong, D. M., J. K. Jones Jr., and E. C. Birney. 1972. Mammals from the Mexican state of Sinaloa. III. Carnivora and Artiodactyla. *J. Mammal.* 53: 48–61.

42. Allen, J. A. 1919. Notes on the synonymy and nomenclature of the smaller spotted cats of tropical America. *Bull. Am. Mus. Nat. Hist.* 41: 341–419.

43. Barlow, J. C. 1965. Land mammals from Uruguay: Ecology and zoogeography. Ph.D. dissertation, University of Kansas, Lawrence.

Serval

Leptailurus serval (Schreber, 1776)

Early European travelers and explorers often named unfamiliar animals after species they already knew, and the serval's name is believed to be derived from the Portuguese word *lobo-cerval*, meaning lynx.[1] The *Concise Oxford Dictionary of Word Origins* states that the word *serval* means lynx or bush cat, dates from the eighteenth century, and is based on the Latin word via French.[2] Molecular analysis has shown that servals are an ancient sister taxon to the lynx group and represent a primitive offshoot of the line leading to the *Panthera* cats (lion, leopard, tiger, jaguar, and snow leopard).[3,4,5] Servals are currently included in the caracal group, along with the African golden cat.[6]

DESCRIPTION

The serval is a tall, lightly built cat with a small, slim face dominated by very large oval-shaped ears. Relative to the rest of its body, the serval has the longest legs of any cat species. Like the lynx, the serval has a comparatively short tail that measures little more than a third of its head and body length.[1,7]

Serval skins are sometimes confused with those of the cheetah, as the two cats have similar spot patterns, consisting of a series of single black dots against a tawny background. But apart from being smaller, the serval has a much shorter tail, and the backs of the serval's ears have a very distinct transverse white bar edged in black.

The serval's coat markings vary in size from fine freckle-sized dots to large, distinct spots that sometimes merge into stripes on the neck and back. In the early 1900s taxonomists thought that these two extremes of coat pattern represented two different species, the servaline and the serval. Now both speckled and spotted forms are considered to be the same species.[7] Black or melanistic servals occur quite frequently in the highland areas of Kenya and Ethiopia. During one survey in the Aberdare Mountains of Kenya, twenty-one different servals were identified, of which eight were almost completely black and five others showed varying degrees of melanism. Most of the black servals were sighted at elevations of 2,440–2,745 meters.[8]

Like the cheetah, the serval is among the more specialized cats. Built for height rather than speed, the serval uses its long legs in combination with its large ears to capture small rodents in long grass. Its long, mobile toes and strong, curved claws also help it hook a mouse hidden in the grass or extract a rat from a burrow.[9] The serval's long legs provide its satellite-dish

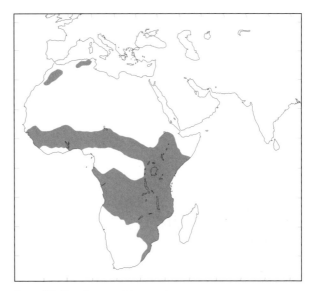

Figure 24. Distribution of the serval.

ears with a raised platform from which to scan the vegetation for sounds of prey. Strictly speaking, it is not the length of the serval's legs that allows it to tower over otherwise similar-sized cat species, but rather the length of its feet. Elongated metatarsal bones in the palms and soles of the serval's feet add considerably to its height. An adult serval stands roughly 60 centimeters tall at the shoulder, which is more than 20 centimeters taller than the otherwise similar-sized ocelot and some 12 centimeters taller than a caracal of the same weight. Compared with the caracal, the serval has much larger ear bullae, reflecting its keen sense of hearing, and a more lightly built skull and less powerful jaws, reflecting its diet of very small prey.[1,7]

DISTRIBUTION

The serval is found only in Africa (fig. 24). It is widely distributed south of the Sahara, and it is still listed for most of the countries from Senegal in the west to Somalia in the east and south to the Republic of South Africa.[10,11,12,13,14] However, the serval has quite specific habitat requirements, so it is locally restricted to smaller areas within this broad geographic range. It is probably extinct in the Cape Province of South Africa.[15] Historically, the serval has also been recorded in Morocco, Algeria, and Tunisia, but today it is believed to be extinct in Algeria, where the last specimen was documented in 1880.[16] Its existence in Morocco and Tunisia is uncertain, as there have been no recorded sightings for thirty years.[12] However, occasional unconfirmed reports of the cat's existence in North Africa offer hope that a few individuals may still survive.[17]

ECOLOGY AND BEHAVIOR

Servals are found in almost all types of grassland in Africa, and their distribution is closely tied to water and its associated vegetation in the form of grasses, reed beds, and marshes. They do not occur in desert or semidesert, but they can live where watercourses penetrate these dryer areas. Servals can also live in forest if it is well interspersed with grassy glades and edges, but they are not found in the dense forests of equatorial West Africa. Provided there is enough food, cover, and water, altitude and cold temperatures do not seem to restrict this cat's distribution; servals have been recorded in bamboo and juniper at elevations of 2,745 meters and on high moorlands in the Aberdare Mountains in Kenya at 3,000 meters.[7,8,12] Servals are also found in the Kamberg Nature Reserve and surrounding areas in Natal, where the elevation ranges from 1,585 to 2,244 meters. Winter temperatures are cold in this part of South Africa, well below those in the warm grass savannas most commonly thought of as typical serval habitat. In the Kamberg Nature Reserve, the mean minimum monthly temperature in July (midwinter) is 0.7°C and heavy frost is common for at least six months of the year, with occasional snowfall.[18] Laboratory tests of servals in a respiratory chamber showed that under cold conditions (10–15°C) they curl up and conserve energy by allowing the body temperature to decline.[19]

The serval is usually described as being strictly nocturnal, but its activity pattern probably reflects human disturbance and patterns of prey activity. Servals may also be less nocturnal in areas where there are many larger nocturnal competitors. Some of the most detailed information on serval behavior comes from Aadje Geertsema's elegant observational study in Tanzania.[20,21,22] Geertsema's study revealed that servals in an undisturbed area of the Ngorongoro Crater hunted mainly in the early morning and late afternoon, with peaks of activity every three hours during the night. Though it was not uncommon to find servals hunting at midday, especially during cool or cloudy weather, they usually chose a shady spot to rest in during the heat of the day, from 1100 to about 1600 hours. This rest period was more pronounced during the dry season, when temperatures were higher. In other areas servals hunt mainly at night. Two radio-collared servals

in the Rustenburg Nature Reserve, South Africa, were predominantly nocturnal, with some limited early morning and late afternoon activity.[23] Servals were also active at night in the Kamberg Reserve in Natal, but the six animals studied with the aid of radiotelemetry moved around during the daytime as well, especially on overcast or misty days.[24] In the Ngorongoro Crater hunting patterns are also affected by weather conditions. Geertsema observed that servals tended to avoid hunting on windy days. They spent the day resting and waited until the wind died down in the early evening. Apparently the wind interfered with the cats' ability to locate prey, obscuring the rustling noises made by rodents in the grass.[20]

When hunting rodents, a serval walks slowly through the grassland, stopping periodically to listen. It may stop and sit for fifteen minutes at a time, scanning the area for sounds of potential prey. Hearing something move in the grass, it stops and locates the exact position of the sound, then after a short, careful stalk, the serval pounces like a fox, leaping into the air and striking the animal with a blow from one or both forefeet. If the initial pounce does not connect, a swift series of stiff-legged bouncing jumps may follow. This capriole jump, in which all four feet are off the ground at the same time, is a characteristic hunting technique. With this jump, the serval can use its forelegs to grab a bird out of the air, then land only on its hind legs while continuing to hold the prey between its forepaws.[9,22] Servals are prodigious leapers, with jumping abilities equal to those of the caracal.[1,11] A single pounce may span 3.6 meters, and they have been seen leaping 2 to 3 meters into the air trying to knock down a bird or an insect in flight.[11]

Geertsema found that some servals developed idiosyncratic hunting patterns and repeatedly returned to hunt in specific areas. One female spent several days walking up and down the same stretch of gravel road, turning at the same place each time. She made frequent pounces to either side of the road. She seemed to be using the road to move quietly through the area. This same female also showed a pattern when hunting abandoned ant mounds where rodents were known to live: "She moved from one mound to another, frequently stopping and/or sitting down in front of a mound for different lengths of time as if expecting to catch something."[22]

Servals react to potential predators, especially hyenas, by hiding or fleeing. A serval's first reaction on detecting a hyena is to crouch and wait; if the hyena approaches too closely, the serval bounds away, tail raised, in a series of darting leaps. Though they do not spend much time in trees, servals can climb well if they have to, and readily take to the trees if they are being pursued by a larger predator. One serval being chased by dogs was observed climbing straight up a eucalyptus tree to a height of over 9 meters before it found a branch.[12,25]

Servals also use their long legs to investigate holes and crevices, and the long, loosely knit metatarsal bones in their feet are well suited to hooking small creatures out of holes.[9,12] One young male was observed standing on his hind legs, systematically poking his front paw into the nest holes of a colony of swallows.[22] Servals also reach deep into holes to catch rodents, and if a mouse evades capture by fleeing down a hole, the cat will often try to dig it out. Angling for prey in a crevice is a common play behavior among captive servals.[9]

Given the serval's preference for wetland habitats, it is not surprising that this cat also hunts in water and does not mind getting its feet wet. Captive servals deftly hook live fish out of water,[26] and in the wild servals have been seen hunting frogs and water birds. One young male was observed to catch and eat at least twenty-eight frogs of various sizes over a three-hour period,[22] and an animal shot in Kenya was found to have a stomach full of crabs.[1]

Servals also learn to use car headlights as a hunting aid at night. They stand or sit beside the road, waiting for a passing car to illuminate the highway. Staring down the lighted portion of the road, they watch for any suitable prey to cross, then bound toward it and pounce. Once they have caught something, they quickly return to the side of the road to eat.[27]

Feeding Ecology
With its long legs and large ears, the serval is a specialized small-mammal catcher, well equipped to capture rodents in tall grass. Though it does occasionally kill larger prey, such as hares, flamingos, duiker, and young antelope, over 90 percent of the serval's diet consists of prey weighing less than 200 grams, or about 2 percent of female body weight. Servals also eat small birds, lizards, snakes, frogs, and insects such as grasshoppers and crickets. In Zimbabwe the multimammate mouse (20–80 grams) and the larger vlei rat (100–200 grams) made up the bulk of the serval's diet, while birds and reptiles were taken only occasionally.[12] In Tanzania the vlei rat was the dominant prey, particularly in the dry season, followed by the pygmy mouse

(2–12 grams) and the unstriped grass mouse (50–100 grams). Indeed, in Tanzania, rodents occurred in 98 percent of all the feces examined, and in almost 90 percent of direct observations of serval kills, the prey was a rodent. Frogs were found in over 75 percent of the scats, but servals were not often seen actually killing frogs, probably because the dense cover in typical frogging areas made it difficult to see the hunt. Like many other cats, servals commonly eat grass, probably as an aid to digestion or as an emetic.[22] In the Kamberg Nature Reserve, scat analysis showed that 80 percent of the cats' diet was made up of rodents weighing less than 127 grams, about 2 percent of female body weight. The remainder of the diet consisted of shrews (13.5 percent), birds (5 percent), reptiles (0.9 percent), and insects (0.7 percent).[18]

Servals kill rodents by pouncing on them, stunning them with a blow from one or both forepaws, then biting them behind the head. Most small prey, including birds, are swallowed whole, on the spot. Larger birds are plucked and eaten more slowly. Snakes are pounced on, hit with several fast blows from the paws, or bitten repeatedly, and are often eaten while still moving. Captive servals have been observed to cache food when the prey is too large to be eaten at one sitting. They scratch grass and leaves over the carcass with raking movements of the front and back paws.[7,9,12,22] They also sometimes play with their food before eating it, throwing it into the air and leaping up to catch it, or pounce again if it is still alive. Younger animals play with prey more often and for longer periods of time.[22]

Interestingly, the serval seems to retain its high pounce and strike-and-bite rodent-killing technique even when attacking larger prey. As one observer noted after watching a serval killing a 7-kilogram Thomson's gazelle fawn, "The method of killing in this case was to spring high above the gazelle and land on it, with all four feet, and bite until dislodged by the violence of the fawn's struggle, when it would circle for a few seconds before making another attack."[8]

Geertsema's study in Tanzania revealed that servals can be remarkably successful predators. In the Ngorongoro Crater about half of their pounces resulted in a meal, and each serval captured between 5,700 and 6,100 prey per year, equivalent to about 3,950 rodents, 260 snakes, and 130 birds per serval per year.[22]

Social Organization
Servals are solitary animals. Odd sightings of groups or pairs have been found to consist of a mother and her

kittens or a mating pair. In Geertsema's study in the Ngorongoro Crater, one adult female occupied a range measuring 9.5 square kilometers, while an adult male's range was 11.6 square kilometers. However, these are minimum range sizes, and the actual range size was probably larger because the study animals were not radio-collared and could not be sighted every day. The ranges of three adult females did not overlap appreciably. Geertsema estimated that servals may reach a density of one per 2.4 square kilometers in optimal habitat. Female servals show strong site fidelity, and one female was observed to occupy the same area for nine years.[21] In the high-elevation grasslands of Natal, ranges were somewhat larger; two adult females used areas of 19.8 and 15.8 square kilometers, and an adult male ranged over 31.5 square kilometers.[28]

The distances covered by servals in their daily travels are not well documented, but from tracks they are known to move at least 3 to 4 kilometers per night.[11] Similar figures were obtained by Geertsema, who followed individual servals during their travels. She estimated that both male and female servals in the Ngorongoro Crater traveled an average of 2.5 kilometers per day.[22] For two males released into Rustenburg Nature Reserve, the total distance moved in a night varied from 0.37 to 6.66 kilometers.[23]

Adult servals scent-mark regularly as they move through their ranges. The most frequent type of scent marking is by urination, and servals have three distinct methods of urine marking. The most commonly observed method involves the cat turning its hindquarters slightly sideways and squirting a few drops of urine onto a bush. Servals also spray urine onto trees and other conspicuous objects. While spraying these kinds of objects, the serval lifts its tail high and makes treading movements with its front feet. Places that are repeatedly sprayed acquire a greasy, powerfully scented deposit.[7] The least commonly observed method involves scraping the ground with the front or hind feet before or after urination.[22]

Adult males urine-mark frequently. Over a twelve-hour period, one male in Ngorongoro averaged forty-six spray marks per hour and forty-one marks per kilometer. Adult females scent-marked approximately half as frequently as adult males, while juvenile and young adult males averaged only two scent marks per hour. Servals increase the frequency of scent marking in a variety of social situations. One young male was observed to scent-mark more frequently (ten times per hour vs. twice per hour) when he moved through a

resident male's range. On another occasion a male followed a female for an hour and forty-five minutes, during which time he marked 94.8 times per hour.[22] Servals also leave their feces in prominent places. Feces are sometimes accompanied by scrapes made with both front and hind feet. There is conflicting evidence as to whether servals use latrines in the wild. One report on captive animals suggests that males defecate at random in the enclosure, whereas females tend to use the same place repeatedly.[7]

Among captive servals, the onset of estrus is characterized by a high rate of urine marking by both male and female.[29] Jonathan Kingdon provides us with a vivid eyewitness account of the behavior of his captive female serval in heat:

A female betrays the onset of her oestrous by a very short, sharp miaow which has considerable carrying power and is repeated in bouts. When approached by a male she may purr and raise her chin as she rubs the side of her mouth and chin against him or the intervening wire. When my solitary female was in oestrus, she would rub the sides of her cheeks against my knee, hand or face and salivate copiously out of the corners of her mouth, so that one became quite wet with spit.[7]

Kingdon went on to describe the vocalizations and scent-marking behavior of his captive female:

When a captive female is in oestrus and on her own, she intersperses bouts of yowling with interminable pacing and frequent but sparing urine squirting at particular points. The vertical tail is always vibrated when this is done and she may smell or even rub her head on the same spot or may lie and roll displaying thereby the most incandescent white of her spotted belly in the typical felid submission posture.[7]

Serval vocalizations seem to be confined primarily to short-range calls used in direct encounters. The vocal repertoire includes the growl, hiss, purr, the wahwah call, and a curious "swallowed meow" that seems to signify friendly recognition.[30,31,32,33]

Despite Buffon's statement that "neither captivity, nor good nor bad treatment will tame or soften the ferocity of this animal,"[34] servals are not known to be particularly fierce fighters. However, these cats do have highly exaggerated aggressive postures and facial expressions. During a confrontation with another serval, the ears are folded back to form a flat plate, displaying the prominent white bars, while the tips of the ears curl over and point toward each other. The two cats arch their backs and stand sideways, fur erect, seemingly on tiptoe on their elongated legs, to present the largest and most intimidating body view. They bare their teeth and make a continuous low mewing sound. Offensive threat displays may also include throwing the head up and down. According to Kingdon, "The dorsal fur bristles, the eyes blaze and ferocious explosive barks and growls are interspersed with long-reaching slashes of the forepaws."[7]

Reproduction and Development

During estrus, which lasts from one to four days,[35,36,37] a male and female serval sometimes travel and rest together. After a gestation period of approximately seventy-four days, females typically give birth to two kittens, but as many as four have been recorded in a litter.[35,37,38] Servals are polyestrous, and young are born at different times of the year, depending on where in Africa they live. In general, births seem to precede the peak breeding season of murid rodents by a month or so.[7] In Botswana servals give birth during the wetter months,[11] while in the Ngorongoro Crater births were observed in September and November, toward the end of the dry season.[21] If the kittens die or are removed soon after birth, captive servals are able to give birth to three or four litters a year.[39] However, when a captive female was allowed a normal-length lactation, the shortest interval between births was 184 days, illustrating that these cats could have two litters a year under optimal conditions.[35] But such a scenario would be exceptional; one litter per year is much more likely. A female in Ngorongoro was known to have had two litters in two and a half years.[22]

In the wild the birth den is usually in dense vegetation, or the female may take over a disused burrow dug by an aardvark or porcupine. The kittens are born blind and helpless, weighing about 250 grams, and they are covered with soft woolly hair, which is somewhat grayer than the fur of adults and patterned with indistinct markings. Their eyes open when they are about nine to thirteen days old.[35,38] When the kittens are about a month old their mother begins to bring food back to the den. Geertsema watched one female carry a mouse for nearly 1.6 kilometers to the spot where her three kittens were hidden in some reeds. When the female was about 50 meters from the den, she began to call, stopping periodically to listen for an answer. The kittens ran out to meet their mother, and one of them

picked up the mouse, while the other two settled down to suckle. When the kittens get a little older, they want to accompany their mother on hunting trips, and it becomes more and more difficult for the female to persuade them to stay behind. Geertsema watched one mother spend over an hour growling and spitting at her kitten before she could get away to hunt.[22]

When a female has very young kittens, her movements are restricted to a small area around the den site; as the young grow, she gradually expands her foraging area and resumes using her previous range. Females with young must step up their hunting efforts, and they spend a major part of the day finding food. They frequently spend twice as much time hunting; as a result, resting time is dramatically decreased. Prey capture rates remain the same per distance traveled whether females have kittens or not, so females with kittens have to travel farther to catch more food. By doubling the normal daily distance (2.5 kilometers per day) traveled, females probably double their food intake.[22]

Young servals acquire their permanent canine teeth when they are about six months old,[35] and are able to hunt for themselves shortly thereafter. When the young are about a year old, adults begin to chase them, and eventually drive them away from their natal area. Males are usually the first to leave; females are sometimes allowed to stay a few months longer.[22]

Data from captivity indicate that female servals may become sexually mature when they are just over a year old. Two captive females gave birth when they were fifteen and sixteen months old.[40] However, two others first came into estrus at twenty-five and twenty-eight months of age, and a captive male was first seen copulating when he was seventeen months old.[41] Though servals have been known to live for twenty years in captivity,[35,42] their reproductive life span is shorter. The record for the oldest mother is held by a female at Switzerland's Basel Zoo, who raised her last litter when she was fourteen.[35] Longevity in the wild is likely to be much less, possibly about ten years; thus females could potentially raise some sixteen to twenty young in a lifetime.

STATUS IN THE WILD

Generally, servals have declined in numbers, but are still quite common in some areas. The last reported sighting of servals in the countries north of the Sahara was more than thirty years ago, and the species' continued existence in Morocco, Algeria, and Tunisia must be in doubt. Servals are widely distributed in savanna and grasslands south of the Sahara, but are declining in numbers in the west and extreme south of Africa.[17] The species is said to be widely distributed in Tanzania.[7] At the southern end of their range in the Cape Province, servals were once found along the coastal belt from Cape Town to the Transkei, but are now thought to be extinct there.[15] In other parts of southern Africa they are still found in areas of suitable habitat.[25] They are common, for example, in the Okavango Delta in Botswana. In western Zimbabwe they are confined to areas where there is permanent water, and are more common toward the east in areas of higher rainfall.[13]

In southern Africa serval are hunted for sport. They are also persecuted for their supposed ability to kill livestock such as goats, sheep, and poultry, and are sometimes caught in traps set for jackal and caracal.[24] However, habitat degradation and the loss of wetlands are also important factors in their decline in southern Africa.[24]

Serval do kill poultry when they get the opportunity, but they are much easier to deter from this habit than other predators. They do not dig under or break through wire netting, but use their long limbs to "fish" for chickens through holes in the wire. They use this same angling technique to pull bait through the wire sides of large live traps.[12] Even though they occasionally raid chicken and duck pens, servals are specialized rodent eaters, and they can play an important role in agricultural areas by keeping rodent numbers down.[11] In fact, agricultural development and the murid rodents that thrive wherever grains are grown are actually thought to have improved serval habitat in some areas.[11] This cat is said to adapt readily to abandoned cultivation and second-growth areas, and as long as it is not persecuted, it may be able to live alongside humans in rural agricultural areas.

To date there has been only a single effort to evaluate the feasibility of reintroducing servals to areas from which they have been extirpated, and in this case the efforts were a qualified success.[23] Two sibling adult males and an unrelated adult male serval, all of which were captive-bred and inexperienced with live prey, were radio-collared and released into the Rustenburg Nature Reserve. The siblings were released first, and their movements and activities were intensely monitored for two to five months. Within a month of their release, the brothers had settled into small (2.1 and 2.7 kilometers) and largely overlapping ranges in the reserve, but they were not often found together. Equipment failure precluded determining whether the siblings remained in the area for an extended period, but they clearly were able to maintain themselves in the wild without the benefit of prior training. The third male, released eight months after the siblings, was accidentally killed twenty days later at a site 17 kilometers from the point of release. Despite this cat's specialized diet and hunting style, the fact that two naive captive-bred servals managed to survive for a few months indicates that the species might eventually be a good candidate for reintroduction programs.

STATUS IN CAPTIVITY

Servals are quite common in zoos; nearly a quarter of the institutions contributing to the ISIS Species Distribution Report have serval exhibits. Servals also breed readily in captivity. Some zoos have bred four or five generations, and almost all the animals held in zoos are captive-bred.[28]

TABLE 26 MEASUREMENTS AND WEIGHTS OF ADULT SERVALS

HB	n	T	n	WT	n	Location	Source
				11.7 (11.6–11.7)	3m	Transvaal	43
				10.5, 10.6	2f	Transvaal	43
850	1f	295	1f	9.1	1f	Transvaal	44
853 (750–920)	5m	283 (250–330)	5m	11.2 (9.8–12.4)	6m	Natal	17
778 (725–820)	5f	264 (255–275)	6f	8.5 (7.0–9.8)	7f	Natal	17
783 (760–820)	3m	323 (310–330)	3m	9.8, 11.6	2m	Botswana	45
780 (753–810)	3f	294 (282–315)	3f	8.8 (8.1–10.0)	3f	Botswana	43

TABLE 26 (*continued*)

HB	n	T	n	WT	n	Location	Source
		314 (280–380)	23m	11.1 (8.6–13.5)	20m	Zimbabwe	11
		290 (254–330)	23f	9.7 (8.6–11.8)	23f	Zimbabwe	11
715 (630–820)	5f	246 (200–280)	5f			Ethiopia	46
590, 760	2m	270, 310	2m			Ethiopia	46
				13 (10–18)	m	East Africa	7
				11 (8.7–12.5)	f	East Africa	7

Note: HB = head and body length (mm), T = tail length (mm), WT = weight (kg). n = sample size. Sex: m = male, f = female, ? = unknown. Mean values are presented only for sample sizes of three or more. Range of values is in parentheses.

TABLE 27 FREQUENCY OF OCCURRENCE OF PREY ITEMS IN THE DIETS OF SERVALS (PERCENTAGE OF SAMPLES)

Prey items	Ngorongoro Crater[22] Scats (n = 56)	Natal[18] Scats (n = 90)	Salisbury District, Zimbabwe[12] Stomach contents (n = 65)
Otomys angoniensis Vlei rat	42.6	94.4	42
Rhabdomys pumilio Four-striped grass mouse	5.1	75.6	1.4
Dasymys incomtus Shaggy swamp or water rat		10.0	1.4
Mastomys natalensis Multimammate mouse	6.1	13.3	42
Tachyoryctes splendens Mole-rat	0.1	10.0	
Tatera sp. Gerbil		2.2	6
Mus minutoides Pygmy mouse	18.5	5.6	6
Dendromus sp. Climbing mouse		3.3	1.4
Myosorex varius Pygmy shrew		41.1	
Amblysomus hottentotus Golden mole		4.4	
Saccostomus campestris Pouched mouse			4
Steatomys pratensis Fat mouse			3
Aethomys chrysophilus Red veld rat			3
Arvicanthus niloticus Unstriped grass mouse	10.1		
Pelomys fallax Groove-toothed rat	7.2		1.4

(*continued*)

TABLE 27 *(continued)*

Prey items	Ngorongoro Crater[22] Scats (n = 56)	Natal[18] Scats (n = 90)	Salisbury District, Zimbabwe[12] Stomach contents (n = 65)
Crocidura sp.	5.6		
White-toothed shrew			
Rattus rattus			1.4
Black rat			
Thryonomys swinderianus			1.0
Cane rat			
Lepus saxatilis			3
Scrub hare			
Unidentified small mammal		10.0	
Birds	12	23.3	15
Reptiles	8	4.4	12
Amphibians	43		1.4
Minimum number of vertebrate prey items	208	433	95

REFERENCES

1. Rosevear, D. R. 1974. *The carnivores of West Africa.* London: Trustees of the British Museum (Natural History).

2. *Concise Oxford Dictionary of Word Origins*, 1986. Oxford: Clarendon Press.

3. Collier, G. E., and S. J. O'Brien. 1985. A molecular phylogeny of the Felidae: Immunological distance. *Evolution* 39: 473–487.

4. O'Brien, S. J., G. E. Collier, R. E. Benveniste, W. G. Nash, A. K. Newman, J. M. Simonson, M. A. Eichelberger, U. S. Seal, D. Janssen, M. Bush, and D. E. Wildt. 1987. Setting the molecular clock in Felidae: The great cats, *Panthera*. In *Tigers of the world: The biology, biopolitics, management, and conservation of an endangered species*, ed. R. L. Tilson and U. S. Seal, 10–35. Park Ridge, NJ: Noyes Publications.

5. Martin, L. D. 1989. Fossil history of the terrestrial Carnivora. In *Carnivore behavior, ecology, and evolution*, ed. J. L. Gittleman, 536–568. Ithaca, NY: Cornell University Press.

6. Pecon-Slattery, J., and S. J. O'Brien. 1998. Patterns of Y and X chromosome DNA sequence divergence during the Felidae radiation. *Genetics* 148: 1245–1255.

7. Kingdon, J. 1977. *East African mammals*. Vol. 3A. Chicago: University of Chicago Press.

8. York, W. A study of serval melanism in the Aberdares and some general behavioral information. In *The world's cats*, vol. 1, ed. R. L. Eaton, 191–197. Winston, OR: World Wildlife Safari.

9. Leyhausen, P. 1979. *Cat behavior: The predatory and social behavior of domestic and wild cats*. New York: Garland STPM Press.

10. Guggisberg, C. A. W. 1975. *Wild cats of the world*. New York: Taplinger.

11. Smithers, R. H. N. 1978. The serval, *Felis serval* Schreber, 1776. *S. Afr. J. Wildl. Res.* 8: 29–37.

12. Smithers, R. H. N. 1983. *The mammals of the southern African subregion*. Pretoria: University of Pretoria.

13. Visser, J. 1976. Status and conservation of the smaller cats of Southern Africa. In *The world's cats*, vol.3, no. 1, ed. R. L. Eaton,

60–66. Seattle: Carnivore Research Institute, University of Washington.

14. Happold, D. C. D. 1987. *The mammals of Nigeria*. Oxford: Clarendon Press.

15. Stuart, C. T. 1985. The status of two endangered carnivores occurring in the Cape Province, South Africa, *Felis serval* and *Lutra maculicollis*. *Biol. Conserv.* 32: 375–382.

16. Kowalski, K., and B. Rzebik-Kowalska. 1991. *Mammals of Algeria*. Warsaw: Polish Academy of Sciences.

17. Nowell, K., and P. Jackson. 1996. *Wild cats: A status survey and conservation action plan*. Gland, Switzerland: International Union for Conservation of Nature and Natural Resources (IUCN).

18. Bowland, J. M., and M. R. Perrin. 1993. Diet of serval *Felis serval* in a highland region of Natal. *S. Afr. J. Zool.* 28: 132–135.

19. Downs, C. T., J. M. Bowland, A. E. Bowland, and M. R. Perrin. 1991. Thermal parameters of serval *Felis serval* (Felidae) and blackbacked jackal *Canis mesomelas* (Canidae). *J. Thermal Biol.* 16: 277–279.

20. Geertsema, A. A. 1976. Impressions and observations of serval behaviour in Tanzania, East Africa. *Mammalia* 40: 13–19.

21. Geertsema, A. A. 1981. The servals of Gorigor. *Wildl. News* 16 (3): 4–8.

22. Geertsema, A. A. 1985. Aspects of the ecology of the serval *Leptailurus serval* in the Ngorongoro Crater, Tanzania. *Neth. J. Zool.* 35(4): 527–610.

23. van Aarde, R. J., and J. D. Skinner. 1986. Pattern of space use by relocated servals, *Felis serval*. *Afr. J. Ecol.* 24: 97–101.

24. Bowland, J. M. 1990. Servals: Wetland cats. *Endangered Wildlife* 1: 4–5.

25. Stuart, C. T., and V. J. Wilson. 1988. *The cats of Southern Africa*. Bulawayo, Zimbabwe: The Chipangali Wildlife Trust.

26. Lousada, A. 1956. Rearing serval cats. *Country Life* 120: 330–331.

27. Scott, K. W. Jr. 1980. Headlights as a hunting aid for servals in Ethiopia and Kenya. *Mammalia* 44: 271–272.

28. Bowland, J. M. 1990. Diet, home range and movement patterns of serval on farmland in Natal. Master's thesis, University of Natal, Pietermaritzburg, Republic of South Africa.

29. Mellen, J. D. 1989. Reproductive behavior of small captive exotic cats (*Felis* spp.). Ph.D. dissertation, University of California, Davis.

30. Peters, G. 1981. Das schnurren der katzen (Felidae). *Säugetierk. Mitt.* 40: 30–37.

31. Peters, G. 1984. On the structure of friendly close range vocalizations in terrestrial carnivores (Mammalia: Carnivora: Fissipedia). *Z. Säugetierk.* 49: 157–182.

32. Peters, G., and M. H. Hast. 1994. Hyoid structure, laryngeal anatomy, and vocalization in felids (Mammalia: Carnivora: Felidae). *Z. Säugetierk.* 59: 87–104.

33. Peters, G. 1987. Acoustic communication in the genus *Lynx* (Mammalia: Felidae): Comparative survey and phylogenetic interpretation. *Bonn. Zool. Beitr.* 38: 315–330.

34. Buffon, G. L. L., Comte de. 1807. *Buffon's natural history.* Vol. 9. London: H. D. Symonds.

35. Wackernagel, H. 1968. A note on breeding the serval cat at Basle Zoo. *Int. Zoo Yrbk.* 8: 46–47.

36. Seager, S. W. J., and C. N. Demorest. 1978. Reproduction of captive wild carnivores. In *Zoo and wild animal medicine*, ed. M. E. Fowler, 667–706. Philadelphia: W. B. Saunders.

37. Mellen, J. D. 1993. A comparative analysis of scent-marking, social and reproductive behavior in 20 species of small cats (*Felis*). *Am. Zool.* 33: 151–166.

38. Mallinson, J. J. J. 1969. The breeding and study of animals at the Jersey Zoo. *Dodo* 6: 26–30.

39. Andrews, P., Hexagon Farm Wild Feline Breeding Facility, 1187 Merrill Road, San Juan Bautista, CA. Personal communication.

40. Eaton, R. L. 1984. Survey of smaller felid breeding. *Zool. Garten* (n.f.) 54: 101–120.

41. Bloxam, Q. M. C. 1973. The breeding of second generation (F.2) serval cat *Felis leptailurus serval.* The Jersey Wildlife Preservation Trust, Tenth Annual Report, 41–43.

42. Tonkin, B. A. 1972. Notes on longevity in three species of felids. *Int. Zoo Yrbk.* 12: 181–182.

43. Thackeray, J. F., and J. A. Kieser. 1992. *Body mass and carnassial length in modern and fossil carnivores.* Annals of the Transvaal Museum, no. 35.

44. Zambatis, N. 1985. Body measurements of a female serval *Felis serval* Schreber, 1776, from the eastern Transvaal. *Koedoe* 28: 169.

45. Smithers, R. H. N. 1971. *The mammals of Botswana.* Museum Memoir no. 4. Salisbury: The Trustees of the National Museums of Rhodesia.

46. Beadles, J. K., and R. H. Ingersol. 1968. An annotated checklist of the mammal fauna of the Chercher Highlands of Ethiopia present in the museum at the College of Agriculture, HSIU. Experimental Station Bulletin no. 51.

Lynx

Lynx

Though fossil members of the lynx genus are well documented throughout the Pleistocene in Europe, Asia, and North America, whether the group had its origins in North America[1,2,3,4] or the Old World[5] remains a matter of debate. The North American fossil lynxlike cat *Felis rexroadensis*, from the late Pliocene, was intermediate in size between the present-day bobcat and puma, and was probably adapted to forest.[4] Another lynxlike cat, *Lynx issiodorensis*, roamed Europe and northern Asia some 2 million years ago. Thought to have its origins in Africa some 4 million years ago, the Issoire lynx is generally believed to be the ancestor of the Eurasian lynx, Canada lynx, Iberian lynx, and bobcat.[5,6] Most of its limb bones were more robust than those of modern lynx species, and in some cases they were comparable to those of the puma. Though it had lynxlike teeth, the Issoire lynx had a larger head, longer neck, and shorter legs than the modern species, giving it much more of a typical *Felis* build than the long-legged lynxes of today.[2,5,6,7]

In the broader context of felid phylogenetics, lynx are sometimes considered to be closely related to the *Felis* species,[8,9] a view that is supported by an analysis of lynx vocalizations.[10] However, genetic analysis suggests that *Lynx* are more closely related to the *Panthera* group, which includes the roaring cats.[11,12,13]

Because the geographic distributions of the Eurasian lynx and the Iberian lynx once overlapped, the taxonomic status of the Iberian lynx has been the subject of considerable interest. Some authors considered it to be a subspecies of the Eurasian lynx.[14,15] However, according to Kurtén and others, both Eurasian and Iberian lynx were living in southwestern Europe during the Pleistocene without evidence of intermediate forms, suggesting that they were already distinct species.[2,5,16,17] By the eighteenth century the geographic distributions of the two species were separate, presumably due to a contraction of their ranges.[18] Morphologically, the two species differ in many respects,[19,20,21] and recent molecular analysis has confirmed that Iberian lynx are genetically distinct from other lynx species.[22] With fewer than about 300 individuals remaining, this finding makes the Iberian lynx the world's rarest felid species.[23]

REFERENCES

1. Hemmer, H. 1976. Fossil history of living Felidae. In *The world's cats*, Vol. 3(2), ed. R. L. Eaton, 1–14. Seattle, Washington: University of Washington.
2. Kurtén, B. 1968. Pleistocene mammals of Europe. Chicago: Aldine.
3. Glass, G. E., and L. D. Martin. 1978. A multivariate comparison of some extant and fossil Felidae. *Carnivore* 1: 80–87.
4. MacFadden, B. J., and H. Galiano. 1981. Late Hemphillian cat (Mammalia: Felidae) from the Bone Valley Formation of central Florida. *J. Paleontol.* 55: 218–226.
5. Werdelin, L. 1981. The evolution of lynxes. *Ann. Zool. Fennici* 18: 37–71.
6. Kurtén, B. 1978. The lynx from Etouaries, *Lynx issiodorensis* (Croizet and Jobert), late Pliocene. *Ann. Zool. Fennici* 15: 314–322.
7. Hendy, Q. B. 1978. The age of the fossils from Baard's quarry, Langebaanweg, South Africa. *Ann. S. Afr. Mus.* 75: 1–24.
8. Hemmer, H. 1978. The evolutionary systematics of living Felidae: Present status and current problems. *Carnivore* 1: 71–79.
9. Tumlison, R. 1987. *Felis lynx. Mammalian Species* 269: 1–8.
10. Peters, G. 1987. Acoustic communication in the Genus *Lynx* (Mammalia: Felidae): Comparative survey and phylogenetic interpretation. *Bonn. Zool Beitr.* 38: 315–330.
11. Collier, G. E., and S. J. O'Brien. 1985. A molecular phylogeny of the Felidae: Immunological distance. *Evolution* 39: 473–487.
12. Wayne, R. K., R. E. Benveniste, D. N. Janczewski, and S. J. O'Brien. 1989. Molecular and biochemical evolution of the Carnivora. In *Carnivore behavior, ecology, and evolution*, ed. J. L. Gittleman, 465–494. Ithaca, NY: Cornell University Press.

13. Janczewski, D. J., W. S. Modi, J. C. Stephens, and S. J. O'Brien. 1995. Molecular evolution of mitochondrial 12s RNA and cytochrome *b* sequences in the Pantherine lineage of Felidae. *Mol. Biol. Evol.* 12: 690–707.
14. Ellermann, J. R., and T. C. S. Morrison-Scott. 1951. Checklist of Palaearctic and Indian mammals. London: British Museum (Natural History).
15. Corbet, G., and J. E. Hill. 1992. *A world list of mammalian species*. London: The Natural History Museum.
16. van den Brink, F. H. 1970. Distribution and speciation of some carnivores. *Mammal. Rev.* 1: 67–78.
17. Kurtén, B., and E. Granqvist. 1987. Fossil pardel lynx (*Lynx pardina spelaea* Boule) from a cave in southern France. *Ann. Zool. Fennici* 24: 39–43.
18. Kratochvil, J. 1968. Survey of the distribution of populations of the genus *Lynx* in Europe. *Acta Sci. Nat. Brno* 4: 5–12.
19. Werdelin, L. 1990. Taxonomic status of the pardel lynx. *Cat News* 13: 18.
20. García-Perea, R., J. Gisbert, and F. Palacios. 1985. Review of the biometrical and morphological features of the skull of the Iberian lynx, *Lynx pardina* (Temminck, 1824). *Säugetierk. Mitt.* 32: 249–259.
21. García-Perea, R. 1992. New data on the systematics of lynxes. *Cat News* 16: 15–16.
22. Beltrán, J. F., J. E. Rice, and R. L. Honeycutt. 1996. Taxonomy of the Iberian lynx. *Nature* 379: 407–408.
23. Gaona, P., P. Ferreras, and M. Delibes. 1998. Dynamics and viability of a metapopulation of the endangered Iberian lynx (*Lynx pardinus*). *Ecol. Monogr.* 68: 349–370.

Canada lynx

Lynx canadensis Kerr, 1792

DESCRIPTION

The Canada lynx and the Eurasian lynx show parallel trends in size reduction, general shortening of the face, and lengthening of the limbs.[1] However, Eurasian lynx are about twice the size of Canada lynx. The size reduction in Canada lynx is thought to represent an adaptation to feeding almost exclusively on snowshoe hares, whereas Eurasian lynx prefer prey the size of roe deer.[2]

Canada lynx are medium-sized cats, weighing approximately 8 to 11 kilograms, and in several respects they resemble bobcats.[3] Both species typically measure less than a meter in length from the nose to the end of the stubby 10–15-centimeter tail. Both species are muscular, leggy, and stand about 48 to 56 centimeters high at the shoulder, with hindlimbs that are longer than the forelimbs, giving them a tipped-forward appearance. The backs of the ears are black at the base, and the ear tips are prominently marked with an elongated tuft of black hair, a character common to all lynx species.

Canada lynx show little geographic variation in size, although, as with bobcats, the sexes are dimorphic, with males slightly larger and heavier than females. The tail tip is completely black in Canada lynx, a character that distinguishes it from the bobcat, whose tail tip is dark only on the top half. Another distinguishing feature of the Canada lynx is its snowshoe-like feet. The fur covering the paws is long and dense, and the paws can be spread widely, thus providing additional support in soft snow. Lynx paws can support twice the weight of bobcat paws.[4] As in other lynx species, the cheeks of the Canada lynx are fringed with a ruff of long hair. The fur is generally unspotted except for the undersides, which are white and mottled with dark spots. It is this long, light-colored belly fur that is valued by the garment industry. Lynx show little color variation, although in Newfoundland they are a brown or buff-gray color in summer and a uniform grayish color in winter, when the fur is thick and silvered over with hoary tips.[5] In other areas, prime winter pelts are more grizzled grayish brown mixed with buff or pale brown.[6,7,8] No melanistic or black phase is reported for Canada lynx, but there are a few records of "blue lynx."[9,10,11]

DISTRIBUTION

The historic range of the lynx in North America extended from treeline in the Arctic south through the boreal forests of Alaska and Canada and into the

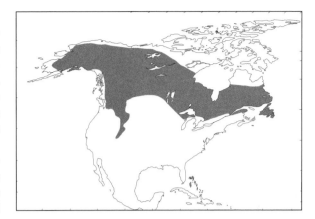

Figure 25. Distribution of the Canada lynx.

northern portions of the United States.[3] Its distribution essentially mirrors that of the snowshoe hare, its principal prey. Within Canada, the lynx still occurs over much of its former range, but it was exterminated from New Brunswick, lower Nova Scotia, and Prince Edward Island, and in the southern provinces it has retreated northward in recent times, apparently in response to timber cutting and habitat changes (fig. 25).[12,13,14,15] Lynx have always been absent from the Great Plains of Alberta, Saskatchewan, and Manitoba. Within the United States, lynx were formerly found at high elevations in the Cascade Mountains of Washington and Oregon and in the Rocky Mountains as far south as Utah.[3,7,16,17,18,19] Lynx are still found in Washington, Idaho, and Montana.[19,20,21] In the Northeast, lynx populations had disappeared by the turn of the twentieth century, except for a small, isolated population in New Hampshire that persisted until the late 1960s.[22] Recently, attempts have been made to reintroduce Canada lynx into New York State.[22,23,24] In other parts of the United States lynx are rare, and their occasional appearances in states as far south as Iowa represent dispersers from population centers in Canada.[25,26,27,28]

ECOLOGY AND BEHAVIOR

Because Canada lynx are so dependent on snowshoe hares as prey, the availability of hares influences all aspects of the natural history of this cat. Lynx are found in a variety of habitat types within the broad belt of boreal forest stretching from Newfoundland to Alaska, but regardless of the habitat type, lynx prefer areas with high hare densities.[4,20,21,29,30,31,32,33,34,35]

Dense forest stands with thickets and tangles of fallen trees and tipped-up roots are used by lynx as shelters from extremely cold temperatures and deep snows.[21,29] In areas where lynx coexist with bobcats and coyotes, lynx are found at higher elevations and in areas with greater snow depth, thus possibly avoiding potential conflicts.[34,35,36,37,38]

Lynx are primarily terrestrial and nocturnal, although they may be found moving about at any time of day.[4,6,39] Snowshoe hares, their principal prey, are basically nocturnal.[40] Much of what is known about lynx movement patterns is derived from tracking individuals in fresh snow. Snow tracking shows that lynx sometimes move rapidly between distant parts of their ranges without stopping or deviating, but when they are hunting, they zigzag, crossing and recrossing areas, circling and probing patches of cover, obviously searching for prey.[36,39,41] Travel rates for lynx range from 0.75 to 1.46 kilometers per hour.[42] At other times lynx may sit or lie in wait, sometimes long enough for the snow to melt and form an ice-encrusted impression of the cat's body. It is not uncommon for a lynx to cover 8 to 9 kilometers a day in these pursuits,[36,39,43] and the distance traveled per day may increase as hare densities decline.[44] Prey are primarily detected by sight, but at other times lynx are apparently first attracted to sounds made by hares.[39]

Feeding Ecology
The daily routine of a lynx differs little from that of other felids, with life revolving largely around finding and catching something to eat. The difference in the lynx's case is that a single prey species, the snowshoe hare, dominates the diet. That the lynx's livelihood was tightly linked to snowshoe hare numbers was first discovered from fur trapping records of the Hudson's Bay Company.[45,46,47] Since the 1950s numerous studies have been initiated to try to understand the relationship between these two species.[35,42,44,48,49,50,51,52,53] The snowshoe hare exhibits a population cycle, in which consecutive highs and consecutive lows occur predictably at about 10-year intervals. Population densities typically peak at 100–400 hares per square kilometer, with recorded maximums of 2,000–4,000. Likewise, when hare populations are at the low in the cycle, densities may be only 3–30 hares per square kilometer. Lynx densities follow the availability of hares, but there is usually a one- or two-year time lag in their response to changes in hare densities.

Hares often make up 60 to 97 percent of the lynx's diet, and at times the cat eats little else.[36,39,42,43,54] On Cape Breton Island, Nova Scotia, for example, lynx were observed attempting to capture prey on 200 occasions, 198 of which involved hares; thirty-four of the thirty-six prey killed were hares.[36] Similarly, snowshoe hares were almost the only prey pursued (94 percent) and killed (91 percent) in the winter by lynx in the southwestern part of the Yukon Territory.[34] Incidental prey in winter often include grouse and squirrels, but lynx also consume carrion or scavenge carcasses, which accounts for the appearance of moose and deer in scats. The summer diets of lynx are more diverse and typically include a large number of small birds and microtine rodents (voles or meadow mice, members of the genus *Microtus*), but hares still contribute more than half the meat consumed.[4,39,54] Similarly, when hare numbers declined in the Yukon, lynx switched to preying more on red squirrels; at one point, squirrels contributed 44 percent of the biomass eaten, although hares remained the preferred prey.[35]

Ungulates do not figure prominently in the lynx's diet other than as carrion, although there are a few references to lynx killing adult mule deer, caribou, and even Dall sheep.[39,54,55,56] A notable exception occurred in Newfoundland, where lynx switched to preying on caribou calves when the hare population crashed.[57] Lynx did not attack the calves in the open, but waited in cover at the edge of the calving ground for an unwary calf to approach. Calves were seized by the neck and dragged into cover, but the lynx were not able to actually kill most of the calves they attacked, and the calves died later of a bacterial infection transmitted in the lynx's saliva. About a quarter of all caribou calf deaths during this period occurred within the first two weeks after birth, when the calves weighed about 10 kilograms. Mortality rates declined as the calves got bigger, and there were few attacks on calves more than five months old. When the snowshoe hare population rebounded, lynx switched back to their main prey, and caribou calf survival rates increased.

Like other felids, lynx employ a variety of methods to capture prey, and their methods may change as conditions vary. In Newfoundland when hare numbers were high, lynx made about 60 percent of kills from ambush, pouncing on hares as they came by,[39] but this method was not effective in Alberta when hare density was low.[43] During a low in hare numbers in the Yukon, lynx hunted more often from ambush than by actively searching for prey. Neither method was more successful than the other, but hunting from ambush was thought to be more energy-efficient during periods of low prey density.[35] In an area of the southern Yukon with relatively high hare densities and dense vegetation, lynx frequently tried to ambush hares, but with little success. This observation suggests, as have others, that lynx hunting success is more dependent on stalking conditions than upon hare densities or habitat type.[4,31,34,57] Indeed, some areas with high hare densities may have such dense vegetation that lynx are less successful in these habitats than in more open areas with lower prey densities.[35,58]

Lynx occasionally hunt cooperatively. Several accounts describe groups of two to four lynx walking single file in the snow across forest openings or areas with low prey abundance, and then fanning out and moving through the area on a common front, flushing hares to other group members. In most cases these are probably family groups.[4,39,58] A researcher in Glacier National Park, Montana, watched an adult lynx circle around a talus slope inhabited by marmots and ground squirrels while another adult and a juvenile concealed themselves among the boulders at the bottom of the slope. The lynx approached openly from above, scattering the marmots and squirrels; one squirrel dashed downslope and into the claws of the adult waiting below. All three cats then fed on the kill.[59] The only other observation of lynx hunting in adult groups is from the Yukon.[35]

Hares may be eaten where killed or taken to another site, which may be close by or several hundred meters away. On Cape Breton Island, lynx first opened the thoracic cavity of hares, then fed on the organs, foreshoulders, and neck, consuming most of the hare while alternating between feeding and resting near the kill. The stomach and intestines were not eaten, nor were the front and hind paws.[36] Estimates of the amount eaten daily by a lynx vary from 600 grams to 1,200 grams, which is equivalent to about one hare every day or every other day.[30,36,39]

Lynx sometimes cache the uneaten parts of their kills, covering them with snow or leaves. On Cape Breton Island, only ten of thirty-four (29 percent) hare carcasses were cached; the remains of the others were left scattered on the surface.[36] In Alberta, caching behavior was related to hunting success. In years when hares were easily caught, twelve caches were found along 195 kilometers of trails, whereas when hares were difficult to catch, no caches were found along 225 kilometers of trails.[43] In the Yukon, lynx typically cached only portions of hares; only one of seven cached carcasses observed was whole. Lynx returned within a day or two to six of these seven carcasses and ate them.[42]

Based on snow tracking observations, lynx kill an average of one hare per day to one every two days,[6,36,39,42,43] but their success rates are highly variable. In the Yukon, when hare numbers were increasing, an individual lynx made six kills in eleven attempts (a success rate of 54.5 percent).[58] When hare numbers in the Yukon were low, success rates of lynx varied from 20 to 22 percent.[42] During a hare population peak in Newfoundland, lynx had a success rate of 42 percent.[39] In other studies, lynx hunting success rates for hares varied from 9 to 36 percent.[31,34,36]

A variety of factors are implicated in the yearly and seasonal differences in lynx hunting success rates, including changing hare densities, individual differences, differences in age or experience, group size, familiarity with the area, and changing environmental conditions. However, as Nellis and Keith[43] and others suggest, success is importantly related to the distance between the lynx and the hare when it begins to run and to the relative speeds attained by predator and prey. How close a lynx can get to a hare depends on its own skill, available cover, the alertness of the hare, and probably other conditions as well. Once the lynx has gotten as close as possible, catching the hare requires speed, which depends on the cat's jump rate and the distance per jump. Results from several studies show lynx leaping 1.5 to 2.5 meters per jump, but they were generally more successful the fewer jumps they had to make.[34,39,43] Lynx on Cape Breton Island, however, made more jumps per successful capture (11.1) than for unsuccessful chases (8.4), covering 24 meters in the chase versus 16.3 meters, respectively.[36]

The highest hunting success rates of lynx are achieved by groups, with the study on Cape Breton Island reporting success rates for groups of one, two, three, and four cats averaging 14 percent, 17 percent, 38 percent, and 55 percent, respectively.[36] The high success rate (42 percent) reported for lynx in Newfoundland[39] may be related to the inclusion of a large amount of group hunting data. In the Yukon lynx hunted in groups of one to five, and while female-kitten groups generally killed hares more frequently than single cats, the return per individual was lower. However, the return per individual for adult groups, in which every cat was an accomplished hunter, was higher than that of single animals.[35]

What effect lynx predation has on snowshoe hare populations depends on where the hare populations are in their cycle. Furthermore, since lynx population density and structure change with the hare cycle, but with a one- to two-year time lag, the effect of predation can be quite variable.[35,42] Studies in Alberta estimate that lynx are a significant factor in overwinter mortality of hares, accounting for about 20 percent of winter losses during a low in the hare cycle.[30] A recent field experiment in the southern Yukon using mammalian predator exclosures resulted in a sixfold increase in hare densities during a low phase of the cycle, with lynx being the most important mammalian predator excluded. The effect of the exclosures on hare densities during the peak phase was negligible.[53] In contrast, the effect of fluctuating hare densities on lynx population dynamics is dramatic at both highs and lows in the hare cycle.

Social Organization

Despite numerous studies of lynx food habits and of the responses of lynx populations to changing prey abundances, remarkably little is known about the social system of the Canada lynx. The Cape Breton study refers to gatherings of lynx at open areas in spruce bogs, where tracks in the snow indicated considerable play activity. These gatherings were apparently frequent enough to suggest that they were more than chance encounters.[36] Gatherings of lynx have not been reported elsewhere, but there are references to Eurasian lynx meeting at a central place for mating purposes.[60,61]

Most studies indicate that lynx are solitary and that the only prolonged association is between a female and her offspring. Lynx spatial arrangements, however, appear to be more variable than those of other felids, and home ranges run the gamut from complete overlap between same-sex adults to exclusive ranges for both males and females.[21,27,30,31,41,44,62,63]

Variations in the land tenure systems of lynx are undoubtedly influenced by the cyclical nature of the prey base. At low hare densities, the system may collapse altogether as lynx abandon their ranges and wander widely in search of food.[62,64,65] Whether any lynx stay on their ranges during such lows is uncertain, but it is suggested that there is a "core population" that maintains territories throughout the cycle.[65,66]

The maintenance of stable spatial arrangements among lynx is also likely to be disrupted by trapping, which occurs regularly across most of the lynx's geographic range. The removal of residents alters any established relationships among neighbors and greatly modifies the age and sex structure of the population.[65,67] The effects of trapping on lynx social dynamics are not clear, but at moderate to high levels of trapping, they are unlikely to be neutral. One study found that lynx numbers increased at high hare densities despite relatively heavy trapping losses (40 percent of the population),[68] whereas in another area a lynx population could not sustain itself even at high hare densities after it had been overexploited by a decade of intense trapping.[33]

Snowshoe hare abundance can fluctuate widely, reaching 2,300 hares per square kilometer one year and then plummeting to 12 per square kilometer a few years later.[69,70] Because lynx are so dependent on hares as food, it is not surprising that lynx densities also fluctuate, varying from 1 to 44.9 lynx per 100 square kilometers, which at the highest densities typically includes adults, yearlings, and kittens.[4,31,33,42,71] Within areas of favorable habitat, lynx can attain, at least for several years, incredibly high densities, up to 44.9 per 100 square kilometers in an untrapped refugium.[65] At low hare densities few young lynx survive, and the remaining adults may concentrate in small, localized pockets or wander widely.

The sizes of areas used by lynx also vary, ranging from 3 to 783 square kilometers, but most lynx ranges are relatively small, measuring 15 to 50 square kilometers. Male ranges are usually larger than female ranges.[3,6,21,33,62] Studies in central Alberta and the Yukon found no significant correlation between lynx home range size and snowshoe hare densities or lynx densities,[31,65] although results from other areas suggest that lynx home range sizes are closely tied to hare densities and that lynx home ranges are typically larger in areas where there are few hares.[44,62]

Range sizes of lynx along the southern periphery of their geographic distribution tend to be larger than those in other parts of their distribution, suggesting that these areas are marginal habitats. Hare populations in the south, primarily in the mountainous regions of the western United States, do not cycle, and hare densities remain low, presumably because of predation.[72,73,74] In central Washington, at lynx densities of two to three per 100 square kilometers, the average home range size of lynx was 39 square kilometers for females and 69 square kilometers for males.[21] These ranges are somewhat smaller than those in Minnesota (51–243 square kilometers),[27] Montana (43–122 square kilometers),[20] and Manitoba (138–221 square kilometers),[63] all areas with low lynx densities.

Through all these changes lynx maintain a solitary

lifestyle, avoiding prolonged associations, but with relatively little strife. In the Northwest Territories, most social interactions between lynx were classified as neutral, with lynx showing neither avoidance nor attraction, even between individuals with extensive home range overlap.[62] This passive system is probably maintained through indirect means, with scent marks providing both the spatial and temporal information needed to reduce the possibility of encounters and to bring animals together.[62,75]

Remarkably little information is available on scent marking by lynx. In Newfoundland adult lynx were found to leave their feces uncovered in prominent locations; some locations contained groups of four to ten scats, all of different ages. When snow cover was absent, lynx often deposited their feces on top of stumps, logs, or moss clumps. Kittens buried their feces. Adults also urinated frequently as they moved about their ranges, with seventeen to twenty urinations per mile being recorded on several occasions.[39] Urine marks probably convey information on the cat's identity, age, and sexual status as well as when the mark was made.

In captivity, a variety of scent-marking behaviors are reported for Canada lynx, including urine spraying by both sexes, cheek and head rubbing on objects, claw raking, and flehmen (open-mouthed grimace) by males; scraping with the hind feet is surprisingly absent.[76,77]

Reproduction and Development

Lynx obviously associate for mating, but the breeding season is short, lasting for only about a month.[6,78] Details of lynx mating behavior are scant, but, as reported for the Eurasian lynx, receptivity is probably preceded by an increase in urine marking and calling, with these advertisements functioning to bring the sexes together at the appropriate time. Female lynx are presumed to be induced ovulators,[29] but this may vary depending on population densities, with females being induced ovulators when mates are sparse and spontaneous ovulators when they are abundant.[79] The estrous cycle is about a month long,[80] and in captivity estrus lasts for three to five days.[81] With a breeding season of approximately a month, females probably have only a single estrous cycle. Gestation length is sixty-three to sixty-four days,[6,81] or possibly as long as seventy days.[29]

Litter sizes in lynx range from one to eight kittens. Unlike most other felids, they show considerable reproductive flexibility. Lynx ovulation rates, pregnancy rates, and litter sizes decrease when hares are scarce and increase when they are abundant.[65,82,83] At a peak in hare abundance (7.4 hares per hectare) in the southwestern Yukon, the mean litter size for adult females was 5.3 and for yearling females, 4.2. When prey densities declined the following year, adult litter size decreased to 4.9, and no yearling females produced kittens. In the third year, when hare density was 1.3 per hectare, no adults or yearlings produced a litter.[80] Similarly, just after a peak in hare abundance in the Northwest Territories, the mean litter size of adult females was 4.0. Two years later there was no sign of successful reproduction.[71] On Cape Breton Island, 67 percent of yearlings bred during a year with high hare densities, but two years later, when hare densities had declined markedly, no yearlings bred.[4] During a low in hare densities in central Alberta, litter size averaged 1.3, increasing to 3.5 as hare densities increased.[31] At the prey low, only 33 percent of adult females conceived, compared with 73 percent when hares were abundant.[82] Even when females do produce kittens during years when prey abundance is low, infant mortality rates are high (60–95 percent), with kittens dying of starvation or nutritional stress–related factors.[4,21,30,65,82]

Reproductive activity in lynx is highly seasonal, with breeding occurring in most areas from March until early April.[6,29,71,80] In central Alberta, conception occurs in April–May.[30] Correspondingly, in most areas young are born in May–June. In the southwestern Yukon, the mean date of birth for adult females was 24 May; yearling females had their young in mid-June.[65] In Newfoundland the birth peak is around 23–24 May.[29]

Little is known about den site selection, but in Alaska three birth dens were found in tangles of blown-down spruce trees or under tree roots, and the sites typically offered good visibility in several directions.[41] Similarly, in north-central Washington, four birth dens were located in mature conifer stands containing large numbers of fallen logs; all the dens had a northern-northeastern exposure.[21]

As in other felids, the arrival of kittens is marked by a characteristic home range contraction and a focus of the female's movements on the den site.[65,71,80] Details of early maternal behavior are not known. At birth the kittens weigh about 175 to 235 grams.[29,65,80] They are born helpless, with closed eyes, folded ears, and a grayish buffy fur that is marked with dark streaks on the back, flanks, and limbs.[84] As with many aspects of the lynx's natural history, kitten growth and development are related to the availability of hares. When food is abundant, kittens grow rapidly, their eyes open by fourteen days of age, and they are weaned by twelve weeks. By midwinter they will weigh 4.5 kilograms. When food is in short supply, growth is retarded and few young survive.[6,65,82]

Kittens begin following their mother at five weeks of age,[80] and are actively participating in the hunt by as early as seven months of age.[4] In Newfoundland young lynx did not attempt to make their own kills until they were nine to ten months old.[29] On Cape Breton Island a young lynx that was suspected of having lost its mother early in the winter had the unusual habit of diving blindly under snow-covered conifer boughs in what was interpreted as an unsuccessful attempt to surprise hares. An increase in the hunting success of lynx on the island from 14 percent in January to 26 percent in April was thought to reflect the improved hunting skills of younger lynx.[36]

Kittens remain with their mother until they are about ten months old, but do not attain adult size until they are two years of age.[4,21] Nevertheless, when prey are abundant, females may breed for the first time at ten months; otherwise, breeding occurs at twenty-two to twenty-three months of age. At high hare densities most female lynx are likely to breed every year, but based on histological differences in reproductive tracts, there is a suggestion that females living in areas where hares are scarce may breed every other year.[3,21] Sexual maturity in males is probably not attained until the second or third year.[29,82] Some young adult females have been observed to establish a breeding range next to or inside the home range of their mothers.[65]

As with other aspects of lynx population dynamics, the pattern of dispersal varies with the snowshoe hare cycle. A recent study of lynx dispersal in the Northwest Territories shows that at high or peak hare numbers the majority of dispersers are yearlings and subadults, whereas at low hare numbers most dispersers are adults, as few young would have survived to dispersal age. Lynx dispersed as early as ten to eleven months of age, but most animals were sixteen to seventeen months old when they left home. In this study, the mean age of dispersing adults was 3.3 years. Dispersal distances averaged 163 kilometers and ranged from 17 to 930 kilometers; mean dispersal distances did not differ by sex, age, or social status.[64]

Lynx have been recorded dispersing over incredibly long distances, and several different studies in different areas report dispersal distances of 100 to 1,000 kilometers.[44,76,85] In the Yukon Territory, eleven dispersing lynx traveled more than 500 kilometers, and two others moved more than 1,000 kilometers.[65]

Mortality rates for young and adult lynx alike vary dramatically depending on the hare cycle, with natural mortality being low when hares are abundant.[42,65,71,80,82] Natural mortality is high everywhere when hares have declined, but longevity may be higher in untrapped areas. In one such refugium at least eight lynx were in residence for more than four years, and one female lived to be fourteen years and eleven months old.[65]

STATUS IN THE WILD
In Canada, the lynx has been extirpated from Prince Edward Island and mainland Nova Scotia. It is considered endangered in New Brunswick. Over the remainder of its range in Canada and the United States, its status is considered satisfactory.

The lynx is managed and trapped for its fur across much of Canada, and the harvest is regulated through trapping concessions, closed seasons, and quotas. There is some concern that lynx populations can be overtrapped during hare declines; proposed solutions include suspension of harvest during the low years of the cycle and the establishment of refuge areas where lynx are not trapped. Habitat modification does not seem to have had a significant effect on lynx populations.[86]

CONSERVATION EFFORTS
Efforts to reestablish Canada lynx in upstate New York have not bseen very successful. Of eighty-three lynx released over three winters, many have died, and there has been no evidence of successful reproduction.[23,24] Similarly, 20 of 41 lynx released near Vail, Colorado, in 1999 died within the first year of release. An additional 55 lynx were released near Vail in 2000.[87,88]

While lynx are abundant in northern Canada and Alaska, there are probably fewer than 200 lynx in the continental United States. In an effort to help protect the lynx, the U.S. Fish and Wildlife Service listed it as a threatened species in 2000. This action will ban hunting or trapping of lynx and prohibit other actions that may be detrimental to the lynx or its habitat.

TABLE 28 MEASUREMENTS AND WEIGHTS OF ADULT CANADA LYNX

HB	n	T	n	WT	n	Location	Source
892 (737–1,067)	96m	104 (50–127)	96 m	10.7 (6.3–17.3)	93m	Newfoundland	5
844 (762–965)	89f	97 (76–122)	95f	8.6 (5.0–11.8)	91f	Newfoundland	5

Note: HB = head and body length (mm); T = tail length (mm); WT = weight (kg). n = sample size. Sex: m = male, f = female, ? = unknown. Mean values are presented only for sample sizes of three or more. Range of values is in parentheses.

TABLE 29 FREQUENCY OF OCCURRENCE OF PREY ITEMS IN THE DIETS OF CANADA LYNX (PERCENTAGE OF SAMPLES)

Prey items	Newfoundland[39] Stomachs and scats ($n = 426$)	Alberta, Canada[31] Scats ($n = 101$) Hares abundant	Alberta, Canada[31] Scats ($n = 123$) Hares scarce
Lepus americanus Snowshoe hare	73	76.2	66.7
Small rodents	14	19.8	4.1
Other rodents	3		10.6
Birds	21	3	8.9
Carrion	20	0.9	5.7
Domestic animals	2		
Miscellaneous animals		3.0	4.1
Minimum number of vertebrate prey items	582	101	123

REFERENCES

1. Kurtén, B., and E. Anderson. 1980. *Pleistocene mammals of North America.* New York: Columbia University Press.

2. Werdelin, L. 1981. The evolution of lynxes. *Ann. Zool. Fennici* 18: 37–71.

3. McCord, C. M., and J. E. Cardoza. 1982. Bobcat and lynx. In *Wild mammals of North America,* ed. J. A. Chapman and G. A. Feldhamer, 728–766. Baltimore: Johns Hopkins University Press.

4. Parker, G. R., J. W. Maxwell, L. D. Morton, and G. E. J. Smith. 1983. The ecology of the lynx (*Lynx canadensis*) on Cape Breton Island. *Can. J. Zool.* 61: 770–786.

5. Saunders, J. K. Jr. 1964. Physical characteristics of the Newfoundland lynx. *J. Mammal.* 45: 36–47.

6. Quinn, N. W. S., and G. Parker. 1987. Lynx. In *Wild furbearer management and conservation in North America,* ed. M. Nowak, J. A. Barker, M. E. Obbard, and B. Malloch, 683–694. Ontario: Ontario Trappers Association.

7. Durant, S. D. 1952. *Mammals of Utah.* University of Kansas Publications, Museum of Natural History, vol. 6. 549 pp.

8. Jackson, H. H. T. 1961. *Mammals of Wisconsin.* Madison: University of Wisconsin Press.

9. Jones, S. V. H. 1923. Color variations in wild animals. *J. Mammal.* 4: 172–177.

10. Schwarz, E. 1938. Blue or dilute mutation in Alaskan lynx. *J. Mammal.* 19: 376.

11. Calahane, V. H. 1947. *Mammals of North America.* New York: Macmillan.

12. Rand, A. L. 1944. The recent status of Nova Scotia furbearers. *Can. Field Nat.* 58: 85–96.

13. DeVos, A., and S. E. Matel. 1952. The status of the lynx in Canada, 1920–1952. *J. Forestry* 50: 742–745.

14. van Zyll de Jong, C. G. 1971. The status and management of the Canada lynx in Canada. In *Proceedings of a symposium on the native cats of North America, their status and management,* ed. S. E. Jorgenson and L. D. Mech, 16–22. Twin Cites, MN: U.S. Department of Interior.

15. Banfield, A. W. F. 1974. *The mammals of Canada.* Toronto: University of Toronto Press.

16. Rust, H. J. 1946. Mammals of northern Idaho. *J. Mammal.* 27: 308–327.

17. Ingles, L. G. 1945. *Mammals of the Pacific states.* Stanford: Stanford University Press.

18. Hoffman, R. S., P. L. Wright, and F. E. Newly. 1969. The distribution of some mammals in Montana. Part 1: Mammals other than bats. *J. Mammal.* 50: 579–604.

19. Nellis, C. H. 1971. The lynx in the Northwest. In *Proceedings of a symposium on the native cats of North America, their status and management,* ed. S. E. Jorgenson and L. D. Mech, 24–28. Twin Cites, MN: U.S. Department of Interior.

20. Brainerd, S. M. 1985. Reproductive ecology of bobcats and lynx in western Montana. Master's thesis, University of Montana, Missoula.

21. Koehler, G. M. 1990. Population and habitat characteristics

of lynx and snowshoe hares in north central Washington. *Can. J. Zool.* 68: 845–851.

22. Brocke, R. H. 1982. Restoration of the lynx *Felis canadensis* in Adirondack Park: A problem analysis and recommendations. Federal Aid Project E-1-3 and W-105-R. New York Department of Environmental Conservation. 77 pp.

23. Brocke, R. H., K. A. Gustafson, and A. R. Major. 1990. Restoration of lynx in New York: Biopolitical lessons. *Trans. N.A. Wildl. Nat. Res. Conf.* 55: 590–598.

24. Brocke, R. H., K. Gustafson, and L. B. Fox. 1991. Restoration of large predators: Potentials and problems. In *Challenges in the conservation of biological resources*, ed. D. J. Decker, M. E. Krasny, G. R. Goff, C. R. Smith, and D. W. Gross, 303–315. San Francisco: Westview Press.

25. Rasmussen, J. L. 1969. A recent record of the lynx in Iowa. *J. Mammal.* 50: 370–371.

26. Gunderson, H. L. 1978. A mid-continent irruption of Canada lynx, 1962–63. *Prairie Nat.* 10: 71–80.

27. Mech, L. D. 1973. Canadian lynx invasion of Minnesota. *Biol. Conserv.* 5: 151–152.

28. Mech, L. D. 1980. Age, sex, reproduction, and spatial organization of lynxes colonizing northeastern Minnesota. *J. Mammal.* 61: 261–267.

29. Saunders, J. K. Jr. 1961. The biology of the Newfoundland lynx (*Lynx canadensis subsolanus*, Bangs). Ph.D. dissertation, Cornell University, Ithaca, New York.

30. Nellis, C. H., S. P. Wetmore, and L. B. Keith. 1972. Lynx-prey interactions in central Alberta. *J. Wildl. Mgmt.* 36: 320–329.

31. Brand, C. J., L. B. Keith, and C. A. Fischer. 1976. Lynx responses to changing snowshoe hare densities in central Alberta. *J. Wildl. Mgmt.* 40: 416–428.

32. Koehler, G. M., M. G. Hornocker, and H. S. Hash. 1979. Lynx movement and habitat use in Montana. *Can. Field Nat.* 93: 441–442.

33. Bailey, T. N., E. E. Bangs, M. F. Portner, J. C. Malloy, and R. J. McAvinchey. 1986. An apparent overexploited lynx population on the Kenai Peninsula, Alaska. *J. Wildl. Mgmt.* 50: 279–290.

34. Murray, D. L., S. Boutin, and M. O'Donoghue. 1994. Winter habitat selection by lynx and coyotes in relation to snowshoe hare abundance. *Can. J. Zool.* 72: 1444–1451.

35. O'Donoghue, M., S. Boutin, C. J. Krebs, D. L. Murray, and E. J. Hofer. 1998. Behavioural responses of coyotes and lynx to the snowshoe hare cycle. *Oikos* 82: 169–183.

36. Parker, G. R. 1981. Winter habitat use and hunting activities of lynx (*Lynx canadensis*) on Cape Breton Island, Nova Scotia. In *Worldwide furbearer conference proceedings*, ed. J. A. Chapman and D. Pursley, 221–248. Falls Church, VA: R. R. Donnelley and Sons.

37. Smith, D. S. 1984. Habitat use, home range, and movements of bobcats in western Montana. Master's thesis, University of Montana, Missoula.

38. Murray, D. L., and S. Boutin. 1991. The influence of snow on lynx and coyote movements: Does morphology affect behavior? *Oecologia* 88: 463–469.

39. Saunders, J. K. Jr. 1963. Movements and activities of the lynx in Newfoundland. *J. Wildl. Mgmt.* 27: 390–400.

40. Bittner, S. L., and O. J. Rongstad. 1982. Snowshoe hares and allies. In *Wild mammals of North America*, ed. J. A. Chapman and G. A. Feldhamer, 146–163. Baltimore: Johns Hopkins University Press.

41. Berrie, P. M. 1973. Ecology and status of the lynx in interior Alaska. In *The world's cats*, ed. R. L. Eaton, 4–41. Winston, OR: World Wildlife Safari.

42. O'Donoghue, M., S. Boutin, C. J. Krebs, G. Zuleta, D. L Murray, and E. J. Hofer. 1998. Functional responses of coyotes and lynx to the snowshoe hare cycle. *Ecology* 79(4): 1193–1208.

43. Nellis, C. H., and L. B. Keith. 1968. Hunting activities and success of lynxes in Alberta. *J. Wildl. Mgmt.* 32: 718–722.

44. Ward, R. M. P., and C. J. Krebs. 1985. Behavioural responses of lynx to declining snowshoe hare abundance. *Can. J. Zool.* 63: 2817–2824.

45. Elton, C. 1933. The Canadian snowshoe rabbit enquiry, 1931–32. *Can. Field Nat.* 47: 63–86.

46. MacLulich, D. A. 1937. *Fluctuations in the numbers of varying hare* (*Lepus americanus*). University of Toronto Studies. Biological Series, no. 43. 136 pp.

47. Elton, C., and M. Nicholson. 1942. The ten-year cycle in numbers of the lynx in Canada. *J. Anim. Ecol.* 11: 215–244.

48. Wing, L. W. 1953. Cycles of lynx abundance. *J. Cycle Res.* 2: 28–51.

49. Moran, P. A. P. 1953. The statistical analysis of the Canadian lynx cycle. *Aust. J. Zool.* 1: 163–173.

50. Keith, L. B. 1963. *Wildlife's ten-year cycle*. Madison: University of Wisconsin Press.

51. Keith, L. B. 1990. Dynamics of snowshoe hare populations. In *Current mammalogy*, ed. H. H. Genoways, 119–195. New York: Plenum Press.

52. Bulmer, M. G. 1974. A statistical analysis of the 10-year cycle in Canada. *J. Anim. Ecol.* 43: 701–718.

53. Krebs, C. J., S. Boutin, R. Boonstra, A. R. E. Sinclair, J. N. M. Smith, M. R. T. Dale, K. Martin, and R. Turkington. 1995. Impact of food and predation on the snowshoe hare cycle. *Science* 269: 1112–1115.

54. van Zyll de Jong, C. G. 1966. Food habits of the lynx in Alberta and Mackenzie District, N.W.T. *Can. Field Nat.* 80: 18–23.

55. Seton, E. T. 1929. *Lives of game animals*. Vol. 1, part 1, *Cats, wolves, and foxes*. New York: Doubleday, Doran.

56. Bailey, V. 1936. *The mammals and life zones of Oregon*. North American Fauna, no. 55. 416 pp.

57. Bergerud, A. T. 1983. Prey switching in a simple ecosystem. *Sci. Am.* 249: 130–141.

58. Major, A. R. 1989. Lynx *Lynx canadensis canadensis* (Kerr) predation patterns and habitat use in the Yukon Territory, Canada. Master's thesis, State University of New York, Syracuse.

59. Barash, D. P. 1971. Cooperative hunting in the lynx. *J. Mammal.* 52: 480.

60. Werner, K. F. 1953. Beiträge zur Freilandbiologie des südosteuropäischen luchses, *Lynx l. lynx* (Linné 1758). *Säugetierk. Mitt.* 1: 104–110.

61. Haglund, B. 1966. Winter habits of the lynx (*Lynx lynx* L.) and wolverine (*Gulo gulo* L.) as revealed by tracking in the snow. *Viltrevy* 4: 1–299.

62. Poole, K. G. 1995. Spatial organization of a lynx population. *Can. J. Zool.* 73: 632–641.

63. Carbyn, L. N., and D. Patriquin. 1983. Observations on home range sizes, movements and social organization of lynx, *Lynx canadensis*, in Riding Mountain National Park, Manitoba. *Can. Field Nat.* 97: 262–267.

64. Poole, K. G. 1997. Dispersal patterns of lynx in the Northwest Territories. *J. Wildl. Mgmt.* 61(2): 497–505.

65. Slough, B. G., and G. Mowat. 1996. Lynx population dynamics in an untrapped refugium. *J. Wildl. Mgmt.* 60(4): 946–961.

66. Breitenmoser, U., B. G. Slough, and C. Breitenmoser-Würsten. 1993. Predators of cyclic prey: Is the Canada lynx victim or profiteer of the snowshoe hare cycle? *Oikos* 66: 551–554.

67. Quinn, N. W. S., and J. E. Thompson. 1985. Age and sex of trapped lynx, *Felis canadensis*, related to period of capture and trapping technique. *Can. Field Nat.* 99: 267–269.

68. Quinn, N. W. S., and J. E. Thompson. 1987. Dynamics of an exploited Canada lynx population in Ontario. *J. Wildl. Mgmt.* 51: 297–305.

69. Keith, L. B., and J. D. Waring. 1956. Evidence of orientation and homing in snowshoe hares. *Can. J. Zool.* 34: 579–581.

70. Green, R. G., and C. A. Evans. 1940. Studies on a population cycle of snowshoe hares on the Lake Alexander area. Part 1, Gross annual census, 1932–1939. *J. Wildl. Mgmt.* 4: 220–238.

71. Poole, K. G. 1994. Characteristics of an unhunted lynx population during a snowshoe hare decline. *J. Wildl. Mgmt.* 58: 608–618.

72. Wolff, J. O. 1980. The role of habitat patchiness in the population dynamics of snowshoe hares. *Ecol. Monogr.* 50: 111–130.

73. Dolbeer, R. A., and W. R. Clark. 1975. Population ecology of snowshoe hares in the central Rocky Mountains. *J. Wildl. Mgmt.* 39: 535–549.

74. Windberg, L. A., and L. B. Keith. 1978. Snowshoe hare populations in woodlot habitat. *Can. J. Zool.* 56: 1071–1080.

75. Brittell, J. D., R. J. Poelker, S. J. Sweeney, and G. M. Koehler. 1989. *Native cats of Washington,* Section III: *Lynx.* Olympia: Washington Department of Wildlife.

76. Wemmer, C., and K. Scow. 1977. Communication in the Felidae with emphasis on scent marking and contact patterns. In *How animals communicate,* ed. T. A. Sebeok, 749–766. Bloomington: Indiana University Press.

77. Mellen, J. D. 1993. A comparative analysis of scent-marking, social and reproductive behavior in 20 species of small cats (*Felis*). *Am. Zool.* 33: 151–166.

78. Tumlison, R. 1987. *Felis lynx. Mammalian Species* 269: 1–8.

79. Kitchener, A. 1991. *The natural history of the wild cats.* Ithaca, NY: Cornell University Press.

80. Mowat, G., B. G. Slough, and S. Boutin. 1996. Lynx recruitment during a snowshoe hare population peak and decline in southwest Yukon. *J. Wildl. Mgmt.* 60: 441–452.

81. Andrews, P., Hexagon Farm Wild Feline Breeding Facility, 1187 Merrill Road, San Juan Bautista, CA. Personal communication.

82. Brand, C. J., and L. B. Keith. 1979. Lynx demography during a snowshoe hare decline in Alberta. *J. Wildl. Mgmt.* 43: 827–849.

83. O'Connor, R. M. 1986. Reproduction and age distribution of female lynx in Alaska, 1961–1971—preliminary results. In *Cats of the world: Biology, conservation, and management,* ed. S. D. Miller and D. D. Everett, 311–325. Washington, DC: National Wildlife Federation.

84. Merriam, C. H. 1886. Description of a newly born lynx. *Bull. Nat. Hist. Soc. New Brunswick* 5: 10–13.

85. O'Donoghue, M., E. Hofer, and F. I. Doyle. 1995. Predator versus predator. *Nat. Hist.* 10: 6–9.

86. Nowell, K., and P. Jackson. 1996. *Wild cats: A status survey and conservation action plan.* Gland, Switzerland: International Union for Conservation of Nature and Natural Resources (IUCN).

87. Byrne, G., and T. Shenk. 1999. Canadian lynx. *Reintroduction News* 18: 15–17.

88. Foster, D. 2000. Lynx thrive after 2 months in the wild. *Denver Rocky Mountain News,* June 30.

Eurasian lynx

Lynx lynx (Linnaeus, 1758)

DESCRIPTION

The Eurasian lynx is also known as the European, boreal, Palearctic, and northern lynx. In his 1842 "Monograph of the Species of Lynx," Edward Blyth describes the Eurasian lynx as neatly as anyone since, saying, "In general, they are light-made animals, with contracted flanks, and rather high on the limbs, and the fur of most of them is in winter long and very dense."[1]

With its short back, stubby tail, and ear tufts, the Eurasian lynx looks like a bobcat, except that it is much larger, longer-legged, and has bigger feet. Eurasian lynx look distinctly "leggy," with exceptionally tall individuals measuring more than 70 centimeters high at the shoulder. The hindlimbs are longer than the forelimbs; this difference, along with other skeletal modifications, appears to be an adaptation for springing.[2] The legs are strong, thick, and powerful-looking. The paws are wide, with well-developed webbing between the toes, and in winter the undersides of the paws are covered with long, dense, shaggy hair. These features are evidently adaptations for moving through deep snow. For the lynx, the "weight load on track," or weight per surface area of the foot, varies from 34 to 60 grams per square centimeter, which means that a lynx's paw supports about three times more weight on snow than that of a forest wildcat.[3,4] Lynx in the Himalaya are distinguishable from other forms in that their foot pads are not covered with fur in the winter.[5]

The tail is short, about one-sixth of the head and body length, and thickly furred; the all-black tip looks chopped off. The large ears are wide at the base and taper to a tip, which is adorned with an erect tuft of black hairs 4 to 7 centimeters long. The backs of the ears have a central silver-gray spot. Long gray and white hairs adorn the cat's lower cheeks, hanging down to form a facial ruff, which in the winter is almost mane-like. The skull is broad, relatively short, and high, with wide-set zygomatic arches, giving the face a flat appearance, which is exaggerated by the facial ruff.

Insulation against the bitter winter cold is provided by long, thick, silky fur, which is densest on the back.[4] The light-colored belly fur, especially that of young animals, is used to make top-quality garments, and it is this soft, beautiful belly fur that makes lynx pelts so valuable.[6] The summer coat is shorter, sparser, and coarser.

Fur color is highly variable in lynx, but the underparts, chest, neck, throat, chin, eyelids, and the insides of the ears and legs are usually white. The lynx's winter coat can be silver-gray, yellowish gray, or grizzled grayish brown. Ashy blue and dark gray coats appear less commonly, although these are thought to be significantly softer than reddish orange skins. Lynx living at more northern latitudes or higher elevations tend to be paler and less spotted than those from farther south, but some variation occurs even locally. Linnaeus, for example, distinguished two color phases of lynx in Sweden, calling one "cat-lynx" and the other "wolf-lynx," the latter being found in dense forests.[7] A dense, woolly underfur, varying in color from ginger-buff or rusty-sandy to grayish or gray-blue, imparts subtle tones to the overall coat color. The shorter, sparser summer coat tends to be more reddish or brownish. Lynx with bright reddish coats are found mainly in southern Europe and the Caucasus, and these also tend to be more vividly spotted than other lynx.

The pattern of spots varies from almost none to highly visible black spots. Himalayan lynx, for example, tend to be paler (isabelline pelage), and in winter often lack the distinct spotting seen in European lynx.[5] Lynx without spots are rare, and a few fuzzy dark spots are usually present on the legs and belly of "unmarked" individuals. More typically, the spots are scattered all over the body. but they vary in number, size, sharpness, tone, and vividness. In addition to spots, lynx are often marked with narrow dark stripes along the spine or back. Several longitudinal blackish brown stripes may also occur on the forehead, between the ears, and on top of the head. The cheeks may also be marked with two or three irregular black lines.

Eurasian lynx are the largest of the bob-tailed cats; they can measure a meter in total length, and may weigh as much as 38 kilograms.[8] An adult male from the Romanian Carpathians reportedly weighed 48 kilograms,[9] and another from the Ukrainian Carpathians weighed 41 kilograms,[10] but such weights are suspect because there are few records of lynx weighing even 30 kilograms. In Sweden, adult male lynx average 17.9 kilograms and females 16.8 kilograms.[11] Similarly, the weights of twenty-two adults from central Russia ranged from 14 to 24 kilograms, but the average weight for males was 19.6 kilograms and for females 17.3 kilograms.[4] Males are usually larger and heavier than females, although in some areas females are nearly equal in size to males. Of all the lynx species, *L. lynx* shows the least amount of sexual dimorphism.[12]

DISTRIBUTION

Lynx were once widespread in the forest and forest-steppe regions of the Old World. Their vast geographic distribution extended from Sweden and Norway in the northwest south to the Iberian Peninsula, eastward through northern Italy, Switzerland, Austria and the Carpathians, Balkans, and Caucasus to Turkey, and east to northern Iraq and Iran. Lynx ranged through northern Europe across Russia to northeastern Siberia, Kamchatka, Sakhalin Island, Manchuria, Korea, northern China, Outer Mongolia, and southward through the Tien Shan to the Kopet Dag of Turkmenistan, northern Afghanistan, and neighboring parts of Pakistan and Kashmir, the Kulun Shan, and southeastern Tibet to Szechwan (fig. 26).[4,5,8,13,14,15]

Within historic time this range has shrunk dramatically, particularly in Europe, where the lynx was eradicated in nine countries and nearly so in another nine.[16,17,18] Lynx populations in Norway, Sweden, Finland, the Czech Republic, Slovakia, Romania, and Poland have rebounded from near extinction, while relict populations have persisted in France, Turkey, southeastern Yugoslavia, and possibly Albania.[15,18] Lynx in Scandinavia, Finland, and Russia expanded their range northward during the 1960s and 1970s.[7,19] Lynx have also been reintroduced successfully into some countries from which they were eradicated.

ECOLOGY AND BEHAVIOR

The Eurasian lynx is a forest-dwelling species, and its habitat use patterns are defined largely by the abundance and distribution of prey, principally several species of small ungulates and arctic hares. Across the northern and central regions of Europe and Russia, these cats use a variety of habitats, including taiga, mixed or deciduous boreal forest, and woodlands, but at the southern limits of their range lynx are found in forest-steppe, reaching far into the steppe along large forested steams. Where mountainous terrain occurs within these regions, lynx also use montane and subalpine forests up to an elevation of 2,500 meters.[4,8,16,17] In the Himalaya, lynx ascend to the highest alpine slopes, up to 4,500 meters in summer, preferring areas with reed beds, willow thickets, and tamarisk in remote valleys.[5] A female with kittens was seen at 5,500 meters in the bleak landscape of Ladakh.[17] Lynx are clearly capable of adjusting to a variety of landscapes, even cultivated ones, if they are not persecuted and adequate food and cover is available.

Lynx habitat in the former Soviet Union is characterized by an abundance of prey, especially arctic hares and small ungulates, inaccessible rocks, and snow cover not deeper than 40 to 50 centimeters. Snow greatly

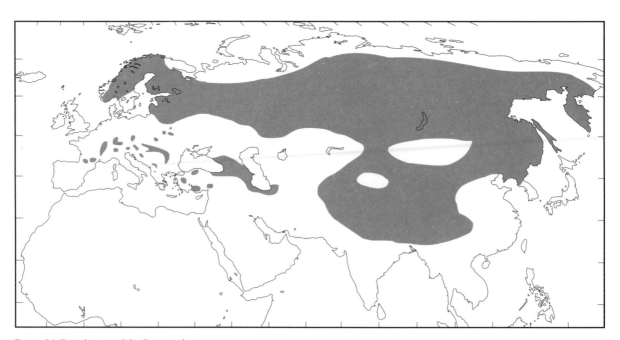

Figure 26. Distribution of the Eurasian lynx.

influences lynx habitat use. Despite their adaptations for moving in snow, lynx find loose, deep snow difficult to deal with and cannot survive in areas with snow depths exceeding 100 centimeters.[4] Deep snow also influences prey movements, and in mountainous parts of the former Soviet Union, lynx are known to migrate up and down the slopes, following ungulates and hares as they move to areas with less snow. Annual winter migrations of lynx also occur in the Ural Mountains; the lynx move from the western to the eastern slopes of the Urals, following roe deer, reindeer, and moose.[4]

Wolves may also influence the habitat use and density of lynx. Guggisberg reports that when wolves invaded eastern Slovakia during World War II, lynx moved out.[17] Similarly, in Russia, lynx are rare where wolves are numerous. In a forest reserve in central Russia two wolves caught and killed a lynx before it could get up a tree, and in another reserve the stomachs of two wolves contained remains of lynx.[4] In several areas, declines in wolf numbers have resulted in lynx numbers increasing.[19,20,21] Snow leopards and leopards may be competitors of lynx in some localities, although there are no records of conflicts.

Eurasian lynx are described as cautious or timid animals, but not cowardly. Like other felids, they are excellent tree climbers, and will use trees to escape if suddenly frightened or pursued. They usually avoid water and cross brooks and streams on logs or rocks, but will swim if pressed. Lynx can live close to humans or their activities and sometimes show up in agricultural villages or towns, but their appearance in these places is usually associated with major declines in natural prey.

Lynx spend the daytime hidden in dense cover, sleeping in a tangle of fallen trees or within a rocky cavern, and emerge in late afternoon. They move intermittently throughout the night, and are most active at dawn and dusk, but will shift to hunting during the daytime while raising kittens or when food is scarce. There are many observations of lynx chasing hares, roe deer, or marmots during the day. They do not, however, appear to hunt in snowstorms, ground blizzards, or on days of inclement weather.[4,11]

Lynx have excellent vision and hearing, and Sludskii reports that they can hear a hare nibbling a twig 50 to 60 meters away.[4] Waldemar Lindemann was able to test the visual acuity of two young hand-raised lynx. They were able to see a mouse at 75 meters, a hare at 300 meters, and a roe deer at 500 meters.[22] Lindemann

also showed experimentally that the lynx has excellent spatial memory and found that "familiar features of the surroundings, its paths, resting places etc. are strongly imprinted."[23]

A hunting lynx moves along logs and fallen trees, climbs cliffs, zigzags and loops through the forest. It moves slowly, often sitting or lying down. When traveling between hunting areas, the lynx follows forest trails made by hares or deer or uses frozen streams. Snow tracking of lynx in central Russia showed that "usually the animal's route runs along ridges between marshes overgrown with forest, through forest islands left intact among clear-cuts, along rocky ridges, particular saddles in the mountains, etc. Moving along its hunting route, the cat regularly approaches some individual large stones lying on the ground, fallen trees, and other prominent objects, from the top of which it surveys the surrounding area."[4] Lynx in the Bialowieza Forest in Poland frequently walk on fallen logs, presumably as a means to increase their field of view.[24] Similarly, lynx in Finland followed well-used prey runways, concentrating their movements in small areas of prey activity, and using short-term "waiting beds," usually on ridges overlooking areas of prey activity or beside well-used prey runways. These seemed to be good places to find and catch hares, roe deer, and other small ungulates in the snow.[19]

Lynx usually hunt alone, but there are a few accounts of two or more lynx hunting together.[4,11,17,20] The most often cited example, in which a pair of lynx flushed a resting musk deer, is based on a reconstruction from tracks in the snow. The two lynx were about 50 meters apart, moving parallel to each other across a slope, when the upslope cat frightened the deer, which immediately bolted downslope, zigzagging past the lunging lynx. The lynx bounded after the deer, making long jumps, but abandoned the chase after about 100 meters. They then resumed searching in the same manner as before, one moving across the slope at a level higher than the other.[4]

Information from snow tracking shows that lynx may travel 7 or 8 kilometers during a single hunt or as much as 20 kilometers in a day, although the average from several areas is about 10 kilometers per day.[3,4,11,25,26] However, these movements pale by comparison with the great distances traveled during times of food shortages. Some Russian accounts describe lynx traveling vast distances, through terrible winter conditions, across treeless areas, and showing up in places hundreds of kilometers from their normal haunts.[4,27] "In years of deep snow cover, hungry lynxes, especially juveniles driven away by their mothers, approach taiga settlements in the Altai and launch attacks on domestic animals, primarily dogs and cats."[4] One winter fifty to sixty dead lynx were found in a single area. By contrast, the lynx's arrival in Kamchatka in the early 1930s, where it was not originally found, coincided with a high population of hares.[4] The lynx's appearance in this case resembles the invasions of Canada lynx into portions of the northern United States.[28,29]

Feeding Ecology

Like other felids, lynx are stalk-and-ambush hunters, using different techniques for different situations.[4,11] Hares are often stalked, with the lynx creeping up slowly on the feeding animal, taking advantage of all cover to get as close as possible. At an opportune moment the lynx leaps, sometimes up to 3 meters, and pounces on its victim. Lynx rarely pursue hares, seldom making more than ten jumps before abandoning the chase. If the snow crust is not thick enough to support the lynx's weight, it will try to ambush hares by hiding near their trails behind stumps or fallen trees. Hunting on thin crust is noisy because the crust caves in with each step. Lynx stalk ungulates and will sometimes chase them for short distances if the snow is deep. Lynx will even kill adult red deer when the snow is deep and sufficiently crusted to support the lynx's weight, but not the deer's[4] although such specific conditions probably occur infrequently.

Lynx take a variety of prey. They feed principally on mammals, mainly herbivores such as wild pigs, beavers, hares, rabbits, and small rodents, but other carnivores and birds are also taken. Differences in the lynx's diet follow a north-south gradient of prey abundance.[24] Hares are more abundant in the taiga and northern boreal forests, and in these regions some 60 to 80 percent of lynx scats contain hare remains. Farther south, in the zone of mixed and deciduous forests, ungulate abundance increases, and larger prey become more important in the cat's diet. Deer constitute 90 to 94 percent of the lynx's diet in the Bialowieza Forest.[30] Birds, such as grouse and capercaillie, are important prey only in boreal and montane forests.[24] The notable exception to this pattern is semi-domesticated reindeer, which are regularly taken by lynx in northernmost Sweden.[11,31]

Whether male and female lynx have different prey preferences is not clear. There were no significant dif-

ferences in the diets of males and females in southeastern Finland, but there were no reindeer or roe deer available there.[19] In Sweden, there were no differences in the occurrence of roe deer and reindeer in the diet of adult male lynx between May–November and December–April (65 and 67 percent), but the diet of adult females showed a significant shift (39 percent in May–November to 67 percent in December–April).[31] In the Swiss Alps, a male and female lynx living in the same area differed in that the male (who weighed 24.5 kilograms) preferred the larger chamois and the female (at 17.0 kilograms) the smaller roe deer.[32] Similarly, adult male lynx in the Bialowieza Forest captured significantly more red deer and fewer small prey than adult female lynx.[30]

Seasonally, the lynx's diet is more varied in the spring and summer, as it feeds on marmots, squirrels, pikas, partridges, pheasants, passerines, kids, fawns, and piglets. As winter progresses and the snow gets deeper, deer become more vulnerable and lynx start to kill more deer. Carrion also becomes more important in the winter diet.

Lynx kill ungulates ranging in size from the 15-kilogram musk deer to 220-kilogram adult male red deer, but show a preference for the smallest ungulate species in the community. When they kill red deer and wild pigs, they usually prey on the young.[24,30,33] Across much of Eurasia the single most important ungulate prey of lynx is the 20-kilogram roe deer. Though the vast geographic ranges of lynx and roe deer mirror each other almost exactly, roe deer do not occur naturally in Finland, and they were introduced to Norway and Sweden sometime after 1900.[34] In these countries lynx prey successfully on the now semi-domesticated reindeer; one account mentions that lynx killed forty-five of the sixty-four reindeer they attacked. The explanation for this high success rate was that these reindeer may have mistaken the lynx for herding dogs.[11]

A more recent study of reindeer and their predators focused on determining first-year mortality of reindeer calves. An amazing total of 1,615 reindeer calves were radio-tagged over four years in two different areas. Reindeer calves two to twelve months old suffered mortality rates of 11 and 14.3 percent; wild carnivores were responsible for 66 and 75 percent of the losses in the two areas, respectively. Lynx accounted for 40 percent of this mortality. Wolverines accounted for 54 percent, but they were twice as abundant as lynx. Most of the calves killed in open, alpine areas were preyed upon by wolverines, whereas lynx were responsible for most of the calves killed in forested areas.[35]

Lynx will also kill and eat other carnivores, and the remains of other carnivores show up in about 4 to 10 percent of lynx stomachs. In the Carpathian Mountains, 12 percent of 38 lynx stomachs contained martens, badgers, foxes, dogs, and wildcats.[36] In Norway, wild carnivores were found in 4 percent of 146 stomachs.[31] Foxes appear to be taken regularly, and one lynx was found to have killed three in a day. In south-central Russia, lynx hunt foxes by chasing them on loose snow, and it is said that where lynx are common no foxes remain by midwinter.[4]

Like other felids, lynx occasionally kill many more animals than they can possibly eat. Most surplus killings have been recorded in situations in which the prey animals were confined and thus vulnerable. A 1948 account records a lynx killing thirty sheep in a pen in one night;[4] on another occasion a lynx killed three of five penned roe deer.[37] In Slovakia, a lynx entered a henhouse one night, killed seventy hens, and was itself killed the following morning.[38] Multiple kills have also been recorded where lynx have been reintroduced to a predator-free area. Under these circumstances, wild prey are naive and clearly more vulnerable to predation. During a study of reintroduced lynx in the Swiss Alps, a radio-tagged female killed four chamois in one day. Urs Breitenmoser, the scientist in charge of the project, remarks that "anecdotal observations indicate that surplus killing was more frequent at an earlier stage of lynx recolonization."[32]

Most cats try to keep their two hind feet planted firmly on the ground while they tackle large prey. Lynx may be an exception. Several anecdotal accounts describe lynx attacking large prey by jumping onto the animal's back, holding on with its claws, and biting the victim's neck or throat. One adult roe deer was seen running with a lynx hanging from its neck.[4,11,17] Trying to subdue a large deer by leaping onto its back is probably not the safest way to kill prey, but it may be the best option in deep snow, where there is no secure purchase for the cat's hind feet. Matjuschkin reported that about 13 percent of 285 lynx killed in the Ural Mountains bore signs of previous injuries to legs and skull, presumably sustained in trying to capture large prey.[20]

The daily food requirement of an adult lynx is at least 1.1 kilograms of meat, usually 1.2 to 1.5 kilograms,[19] which is about 5 to 10 percent of the animal's body weight. In zoos lynx are usually fed about 1.5 kilo-

grams of meat a day. This is similar to the maximum amount of meat found in the stomachs of lynx killed in the wild. In Finland four stomachs each contained 1.2 kilograms of meat.[19] Food in the stomach of a 17-kilogram wild lynx from Russia weighed 1.1 kilograms, and in Siberia another lynx had eaten three to four squirrels estimated to weigh a total of 0.8 to 1.1 kilograms.[4] Lynx in the Bialowieza Forest consume, on average, about 2 kilograms of food daily.[30]

Lynx occasionally eat only a portion of a large kill, but their abandonment of kills may be related to disturbance or competition from scavengers. In Switzerland, lynx abandoned over a third of their ungulate kills when the carcass was only half eaten. Carcass utilization was higher in undisturbed areas; near civilization it dropped to 62 percent.[39] Large carcasses attract wolves, wolverines, wild pigs, and foxes. Lynx sometimes try to hide uneaten prey, covering it with dry grass, twigs, or snow. In the Bialowieza Forest lynx kills were often fed on by scavengers, most frequently by wild pigs.[21]

Prey utilization by lynx in the Bialowieza Forest differed by sex and age class, with family groups consuming a deer in a short time; sometimes small prey were killed and eaten while the group was still feeding on the deer carcass. Adult males typically fed on a deer, then left before it was consumed and traveled widely, often making another kill and feeding on it for a few days before returning to the previous kill.[30]

Data on 101 ungulate kills and 5 hare kills in the Bialowieza Forest show that time spent feeding on kills varied depending on the size of the prey and the age and number of lynx feeding.[30] Lynx spent an average of 32 hours (1.3 days) consuming a hare, while the average time for an adult female red deer was 92 hours (3.8 days). Adult roe deer were eaten in 3 days, and utilization rates for ungulate carcasses were generally high, commonly exceeding 75 percent.

In Sweden, lynx are reported to kill a roe deer every six days.[40] Similarly, in the northern Alps, adult lynx killed one ungulate every 6.6 days, and a female with two ten-month-old young killed one ungulate every 2.7 days.[32,39] The frequency of killing smaller prey is higher, in some cases approaching a hare a day.[11] In the Bialowieza Forest, the average time between leaving a deer kill and making another was 2.25 days.[30] In most cases lynx spent 0.5 to 5 days hunting deer before making another kill. Remarkably, a female with three kittens spent an average of only ten hours between leaving a carcass and killing another deer. The killing rates of lynx in the Bialowieza Forest are estimated at 43 deer per year for subadult lynx and females without young and 76 deer per year for adult males. The rate of killing by females with young increased with litter size, from 69 per year for a female with one young to 190 per year for a female with three young. Overall, lynx average a deer kill every 5.4 days.[30]

Lynx are fairly proficient hunters. Snow tracking data from a variety of locations show that 18 to 43 percent of attacks on hares are successful; the success rate on grouse is about 25 to 30 percent.[4,11,19,41,42] Lynx were almost twice as successful catching hares in southern Sweden than they were in the north, a difference that was attributed to soft, deep snow, which impeded capture. In Sweden, 70 percent of attacks on semi-domesticated reindeer and 52 percent of attacks on roe deer were successful,[11] although such high success rates on ungulates are rather unusual.

Haglund's data for lynx in Sweden show that 70 percent of their successful hunts involved chases of 20 meters or less.[11] Surprisingly, in longer chases (200 to 300 meters) of reindeer and hares, lynx were quite successful (67 percent and 100 percent respectively), which Haglund suggests is related to the lynx assessing prey body condition and pursuing for longer distances only in situations in which there was a high probability of capture. Isolated reindeer and those standing at the edge of a herd were taken more often, and most reindeer killed were young animals.

The effect of lynx predation on natural prey populations is largely unknown. In the northern Alps, where lynx density was estimated at 1.2 per 100 square kilometers, each lynx annually consumes some sixty roe deer or chamois, amounting to 3 to 9 percent of the ungulate population.[39] In 1991–1996, the winter density of lynx in Poland's Bialowieza Forest was estimated at 2.4 to 3.2 per 100 square kilometers. Lynx predation accounted for 15 to 32 percent of the annual mortality of red deer and 41 to 43 percent of the annual mortality of roe deer. Indeed, lynx predation was the single most important cause of roe deer mortality, and during this period lynx predation limited the roe deer population.[24,30] In one winter lynx killed an estimated 23 percent of a hare population in the southern taiga of the Upper Volga River region, although such losses were judged to be insignificant at the time.[42]

Social Organization
Although the evidence is meager, lynx appear to have a social organization that is similar to that of other soli-

tary felids, in which males occupy large home ranges and one or more females reside within each male's area. The overlap of neighboring female home ranges is small, suggesting that they occupy fairly exclusive areas. Overlap of male ranges appears to be greater, although males typically avoid each other.[11,20,43,44,45] This arrangement, along with the prey base, sets limits on the number of residents. Lynx densities are typically low, about one to three adults per 100 square kilometers.[4,20,43,46] The highest reported lynx densities are from the mixed forests of Russia's central mountains, where they averaged 5 per 100 square kilometers over a twenty-year period; densities varied from 1.7 to 5.6 per 100 square kilometers over that period.[3] Over a 125-year period in the Bialowieza Forest, lynx numbers were high at three times, with densities of 2–3, 4–6, and 2–5 lynx per 100 square kilometers recorded. During the lows, lynx densities were less than 1 per 100 square kilometers.[21]

Based on snow tracking data, home range sizes of lynx vary from as little as 20 square kilometers in a densely populated area in the Carpathians to more than 2,000 square kilometers in northern Sweden.[17,40] However, Haglund tracked a male lynx in Sweden whose home range measured 300 square kilometers.[11] In the Volga River region of Russia, the home ranges of two males were 130 and 250 square kilometers, and that of a female was 70 square kilometers.[44] The ranges of five radio-tagged males in Poland's Bialowieza Forest averaged 165 square kilometers in autumn–winter, 143 square kilometers in spring–summer, and 248 square kilometers on an annual basis.[45] This size difference between seasonal and annual ranges was associated both with males shifting their ranges to include those of more females and with their extensive travels just before and during the breeding season (December–March). For five adult females, home range sizes averaged 94 square kilometers in autumn–winter, 55 square kilometers in spring–summer, and 133 square kilometers on an annual basis. Female lynx in the Bialowieza Forest showed more site fidelity than males and rarely shifted ranges.

In Switzerland, Urs Breitenmoser radio-tracked an expanding population of reintroduced lynx and found that the home ranges of animals on the expanding edge of the population were about three times smaller than the ranges of animals living in the center of the population. Two males in the center had home ranges of 275 square kilometers and 450 square kilometers, compared with 135 square kilometers for a male at the front. Similarly, the average range size for three females at the front was 72 square kilometers, compared with an average of 209 square kilometers for five females in the center.[39,43] Breitenmoser speculates that at the leading edge of the lynx population expansion, ungulate prey are naive to predators and thus more vulnerable. Under these circumstances, lynx can exist in smaller ranges. However, as prey densities decline because of heavy predation and the prey learn about predators, they become harder to capture, and lynx must expand their ranges to meet their energy requirements. Hence the densities of lynx in the center are lower than at the front.

Lynx densities and social systems may, however, be different in regions where lynx depend primarily on hares for food. Hare populations are cyclical, and during periods of extremely low numbers the cats are likely to abandon their home ranges. Observations of mass migrations of lynx in 1969–1973 in western Siberia and northern Kazakhstan coincided with long-term population declines of hares and unusually deep snow in the subzone of pine-birch forests.[27] Under such dire circumstances the social system is likely to collapse; animals will wander widely in search of food, and many young and adult cats will die. The survivors, if there are any, or immigrants will form the nucleus of the population as it recovers. Such a situation has also been described for the Canada lynx.[47,48]

Extensive movements, or roaming, has also been noted for male lynx during the mating season.[11,43,44,45,46] Where female densities are low, males might be expected either to travel widely in search of mating opportunities or to stay at home and try to monopolize access to females.[49] These predictions are supported by observations of male lynx in Switzerland. One radio-tagged male in the Jura Mountains, whose home range overlapped those of two females, did not roam during the mating season, whereas two other males traveled well outside their normal ranges to visit neighboring females.[43]

Lynx indicate occupancy of their home ranges and communicate with their neighbors principally through scent marks. A lynx regularly visits most parts of its range, passing through sections every seven to ten days and covering the entire area every fifteen to thirty days.[4] A variety of scent marks, including scrapes, urine, and feces, are deposited about the range. Feces may be buried, although along territorial boundaries they are often left in the open, on a prominent place such as the top of a rock. Territorial marking may be particularly intense during the mating season.[23,45]

Lynx have ten to twelve vocalizations and, while a few of these are common to all cats, the majority of these signals and their structures are similar to those in the genus *Felis,* rather than those of the *Panthera* cats.[50,51] Like other cats, lynx mew, spit, hiss, and growl; they also yowl, chatter, wah-wah, gurgle, and purr. The yowl probably represents a mild threat. It is used by females when they are being pestered by their kittens, and has been heard in captivity when two animals are waiting to be fed. Lynx "chatter" when they are close to prey that is out of reach, just as domestic cats do when they see a bird through a window. The "gurgle" is a friendly close-contact call used during courtship and mating and by females with kittens. The "purr" is also a friendly close-contact sound. It is effective only at very close range, and is used by mothers nursing or licking their kittens.

In the wild, lynx are rarely heard except during the mating season, between January and April.[4,52,53,54] Both males and females vocalize. The female's call has been described as "a loud powerful cat-like yowl repeated up to a dozen times, followed by a pause before the sequence is repeated again." Males are said to have a deeper, hoarse growling call,[55] or a "muted, almost bearlike purr."[17] Others describe the female call as a "raucous loud meow,"[20] which is technically more correct. Though these mating calls may sound like yowls and growls, vocalization expert Gustav Peters says these mating calls are really "a series of intense mews."[51]

During the early part of the mating season most of the calling goes on at night, but as the breeding season progresses, lynx become more active and move more during the daytime. Young lynx, which up to now had been traveling with their mother, begin the process of separation.[4]

Reproduction and Development

A female in estrus rolls on her back, meowing loudly. According to observations of captive lynx, estrus lasts anywhere from four to seven days[56] or seven to ten days.[57] The peak of estrus lasts one to two days. Males rarely eat while they are courting receptive females.[54] The pair mate frequently, and coitus is brief; during intromission the male grasps the skin on the back of the female's neck with his teeth and vocalizes.

A study of reproductive tracts from harvested lynx suggests that despite the rather long mating season,

"European lynx are not truly polyestrous and do not have more than one ovulation wave per season."[58] However, lynx will cycle again if they lose their first litter soon after birth, and there are records of captive females having two litters in one year.[56]

Data collected from harvested lynx carcasses in Norway show that ovulation rates of Eurasian lynx do not change with age, physical condition, or prey availability.[58] In contrast, the ovulation rate of Canada lynx is clearly correlated with snowshoe hare abundance, and is significantly lower during hare declines.[59] This difference between the species may be governed by the nature of their food supply. Canada lynx are tied to a single prey species—the snowshoe hare—but Eurasian lynx feed on a greater variety of prey, and can switch to roe deer or birds and other mammals during times of low hare numbers.

Gestation lasts sixty-seven to seventy-four days.[4,60] Toward the end of the gestation period, the female selects a secluded den site for the birth of her kittens. Only a few wild den sites have been described, and they tend to be beneath low overhanging branches of conifers, among the roots at the base of a tree, or in rock piles and crevices. Shaposhnikov described a den found amid the roots of an old birch tree in south-central Russia: "Feathers of hazel grouse and capercaillie and the wool of musk and roe deer were found in the bedding along with rotten wood, and also a small quantity of dry grass. Along the sides of the den were bones of birds and arctic hare. To one side of the hollow lay the remains of musk deer (hooves and wool), quill feathers of capercaillie . . . and summer wool of arctic hare."[4]

Females give birth to one to four kittens. The average size of twenty-two litters was 2.46.[4,55,58,60] Kittens weigh 245 to 430 grams at birth. For the first few weeks they are covered with "soft, downy, greyish-brown fur with only vague indications of spots."[56,60] The spots gradually become more distinct and are quite pronounced by the eleventh week. By the time young lynx are fourteen weeks old, they are the same color as adults.

Young lynx develop at a much slower rate than wildcats.[11,19,23] Lynx kittens open their eyes at ten to twelve days, and they start to eat solid food between six and seven weeks of age.[4,55,60] In the Ostrava Zoo (Slovakia), a female began to bring her litter out of the den during the daytime when they were forty-nine days old. By this age the kittens could groom themselves and were beginning to show an interest in solid food, but could not yet bite through the skin of a rabbit. The kittens began play-fighting at twelve weeks of age.[60] At another zoo a lynx kitten was quite independent by fourteen weeks and could climb 6 meters up into an oak tree.[55]

In the wild, mothers spend most of the early den phase close to their young. In Switzerland the home ranges of two radio-tagged females shrank to 6 square kilometers and 9 square kilometers when they gave birth to young, but after three months, when the kittens were able to travel, their ranges increased to 18.5 square kilometers and 84 square kilometers, respectively.[61] In the Bialowieza Forest, female ranges were smallest during the two months following the birth of young, when range sizes measured only 10 square kilometers.[45]

Lynx abandon the birth den when their kittens are two to three months old, but the young are not completely weaned until five to six months of age.[23] They continue to travel with their mother until they are ten months old, and the family separates only when the next mating season begins. There is one observation of a mother still traveling with a two-year-old young.[4]

Though the young lynx are essentially independent by ten to eleven months of age, most do not become sexually mature until their second or third year.[52,62] In Norway, a detailed study of lynx reproduction using information from over three hundred harvested animals showed that females reach sexual maturity earlier than males. Half the females were fertile by the time they were a year old, the rest by two years of age. At two, only half the males were fertile, but by three years of age all males were able to father offspring.[58]

When a young lynx separates from its mother, it must leave her range and search for an unoccupied area. Depending on the local circumstances, dispersers may be lucky enough to find a vacant spot close to their natal range or may have to travel hundreds of kilometers. Just getting to dispersal age may also be fortuitous. In Switzerland, eight of fourteen young lynx disappeared by their first winter, and only six remained with their mother until they were ten months old. These six subadults were radio-collared and followed as they dispersed some 25 to 92 kilometers from their natal range. The radio collar of one animal failed, but four of the other five dispersing young died within eight months of independence. The remaining female was still alive one year after separating from her mother.[43]

Mortality among resident lynx in the Swiss Jura was also high; of seven adults, one was killed by a car and two were shot by hunters. Thirty-seven of fifty-nine (63 percent) lynx found dead in Switzerland were killed by humans, eighteen in traffic accidents and sixteen shot.[43] Mortality among Bialowieza Forest lynx was also largely human-related. Between 1978 and 1994, eleven cases of mortality were recorded in radio-tagged cats: six lynx were poached, two were shot, one was rabid, and two died of natural causes. The annual mortality rate of radio-tagged subadult and adult lynx was 0.372; natural mortality was low, on average 5 percent per year.[21]

In captivity, lynx have lived for twenty-one years and ten months.[63]

STATUS IN THE WILD

Eradicated from many parts of their former range in Europe, intensively hunted for their fur, and considered a threat to other wildlife populations, lynx currently are restricted to forested areas in France, Sweden, Norway, Finland, Poland, the Carpathians, the Czech Republic, Slovakia, Romania, and the Balkans.[18] Lynx were thought to have gone extinct in France,[25] but others argue that a relict population has survived in the Pyrenees.[64,65,66,67] Lynx populations in Sweden, Norway, and Finland appear to be stable or increasing slightly; while estimates vary, there may be five hundred in each country.[18] In Poland, lynx are found in two widely separated areas, in two populations that have been separated for over two centuries. Possibly a hundred lynx exist in large forest tracts in the northeast, including the Masurian Lakeland and Bialowieza Forest, and perhaps two hundred remain in the remote parts of the Carpathian Mountains in the southeastern part of the country.[68] In the adjoining Slovakian Carpathians lynx numbers are estimated in the hundreds.[69] Within the Romanian Carpathians lynx numbers have been estimated at 1,500, but this figure is thought to be an overestimate.[18] The lynx had disappeared from northwestern Italy by the early twentieth century, but since 1982 several sightings of lynx and indirect evidence (tracks) have been reported in two areas in the Italian Alps.[70,71] These lynx are thought to represent spontaneous reimmigrations of individuals traveling from Switzerland and Slovenia (Yugoslavia); lynx were reintroduced into Switzerland in 1971 and into Yugoslavia in 1973.[72] The status of the lynx in Turkey is unknown, but within the widely scattered forests where the cat still occurs, its numbers are thought to be declining.[15] The largest population of *Lynx lynx* is in Russia, where there are an estimated 36,000–40,000 individuals.[73]

Lynx in Western Europe are seriously threatened; they are extinct in most countries and exist only as small isolated populations in others. Habitat fragmentation, loss of prey, and a variety of human-related causes of mortality are the major causes of the cat's decline. In some countries there are hunting seasons for lynx.[18]

Lynx in Ladakh are threatened by human activities, habitat loss, poaching, and snaring. A small number of lynx, estimated at fourteen to sixteen, live in the Numra Valley, where they exist on shrub-covered islands in the riverbeds. Shrub forest is the only source of fuel for local people, and biologists predict that if the present use pattern continues, the shrub will be gone in ten to fifteen years.[74]

CONSERVATION EFFORTS

Lynx are afforded legal protection in most European countries, and in those countries where the cats can be hunted or trapped, there are restrictions on when they can be taken. Lynx have become established in the Alps, French Jura, and Vosges Mountains as a result of immigration from neighboring countries and reintroductions.[18,75] The reintroduction of just three male and three female lynx into Slovenia has been incredibly successful. Since 1978 hunters have shot about two hundred lynx in the territory, and the population size is currently estimated at 150 to 200.[76]

Lynx have been reintroduced at sites in Switzerland, France, Yugoslavia, Austria, and Slovakia. Three of nine planned lynx reintroductions in Europe have been judged successful; for two it is too early to tell, and four have not been successful. There have also been four illegal reintroductions, of which two failed and the fate of the others is unknown.[77,78] The reintroductions have spawned heated conflicts between conservationists on one side and hunters and farmers on the other. Some opposition in France and Switzerland resulted in killings of lynx.[79,80,81,82,83] In Slovenia, reintroduced lynx wiped out two colonies of mouflon sheep in hunting enclosures.[76] In Austria, lynx preyed heavily on red deer concentrated around feeding stations.[84] In the Swiss Alps, predation on domestic sheep and goats was highest at the expanding edge of the lynx population.[32]

TABLE 30 MEASUREMENTS AND WEIGHTS OF ADULT EURASIAN LYNX

HB	n	T	n	WT	n	Location	Source
1,218 (920–1,480)	15m	180 (120–220)	15m	17.4 (11.7–21.0)	7m	Romania	9
1,170 (1,050–1,300)	14f	187 (170–210)	14f	16.1 (13.0–20.0)	9f	Romania	9
1,000 (760–1,080)	16m	202 (170–240)	16m	19.6 (16.3–23.5)	10m	Russia	4
900 (850–1,000)	21f	196 (180–235)	21f	17.3 (14.0–21.5)	12f	Russia	4
				17.9	m	Sweden	18
				16.8	f	Sweden	11
				21.7 (19.0–25.0)	5m	Poland	45
				17.0 (16.5–19.5)	3f	Poland	45
865	1m	202	1m			Kashmir	85
1,030	1m	225	1m			Pakistan	5

Note: HB = head and body length (mm), T = tail length (mm), WT = weight (kg). n = sample size. Sex: m = male, f = female, ? = unknown. Mean values are presented only for sample sizes of three or more. Range of values is in parentheses.

TABLE 31 FREQUENCY OF OCCURRENCE OF PREY ITEMS IN THE DIETS OF EURASIAN LYNX (PERCENTAGE OF SAMPLES)

Prey items	Bialowieza Forest, Poland[4] 1947–1951 Scats (n = 126)	Bialowieza Forest, Poland[30] 1985–1996 Scats (n = 127)	SE Finland[19] Stomachs (n = 88)	Norway[31] Stomachs (n = 146)	Caucasian Preserve, Russia[4] Scats (n = 136)	Sweden[11] Scats, stomachs, kills (n = 158)
Capreolus capreolus Roe deer	28.6	8.7		21.9	3.7	20.3
Cervus elaphus Red deer		5.5			8.8	
Unidentified deer	1.6	77.4		5.5		
Rupricapra rupricapra Chamois					17.6	
Capra sp. Tur					19.1	
Rangifer tarandus Reindeer				39.0		34.2
Sus scrofa Wild pig	4.0	3.9			4.4	
Lepus sp. Hare	38.9	11.0	79.5	24.0	0.7	24.1
Rodents	73.0	3.9	3.2	9.6	40.4	
Birds	7.1	3.9	7.4	13	8.8	13.3
Domestic animals			4.9	6.2		
Carnivores			0.8	4.8		1.3
Miscellaneous						6.3
Minimum number of vertebrate prey items	193	141	89	181	141	158

REFERENCES

1. Blyth, E. 1842. A monograph on the species of lynx. *J. Asiatic Soc. Bengal* 11: 740–760.

2. Mandal, A. K., and S. K. Talukder. 1975. Skeletal differences in the appendicular skeleton of the lynx and the caracal (Felidae: Carnivora) in relation to ecology. *Anat. Anz.* 137: 447–453.

3. Iurgenson, P. B. 1955. [Ecology of the lynx in forests of the central zone of the USSR.] (In Russian, English summary.) *Zool. Zh.* 34: 609–620.

4. Heptner, V. G., and A. A. Sludskii. 1992. *Mammals of the Soviet Union*. Vol. 2, part 2, *Carnivora (Hyaenas and cats)*. English translation, sci. ed. R. S. Hoffmann. Washington, DC: Smithsonian Institution Libraries and National Science Foundation.

5. Roberts, T. J. 1977. *The mammals of Pakistan*. London: Ernest Benn.

6. Quinn, N. W. S., and G. Parker. 1987. Lynx. In *Wild furbearer management and conservation in North America*, ed. N. Novak, J. A. Baker, M. E. Obbard, and B. Malloch, 683–694. Ontario: Ontario Trappers Association.

7. Curry-Lindahl, K. 1969. The former occurrence of the lynx (*Lynx lynx lynx*) in Scandinavia. *Mammalia* 33: 140–144.

8. Tumlison, R. 1987. *Felis lynx. Mammalian Species* 269: 1–8.

9. Vasiliu, G. D., and P. Decei. 1963. Über den luchs (*Lynx lynx*) der rumänischen Karpaten. *Säugetierk. Mitt.* 12: 155–183.

10. Tur'anin, I. I., and I. I. Kol'usev. 1968. Occurrence of the lynx in the Ukrainian Carpathians. *Acta Sci. Nat. Brno* 2(5/6): 49–52.

11. Haglund, B. 1966. Winter habits of the lynx (*Lynx lynx* L.) and wolverine (*Gulo gulo* L.) as revealed by tracking in the snow. *Viltrevy* 4: 1–299.

12. Werdelin, L. 1981. The evolution of lynxes. *Ann. Zool. Fennici* 18: 37–71.

13. Corbet, G. B., and J. E. Hill. 1991. *A world list of mammalian species*, 3rd ed. Oxford: Oxford University Press.

14. van den Brink, F. H. 1970. Distribution and speciation of some carnivores. *Mammal Rev.* 1: 67–78.

15. Serez, M. 1992. Evolution of lynx population in Turkey. In *The situation, conservation needs and reintroduction of lynx in Europe*, 26–29. Environmental Encounters, no. 11. Strasbourg: Council of Europe Press.

16. Kratochvil, J. 1968. Recent distribution of the lynx in Europe. *Acta Sci. Nat. Brno* 2(5): 1–74.

17. Guggisberg, C. A. W. 1975. *Wild cats of the world*. New York: Taplinger.

18. Breitenmoser, U., and C. Breitenmoser-Würsten. 1990. *Status, conservation needs and reintroduction of the lynx (Lynx lynx) in Europe*. Nature and Environment Series, no. 45. Strasbourg: Council of Europe.

19. Pulliainen, E. 1981. Winter diet of *Felis lynx* L. in SE Finland as compared with the nutrition of other northern lynxes. *Z. Säugetierk.* 46: 249–259.

20. Matjuschkin, E. N. 1978. *Der luchs*. Wittenberg Lutherstadt: A. Zismsen.

21. Jedrzejewski, W., B. Jedrzejewska, H. Okarma, K. Schmidt, A. N. Bunevich, and L. Milkowski. 1996. Population dynamics (1869–1994), demography, and home ranges of lynx in Bialowieza Primeval Forest (Poland and Belarus). *Ecography* 19: 122–138.

22. Lindemann, W. 1950. Beobachtungen an wilden und gezähmten Luchsen. *Z. Tierpsychol.* 7: 217–239.

23. Lindemann, W. 1955. [Über die jugendentwicklung beim luchs (*Lynx l. lynx* Keer.) und bei der wildkatze (*Felis s. silvestris* Schreb.).] (In German, with English summary.) *Behaviour* 8: 1–45.

24. Jedrzejewski, W., K. Schmidt, L. Milkowski, B. Jedrzejewska, and H. Okarma. 1993. Foraging by lynx and its role in ungulate mortality: The local (Bialowieza Forest) and the Palaearctic viewpoints. *Acta Theriologica* 38: 385–403.

25. Schauenberg, P. 1969. Le lynx *Lynx lynx* (L.) en Suisse et dans les pays voisins. *Rev. Suisse Zool.* 76: 257–287.

26. Goszczynski, J. 1986. Locomotor activity of terrestrial predators and its consequences. *Acta Theriologica* 31: 79–95.

27. Azarov, V. I. 1976. [Distribution and migrations of *Felis lynx* in the south of West Siberia and in North Kazakhstan.] (In Russian, with English summary.) *Zool. Zh.* 55: 624–628.

28. Gunderson, H. L. 1978. A mid-continent irruption of Canada lynx, 1962–63. *Prairie Nat.* 10: 71–80.

29. Mech, L. D. 1980. Age, sex, reproduction, and spatial organization of lynxes colonizing northeastern Minnesota. *J. Mammal.* 61: 261–267.

30. Okarma, H., W. Jedrzejewski, K. Schmidt, R. Kowalczyk, and B. Jedrzejewska. 1997. Predation of Eurasian lynx on roe deer and red deer in Bialowieza Primeval Forest, Poland. *Acta Theriologica* 42: 203–224.

31. Birkeland, K. H., and S. Myrberget. 1980. The diet of the lynx *Lynx lynx* in Norway. *Fauna Norv. Ser. A* 1: 24–28.

32. Breitenmoser, U., and H. Haller. 1993. Patterns of predation by reintroduced European lynx in the Swiss Alps. *J. Wildl. Mgmt.* 57: 135–144.

33. Okarma, H. 1984. The physical condition of red deer falling prey to the wolf and lynx and harvested in the Carpathian Mountains. *Acta Theriologica* 29: 283–290.

34. Kvam, T. 1990. Ovulation rates in European lynx, *Lynx lynx* (L.), from Norway. *Z. Säugetierk.* 55: 315–320.

35. Bjärvall, A. 1992. Lynx and reindeer management in Sweden. In *The situation, conservation needs and reintroduction of lynx in Europe*, 40–42. Environmental Encounters, no. 11. Strasbourg: Council of Europe Press.

36. Lindemann, W. 1956. Der Luchs und seine Bedeutung im Haushalt der Natur. *Kosmos* 52: 187–193.

37. Kossak, S. 1989. Multiple hunting by lynx and red fox and utilization of prey by some carnivores. *Acta Theriologica* 34: 505–512.

38. Hell, P. 1968. Population density of the lynx in the Czechoslovakian Carpathians. *Acta Sci. Nat. Brno* 2(5/6): 57–64.

39. Breitenmoser, U., and H. Haller. 1987. Zur nahrungsökologie des luchses *Lynx lynx* in den schweizerischen Nordalpen. *Z. Säugetierk.* 52: 168–191.

40. Jonnson, S. 1980. Erforschung und Erhaltung des Luchses in Schweden. In *Der Luchs in Europa*, ed. A. Festetics, 170–180. Greven: Kilda-Verlag.

41. Pulliainen, E., and V. Hyypiä. 1975. [Winter food and feeding habits of lynxes (*Lynx lynx*) in southeastern Finland.] (In Finnish, with English summary.) *Suomen Riista* 26: 60–63.

42. Zheltukhin, A. S. 1986. [Biocoenotic relationships of the European lynx (*Lynx lynx*) in the southern taiga of the Upper Volga.] (In Russian, with English summary.) *Zool. Zh.* 65: 259–271.

43. Breitenmoser, U., P. Kaczensky, M. Dötterer, C. Breitenmoser-Würsten, S. Capt, F. Bernhart, and M. Liberek. 1993. Spatial organization and recruitment of lynx (*Lynx lynx*) in a re-introduced population in the Swiss Jura Mountains. *J. Zool.* (Lond.) 231: 449–464.

44. Zheltukhin, A. S. 1984. [Daily activity and sizes of home

ranges of the lynx in the southern taiga of the upper Volga USSR River region.] (In Russian, with English summary.) *Byull. Mosk. Obshkch. Ispyt. Prir.* (Otd. Biol.) 89: 54–62.

45. Schmidt, K., W. Jedrzejewski, and H. Okarma. 1997. Spatial organization and social relations in the Eurasian lynx population in Bialowieza Primeval Forest, Poland. *Acta Theriologica* 42: 289–312.

46. Haller, H., and U. Breitenmoser. 1986. Zur Raumorganisation der in den Schweizer Alpen wiederangesiedelten Population des Luchses (*Lynx lynx*). *Z. Säugetierk.* 51: 289–311.

47. Breitenmoser, U., B. G. Slough, and C. Breitenmoser-Würsten. 1993. Predators of cyclic prey: Is the Canada lynx victim or profiteer of the snowshoe hare cycle? *Oikos* 66: 551–554.

48. Poole, K. G. 1994. Characteristics of an unharvested lynx population during a snowshoe hare decline. *J. Wildl. Mgmt.* 58: 608–618.

49. Sandell, M. 1989. The mating tactics and spacing patterns of solitary carnivores. In *Carnivore behavior, ecology and evolution*, ed. J. L. Gittleman, 164–182. Ithaca, NY: Cornell University Press.

50. Peters, G. 1984. On the structure of friendly close range vocalizations in terrestrial carnivores (Mammalia: Carnivora: Fissipedia). *Z. Säugetierk.* 49: 157–182.

51. Peters, G. 1987. Acoustic communication in the genus *Lynx* (Mammalia: Felidae)—comparative survey and phylogenetic interpretation. *Bonn. Zool. Beitr.* 38: 315–330.

52. Bürger, M. 1966. Breeding of the European lynx at Magdeburg Zoo. *Int. Zoo Yrbk.* 6: 182.

53. Stehlik, J. 1978. Zur Ethologie, insbesondere zur Fortpflanzung von Luchsen in Gefangenschaft. In *Der Luchs in Europa*, ed. A. Festetics, 196–215. Greven: Kilda-Verlag.

54. Stehlik, J. 1983. Le comportement sexuel du lynx boréal (*Lynx lynx*). *Mammalia* 47: 483–491.

55. Wayre, P. 1968. Breeding the European lynx *Felis l. lynx* at the Norfolk Wildlife Park. *Int. Zoo Yrbk.* 9: 95–96.

56. Andrews, P., Hexagon Farm Wild Feline Breeding Facility, 1187 Merrill Road, San Juan Bautista, CA. Personal communication.

57. Seager, S. W. J., and C. N. Demorest. 1986. Reproduction of captive wild carnivores. In *Zoo and wild animal medicine*, 2nd ed., ed. M. E. Fowler, 667–706. Philadelphia: W. B. Saunders.

58. Kvam, T. 1991. Reproduction in the European lynx, *Lynx lynx*. *Z. Säugetierk.* 56: 146–158.

59. Brand, C. J., and L. B. Keith. 1979. Lynx demography during a snowshoe hare decline in Alberta. *J. Wildl. Mgmt.* 43: 827–849.

60. Kunc, L. 1970. Breeding and rearing the Northern lynx *Felis l. lynx* at Ostrava Zoo. *Int. Zoo Yrbk.* 10: 83–84.

61. Cat News. 1991. Female lynx range and cub mortality. *Cat News* 15: 14–15.

62. Hemmer, H. 1979. Gestation period and postnatal development in felids. *Carnivore* 2: 90–100.

63. Jones, M. L. 1977. Record keeping and longevity of felids in captivity. In *The world's cats*, vol. 3, no. 3, ed. R. L. Eaton, 132–138. Seattle: Carnivore Research Institute, Burke Museum, University of Washington.

64. Beaufort, F. 1965. Lynx des Pyrénées, *Felis* (L.) *lynx lynx* (L.). *Mammalia* 29: 598–601.

65. Beaufort, F. 1968. Survivance du lynx dans le Parc National des Pyrénées occidentales. *Mammalia* 32: 207–210.

66. Navarre, H. 1976. Observations récentes sur le lynx dans les Pyrénées occidentales. *Mammalia* 40: 518–519.

67. Chazel, L. 1989. Notes sur la survivance du lynx dans les Pyrénées françaises. *Mammalia* 53: 461–464.

68. Okarma, H. 1992. Status, distribution and numbers of lynx in Poland. In *The situation, conservation needs and reintroduction of lynx in Europe*, 23–25. Environmental Encounters, no. 11. Strasbourg: Council of Europe Press.

69. Hell, P. 1992. Managing the lynx population in Czechoslovakia. In *The situation, conservation needs and reintroduction of lynx in Europe*, 36–39. Environmental Encounters, no. 11. Strasbourg: Council of Europe Press.

70. Guidali, F., T. Mingozzi, and G. Tosi. 1990. Historical and recent distribution of lynx (*Lynx lynx* L.) in northwestern Italy, during the nineteenth and twentieth centuries. *Mammalia* 54: 587–596.

71. Ragni, B., M. Possenti, F. Guidali, T. Mingozzi, and G. Tosi. 1992. Status of the lynx in Italy. In *The situation, conservation needs and reintroduction of lynx in Europe*, 74–76. Environmental Encounters, no. 11. Strasbourg: Council of Europe Press.

72. Breitenmoser, U. 1983. Zur Wiedereinbürgerung und Ausbreitung des Luchses (*Lynx lynx* L.) in der Schweiz. *Schweiz. Zeitschr. Forstwesen* 134: 207–222.

73. Zheltukhin, A. 1992. Distribution and numbers of lynx in the Soviet Union. In *The situation, conservation needs and reintroduction of lynx in Europe*, 19–22. Environmental Encounters, no. 11. Strasbourg: Council of Europe Press.

74. Chundawat, R. S. 1990. Lynx survey in Nubra Valley, Ladakh. *Wildl. Inst. India Newsl.* 5(2): 42–44.

75. Yalden, D. W. 1993. The problems of reintroducing carnivores. *Symp. Zool. Soc. Lond.* 65: 289–306.

76. Cop, J. 1992. Reintroduction of lynx in Yugoslavia. In *The situation, conservation needs and reintroduction of lynx in Europe*, 60–62. Environmental Encounters, no. 11. Strasbourg: Council of Europe Press.

77. Tassi, F. 1991. Will the lynx return to central Italy? *Cat News* 15: 12–14.

78. Wotschikowsky, U., and G. Kerger. 1992. Summary of experiences on lynx reintroduction in Europe. In *The situation, conservation needs and reintroduction of lynx in Europe*, 43–49. Environmental Encounters, no. 11. Strasbourg: Council of Europe Press.

79. Herrenschmidt, V. 1989. Lynx (*Lynx lynx*) reintroduction in France. *Felid* 4: 20.

80. Herrenschmidt, V., and J.-M. Vandel. 1992. The reappearance of the lynx in France. In *The situation, conservation needs and reintroduction of lynx in Europe*, 56–59. Environmental Encounters, no. 11. Strasbourg: Council of Europe Press.

81. Cat News. French hunters call for lynx control. 1990. *Cat News* 13: 17–18.

82. Boegli, J. P. 1992. The lynx and hunting. In *The situation, conservation needs and reintroduction of lynx in Europe*, 63–65. Environmental Encounters, no. 11. Strasbourg: Council of Europe Press.

83. Grosjean, D. 1992. Impact of lynx on farming. In *The situation, conservation needs and reintroduction of lynx in Europe*, 66–70. Environmental Encounters, no. 11. Strasbourg: Council of Europe Press.

84. Gossow, H., and P. Honsig-Erlenburg. 1986. Management problems with re-introduced lynx in Austria. In *Cats of the world: Biology, conservation, and management*, ed. S. D. Miller and D. D. Everett, 77–83. Washington, DC: National Wildlife Federation.

85. Ward, A. E. 1923. Game animals of Kashmir and adjacent hill provinces. *J. Bombay Nat. Hist. Soc.* 29: 23–35.

Iberian lynx

Lynx pardinus (Temminck, 1827)

DESCRIPTION

The Iberian lynx is a medium-sized cat. Its adult weight is 8 to 15 kilograms, or about half that of the Eurasian lynx, and it is thus closer in size to the New World lynx species (bobcat and Canada lynx) than to its Old World relative. It is nevertheless recognizable as a lynx by its short tail, short body, long legs, tufted ears, and relatively small head.[1] The cat stands 40 to 50 centimeters high at the shoulder. The sexes are dimorphic, with adult males being about 27 percent heavier than adult females; males are also typically longer than females. Both sexes have prominent facial whiskers (ruff), and the ears are tipped with long, erect tufts of black hair, which are longer in males than in females (4.9 vs. 3.8 centimeters). The backs of the ears are black at the tip with a whitish triangular area near the base.

Of all the lynx, the Iberian lynx has the most heavily spotted coat. It also differs from other lynx in that its coat is described as relatively sparse, short, and coarse. Its basic coat color is bright yellowish red or tawny overlaid with dark brown or black spots, while the underparts are white. On the flanks the spots appear as several parallel rows extending from the shoulder to the groin. However, the size, shape, and pattern of the spots may vary geographically, and three pelage patterns are recognized.[1] Researchers have noted that all the lynx captured lately in the Coto Doñana area of Spain are marked with large and distinct black lines and spots, whereas Iberian lynx from elsewhere have small and poorly defined black spots, although both forms occurred in the Doñana area until about 1960. In fact, the spot patterns of lynx from the Doñana area are remarkably uniform, a feature that has been attributed to a loss of genetic variation in the Doñana population.

DISTRIBUTION

In the mid-nineteenth century lynx were reportedly found in all parts of the Iberian peninsula, although their abundance varied regionally.[2] By the early twentieth century they had disappeared from northern Spain, but were still abundant in the central and southern regions. However, lynx numbers were reduced even further following the initiation of the "wheat programme" in the 1940s in Portugal, the large-scale conversion of native forest to pine and eucalyptus plantations in both Spain and Portugal, and myxomatosis epidemics among rabbit populations in the 1950s and 1960s. By the 1970s the lynx's range was

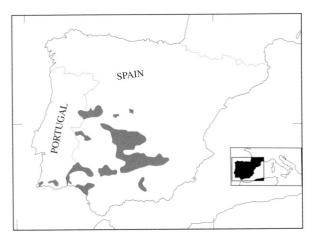

Figure 27. Distribution of the Iberian lynx.

limited to the southwestern quarter of the peninsula (fig. 27).

A 1987–1988 survey indicated that the total lynx population in Spain was only 880 to 1,150 animals, with possibly another 40 to 60 individuals in Portugal.[3] These individuals were widely distributed among forty-eight sites within ten central and southwestern areas in Spain and three sites in Portugal. Most of these sites are small (91 percent are less than 500 square kilometers), and only eight are thought to contain more than a couple of dozen individuals. The four largest areas (Sierra Morena Central and Oriental, Montes de Toledo, and Villuercas y Monfragüe) account for more than half of the range occupied by lynx in Spain.

The change in the Iberian lynx's range from 1960 to 1990 has been dramatic. Within Spain, it now occurs in only eight of the thirty regions it occupied in 1960. Furthermore, lynx have not recolonized unoccupied portions of their former range, and those populations that do remain are being increasingly fragmented and genetically isolated. About 65 percent of the total estimated population occurs in just two areas in south-central Spain (Sierra Morena and Montes de Toledo). An estimated fifty to sixty animals occur in a 1,000-square-kilometer area in southwestern Spain; this area includes the Doñana National Park (570 square kilometers).[3,4]

ECOLOGY AND BEHAVIOR

Most of what has been published on the ecology and behavior of the Iberian lynx comes from a long-term field study conducted at the Doñana Biological Reserve, a 70-square-kilometer area within the National Park.[5] The first accounts (1950s and 1960s) of lynx natural history were made by José Antonio Valverde.[6,7] These were followed by more intensive studies on food habits by Miguel Delibes,[8,9] and information on density, social organization, dispersal, activity patterns, mortality, and energetics were collected by Delibes and his co-workers.[4,10,11,12,13,14,15,16,17,18,19,20] Between 1983 and 1992, studies in Doñana incorporated radio telemetry, with a total of thirty-six lynx being monitored.

Across their geographic distribution, lynx species in general seem to prefer areas with dense cover, although the type of habitat may vary considerably. The Iberian lynx is apparently no exception, being most abundant where habitat diversity is high and the vegetative cover is a mosaic of open forest mixed with extensive areas of dense bush or shrubs (matorral). The cat was formerly found in deciduous and coniferous forest, but it is currently confined to mountainous areas with Mediterranean vegetation at elevations between 400 and 1,300 meters, although it is occasionally found at higher and lower elevations in the central mountains.[2] The only exception is in southwestern Spain, where the lynx has established itself in the lowland Mediterranean forests, scrublands (maquis), and marshes of the Doñana region.[4]

Studies of lynx in Doñana show that their habitat use patterns are related primarily to environmental variables and seasonal differences in prey availability and vulnerability.[4,16] Use of dense scrublands (maquis), for example, is high in both summer and winter. More than 90 percent of lynx summer daytime rest sites were in dense heath thickets, presumably for relief from high temperatures and humidity. Similarly, scrublands were also favorite daytime rest sites of lynx in the winter, probably because they provide protection from cold and rain. The maquis is also used in the spring for den sites by females with kittens. However, lynx hunt mainly in the open pastures and scrub-forest edge between the scrublands and the marshes. This pasture and edge area (vera) is the zone of highest rabbit abundance and the preferred habitat of fallow deer as well.[9,15,21] Many mallard ducks are taken by lynx in spring, when the ducks leave the marshes to breed and nest in the small pools of the scrublands. Such behavior appears to increase duck vulnerability, as predation on waterfowl by lynx is normally less during the winter, even though large numbers of waterfowl congregate on the marshes.[8,9]

Lynx in Doñana are generally nocturnal, but there is a fair amount of individual and seasonal variation in their activity patterns.[19] Most (38 percent) of the variation in nocturnal activity reflected individual differences. Photoperiod was also an important (29 percent) source of variation, with lynx being more active during day and night as day length decreased. Seasonal variation ranked third (21 percent), and was most often seen as influencing the level of diurnal activity. For example, during the summer, adult lynx are primarily nocturnal, and activity levels are high around sunset and sunrise, which corresponds to the times when lynx are moving from rest sites to hunting areas or back again. In the winter, however, adult lynx were commonly found moving about during the daytime, and no regular pattern of activity was evident. Irregularity in activity patterns was, however, more common for juveniles than for adult lynx. In general, the activity patterns of lynx are closely synchronized with those of their major prey, the rabbit.

Feeding Ecology

Studies of lynx food habits in the mountains of central Spain found rabbit remains in more than three-quarters of all fecal ($n = 37$) and stomach ($n = 56$) samples examined, and rabbits contributed almost 85 percent of the total amount of food consumed.[22,23] Rodents and birds, principally red-legged partridge, are important secondary prey. An examination of a large number ($n = 71$) of wildcat stomachs from the same area revealed that wildcats prey more intensively on small rodents than do lynx, although rabbits still account for 63 percent of the total amount of food eaten by wildcats.[23]

The lynx in Doñana National Park is described as a specialized predator of medium-sized to small terrestrial vertebrates, although the vast majority of its prey weigh about 1 kilogram. Studies of lynx food habits in 1973–1975 and again in 1983–1984 showed the same general pattern; the staple year-round prey for lynx is the rabbit, occurring in 73 to 88 percent of all scats examined.[9,16,22] In terms of amount eaten, rabbits contribute 75 to 93 percent of the lynx's diet. Birds, principally ducks and geese, rank a distant second in terms of frequency of occurrence (19 percent) in scats. Predation on geese was higher in 1983–1984 than previously, but drought conditions in 1983 were thought to have increased the vulnerability of geese overwintering on the marshes.[16] Normally, lynx predation on waterfowl is greatest in the spring, and is then largely confined to upland-nesting mallards. Ungulates, including fallow and red deer, do not appear to be a major part of the lynx diet except in the fall–winter period. A variety of other animals, including snakes, lizards, and rats, occur infrequently in lynx scats from Doñana. Small mammals used to occur infrequently in the cat's diet, but habitat changes in the park have apparently been favorable for small mammals, and they now occur more frequently in scats.[8]

While rabbits are the mainstay for lynx in Doñana National Park, the relative frequency of rabbits in the diet varies seasonally. Rabbits attain maximum densities in May–June or June–July, then decline over the summer, reach minimum densities in the fall (October), and increase again following the onset of rains in the winter.[16,24] The density at the peak can be four or more times higher than at the minimum (e.g., eight vs. two rabbits per square kilometer). Strangely, predation on rabbits does not follow their relative abundance: the highest frequency of rabbits in the lynx's diet occurs in the fall. This finding has been attributed to an increase in vulnerability of young rabbits and, more importantly, to the effects of myxomatosis, a disease that affects rabbits almost exclusively in the summer.[9] Observations of lynx playing (catch-release) with rabbits occurred when the incidence of myxomatosis was high, and in a few cases the cat let the rabbit escape. Aldama and Delibes suggest that these incomplete predatory sequences were related to an abundance of easily captured prey—namely, rabbits.[24] However, from October to February, rabbit densities are low, and those that have survived are mostly healthy adults, forcing lynx to look for alternative prey, the most important of which are ungulates.

Lynx predation on ungulates occurs mainly in the fall–winter period and is largely confined to fawns and juvenile deer (less than one year old).[9,11] The timing corresponds to the initiation of the rut and the consequent disruption of doe-fawn relations, which is thought to increase the vulnerability of young deer. Lynx predation is greater on fallow deer than on red deer, even though red deer are more abundant, suggesting that lynx prefer fallow deer, or that they are more vulnerable. Fallow deer are, however, strongly associated with the more open ecotonal habitat between the scrublands and marshes, which is thought to increase their chances of being located and ambushed by lynx. Red deer spend more time in the dense scrublands, where stalk-and-ambush hunting is apparently more difficult.

Red deer are also larger than fallow deer, and prey size appears to be an important component of lynx predation. Among twenty-four deer killed by lynx in Doñana, only three were adults, and those were fallow deer,[11] although an early account by Valverde indicates that adult female red deer are occasionally taken by lynx.[7] Adult male red deer are probably too large to be taken, although fawns are not. About 10 percent of red deer fawn mortality is probably attributable to lynx predation, whereas lynx may account for 40 to 50 percent of fallow deer fawn mortality in Doñana. However, some lynx-killed fawns were in extremely poor physical condition, suggesting that lynx predation may be partially compensating for fawn mortality that would otherwise be attributable to starvation.[9]

Lynx kill deer with one or more bites to the throat, crushing the larynx so that the animal dies from suffocation.[11] They kill rabbits with a bite to the base of the skull or nape, which results in cervical dislocation and spinal cord damage. These techniques are commonly used by felids to kill prey, with the throat bite being used on prey that are larger than the cat. Lynx drag their deer kills into dense cover before beginning to feed. Feeding usually begins on the thighs and then proceeds to the shoulder and neck; when the stomach cavity is opened, the gastrointestinal tract is removed and set aside. With rabbits, feeding begins at the head and continues until the entire animal is eaten.[9]

With deer, the amount eaten per meal is about 1 kilogram, although little remained of a yearling female fallow deer (20–25 kilograms) after three days of feeding by three lynx.[15] Similarly, only skin and bones remained of an 18–20-kilogram young male fallow deer after three days of feeding by the same three lynx. In the first case, the feeding group consisted of an adult female, her dependent son, and her independent daughter from a previous litter. In the second case, which occurred about a year later, this same adult female and her now independent son were seen sharing the kill; the independent daughter, who had settled in an adjoining area, was observed near the kill, but it was uncertain whether she also fed on the carcass. On its own, a lynx will feed on a deer carcass for several days, but the number of meals depends on the size of the kill and how long it takes scavengers, principally wild pigs, to find the carcass. Like other felids, lynx will rake soil, branches, and other debris over what remains of a large kill when leaving it, presumably in an attempt to hide the carcass from scavengers until the cat returns.[11] Some meat may also be lost to red foxes, although lynx and fox diets show little overlap except during the fox breeding period, when foxes are feeding extensively on rabbits.[12]

Lynx obtain most of their energy needs from rabbits. Based on captive feeding trials, the maintenance diet for a male lynx is estimated at 912 kilocalories per day, compared with 673 kilocalories per day for a female.[14] This amount converts, for a lynx feeding solely on rabbits, to a male needing 379 rabbits per year and a nonreproductive female, 277 per year. However, since lynx do not feed exclusively on rabbits, the number consumed annually should be somewhat less, although the number is probably close to the mark because the increased energy demands of females with kittens would most likely be largely met by rabbits.

What effect lynx predation has on the rabbit population in Doñana is not known, although Delibes has estimated that annually lynx may remove 3.5 percent of the population.[9] While this percentage is low, he argues that predation is nevertheless an important factor because it is heaviest when rabbit numbers are low.

Social Organization

The spatial arrangement of lynx home ranges in Doñana National Park is similar to that of other felids in that there is little range overlap for resident animals of the same sex, although each male's territory typically overlaps only one of the smaller female territories.[20] Other than females with young and associations for mating, lynx were essentially solitary. Based on radio-tracking data, annual territory size averaged 10.3 square kilometers for resident males and 8.7 square kilometers for resident females. As with other felids, the range sizes of female Iberian lynx are greatly reduced when they have small kittens; one female restricted her movements to an area of only 1.7 square kilometers during the first months of her kittens' lives. Estimates of lynx density in the park vary from ten to eighteen per 100 square kilometers.[12] However, densities in buffer areas adjacent to the park are estimated at only two to four per 100 square kilometers.[4]

Occupancy of ranges by lynx appears to be indicated primarily by scent marking, principally the deposition of urine and feces. Lynx leave their feces uncovered at nonrandom locations within their ranges, preferentially depositing them on narrow human-made tracks through the vegetation and at intersections of deer trails and tracks.[13] The density of feces was also higher in areas of home range overlap, suggesting the importance of scent marks as a type of advertisement of occupancy. A few residents have, however, been forced out of their ranges by other lynx, and at least one was severely injured in the process.[20] Social status appears to have a strong effect on mortality rates, and non-territory holders suffer greater mortality rates than do residents.[18]

It is not known whether lynx spend a disproportionate amount of time in the areas that are more intensively scent-marked, but they travel extensively and thus probably visit most parts of their ranges on a regular basis. One adult male, for example, traveled an average of 9.3 kilometers per day over a four-day tracking period, and the distance he traveled per day (mostly at night) varied from 5.9 to 13.6 kilometers.[25] The average distance traveled per day for males was 8.7 kilometers, compared with 6.4 kilometers for females.[20] The greater distances traveled by males are probably related to their slightly larger ranges and their need to patrol the area and check on the reproductive status of any females residing within their territories.

As only residents were observed to breed, there was considerable activity associated with acquiring and maintaining territories in the optimal habitat (vera), which was located within the park.[20] Some established residents were ousted from their territories by younger adults, and boundary disputes, some of which lasted for several months, were a regular feature of home range dynamics. Territorial boundaries often coincided with roads and trails, and they were intensively scent-marked by both sexes. Interestingly, females that acquired the territory of another female, whether by takeover, inheritance, or filling a vacancy, essentially occupied the same space used by the previous owner. One female was known to have occupied a territory for 5.2 years, and for five other females, the minimum time of occupancy was 2.3 years. The length of tenure for males appears to be shorter. Minimum occupancy times of 4.0 and 2.6 years were recorded for two males, but on average the minimum occupancy time for males was 1.5 years. Some lynx were able to establish themselves in territories by two years of age, but acquisition of a territory in the optimal vera habitat was almost invariably accomplished only by older cats, both females (three to seven years old) and males (four to seven years old).

Reproduction and Development

There are no details available on the mating behavior of Iberian lynx, although a few observations suggest that mating begins in January and February. Following a gestation period of sixty-three to seventy-three days, young are born in March and April, although breeding can take place in any month of the year.[6,8] Litter size varies from one to four kittens, but the most common size is two. For one female, the interval between consecutive births was about fifteen months.[15]

Young lynx remain in their natal ranges until dispersal, which begins in their second winter or when they are about twenty months old. Aldama and Delibes reported that a twenty-one-month-old female lynx was still living in her natal range, but by twenty-six months of age she had established her own territory in an area adjoining her mother's territory. A six-month-old male was still located with his mother about 75 percent of time, but at eighteen months of age he was fully independent, and at twenty-three months he began making exploratory (pre-dispersal) trips outside his natal range.[15] Three females had established themselves on territories by twenty-four to twenty-five months of age, and, following dispersal, four males first acquired territories when they were twenty-four, twenty-five, twenty-six, and twenty-nine months old.[20]

The direction that dispersers in Doñana National Park can take is restricted by the Guadalquivir River, but some lynx have managed to establish themselves in unprotected areas more than 30 kilometers from the park. These greater dispersal distances are typically associated with males. However, animals that disperse outside the park suffer high rates of mortality, principally due to human activities.[18]

There is little information on the longevity of Iberian lynx, although one skull in the collection of the Estación Biológica de Doñana was estimated from counts of tooth annuli (annual rings, like those of a tree) to be fourteen years old.[26]

STATUS IN THE WILD

The Iberian lynx is critically endangered, and some feel that it is probably the most endangered carnivore in Europe. Lynx populations on the Iberian Peninsula have been greatly reduced, and lynx currently exist in small, isolated, and highly fragmented areas.[3] These localized populations are vulnerable to extinction simply by virtue of their small size, as a single epidemic could wipe out the few remaining individuals. Any deterioration in habitat quality will also reduce the capacity of the area to support those lynx that are there. Some areas are no longer suitable for lynx due to loss of habitat. The conversion of bush and heath forests to pine and eucalyptus plantations has significantly reduced rabbit populations and consequently lynx populations. Rabbit numbers have also declined due to myxomatosis, and their numbers have been further reduced since the arrival of viral hemorrhagic pneumonia in Spain in 1988.[27,28]

Few Iberian lynx die of natural causes. About three-quarters of all lynx mortality is attributable to human-related activities such as shooting, poaching, poisoning, snaring, or trapping.[3] In some cases the deaths are accidental, and are related to lynx getting caught in snares set for rabbits, being hit trying to cross highways, or falling into artesian wells and drowning.

Even within Doñana National Park, illegal trapping and other human-related activities are a significant source of lynx mortality. In fact, the annual mortality rate of lynx in the park is similar to that of some harvested felid populations.[18] Between 1983 and 1989, for example, twenty-four lynx (eleven radio-tagged) died in the park and another six in the surrounding area. Only three of these animals died from natural causes; the remaining deaths were related to a variety of human activities. The high mortality rates of adult lynx in Doñana have been shown to be an important parameter in an analysis of risk of extinction.[29]

CONSERVATION EFFORTS

The Spanish National Nature Conservation Institute (ICONA), in collaboration with the Consejo Superior de Investigaciones Científicas (CSIC), has issued a management plan for the lynx in Doñana National Park.[30] The measures include increasing rabbit numbers within the park through habitat improvements and the removal of ungulates to other areas, thus decreasing competition with rabbits for food.[31] In areas surrounding the park, efforts are being made to reduce lynx traffic fatalities, eliminate trapping of rabbits and other carnivores, and initiate a campaign on environmental awareness.

As part of its recovery plan, ICONA has proposed similar conservation measures for other areas of Spain that still contain sizable lynx populations.[2] The aim of the plan is, first, to stop the population decline, and second, to increase lynx densities and promote genetic exchange via corridors. An analysis of habitat use by radio-tagged lynx in the Doñana region showed that mediterranean scrubland was strongly preferred by residents, whereas pine plantations were also important during and after dispersal. That dispersing animals used lower-quality habitats such as pine plantations is encouraging because these habitats also are suitable for compatible human use. These results suggest that dispersal between resident lynx populations could be promoted by establishing a matrix of intervening patches of lower-quality habitat. However, dispersing lynx avoided open habitats, and thus it will be important to consider not only the spatial arrangement of the patches, but also whether lynx can or will move between patches.[32]

Efforts to conserve the Iberian lynx also include plans to establish a captive breeding program, utilizing lynx that have been injured but cannot be returned to the wild, with a view to eventually reintroducing animals to formerly occupied range.

TABLE 32 MEASUREMENTS AND WEIGHTS OF ADULT IBERIAN LYNX

HB	n	T	n	WT	n	Location	Source
787	6m	148	6m	12.8	6m	Doñana NP	1
(747–820)		(125–160)		(11.1–15.9)			
720	6f	143	6f	9.3	4f	Doñana NP	1
(682–754)		(127–160)		(8.7–9.9)			
752	1m	138	1m	7.0, 14.0	2m	Spain	33
710, 775	2f	150, 154	2f	9.6	3f	Spain	33
				(9.2–10.0)			

Note: HB = head and body length (mm); T = tail length (mm); WT = weight (kg). n = sample size. Sex: m = male, f = female, ? = unknown. Mean values are presented only for sample sizes of three or more. Range of values is in parentheses.

TABLE 33 FREQUENCY OF OCCURRENCE OF PREY ITEMS IN THE DIETS OF IBERIAN LYNX (PERCENTAGE OF SAMPLES)

Prey items	Coto Doñana, Spain[9] Scats (n = 1,537)
Oryctolagus cuniculus	88.3
Old World rabbit	
Lepus capensis	0.3
Hare	
Unidentified lagomorphs	0.3
Eliomys quercinus	0.8
Dormouse	
Rattus sp.	0.4
Black rat	
Apodemus-Mus spp.	1.2
Field-house mouse	
Unidentified small mammals	0.9
Cervus elaphus	1.2
Red deer	
Dama dama	3.1
Fallow deer	
Unidentified ungulates	1.0
Ducks	17.7
Birds	5.0
Reptiles	0.1
Minimum number of vertebrate prey	1,855

REFERENCES

1. Beltrán, J. F., and M. Delibes. 1993. Physical characteristics of Iberian lynxes (*Lynx pardinus*) from Doñana, southwestern Spain. *J. Mammal.* 74: 852–862.

2. ICONA. 1990. Status and conservation of the pardel lynx (*Lynx pardina* Temminck, 1824) in the Iberian peninsula. Convention on the Conservation of European Wildlife and Natural Habitats, 1–19. Strasbourg: Council of Europe Press.

3. Rodríguez, A., and M. Delibes. 1992. Current range and status of the Iberian lynx *Felis pardina* Temminck, 1824 in Spain. *Biol. Conserv.* 61: 189–196.

4. Palomares, F., A. Rodríguez, R. Laffitte, and M. Delibes. 1991. The status and distribution of the Iberian lynx *Felis pardina* (Temminck) in Coto Doñana area, SW Spain. *Biol. Conserv.* 57: 159–169.

5. Beltrán, J. F. 1987. Base bibliográfica de especies amenazadas: El lince ibérico (*Lynx pardina* Temminck, 1824). Agencia de medio Ambiente, Junta de Andalucía.

6. Valverde, J. A. 1957. Notes écologiques sur le lynx d'Espagne *Felis lynx pardina* Temminck. *Terre Vie* 1957: 51–67.

7. Valverde, J. A. 1964. Rémarques sur la structure et l'évolution des communautés de vertébrés terrestres I. Structure d'une communauté. II. Rapports enrte prédateurs et proies. *Terre Vie* 1964: 121–154.

8. Delibes, M., F. Palacios, J. Garzon, and J. Castroviejo. 1975. Notes sur l'alimentation et la biologie du lynx pardelle, *Lynx pardina* (Temminck, 1824), en Espagne. *Mammalia* 39: 387–393.

9. Delibes, M. 1980. Feeding ecology of the Spanish lynx in the Coto Doñana. *Acta Theriologica* 25: 309–324.

10. García-Perea, R., J. Gisbert, and F. Palacios. 1985. Review of the biometrical and morphological features of the skull of the Iberian lynx, *Lynx pardina* (Temminck, 1824). *Säugetierk. Mitt.* 32: 249–259.

11. Beltrán, J. F., C. San José, M. Delibes, and F. Braza. 1985. An analysis of the Iberian lynx predation upon fallow deer in the Coto Doñana, SW Spain. Transactions XVIIth Congress of International Union Game Biologists, Brussels, 961–967.

12. Rau, J. R., J. F. Beltrán, and M. Delibes. 1985. Can the increase of fox density explain the decrease in lynx numbers at Doñana? *Rev. Ecol. (Terre Vie)* 40: 145–150.

13. Robinson, I. H., and M. Delibes. 1988. The distribution of faeces by the Spanish lynx (*Felis pardina*). *J. Zool.* (Lond.) 216: 557–582.

14. Aldama, J. J., J. F. Beltrán, and M. Delibes. 1991. Energy expenditure and prey requirements of free-ranging Iberian lynx in southwest Spain. *J. Wildl. Mgmt.* 55: 635–641.

15. Aldama, J. J., and M. Delibes. 1991. Observations of feeding groups in the Spanish lynx (*Felis pardina*) in the Doñana National Park, SW Spain. *Mammalia* 55: 143–147.

16. Beltrán, J. F., and M. Delibes. 1991. Ecología trófica del lince ibérico en Doñana durante un período seco. *Doñana Acata Vertebr.* 18: 113–122.

17. Beltrán, J. F., J. J. Aldama, and M. Delibes. 1992. Ecology of the Iberian lynx in Doñana, southwestern Spain. In *Global trends in wildlife management*, ed. B. Bobek, K. Perzanowski, and W. Regelin, 331–334. Krakow-Warszawa: Swiat Press.

18. Ferreras, P., J. J. Aldama, J. F. Beltrán, and M. Delibes. 1992. Rates and causes of mortality in a fragmented population of Iberian lynx *Felis pardina* Temminck, 1824. *Biol. Conserv.* 61: 197–202.

19. Beltrán, J. F., and M. Delibes. 1994. Environmental determinants of circadian activity of free-ranging Iberian lynxes. *J. Mammal.* 75: 382–393.

20. Ferreras, P., J. F. Beltrán, J. J. Aldama, and M. Delibes. 1997. Spatial organization and land tenure system of the endangered Iberian lynx (*Lynx pardinus*). *J. Zool.* (Lond.) 243: 163–189.

21. Beltrán, J. F. 1991. Temporal abundance pattern of the wild rabbit in Doñana, SW Spain. *Mammalia* 55: 591–599.

22. Rogers, P. M. 1978. Predator-prey relationships between rabbit and lynx in southern Spain. *Terre Vie* 32: 83–87.

23. Aymerich, M. 1982. Etude comparative des régimes du lynx pardelle (*Lynx pardina* Temminck, 1824) et du chat sauvage (*Felis silvestris* Schreber, 1777) au centre de la péninsule Ibérique. *Mammalia* 46: 515–521.

24. Aldama, J. J., and M. Delibes. 1991. Field observations of Spanish lynxes (*Felis pardina*) playing with prey in Doñana, southwest Spain. *J. Zool.* (Lond.) 225: 683–684.

25. Delibes, M., and J. F. Beltrán. 1984. Ecología del lince ibérico en el Parque Nacional de Doñana. *Quercus* 14: 4–9.

26. Zapata, S. C., R. García-Perea, J. F. Beltrán, P. Ferreras, and M. Delibes. 1997. Age determination of Iberian lynx (*Lynx pardinus*) using canine radiograph and cementum annuli enumeration. *Z. Säugetierk.* 62: 119–123.

27. Argüello, J. L., J. L. Llanos, and A. Perez-Ordoyo. 1988. Enfermedad vírica hemorrágica del conejo en España. *Med. Vet.* 5: 645–650.

28. Villafuerte, R., C. Calverte, C. Gortázar, and S. Moreno. 1994. First epizootic of rabbit haemorrhagic disease in free living populations of *Oryctolagus cuniculus* at Doñana National Park, Spain. *J. Wildl. Dis.* 30: 176–179.

29. Gaona, P., P. Ferreras, and M. Delibes. 1998. Dynamics and viability of a metapopulation of the endangered Iberian lynx (*Lynx pardinus*). *Ecol. Monogr.* 68: 349–370.

30. Aymerich, M. 1992. Management of a lynx population in the Doñana National Park. In *The situation, conservation needs, and reintroduction of lynx in Europe*, 33–35. Environmental Encounters, no. 11. Strasbourg: Council of Europe Press.

31. Moreno, S., and R. Villafuerte. 1995. Traditional management of scrubland for the conservation of rabbits *Oryctolagus cuniculus* and their predators in Doñana National Park, Spain. *Biol. Conserv.* 73: 81–85.

32. Palomares, F., M. Delibes, P. Ferreras, J. M. Fedriani, J. Calzada, and E. Revilla. 2000. Iberian lynx in a fragmented landscape: Predispersal, dispersal, and postdispersal habitats. *Conserv. Biol.* 14: 809–818.

33. García-Perea, R. 1991. Variabilidad morfológica del género *Lynx* Kerr, 1792 (Carnivora: Felidae). Ph.D. dissertation, University Complutense, Madrid, Spain.

Bobcat

Lynx rufus (Schreber, 1777)

DESCRIPTION

The bobcat's common name is derived from its bobbed tail, but it is also known by a number of other names, including wildcat, bay lynx, lynx cat, pallid bobcat, red lynx, *chat sauvage,* and *gato monte.* The bobcat is roughly the size of a cocker spaniel, but is generally more muscular and has much longer legs. This cat has long legs relative to its body length, a small head, and a short tail. The tail is about 14 centimeters long, white underneath and marked with dark bands above. The large ears are tipped with a short tuft of black hairs, and the backs of the ears are black with a prominent white spot. A ruff of fur flares from the animal's cheeks and neck, and the large eyes are ringed with white.[1,2]

Bobcat fur is thick and soft and is much in demand by the fur industry. The pelts are used for coats and jackets and for trimming other fur garments, but it does not wear as well as the fur of mustelids, such as mink or sable.[3] The background color of the coat varies from buff, brown, reddish or yellowish brown to light gray and is streaked or spotted with black or dark brown, giving the cat a mottled appearance. The fur on the belly and inside of the limbs is white and is marked with black or dark brown spots or bars. Both melanistic and albino bobcats have been reported; a Texas zoo kept an albino bobcat for several years,[4] and there are ten reports of black bobcats, all from southern Florida.[5,6]

Adult male bobcats are typically longer and 30 to 40 percent heavier than females;[2] the record adult male weighed 26.8 kilograms, whereas the largest adult female on record was 15.9 kilograms.[4] However, weight and other physical dimensions vary with age, season, and geographic location. Bobcats at northern latitudes are generally larger than those from the southern part of their range. For example, in a small sample of bobcats from Oklahoma, the average weight of adult males was 8.9 kilograms and that of adult females was 5.8 kilograms,[7] whereas in northern Minnesota, the average winter weight for males was 13.0 kilograms and for females, 9.2 kilograms.[8]

Sexual dimorphism is also evident in skull dimensions. The skulls of males are larger and have more prominent ridges than those of similar-aged females.[2,9,10] While bobcat and domestic cat skulls appear to be roughly the same size, bobcat skulls are shorter, wider, and more sharply ridged; the bobcat also has two fewer teeth than the domestic cat.[11]

The bobcat and the Canada lynx are similar in appearance and quite difficult to tell apart. Both have tufted ears, short tails, relatively small heads, and long,

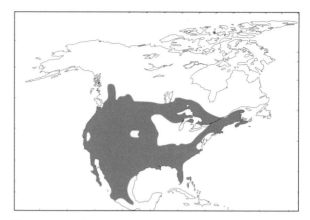

Figure 28. Distribution of the bobcat.

stout legs. However, the lynx has longer ear tufts and a solid black tail tip, whereas the tip of the bobcat's tail is black above and light below. Bobcats have smaller feet and lack the lynx's hairy foot pads, suggesting that bobcats are not as well adapted as lynx for living in areas with deep, soft snow.[12] Furthermore, studies of bobcat energetics in New York and New Hampshire show that these cats have relatively poor thermoregulatory abilities.[13,14] Indeed, the combination of deep snow and extremely cold temperatures probably limits the bobcat's northern distribution.[2,11]

DISTRIBUTION

The bobcat is widely distributed from British Columbia in the west across southern Canada to Nova Scotia in the east, and southward through much of the United States and into central Mexico (fig. 28).[4,15,16] Historically, the cat occurred in all forty-eight contiguous U.S. states, but it is now absent from several intensively cultivated midwestern states as well as the densely populated areas of some eastern states. In 1987, for example, a bobcat was shot while raiding a henhouse in Ohio; it was only the fifth specimen to be documented in Ohio since the early 1970s. While bobcats were disappearing from some parts of the United States, they were at the same time invading more northerly areas as farming, logging, and other human activities opened up previously unbroken coniferous forests. Bobcats now occur in northern Minnesota, southern Ontario, Manitoba, and on Cape Breton Island, Nova Scotia.[2,11,15,17]

ECOLOGY AND BEHAVIOR

Bobcats are found in a wide variety of habitats, including swamps, boreal coniferous forest, and mixed hardwood forest in the north; chaparral, sagebrush-grasslands, and desert scrub in the west; and bottomland hardwoods, brushlands, and mixed agricultural-forest areas in the south. While the cat is obviously adaptable and is frequently labeled as a habitat generalist, numerous studies indicate that bobcats prefer areas with dense cover or uneven, broken terrain. Dense cover provides not only concealment and escape cover but also relief from extremes of temperature and wind. In the north, deer, hares, and bobcats frequently use closed-canopy coniferous forest during the winter because temperatures are slightly warmer and snow depth is less beneath the shelf of branches.[2,8,18,19] Bobcats often avoid areas with sparse understories.[20] Snow depths greater than 13 to 15 centimeters limit the cats' movements, forcing them to modify their travel routes and choice of habitats used.[2,20,21,22] In many parts of their range bobcats often use ledges, bluffs, breaks, or rocky outcrops.[2,23,24,25,26] These features offer protection from inclement weather, serve as sheltered rest sites or birth dens, and may be good hunting sites. Broken terrain is especially important as escape and thermal cover for bobcats living in the northern prairies.[27,28] In the South and Southeast, bobcats prefer bottomland hardwood forests and early to mid-successional habitat mosaics with dense patches of grass, palmetto, and briar. They usually avoid open understories unless these areas are small and situated next to or within preferred habitats.[29,30,31,32,33,34] The requisite features of bobcat habitat typically include areas with abundant rabbit and rodent populations, dense cover, and shelters that function as escape cover or as den sites. The habitat use patterns of bobcats may, however, vary as the cats adjust to seasonal changes in environmental conditions and resource availability within and between habitats. In some cases habitat use patterns may also differ by sex.

Bobcats share many habitats with other carnivores. Coyotes and pumas are known to kill bobcats occasionally,[25,35] so the obvious question is whether these two predators limit bobcat distribution and density; indirect evidence suggests that the answer is yes. Bobcats apparently declined as coyotes moved into upper New York State and Maine,[36,37,38] and in the western United States bobcat numbers increased when coyotes were extirpated.[39,40] Coyotes and bobcats use similar habitats and eat similar food, and the two species may be in direct competition for resources, especially in winter when food is in short supply. Coyotes may also reduce deer densities, thereby indirectly lowering habitat quality for bobcats. When resources are not limiting, subtle differences in habitat use and diet probably serve to keep the two species apart.[41] Coyotes have more catholic feeding habits and make their living in more open grassland habitats, whereas bobcats are carnivorous and prefer areas with dense cover. Pumas and bobcats use similar habitats, and while both species will take deer, bobcats are no match for pumas in disputes over deer carcasses.

Bobcats also live sympatrically with the similar-sized ocelot in southern Texas. While both species tend to be active at the same time, they differ somewhat in their habitat use patterns. Ocelots restrict their activities to areas with dense cover, which they use intensively, whereas bobcats use both open and closed habitats.[42]

Bobcats are good climbers and will climb a tree if pursued by dogs or if charged seriously by deer, but they spend most of their time on the ground. They can also swim well but do not often venture freely into water, although a captive pair of kittens readily took to water to catch fish, to defecate, and simply to play.[43] Bobcats are primarily crepuscular, being most active in the few hours before and after sunset and sunrise. But, not surprisingly, there are exceptions; while some studies have found the cats to be primarily nocturnal, others report that they may be active at any time of the day, or that they are arrhythmic. In some areas bobcats are more active during the daytime in winter, probably because they must spend more time searching for food. Daytime temperatures above 26°C may also promote more nocturnal activity.[24] In most studies the bobcat's pattern of activity appears to coincide with that of its major prey.

In general, male bobcats travel farther than females, and movement patterns also vary by season and region. Estimates of distance traveled by radio-tagged bobcats range from as little as 2.6 kilometers to 18.5 kilometers per day, with longer distances occurring during the mating season.[44,45,46,47] Estimates of distances traveled based on snow tracking are similar to the figures derived from radio-tracking.[2]

The daily movements of bobcats are sometimes expressed as the straight-line distance between rest sites on consecutive days. While this calculation often underestimates the total distance traveled per day, it will, as long as an animal regularly changes its daytime rest sites, generally indicate differences in home range size.[33,48] In the few studies that have measured rates of travel, bobcats appeared to move slowly (0.1 to 0.6 kilometers per hour),[7,49,50] although overall rates of

2.2 kilometers per hour were recorded for bobcats in western Arkansas, and even faster rates were noted for cats moving between areas.[34] Many studies also report that males move farther and at a faster rate than females, and such differences are probably a reflection of larger male home ranges. While females commonly travel less, they appear to use their smaller ranges more intensively.

Feeding Ecology

Bobcats, like other felids, require a high-protein diet and, as such, are exclusively meat eaters. They use both sit-and-wait (ambush) and mobile hunting techniques to obtain their food. Bobcats using the ambush technique wait at lookouts or at the junctions of well-used game trails for prey to pass. They seem to be patient hunters; there are observations of bobcats waiting at burrow entrances for several hours after a missed attempt on a prairie dog. Bobcats using the mobile technique patrol their ranges on roads, trails, footpaths, and lanes, crossing and recrossing areas, looking and listening for prey. Describing a bobcat's movements through the snow, Clair Rollings wrote:

> The bobcat constantly haunted trails of the varying hare, and searched carefully through thickets, under windfalls, and about upturned roots. On the trail it usually advances by a steady trot, but stops often as if to survey the trail ahead or to watch some movement. It then may continue if nothing special has been seen; or it may crouch and slink forward (indicated by irregular tracks and deep snow drag); or it may suddenly leap in pursuit of observed prey. If the victim is not captured after a short burst of speed, the chase usually is abandoned.[51]

Bobcats rely chiefly on sight and hearing to detect their prey, as Hall and Newsom noted:

> Constantly on the alert for sound or movement, a bobcat would often stop and sit in the road, peering intently into the roadside vegetation. Sometimes this position would be held for five to ten minutes before the animal moved. If the object of investigation seemed to be a potential food item, a sitting bobcat would assume a crouched position, often followed by a pounce into the roadside cover.[46]

Hope Ryden watched a semi-tame female bobcat hunting and saw several attempts at prey capture.[52] On one occasion the female sprang from her hiding place in a palmetto clump in an unsuccessful attempt to catch a cottontail rabbit; twice she was seen chasing gray squirrels, once on the ground and once in a tree. She would walk slowly along trails, stopping to listen intently at any sound, then stalking in the direction of the sound. One day the scuttling of a skink caught her attention and, after stalking to within 1.5 meters, she pounced on the spot with her feet and pushed her nose into the grass. She caught and killed the lizard, but did not eat it. Another time she stalked an armadillo but, on seeing what it was, walked away.

The mere flicker of a feather or the slight turn of a tuft of fur caught on a branch will attract the cat's attention. Fur trappers capitalize on this fact by using tufts of fur, bunches of feathers, or a ball of silver paper to lure bobcats to a trap site.

Once prey is detected, the bobcat's stalk is slow and deliberate; the cat uses whatever cover is available to slink forward so that it can get as close as possible before making a final rush. Most attacks are launched from 10 meters or less. One observer found tracks in the snow indicating that a bobcat had stalked to "within a leap or two of a deer by crawling among the cliffs."[53] However, bobcats rarely pursue an animal if their initial rush misses the target.

Cooperative hunting in bobcats appears to be rare, although one courting pair was tracked through the snow to several spruce plantations where snowshoe hares were common. In each area "the cats moved through the plantation about 10 to 15 meters apart and appeared to alternate stopping as the other moved forward 15 to 20 meters."[54] There is also an observation in central Arizona of an unsuccessful attack by two bobcats on a javelina.[55]

Across much of its geographic range the bobcat specializes in lagomorphs; bobcat densities are usually high where rabbits and hares are abundant.[25] In some areas lagomorphs constitute as much as 90 percent of the bobcat's diet, with the majority contributed by cottontail rabbits.[56] Cottontails may be easier to catch because they tend to freeze, rather than run as hares do.[48] Cottontails also tend to live in brushy habitats, where they may be more easily ambushed. Snowshoe hares are more prominent in the bobcat diet across the northern portions of the cat's geographic range.[2]

In some areas lagomorph populations fluctuate markedly, and during declines bobcats are forced to change their diets to include more rodents and other alternative prey. These swings in rabbit and hare abundance can have a profound influence on the social systems and population dynamics of bobcats.[28,56] During a severe and prolonged decline of lagomorphs in southeastern Idaho, the bobcats' social system broke down; cats abandoned their home ranges, kitten mortality increased, reproduction was reduced or curtailed, and some adults died of starvation.[26]

Although the bobcat's diet is dominated by rabbits or hares throughout most of its range, deer and various species of rodents are also important food sources, depending on season and geographic location. In Texas, Arizona, and California, for example, cotton rats, wood rats, and kangaroo rats are a significant part of the bobcat diet.[57,58,59,60] In western Washington State 42 percent of bobcat stomachs contained mountain beavers, while only 26 percent contained snowshoe hares; the diets of cats in eastern Washington were more varied.[61] The bobcat's summer diet in Oregon's western Cascades was also varied; snowshoe hare was the most frequently occurring (28 percent) prey in scats, but the remains of black-tailed deer, mountain beaver, pocket gopher, and passerine birds all occurred in more than 10 percent of the scats examined.[44] In early winter, opossums were the most frequently occurring prey in bobcat stomachs from eastern Kentucky.[62] In Florida and on the southeastern coastal plain, cotton rats appear to be almost as important as rabbits in the bobcat diet.[2,63] Adult deer do not figure prominently in the cat's diet in the Southeast,[63] except in Florida.[64,65] The bobcat is, however, a serious predator of fawns.[65,66,67]

Deer are important in the bobcat diet across the northeastern United States, occurring in 16 to 35 percent of samples (stomachs, feces) in this region.[63] This proportion may be much higher in the winter, when deep, soft snow limits the cats' movements and extremely low temperatures increase their thermoregulatory costs. Some deer are obtained as carrion while others represent actual kills by bobcats. There is a suggestion that bobcat survival in the Adirondacks of upstate New York depends on finding a deer carcass or making a deer kill early in the winter. Of ninety-three bobcat carcasses from this area examined in the winter, deer remains occurred in 72 percent of the stomachs. A deer kill or carcass may give the cat the edge that it needs to survive with enough reserves so that it can hunt deer during the latter parts of the winter when deer become more vulnerable.[68]

The food habits of bobcats in Maine, Arkansas, and Nova Scotia differ among sex and age classes, and it

has been suggested that these differences may serve to reduce competition for limited resources.[20,69,70,71] In contrast, the diets of adult bobcats in North Dakota did not differ, even though males there are larger than females.[72]

While the majority of prey taken by bobcats are small, weighing less than 2 kilograms, there is now a substantial body of evidence showing that bobcats can single-handedly kill prey weighing about ten times their own body weight.[2] In a sample of thirty-seven deer killed by bobcats in Vermont, six weighed less than 23 kilograms, twenty-two between 23 and 45 kilograms, and eight between 45 and 67 kilograms. The largest deer killed was a 68-kilogram buck.[73] Similar observations were reported for thirty-four deer killed by bobcats in Maine.[74] Large prey such as deer are killed with rapid bites to the throat, neck, or base of the skull. Occasionally, even small cats (5–6 kilograms) succeed in killing an adult deer. Since most attacks are directed at the throat, death most likely results from suffocation or hemorrhage.

In the northern United States predation on adult deer by bobcats occurs most frequently in the winter, when deep snow or nutritional stress increases the deer's vulnerability to predation. Some accounts suggest that bobcat attacks are often directed at deer that are bedded down. The kill is not always instantaneous, however; there are a few eyewitness accounts of deer bounding along with a bobcat straddling the deer's back or clinging to its throat.[4] Most bobcat predation on deer, however, is on fawns, which are quickly killed by a neck or throat bite.

Rodents are pounced on and pinned by the cat's front feet and killed by a bite to the nape or head. Small prey may be eaten on the spot or carried to a secluded spot before being consumed. Females with small kittens sometimes take food back to the den. In captivity, bobcats rarely pluck birds smaller than a blackbird before starting to eat. While they do pluck feathers from larger birds, they pluck much less intensively than do ocelots or pumas. Bobcats invariably start at the head when beginning to feed on small birds.[75]

Deer are usually fed on where killed or moved only a short distance because dragging a large carcass is too difficult for the cat. Bobcats generally start feeding on the hindquarters of deer. The remains are cached or covered with whatever material is available, including snow, leaves, soil, or deer hair. Whether the cat stays near the carcass and for how long appears to depend on many factors, including the cat's fat reserves, winter temperatures, snow conditions, and disturbance. Decomposition rate is also important, as high heat and humidity may render carcasses unpalatable in a day or two.[64] During periods of extreme cold or loose, deep snow, a bobcat will often remain near the carcass, alternating feeding and resting. In the winter of 1978–1979 bobcats in the Adirondacks stayed an average of 12.6 days with each deer carcass.[68]

Bobcats also prey on domestic stock, including chickens, turkeys, piglets, sheep, and goats, but depredation on livestock does not appear to be significant except in localized situations.[4] In some circumstances, however, a bobcat may cause havoc in henhouses or lambing areas by killing large numbers of chickens or lambs in a single night. At other times, ranchers may suffer substantial losses of livestock to a bobcat over a month or two before managing to capture the cat.

There is little information on bobcat hunting success rates, although they obviously vary depending on type and abundance of prey. In South Carolina, of eight observed attempts at prey capture, three were successful (37.5 percent), with the bobcat managing to capture two cotton rats and a cottontail rabbit.[45] On several occasions bobcats in Louisiana were seen vainly trying to catch prey; in each attempt the prey was presumably small, since the cat was seen to pounce but no intended victim was seen.[46] Another report estimated that only one out of six attempts to capture rabbits and rodents (17 percent) was successful. The cat's success rate on adult deer is most certainly less than that when it is preying on rodents.

Social Organization

The bobcat, like most other felids, essentially lives a solitary lifestyle. While individuals may occasionally encounter conspecifics within their home ranges, most associations are brief, lasting for a few hours to several days in the case of mating pairs.[2,11] An anecdotal account that notes "the tracks of eleven Wild Cats in one drove" and says that "it is a common thing to see three, four or even six at one time"[76] is rather similar to a reference to "droves" of seven and eleven lynxes.[2] Such gatherings appear to be unusual, although they are reminiscent of the reported congregations of Eurasian lynx at "rendezvous" sites during the mating period.[77] In general, the only prolonged association among bobcats is between a female and her young. In one study, social interaction between pairs outside of the breeding season led to speculation that under some circumstances pairs may form a persistent but loose bond.[33] There are also observations of adult males jointly using a rest site during a period of inclement weather, suggesting some degree of social tolerance.[48] The varying degree of home range overlap between adults of the same sex also suggests some flexibility in social-spatial arrangements.

The bobcat's social-spatial system is fairly similar across much of its geographic distribution. Adult females occupy relatively small ranges that overlap very little with those of neighboring females. Adult male ranges are large and typically include one to several female home ranges, but among male ranges the amount of overlap is quite variable, ranging from none to extensive. In one Californian study, the home ranges of both males and females overlapped extensively.[24,60] At the Archbold Biological Station in south-central Florida, there was little overlap between the ranges of same-sex individuals. Males and females tended to be associated as pairs; even when a male's range overlapped the ranges of more than one female, he appeared to have a closer relationship with one female.[33]

Despite the hundreds of published studies, our understanding of the bobcat's land tenure system is much less complete than it is for some of the less-studied felids such as the ocelot. The problem seems to be that the bobcat lives in a variety of habitats at a great variety of population and prey densities, and many study populations are harvested at some level. In addition, almost all the studies have been relatively short-term and thus lack information on genetic relatedness. New information on the land tenure systems of pumas and tigers shows that daughters often settle next to their mothers, sometimes partially overlapping their mothers' ranges. This pattern results in clusters of related females with partially overlapping ranges. The apparent territorial boundaries appear to change over the short term. but are actually quite stable in the long term. The bobcat social system may be similar.

In situations in which stable unhunted populations live in areas with adequate prey and sufficient rest sites, one might expect a typical system to consist of one male's range overlapping the ranges of one or two females. At the other extreme, the studies that have shown major overlap in male ranges have been conducted at sites where bobcats are harvested,[8] or where rest sites are a serious limiting factor.[48] The widely varying land tenure systems that have shown up in bobcat studies ought, perhaps, to be regarded simply as a series of snapshots of an adaptable predator living under a wide variety of social and environmental conditions. Only a study of an unharvested population in which individuals are known and followed over their lifetimes will reveal the whole picture.

There is considerable variation in the size of home ranges, from 60 hectares for female bobcats in southern California[78] to 32,570 hectares for male bobcats in upstate New York.[68] Males typically have ranges that are two to three times larger than those of females, and the home ranges of bobcats in northern and western portions of the United States are consistently larger than those in the south. This geographic variation may be related to climate in that the warmer southern regions probably provide a more consistent year-round prey base than other parts of the country. In the bottomland hardwood forests of southern Louisiana, for example, with abundant prey and no hunting pressure, the home ranges of adult males measured only 4.9 square kilometers, and those of adult females 0.9 square kilometers.[46] At Archbold Biological Station in south-central Florida, the average home range size for males was 25.5 square kilometers and for females, 14.5 square kilometers. Two females at Archbold occupied essentially the same ranges for more than five years.[33]

The largest and most variable home ranges are recorded at the northern limits of the bobcat's distribution. In the Adirondacks, male ranges averaged 325 square kilometers, whereas those of females averaged 86 square kilometers. These range sizes exceed all other estimates for bobcats, but in this region the cats rely primarily on white-tailed deer to meet their energy requirements and thus must travel extensively. In the neighboring Catskill region, where deer and rabbit densities are higher than in the Adirondacks, adult male bobcat ranges measured only 36 square kilometers; that of an adult female was 31 square kilometers.[68]

Changes in prey abundance can markedly influence the size of a bobcat's home range. During a period of high lagomorph populations in southeastern Idaho, home range sizes measured 20.4 square kilometers for males and 11.6 square kilometers for females. When lagomorph populations plummeted, male ranges increased to 123 square kilometers and those of females to 69.7 square kilometers. With greatly increased home range sizes, there was a corresponding decrease in bobcat density in the study area.[26]

Increasing range sizes and declining densities are also reported for bobcats at the Savanna River Plant (SRP) in South Carolina, but here the changes have been long-term. From a mosaic of old fields, early successional forests, and abandoned small towns and farms in the 1950s and 1960s, a sizable portion of the habitat was gradually converted through succession and management practices to large pine plantations, often with limited undergrowth, resulting in a decreased prey base, increased home ranges, and thus reduced bobcat densities.[79,80] Such effects on bobcat populations at SRP are thought to parallel what has happened to bobcats across much of the Southeast.[31]

Bobcat density is variable over time and space, primarily as it relates to prey density and the amount of home range overlap. Density can also change markedly in areas where bobcats are harvested. Over a three-year period in southeastern Idaho during which lagomorph populations declined precipitously, the bobcat density decreased from about nine bobcats per 100 square kilometers to fewer than one per 100 square kilometers.[26] In parts of the southwestern and southeastern United States where rabbit and rodent populations are high, bobcat densities may be greater than one cat per square kilometer. Bobcat densities in parts of the northern and northeastern United States, where the cats must travel widely to find enough prey, are about thirty times less than in the better areas.[2]

The spatial arrangement of bobcat ranges appears to be a form of territoriality in that adults tend to have well-defined home ranges that are not often used by other cats of the same sex. In cases in which home ranges overlap, use of common ground is usually not simultaneous. Where resident bobcats are removed annually by trapping, the system of spatial separation may be disrupted.[33,81] There is little evidence to suggest that bobcats actively defend their ranges, although such behavior could easily go unobserved. More likely, the bobcats indicate occupancy of ranges and manage to avoid encounters principally via a combination of olfactory and visual marks. At other times these marks may also serve to bring animals together for mating.[82,83]

While moving about their home ranges, bobcats mark the area with scent, deposited as urine, anal gland secretions, and feces. Urine may be squirted or sprayed backward onto vertical objects, or the cat may squat-urinate; both sexes mark in this manner. These marks are deposited alone or in varying combinations on trees, bushes, or other objects. Scent may also be used in conjunction with scrapes. Scrapes are made with a backward raking motion of the hind feet and appear as rectangular patches of bare soil. These bare patches are sometimes marked with feces or urine. Similarly, bobcats may routinely sharpen their claws on a specific tree or log, which combines their scent with a visual mark. Most marks are placed along roads, trails, and other paths, as bobcats readily use these as travel lanes when moving about their ranges. However, the distributions and types of scent marks are not necessarily uniform, and there may be seasonal and sex or age differences in marking behavior as well.

Observations from several studies suggest that bobcats use scent marks to delineate the boundaries of their home ranges, as indicated by the greater intensity of marking along boundaries.[33,45] Scrapes appear to be the most frequent type of mark used, often combined with either urine or feces. At some locations large numbers of feces may accumulate to form what have been called toilets, depositories, or scent posts.[2] Feces, when left uncovered, are usually deposited at conspicuous and prominent sites. However, adults, young kittens just out of the den, females with small kittens, and juveniles sometimes bury their feces.[33,56] In this case presumably the action is simply elimination, although the burying of feces by females with nursing kittens may be interpreted as a strategy to avoid attracting attention. Conversely, other researchers have found that females make more scrapes and leave their feces uncovered around dens, which could be interpreted as a strategy to let others know that the area is occupied.[84]

Some variation in marking behavior may also be related to the weather, as feces disappear rapidly during the rainy season, which is also a time when dung beetle activity is high. The odor of urine marks also fades, and thus bobcats must regularly traverse their ranges to freshen old marks and deposit new ones. In this regard, one study found that in six cases, five to fourteen days elapsed between the disappearance of a resident and the appearance of a new cat in the vacant area.[33] Other studies report that vacancies were filled in two days, ten days, eleven days,[24] four weeks,[34] or two to three months.[85] The time lag between the death or disappearance of a resident and the arrival of a new resident probably depends on the number and sex of cats waiting for an opening. In some cases the vacant areas are simply annexed by neighbors. Vacant female ranges are taken over by other adult females, and likewise, males replace males.

An increase in the frequency of scent marking is also associated with the breeding season, with feces left uncovered and scrapes marked with urine peaking at this time.[33,86] During the mating period the feces and urine of females are thought to contain chemical information advertising their reproductive status. Females may also give vocal signals of their sexual receptivity. Some observations of captive female bobcats suggest that they vocalize more often during suspected heat periods,[87] but other observers report no change in calling frequency.[88] In the wild, caterwauling seems to be common during the mating season; the calls can be heard from a mile away.[4] These loud, long-distance calls serve to bring animals together for mating and are one of about a dozen signal types identified in the bobcat's vocal repertoire.[89,90]

The long-distance call is classified in the general category of "mew": a relatively short, high-pitched call that varies in amplitude, tonality, and pitch. Some forms of this call are close-contact types—used, for example, by female bobcats with mobile kittens—but mews occur in a variety of behavioral contexts. The long-distance call is described as a series of intense mews with fairly regular intervals between the calls.[89]

Besides these different forms of the mew, bobcat vocalizations also include the spit, hiss, growl, yowl, purr, snort, chatter, gurgle, and wah-wah call. Some of these vocalizations are common to all cat species, whereas calls such as the gurgle, wah-wah, yowl, chatter, and snort are more restricted. Some specific vocalizations are likely to be associated with courtship and mating, and there may be additional calls in agonistic situations, but the ten to twelve signal types identified for bobcats are nevertheless similar to the number recorded for other felids.[89]

Reproduction and Development

Bobcats are seasonally polyestrous; females go through several estrous cycles in a season if they do not become pregnant. Many studies of bobcat reproduction have relied on carcasses of trapped animals and thus are based on indirect evidence, such as counts of corpora lutea and placental scars. The former show the number of eggs the female has ovulated; the latter indicate the number of embryos that were attached to the uterine wall. An examination of the reproductive tracts of harvested cats showed that, unless they were impregnated, females went through about three estrous cycles in a season. Bobcats appear to be spontaneous ovulators, although it has also been suggested that copulation may sometimes induce or hasten ovulation.[71,81]

Females become sexually mature before the breeding season of their second year, and they may breed as early as nine to twelve months of age.[15] Males are generally not capable of breeding until their second winter, and the earliest detected age of sperm production is 1.5 years.[71] The average estrous cycle lasts about forty-four days, and the female is receptive for five to ten days.[81,88] If a pregnancy is lost or a litter dies soon after birth, the female can cycle again and produce another litter. While some mating activity is reported to occur as early as November–December and as late as August–September, the peak breeding season in the bobcat appears to be February–April.[15,91,92] Breeding activity tends to occur earlier in the southern portion of the bobcat's range; it has been suggested that breeding may occur at any time of the year in southern populations.[33,71,93] In Florida, one semi-tame female produced two litters in one year, but this appears to be unusual.[94]

Whether a female becomes pregnant or not apparently depends not only on her age, but also on prey density and bobcat density. Yearling and two-year-old females often have lower pregnancy rates than older females,[7,95] although, if prey populations are high, even juvenile females mate and give birth. When prey densities are low, fewer young females breed.[26,96] There is also evidence to suggest that at high bobcat densities, fewer females breed.[24]

Despite the fact that there are many bobcats in zoos and wildlife parks, there are few observations of their courtship and mating behavior. Mehrer reports that among the bobcats he maintained in captivity, there was little interaction between males and females during nonreproductive periods, although females were extremely vehement in repelling males that approached too closely.[88] However, with the onset of estrus, the behavior of females changed to include more pacing, and they showed more "affectionate" movements, such as squirming, wriggling, stretching, and rolling. These motions were accompanied by a dramatic increase in the frequency of urination and a more or less continuous rubbing of the head and shoulders against every available object in the cage. At this point a female's behavior toward a male became rather "friendly"; she actively sought him out, brushing her cheeks against his and presenting her anal area to him. She also crawled in a circle around the male in lordosis (the mating posture, in which the female is on her elbows and her hindquarters are elevated). The male's response to these advances was generally passive. No vocalization was heard from either sex. Eventually the female stopped squirming, wriggling, and rolling and assumed a coital position, the point of complete sexual receptivity.

In a typical mating sequence, the male approaches the female, grips the scruff of her neck with his teeth, and mounts, his legs straddling her sides. The female holds her tail to one side, exposing her genitals. The male extends his hindquarters posteriorly, arches his back, lowers his genitals toward those of the female, and begins pelvic thrusting. At intromission females either make no sound or give a low, barely audible growl—the copulatory cry. Following a brief copulation, the female stands, displacing the male from her back, and he retreats from the immediate area. Both then engage in grooming their own anogenital area. The entire sequence from mounting through copulation is usually over in less than five minutes. After a refractory or rest period the pair again go through a courtship sequence and mate; Mehrer reports that during the estrous period the number of copulations varied from one to sixteen per day.[88]

Outside of a glimpse of mating behavior reported by Guggisberg,[1] the only information we have on bobcat courtship in the wild comes from a study conducted in Massachusetts more than twenty years ago, in which Chet McCord reconstructed the activities of consorting pairs by following their tracks through the snow.[54] McCord describes signs of play—running encounters in which the two animals ran parallel to each other, then one "looped out to the side and came back to meet the other"—and an activity he calls "bumping," in which the two walk side by side, bumping each other, while the male seems to be trying to secure a neck grip. He found several copulation sites, areas about 100 centimeters across where the snow was trampled and there were signs of body impressions, and often small tufts of hair, which probably were related to the neck grip by the male. McCord suggests that the body impressions next to the tracks may indicate where the female rolls in the snow after copulating. On one occasion a female in heat was followed by three other bobcats, two of which were unmarked and the third a tagged male. On another occasion a mating pair was followed at a distance by a third bobcat. Snow tracking indicated two to five possible copulations per bout of activity, a frequency that is less than that reported for the larger cats.

Gestation lasts about sixty-three days. Average litter sizes range from 2.5 to 3.9,[2] but as many as 6 kittens have been observed.[92] Of the larger litter sizes that have been reported, several are based on counts of corpora lutea and placental scars, and as such are probably overestimates. Generally, young females tend to have smaller litters than older females.[95,96] Shortly before giving birth, the female selects a well-hidden site—typically a rock pile, cave, brush pile, or hollow tree—as a natal den, but abandoned buildings and even a beaver lodge have been used.[48,97] There are reports of birth weights ranging from 128 grams to 800 grams,[92,98] although Young cited 280–340 grams as being common.[4] Kittens are blind and helpless at birth, and their eyes remain closed until they are three to eleven days old. Their fur is mottled or dark-spotted at birth. The female stays with her young for the first two days, sustaining herself by eating the placenta, feces, and any stillborn young. The kittens grow rapidly, and in the first month after birth they may gain 10 grams or more per day.[99,100] The young are nursed for about three months, and the female begins bringing solid food back to the den during the seventh or eighth week.

The birth of kittens is typically marked by a rapid change in the movement patterns of the female, with the natal den becoming the focal point of her activity. For the first couple of months her movements tend to be restricted; while she may still be visiting many parts of her pre-parturition range, she must return to the den. Furthermore, the provisioning of kittens can be a demanding task. In Idaho, female bobcats with dependent young had difficulty feeding their kittens when they were forced to rely on small rodents because rabbit numbers were low. Indeed, many kittens died of starvation during the lagomorph decline. Females not only had to travel greater distances to find food, but the small prey also meant that multiple trips were required. These increased energy costs were more than could be afforded by females with kittens in dens.[26,56] In California, two of three collared juveniles died of malnutrition during a prey decline.[60]

Kittens in dens also appear to be vulnerable to being killed, as suggested by observations that females with small kittens regularly change den sites. During the first month or two after birth, female bobcats at Archbold Biological Station in south-central Florida moved their kittens short distances to a new den every one to six days.[33] Females with two- to four-month-old kittens changed den sites at the same rate, but now the young were mobile and the sites were more widely dispersed about the female's range. When traveling between den sites, the mother would lead, and the kittens followed single file. Kittens begin to accompany their mother on hunts when they are three to five months old, although sometimes the female hunts alone. Kittens are dependent on their mother until about seven

months of age, after which they spend progressively more time away from her, although some mother-young associations may last a year or more.[7,101,102]

Young males grow faster than females; by six months of age a male can be nearly 20 percent heavier than his sister.[81] Females tend to reach their adult size and weight by the time they are two and a half years old, but males continue to grow and put on muscle until they are three and a half years old.[11,95]

Prior to attaining adult size and weight, young bobcats leave their natal ranges and often wander widely in search of suitable unoccupied habitat, becoming part of a transient or floating population. The age of dispersal is variable; some young leave as early as nine months of age, whereas others may reach almost two years of age before dispersing. The pattern of dispersal is also variable; some juveniles suddenly leave their natal ranges and rapidly travel many kilometers, whereas for others the process may take several months. Occasionally, an individual establishes residency in its natal range, but this is usually associated with the death or disappearance of its mother or father. For most dispersers, finding a suitable vacant range takes much longer, although it is important to get settled as soon as possible because residency appears to be a prerequisite for successful reproduction.[26]

At Archbold Biological Station two ten-month-old bobcats restricted their movements to areas at the periphery of their mother's range prior to dispersing three to four months later. Their mother's increasing aggressiveness during the breeding season and her subsequent pregnancy was thought to have prompted the young to move to the edge of her range.[33] However, while maternal intolerance, aggression by breeding males, and competition for resources undoubtedly play a role in encouraging young to disperse, the timing of dispersal is probably influenced by a variety of social and environmental circumstances.

Observations from several studies suggest that dispersal is a gradual process, with subadults making short, exploratory forays outside the natal range, then remaining in these areas for a few days to several months before moving again to new areas.[26,101,102] In one area bobcats spent five to ten months looking for a place to live, whereas in another area dispersal was over in two to six days. The length of time spent searching for a suitable site varies, largely according to the density and territory size of adults and the disappearance rate of residents.

Information on other aspects of dispersal, such as

distances and routes traveled or the fate of dispersers, is patchy and derived from only a few studies. The maximum recorded dispersal distance is 182 kilometers,[103] and there are a few other records of dispersers traveling more than 100 kilometers; these long journeys are typically made by subadult males and are apparently related to severe declines in the availability of lagomorphs.[56,103] Intermediate dispersal distances of 20 to 40 kilometers appear to be fairly common,[26,27,85,102] and in several cases the cats dispersed less than 10 kilometers.[101]

Bobcats have a relatively high reproductive potential. Females typically reach sexual maturity by eighteen to twenty-four months of age, then reproduce annually for six to eight years or more.[2] With litter sizes commonly approaching three, a potential lifetime output of eighteen to twenty-four young is probably not an unreasonable estimate for females in unharvested populations.

The age of bobcats in the wild may be estimated by various techniques; the most reliable estimates are derived by counting annuli in the teeth of harvested animals.[104,105,106] From 1978 to 1992, Matson's laboratory sectioned the teeth of almost 90,000 bobcats. The oldest individual recorded was twenty-three years old; this individual was harvested in New Mexico in 1986.[107] There are few data available on adult survival rates from unexploited populations, although data from southern California and southeastern Idaho suggest that there are likely to be more older bobcats in non-hunted populations.[24,26] Adults appear to be fairly long-lived, and some ten- to seventeen-year-old cats appear in harvested populations.[108] There are records of captive bobcats living to twenty-five and thirty-two years of age.[109,110]

STATUS IN THE WILD

In 1975 the Convention on International Trade in Endangered Species (CITES) listed the bobcat on appendix II, thus classifying it as a species that was not currently threatened with extinction, but might become so unless trade were strictly regulated. The CITES listing of bobcats was prompted by a large increase in the demand for their fur, which followed on the heels of the ban on commercial trade in pelts of cats listed on appendix I. With trade in leopard, jaguar, and cheetah pelts now banned, fur buyers focused on other cat species as substitutes.[111] As the prices of bobcat pelts rose to record heights, trapping pressure increased. In Missouri, for example, the bobcat har-

vest increased from 91 cats in 1970–1971 to 1,107 in 1976–1977, while pelt prices increased from $4.00 to $46.00 during the same period.[112] By 1979 the price of bobcat pelts had risen still higher, to an average of $125.00, and a quality skin might bring $250.00 or more.

As pelt prices soared, more and more bobcats were trapped for their skins. To implement the regulations of CITES, each state was required to provide documentation concerning the status of the bobcat.[113] This posed a problem, as bobcats are reclusive and almost impossible to census, and many states could not produce the information. Wildlife departments began tagging pelts and requiring that lower jaws and teeth be handed in for analysis; these regulations provided some much-needed data on the sex and age classes of the harvested segment of the population.[114] To safeguard bobcat populations from overexploitation, state agencies were required to show that existing harvest intensities were not detrimental.[111] This meant that agencies had to obtain information on population status, and thus numerous small-scale, short-term studies of bobcats began in almost every state.[115]

Not unexpectedly, the data available on wild populations and information on the number of bobcats harvested vary enormously from state to state. For instance, between 1979 and 1986, fewer than 40 bobcats were harvested each year in Massachusetts and in New Hampshire, but more than 10,000 were taken annually in California. Texas holds the record for the number of bobcats harvested: 17,686 were killed during the 1985–1986 season. In 1987 the fur harvest in the United States and Canada was estimated at 90,000 to 100,000 skins per year.[116]

Currently the official consensus is that most bobcat populations in North America are either stable or increasing; but many field biologists who have worked on bobcats do not believe the situation is that simple, including Robert E. Rolley of the Indiana Department of Natural Resources. "Current estimates of population size are not precise," Rolley says, "and the exact relationship of population size and rates of reproduction and mortality are largely unknown. Therefore harvest quotas have been influenced more by tradition and politics than by determinations of optimum sustained yields."[11] Roughly half of the U.S. bobcat harvest is currently used within the United States.

There is no information available on the status of bobcats in Mexico, but loss of habitat has prompted concern for a subspecies in south-central Mexico (*L.*

rufus escuinapae), resulting in this subspecies being placed on appendix I of CITES.

CONSERVATION EFFORTS

Bobcats have been reintroduced to Cumberland Island, Georgia, in an attempt to restore a native predator to that ecological community; preliminary observations indicate that the cats are surviving and reproducing.[117] A reintroduction of bobcats to New Jersey has also met with some success; besides settling and reproducing, the cats appear to be expanding their range.[118]

TABLE 34 MEASUREMENTS AND WEIGHTS OF ADULT BOBCATS

HB	n	T	n	WT	n	Location	Source
841.2 (698–1,003)	13m	138.9 (114–178)	13m	10.1 (4.5–15.7)	16m	Minnesota	22
754.4 (635–902)	12f	125.5 (98–171)	12f	8.9 (3.6–18.2)	15f	Minnesota	22
773.8 (695–863)	19m	159.6 (139–198)	19m	11.8 (8.4–14.8)	32m	Michigan	119
734.4 (627–952)	16f	146.4 (132–157)	16f	8.8 (7.3–11.8)	24f	Michigan	119
735.4 (603–927)	21m	142.7 (114–171)	21m	9.3 (5.6–11.4)	21m	North Carolina	4
623.5 (508–724)	26f	129.7 (114–165)	26f	6.2 (4.2–10.5)	26f	North Carolina	4
725.1 (636–864)	12m	145 (121–170)	12m	8.9 (7.2–11.5)	12m	Kentucky	62
647.6 (577–864)	8f	128.4 (90–158)	8f	6.0 (5.3–7.3)	8f	Kentucky	62
775 (753–818)	6m	158.3 (139–181)	6m	9.5 (9.0–10.5)	6m	Florida	33
715 (679–748)	7f	157.4 (138–182)	7f	8.0 (5.8–9.9)	7f	Florida	33

Note: HB = head and body length (mm), T = tail length (mm), WT = weight (kg). n = sample size. Sex: m = male, f = female, ? = unknown. Mean values are presented only for sample sizes of three or more. Range of values is in parentheses.

TABLE 35 FREQUENCY OF OCCURRENCE OF PREY ITEMS IN THE DIETS OF BOBCATS (PERCENTAGE OF SAMPLES)

Prey items	Baja California Sur, Mexico[120] Scats (n = 188)	Florida[33] Scats (n = 146)	Florida[63] Stomachs (n = 413)	Michigan[119] Stomachs (n = 125)	Eastern Washington[61] Stomachs (n = 123)
Odocoileus virginianus White-tailed deer			2.4	26.7	12.1
Lagomorphs					21.6
Sylvilagus sp. Cottontail rabbit	28.2	36.5	4.4	21.9	
Sylvilagus palustris Marsh rabbit		6.6	3.0		
Lepus americanus Snowshoe hare				16.2	
Lepus californicus Black-tailed jackrabbit	26.0				
Unknown lagomorphs	19.7		20.4		

TABLE 35 *(continued)*

Prey items	Baja California Sur, Mexico[120] Scats (n = 188)	Florida[33] Scats (n = 146)	Florida[63] Stomachs (n = 413)	Michigan[119] Stomachs (n = 125)	Eastern Washington[61] Stomachs (n = 123)
Erethizon dorsatum Porcupine				8.6	1.7
Mephitis mephitis Striped skunk				1.0	
Sigmodon hispidus Cotton rat		23.9	29.4		
Procyon lotor Raccoon		0.7			
Didelphis virginiana Opossum		1.7			
Chaetodipus sp. Pocket mouse	19.1				
Tamiasciurus hudsonicus Red squirrel					15.5
Peromyscus sp. White-footed mouse	4.7				6.0
Neotoma spp. Wood rat	4.7		1.0		
Other rodents and insectivores	11.6	21.0	9.3	17.1	24.2
Unknown mammals		0.7	6.9		
Birds	12.2	16.9	23.6	7.6	15.5
Lizards	9.0				
Snakes	5.3		0.4		
Scorpion	1.1				
Plant material			13.6		5.1
Minimum number of vertebrate prey items	252	301	432	105	116

REFERENCES

1. Guggisberg, C. A. W. 1975. *Wild cats of the world.* New York: Taplinger.

2. McCord, C. M., and J. E. Cardoza. 1982. Bobcat and lynx. In *Wild mammals of North America,* ed. J. A. Chapman and G. E. Feldhamer, 728–766. Baltimore: Johns Hopkins University Press.

3. Funderburk, S. 1986. International trade in U.S. and Canadian bobcats, 1977–1981. In *Cats of the world: Biology, conservation, and management,* ed. S. D. Miller and D. D. Everett, 489–501. Washington, DC: National Wildlife Federation.

4. Young, S. P. 1978. *The bobcat of North America.* Lincoln: University of Nebraska Press.

5. Ulmer, F. A. Jr. 1941. Melanism in the Felidae, with special reference to the genus *Lynx. J. Mammal.* 22: 285–288.

6. Regan, T. W., and D. S. Maehr. 1990. Melanistic bobcats in Florida. *Fla. Field Nat.* 18: 84–87.

7. Rolley, R. E. 1983. Behavior and population dynamics of bobcats in Oklahoma. Ph.D. dissertation, Oklahoma State University, Stillwater.

8. Berg, W. E. 1979. Ecology of bobcats in northern Minnesota. In *Bobcat research conference proceedings,* ed. L. G. Blum and P. C. Escherich, 55–61. National Wildlife Federation Scientific and Technical Series, no. 6.

9. Schmidly, D. J., and J. A. Read. 1986. Cranial variation in the bobcat (*Felis rufus*) from Texas and surrounding states. Occasional Papers/The Museum, Texas Tech University, no. 101. 39 pp.

10. Sikes, R. S., and M. L. Kennedy. 1992. Morphological variation of the bobcat (*Felis rufus*) in the eastern United States and its association with selected environmental variables. *Am. Midl. Nat.* 128: 313–324.

11. Rolley, R. E. 1987. Bobcat. In *Wild furbearer management and conservation in North America,* ed. M. Novak, J. A. Baker, M. E. Obbard, and B. Malloch, 671–681. Ontario: Ontario Trappers Association.

12. Parker, G. R., J. W. Maxwell, L. D. Morton, and G. E. Smith. 1983. The ecology of the lynx (*Lynx canadensis*) on Cape Benton Island. *Can. J. Zool.* 61: 770–786.

13. Mautz, W. W., and P. J. Pekins. 1989. Metabolic rate of bobcats as influenced by seasonal temperatures. *J. Wildl. Mgmt.* 53: 202–205.

14. Gustafson, K. A. 1984. The winter metabolism and bioenergetics of the bobcat in New York. Master's thesis, State University of New York, Syracuse.

15. Larivière, S., and L. R. Walton. 1997. *Lynx rufus. Mammalian Species* 563: 1–8.

16. López-González, C. A., A. González-Romero, and J. W. Laundré. 1998. Range extension of the bobcat (*Lynx rufus*) in Jalisco, Mexico. *Southwest. Nat.* 43: 103–105.

17. Banfield, A. W. F. 1974. *The mammals of Canada.* Toronto: University of Toronto Press.

18. Fuller, T. K., W. E. Berg, and D. W. Kuehn. 1985. Bobcat home range size and daytime cover-type use in north central Minnesota. *J. Mammal.* 66: 568–571.

19. Koehler, G. M., and M. G. Hornocker. 1989. Influences of seasons on bobcats in Idaho. *J. Wildl. Mgmt.* 53: 197–202.

20. Litvaitis, J. A., A. G. Clark, and J. H. Hunt. 1986. Prey selection and fat deposits of bobcats (*Felis rufus*) during autumn and winter in Maine. *J. Mammal.* 67: 389–392.

21. Marston, M. A. 1942. Winter relations of bobcats and white-tailed deer in Maine. *J. Wildl. Mgmt.* 6: 328–337.

22. Petraborg, W. H., and V. E. Gunvalson. 1962. Observations on bobcat mortality and bobcat predation on deer. *J. Mammal.* 43: 430–431.

23. Bailey, T. N. 1979. Den ecology, population parameters and diet of eastern Idaho bobcats. In *Bobcat research conference proceedings,* ed. L. G. Blum and P. C. Escherich, 62–69. National Wildlife Federation Scientific and Technical Series, no. 6.

24. Zezulak, D. S., and R. G. Schwab. 1979. A comparison of density, home range and habitat utilization of bobcat populations at Lava Beds and Joshua Tree National Monuments, California. In *Bobcat research conference proceedings,* ed. L. G. Blum and P. C. Escherich, 74–79. National Wildlife Federation Scientific and Technical Series, no. 6.

25. Anderson, E. M. 1990. Bobcat diurnal loafing sites in southeastern Colorado. *J. Wildl. Mgmt.* 54: 600–602.

26. Knick, S. T. 1990. Ecology of bobcats relative to exploitation and a prey decline in southeastern Idaho. *Wildl. Monogr.* 108: 1–42.

27. Robinson, W. B., and E. F. Grand. 1958. Comparative movements of bobcats and coyotes as disclosed by tagging. *J. Wildl. Mgmt.* 22: 117–122.

28. Giddings, B. J., G. L. Risdahl, and L. R. Irby. 1990. Bobcat habitat use in southeastern Montana during periods of high and low lagomorph abundance. *Prairie Nat.* 22: 249–258.

29. Labisky, R. F., and D. R. Progulske Jr. 1982. Spatial distribution of bobcats and gray foxes in eastern Florida. Technical Report No. 4. School of Forest Resources and Conservation, Institute of Food and Agricultural Sciences, University of Florida.

30. Rolley, R. E., and W. D. Warde. 1985. Bobcat habitat use in southeastern Oklahoma. *J. Wildl. Mgmt.* 49: 913–920.

31. Fendley, T. T., and D. E. Buie. 1986. Seasonal home range and movement patterns of the bobcat on the Savannah River Plant. In *Cats of the world: Biology, conservation, and management,* ed. S. D. Miller and D. D. Everett, 237–259. Washington, DC: National Wildlife Federation.

32. Heller, S. P., and T. T. Fendley. 1986. Bobcat habitat on the Savannah River Plant, South Carolina. In *Cats of the world: Biology, conservation, and management,* ed. S. D. Miller and D. D. Everett, 415–423. Washington, DC: National Wildlife Federation.

33. Wassmer, D. A., D. D. Guenther, and J. N. Layne. 1988. Ecology of the bobcat in south-central Florida. *Bull. Fla. State Mus., Biol. Sci.* 33(4): 159–228.

34. Rucker, R. A., M. L. Kennedy, G. A. Heidt, and M. J. Harvey. 1989. Population density, movements, and habitat use of bobcats in Arkansas. *Southwest. Nat.* 34: 101–108.

35. Koehler, G. M., and M. G. Hornocker. 1991. Seasonal resource use among mountain lions, bobcats, and coyotes. *J. Mammal.* 72: 391–396.

36. Major, J. T., and J. A. Sherburne. 1987. Interspecific relationships of coyotes, bobcats, and red foxes in western Maine. *J. Wildl. Mgmt.* 51: 606–616.

37. Litvaitis, J. A., and D. J. Harrison. 1989. Bobcat-coyote niche relationships during a period of coyote population increase. *Can. J. Zool.* 67: 1180–1188.

38. Diebello, F. J., S. M. Arthur, and W. B. Krohn. 1990. Food habits of sympatric coyotes, *Canis latrans,* red foxes, *Vulpes vulpes,* and bobcats, *Lynx rufus,* in Maine. *Can. Field Nat.* 104: 403–408.

39. Nunley, G. L. 1978. Present and historical bobcat population trends in New Mexico and the West. *Proc. Vert. Pest Conf.* 8: 77–84.

40. Robinson, W. B. 1961. Population changes of carnivores in some coyote-control areas. *J. Mammal.* 42: 510–515.

41. Witmer, G. W., and D. S. DeCalesta. 1986. Resource use by unexploited sympatric bobcats and coyotes in Oregon. *Can. J. Zool.* 64: 2333–2338.

42. Tewes, M. E. 1986. Ecological and behavioral correlates of ocelot spatial patterns. Ph.D. dissertation, University of Idaho, Moscow.

43. Yoakum, J. 1964. Observations on bobcat-water relationships. *J. Mammal.* 45: 477–479.

44. Toweill, D. E. 1986. Resource partitioning by bobcats and coyotes in a coniferous forest. Ph.D. dissertation. Oregon State University, Corvallis.

45. Marshall, A. D., and J. H. Jenkins. 1966. Movements and home ranges of bobcats as determined by radio-tracking in the upper coastal plain of west-central South Carolina. *Proceedings of the annual conference of the Southeastern Association of Game and Fish Commissioners* 20: 206–214.

46. Hall, H. T., and J. D. Newsom. 1978. Summer home ranges and movements of bobcats in bottomland hardwoods of southern Louisiana. *Proceedings of the annual conference of the Southeastern Association of Fish and Wildlife Agencies* 30: 427–436.

47. Buie, D. E., T. T. Fendley, and H. McNab. 1979. Fall and winter home ranges of adult bobcats on the Savannah River Plant, South Carolina. In *Bobcat research conference proceedings,* ed. L. G. Blum and P. C. Escherich, 42–46. National Wildlife Federation Scientific and Technical Series, no. 6.

48. Bailey, T. N. 1974. Social organization in a bobcat population. *J. Wildl. Mgmt.* 38: 435–446.

49. Guenther, D. D. 1982. Home range, social organization, and movement patterns of the bobcat, *Lynx rufus,* from spring to fall in south-central Florida. Master's thesis, University of South Florida, Tampa.

50. Shiflet, B. L. 1984. Movements, activity, and habitat use of the bobcat in upland mixed pine-hardwoods. Master's thesis, Louisiana State University, Baton Rouge.

51. Rollings, C. T. 1945. Habits, foods and parasites of the bobcat in Minnesota. *J. Wildl. Mgmt.* 9: 131–145.

52. Ryden, H. 1981. Following the shadowy trail of the cat that walks by itself. *Smithsonian* 12: 36–47.

53. Koehler, G. M. 1988. Bobcat bill of fare. *Nat. Hist.* 12/88: 48–56.

54. McCord, C. M. 1974. Selection of winter habitat by bobcats (*Lynx rufus*) on the Quabbin Reservation, Massachusetts. *J. Mammal.* 55: 428–437.

55. Foldesh, W. E. 1982. An attack by bobcats on adult javelina. *Southwest. Nat.* 27: 457.

56. Bailey, T. N. 1972. Ecology of bobcats with special reference to social organization. Ph.D. dissertation, University of Idaho, Moscow.

57. Beasom, S. L., and R. A. Moore. 1977. Bobcat food habit response to a change in prey abundance. *Southwest. Nat.* 21: 451–457.

58. Leopold, B. D., and P. R. Krausman. 1986. Diets of three predators in Big Bend National Park, Texas. *J. Wildl. Mgmt.* 50: 290–295.

59. Jones, J. H., and N. S. Smith. 1979. Bobcat density and prey selection in central Arizona. *J. Wildl. Mgmt.* 43: 666–672.

60. Zezulak, D. S. 1981. Northeastern California bobcat study. California Department of Fish and Game Report, Federal Aid in Wildlife Restoration Project W-54-R-12, job IV-3.

61. Knick, S. T., S. J. Sweeney, J. R. Alldredge, and J. D. Brittell. 1984. Autumn and winter food habits of bobcats in Washington State. *Great Basin Nat.* 44: 70–74.

62. Frederick, R. B., T. L. Edwards, D. J. Painter, and J. Whitaker. 1989. Bobcat densities and population dynamics in Kentucky. Final Report: P-R Project, W-45–19, Study B-R-I. Eastern Kentucky University and Kentucky Department of Fish and Wildlife Resources.

63. Maehr, D. S., and J. R. Brady. 1986. Food habits of bobcats in Florida. *J. Mammal.* 67: 133–138.

64. Land, E. D. 1991. Big Cypress deer/panther relationships: Deer mortality. Final report—1 July 1986–30 June 1991 (Study No. E-1-11 II-E-5b). Florida Game and Fresh Water Fish Commission, Tallahassee.

65. Labisky, R. F., and M. C. Boulay. 1998. Behaviors of bobcats preying on white-tailed deer in the Everglades. *Am. Midl. Nat.* 139: 275–281.

66. Barick, F. B. 1969. Deer predation in North Carolina and other southeastern states. In *White-tailed deer in the southern forest habitat*, ed. L. K. Halls, 25–31. Symposium Proceedings, South Forest Experiment Station, Nacogdoches, Texas.

67. Epstein, M. B., G. A. Feldhamer, and R. L. Joyner. 1983. Predation on white-tailed deer fawns by bobcats, foxes, and alligators: Predator assessment. *Proceedings of the annual conference of the Southeastern Association of Fish and Wildlife Agencies* 37: 161–172.

68. Fox, L. B. 1990. Ecology and population biology of the bobcat, *Felis rufus* in New York. Ph.D. dissertation, State University of New York, Syracuse.

69. Litvaitis, J. A., C. L. Stevens, and W. W. Mautz. 1984. Age, sex, and weight of bobcats in relation to winter diet. *J. Wildl. Mgmt.* 48: 632–635.

70. Matlacak, C. R., and A. J. Evans. 1992. Diet and condition of bobcats, *Lynx rufus*, in Nova Scotia during autumn and winter. *Can. J. Zool.* 70: 1114–1119.

71. Fritts, S. H., and J. A. Sealander. 1978. Diets of bobcats in Arkansas with special reference to age and sex differences. *J. Wildl. Mgmt.* 42: 533–539.

72. Trevor, J. T., R. W. Seabloom, and S. H. Allen. 1989. Food habits in relation to sex and age of bobcats from southwestern North Dakota. *Prairie Nat.* 21: 163–168.

73. Foote, L. E. 1945. The Vermont deer herd: A study in productivity. Vermont Fish and Game Service, Federal Aid in Wildlife Restoration Project No. 1-R, State Bulletin, Pittman-Robertson Series, no. 13. 125 pp.

74. Marston, M. A. 1948. Cats kill deer. *J. Mammal.* 29: 69–70.

75. Leyhausen, P. 1979. *Cat behavior: The predatory and social behavior of domestic and wild cats.* New York: Garland STPM Press.

76. Seton, E. T. 1929. *Lives of game animals.* Vol. 1, part 1, *Cats, wolves, and foxes.* New York: Charles Scribner's Sons.

77. Lindemann, W. 1955. Über die Jugendentwicklung beim Luchs (*Lynx L. lynx. Kerr.*) und bei der Wildkatze (*Felis s. silvestris* Schreb.). *Behaviour* 8: 1–45.

78. Lembeck, M. 1978. Bobcat study, San Diego County, California. Federal Aid for Endangered, Threatened and Rare Wildlife, Nongame Wildlife Investigations, Project E-W-2, Study IV, Job 1.7. Mimeographed, 22 pp.

79. Provost, E. E., C. A. Nelson, and A. D. Marshall. 1973. Population dynamics and behavior in the bobcat. In *The world's cats*, vol. 1, ed. R. L. Eaton, 42–67. Winston, OR: World Wildlife Safari.

80. Jenkins, J. H., E. E. Provost, T. T. Fendley, J. R. Monroe, I. L. Brisbin Jr., and M. S. Lenarz. 1979. Techniques and problems with a consecutive twenty-five year furbearer trapline census. In *Bobcat research conference proceedings*, ed. L. G. Blum and P. C. Escherich, 92–96. National Wildlife Federation Scientific and Technical Series, no. 6.

81. Crowe, D. M. 1975. A model for exploited bobcat populations in Wyoming. *J. Wildl. Mgmt.* 39: 408–415.

82. Macdonald, D. W. 1980. Patterns of scent marking with urine and faeces amongst carnivore communities. *Symp. Zool. Soc. Lond.* 45: 107–139.

83. Macdonald, D. W. 1985. The carnivores: Order Carnivora. In *Social odours in mammals*, vol. 2, ed. R. E. Brown and D. W. Macdonald, 619–722. Oxford: Clarendon Press.

84. Bailey, T. N. 1981. Factors of bobcat social organization and some management implications. In Worldwide furbearer conference proceedings: August 3–11, 1980, Frostburg, Maryland, ed. J. A. Chapman and D. Pursley, 984–1000.

85. Hamilton, D. A. 1982. Ecology of the bobcat in Missouri. Master's thesis, University of Missouri, Columbia.

86. Conner, M. C., R. F. Labisky, and D. R. Progulske Jr. 1983. Scent-station indices as measures of population abundance for bobcats, raccoons, gray foxes, and opossums. *Wildl. Soc. Bull.* 11: 146–152.

87. Colby, E. D. 1974. Artificially induced estrus in wild and domestic felids. In *The world's cats*, vol. 2, ed. R. L. Eaton, 126–147. Winston, OR: World Wildlife Safari.

88. Mehrer, C. F. 1975. Some aspects of reproduction in captive mountain lions *Felis concolor*, bobcats *Lynx rufus* and lynx *Lynx canadensis*. Ph.D. dissertation, University of North Dakota, Grand Forks.

89. Peters, G. 1987. Acoustic communication in the genus *Lynx* (Mammalia: Felidae)—comparative survey and phylogenetic interpretation. *Bonn. Zool. Beitr.* 38: 315–330.

90. Peters, G. 1984. On the structure of friendly close range vocalizations in terrestrial carnivores (Mammalia: Carnivora: Fissipedia). *Z. Säugetierk.* 49: 157–182.

91. Duke, K. L. 1954. Reproduction in the bobcat (*Lynx rufus*). *Anat. Rec.* 120: 816–817.

92. Gashwiler, J. S., W. L. Robinette, and O. W. Morris. 1961. Breeding habits of bobcats in Utah. *J. Mammal.* 42: 76–83.

93. Blankenship, T. L., and W. G. Swank. 1979. Population dynamic aspects of the bobcat in Texas. In *Bobcat research conference proceedings*, ed. L. G. Blum and P. C. Escherich, 116–122. National Wildlife Federation Scientific and Technical Series, no. 6.

94. Winegarner, C. E., and M. S. Winegarner. 1982. Reproductive history of a bobcat. *J. Mammal.* 63: 680–682.

95. Parker, G. R., and G. E. J. Smith. 1983. Sex- and age-specific reproductive and physical parameters of the bobcat (*Lynx rufus*) on Cape Breton Island, Nova Scotia. *Can. J. Zool.* 61: 1771–1782.

96. Rolley, R. E. 1985. Dynamics of a harvested bobcat population in Oklahoma. *J. Wildl. Mgmt.* 49: 283–292.

97. Lovallo, M. J., J. H. Gilbert, and T. M. Gehring. 1993. Bobcat, *Felis rufus*, dens in an abandoned beaver, *Castor canadensis*, lodge. *Can. Field Nat.* 107: 108–1109.

98. Peterson, R. L. 1966. *The mammals of eastern Canada.* Toronto: Oxford University Press.

99. Scott, P. P. 1976. Diet and other factors affecting the development of young felids. In *The world's cats*, vol. 3, no. 2, ed. R. L. Eaton, 166–179. Seattle: Carnivore Research Institute, University of Washington.

100. Hemmer, H. 1979. Gestation period and postnatal development in felids. *Carnivore* 2: 90–100.

101. Kitchings, J. T., and J. D. Story. 1984. Movements and dispersal of bobcats in east Tennessee. *J. Wildl. Mgmt.* 48: 957–961.

102. Griffith, M. A., D. E. Buie, T. T. Fendley, and D. A. Shipes. 1980. Preliminary observations of subadult bobcat movement behavior. *Proceedings of the annual conference of the Southeastern Association of Fish and Wildlife Agencies* 34: 563–571.

103. Knick, S. T., and T. N. Bailey. 1986. Long-distance movements by two bobcats from southeastern Idaho. *Am. Midl. Nat.* 116: 222–223.

104. Conley, R. H., and J. H. Jenkins. 1969. An evaluation of several techniques for determining the age of bobcats (*Lynx rufus*) in the Southeast. *Proceedings of the annual conference of the Southeastern Association of Game and Fish Commissioners* 23: 104–110.

105. Crowe, D. M. 1972. The presence of annuli in bobcat tooth cementum layers. *J. Wildl. Mgmt.* 36: 1330–1332.

106. Mahan, C. J. 1979. Age determination of bobcats (*Lynx rufus*) by means of canine pulp cavity ratios. In *Bobcat research conference proceedings*, ed. L. G. Blum and P. C. Escherich, 126–129. National Wildlife Federation Scientific and Technical Series, no. 6.

107. Matson, G., and J. Matson. 1993. Progress Report no. 13. Matson's Laboratory, Milltown, Montana.

108. Fox, L. B., and J. S. Fox. 1982. Population characteristics and food habits of bobcats in West Virginia. *Proceedings of the annual conference of the Southeastern Association of Fish and Wildlife Agencies* 36: 671–677.

109. Carter, T. D. 1955. Remarkable age attained by a bobcat. *J. Mammal.* 36: 290.

110. Jones, M. L. 1977. Record keeping and longevity of felids in captivity. In *The world's cats*, vol. 3, ed. R. L. Eaton, 132–138. Seattle: Carnivore Research Institute, University of Washington.

111. McMahan, L. R. 1986. The international cat trade. In *Cats of the world: Biology, conservation, and management*, ed. S. D. Miller and D. D. Everett, 461–488. Washington, DC: National Wildlife Federation.

112. Erickson, D. W., D. A. Hamilton, and F. B. Sampson. 1981. The status of the bobcat (*Lynx rufus*) in Missouri. *Trans. Missouri Acad. Sci.* 15: 49–60.

113. Johnson, M. K. 1980. New treaty arouses management issues. *Wildl. Soc. Bull.* 8: 152–156.

114. Mitchell, R. M. 1983. Export of bobcats taken in 1982–83 season. *Federal Register* 48: 7604–7608.

115. Blum, L, G., and P. C. Escherich, eds. 1979. *Bobcat research conference proceedings*. National Wildlife Federation Scientific and Technical Series, no. 6.

116. Theobald, A., and D. R. Pierson. 1987. Survey of lynx and bobcat harvest data, by population estimates and current research, as provided by individual state departments of fish and wildlife. Fauna and Flora Preservation Society, Boston, Massachusetts. Mimeographed, 22 pp.

117. Warren, R. J., M. J. Conroy, W. E. James, L. A. Baker, and D. R. Diefenbach. 1990. Reintroduction of bobcats on Cumberland Island, Georgia: A biopolitical lesson. *Trans. N. Am. Wildl. Nat. Res. Conf.* 55: 580–589.

118. Turbak, G. 1994. Bounce-back bobcat. *Wildl. Conserv.* 97(6): 22–31.

119. Erickson, A. W. 1955. An ecological study of bobcat in Michigan. Master's thesis, Michigan State University, East Lansing.

120. Delibes, M., M. C. Blázquez, R. Rodríguez-Estrella, and S. C. Zapata. 1997. Seasonal food habits of bobcats (*Lynx rufus*) in subtropical Baja California Sur, Mexico. *Can. J. Zool.* 74: 478–483.

Pampas cat

Oncifelis colocolo (Molina, 1782)

In Argentina and Chile the pampas cat is known as the *gato pajero*, or "grass cat," *pajero* being the local name for pampas grass. This cat's scientific name, *colocolo*, has been the subject of much confusion, and the binomial has been temporarily attached to at least two other cat species. The name was probably connected with the early Araucanian hero Colocolo.[1,2]

Molecular analysis suggests that about 5 to 6 million years ago, the pampas cat (*Oncifelis colocolo*), oncilla (*Leopardus tigrinus*), Geoffroy's cat (*Oncifelis geoffroyi*), and kodkod (*Oncifelis guigna*) split from the other small South American cats in the ocelot lineage. The pampas cat diverged early, about 5.3 million years ago, which is about the same time the Andean mountain cat (*Oreailurus jacobitus*) diverged from a common ancestor with the ocelot (*Leopardus pardalis*) and margay (*Leopardus weidii*). In the most recent split, about 4 million years ago, the oncilla, Geoffroy's cat, and kodkod diverged from a common ancestor with the pampas cat.[3]

DESCRIPTION

Pampas cats look like heavy-set house cats; their long hair makes them appear larger than they really are. The tail is short, only half the length of the head and body. The face is broad and sometimes marked with two conspicuous eye stripes. The backs of the pointed ears are black with grayish-white central spots or gray and unmarked. The tail is full and ringed with brown or black, but the rings are not always distinct.[4]

The color, pattern, and even texture of this cat's coat vary considerably, and specimens from the extremes of its range can look like different species. In some areas the coat is short, soft, and vividly spotted and striped, whereas in other areas the fur is long, coarse, and almost unmarked. On some animals the long hairs on the back form a sort of mane, which may be erected when the cat is frightened or nervous, giving it a larger and more formidable appearance. The background coat color varies from yellowish white to grayish brown to silvery gray through all shades in between. Some animals are dark with red-gray spots or broad transverse streaks on the sides, whereas others are almost completely unpatterned, except for distinctive brown bands on the forelimbs and hindlimbs.[1,4,5] The banding on the limbs may in fact be a diagnostic feature.[6]

García-Perea examined eighty-six museum specimens of *F. colocolo*, evaluating standard morphological variations in the skull, jaw, teeth, and coat pattern.

Figure 29. Distribution of the pampas cat.

She came to the conclusion that the animal known as the pampas cat is actually three closely related species,[7] and that the level of variation of bones in the skull indicates that those species have been separated for some time. She also suggests that the pampas cat has been incorrectly included in the genus *Oncifelis* and believes that it should be placed in its own genus, *Lynchailurus*, as discussed by Allen.[8] These views are supported by the phylogenetic analysis, which suggests that the current lineage of pampas cat split from a common ancestor about 1.7 million years ago and that subsequent geographic isolation has divided the cat into two or possibly three species.

DISTRIBUTION

The pampas cat ranges from the mountainous areas of southern Ecuador and Peru to central, western, and southern Brazil, parts of Bolivia, central Chile, Paraguay, Uruguay, and Argentina to southern Patagonia (fig. 29).[9,10,11,12]

ECOLOGY AND BEHAVIOR

The pampas cat is found in a greater variety of habitats than any other South American cat. It is typically associated with the pampas, or open grasslands, of Argentina and Uruguay[13,14] but it also occurs in the thorn forest and scrub of the Paraguayan Chaco, the open woodlands and grasslands of central Brazil, and Chilean cloud forests.[6] The species has also been reported, albeit rarely, in the floodplain areas of the Brazilian Pantanal.[12,15] In the Andes Mountains this cat has been recorded living at altitudes as high as 4,800 meters,[16] and it is also is found in the semiarid cold deserts of Patagonia.[11,17]

The pampas cat is thought to be nocturnal and mainly terrestrial, but little is known of its habits. However, judging from its broad distribution across such a wide range of habitats, this cat is clearly a generalist, and it probably eats just about any small vertebrate it can catch. A captive male pampas cat in Brazil's Parque Zoológico de Goiânia was quite adept at tree climbing and often rested draped over the highest fork of a tree in his cage.[12] Pampas cats are thought to feed on small mammals, especially guinea pigs, as well as ground birds such as tinamous.[4,18] Pearson reports that the cat hunts mountain viscachas at night in the altiplano of southern Peru.[16] In Argentina the pampas cat has been seen raiding the nests of Magellan penguins,[19] and there are accounts of it attacking domestic poultry.

The vocal repertoire of the pampas cat appears similar to that of other small felids, and includes a hiss, spit, growl, meow, gurgle, and purring.[20]

One captive female mated for the first time at two years of age. Litter size reportedly varies from 1 to 3 kittens, but among thirteen litters born in captivity, the average litter size was 1.31. These thirteen litters showed no indication of a seasonal birth peak.[21,22] One newborn at the Cincinnati Zoo in Ohio weighed 132 grams.[23]

STATUS IN THE WILD

There is very little information on the pampas cat's status in the wild. There are no population estimates from any of the countries in this cat's range. Habitat destruction is believed to be one of the major threats to the species; however, the extent of this threat is vague. Sport hunting is also considered to be a threat, but this too is difficult to quantify. In central Chile, cover, in the form of thickets, is becoming rarer, while hunters and their dogs are becoming more common. Chile does, however, have strong hunting laws and good enforcement.[24,25] In Salta Province, Argentina, this cat is reported to be rare and endangered.[13]

Despite the fact that skins of the pampas cat are reported to have no commercial value, a considerable number of pelts are known to have entered the international fur trade. Between 1976 and 1979, 78,239 specimens, with a value of US$1.8 million, were reported to have been exported from Buenos Aires, Argentina. However, to put these numbers into perspective, this represented less than 1 percent of the total value of Argentina's wildlife exports during this period.[26] The number of skins in trade decreased sharply in the 1980s, dwindling to 361 in 1983 and none in 1984. This sharp decline coincides with the instigation of legislation prohibiting hunting, trade, and commercial export in Argentina.

STATUS IN CAPTIVITY

The pampas cat is poorly represented in captivity, and many of the pampas cats in North American zoos are believed to be the offspring of what was probably a brother-sister pair. There is no studbook or Species Survival Plan for this species.

TABLE 36 MEASUREMENTS AND WEIGHTS OF ADULT PAMPAS CATS

HB	n	T	n	WT	n	Location	Source
610 (559–670)	4?	297 (290–322)	4?			Chile	27
596 (535–650)	5?	268 (230–284)	5?			Argentina	9
504 (423–610)	6?	270 (240–330)	6?	2.93 (1.7–3.65)	3?	Brazil	12
490	1f	220	1f			Argentina	17
790	1?	270	1?			Argentina	7
510	1?	270	1?			Ecuador	7
532	1f	292	1f			Uruguay	9
				2.95	1?	Uruguay	5

Note: HB = head and body length (mm), T = tail length (mm), WT = weight (kg). n = sample size. Sex: m = male, f = female, ? = unknown. Mean values are presented only for sample sizes of three or more. Range of values is in parentheses.

REFERENCES

1. Cabrera, A., and J. Yepes. 1960. *Mamíferos sud-americanos*. Buenos Aires: Compañia Argentina de Editores.

2. Osgood, W. H. 1943. The mammals of Chile. Field Museum of Natural History, Publication 542, Zoological Series, vol. 30. 268 pp.

3. Johnson, W. E., J. Pecon-Slattery, E. Eizirik, J.-H. Kim, M. Menotti-Raymond, C. Bonacic, R. Cambre, P. Crawshaw, A. Nunes, H. N. Seuánez, M. A. Martins Moreira, K. L. Seymour, F. Simon, W. Swanson, and S. J. O'Brien. 1999. Disparate phylogeographic patterns of molecular genetic variation in four closely related South American small cat species. *Mol. Ecol.* 8(suppl.): S79–S94.

4. Guggisberg, C. A. W. 1975. *Wild cats of the world*. New York: Taplinger.

5. Barlow, J. C. 1965. Land mammals from Uruguay: Ecology and zoogeography. Ph.D. dissertation, University of Kansas, Lawrence.

6. Redford, K. H., and J. F. Eisenberg. 1992. *Mammals of the Neotropics*. Vol. 2, *The Southern Cone*. Chicago: University of Chicago Press.

7. García-Perea, R. 1994. The pampas cat group (Genus *Lynchailurus* Severtzov, 1858). (Carnivora: Felidae), a systematic and biogeographic review. *Am. Mus. Novitates* 3096: 1–36.

8. Allen, J. A. 1919. Notes on the synonymy and nomenclature of the smaller spotted cats of tropical America. *Bull. Am. Mus. Nat. Hist.* 41: 341–419.

9. Cabrera, A. 1961. Los félidos vivientes de la república Argentina. *Revista del Museo Argentino de Ciencias Naturales "Bernardino Rivadavia," Ciencias Zoológicas* 6: 161–247.

10. Ximénez, A. 1961. Nueva subespecie del gato pajero en el Uruguay. *Comunicaciones Zoológicas del Museo de Historia Natural de Montevideo* 88: 1–8.

11. Texera, W. A. 1973. Distribución y diversidad de mamíferos y aves en la provincia de Magallanes. *Anal. Inst. Patagonia, Punta Arenas (Chile)* 4, no. 1–3: 321–333.

12. Silveira, L. 1995. Notes on the distribution and natural history of the pampas cat, *Felis colocolo*, in Brazil. *Mammalia* 59: 284–288.

13. Mares, M. A., R. A. Ojeda, and M. P. Kosco. 1981. Observations on the distribution and ecology of the mammals of Salta Province, Argentina. *Ann. Carnegie Mus.* 50: 151–206.

14. Olrog, C. C. 1979. Los mamíferos de la selva húmeda, cerro Calilegua, Jujuy. *Acta Zool. Lilloana* 33: 9–14.

15. Miller, F. W. 1930. Notes on some mammals of southern Matto Grosso, Brazil. *J. Mammal.* 11: 10–23.

16. Pearson, O. P. 1951. Mammals in the highlands of southern Peru. *Bull. Mus. Comp. Zool.* 106: 117–174.

17. Daciuk, J. 1974. Notas faunísticas y bioecológicas de Península Valdés y Patagonia. XII. Mamíferos colectados y observados en la Península Valdés y zona litoral de los Golfos San José y Nuevo (Provincia de Chubut, República Argentina). *Physis* secc. C, 33: 23–39.

18. Ilhering, H. 1911. Os mamíferos do Brasil Meridional. *Revista do Museu Paulista* 8: 147–272.

19. Mellen, J. D. 1991. Little-known cats. In *Great cats*, ed. J. Seidensticker and S. Lumpkin, 170–179. Emmaus, PA: Rodale Press.

20. Peters, G. 1984. On the structure of friendly close range vocalizations in terrestrial carnivores (Mammalia: Carnivora: Fissipedia). *Z. Säugetierk.* 49: 157–182.

21. Mellen, J. D. 1993. A comparative analysis of scent-marking, social and reproductive behavior in 20 species of small cats (*Felis*). *Am. Zool.* 33: 151–166.

22. Eaton, R. L. 1984. Survey of smaller felid breeding. *Zool. Garten* (n.f.) 54: 101–120.

23. Callahan, P., Curator, Cincinnati Zoo, Ohio. Personal communication.

24. Iriarte, J. A., and F. M. Jaksic. 1986. The fur trade in Chile: An overview of seventy-five years of export data (1910–1984). *Biol. Conserv.* 38: 243–253.

25. Miller, S. D., J. Rottmann, K. J. Raedeke, and R. D. Taber. 1983. Endangered mammals of Chile: Status and conservation. *Biol. Conserv.* 25: 335–352.

26. Mares, M. A., and R. A. Ojeda. 1984. Faunal commercialization and conservation in South America. *Bioscience* 34: 580–584.

27. Wolffsohn J. A. 1923. Medidas máximas y mínimas de algunos mamíferos chilenos colectados entre las años 1896 y 1917. *Revista Chilena Historia Natural* 27: 159–167.

Geoffroy's cat

Oncifelis geoffroyi (d'Orbigny and Gervais, 1844)

Also known as *gato montes,* or "mountain cat," Geoffroy's cat was named after the French naturalist Geoffroy St. Hilaire. It was originally thought to belong to the same species as the kodkod, but was later given its own species.[1] Recent genetic studies have partly vindicated the early taxonomists and shown that Geoffroy's cat and the kodkod are indeed closely related.[2]

DESCRIPTION

Geoffroy's cat is about the size of a domestic cat, but with a shorter tail and a more flattened head. Individuals from the extreme southern portion of the species' range are much larger than those from the north. The backs of the ears are black with a central white spot. The background color of the fur varies from smoky gray to lion-colored, with many intermediate shades. The four subspecies vary considerably in fur coloration and body size. Melanistic forms are common in this species; the melanism is due to a dominant autosomal allele.[3] The belly fur is white or cream-colored, and the body is covered with numerous small (15 to 20 millimeters in diameter) black spots; on the sides and limbs these spots tend to coalesce into transverse bands. The tail is ringed with dark bands. The cheeks are marked with two dark streaks, and several dark longitudinal lines occur on the crown and neck.[1,3,4] After that of the bobcat, the pelt of Geoffroy's cat is the world's most frequently traded cat skin.[5]

DISTRIBUTION

Geoffroy's cat is found from sea level up to an elevation of 3,300 meters in the Andes of southern Bolivia and northwestern Argentina, across southern Brazil to the Paraguayan Chaco, Uruguay, and south through Argentina and bordering areas of southern Chile to Patagonia and the Strait of Magellan (fig. 30).[5,6,7,8]

ECOLOGY AND BEHAVIOR

Geoffroy's cats are found in a wide variety of temperate and subtropical habitats, including pampas grasslands and marsh-grassland mosaics in Buenos Aires Province,[9] mesquite brush in the Paraguayan Chaco[10] and xeric shrublands in the foothills of the Andes in Argentinean Patagonia.[11] In neighboring Chile they use arid steppe uplands, but prefer areas with trees or trees mixed with shrubs.[1,5] Over 75 percent of all radiotelemetry locations of Chilean Geoffroy's cats were in areas of dense cover.[12] In Uruguay, the cats prefer open

Figure 30. Distribution of Geoffroy's cat.

woodlands, brushy areas, and remnants of open savannas associated with marshes. They were also observed to use trails made by capybaras in the dense undergrowth along lagoons.[13] Geoffroy's cats have been known to use cavities in tree roots as birth dens, and one individual was observed to spend the day in a small cave.[13] Other daytime retreats include burrows of larger mammals and tree cavities.

Geoffroy's cats spend most of their time on the ground, though they can also climb extremely well.[14] In captivity, Geoffroy's cats are less arboreal than other small South American cats such as the margay, oncilla, and ocelot. Captive Geoffroy's cats sometimes tunnel under leaf litter and leap out from this hiding place to "capture" moving objects. They also sit upright on their haunches or stand on the hind feet using the tail as a balancing aid. One individual was seen to hold this balancing position for 10 minutes.[3] A similar stance is used by prairie dogs, meerkats, and many mongoose species to check for predators or to scan a wide area.

In Torres del Paine National Park, Chile, Geoffroy's cats use the crooks of trees as defecation sites.[12] Ninety-three percent of all feces found in the park were in arboreal middens in old Chilean beech trees

(*Nothofagus*) some 3 to 5 meters above the ground, usually where the main trunk split into several branches. These tree middens were often reused. Similarly, in the almost treeless landscape of the Ernesto Tornquist Provincial Park, Buenos Aires Province, 18 percent of 190 Geoffroy's cat scats were found in the crooks of trees. Of twenty-seven marking sites, 62 percent were reused.[9]

Captive studies have shown that these cats are mainly nocturnal, with major activity periods occurring after sunset and before sunrise.[3,15] In Chilean Patagonia, radio-tagged Geoffroy's cats were most active at night; daytime activity was limited to the early morning or late afternoon.[12]

Feeding Ecology

Information on the food habits of Geoffroy's cat is limited, but its diet appears to consist largely of small rodents and birds. A hare was also recorded from the stomach of a male cat collected in Uruguay.[13] The remains of small birds, rodents, frogs, fish, and coypu were found in the stomachs of cats from Uruguay. Another stomach contained five rats and three small birds.[5,16] A preliminary analysis of ninety scats from Tornquist Provincial Park showed that small mammals occurred in 80 percent of scats and birds in 50 percent.[9] In northeastern Argentina a female Geoffroy's cat was seen at 0600 hours, trying to carry a sereima into a tree. She was unsuccessful, and when checked on again an hour later, she had dragged the bird into a nearby burrow. Sereimas are large, diurnal, running birds that stand almost a meter high.[17] The diets of Geoffroy's cats in northwestern Argentina were dominated by hares and European rabbits; cricetine rodents were consumed less often than expected based on their densities.[18]

The fish and frog remains found in Geoffroy's cats collected from Uruguay and Brazil lend support to the anecdotal accounts of this species being a fishing cat.[16] In captivity, Geoffroy's cats have no aversion to water and will readily "fish" for food.[3] This observation supports those made by Weigel, who remarks that the local people refer to the Geoffroy's cat as the fishing cat and say that it readily enters water.[19]

In southern Chile, studies by Johnson and Franklin have revealed that Geoffroy's cats feed extensively on hares. Overall, hares occurred in more than 50 percent of all feces (*n* = 325) examined, although the frequency of occurrence varied by season. In the spring, hares were found in 79 percent of scats, rodents in 18 percent, and the remainder (3 percent) contained birds. In the winter, the percentage of scats containing hares declined to 41 percent, but those containing rodents increased to 50 percent, and the remainder contained birds.[12]

Social Organization

Little is known of the social organization of Geoffroy's cat, but it is likely to be solitary.[20] In Paraguay, a sub-adult female radio-tracked for about three weeks moved over an area of less than 2 square kilometers.[10] In southern Chile, range sizes of radio-tagged cats were considerably larger.[12] One adult female's range measured 6.51 square kilometers, while another used an area of 2.33 square kilometers; the two largest ranges of adult males measured 10.89 square kilometers and 12.41 square kilometers.

The vocal repertoire of Geoffroy's cat has not been described, although individuals caught in traps have snarled, hissed, and spit. The cats also gurgle, which is a friendly, close-contact call.[21]

Reproduction and Development

In captivity there are records of both males and females first reproducing at eighteen months of age, but another captive study records a much later sexual maturity, in which one female's first estrus did not occur until she was twenty-two months old. Zoo records show that it is not uncommon for ten-year-old females to have young, and the record for the oldest Geoffroy's cat to give birth and rear a litter is held by a thirteen-year-old.[3]

Captive Geoffroy's cats in North American zoos exhibit estrus and breed year-round, but the majority of estrous periods occur between February and August, resulting in most young being born between April and October. In the Southern Hemisphere, estrus and the timing of birth are reversed, with most births recorded between December and May.[12,17] Estrous periods lasted from one to twelve days, and the duration of estrus varied for individual females, with the female's age appearing to affect estrus length. The length of time between heat periods is estimated to vary from twenty-three to thirty-nine days. A pre-estrous period, indicated by a loss of appetite and lower levels of interactive and affiliative behavior with other cats, begins about two weeks before estrus.[3]

Several observers have noted that in captivity, copulation occurs on a high ledge or shelf. Copulations are typically brief (two to seventy-five seconds) and occur frequently, 8 to 150 times a day.[3] Mating behavior includes a neck bite.[22]

In captivity, gestation length ranges from sixty-two to seventy-six days, and female Geoffroy's cats have been observed to pluck out their fur and use it to line the birth den. Litter size varies from 1 to 3 kittens; the average of ninety-five litters born in captivity is 1.5.[3,22,23,24,25] In northern Argentina a female was found in a burrow with three kittens,[17] and in southern Chile two females were seen with one kitten each.[12]

Kittens are born with their eyes closed; they are opened eight to nineteen days later. Development is slow compared with that of domestic kittens.[23,24] By the time the kittens are three to four weeks old, they are quite mobile and initiate play with siblings and their mother. In one captive study, the mother brought live cockroaches back to the den for the young to play with.[3] By six to seven weeks of age the kittens are eating solid food, and weaning begins at about seven weeks. At fifty-nine days kittens were first seen to sit up like prairie dogs. Kittens weigh 65 to 90 grams at birth and gain weight rapidly, tripling their weight by two weeks of age. By the time they are six months old, they are nearly as large as their mother. In captivity the interbirth interval is 12.1 months.[3,25]

In southern Chile, two males dispersed more than 25 kilometers from what were presumed to be their natal ranges.[12]

STATUS IN THE WILD
With regard to habitat and diet, Geoffroy's cat is a versatile species, a generalist compared with the similar-sized margay. Geoffroy's cat is apparently tolerant of moderate deforestation, but clearing of large tracts of chaco forest for cattle ranches has removed large areas of suitable habitat. Habitat loss is regarded as a threat to the species, but the most serious problem is hunting.[26,27]

Geoffroy's cat has the dubious distinction of having the world's second most frequently traded cat pelt. It takes at least twenty-five skins of this cat to make a fur coat.[4] Beginning in 1978, the species was increasingly heavily exploited, and in 1979 and 1980 over a quarter of a million Geoffroy's cat skins were traded in the

international marketplace. In 1981, West Germany alone imported over 70,000 Geoffroy's cat skins.[28]

Throughout South America there are large differences among countries with regard to regulation, enforcement, and reporting of number of skins traded. Many of the fur trade statistics, especially those detailing "country of origin," cannot be taken at face value because skins are often transferred to neighboring countries for export. The major reported sources of Geoffroy's cat skins in 1979 and 1980 were Paraguay and, to a lesser extent, Argentina. However, this cat's distribution in Paraguay is small, whereas it is widely distributed in Argentina; it is likely that many skins were illegally shipped across the border from Argentina, then re-exported from Paraguay.[28]

In Chile, Geoffroy's cat has been legally protected from hunting and commercialization since 1972, and just under three thousand wild cat skins have been exported from Chile since recordkeeping began in 1910. In neighboring Argentina, the situation is very different. The wildlife trade is a multimillion-dollar business, and Geoffroy's cat is the most heavily traded species. Over 340,000 Geoffroy's cat pelts, with a declared value of US$8.6 million, were exported from Buenos Aires between 1976 and 1979.[29,30,31]

The trade data indicate that West Germany was the major consumer of skins, but in 1986 the European Economic Community (EEC), of which West Germany is a member, prohibited the import of Geoffroy's cat from Argentina, Bolivia, Brazil, Chile, Paraguay, and Uruguay.

STATUS IN CAPTIVITY
Geoffroy's cat is not very well represented in zoo collections, but it does breed well in captivity. As of June 1989, there were forty-five cats in institutions participating in the International Species Inventory System (ISIS). In a 1988 study, Foreman found that the captive population was not seriously inbred, but suggested that inbreeding could become a problem in the future. One of the more unusual demands on the captive population of Geoffroy's cat has been created by a recent boom in the exotic pet trade. This cat's tractable nature and attractive pelt has resulted in a demand by the private sector for Geoffroy's cat–domestic cat hybrids, known as "Safari cats."[3]

TABLE 37 MEASUREMENTS AND WEIGHTS OF ADULT GEOFFROY'S CATS

HB	n	T	n	WT	n	Location	Source
701 (570–880)	7m	327 (300–370)	7m			Chile	6
537 (500–580)	3f	260 (250–280)	3f			Chile	6
628 (540–700)	4m	349 (325–375)	4m	4.9 (4.2–6.5)	4m	Chile	32
620 (535–745)	5f	348 (288–370)	5f	4.5 (3.5–4.9)	5f	Chile	32
440, 500	2m	340, 400	2m			Bolivia	33
430, 435	2f	260, 265	2f			Argentina	14
640, 665	2?	270, 275	2?			Argentina	14
492 (480–510)	3?	267 (250–280)	3?			Argentina	14
762 (665–850)	18?	285 (230–332)	18?	2.5 (2.2–2.8)	6?	Argentina	7
683 (630–740)	4m	335 (300–360)	4m	6.2 (4.3–7.8)	4m	Argentina	9
628 (610–650)	4f	302 (300–310)	4f	4.0 (3.5–4.3)	4f	Argentina	9
				3.7 (3.2–4.1)	5m	Uruguay	8
				3.1 (2.6–3.4)	5f	Uruguay	8
				5.2 (3.6–6.0)	5m	Uruguay	13

Note: HB = head and body length (mm), T = tail length (mm), WT = weight (kg). n = sample size. Sex: m = male, f = female, ? = unknown. Mean values are presented only for sample sizes of three or more. Range of values is in parentheses.

TABLE 38 FREQUENCY OF OCCURRENCE OF PREY ITEMS IN THE DIETS OF GEOFFROY'S CATS (PERCENTAGE OF SAMPLES)

Prey items	Torres del Paine NP, Chile [12] Scats (n = 325)
Lepus capensis Hare	67.4
Akodon sp. Field or grass mouse	16.9
Auliscomys micropus Leaf-eared mouse	4.9
Chelemys macronyx Greater long-clawed mouse	0.9
Eligmondontia typus Highland desert mouse	1.2
Oryzomys longicaudatus Rice rat	8.3
Phyllotis darwini Leaf-eared mouse	0.6
Reithrodon physodes Coney rat	1.5

(continued)

TABLE 38 *(continued)*

Prey items	Torres del Paine NP, Chile [12] Scats ($n = 325$)
Unidentified rodents	1.5
Unidentified mammals	5.2
Birds	8.0
Minimum number of vertebrate prey items	379

REFERENCES

1. Guggisberg, C. A. W. 1975. *Wild cats of the world.* New York: Taplinger.

2. Pecon-Slattery, J., W. E. Johnson, D. Goldman, and S. J. O'Brien. 1994. Phylogenetic reconstruction of South American felids defined by protein electrophoresis. *J. Mol. Evol.* 39: 296–305.

3. Foreman, G. E. 1988. Behavioral and genetic analysis of Geoffroy's cat (*Felis geoffroyi*) in captivity. Ph.D. dissertation, Ohio State University, Columbus.

4. Ximénez, A. 1975. *Felis geoffroyi. Mammalian Species* 54: 1–4.

5. McMahan, L. R. 1986. The international cat trade. In *Cats of the world: Biology, conservation, and management,* ed. S. D. Miller and D. D. Everett, 461–488. Washington, DC: National Wildlife Federation.

6. Texera, W. A. 1974. Nuevos antecedentes sobre mamíferos de Magallanes. *Anal. Inst. Patagonia, Punta Arenas (Chile)* 5: 189–192.

7. Redford, K. H., and J. F. Eisenberg. 1991. *Mammals of the Neotropics.* Vol. 2, *Mammals of the southern Neotropics: Chile, Argentina, Uruguay, Paraguay.* Chicago: University of Chicago Press.

8. Ximénez, A. 1973. Notas sobre félidos neotropicales III. *Papeis Avulsos de Zoologia* (São Paulo) 27: 31–43.

9. Lucherini, M., L. Soler, C. Manfredi, A. Desbiez, and C. Marull. 2000. Geoffroy's cat in the Pampas grasslands. *Cat News* 33: 22–24.

10. Berrie, P. M. 1978. Home range of a young female Geoffroy's cat in Paraguay. *Carnivore* 1: 132–133.

11. Rabinovich, J., A. Capurro, P. Folgarait, T. Kitzberger, G. Kramer, A. Novaro, M. Puppo, and A. Travaini. 1987. Estado del conocimiento de 12 especies de la fauna silvestre Argentina de valor comercial. Unpublished CONICET report to IUCN, Buenos Aires.

12. Johnson, W. E., and W. L. Franklin. 1991. Feeding and spatial ecology of the *Felis geoffroyi* in southern Patagonia. *J. Mammal.* 72: 815–820.

13. Barlow, J. C. 1965. Land mammals from Uruguay: Ecology and zoogeography. Ph.D. dissertation, University of Kansas, Lawrence.

14. Cabrera, A. 1961. Los félidos vivientes de la república Argentina. *Revista del Museo Argentino de Ciencias Naturales "Bernardino Rivadavia," Ciencias Zoológicas* 6: 161–247.

15. Mellen, J. D. 1989. Reproductive behavior of small captive exotic cats (*Felis* spp.). Ph.D. dissertation, University of California, Davis.

16. Ximénez, A. 1982. Notas sobre félidos neotropicales VIII. *Revista Nordest. Biol.* 5: 89–91.

17. Yanosky, A. A., and C. Mercolli. 1994. Notes on the ecology of *Felis geoffroyi* in northeastern Argentina. *Am. Midland Nat.* 132: 202–204.

18. Novaro, A. J., M. C. Funes, and R. S. Walker. 2000. Ecological extinction of native prey of a carnivore assemblage in Argentine Patagonia. *Biol. Conserv.* 92: 25–33.

19. Weigel, I. 1972. Small felids and clouded leopards. In *Grzimek's animal life encyclopedia,* vol. 12, *Mammals* III, ed. H. C. B. Grzimek, 281–332. New York: Van Nostrand Reinhold.

20. Gittleman, J. L. 1989. Carnivore group living: Comparative trends. In *Carnivore behavior, ecology, and evolution,* ed. J. L. Gittleman, 183–207. Ithaca, NY: Cornell University Press.

21. Peters, G. 1984. On the structure of friendly close range vocalizations in terrestrial carnivores (Mammalia: Carnivora: Fissipedia). *Z. Säugetierk.* 49: 157–182.

22. Kachuba, M. 1977. Sexual behavior and reproduction in captive Geoffroy's cats (*Leopardus geoffroyi* d'Orbigny and Gervais 1844). *Zool. Garten* (n.f.) 47: 54–56.

23. Scheffel, W., and H. Hemmer. 1975. Breeding Geoffroy's cat in captivity. *Int. Zoo Yrbk.* 15: 152–154.

24. Anderson, D. 1977. Gestation period of Geoffroy's cat bred at Memphis Zoo. *Int. Zoo Yrbk.* 17: 164–166.

25. Law, G., and H. Boyle. 1984. Breeding the Geoffroy's cat at Glasgow Zoo. *Int. Zoo Yrbk.* 23: 191–195.

26. Koford, K. B. 1973. Spotted cats in Latin America: An interim report. *Oryx* 12: 37–39.

27. Melquist, W. E. 1984. Status survey of otters (Lutrinae) and spotted cats (Felidae) in Latin America. Report to IUCN, Gland, Switzerland. 269 pp.

28. Broad, S. 1987. The harvest of and trade in Latin American spotted cats (Felidae) and otters (Lutrinae). Cambridge: IUCN Conservation Monitoring Centre.

29. Iriarte, J. A., and F. M. Jaksic. 1986. The fur trade in Chile: An overview of seventy-five years of export data (1910–1984). *Biol. Conserv.* 38: 243–253.

30. Mares, M. A., and R. A. Ojeda. 1984. Faunal commercialization and conservation in South America. *Bioscience* 34: 580–584.

31. Miller, S. D., J. Rottmann, K. J. Raedeke, and R. D. Taber. 1983. Endangered mammals of Chile: Status and conservation. *Biol. Conserv.* 25: 335–352.

32. Johnson, W., research scientist, Laboratory of Genomic Diversity, National Cancer Institute, FCRDC, Frederick, MD. Personal communication.

33. Allen, J. A. 1919. Notes on the synonymy and nomenclature of the smaller spotted cats of Neotropical America. *Bull. Am. Mus. Nat. Hist.* 41: 341–419.

Kodkod

Oncifelis guigna (Molina, 1782)

The word *kodkod* is the Araucanian Indian name for this cat.[1] In Chile and Argentina the kodkod is commonly called *guiña*. Recent genetic analysis indicates that the kodkod is closely related to Geoffroy's cat.[2]

DESCRIPTION

Along with the oncilla, the diminutive kodkod shares the distinction of being the smallest cat in the Western Hemisphere. About the size of a tiny house cat, this 1.5–2.8-kilogram felid is quite similar in appearance to Geoffroy's cat. Its buff or gray-brown coat is heavily marked with small, round black spots, which also cover the belly. The spots on the kodkod's head and neck sometimes form broken streaks, whereas in Geoffroy's cat the markings on the head and shoulders form more distinct stripes. The kodkod's tail is short — about half its head and body length—bushy, and marked with a series of narrow black bands. The backs of the low-set ears are black with a white central spot. Melanistic individuals are not uncommon; their dark coat markings are visible in bright sunlight.[1,3,4,5]

DISTRIBUTION

The entire geographic distribution of the kodkod is limited to an area of Chile and Argentina roughly the size of Texas (fig. 31). In Chile it is found in the central and southern regions, from Santiago Province south to the islands of Chiloé and the Guaitecas; in Argentina it is confined to a small area of the eastern slopes of the Andes, in the provinces of Neuquén, Río Negro, Chubut, and Santa Cruz.[1,3,4,5,6,7]

ECOLOGY AND BEHAVIOR

Kodkods are forest dwellers, inhabiting the montane and coniferous forests on both slopes of the southern Andes at elevations below about 2,000 meters. Wooded and semi-open areas along the Central Valley are also used by the cat.[1,3,8] Until recently the kodkod was one of the world's least known felids, but a six-month (1997–1998) study on Chiloé Island, off the coast of Chile, has given us a glimpse into this cat's lifestyle.[9] Jim Sanderson radio-collared five male and two female kodkods and followed their movements in the deep ravines and broken terrain of Chiloé's temperate rain forest.

The cats were as likely to be active during the day as at night. A male kodkod was found hunting during the daytime from a forest edge, preying on free-ranging young chickens in a nearby field. The cats made some

Figure 31. Distribution of the kodkod.

long-distance movements shortly before dawn or just after sunset. They also made long-distance movements during the daytime, but only under cover of vegetation. One male traveled 5 kilometers in an evening. On two occasions a male kodkod was seen crossing a road during the daytime, but only late in the afternoon when the shadows of trees extended across the road. Nighttime rest sites were in thick piles of live or dead vegetation, often consisting of seemingly impenetrable bamboo. Daytime rest sites were in dense vegetation in ravines, along streams with heavy cover, and in piles of dead gorse, an exotic shrub. Cats were also seen resting on stumps of fallen trees, and those found resting on branches in relatively open forest were often mobbed by caracaras and Southern lapwings. On a single occasion a kodkod was discovered resting in an orchard tree in an otherwise open field.

Kodkods were observed to be excellent climbers, easily able to climb trees more than a meter in diameter. The cats were not seen to hunt in trees, but they did use branches on the steep sides of ravines while stalking prey. Deep forested ravines with streams and near-vertical forested strips along the coast were frequently used habitats. Agricultural fields, pastures, and isolated forest tracts within kodkod home ranges were not used, but vegetated depressions or narrow riparian strips in otherwise open ravines were used as travel corridors between forest tracts.

Feeding Ecology

The kodkod was found to be a secretive, terrestrial, stalking predator of birds, lizards, and rodents in the ravines and forested areas. Prey remains at suspected kill sites and actual observations of kills showed that kodkods fed on a variety of birds, including Austral thrush, Southern lapwing, chucao tapaculo, huet-huet, domestic geese, and chickens, as well as the Chiloé lizard. The thrush, tapaculo, and huet-huet often skulk in thick vegetation, rarely leaving the ground. Predation on birds that feed diurnally on the ground, chickens, and small rodents has also been reported by others.[3,8,10,11,12]

Social Organization

The telemetry data suggest that kodkods have a social organization similar to that of many other felid species, in which males occupy large ranges that overlap the smaller home ranges of one or more resident females. In one area on Chiloé Island, the home ranges of three collared males did not overlap, nor was there any overlap in the home ranges of two collared females residing within one male's range. In this area, the male's range measured 2.5 square kilometers, while those of the two females measured 0.73 and 0.48 square kilometers. In another area, a male's range measured 1.1 square kilometers. The home ranges of the radio-collared females did not change over the six-month period, whereas within a month of a resident male's death, a neighboring male expanded his territory to include the area occupied by the previous resident.[9] The mean home range size of five kodkods (three males, two females) radio-tracked in the pristine forests in Laguna San Rafael National Park, Chile, was estimated at 1.5 square kilometers, with no significant differences between the sexes.[13]

STATUS IN THE WILD

The kodkod is rare in Argentina, and it is reported to be endangered in the agricultural heartland of central Chile due to destruction of its woodland habitat and overhunting. It may be slightly more abundant in south-central Chile, where these pressures are not so great, but its status is largely unknown.[14,15] In 1966 it was reported to be locally abundant in Malleco Province in Chile, and to be commonly found near human habitation. In this area the kodkod is said to attack livestock, especially young goats, so it is hunted and killed wherever its presence is suspected.[3] The kodkod does kill poultry, but given its small size, it seems unlikely that this tiny cat is a significant predator of goats.

Because the kodkod is so small, its pelt has been of little interest to the international fur trade, though the skins sometimes appear in local trade.[14] In 1983, Argentina listed the kodkod as vulnerable, and shortly thereafter, in 1986, enacted legislation to prohibit international trade and reinforce an export ban on all native cats.[14]

In Chile, habitat destruction is listed as the principal reason for the kodkod's decline, with hunting as the second most important. Customs data from Chile indicate that there has been little international trade in cats since the mid-1970s; however, there are local reports of large-scale hunting, which may mean that the skins are being used within the country.[15] Reports also indicate that the kodkod has been heavily overhunted in the past. The species currently is on CITES appendix II and is fully protected in Argentina and Chile.[16]

STATUS IN CAPTIVITY

There are no kodkods in North American zoos, and nothing is known of their behavior in captivity.

TABLE 39 MEASUREMENTS AND WEIGHTS OF ADULT KODKODS

HB	n	T	n	WT	n	Location	Source
470 (460–480)	1m, 2f	227 (220–235)	1m, 2f	2.23 (2.08–2.50)	1m, 2f	Chile	3
440 (418–480)	4m	225 (220–230)	4m			Chile	17
412 (390–450)	3f	218 (195–250)	3f			Chile	17

(continued)

TABLE 39 *(continued)*

HB	n	T	n	WT	n	Location	Source
470	5m	233	5m	2.18	5m	Chiloé Island	9
(430–490)		(210–250)		(1.7–2.8)			
430, 450	2f	210, 225	2f	1.5, 1.7	2f	Chiloé Island	9
480	1m	230	1m			Chile	18
510	1f	210	1f			Chile	18
424	1m	241	1m			Argentina	12
386	3f	208	3f	1.40	3f	Chile	13
(374–397)		(203–211)		(1.30–1.48)			
427	1m	213	1m	2.97	1m	Chile	13

Note: HB = head and body length (mm), T = tail length (mm), WT = weight (kg). *n* = sample size. Sex: m = male, f = female, ? = unknown. Mean values are presented only for sample sizes of three or more. Range of values is in parentheses.

REFERENCES

1. Osgood, W. H. 1943. The mammals of Chile. Field Museum of Natural History, Publication 542, Zoological Series, vol. 30. 268 pp.

2. Pecon-Slattery, J., W. E. Johnson, D. Goldman, and S. J. O'Brien. 1994. Phylogenetic reconstruction of South American felids defined by protein electrophoresis. *J. Mol. Evol.* 39: 296–305.

3. Greer, J. K. 1965. Mammals of Malleco Province Chile. *Pub. Mus. Mich. St. Univ.: Biol. Ser.* 3: 49–152.

4. Nowak, R. M. 1991. *Walker's mammals of the world*, 5th ed. Vol. 2. Baltimore: Johns Hopkins University Press.

5. Redford, K. H., and J. F. Eisenberg. 1992. *Mammals of the Neotropics*. Vol. 2, *The southern cone*. Chicago: University of Chicago Press.

6. Cabrera, A. 1961. Los félidos vivientes de la república Argentina. *Revista del Museo Argentino de Ciencias Naturales "Bernardino Rivadavia," Ciencias Zoológicas* 6(5): 161–247.

7. Melquist, W. E. 1984. Status survey of otters (Lutrinae) and spotted cats (Felidae) in Latin America. Report to IUCN, Gland, Switzerland. 269 pp.

8. Cabrera, A., and J. Yepes. 1960. *Mamíferos sud-americanos.* 2 vols. Buenos Aires: Compañia Argentina de Editores.

9. Sanderson, J. G., M. E. Sunquist, and A. W. Iriarte. In press. Natural history and landscape-use of guignas (*Oncifelis guigna*) on Isla Grande Chiloé, Chile. *J. Mammal.*

10. Miller, S. D., and J. Rottmann. 1976. *Guía para el reconocimiento de mamíferos chilenos.* Santiago: Editora Nacional Gabriela Mistral.

11. Housse, P. R. 1953. *Animales salvajes de Chile.* Santiago: Ediciones Universidad de Chile.

12. Koslowsky, J. 1904. Dos mamíferos de Patagonia, cazados en el Valle del Lago Blanco (territorio del Chubut). *Rev. Mus. La Plata* 11: 129–132.

13. Dunstone, N., L. Durbin, I. Wyllie, S. Rose, and G. Acosta. 1998. Ecology of the kodkod in Laguna San Rafael National Park, Chile. *Cat News* 29: 18–20.

14. Broad, S. 1987. The harvest of and trade in Latin American spotted cats (Felidae) and otters (Lutrinae). Cambridge: Wildlife Trade Monitoring Unit, IUCN Conservation Monitoring Centre.

15. Miller, S. D., J. Rottmann, K. J. Radedeke, and R. D. Taber. 1983. Endangered mammals of Chile: Status and conservation. *Biol. Conserv.* 25: 333–352.

16. Nowell, K., and P. Jackson. 1996. *Wild cats: A status survey and conservation action plan.* Gland, Switzerland: International Union for Conservation of Nature and Natural Resources (IUCN).

17. Allen, J. A. 1919. Notes on the synonymy and nomenclature of the smaller spotted cats of tropical America. *Bull. Am. Mus. Nat. Hist.* 41: 341–419.

18. Wolffsohn, J. A. 1923. Medidas máximas y mínimas de algunos mamíferos chilenos colectados entre los años 1896 y 1917. *Revista Chilena Historia Natural* 27: 159–167.

Andean mountain cat

Oreailurus jacobitus (Cornalia, 1865)

The Andean mountain cat is one of the least known felids in South America. Everything that is known of this cat comes from a few museum skins and skulls and a few observations of the cat in the wild. DNA extracted from nine skins indicates that this cat is a distinct species belonging to the ocelot lineage. It diverged from ocelots and margays about 5.3 million years ago.[1]

DESCRIPTION

About the size of a large house cat, the Andean mountain cat has long, thick fur. Its coat is pale silvery gray, spotted and striped with blackish or brownish markings. The underparts are white, marked with dark spots. The tail is long and bushy, banded with about seven dark rings. The legs are banded with two to three black bars.[2,3]

"In general coloration and coat, these specimens are reminiscent of the Snow Leopard (*Uncia*)," wrote the taxonomist R. I. Pocock in 1941, "suggesting rocky hills, not jungle or forest, as their habitat. The coat is very full and soft, about 40 mm long on the back and 35 mm on the uniformly bushy tail."[2] The mountain cat's skull has inflated ear bullae, the anterior chamber being somewhat larger than the posterior.[4,5]

DISTRIBUTION

The Andean mountain cat is a rare felid with a very restricted distribution. It is confined to the high Andes of southern Peru, southwestern Bolivia, northeastern Chile, and northern Argentina (fig. 32).[6,7,8] In 1943 Osgood remarked that the cat's distribution roughly coincided with that of the chinchilla, and indeed, before the chinchilla was almost extirpated for its fur, this was probably true.[1]

ECOLOGY AND BEHAVIOR

The Andean mountain cat is confined to the high, rocky, generally treeless zone of the Andes. Most of the specimens in museum collections were obtained at elevations above 3,000 meters, and in Peru one was collected at 5,100 meters in a barren expanse of rocks with scattered clumps of grass and small bushes.[3]

One reported observation of the cat was on the mountainous altiplano, or plateau, at an elevation of 4,250 meters in the Cumbres Calchaquíes, Province Tucumán, Argentina.[5] The cat was seen on a rocky hillside in an area dotted with numerous permanent and ephemeral lakes. The climate in this area is very cold, with minimum daily temperatures frequently at

Figure 32. Distribution of the Andean mountain cat.

or below 0°C. Arid and windswept, the altiplano gets little rain; most of the moisture falls as snow during the summer. The vegetation consists of cold-hardy grasses, prostrate cushion plants, some minute flowering plants, and a few scattered shrubs.

Although there is no information on the mountain cat's feeding habits, it probably eats any small mammal, bird, or lizard it can catch. In the altiplano there is a surprisingly diverse array of potential prey, including rabbits, mountain viscachas, hairy armadillos, and several rodent species. A variety of ground-dwelling birds, such as seed snipes, earth creepers, and several species of ducks, geese, and wading birds, also frequent the altiplano.

The scientists who were lucky enough to see the elusive mountain cat in Argentina managed to follow it at close range (20 to 30 meters) for two hours. During this time the cat went down to a lake to drink. A flock of ducks on the lake followed the cat's movements as it edged around the water. Later, a passing gray fox saw the cat and immediately fled, bristling and looking over its shoulder at the cat as it ran away; the fox obviously considered the cat to be a potential predator, although the cat showed no interest in pursuit. The cat also rested for about twenty minutes in a cavelike shelter formed by a large rock.

Another observation (November 1988) took place near the Salar de Surire at an elevation of about 4,600 meters in the Chilean Puna.[9] Günter Ziesler, a wildlife photographer, was watching a colony of mountain viscachas in an area of boulders near a spring. The cat appeared early in the morning, shortly after sunrise; it had evidently come to hunt. Ziesler watched for an hour as the cat searched unsuccessfully for prey among and under the rocks. It was not in the least shy and paid him no attention as long as he remained 20 to 30 feet away. Ziesler also recounts an occasion when a mountain cat killed a viscacha directly in front of the guardhouse in the Vicuña Reserve Pampa Galeras in Peru; the guards threw stones at the cat to drive it away and killed it.[10] Ten years later (November 1998), Jim Sanderson also saw an Andean mountain cat at Salar de Surire. The cat was seen on three different days, sometimes from as close as 3 meters. On each occasion the cat was hunting in a colony of mountain viscachas.[11]

A fourth observation was of a single cat, stalking viscachas at 4,300 meters elevation on Hacienda Cala Cala in Peru, near Azángaro.[12]

Beyond these few observations and the fact that the only times the cat was seen it was active during the day, little can be surmised about the biology and behavior of this species. In a recent forty-one-day survey of a site in northwestern Argentina that has been proposed for a national park (Anconquija National Park), no cats were seen, even though five sample areas were searched intensively. A skull identified as that of an Andean mountain cat was found. Scats that were thought to be from Andean mountain cats were most commonly found in areas of rocky, steep terrain that were occupied by mountain viscachas.[13]

There are no Andean mountain cats in captivity, and thus nothing is known of litter size, growth and development of young, or longevity.

STATUS IN THE WILD

Virtually the only proof that the Andean mountain cat is not extinct comes from the periodic appearance of fresh skins in the fur markets of Buenos Aires. The species is, however, very rare. Any existing populations are probably isolated from one another because its mountainous habitat areas are separated by deep, human-inhabited valleys that would act as dispersal barriers for a high-altitude species.[5]

Despite its rarity, the Andean mountain cat is still hunted illegally for its beautiful fur. The loss of even a few individuals from an already small population could be disastrous, and this species is probably in great danger of extinction.

The Andean mountain cat is protected from hunting and commercialization in Chile and Peru.[14] In 1986, legislation was enacted in Argentina to protect the cat from hunting, exploitation, commercialization, trade, and export. In the same year Bolivia effected a three-year moratorium on capture, commercialization, and export of a list of species, including *O. jacobitus*. The species is now listed on appendix 1 of CITES for all four countries in which it is believed to occur.

TABLE 40 MEASUREMENTS AND WEIGHTS OF ADULT ANDEAN MOUNTAIN CATS

HB	n	T	n	WT	n	Location	Source
600	1?	430	1?			Chile	2
640	1?	480	1?			Chile	15
577	1?	413	1?	4.0	1?	Peru	16

Note: HB = head and body length (mm), T = tail length (mm), WT = weight (kg). n = sample size. Sex: m = male, f = female, ? = unknown.

REFERENCES

1. Johnson, W. E., M. Culver, J. A. Iriarte, E. Eizirik, K. L. Seymour, and S. J. O'Brien. 1998. Tracking the evolution of the elusive Andean mountain cat (*Oreailurus jacobita*) from mitochondrial DNA. *J. Hered.* 89: 227–232.

2. Osgood, W. H. 1943. *The mammals of Chile.* Field Museum of Natural History, Publication 542, Zoological Series, vol. 30. 268 pp.

3. Pearson, O. P. 1957. Additions to the mammalian fauna of Peru and notes on some other Peruvian mammals. *Breviora* 73: 1–7.

4. Kuhn, H. J. 1973. Zur Kenninis der Andenkatze, *Felis (Oreailurus) jacobita* Cornalia, 1865. *Säugetierk. Mitt.* 21(4): 359–364.

5. Scrocchi, G. J., and S. P. Halloy. 1986. Notas sistemáticas, ecológicas, etológicas y biogeográficas sobre el gato Andino *Felis jacobita* Cornalia (Felidae, Carnivora). *Acta Zool. Lilloana* 38: 157–170.

6. Cabrera, A. 1961. Los félidos vivientes de la república Argentina. Revista del Museo Argentino de Ciencias Naturales "Bernardino Rivadavia," Ciencias Zoológicas 6(5): 161–247.

7. Cabrera, A., and J. Yepes. 1960. *Mamíferos sud-americanos.* 2 vols. Buenos Aires: Compañia Argentina de Editores.

8. Redford, K. H., and J. F. Eisenberg. 1992. *Mammals of the Neotropics*. Vol. 2, *The southern cone*. Chicago: University of Chicago Press.

9. Ziesler, G. 1992. Erinnerung an eine Andenkatze. *ANIMAN Mensch und Natur* 38: 68–79.

10. Ziesler, G., wildlife photographer, Am Riesenanger 7, D-8958 Füssen, Germany. Personal communication.

11. Sanderson, J., landscape ecologist, Conservation International, Washington, DC. Personal communication.

12. Grimwood, I. R. 1969. *Notes on the distribution and status on some Peruvian mammals*. Special publication no. 21. Bronx, NY: New York Zoological Society. 86 pp.

13. Lucherini, M., D. Sana, and D. Birochio. 1999. The Andean mountain cat (*Oreailurus jacobita*) and the other wild carnivores in the proposed Anconquija National Park, Argentina. Società Zoologica "La Torbiera," Scientific Report no. 5: 1–30.

14. Fuller, K. S., B. Swift, A. Jorgenson, and A. Brautigam. 1985. *Latin American wildlife trade laws*, 2nd ed. Washington, DC: World Wildlife Fund-U.S.

15. Pine, R. H., S. D. Miller, and M. L. Schamberger. 1979. Contributions to the mammalogy of Chile. *Mammalia* 43: 339–376.

16. Miller, S. D., and J. Rottmann. 1976. *Guía para el reconocimiento de mamíferos Chilenos*. Santiago: Editoria Nacional Gabriela Mistral.

Manul

Otocolobus manul (Pallas, 1776)

The manul, or Pallas's cat, was discovered by the German explorer and naturalist Peter Simon Pallas. This distinctive felid, with its short legs and long hair, cannot be easily confused with any of the other cats. Its popular Russian name means "steppe cat" or "rock wildcat," and another name that is often used, *manul*, is derived from the Mongolian.[1] It is also called "steppe cat" (*steppenkatze*) in German.[2]

At different times this cat has been variously thought to be a member of the lynx family, a member of the wildcat family, or in a genus by itself.[3,4,5] The manul was once thought to be the ancestor of domestic long-haired breeds such as the Persian, but this theory has since been abandoned. Recent genetic studies place the manul early in the domestic cat lineage, from which it probably separated before the jungle cat, sand cat, black-footed cat, and African wildcat. Evidence for this early split from the rest of the domestic cat line comes from the presence or absence of a retrovirus. Endogenous retroviral gene families are present in the chromosomal DNA of several felid species. Studies of these retroviruses show that the RD-114 retroviral genes were introduced into the ancestors of the modern domestic cat some 6 to 8 million years ago.[6,7] All members of the domestic cat lineage except the manul have RD-114 genes, suggesting that the manul split off from this lineage before the genes were introduced.[8]

Despite, or perhaps because of, the fact that the manul was the first to separate from the main stem of the domestic cat group, it is the most advanced, or specialized, of those cats. Many authors consider it to be "the culmination of the evolutionary series of modern cats,"[1] even more specialized than the closely related sand cat. Indeed, K. A. Satunin, a Russian scientist, considers the manul to be "an extreme development of the cat type as manifested by the great roundness and shortness of its skull, size of its eyes, etc. Thus I place the manul on one end and the cheetah on the other end of the series of cats described by me, since the cheetah lacks some of the characteristic traits of this family."[2]

DESCRIPTION

About the size of a domestic cat, the manul is a squat, rather short-legged felid with a thick, bushy tail that is about half the length of its head and body. Its coat is long, and its fur is so thick that it makes the 2–4-kilogram animal look much larger than it really is. It has a broad head with a low forehead and a face that appears flattened, like that of a pug or Pekingese dog. The ears are short, set very wide apart and low on the sides of the head—so low that the top of the ear is level with the outer corner of the eye. The eyes are large and face almost directly forward. The claws are very short.[1,3,9,10]

The skull of the manul differs markedly from those of other small felids, but has the closest resemblance to that of the sand cat.[1] The cranial portion is very wide, and the muzzle is short and deeply sloped. The palate is short, only slightly wider than it is long, and the ear bullae are large. The teeth are also unusual in that there are only twenty-eight; the canines are large, and the first upper premolar is absent.[2,11]

The general coloration is grizzled or silvery buff, although the fur of some forms is rusty red or ginger. The tail is marked with a black tip and from four to seven narrow black rings. The rest of the body is unmarked except for several dark transverse stripes on the loins and back and one or two dark horizontal stripes on the forelegs. The chin and upper parts of the throat are white, becoming brownish or dark gray, and the fur is longer and more silky on the chest and belly. The backs of the ears are grayish, buff, or rust. The face is marked with blackish spots on the crown, and two dark stripes on the cheeks extend downward from the outer corner of each eye. The fur between the stripes is white. There is white around the eyes, surrounded by a dark rim, giving the cat a "spectacled" appearance;[1,2,3,9,12] and Pocock remarked that "the [fur] pattern on the face is very clearly disruptive."[11]

In captivity manuls have a unique motion when traveling across steep cliffs and rocky ledges in their exhibit. The cats observed by Jill Mellen "did not overtly leap from ledge to ledge, but instead appeared to 'flow' from perch to perch on stocky little legs."[13]

DISTRIBUTION

The manul is distributed from the Caspian Sea in the west through southern Turkmenistan, Iran, Afghanistan, Baluchistan, Kashmir, western and central China, Inner Mongolia, and Mongolia (fig. 33).[1,3,9,11,12,14,15,16]

ECOLOGY AND BEHAVIOR

The manul lives in central Asia in uplands, hilly areas, and steppes with rocky outcrops as well as semidesert areas. In a few places where these habitats exist at higher altitudes, such as the Tien Shan, Gobi Altai, and the Palmirs, the cat is found at elevations of

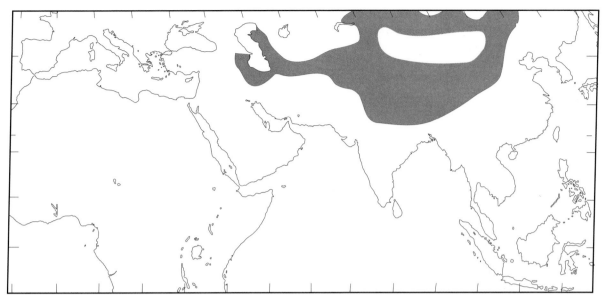

Figure 33. Distribution of the manul.

3,000–4,000 meters, but most records come from lower elevations. In western areas of the former Soviet Union it is found at 1,000–1,500 meters elevation in steppe vegetation (*Artemisia, Festuca, Stipa*). In Ladakh the cat is found in barren, stony valleys and hilly terrain above the treeline, from 3,600 meters to 4,800 meters elevation.[1,9]

Typical habitat for the manul is characterized by an extreme continental climate—little rainfall, low humidity, and a wide range of temperatures. In central Asia the winter air temperature is commonly −50°C, and snowfall is light and uneven. These cats seem to be unable to negotiate deep, loose snow, and though they can survive occasional short periods of heavy snow, they rarely live in areas where the maximum mean ten-day snow cover depth exceeds 10 centimeters. As a general rule, a continuous snow cover of 15 to 20 centimeters marks the ecological limit for this species. In winter manuls become fat and much less mobile; as they are unable to run through snow, this time of year presents the best opportunity to hunters. Two nineteenth-century Russian authors mention that shepherds and Kirgizians would chase manuls through snow, or follow their tracks to a den, upon which they would kill the cats with sticks or stone them to death.[1]

Manuls spend the day in caves, rock crevices, or marmot burrows, emerging in late afternoon to begin hunting. Observations of a manul "at midday stretched out on a boulder warming itself in the sun"[1] and "basking on a little patch of sand just below an overhanging bush"[11] suggest that these cats sometimes sunbathe just as the sand cat and jungle cat do.

Manuls hunt by stalking or creeping up on prey; they are not good or particularly fast runners. They hunt mostly by sight, using the sparse vegetation as stalking cover. The low-set ears and flat forehead are adaptations for hunting in open terrain, allowing the cat to peer over rocks or low bushes without exposing too much of its head.[11] Tamed individuals hunting for voles and gerbils not only managed to catch those animals running on the surface, but also ambushed prey by hiding near burrow exits.[1]

The cat's pale, shaggy fur helps it blend into its surroundings, and the species has a remarkable ability to hide in plain view. Several authorities have commented on this characteristic hiding behavior, including the well-known Russian biologist A. A. Sludskii. "It is surprising how such a big animal can render itself instantly invisible," he writes. "Even knowing the places where a cat is hiding, it is very difficult to find."[1] Given the cat's poor running ability and the fact that it lives in open, sparsely vegetated areas, a combination of camouflage and hiding behavior is its best escape option. However, when approached or "frightened by a pursuer it sits, lies on its back, or often turns to attack, fiercely defending itself."[1]

Feeding Ecology
Manuls feed largely on pikas, gerbils, voles, mouselike rodents, and chukar partridge; they sometimes catch

Tolai hares or young marmots. Pikas, or mouse hares as they are sometimes known, weigh 100 to 400 grams and seem to be a favorite food; one cat had the remains of five Mongolian pikas in its stomach. Other specimens have been collected after having killed similarly impressive numbers of prey. One male cat had sixteen Brandt's voles, weighing a total of 410 grams, in its stomach, another had just eaten two Daurian pikas, five Brandt's voles, and one Daurian hamster. Pikas were found in 89 percent of 502 scats from western trans-Baikal; small rodent remains were found in 44 percent, ground squirrels in 3 percent, and hares and birds each in 2 percent.[1] In Ladakh a scientist trapping for pikas at 3,300 meters came upon a manul in a small cave. From the scattered feathers, the cat had obviously been eating a chukar partridge. Since most pikas and partridges are active during the daytime, this cat is likely to be quite diurnal. Indeed, in Ladakh, where pikas are their main prey, the cats are known to hunt during the day.[9]

Social Organization

The few observations of manuls in the wild suggest that they are solitary. There are few descriptions of manul vocalizations. Pocock describes some of the sounds made by a captive animal: "Its 'spit' was a short, sharp 'ts, ts, ts,' projected through closed lips, and its sexual call was a combination of the bark of a small dog and the 'hoot' of an owl."[11] The manul also has a unique "lip quiver," probably a threat display. The cat raises the upper lip on one side of its muzzle, exposing the canine, then rapidly raises and lowers the lip for about five seconds. Males spray urine, and both sexes are reported to cover their feces.[13,17]

Reproduction and Development

Observations in captivity suggest that the manul has a short estrus, with the period of sexual receptivity lasting for only twenty-six to forty-two hours. The gestation period is sixty-six to sixty-seven days,[13] or seventy-four to seventy-five days.[18] As might be expected of a cat that lives in such a seasonally harsh climate, the manul is a seasonal breeder; most litters are born in April and May. In the trans-Baikal region the manul comes into heat in February: "At that time calls of the cat are heard frequently at night. Several males follow a female in estrus and there are sometimes serious fights among them."[1]

Manuls have large litters; two to four kittens are common,[13,19] and as many as five or six is not unusual.[1,19,20] There is even one record of eight kittens in a litter.[1] Such large litters are not uncommon for felids living in highly seasonal environments where prey such as pikas, hares, and small rodents may undergo major population cycles or fluctuations. In Utah, for example, the litter size of bobcats ranges from one to six;[21] likewise, one to four is the most common litter size for Eurasian lynx, but as many as six have been recorded.[1] Given the diet and litter size of the manul and the highly seasonal climate in its range, its populations are likely to undergo changes similar to those of the lynx and bobcat. Exceptionally long winters, deep snow, or prolonged periods of glaze ice can cause these cats to starve to death, and such winters occur roughly twice a decade.[1] During years when prey numbers crash, females probably have smaller litter sizes and few kittens survive, but when prey numbers rise, litter size will increase, as will survivorship.

Manuls use dens year round to protect themselves from the summer heat and severe winter cold. Dens and nests have been found in rock fissures, under large boulders, and in the abandoned burrows of foxes, badgers, and marmots. Nests contain dried vegetation, pieces of rodent skin, bird feathers, and other pieces of prey that the mother has brought back for her kittens.[1] Descriptions of den sites containing kittens are rare, but in Mongolia three nesting dens with kittens were found among rock crevices, and in another area four kittens were found "in a niche formed by the disintegration of a block of montane rock." There was no bedding in this particular den, only the bones of small rodents.[1]

Kittens are born blind and helpless, covered in dense, very fuzzy fur. Some longer hairs stand out along the back.[1] One male kitten weighed 89 grams at birth; its head and body measured 152 millimeters, while its tail was 55 millimeters.[18] Another newborn found in the wild had a head and body length of 123 millimeters and a tail length of 31 millimeters. One female kitten had a head and body length of 123 millimeters and a tail length of 55 millimeters.[10] At the age of two months, when they weigh about 500 to 600 grams, the kittens molt, exchanging their juvenile coats for long adult fur. Kittens born in April and May begin hunting voles by the end of August. By October, young of the year have almost reached adult size and may weigh 4 kilograms.[1]

Manuls have a high reproductive potential. Given

that they can give birth annually to large litters of kittens, which are able to hunt when five months old and are adult size at six or seven months of age, this species is perfectly designed to expand its population rapidly in a short time. Judging from a single captive animal that lived to be 11.2 years old,[22] the manul's lifespan is probably similar to that of the domestic cat, or roughly eight to ten years in the wild. If a female produces her first litter at two years of age and breeds annually thereafter, she could, assuming a litter size of four and no mortality, potentially rear twenty-four to thirty-two kittens in a lifetime. Such numbers are likely to be attained only under optimum conditions; under normal conditions, a female will do well to rear half these numbers.

STATUS IN THE WILD

Much of the information on the status of the manul comes from records of the animal's pelt in the fur trade, although a Canadian team reported recently that the cat was commonly seen in the Arjin Mountains Nature Reserve of western China.[23] Tan Bangjie believes that in China it is more numerous than the desert cat (*F. bieti*) because there are more manul furs in the market.[16] In Tibet 1,000 skins were sold in 1977.[15] China is a signatory to CITES, and the manul is listed as a protected species in China because it is known to eat large quantities of rodents. However, China has little money for enforcement and protection, so the cat's protected status exists largely on paper. Afghanistan, India, Iran, Pakistan, and Russia are also parties to the CITES agreement, but these countries are similarly short of funds for law enforcement and protection. The People's Republic of Mongolia has not signed the CITES agreement, and hunting and shooting for furs

is permitted under a regulated harvest. Mongolia is the main exporter of manul pelts; between 1978 and 1988 at least 4,356 skins were exported from the country.[24] The average minimum world trade in skins is estimated at an annual 2,000 skins. The main importing country is the Federal Republic of Germany, but Austria, Finland, and Italy also import pelts.[25]

STATUS IN CAPTIVITY

Captive manuls are reported to be quite friendly. "The manul is markedly different in both behavior and appearance from the majority of the specimens of the genus *Felis* kept in captivity," Pocock notes, adding that when they are not yet tamed they show "no fear or desire to hide from spectators."[26]

The manul's captive status is precarious. Though it is a highly desirable exhibit animal and much sought after by zoos, it breeds poorly in captivity, and its offspring seem to suffer high mortality rates, due primarily to *Toxoplasma gondii* infection. In an effort to understand the nature of this infection, efforts are currently under way to gather information on parasite loads and physiological and genetic parameters of manuls in Mongolia. This effort is the first study of the manul in the wild.[27]

As of 1989 only ten manuls were held in institutions participating in ISIS.[13] According to Jill Mellen's survey of small cats in captivity, virtually all manuls born in North America are the offspring of two wild-caught individuals, and the only pair in a breeding situation are related and probably past reproductive age.[13] However, a few manuls may still be found in Chinese zoos; in 1984 there were four in the Urumqi Zoo and four in the Beijing Zoo.[16] The species has no studbook and no Species Survival Plan.

TABLE 41 MEASUREMENTS AND WEIGHTS OF ADULT MANULS

HB	n	T	n	WT	n	Location	Source
535	1m	280	1m	4.3	1m	Lake Balkhash	1
500–620	?	230–310	?	2.5–4.5	?	Russia	1
520	1?	310	1?			trans-Caucasus	2
650 (preserved skin)	1m	281	1m			trans-Caspian	11
600 (preserved skin)	1f	300	1f			trans-Caspian	11
460, 500	2m	206, 225	2m			Tibet	11

Note: HB = head and body length (mm), T = tail length (mm), WT = weight (kg). n = sample size. Sex: m = male, f = female, ? = unknown. Mean values are presented only for sample sizes of three or more. Range of values is in parentheses.

REFERENCES

1. Heptner, V. G., and A. A. Sludskii. 1992. *Mammals of the Soviet Union*. Vol. 2, part 2, *Carnivora (Hyaenas and cats)*. English translation, sci. ed. R. S. Hoffmann. Washington, DC: Smithsonian Institution Libraries and the National Science Foundation.

2. Ognev, S. I. 1962. *Mammals of U.S.S.R. and adjacent countries*. Vol. 3, *Carnivora, Fissipedia and Pinnipedia*. Washington, DC: Israel Program for Scientific Translations.

3. Guggisberg, C. A. W. 1975. *Wild cats of the world*. New York: Taplinger.

4. Hemmer, H. 1978. The evolutionary systematics of living Felidae: Present status and current problems. *Carnivore* 1: 71–79.

5. Wozencraft, W. C. 1993. Order Carnivora. In *Mammal species of the world*, 2nd ed., ed. D. E. Wilson and D. M. Reeder, 279–348. Washington, DC: Smithsonian Institution Press.

6. Collier, G. E., and S. J. O'Brien. 1985. A molecular phylogeny of the Felidae: Immunological distance. *Evolution* 39: 473–487.

7. O'Brien, S. J. 1986. Molecular genetics in the domestic cat and its relatives. *Trends Genet.* 2: 137–142.

8. Wayne, R. K., R. E. Benveniste, D. N. Janczewski, and S. J. O'Brien. 1989. Molecular and biochemical evolution of the Carnivora. In *Carnivore behavior, ecology, and evolution*, ed. J. L. Gittleman, 465–494. Ithaca, NY: Cornell University Press.

9. Roberts, T. J. 1977. *The mammals of Pakistan*. London: Ernest Benn.

10. Blonk, H. L., and R. Lomanlaan. 1965. Einige bemerkungen über den Manul, *Otocolobus manul* (Pallas, 1776). *Säugetierk. Mitt.* 13: 163–165.

11. Pocock, R. I. 1939. *The fauna of British India including Ceylon and Burma*. Vol. 1, *Mammalia*. London: Taylor and Francis.

12. Novikov, G. A. 1962. *Carnivorous mammals of the fauna of the USSR*. Jerusalem: Israel Program for Scientific Translations.

13. Mellen, J. D. 1989. Reproductive behavior of small captive exotic cats (*Felis* spp.). Ph.D. dissertation, University of California, Davis.

14. Mallon, D. P. 1985. The mammals of the Mongolian People's Republic. *Mammal Rev.* 15: 71–102.

15. Wang, Z.-Y. and S. Wang. 1986. Distribution and recent status of the Felidae in China. In *Cats of the world: Biology, conservation, and management*, ed. S. D. Miller and D. D. Everett, 201–209. Washington, DC: National Wildlife Federation.

16. Tan, B. 1984. The status of felids in China. In The plight of the cats: Proceedings of the meeting and workshop of IUCN/SSC Cat Specialist Group at Kanha National Park, Madhya Pradesh, India, ed. P. Jackson, 33–47. Unpublished report, IUCN/SSC Cat Specialist Group, Bougy-Villars, Switzerland.

17. Wemmer, C., and K. Scow. 1977. Communication in the Felidae with emphasis on scent marking and contact patterns. In *How animals communicate*, ed. T. A. Sebeok, 749–766. Bloomington: Indiana University Press.

18. Schauenberg, P. 1978. Note sur la reproduction du manul *Otocolobus manul* (Pallas, 1776). *Mammalia* 42: 355–358.

19. Eaton, R. L. 1984. Survey of smaller felid breeding. *Zool. Garten* (n.f.) 54: 101–120.

20. Seager, S. W. J., and C. N. Demorest. 1978. Reproduction in captive wild carnivores. In *Zoo and wild animal medicine*, ed. M. E. Fowler, 667–706. Philadelphia: W. B. Saunders.

21. Gashwiler, J. S., W. L. Robinette, and O. W. Morris. 1961. Breeding habits of bobcats in Utah. *J. Mammal.* 42: 76–84.

22. Jones, M. L. 1977. Record keeping and longevity of felids in captivity. In *The world's cats*, vol. 3, no. 3, ed. R. L. Eaton, 132–138. Seattle: Carnivore Research Institute, Burke Museum, University of Washington.

23. Cat News. 1987. Cats in Xinjiang Nature Reserve, China. *Cat News* 6: 33.

24. Cat News. 1989. Mongolia exports manul skins. *Cat News* 11: 20.

25. McMahan, L. R. 1986. The international cat trade. In *Cats of the world: Biology, conservation, and management*, ed. S. D. Miller and D. D. Everett, 461–488. Washington, DC: National Wildlife Federation.

26. Pocock, R. I. 1907. On Pallas's cat. *Proc. Zool. Soc. Lond.* 1907: 299–306.

27. Brown, M., and B. Munkhtsog. 2000. Ecology and behaviour of Pallas's cat in Mongolia. *Cat News* 33: 22.

Leopard cat

Prionailurus bengalensis (Kerr, 1792)

In China the leopard cat is sometimes known as *chin-ch'ien mao*, or "money cat," because its spots are said to look like Chinese coins.[1] This small, slim spotted cat is found in twenty-one Asian countries and varies so much in coloration and size that it was originally thought to be several different species and given many different names, including Jerdon's cat, Elliot's cat, Sumatra cat, Java cat, and Chinese cat.[2]

In 1965, rumors of a new and different kind of cat came to the attention of scientists. The house-cat-sized animal was unique to the island of Iriomote, off the coast of Taiwan. In 1967, after examining skins and skulls, scientists declared the cat a new species—the Iriomote cat.[3] However, recent DNA studies have shown that the Iriomote cat is an island subspecies of the leopard cat.[4]

DESCRIPTION

The leopard cat is about the size of a domestic cat, but has longer legs and looks like a diminutive, more slender version of its namesake. The leopard cat's head is relatively small, with a short, narrow muzzle and moderately long, rounded ears. The tail is about 40 to 50 percent as long as the head and body. Leopard cats from northern China and the Amur region of the former Soviet Union are much larger than those from Southeast Asia; indeed, a slim, normal-sized 2.5-kilogram leopard cat from Sumatra would look like another species alongside two record heavyweight cats from Russia of 8.2 and 9.9 kilograms. However, the weights of northern leopard cats fluctuate seasonally and from year to year, with individuals generally putting on weight before winter and becoming much thinner by spring. In years when rodent numbers are high, leopard cats have been described as "very obese."[5]

Cats from the north are pale silvery gray, whereas those from the south are darker, being more ochre-yellow or brownish. The coat texture is soft, and individuals from the north have long, full coats.[5,6,7,8]

"It is useless to lay down, as in Jerdon, a very accurate description of the markings of this cat," Robert Sterndale remarks in his 1884 treatise on Indian mammals, "for it varies to such an extent as to have given rise to at least sixteen synonymous names."[9] In general, the background color of the coat is tawny and the underparts white, but the color and pattern of markings are both, as Sterndale said, very variable. Black spots of varying size and shape mark the body and limbs; sometimes the body markings coalesce to form lines, and commonly there are two to four rows of elongated spots along the back. The tail is spotted, and there are a few indistinct rings near the black tip. The head is marked with two prominent dark stripes that extend from the inner corner of each eye to the base of the ear; two or three less distinct stripes also occur on the crown. A white streak extends from the inner corner of each eye toward the nose; in some forms this streak extends upward to the middle of the forehead. The muzzle is white, and streaks of white extend onto the cheeks, where they are bordered by two black lines, the lower of which may join a black bar across the throat. The backs of the ears are black with a brilliant white central spot. The feet are narrower and longer than those of the marbled cat, and there are well-defined webs between the toes.[1,2,5,10,11,12]

Though the leopard cat is much smaller and slighter than the fishing cat, both have similar coat patterns and a great affinity for water; thus the two species are sometimes confused. Leopard cats are excellent swimmers, completely at ease in the water. Indeed, the type specimen was said to have been captured when it swam to a ship anchored in the Bay of Bengal.[6] In Sumatra one young cat was seen playing belly-deep at the edge of a small stream; it eventually swam confidently into the swift-flowing deep water and crossed to the other side.[13] Captive leopard cat kittens spend much time playing in water, and in Borneo two young males kept as pets began playing in a small pond when they were only two months old. According to the leopard cats' owners, "they tried to catch water weeds or played with each other, falling over and getting thoroughly wet. Frequently they swam right across the pond."[14]

DISTRIBUTION

The leopard cat has the broadest geographic distribution of all the small Asian cats. It is found in forest areas throughout Southeast Asia, including Indonesia, the Philippines, Borneo, Malaysia, Thailand, Myanmar, Laos, Cambodia, China, and Taiwan. In the northeast it occurs in Korea and the Amur basin of the former Soviet Union. In the west it is known from Bangladesh, Assam, and across the foothills of the Himalaya to Jammu and Kashmir and northern Pakistan. In peninsular India the leopard cat is found in the western Ghats as far south as Coorg; it is also known from other forested regions in eastern India, but appears to be extremely rare or absent from the southern, mid-central, and arid western zones (fig. 34).[5,6,8,12,15,16,17,18]

ECOLOGY AND BEHAVIOR

Leopard cats live in habitats from lowland tropical evergreen rainforest and plantation forests at sea level to moist temperate and dry coniferous forests in the Himalayan foothills at elevations of 1,000 to 3,000 meters. The species also does well in farmland environments and on coastal islands. Leopard cats are widespread in China and occupy temperate, subtropical, and tropical habitats. In the Russian Far East the species is known as the "Amur forest cat" and is commonly associated with rivers, river valleys, forested ravines, and coastal habitats, where it lives in deciduous broad-leaved forests.[2,5,8,12,17,19] This cat's small, narrow feet make moving through deep snow difficult, and in the Russian Far East it lives only in areas where winter snow cover is typically less than 10 centimeters deep.[5]

In the southern portion of their range leopard cats are always associated with some type of forest cover; they also do well in modified habitats such as rubber plantations, oil palm plantations, areas of shifting cultivation, and villages. Their usual absence from arid, treeless areas suggests a dependency on cover or water, but more likely reflects the absence of suitable small rodent prey.

In 1939 Pocock remarked that the leopard cat is "not often seen owing to its liking for dense cover."[6] Radio-collared leopard cats in Thailand's Huai Kha Khaeng Wildlife Sanctuary did not use areas in the mosaic of forest types in the sanctuary equally. Dry deciduous dipterocarp forest, a fire-maintained habitat with little understory cover, was visited only occasionally by the radio-tagged cats. They preferred the mixed deciduous and dry evergreen forest habitats (the evergreen type is found at lower elevations in association with watercourses). These habitats not only offered more cover than the dipterocarp forest, but also harbored more prey.[20,21]

Most of the early anecdotal reports suggest that the leopard cat is strictly nocturnal, but radiotelemetry studies in two national parks in Thailand found that leopard cats were just as likely to be active during the day as at night.[20,22] In Huai Kha Khaeng, three of the four tagged leopard cats were active for nearly half the hours of daylight, and one cat's activity levels peaked about midday.[20] Radio-tagged leopard cats in Tabin Wildlife Reserve, Sabah, were mainly nocturnal but they were occasionally active during the day, especially in the wet season.[23]

Leopard cats are agile climbers and can be quite arboreal in their habits. In the oil palm plantations bordering Tabin Wildlife Reserve in Sabah, leopard cats seemed quite at ease 3 to 4 meters off the ground as they moved lightly and easily among the palm fronds hunting rodents. In ten of eleven attempts to locate the rest sites of radio-tagged leopard cats, the cats were found resting in dense, thorny undergrowth on the ground.[23] In Thailand, radio-tagged leopard cats occasionally rested in trees, although they preferred resting in dense cover and moving on the ground.[20] Leopard cats in the East Berlin Zoo sleep at the ends of tree branches rather than in nest boxes.[24]

Feeding Ecology

Leopard cats feed on a variety of small prey, including mammals, lizards, amphibians, birds, and insects. In Java the cat's diet was found to consist mainly of small ground-living mammals, principally rats and mice, although scats also contained large numbers of leaves of one species of herb.[25] In Pakistan, leopard cats feed primarily on small birds and secondarily on wood mice and flying squirrels.[8] In Huai Kha Khaeng, Thailand, Rabinowitz identified fourteen prey species in leopard cat feces, but small mammals, principally rats, were the dominant prey.[20] In Kaeng Krachan National Park, Thailand, rats and mice were the main prey, but the cats also took tree shrews and hares. Langur remains were found in one scat.[22] Rats were also the dominant prey found in leopard cat feces from Tsushima Island, Japan, along with moles, birds, amphibians, and a large number of insects.[26] On Iriomote Island, some ninety-five prey species were identified from 849 scats. Rats were the dominant prey, but flying foxes and skinks

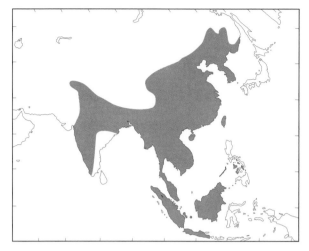

Figure 34. Distribution of the leopard cat.

were also important. Iriomote leopard cats also took birds, insects, crabs, and amphibians.[27,28,29] Leopard cats have been seen in caves feeding on fallen bats and swifts, and in some areas the species is notorious for attacking and killing domestic poultry.[12] In Tabin, an analysis of fecal samples indicated that mammals formed the bulk of the cat's diet (96 percent of samples), with rats being the main prey (89 percent). Reptiles and amphibians were the second most frequently occurring prey in feces (19 percent).[23]

Laboratory experiments by Paul Leyhausen and other researchers show that leopard cats and other small cats capture prey with a combination of vision and vibrissae (whiskers). Though blind in one eye, one of Leyhausen's captive leopard cats was still able to capture mice—even when they ran to its blind side. Captive leopard cats kill animals such as rats and mice with a nape bite. During a capture attempt, these cats tend to hold on to struggling prey, rather than dropping it and re-attacking.[30] This behavior is similar to that observed in fishing cats, flat-headed cats, servals, and caracals. It is thought to be characteristic of felids that prey on fish and birds because, unlike a rodent, once released, a bird or fish may not be easy to recapture. Like most felids, leopard cats pluck birds larger than a blackbird before eating them.[30]

In Borneo, leopard cats and other nocturnal predators such as owls are often seen hunting in oil palm plantations. On one plantation bordering Tabin Wildlife Reserve in Sabah, we were able to watch an adult male leopard cat hunting rodents. From its perch near the base of a low-hanging palm frond, the cat spotted a rat moving in some ground creeper. With a long bound, it sprang from the tree and pounced on the rat, which had by then disappeared under the mat of vegetation. After a few seconds of rummaging around under the creeper, the cat raised its head, holding the rat in its mouth, and, without pausing, began to chew. In twenty seconds the event was over; the rodent had been devoured headfirst, and the cat was moving on, pushing its head under the creeping vines that carpeted the ground, sometimes becoming half-submerged.

Rajaratnam observed leopard cats foraging on twenty-three occasions; a kill was recorded on six of those occasions. The cats were active hunters, walking slowly with head held level but moving it from side to side as if scanning the environment. Upon detecting a rodent, the cats would freeze, crouch, and then dart forward, staying low to the ground. They pinned the prey with the front paws while simultaneously grabbing it with the mouth. All kills (five rats, one beetle) were immediately consumed.[23]

Social Organization

Rajaratnam's study of leopard cats in Tabin is the most comprehensive study to date.[23] It involved ten radio-tagged cats, many of which were tracked for a year or more. The spatial arrangement of these cats resembled that of other solitary-living felids. Adult males had larger home ranges than adult females. and each male's range overlapped one or more female ranges. There was little overlap in home ranges of same-sex cats. The mean home range size for four adult males was 3.5 square kilometers, while the ranges of three adult females averaged 2.1 square kilometers. Rajaratnam estimated the density of leopard cats in his study area at 37.5 adults/100 square kilometers.

Rabinowitz's study in Thailand monitored radio-tagged animals; while he followed three adult males and one adult female, only the female was tracked for more than a year. One male, tracked for about two and a half months, moved over two areas totaling 7.5 square kilometers. The female leopard cat used a total area of 6.6 square kilometers during the thirteen months she was tracked, but on average she used an area of only about 2 square kilometers in any single month. Seasonally, the female's movements were smallest during the cold, dry months of November–February and largest during the wet-season months of May–October.[20] In Kaeng Krachan National Park in southern Thailand, an adult male used an area of 5.4 square kilometers, while a female's range was 2.5 square kilometers.[22] In the broad-leaved evergreen forest on Iriomote Island, the average home range size for male leopard cats was 2.96 square kilometers, while the average for females was 1.75 square kilometers.[31]

Leopard cats indicate occupancy of ranges, as do other cats, by scent marking and by leaving conspicuous marks around their ranges. Rabinowitz found scrapes associated with the feces of leopard cats on roads and trails in Huai Kha Khaeng Wildlife Sanctuary, but these signs appeared infrequently.[20]

In captivity, both males and females spray urine. Their feces are left scattered and sometimes buried. They also mark objects in their enclosures by rubbing the head on them or raking them with the claws.[32]

The vocal repertoire of the leopard cat includes the typical growl, hiss, spit, meow, purr, and gurgle.[32,33,34]

All of these calls are associated with agonistic or friendly situations and are used at close range.

Reproduction and Development

After a gestation period of sixty to seventy days,[5,35] the female leopard cat usually gives birth to two or three kittens.[24,36,37,38] Occasionally larger litters are born, but these are rare.[5,25] The kittens weigh 75 to 130 grams at birth, and they open their eyes ten to fifteen days after they are born.[24,36,37,38] In the wild, birth dens have been found in the hollow of a fallen tree, among bushes, and between rocks.[39] Kittens usually double their weight by the time they are two weeks old, and at five weeks they are about four times their birth weight. Their permanent canines erupt at about four weeks, which coincides with their beginning to eat solid food.[38] The ability to eat meat results in a rapid weight gain;[24] by thirteen weeks there is a tenfold increase over birth weight, and at thirty-seven weeks the young are almost as large as their parents.[38] As with most felids, males grow faster than females.

Several zoos report that the male can be left with the female during the birth and rearing of the young.[14,24,36] One report from the West Berlin Zoo documents the male's progressively active involvement with three litters of kittens. When the first litter was born, the female was reluctant to let the male near the kittens until they were a month old, but by the third litter the male was an active participant from the first day after birth onward. He defended the young against keepers and carried chunks of meat to the nest box.[36]

In Java records of twenty-seven litters showed no seasonality, and birth dates were spread evenly over the year.[25] In India breeding takes place in spring and summer,[11] and in Russia kittens appear in the second half of May.[5]

There are varying reports of the age of first reproduction in leopard cats. Most observations of captive animals record first litters being born to two- to three-year-old females,[24,40,41] although these observations may be related to incompatible pairs or to the stress of captivity. In a captive setting where the cats were isolated from humans, a female leopard cat reached sexual maturity just before she was a year old and had her first litter at thirteen to fourteen months.[42] In captivity leopard cats are known to have had two litters in one year, but in the wild they are more likely to breed only once a year.

Of all the Asian wild cats, leopard cats are said to be the most difficult to tame; the few successes have been with kittens obtained at a very early age. Even month-old kittens may become unhandleable and intolerant of one another by one year of age.[11,14,24,39,43]

Leopard cats have been known to hybridize with domestic cats and produce fertile viable offspring, which have been used in biomedical research. Captive animals have lived for thirteen years.[44]

STATUS IN THE WILD

The leopard cat is able to live near human settlement and, though it prefers forest, seems able to adapt to secondary forest and successional vegetation. Broad-scale habitat modification and forest clearance for agriculture, tea plantations, and exotic tree plantations are considered to be major threats to this cat. Cleared areas replanted in exotic trees and plantation crops often lack the understory necessary for the cat and its prey to survive.

The leopard cat is heavily hunted in many parts of its range, and leopard cat skins figure prominently in the fur trade. In China, where the cat is most abundant in the subtropical regions and less common in the arid areas of the north and northwest, there is an average annual harvest of some 150,000 pelts. Chinese records show that the highest recorded harvest was in 1963, when approximately 230,000 cats were harvested. The numbers decreased somewhat in the following years, but in both 1980 and 1981 over 200,000 leopard cat skins originated in China alone. Many of the skins originating in China are exported to Japan.[45,46]

According to a statement made by Dr. Lu Houji at the 1989 meeting of the IUCN Cat Specialist Group, the Chinese government has set an annual harvest quota of 150,000 leopard cats. Leopard cat skins are sold within China by the Fur Trade Company in Beijing, and are sold as skins and finished garments in many other parts of Asia.[47] Some thirty-six leopard cat skins are required to make one full-length coat, and such coats are frequently sold in tourist shops in Kathmandu, Nepal, and in Kashmir.[48] In 1986, after a survey of large mammals in Sumatra, Santiapillai reports that the future of the leopard cat in Sumatra appears to be linked to the protection of the Sumatran tiger. He found that the leopard cat is widely distributed in Sumatra, where it is not hunted for food or its skin; however, the young are captured and sold as pets, especially in the province of Bengkulu.[17] The species

is said to be declining in Bangladesh,[49] "reduced and vulnerable" in India,[50] and common in Thailand.[12] The range of the leopard cat in Russia is restricted to the Amur region of the Far East, and hence the population is not large.[5] Pelts of Amur leopard cats were formerly exported to China, where they were used to make collars, hats, and jacket linings, but in recent years the number captured has declined. At the peak 1,000 to 2,000 skins were tanned, but more recently the number has dropped to 100 to 300 skins. Sludskii believes that "the range is shrinking and the population in many parts dropping rapidly; the Amur cat could easily disappear altogether. Measures for its protection should be implemented, at least in those areas where the animal faces extinction."[5]

In 1985, CITES approved a request from the Chinese government to move the Chinese population of the leopard cat from appendix I to appendix II.[51] In 1994, CITES voted to downlist *Prionailurus bengalensis bengalensis* for all range countries except Bangladesh, India, and Thailand, whose populations remain on appendix I.[52]

STATUS IN CAPTIVITY

It is likely that a large, but unknown, number of leopard cats live in captivity in Asian and European zoos, and an equally large number are probably kept as pets in both the United States and Asia. However, the species is not well represented in ISIS zoo collections.

TABLE 42 MEASUREMENTS AND WEIGHTS OF ADULT LEOPARD CATS

HB	n	T	n	WT	n	Location	Source
584 (540–660)	4m	269 (245–310)	4m	2.7 (2.0–3.1)	3m	China	53
520 (460–550)	6f	241 (220–260)	6f	2.2 (1.7–2.5)	5f	China	53
489 (450–560)	11m	250 (200–300)	11m	2.1–3.8	11 m	Southern China	19
640, 665	2m	300, 315	2m	6.2, 7.0	2m	Northern China	19
547 (508–615)	7m	295 (241–310)	7m	3.2 (2.7–3.6)	4m	India	6
505 (488–528)	3f	290 (279–295)	3f	2.7, 2.8	2f	India	6
583 (570–600)	3m	243 (200–270)	3m	3.3 (3.0–3.5)	3m	Thailand	22
474 (455–500)	4m	220 (208–245)	4m	2.5 (2.1–2.9)	4m	Sabah	23
463 (460–470)	3f	208 (206–210)	3f	2.1 (2.0–2.3)	3f	Sabah	23
435	1m	220	1m	1.7	1m	Borneo	54
655 (600–750)	9m	273 (235–310)	9m	2.5–7.1	10m	Russia	5
610–620	4f	235–295	4f	3.2–4.5	4f	Russia	5
546 (430–625)	12m	226 (172–265)	12m	0.99 (0.74–1.45)	12m	Peninsular Malaysia	55
513 (388–655)	8f	214 (178–235)	8f	0.90 (0.55–1.48)	8f	Peninsular Malaysia	55

Note: HB = head and body length (mm), T = tail length (mm), WT = weight (kg). n = sample size. Sex: m = male, f = female, ? = unknown. Mean values are presented only for sample sizes of three or more. Range of values is in parentheses.

TABLE 43 FREQUENCY OF OCCURRENCE OF PREY ITEMS IN THE DIETS OF LEOPARD CATS (PERCENTAGE OF SAMPLES)

Prey items	Huai Kha Khaeng Wildlife Sanctuary, Thailand[20] Scats (n = 52)	Tsushima Island, Japan[26] Scats (n = 230)
Muridae	65.3	73
Mice		
Talpidae		16
Moles		
Cannomys badius	7.7	
Bay bamboo rat		
Callosciurus sp.	5.7	
Tricolored squirrels		
Petaurista petaurista	1.9	
Giant flying squirrel		
Menetes berdmorei	5.7	
Berdmore's palm squirrel		
Tupaia glis	1.9	
Tree shrew		
Hylomys suillus	1.9	
Lesser gymnure		
Arctonyx collaris	1.9	
Hog badger		
Carrion	1.9	
Reptiles	9.6	3.8
Amphibians		10
Birds	1.9	41.7
Fish		6.5
Crab	1.9	
Insects		43.9
Plant material	48	92.6
Minimum number of vertebrate prey	58	575

REFERENCES

1. Allen, G. M. 1938. *The mammals of China and Mongolia.* Washington, DC: American Museum of Natural History.

2. Guggisberg, C. A. W. 1975. *Cats of the world.* New York: Taplinger.

3. Imaizumi, Y. 1967. A new genus and species of cat from Iriomote, Ryukyu Islands. *J. Mammal Soc. Jpn.* 3: 74–105.

4. Johnson, W. E., F. Shinyashiki, M. Menotti Raymond, C. Driscoll, C. Leh, M. Sunquist, L. Johnston, M. Bush, D. Wildt, N. Yuhki, and S. J. O'Brien. 1999. Molecular genetic characterization of two insular Asian cat species, Bornean bay cat and Iriomote cat. In *Evolutionary theory and processes: Modern perspectives, Essays in Honour of Eviatar Nevo,* ed. S. P. Wasser, 223–248. Dordrecht: Kluwer Academic Publishers.

5. Heptner, V. G., and A. A. Sludskii. 1992. *Mammals of the Soviet Union.* Vol. 2, part 2, *Carnivora (Hyaenas and cats).* English translation, sci. ed., R. S. Hoffmann. Washington, DC: Smithsonian Institution Libraries and the National Science Foundation.

6. Pocock, R. I. 1939. *The fauna of British India, including Ceylon and Burma.* Vol. 1, *Mammalia.* London: Taylor and Francis.

7. Dobroruka, L. J. 1971. Individual variation of the Amur leopard cat, *Prionailurus bengalensis euptilurus* (Elliot, 1871), from Korea. *Vestnik Ceskoslovenske Spolecnosti Zoologicke* 35: 9–10.

8. Roberts, T. J. 1977. *The mammals of Pakistan.* London: Ernest Benn.

9. Sterndale, R. A. 1884. *Natural history of the Mammalia of India and Ceylon.* Calcutta: Thacker and Spink.

10. Pocock, R. I. 1932. The marbled cat (*Pardofelis marmorata*) and some other Oriental species, with the definition of a new genus of Felidae. *Proc. Zool. Soc. Lond.* 1932: 741–766.

11. Prater, S. H. 1971. *The book of Indian animals,* 3rd (revised) edition. Bombay: Bombay Natural History Society.

12. Lekagul, B., and J. A. McNeely. 1977. *Mammals of Thailand.* Bangkok: Association for the Conservation of Wildlife.

13. Sunquist, F. C. Personal observation.

14. Birkenmeier, E., and E. Birkenmeier. 1971. Hand-rearing the leopard cat. *Int. Zoo Yrbk.* 11: 118–121.

15. Lyon, M. W., Jr. 1911. Mammals collected by Dr. W. L. Abbott on Borneo and some of the small adjacent islands. *Proc. U.S. Nat. Mus.* 40: 53–153.

16. McCullough, D. R. 1974. *Status of larger mammals in Taiwan.* World Wildlife Fund Report. Taipei, Taiwan: Tourism Bureau.

17. Santiapillai, C., and H. Supraham. 1985. On the status of the leopard cat (*Felis bengalensis*) in Sumatra. *Tigerpaper* 12: 8–13.

18. Khan, M. A. R. 1985. *Mammals of Bangladesh: A field guide*. Dhaka, Bangladesh: Nazma Reza.

19. Tan, B. 1984. The status of felids in China. In The plight of the cats: Proceedings of the meeting and workshop of the IUCN/SSC Cat Specialist Group at Kanha National Park, Madhya Pradesh, India, ed. P. Jackson, 33–47. Unpublished report, IUCN/SSC Cat Specialist Group, Bougy-Villars, Switzerland.

20. Rabinowitz, A. 1990. Notes on the behavior and movements of leopard cats, *Felis bengalensis*, in a dry tropical forest mosaic in Thailand. *Biotropica* 22: 397–403.

21. Walker, S., and A. Rabinowitz. 1992. The small mammal community of a dry tropical forest in central Thailand. *J. Tropical Ecol.* 8: 57–71.

22. Grassman, L. I., Jr. 1998. Movements and prey selection of the leopard cat (*Prionailurus bengalensis*) in a subtropical evergreen forest in southern Thailand. Società Zoologica "La Torbiera" Scientific Report no. 4: 9–21.

23. Rajaratnam, R. 2000. Ecology of the leopard cat (*Prionailurus bengalensis*) in Tabin Wildlife Reserve, Sabah, Malaysia. Ph.D. dissertation, Universiti Kebangsaan Malaysia, Bangi, Malaysia.

24. Dathe, H. 1968. Breeding the Indian leopard cat at East Berlin Zoo. *Int. Zoo Yrbk.* 8: 42–44.

25. Hoogerwerf, A. 1970. *Udjung Kulon, the land of the last Javan rhinoceros*. Leiden: E. J. Brill.

26. Inoue, T. 1972. The food habit of Tsushima leopard cat, *Felis bengalensis* ssp., analysed from their scats. *J. Mammal Soc. Jpn.* 5: 155–169.

27. Yasuma, S. 1981. Feeding behaviour of the Iriomote cat (*Prionailurus iriomotensis* Imaizumi, 1967). *Bull. Tokyo Univ. Forests* 70: 81–140.

28. Yasuma, S. 1984. The Iriomote cat. In The plight of the cats: Proceedings of the meeting and workshop of the IUCN/SSC Cat Specialist Group at Kanha National Park, Madhya Pradesh, India, ed. P. Jackson, 49–54. Unpublished report, IUCN/SSC Cat Specialist Group, Bougy-Villars, Switzerland.

29. Yasuma, S. 1988. Iriomote cat: King of the night. *Animal Kingdom* 91(6): 12–21.

30. Leyhausen, P. 1979. *Cat behavior: The predatory and social behavior of domestic and wild cats*. New York: Garland STPM Press.

31. Izawa, M., T. Doi, and Y. Ono. 1989. Social system of the Iriomote cat (*Felis iriomotensis*). Abstracts 5th International Theriological Congress 2: 608. Rome.

32. Wemmer, C., and K. Scow. 1977. Communication in the Felidae with emphasis on scent marking and contact patterns. In *How animals communicate*, ed. T. A. Sebeok, 749–766. Bloomington: Indiana University Press.

33. Peters, G. 1984. On the structure of friendly close range vocalizations in terrestrial carnivores (Mammalia: Carnivora: Fissipedia). *Z. Säugetierk.* 49: 157–182.

34. Peters, G., and M. H. Hast. 1994. Hyoid structure, laryngeal anatomy, and vocalizations in felids (Mammalia: Carnivora: Felidae). *Z. Säugetierk.* 59: 87–104.

35. Hemmer, H. 1979. Gestation period and postnatal development in felids. *Carnivore* 2: 90–100.

36. Frese, R. 1980. Some notes on breeding the leopard cat (*Felis bengalensis*) at West Berlin Zoo. *Int. Zoo Yrbk.* 20: 220–223.

37. Acharjyo, L. N., and Ch. G. Mishra. 1980. A note on the breeding of the leopard cat (*Felis bengalensis*) in captivity. *J. Bombay Nat. Hist. Soc.* 77: 127–128.

38. Acharjyo, L. N., and Ch. G. Mishra. 1983. Further notes on the birth and growth of the leopard cat (*Felis bengalensis*) in captivity. *J. Bombay Nat. Hist. Soc.* 80: 207–208.

39. Lim, B. L., and I. A. Rahman bin Omar. 1961. Observations on the habits in captivity of two species of wild cats, the leopard cat and the flat-headed cat. *Malayan Nature J.* 15: 48–51.

40. Pohle, Von C. 1973. Zur zucht von Bengalkatzen (*Felis bengalensis*) im Tierpark Berlin. *Zool. Garten* 43: 110–126.

41. Eaton, R. L. 1984. Survey of smaller felid breeding. *Zool. Garten* (n.f.) 54: 383–400.

42. Schauenberg, P. 1979. Note sur la reproduction du chat du Bengale. *Mammalia* 43: 127–128.

43. Gee, E. P. 1962. A leopard cat (*Felis bengalensis* Kerr) in captivity. *J. Bombay Nat. Hist. Soc.* 59: 641–642.

44. Acharjyo, L. N., and S. K. Patnaik. 1984. A note on the longevity of two species of wild carnivores in captivity. *J. Bombay Nat. Hist. Soc.* 81: 461–462.

45. Lu, H., and H. Sheng. 1986. The status and population fluctuation of the leopard cat in China. In *Cats of the world: Biology, conservation, and management*, eds. S. D. Miller and D. D. Everett, 59–62. Washington, DC: National Wildlife Federation.

46. Wang, Z.-Y., and S. Wang. 1986. Distribution and recent status of the Felidae in China. In *Cats of the world: Biology, conservation, and management*, eds. S. D. Miller and D. D. Everett, 201–209. Washington, DC: National Wildlife Federation.

47. Lu, H. 1989. Problems of conserving cats in China. *Felid* 4: 7.

48. Barnes, L. 1989. Illegal furs on Durbar Marg. *Himal* 2: 25–26.

49. Khan, M. A. R. 1986. The status and distribution of the cats in Bangladesh. In *Cats of the world: Biology, conservation, and management*, eds. S. D. Miller and D. D. Everett, 43–49. Washington, DC: National Wildlife Federation.

50. Panwar, H. S. 1984. Conservation of wild cats in India. In The plight of the cats: Proceedings of the meeting and workshop of the IUCN/SSC Cat Specialist Group at Kanha National Park, Madhya Pradesh, India, ed. P. Jackson, 63–80. Unpublished report, IUCN/SSC Cat Specialist Group, Bougy-Villars, Switzerland.

51. Cat News. 1985. *Felis b. bengalensis* (China) moved to CITES Appendix II. *Cat News* 3: 12.

52. Nowell, K., and P. Jackson. 1996. *Wild cats: A status survey and conservation action plan*. Gland, Switzerland: International Union for Conservation of Nature and Natural Resources (IUCN).

53. Shaw, T. H. 1962. *Economic fauna of China: Mammals*. Beijing: Scientific Press.

54. Davis, D. D. 1962. Mammals of the lowland rain-forest of north Borneo. *Bull. Nat. Mus. Singapore* 31: 1–129.

55. Lim, B. L. 1999. The distribution, food habits and parasite patterns of the leopard cat (*Prionailurus bengalensis*) in Peninsular Malaysia. *J. Wildl. Parks* 17: 17–27.

Flat-headed cat

Prionailurus planiceps (Vigors and Horsfield, 1827)

The flat-headed cat is closely related to the leopard cat,[1] but, unlike its very feline-looking cousin, this peculiar little cat more closely resembles a mustelid. Short legs, a long head with tiny, low-set ears, and a short tail combine to give it a most uncatlike appearance. In fact, in some ways it looks more like an otter or a civet.

DESCRIPTION

The flat-headed cat's distinctly elongated and flattened head and its small, rounded ears make it one of the more easily recognizable small cats. It has long, narrow feet like the bay cat, but the latter has a longer tail and lacks white on the chin and chest. Facially, the flat-headed cat bears a vague resemblance to the much larger fishing cat, and both species share with the cheetah the uncommon characteristic of having so-called nonretractile claws. This description is not technically correct because the claws do retract, but the covering sheaths are so reduced in size that some two-thirds of the claw is left protruding.[2]

The flat-headed cat's long fur is thick and soft. The fur is reddish brown on top of the head, dark roan brown on the body, and mottled white on the underbelly. Many of the body hairs are tipped with white or gray. The face is lighter in color than the body, and the muzzle and chin are white. Two prominent whitish buff streaks run on either side of the nose between the eyes. The tail is short, measuring only a quarter to a third of the cat's head and body length.[3,4,5]

The eyes of the flat-headed cat are set farther forward and closer together than those of other cats, giving it better stereoscopic vision. The teeth are unusual in that the tooth rows are nearly parallel, all the teeth are pointed, and the first and second upper premolars are large. Thus, the front portion of this cat's mouth is specialized for seizing and gripping slippery prey, while its well-developed sagittal crest and strong zygomatic arches indicate great biting power.[5,6] In short, the flat-headed cat is almost better designed for finding and catching food in water than the larger fishing cat.

DISTRIBUTION

The flat-headed cat's range is southern Thailand, Malaysia, Sumatra, and Borneo (fig. 35).[5,7,8,9]

ECOLOGY AND BEHAVIOR

Almost all the available information on the flat-headed cat comes from five or six animals in captivity and fewer than twenty specimens collected from the

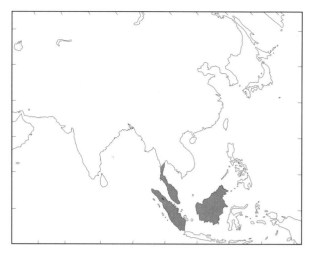

Figure 35. Distribution of the flat-headed cat.

wild. The flat-headed cat's morphological specializations suggest that it is a cat whose diet is composed largely of fish, and thus that its distribution is closely associated with water. In the wild, specimens have been collected in disturbed primary and secondary forests, along rivers and streams, and in flooded areas.[7,8] However, Khan suggests that in Malaysia the flat-headed cat may also live in oil palm plantations.[10] Anecdotal historical accounts report that the flat-headed cat is nocturnal, but in captivity an adult female was crepuscular, being most active between 1800 and 2200 hours and 0800 and 1130 hours.[11]

Two flat-headed cats were seen by spotlight at 2300 hours along the Merang River in southeastern Sumatra. The cats were on opposite banks and 100 meters apart.[12] Flat-headed cats have been seen on mudbanks and along rivers, where they were probably hunting. The stomach of one animal contained the remains of fish. Another account reports them hunting for frogs and fish, and the diet is also thought to include crustaceans.

Captive animals show a great affinity for water. When a captive kitten was given a large bowl of water, it immediately jumped in and began to play. The youngster would submerge its head completely to depths of at least 12 centimeters to seize pieces of fish, and it sometimes played in the water for hours. It also caught live frogs, but ignored sparrows that were put in its cage. This kitten "washed" its food in water,[6] and in another captive situation, adult flat-headed cats were seen to grope on the bottom of a pool with their forepaws spread wide, much like a raccoon. Furthermore, these adults were much more excited by a mouse in their bathtub than one on dry land; by standing either in the water or next to the tub, they would try to fish out the mouse with their teeth or paws.[13] When presented with food, the kitten always carried it at least 2 meters away from the place where it was offered, a potentially meal-saving behavior for an animal that feeds on fish and frogs—the chances of recapturing a wriggling fish are better if the escape does not occur right next to the water.[6]

In captivity adult flat-headed cats kill rats and mice with a nape bite, but quickly let go and toss the rodent away between bites, repeating the action again and again.[13] In the wild they may also feed on rats; it has been suggested that flat-headed cats can survive in oil palm plantations by hunting rodents.[10]

Flat-headed cats are presumably solitary, like other felids, and, again like other cats, they probably maintain their ranges by scent marking. In captivity, both males and females spray urine—but in a rather unusual manner. Most cats point their rear ends at a tree or bush, raise their tails to a vertical or upward position, and spray. The flat-headed cat, by contrast, raises its tail to half-mast, crouches with its hind legs, and walks forward in this position, leaving a trail of urine.[13]

The vocalizations of a flat-headed kitten resembled those of the domestic cat, although Muul and Lim described the kitten's calls as being "more vibrating and comparable to the sound made by pulling a thumb along the teeth of a comb."[6] The vocal repertoire of adults has not been analyzed completely, but they do purr and give other short-range vocalizations.[14,15]

Only two zoos are on record as having successfully bred the flat-headed cat: the Rotterdam Zoo (Netherlands) and Louisiana Purchase Zoo (Monroe, Louisiana). There are only three litters recorded; one consisted of two kittens and the others each contained a singleton.[16] Lincoln Park Zoo in Chicago had nine flat-headed cats in its collection, and three lived to fourteen years of age.[16]

STATUS IN THE WILD

The flat-headed cat appears to be a very rare and elusive species, although its skins are commonly seen in native longhouses in the interior of Sarawak.[17] It may be especially vulnerable because there is a suggestion that its distribution is closely tied to watercourses, and habitats along rivers are often the first to be developed or exploited by humans. However, if the reports of increased sightings of flat-headed cats near oil palm plantations in Malaysia are confirmed,[10] this cat may be more adaptable than its morphological specializations would indicate. The sightings of flat-headed cats in secondary lowland forest in Sumatra also suggest some tolerance of modified habitats.[12]

TABLE 44 MEASUREMENTS AND WEIGHTS OF ADULT FLAT-HEADED CATS

HB	n	T	n	WT	n	Location	Source
508	1m	152	1m	2.1	1m	captive	3
470	3f	149	4f	1.7	3f	Borneo	18
(455–490)		(130–169)		(1.5–1.9)			
446, 505	2m	135, 149	2m	1.8, 2.2	2m	Borneo	18
465, 485	2m	128, 130	2m	1.5, 2.1	2m	Peninsular Malaysia	6
521	1m	143	1m	1.8	1m	Sumatra	12

Note: HB = head and body length (mm), T = tail length (mm), WT = weight (kg). n = sample size. Sex: m = male, f = female, ? = unknown. Mean values are presented only for sample sizes of three or more. Range of values is in parentheses.

REFERENCES

1. Collier, G. E., and S. J. O'Brien. 1985. A molecular phylogeny of the Felidae: Immunological distance. *Evolution* 39: 473–487.

2. Pocock, R. I. 1932. The marbled cat (*Pardofelis marmorata*) and some other Oriental species, with the definition of a new genus of the Felidae. *Proc. Zool. Soc. Lond.* 1932: 741–766.

3. Lim, B. L., and A. Rahman. 1961. Observations on the habits in captivity of two species of wild cats, the leopard cat and the flat-headed cat. *Malayan Nature J.* 15: 48–51.

4. Guggisberg, C. A. W. 1975. *Wild cats of the world.* New York: Taplinger.

5. Lekagul, B., and J. A. McNeely. 1977. *Mammals of Thailand.* Bangkok: Association for the Conservation of Wildlife.

6. Muul, I., and B. L. Lim. 1970. Ecological and morphological observations of *Felis planiceps. J. Mammal.* 51: 806–808.

7. Muul, I., and B. L. Lim. 1971. New locality records for some mammals of West Malaysia. *J. Mammal.* 52: 430–436.

8. Payne, J., C. M. Francis, and K. Phillips. 1985. *A field guide to the mammals of Borneo.* Kuala Lumpur: The Sabah Society.

9. Medway, L. 1969. *The wild mammals of Malaya.* Oxford: Oxford University Press.

10. Cat News. 1986. Notes for the record. *Cat News* 5: 11.

11. Schaffer, N., and M. Rosenthal. [No date.] Report on the flat-headed cat reproductive projects initially funded from support from the Institute of Museum Services, Special Conservation Project. Mimeographed. 96 pp.

12. Bezuijen, M. R. 2000. The occurrence of the flat-headed cat *Prionailurus planiceps* in south-east Sumatra. *Oryx* 34: 222–226.

13. Leyhausen, P. 1979. *Cat behavior: The predatory and social behavior of domestic and wild cats.* New York: Garland STPM Press.

14. Peters, G. 1981. Das schnurren der katzen (Felidae). *Säugetierk. Mitt.* 29: 30–37.

15. Peters, G. 1984. On the structure of friendly close range vocalizations in terrestrial carnivores (Mammalia: Carnivora: Fissipedia). *Z. Säugetierk.* 49: 157–182.

16. Rosenthal, M., curator of mammals, Lincoln Park Zoo, Chicago, Illinois. Personal communication.

17. Bennett, E., zoologist, NYZS/The Wildlife Conservation Society. Personal communication.

18. Lyon, M. W. Jr. 1911. Mammals collected by Dr. W. L. Abbott on Borneo and some of the small adjacent islands. *Proc. U.S. Nat. Mus.* 40: 53–146.

Rusty-spotted cat

Prionailurus rubiginosus (Geoffroy, 1831)

The diminutive rusty-spotted cat is closely related to the leopard cat. It has been called the hummingbird of the cat family—a fairly apt description, as not only is this miniature cat about half the size of a domestic cat, but it is also extremely agile and active.

DESCRIPTION

The rusty-spotted cat has short brownish gray fur tinged with a rufous color. In Sri Lanka the coat is more russet than gray. The face is marked with two dark streaks on each cheek and four dark stripes that extend from above the eyes backward between the ears and to the shoulders. On the back and flanks, lines of elongated rust-brown blotches and spots pattern the fur. The belly, chest, and throat are white, marked with large dark spots and bars. The ears are small and rounded, and the tail is about half the length of the head and body. The soles of the feet are black.[1,2,3]

DISTRIBUTION

The rusty-spotted cat was originally thought to be confined to Sri Lanka and southern India, with a distribution extending some 110 kilometers north of Bombay and as far east as Seoni in Madhya Pradesh.[1,2,4,5] However, recent reports have extended the species' range farther to the west and some 1,600 kilometers north (fig. 36). In 1975 the rusty-spotted cat was collected near Udhampur, in the region of Jammu and Kashmir, a disputed territory in the far north of India on the western rim of the Tibetan plateau.[6] Later the cat was reported from the Dangs forest in Gujarat.[7] Then in 1989 and 1990, rusty-spotted cats were seen on three different occasions in the western portion of the Gir Wildlife Sanctuary and National Park, extending the range still farther to the west.[8] In 1992 a rusty-spotted cat was found dead beside a road near Udaipur in Rajasthan.[9] A live and a dead cat have also been reported in Panna district, Madhya Pradesh.[10] Two kittens were found on a road in Orissa in 1995, which is the first record of rusty-spotted cats in this state.[11]

ECOLOGY AND BEHAVIOR

In India the rusty-spotted cat is found in moist and dry deciduous forests, tropical thorn forest, scrub forest, grasslands, arid shrublands, rocky areas, and hill slopes. Sightings of the cat are most frequently reported from teak, bamboo, grassy areas, and dry thorny vegetation.[2,3,8,12] The young female collected in Jammu was found in open scrub forest with low thorny bushes and

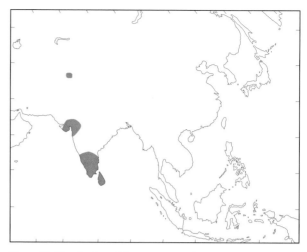

Figure 36. Distribution of the rusty-spotted cat.

stunted trees.[6] In Sri Lanka the species is found from sea level to elevations of 2,100 meters in humid forest, in low scrub, on mountaintops, and in arid coastal belts.[13,14]

A hundred years ago two naturalists, R. A. Sterndale and T. C. Jerdon, independently kept rusty-spotted cats as pets. They later recorded their incidental observations, and today almost everything that we know of this tiny cat's behavior comes from these two accounts.[1,15] Both authors obtained their pets as kittens and wrote that they tamed easily. The cats were noticeably active. "The grace and agility of their motions was most striking," Sterndale wrote. He observed them climbing tents and trees with far greater ease than a domestic cat and said they would "dart like a squirrel up the walls of the tent onto the roof."[1]

Despite the fact that they weigh only a few pounds, rusty-spotted cats are reputed to be extremely fierce. "For its size," de Alwis maintains, "it is singularly vicious."[13] On one occasion T. C. Jerdon introduced his eight-month-old pet rusty-spotted cat into a room where there was a gazelle fawn: "The little creature flew at it the moment it saw it, seized it by the nape, and was with difficulty taken off."[15]

Though few species of small cats have been studied in the wild, considerable information on reproduction and behavior has accrued for many species from captive studies. Rusty-spotted cats are an exception. There are so few of them in zoos that we still know very little about the species. In North America, the Cincinnati Zoo is the only institution to have kept and bred these cats for any length of time. The rusty-spotted cats at the Cincinnati Zoo are primarily nocturnal, but tend to have bursts of activity during the day.[16] They pace very rapidly, and their quick, darting movements make them look like a speeded-up version of the other small cats. In the wild, rusty-spotted cats are thought to be mainly, but not completely, nocturnal and spend the daytime resting in a hollow log or dense cover.[14]

The rusty-spotted cat's diet consists mainly of birds and small mammals, and possibly insects, lizards, and frogs. It is also known to kill domestic chickens and ducks when the opportunity arises.[14] In captivity it is reported to have a tremendous appetite; a cat weighing 5 pounds will eat 4 to 6 ounces of meat mixture and a dead mouse or chick every day.[16]

Early reports suggested that the rusty-spotted cat might be partially arboreal, but recent sightings of these cats have all been on the ground.[6,8,12,17] Though the rusty-spotted cat is reputed to be a fierce fighter, it is very small, and thus a potential meal for almost any other predator, including foxes, jackals, and other larger cats. In all likelihood this tiny cat hunts mostly on the ground and uses its superb climbing abilities to escape predation.

In captivity both males and females scent-mark by spraying urine. Estrus lasts about five days. Copulation follows the typical sequence for small cats, including a nape bite and straddling. Mounts are frequent (7.64 per hour), but intromission is brief, lasting less than a minute.[18,19] For very small felids courtship and mating is quite likely to be a period of increased vulnerability to predation. In Africa the tiny black-footed cat (*Felis nigripes*) has a thirty-six-hour estrus, and the female is receptive to the male for only five to ten hours. A reduced period of receptivity and brief copulations may be just some of the ways in which small cats reduce their chances of becoming a meal for another carnivore.

After a gestation period of sixty-six to seventy days, the female gives birth to one or two kittens; for nine litters born at the Cincinnati Zoo, the mean litter size was 1.55.[18] The young are blind at birth and weigh about 60 to 77 grams.[16] In captivity, births are not confined to any particular season. The only information from the wild comes from Sri Lanka, where a litter of two-week-old kittens was found in early February. The den was a shallow cave beneath a small rock among a field of tea bushes. The site was close to a steep, rocky patch of virgin jungle. The kittens' eyes were not yet open, and their fur was a dark earth-brown with a slight reddish tinge and marked with dusky black spots arranged in longitudinal lines. Very young kittens show no signs of the characteristic rusty spots, but the color develops as they grow older.[20] One female rusty-spotted cat reached sexual maturity at sixty-eight weeks of age.[18] The oldest rusty-spotted cat in captivity is twelve years old.[21]

STATUS IN THE WILD

It has been reported that the rusty-spotted cat is not an adaptable species.[13] However, in southern India, rusty-spotted cats were recently discovered to be living among the rafters of abandoned houses. The houses were in a thickly populated area some distance from forest cover.[22] Adaptable or not, these small cats are often killed by local people. In Sri Lanka adult rusty-spotted cats are frequently mistaken for baby leopards and killed. In some parts of Sri Lanka and India the flesh of the rusty-spotted cat is considered edible, and a fair number of cats are taken for this purpose.[13,14]

In 1987, Chavan estimated that this cat was "near extinction" in Gujarat State in India and that there were perhaps fifty individuals left.[7] A few years later an informal survey of forty-five villages in the Dangs forest in Gujarat found that the cat may not be quite so rare as previously believed, since almost every village reported having seen the cat.[12] Apart from the fact that it is considered to be rare, there is very little information on the status of the rusty-spotted cat from other parts of its range in India and Sri Lanka.

STATUS IN CAPTIVITY

The rusty-spotted cat does not seem to fare well in captivity. These cats must be vaccinated against feline enteritis immediately after arrival or capture, otherwise they contract this disease as a matter of routine.[13] Certainly they are rarely seen in zoos. The Frankfurt, Cincinnati, and Colombo (Sri Lanka) zoos currently hold the majority of the small captive population.

TABLE 45 MEASUREMENTS AND WEIGHTS OF ADULT RUSTY-SPOTTED CATS

HB	n	T	n	WT	n	Location	Source
370	1f	200	1f			Jammu	6
383, 470	2?	250, 298	2?	1.1, 1.6	2?	Sri Lanka	14
350–480	?	150–250	?			?	5
406–457	?	240	1?			?	2
				0.9 (0.8–1.1)	3m	captive	21, 23
				~0.9	1f	captive	21, 23

Note: HB = head and body length (mm), T = tail length (mm), WT = weight (kg). *n* = sample size. Sex: m = male, f = female, ? = unknown. Mean values are presented only for sample sizes of three or more. Range of values is in parentheses.

REFERENCES

1. Sterndale, R. A. 1884. *Natural history of the Mammalia of India and Ceylon.* Calcutta: Thacker, Spink, & Co.

2. Guggisberg, C. A. W. 1975. *Wild cats of the world.* New York: Taplinger.

3. Pocock, R. I. 1939. *The fauna of British India, including Ceylon and Burma.* Vol. 1, *Mammalia.* London: Taylor & Francis.

4. Abulali, H. 1945. Northern limits of the rusty-spotted cat (*Prionailurus r. rubiginosus* Geoff.). *J. Bombay Nat. Hist. Soc.* 45: 600–601.

5. Weigel, I. 1972. Small felids and clouded leopards. In *Grzimek's animal life encyclopedia,* vol. 12, *Mammals III,* ed. H. C. B. Grzimek, 281–332. New York: Van Nostrand Reinhold.

6. Chakraborty, S. 1978. The rusty-spotted cat, *Felis rubiginosa* I. Geoffroy, in Jammu and Kashmir. *J. Bombay Nat. Hist. Soc.* 75: 478–479.

7. Chavan, S. A. 1987. Status of wild cats in Gujarat. *Tigerpaper* 14: 21–24.

8. Pathak, B. J. 1990. Rusty-spotted cat *Felis rubiginosa* Geoffroy: A new record for Gir Wildlife Sanctuary and National Park. *J. Bombay Nat. Hist. Soc.* 87: 8.

9. Tehsin, R. 1994. Rusty-spotted cat (*Felis rubiginosa* Geoffroy) sighted near Udaipur. *J. Bombay Nat. Hist. Soc.* 91: 136.

10. Digveerendrasinh. 1995. Occurrence of the rusty spotted cat (*Felis rubiginosa*) in Madhya Pradesh. *J. Bombay Nat. Hist. Soc.* 92: 407–408.

11. Acharjyo, L. N., K. L. Purohit, and S. K. Patnaik. 1997. Occurrence of the rusty spotted cat (*Felis rubiginosa*) in Orissa. *J. Bombay Nat. Hist. Soc.* 94: 554.

12. Worah, S. 1990. Rusty spotted cat *Felis rubiginosa. Cat News* 12: 12.

13. de Alwis, W. L. E. 1973. Status of Southeast Asia's small cats. In *The world's cats,* vol. 1, ed. R. L. Eaton, 198–208. Winston, OR: World Wildlife Safari.

14. Phillips, W. W. A. 1984. *Manual of the mammals of Sri Lanka,* 2nd ed. Colombo: Aitken Spence.

15. Jerdon, T. C. 1874. *The mammals of India: A natural history of all the animals known to inhabit continental India.* London: John Wheldon.

16. Callahan, P. 1991. The rusty spotted cat. *Cat Tales: Newsletter of the International Society for Endangered Cats.* Columbus, OH.

17. Chavan, S. A., C. D. Patel, S. V. Pawar, N. S. Gogate, and N. P. Pandya. 1991. Sighting of the rusty spotted cat *Felis rubiginosa* (Geoffroy) in Shoolpaneshwar Sanctuary, Gujarat. *J. Bombay Nat. Hist. Soc.* 88: 107–108.

18. Mellen, J. D. 1989. Reproductive behavior of small captive exotic cats (*Felis* spp.). Ph.D. dissertation. University of California, Davis.

19. Mellen, J. D. 1993. A comparative analysis of scent-marking, social and reproductive behavior in 20 species of small cats (*Felis*). *Am. Zool.* 33: 151–166.

20. Phillips, W. W. A. 1950. On the young of the Ceylon rusty-spotted cat (*Prionailurus rubiginosus phillipsi* Pocock). *J. Bombay Nat. Hist. Soc.* 49: 297–298.

21. Callahan, P., head cat keeper, Cincinnati Zoo, Cincinnati, OH. Personal communication.

22. Cat News. 1992. Rusty spotted cats living in abandoned houses. *Cat News* 16: 19.

23. Dresser, B., director of research, Center for Reproduction of Endangered Wildlife, Cincinnati Zoo, Cincinnati, OH. Personal communication.

Fishing cat

Prionailurus viverrinus (Bennett, 1833)

Many cats catch and eat fish when the opportunity presents itself, but the fishing cat is the only species to have been named for its habits and diet. Early zoologists were struck by this cat's resemblance to the viverrid family, particularly the large Indian civet (*Viverra zibetha*), hence its Latin name—*Prionailurus viverrinus*.[1]

DESCRIPTION

The fishing cat belongs to a group that includes the rusty-spotted cat, flat-headed cat, and leopard cat; all are characterized by conspicuous stripes and spot patterns on the head and body. Recent immunological and DNA studies confirm taxonomists' earlier impression that the fishing cat is closely related to the leopard cat.[2] The two cats also share several physical characteristics, including similarly spotted coats, long, narrow skulls, and small, rounded, black-backed ears with prominent white patches. But here the resemblance ends. The powerful, stocky fishing cat and the slim, gracile leopard cat look as different as a shot-putter and a hurdler.

Rather than the lithe, long-legged grace that one normally associates with a small cat, the fishing cat projects an aura of power and strength. Its deep-chested body and comparatively short legs give it the look of a much bigger cat, and it is not surprising that villagers sometimes kill fishing cats, mistaking them for leopards.[3]

The fishing cat is about twice the size of a large domestic cat. Its small, rounded ears are set well back on its elongated face.[4] The toes on the front feet are partially webbed, and the tips of the claws protrude from their sheaths even when fully retracted.[5] The tail is comparatively short, about one-third of the cat's head and body length, and it is unusually thick and muscular near the body. As the fishing cat is known to be a strong swimmer, even in deep water, it is not unreasonable to suppose that the tail is used as a rudder.[1,6,7] The cat's short, coarse fur is mouse gray or olive brown and covered with small black spots. The underside of the body is white, and there are two dark collars on the throat. On the face, back, and neck the spots merge into short streaks or lines. The backs of the ears are black with small white central spots. The short tail is marked with five or six black rings and a black tip.[1,8]

DISTRIBUTION

The fishing cat has a limited and discontinuous distribution in Asia. It is very rare in the Indus Valley of

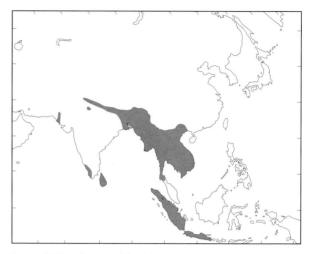

Figure 37. Distribution of the fishing cat.

Pakistan, and there may be scattered populations in coastal areas of Kerala in southwestern India and Sri Lanka. Its main stronghold is the Himalayan foothill region of India, Nepal, and Assam, and then south through Bangladesh, Myanmar, and northern Thailand to Vietnam. It is also found in Sumatra and Java (fig. 37).[6,7,9,10,11] There are a few specimens from peninsular Malaysia, Singapore, and Kalimantan, but whether these represent escaped pets or relicts is uncertain.[12]

ECOLOGY AND BEHAVIOR

The fishing cat lives near water in thick cover in habitats such as mangroves, marshes, and the densely vegetated areas along watercourses. In Sri Lanka, India, and Nepal it is found in forest, scrub, reed beds, and tallgrass areas. The only radio-tracking study of fishing cats to date took place in the terai grasslands of southern Nepal. There, the cats spent most of their time in dense tall and short grasslands, sometimes well away from water; they were active only at night.[13] Fishing cats are not often seen in the wild, and they are thought to be primarily nocturnal.

Early naturalists maintained that the fishing cat was reluctant to enter water, but the animal's swimming abilities are now firmly established. It is very much at home in the water and can swim long distances, even under water. Roberts records one individual pursued by dogs that was seen to swim "a considerable distance down a narrow channel without exposing any part of its body. It appeared to have its eyes open the whole time and propelled itself with powerful strokes of its hind feet." Roberts also remarks on the fact that a captive fishing cat enjoyed swimming: "I observed it swimming with its head well clear of the water and using both fore- and hind legs with the tail acting as a rudder."[6]

Feeding Ecology

Given its powerful build and strong swimming abilities, it is not surprising to find that the fishing cat takes a wide range of prey. It has been observed crouching on rocks and sandbanks along rivers, using its paw to scoop out fish,[11] and it will swim under water to catch coots and ducks.[6] In Keoladeo Ghana National Park, India, an Indian graduate student watched for five hours while a fishing cat hunted along the edge of a small canal. The cat came to the canal at 1945 hours in the evening and sat at the edge of the water. It pounced on a frog, ate it, then moved to another spot, where it sat, concentrating on the water. Over the next four hours the cat changed hunting locations roughly every fifteen minutes, but did not catch anything. Then, just before midnight, it dived into the water and thrashed around with its forelimbs. Putting its head under the surface, it grabbed something and ran out of the water onto the bank with its prize.[14]

Despite the fact that the fishing cat does catch and eat fish, its teeth are not specially adapted for catching fish or crushing mollusks.[8] Rather, like most felids, it has teeth suited for killing any mammal, bird, or reptile it can catch. This powerful cat is reported to be a formidable hunter, and historical accounts mention fishing cats killing calves, dogs, and even young children.[7] A large male fractured a dog's jaw with a blow from its paw,[6] and, in what can only be an exceptional situation, a newly caught male broke through the partition of a cage and attacked and killed a female leopard twice his own size.[7] There are several records of fishing cats killing chital fawns,[13,15] and one was seen scavenging a cow carcass in Keoladeo Ghana National Park.[16] In a sample of nine fishing cat scats from Keoladeo, fish were the most frequently found prey, followed by birds and small mammals.[14] These findings lend support to reports that, in addition to fish, these cats also eat small mammals, snakes, snails, crustaceans, and birds.

Captive fishing cats bite hens and ducks first in the shoulder area, then use both paws to draw the prey close enough to deliver a killing bite to the head. Birds larger than a blackbird are plucked before being eaten.[17]

Social Organization

The fishing cat appears to be a solitary hunter, and there is little information on its social organization or mating behavior in the wild. Limited telemetry data suggest that these cats follow the usual felid land tenure pattern in which a male's range overlaps the smaller ranges of several females. In Chitwan National Park, Nepal, radio-tagged females used areas of 4 to 6 square kilometers, while a male's range was three or four times larger, about 16 to 22 square kilometers.[13]

Among the felids there is a general uniformity in the types of indirect and direct signals used in communication, although the vocal repertoire and scent marking patterns of fishing cats are not well known. Both males and females utter a chuckling call, described as "eh-eh-eh," and kittens have been heard to mew and give a birdlike "chirrup."[18] Adult fishing cats are also likely to gurgle, as this vocalization is known from other members of its taxonomic group.[19] Both sexes scent-mark by spraying urine, cheek rubbing, and head rubbing.[20,21]

In zoos, fishing cats have a reputation for being extremely wary and aggressive, but people who have kept them as pets report that they become quite tame and affectionate. Several different zoos have found that fishing cats seem to tolerate living in groups. In the Colombo Zoo in Sri Lanka two males, three females, and two juveniles lived together peacefully.[3] E. D. W. Jayewardene, who kept both jungle cats and fishing cats as pets, observed that "unlike the Jungle cats which, unless fed simultaneously, would fight savagely and violently over their food, the Fishing cats never quarrelled at feeding time."[22] Captive fishing cats have lived for ten years.[23]

Reproduction and Development

Most observations of kittens in the wild date from March–April, suggesting that mating takes place in January–February, although young may be born at other times of the year.[24,25,26] Two den sites have been found in the wild, and both consisted of rough nests in dense patches of reeds. The remains of a coot and a wood sandpiper were found at one of the dens.[6]

Litters consist of two to three kittens. In captivity, the average litter size of thirteen litters was 2.61;[20] two litters of two[27] and a single litter of two have also been reported.[22] The gestation period is approximately sixty-three to seventy days;[27,28] a ninety- to ninety-five-day[10] gestation appears to be an overestimate. Young fishing cats weigh about 170 grams at birth, and kittens at the Philadelphia Zoo were able to walk and climb over objects by the time they were twenty-nine days old. By two months of age the kittens regularly played in their water dish, and at three months they were wrestling violently with each other and leaping 60 centimeters up the wall while chasing flies. These captive kittens were first observed eating solid food at fifty-three days of age, but continued to suckle for about six months, at which time they were roughly three-quarters the size of their mother. They reached adult size at eight and half months.[27] Fishing cats shed their milk teeth as early as six and a half months and have acquired their adult canines by the time they are eleven months old.[27] One female became sexually mature at fifteen months.[20]

STATUS IN THE WILD

The fishing cat's association with wetlands, marshes, and grasslands does not bode well for its survival, since these areas are in increasing demand by people. The rapid conversion of wetland and floodplain habitat to agriculture has had a serious effect on the fishing cat in many parts of its range. Fishing cats are gradually disappearing from areas near villages in Bangladesh due to large-scale habitat destruction.[29] In 1982 a two-and-a-half-month status survey of cats in Sikkim and North Bengal did not find any conclusive evidence of the fishing cat's presence.[30] In Pakistan it is now considered very rare and fast disappearing because of increased cultivation along the Indus River and ever-expanding human exploitation of remaining swamp areas.[6] The fishing cat also appears to have disappeared from the western coast of India.[31] The situation is much the same in Sri Lanka as land development programs convert forests and wetlands to agricultural uses.

Although the main threat to the fishing cat comes from habitat loss, it is also considered edible, and its skin is still esteemed by the fur trade. In 1991, eighty fishing cat skins, along with the skins of a tiger and a leopard, were found wrapped in a package deposited in a culvert in Silguri in North Bengal.[32] Fishing cat numbers have also been reduced by live capture. According to records of Thailand's Royal Forestry Department, 448 fishing cats were declared for export between 1967 and 1971.[33] Fishing cats are also killed when caught raiding poultry sheds, and some villagers believe they kill young domestic stock.

Large body size, a sought-after spotted pelt, and a distribution closely tied to wetlands and grasslands suggest that the fishing cat will undoubtedly suffer further contraction of its already disjunct geographic range. However, Khan reports that in some plantations and forests of southwestern Bangladesh the fishing cat is still a common predator.[29] In 1988–1989 four fishing cats were killed by villagers in a small wetland near Calcutta. The news caused great excitement because these cats were reportedly abundant in the area a hundred years ago, but there have been few confirmed sightings until now. Forest department officials now think these cats may be quite common in the *Typha-Imperata* wetlands in the Howra district near Calcutta. A local conservation organization, The Indian Society for Wildlife Research, is carrying out a fishing cat survey and has also launched a public education program to promote conservation awareness.[34]

STATUS IN CAPTIVITY

Fishing cats are not common in zoos; a 1988 census found only thirty-three individuals in North American and European zoos. Most of these animals are related to stock originally bred at the Rotterdam Zoo, and the population is probably inbred.[28] The few zoos that do keep fishing cats have found that when provided with a pond and live fish to catch, these cats make striking exhibits. Some zoos have found that fishing cats seem to be unusually tolerant of one another, so that several adults can be kept in the same enclosure.

TABLE 46 MEASUREMENTS AND WEIGHTS OF ADULT FISHING CATS

HB	n	T	n	WT	n	Location	Source
725–780	?	250–290	?	7–11	?	Thailand	10
775	1m	300	1m			Sri Lanka	8
724	3m	279	3m			Sri Lanka	8
660	3f	254	3f			Sri Lanka	8
658–857	?	254–280	?	6.4–11.8	?	Sri Lanka	4
720	1m	288	1m			Pakistan	6
711	1m	279	1m	14.5	1m	India	26
660	1m	240	1m	16.0	1m	India	16

TABLE 46 (continued)

HB	n	T	n	WT	n	Location	Source
648, 743	2f	242, 251	2f	5.1, 6.8	2f	Nepal	13
724, 762	2?	241, 267	2?			Nepal	4
1,150	1?	400	1?			Java	11
570–770	?	200–260	?			Java	35

Note: HB = head and body length (mm), T = tail length (mm), WT = weight (kg). n = sample size. Sex: m = male, f = female, ? = unknown. Mean values are presented only for sample sizes of three or more. Range of values is in parentheses.

REFERENCES

1. Guggisberg, C. A. W. 1975. *Wild cats of the world.* New York: Taplinger.

2. Collier, G. E., and S. J. O'Brien. 1985. A molecular phylogeny of the Felidae: Immunological distance. *Evolution* 39: 473–487.

3. de Alwis, W. L. E. 1973. Status of Southeast Asia's small cats. In *The world's cats,* vol. 1, ed. R. L. Eaton, 198–208. Winston, OR: World Wildlife Safari.

4. Phillips, W. W. A. 1984. *Manual of the mammals of Sri Lanka,* 2nd ed. Colombo: Aitken Spence.

5. Pocock, R. I. 1932. The marbled cat (*Pardofelis marmorata*) and some other Oriental species, with the definition of a new genus of the Felidae. *Proc. Zool. Soc. Lond.* 1932: 741–766.

6. Roberts, T. J. 1977. *The mammals of Pakistan.* London: Ernest Benn.

7. Sterndale, R. A. 1884. *Natural history of the Mammalia of India and Ceylon.* Calcutta: Thacker, Spink.

8. Pocock, R. I. 1939. *The fauna of British India, including Ceylon and Burma.* Vol. 1, Mammalia. London: Taylor and Francis.

9. Corbet, G. B., and J. E. Hill. 1992. *The mammals of the Indomalayan region: A systematic review.* Oxford: Oxford University Press.

10. Lekagul, B. M. D., and J. A. McNeely. 1977. *Mammals of Thailand.* Bangkok: Association for the Conservation of Wildlife.

11. Hoogerwerf, A. 1970. *Udjung Kulon: The land of the last Javan rhinoceros.* Leiden: E. J. Brill.

12. Van Bree, P. J. H., and M. K. M. Khan. 1992. On a fishing cat, *Felis (Prionailurus) viverrina* Bennett, 1833, from continental Malaysia. *Z. Säugetierk.* 57: 179–180.

13. Smith, J. L. D., associate professor, Department of Fisheries and Wildlife, University of Minnesota, St. Paul, Minnesota. Personal communication.

14. Mukherjee. S. 1989. Ecological separation of four sympatric carnivores in Keoladeo Ghana National Park, Bharatpur, Rajasthan, India. Master's thesis, Wildlife Institute of India, Dehra Dun. 83 pp.

15. Singh, A. 1982. *Prince of Cats.* London: Jonathan Cape.

16. Haque, M. N., and V. S. Vijayan. 1993. Food habits of the fishing cat *Felis viverrina* in Keoladeo National Park, Bharaptur, Rajasthan. *J. Bombay Nat. Hist. Soc.* 90: 498–500.

17. Leyhausen, P. 1979. *Cat behavior: The predatory and social behavior of domestic and wild cats.* New York: Garland STPM Press.

18. Ulmer, F. A. Jr. 1966. Voices of the Felidae. *Int. Zoo Yrbk.* 6: 259–262.

19. Peters, G. 1984. On the structure of friendly close range vocalizations in terrestrial carnivores (Mammalia: Carnivora: Fissipedia). *Z. Säugetierk.* 49: 157–182.

20. Mellen, J. D. 1993. A comparative analysis of scent-marking, social and reproductive behavior in 20 species of small cats (*Felis*). *Am. Zool.* 33: 151–166.

21. Wemmer, C., and K. Scow. 1977. Communication in the Felidae with emphasis on scent marking and contact patterns. In *How animals communicate,* ed. T. A. Sebeok, 749–766. Bloomington: Indiana University Press.

22. Jayewardene, E. D. W. 1975. Breeding the fishing cat in captivity. *Int. Zoo Yrbk.* 8: 150–152.

23. Dover, C. 1933. The duration of life of some Indian mammals. Miscellaneous Notes, no. 1. *J. Bombay Nat. Hist. Soc.* 36: 244–250.

24. Bhattacharyya, T. 1992. A brief note on some observations on the breeding biology of fishing cat (*Felis viverrina*). *Tigerpaper* 14(2): 20–21.

25. Datye, H. S. 1993. First record of the fishing cat *Felis viverrina* Bennet in Dalma Wildlife Sanctuary and Chhotanagpur plateau of Bihar. *J. Bombay Nat. Hist. Soc.* 90: 90.

26. Macdonald, A. St. J. 1950. The fishing cat (*Prionailurus viverrinus* Bennett). *J. Bombay Nat. Hist. Soc.* 49: 298.

27. Ulmer, F. A., Jr. 1968. Breeding fishing cats at Philadelphia Zoo. *Int. Zoo Yrbk.* 8: 49–55.

28. Mellen, J. D. 1989. Reproductive behavior of small captive exotic cats (*Felis* spp.). Ph.D. dissertation, University of California, Davis.

29. Khan, M. A. R. 1986. The status and distribution of the cats in Bangladesh. In *Cats of the world: Biology, conservation, and management,* ed. S. D. Miller and D. D. Everett, 43–49. Washington, DC: National Wildlife Federation.

30. Biswas, B., and R. K Ghose. 1982. Progress report on "Pilot Survey" of the World Wildlife Fund-India/Zoological Survey of India collaborative project on the "Status survey of the lesser cats in eastern India." [Project No. IUCN 1357-India]. Zoological Survey of India, Calcutta. 52 pp.

31. Cat News. 1986. Some notes for the record. *Cat News* 5: 11.

32. Cat News. 1992. Rampant skin trade in India. *Cat News* 16: 25.

33. Royal Forestry Department. 1972. Cited in S. R. Humphrey and J. R. Bain (1990), *Endangered Animals of Thailand.* Gainesville, Florida: Sandhill Crane Press.

34. Cat News. 1989. Cats around Calcutta. *Cat News* 11: 16.

35. Weigel, I. 1972. Small felids and clouded leopards. In *Grzimek's animal life encyclopedia,* vol. 12, Mammals III, ed. H. C. B. Grzimek, 281–332. New York: Van Nostrand Reinhold.

African golden cat

Profelis aurata (Temminck, 1827)

The African golden cat is known as "boy of the leopard" or "the leopard's brother" because local people believe that this cat follows the leopard.[1] People consider the golden cat to be very fierce and fear it, and in many parts of Africa it is the subject of tribal superstition. In Cameroon, for example, pygmy tribes carry the cat's tail to ensure good fortune when hunting elephants.[2] Golden cat skins are also used locally during circumcision rites, or to wrap up valuable objects.[1]

Interestingly, the similarly named Asian golden cat is also considered to be extremely fierce, and some local tribes attribute supernatural powers to that cat or its parts.[3] However, the evolutionary connection between the two species of golden cats has been the subject of dispute. Some have argued, on the basis of differences in skull and dental characteristics, that there is no direct affiliation, and assign the cats to different genera (*Profelis* and *Catopuma*).[4,5] Immunological and chromosomal studies suggest that both golden cats were part of an early radiation in the *Panthera* lineage that split off some 6 million years ago,[6,7] but more recent analyses place the African golden cat in the caracal group, along with the serval.[8]

DESCRIPTION

The African golden cat is about twice the size of a large domestic cat and robustly built, weighing 8 to 16 kilograms. As with other cats, males are larger and heavier than females. This cat might better be called the cat of many colors, as its fur varies from marmalade orange-red to sepia-gray, and each color phase may be spotted all over, unspotted, or somewhere in between.[1,9] The throat, chest, and undersides are invariably white or whitish, and the belly is marked with bold dark spots or blotches. Weigel suggested that the difference in spot patterns of golden cats follows a transcontinental cline because those individuals from western Africa tended to be heavily spotted, whereas those from eastern Africa were more likely to be unspotted.[10] Support for this east-west theory has not been universal, although after examining 175 golden cat pelts, van Mensch and van Bree concluded there were two distinct races.[1] Others argue that the evidence is incomplete and suggest that the cat is simply a highly polymorphic species.[9,11] To make matters even more confusing, the coat color of a captive animal in the London Zoo was observed to change from red to gray over a period of four months.[1] A variety of reasons have been put for-

Figure 38. Distribution of the African golden cat.

ward to explain such changes,[12,13,14] but differences in coat coloring do not appear to be linked to age, sex, or season.[1,9]

The golden cat has a round face and a heavy muzzle. It has small, blunt, untufted ears that are almost completely black on the back. Its tail is short, only about a third of its head and body length, and may be distinctly banded, unbanded, or anything in between. Some individuals are marked with dark spots or stripes on the head, but otherwise the golden cat has no obvious facial markings except for small whitish patches above the eyes and on the lower parts of the cheeks. Melanistic and partially black golden cats have been seen.[1,9]

Despite the fact that this cat has so many different coat patterns, a golden cat pelt has one distinguishing feature: The fur, from just in front of the shoulders to the crown of the head, changes direction and points forward. The junction of the change in direction of the hair pattern is marked by whorls and a low, crest-like ridge.[1,11]

DISTRIBUTION

The golden cat is found in the tropical forest region of equatorial Africa from Senegal, Sierra Leone, and Liberia in the west through the Central African Republic and the Democratic Republic of the Congo (formerly Zaire) to Uganda and Kenya in the east. Its southern limit is northern Angola (fig. 38).[1,9] While its presence has not been confirmed from several countries within these boundaries, this is thought to reflect insufficient knowledge rather than the cat's absence.[1]

ECOLOGY AND BEHAVIOR

Little is known of the biology and natural history of the African golden cat other than what can be inferred from occasional sightings, a few scats, and the records of collectors. The golden cat seems to be able to live in almost every type of forest, including primary forest, secondary vegetation, recently logged forest with a dense understory, and riverine forest where watercourses penetrate more open habitat.[9] It is also known from montane forest, alpine moorland, and bamboo forest at elevations of 2,000–3,000 meters.[2,13,15] More typically the cat is found in forested areas with very dense, moist secondary undergrowth, often along rivers.[9]

While some authorities suggest that the golden cat is arboreal,[11,16] its stocky build and rather short tail, combined with its presence in alpine moorland, would suggest that it is primarily a terrestrial hunter. There are several observations of golden cats hunting during the daytime, but based on the activity patterns of its reported prey, this species is likely to be primarily crepuscular and nocturnal.

Feeding Ecology

The available information on the golden cat's diet indicates that it feeds primarily on small mammals and birds. In the Ruwenzori Mountains in East Africa, golden cats live mainly on groove-toothed rats, swamp rats, hyraxes, and duikers, all of which are terrestrial and primarily diurnal or crepuscular in their habits.[9] In another forest reserve the cats' feces contained the remains of duikers, monkeys, rodents, and birds. Golden cats are clearly not averse to tackling medium-sized prey such as duikers, and they are known to raid chicken coops and kill sheep and goats.[9] They probably take guinea fowl, francolins, and other ground-foraging birds opportunistically; the stomach of a male golden cat killed in Senegal contained feathers, claws, and the gizzard of an unidentified bird.[17] In the Ituri Forest, Democratic Republic of the Congo, an analysis of sixty golden cat scats showed that small to medium-sized rodents made up nearly 70 percent of prey items. The mean weight of prey consumed was 1.4 kilograms. Less than 5 percent of the prey items in golden cat scats were medium-sized ungulates and primates. Birds were recorded in 18 percent of scats.[18] In

the Central African Republic, small duikers and rodents ranked first and second, respectively, in their biomass contribution to the golden cat diet.[19] Captive cats have been observed to eat birds eagerly, always plucking them first.[16,20]

Throughout most of its geographic range the golden cat shares its habitat with the leopard. Though the diets of the two cats may overlap, small prey such as rodents and birds are probably more important to the golden cat than they are to the leopard.

Social Organization

Apart from the fact that the golden cat is solitary, nothing is known about this animal's behavior, social life, or land tenure system. Like other felids, males and females probably maintain spatially or temporally separate home ranges, and do so by a combination of scent marks, scrapes, and feces. The observation that the golden cat does not cover its feces, but leaves them exposed on trails and paths, supports this view.[9]

The vocal repertoire of golden cats is thought to be extensive,[21] although it is unlikely to exceed the twelve vocalization types recorded for most felids.[22] Besides hissing, meowing, and growling, golden cats probably purr, and in close-contact situations they gurgle.[23,24]

Reproduction and Development

Outside of an observation in the Ituri Forest of a female with a single nursing kitten in a den in a fallen hollow log,[18] what is known about reproduction in African golden cats is derived entirely from captive animals held at the Max Planck Institute in Germany.[19,20] Two litters of two kittens each were born at the Institute following a seventy-five-day gestation, and their fur was dark gray or grayish brown. The newborn kittens varied in weight from 180 to 235 grams. Their eyes were completely open by day six, and thereafter they exhibited rapid development of motor skills. One female kitten was standing at ten days of age and walking well at thirteen days. By sixteen days she was able to climb into the nest box, scaling a wall 40 centimeters high. At 19 days both kittens made their first attempt to jump onto a low tree stump. At forty days they were chewing pieces of meat off chickens and mice, and shortly thereafter they were eating whole animals. In comparison with other small felids, golden cat kittens are advanced in physical agility and in other respects as well. By twelve weeks of age the male kitten weighed 2.9 kilograms and the female 2.5 kilograms, although the female was somewhat more advanced in her development than the male. Her permanent dentition started to appear at fourteen weeks, and his lagged about a month behind. The female also showed signs of sexual maturity at eleven months, whereas the first signs for the male occurred at eighteen months of age. In terms of absolute size, however, the male grew faster, and at six months of age he was as large as his mother; his sister was still smaller than their mother at eleven months of age.

One golden cat at the Institute came into estrus at eleven months of age, and a male sired his first litter at eighteen months. The only other record is of a captive female who first reproduced at four years of age.[25] The longevity record for golden cats in captivity is just over twelve years.[26]

STATUS IN THE WILD

As might be expected from the paucity of even basic information on the African golden cat, there is no reliable information on its status in the wild. In many countries of equatorial Africa golden cats are listed as rare,[1] although Rosevear believes that they are either common or easily trapped because, compared with those of other African cats, there are a large number of golden cat skins in museum collections.[11] In contrast, Kingdon reports that golden cat skins are relatively rare in collections, but that the cat may not be as rare as generally believed. In Uganda, for example, he found it to be "locally common" in previously logged forests with dense secondary growth.[9] In 1987, Wilson reported that golden cats appeared to be common in the Azagny and Taï National Parks in Ivory Coast.[27] Tracks were often seen, and cats were heard calling at night. That the cat does well in secondary forest, combined with its ability to survive on small rodents, would suggest that it is in less danger of extinction than many other small cats. The long-range forecast for the golden cat is nevertheless not terribly optimistic, because humans are reclaiming these second-growth areas and golden cats are being killed while raiding poultry sheds or going after domestic sheep and goats.

STATUS IN CAPTIVITY

Of the 343 zoos participating in the ISIS species distribution program, only a few have African golden cats in their collections.

TABLE 47 MEASUREMENTS AND WEIGHTS OF ADULT AFRICAN GOLDEN CATS

HB	n	T	n	WT	n	Location	Source
657	4?	349	4?			West Africa	11
860	3?	300	3?			Cameroon	11
792	16?	292	15?	8.5	5?	Africa	1
(616–1,010)		(163–370)		(5.3–12.0)			
910	1m	310	1m			Senegal	17
780	1m	330	1m			Ivory Coast	28
935	1m	325	1m	9.75	1m	Guinea	29

Note: HB = head and body length (mm), T = tail length (mm), WT = weight (kg). n = sample size. Sex: m = male, f = female, ? = unknown. Mean values are presented only for sample sizes of three or more. Range of values is in parentheses.

TABLE 48 FREQUENCY OF OCCURRENCE OF PREY ITEMS IN THE DIETS OF AFRICAN GOLDEN CATS (PERCENTAGE OF SAMPLES)

Prey items	Ituri Forest, Democratic Republic of the Congo[18] Scats (n = 60)	Dzanga-Ndoki NP, Central African Republic[19] Scats (n = 17)
Neotragus batesi Dwarf or pygmy antelope	6.7	
Cephalophus monticola Blue duiker	25.0	23.5
Cephalophus dorsalis Bay duiker	1.7	

(continued)

TABLE 48 (continued)

Prey items	Ituri Forest, Democratic Republic of the Congo[18] Scats (n = 60)	Dzanga-Ndoki NP, Central African Republic[19] Scats (n = 17)
Cephalophus callipygus Peter's duiker		17.6
Cercopithecus sp. Guenons	5.0	5.9
Small rodents	51.7	11.8
Large rodents	8.3	
Squirrels	10.0	7.1
Protoxerus stangeri Oil palm squirrel	1.8	
Cricetomys emini Giant rat	5.0	11.8
Rhynchocyon cirnei Checkered elephant shrew	11.7	
Atherurus africanus Brush-tailed porcupine		11.8
Insectivora		5.9
Unidentified mammals	13.4	11.8
Unidentified birds	18.4	
Minimum number of vertebrate prey items	99	21

REFERENCES

1. van Mensch, P. J. A., and P. J. H. van Bree. 1969. On the African golden cat, *Profelis aurata* (Temminck, 1827). *Biologica Gabonica* 5: 235–269.

2. Guggisberg, C. A. W. 1975. *Wild cats of the world.* New York: Taplinger.

3. Lekagul, B., and J. A. McNeely. 1977. *Mammals of Thailand.* Bangkok: Association for the Conservation of Wildlife.

4. Hemmer, H. 1978. The evolutionary systematics of living Felidae: Present status and current problems. *Carnivore* 1: 71–79.

5. Groves, C. 1982. Cranial and dental characteristics in the systematics of Old World Felidae. *Carnivore* 5: 28–39.

6. Collier, G. E., and S. J. O'Brien. 1985. A molecular phylogeny of the Felidae: Immunological distance. *Evolution* 39: 473–487.

7. Wayne, R. K., R. E. Benveniste, D. N. Janczewski, and S. J. O'Brien. 1989. Molecular and biochemical evolution of the Carnivora. In *Carnivore Behavior, Ecology, and Evolution,* ed. J. L. Gittleman, 465–494. Ithaca, NY: Cornell University Press.

8. Pecon-Slattery, J., and S. J. O'Brien. 1998. Patterns of Y and X chromosome DNA sequence divergence during the Felidae radiation. *Genetics* 148: 1245–1255.

9. Kingdon, J. 1977. *East African Mammals.* Vol. 3A. Chicago: University of Chicago Press.

10. Weigel, I. 1961. Das Fellmuster der wildlebenden Katzenarten und der Hauskatze in vergleichender und stammesgeschichtlicher Hinsicht. *Säugetierk. Mitt.* 9: 1–120.

11. Rosevear, D. R. 1974. *The carnivores of West Africa.* London: Trustees of the British Museum (Natural History).

12. Pocock, R. I. 1907. Notes upon some African species of the genus *Felis* based upon specimens recently exhibited in the Society's gardens. *Proc. Zoo. Soc. Lond.* 1907: 656–677.

13. Brooks, A. C. 1962. Uganda's small mammals. II. The small cats. *Wildl. Sport* 3(2): 8–11.

14. Dekeyser, P. L. 1945. A propos des chats de l'Afrique Noire Française. *Mammalia* 9: 51–60.

15. Bourdelle, E., and G. Babault. 1931. Note sur une forme particulière de Félidé de la région de Kivu (*Felis aurata,* Temminck = *Profelis aurata,* Pocock). *Bull. Mus. Hist. Nat.* (Paris) 2(3): 294–297.

16. Blonk, H. L. 1965. Einiges uber die afrikanische Goldkatze, *Profelis aurata aurata* (Temminck, 1827). *Säugetierk. Mitt.* 13: 132–133.

17. Gaillard. 1969. Sur la présence du chat doré (*Felis aurata* Temm.) et du caracal (*Felis caracal* Schreb.) dans le sud du Sénégal. *Mammalia* 33: 350–351.

18. Hart, J. A., M. Katembo, and K. Punga. 1996. Diet, prey selection and ecological relations of leopard and golden cat in the Ituri Forest, Zaire. *Afr. J. Ecol.* 34: 364–379.

19. Ray, J. C., and M. E. Sunquist. 2001. Trophic relations in a community of African rainforest carnivores. *Oecologia* 127: 395–408.

20. Leyhausen, P. 1979. *Cat behavior: The predatory and social behavior of domestic and wild cats.* New York: Garland STPM Press.

21. Tonkin, B. A., and E. Kohler. 1978. Breeding the African golden cat in captivity. *Int. Zoo Yrbk.* 18: 147–50.

22. Peters, G. 1991. Vocal communication in cats. In *Great Cats,* ed. J. Seidensticker and S. Lumpkin, 76–77. Emmaus, PA: Rodale Press.

23. Peters, G. 1984. On the structure of friendly close range vo-

calizations in terrestrial carnivores (Mammalia: Carnivora: Fissipedia). *Z. Säugetierk.* 49: 157–182.

24. Peters, G., and M. H. Hast. 1994. Hyoid structure, laryngeal anatomy, and vocalization in felids (Mammalia: Carnivora: Felidae). *Z. Säugetierk.* 59: 87–104.

25. Eaton, R. L. 1984. Survey of smaller felid breeding. *Zool. Garten* (n.f.) 54: 101–120.

26. Jones, M. L. 1977. Record keeping and longevity of felids in captivity. In *The world's cats*, vol. 3, no. 3, ed. R. L. Eaton, 132–138.

Seattle: Carnivore Research Institute, Burke Museum, University of Washington.

27. Wilson, V. 1987. Cats in Ivory Coast. *Cat News* 6: 33.

28. Bellier, L., P. J. H. van Bree, and J. Vissault. 1972. Quelques données nouvelles concernant le chat doré d'Afrique, *Profelis aurata* (Temminck, 1827) en Côte d'Ivoire. *Biologia Gabonica* 8(2): 191–192.

29. Brugiere, D. 2001. Range expansion of African golden cat in Guinea. *Cat News* 35: 14–15.

Puma

Puma concolor (Linnaeus, 1771)

Puma, mountain lion, and cougar are just some of the more common names this cat is known by, and the species is listed in the dictionary under more names than any other mammal in the United States.[1,2] In years past, the puma's many different names caused some confusion, and people believed that the various names represented several different animals.

Columbus was one of the first to call this cat a "lion" because its tawny coat resembled that of the African lion. Later, others assumed that males of the species were fierce, elusive creatures because explorers had seen only maneless "female" skins. The name "lion," or *león*, is widely used through much of Spanish-speaking South and Central America, while in Brazil the cat is called *leão*. The name *puma* first appeared in 1609, when Garcilasso de la Vega, the son of a Spanish conquistador and an Incan princess, wrote, "Lions are met with, though they are not so large nor so fierce as those of Africa. The Indians call them puma."[3]

The name *cougar* appears to have been derived from a word used by the German geographer Georg Marcgrave in 1648. Marcgrave used the Guarani word *cuguacuarana* to refer to the puma, but this was eventually shortened to "cuguacuara."[3] Later, the French naturalist Georges Buffon, who wrote about a variety of animals he had never seen, dubbed the cat "cuguar," which is his own contraction of *cuguacuarana*.[4] The original meaning of *cuguacuarana* is obscure and may be further confused by a three-hundred-year-old typo. Marcgrave was said to have incorrectly transcribed *sassúarána*, a Tupi Indian word for "false deer," to "cuguacuarana."[3]

The name *panther* is used as a general word for a cat of uniform color, and is most commonly applied to the black leopard of Asia. Early colonists in Virginia and Pennsylvania often wrote of the panther, a name that later became corrupted to "painter" in the southern United States. Another slightly more fanciful name is *catamount*, a shortened version of "cat-of-the-mountain," which is, in turn, a translation of the Spanish *gato monte*.

Today, the cat is called puma almost everywhere in South America, but a variety of local and regional names also exist. In North America the name puma is commonly used among the scientific community, but cougar and mountain lion seem to be more common with the general public. Theodore Roosevelt summed up the situation well in 1901 when he wrote:

No American beast has been the subject of so much loose writing or of such wild fables as the cougar. Even its name is unsettled. In the Eastern States it is called panther or painter; in the Western States, mountain lion, or toward the South, Mexican lion. The Spanish-speaking people call it simply lion. It is, however, sometimes called cougar in the West and Southwest of the United States, and in South America, puma.[3]

DESCRIPTION

Is the puma a member of the big cat group or, as Werdelin has suggested, does it just "think" it is, having attained the large body size of big cats while retaining the cranial proportions of small cats?[5] Scientists have argued over the subject for years, and before molecular geneticists began to study felid phylogeny, the debate resulted in the puma being included in the small cat group (*Felis*). The reasons included the shape of the puma's rhinarium (nose), the morphology of its feet, and the shape of its pupils, all of which are similar to those of small cats.[6] Pumas also resemble the smaller cats in that they have a short, wide skull and a short face (in terms of the distance from the eyes to the end of the nose). Furthermore, pumas do not roar in the manner of lions and leopards, but purr like the smaller cats.[7,8]

The fossil record shows that pumalike cats were common during the early Pleistocene in North America, and that in some areas they lived alongside lions, jaguars, and a cheetahlike cat.[9,10,11] In 1979 paleontologist Daniel Adams reported that "cheetahs and pumas may have had a common ancestor in the Miocene of North America."[12] However, recent molecular analysis indicates that today's North American pumas derive from a recent replacement and recolonization by a small number of founders that had their origins in eastern South America 200,000 to 300,000 years ago. The recolonization of North America by pumas was coincident with a massive late Pleistocene extinction event that probably extirpated pumas from that continent.[13] The most recent classification has the cat in its own genus (*Puma*), where it was also placed by Pocock and others.[6,14,15]

From a layperson's point of view, pumas do bear a closer resemblance to cheetahs than to the big cats. Both pumas and cheetahs have small, rounded heads, slim, lanky bodies, and moderately long limbs. Like cheetahs, pumas are gentle, retiring cats, more eager to flee than fight, and both species rarely confront humans.[16,17]

Now that the jaguar has been extirpated from the

southwestern United States, the puma has become the largest native North American cat. However, the size of this cat is frequently overestimated, and documentation is lacking for some of the largest specimens claimed by hunters. *Sports Afield Hunting Annual* reported that one such giant puma weighing 170 kilograms was killed in 1958 in the Chaco region of Paraguay. A more likely record holder was an Arizona puma killed in 1917 by a predator hunter. This cat was certified to the U.S. Biological Survey at 125 kilograms with its intestines removed.[4,18]

The weights of adult pumas vary considerably over their vast geographic range.[19] Pumas from Chile and Canada, the southern and northern limits of the species' range, weigh roughly twice as much as those found in the tropics. The smallest pumas are found in equatorial rainforests, where there are records of adult males from Peru weighing only 28 to 30 kilograms, whereas adult males from Canada and Chile weigh 65 to 85 kilograms.[20,21,22]

Adult males commonly weigh 40 to 60 percent more than females, and are larger in all body measurements than females.[23,24] A recent analysis of 1,201 puma skulls from across the geographic range shows that males are significantly larger than females for all nineteen characters measured. This sexual variation in size does not, however, follow a geographic pattern, nor does the dimorphism correlate with environmental variables. The causes of the variation are thought to be associated with intraspecific and interspecific interactions, with sexual selection being the most likely explanation for the size dimorphism.[25] Within individuals, some skull variation is also associated with age, as both sexes show growth of the cranium throughout most of the life span.[26]

Compared with other large cats, the puma has unusually long hind legs, which are thought to be an adaptation for jumping.[27] One account describes a female puma, sitting near her kill, leaping over a 2-meter-high mesquite bush and catching a vulture in midair as it was about to land on the shrub.[28] The powerful hind legs also work in unison, enabling a running cat to put on a burst of high speed that may last for a few hundred yards. Showing little regard for the desert terrain, one puma overtook and killed a javelina in a 200-meter chase.[29] In California, pumas have been seen leaping boulders and dodging clumps of vegetation while chasing, and eventually catching, jackrabbits. Occasionally they even manage to catch the swift pronghorn.[30,31] Hunters' stories also tell of the puma's amazing ability to leap 20 feet straight up a cliff, and pumas chased by dogs have made downhill leaps 30 and 40 feet long. Interestingly, the puma also possesses a relatively long spinal column, which provides increased lumbar flexion while running. This characteristic is shared by the cheetah, but the puma usually relies more on ambushing its prey than on running it down.

The puma is a plain-colored cat, and its coat color varies from grizzled gray to dark brown, with intermittent shades of buff, tawny, and cinnamon red. The pelage color also varies geographically, with pumas from warm, humid areas tending to be darker than those from elsewhere; cats inhabiting drier habitats are light-colored.[32] The color along the back is more intense than on the shoulders and sides. The underparts are whitish, as are the chin and throat. The sides of the white muzzle are framed in black. The ears are small, rounded, and black on the back. The long, cylindrical tail has a black tip.

Melanistic pumas, or "black panthers" as they are often called, have reportedly been shot in South America.[4] In North America there are literally thousands of reported sightings of black pumas, but none of these has ever been authenticated.[23] Though people regularly report seeing black pumas and sometimes claim to have shot them, no museum skins exist. Despite this, sightings of black panthers continue to crop up year after year in newspaper reports. In Florida, where only fifty or so pumas exist, black panthers are the most commonly seen cat. Biologists insist that there are no black panthers in Florida, and maintain that they should know, because most of Florida's pumas have been radio-collared, photographed, and followed since birth.[33,34] Throughout the puma's range, officials of state wildlife agencies remain skeptical and ascribe the sightings to large house cats, excited observers, or poor light conditions; however, others continue to believe in the beast, arguing that so many observers cannot be wrong.

DISTRIBUTION

The geographic range of the puma is the largest of any terrestrial mammal in the Western Hemisphere. Historically, the cat was found from northern British Columbia across the southern portions of the Canadian provinces to New Brunswick, south through all of the United States, through Central America, and into South America to the southern tip of Chile.[35] Pumas were extirpated from the eastern United States by the late 1890s; with the exception of a small population in southern Florida, the cat no longer occurs east of

Texas (fig. 39).[23,36] However, some people believe that small, isolated puma populations still exist in remote parts of the cat's former range, or even that these populations are expanding. This belief has been fueled by actual specimens as well as by an increase in reports of sightings or sign of pumas in parts of the United States and Canada where the cat has not been found for some time.[36,37,38,39,40,41] Others have argued, especially in regard to eastern North America, that these cats are most likely escapees or released animals.[2] The puma's distribution in Central and South America was once extensive, and while it is still reported for most countries, its range has been reduced by habitat loss, overhunting of its prey, and direct persecution.[42,43,44,45,46]

ECOLOGY AND BEHAVIOR

Pumas live in a wide variety of habitats, including tropical rainforests, seasonally flooded savannas, semiarid scrub, and high mountains—from sea level up to elevations of 5,800 meters in southern Peru.[17,23,44] The fact that its habitats are so different across its broad geographic range reflects the puma's adaptability to a wide range of vegetative and environmental conditions.

An essential component of puma habitat is stalking cover, which can take many forms, including rocks, cliffs, sagebrush, or trees. In Idaho, Seidensticker and his colleagues concluded that pumas preferred areas that contained diverse habitats and topography, including dense stands of fir, open pine forests, and sagebrush-grassland openings, as well as bluffs and talus slopes.[47] In Wyoming, pumas preferred the steep, rugged slopes of canyonland habitats with mixed conifer and mountain mahogany cover. These habitats contained tall, dense overstory and understory cover, high relief, and abundant prey, all of which are important for resting, stalking, and feeding on kills. The cats generally avoided sagebrush grasslands.[48] In southern Utah, pumas avoided using agricultural lands, open meadows, and other openings, most probably because these areas lacked suitable stalking cover. Females with kittens used high-elevation sites within ancient lava flows and showed a preference for mixed aspen-spruce-fir and spruce-fir habitats with dense understories containing large lava boulders. The numerous cavities in these areas probably provide good protection for young. Seasonal differences in habitat use were related to the movement of prey—primarily mule deer—from high elevations to lower ones as snow depths increased higher up, forcing the deer to lower elevations. Intensively used areas were characterized

Figure 39. Distribution of the puma.

by dense overstory and understory vegetation with limited horizontal visibility.[49]

In southern Florida pumas spend their time in hardwood hammocks, pine flatwoods, cypress swamps, and cabbage palm woodlands. They use drier upland oak and pine forests more often than wetter mixed swamp forests and sawgrass marshes. During the daytime Florida pumas seek safe, shady sleeping spots, often resting in tall, dense clumps of saw palmetto.[50,51]

Habitat choice may also be influenced by competitors, although the findings are equivocal. In Manu National Park, Peru, pumas avoid waterside habitats and other densely forested areas that are the favorite haunts of the larger jaguar.[20] In the central-western portion of Brazil's Pantanal, pumas also use the drier habitats, avoiding the wetter areas frequented by jaguars.[52] In the southern Pantanal, however, both pumas and jaguars use gallery forest, tree islands, and blocks of semideciduous forest.[53] Jaguars and pumas in Iguaçu National Park, Brazil,[54] and in the Venezuelan llanos use many of the same forest types, but in the llanos pumas use more open habitats than jaguars.[55]

Although pumas are terrestrial, they can swim and climb trees when they need to, and they commonly take refuge in trees when pursued by dogs. These cats can be found hunting at any time of the day or night, but in most areas their activity peaks around dawn and dusk, and they rest during the middle of the day. Their activities coincide with those of their major prey, so the details of their hunting periods vary seasonally and from place to place. In the Idaho Primitive Area they are active in the daytime during summer to take advantage of the abundant diurnal ground squirrels.[47] In many areas, females with young sometimes hunt during the day, especially when the young are older and their demands for food are greater.[56] Pumas also become more nocturnal near, and shy away from, areas of logging operations or timber sales.[57] Weather is less of an influence on their movements than might be expected. Pumas in Idaho hunted during snowfall and light rain; the only time they sought shelter was during periods of heavy rain.[47]

Pumas travel extensively while hunting. Seidensticker reports that "pumas zigzagged through thickets, moved around large openings, under rock overhangs, up and down little ravines, and back and forth across small creeks." He adds that pumas were "constantly moving through the country in a way that optimized encounters with prey and provided them with the best possible positions in terms of cover from which to launch attacks."[47]

There are few measurements of the actual distances covered by pumas during daily activities, but males generally travel farther than females, and the travel distances of females vary with the age of their young. On several occasions Musgrave knew "an old 'tom' to cover more than 32 kilometers in a single night, traveling along the top of a high ridge and crossing over the peaks or highest spots as it reached them."[18] In New Mexico two adult males traveled 5.2 and 7.9 kilometers in a day, whereas the distances moved by four females with small kittens were much shorter: 1.0, 1.2, 2.5, and 3.1 kilometers in a day.[58] Pumas in the Santa Ana Mountains of southern California traveled an average of 6.4 kilometers per day, with most travel occurring at night. When hunting, the cats exhibited a punctuated movement pattern. Long periods of waiting at one location were followed by rapid movement to another location, where the cat again sat for a long time (an average of forty-two minutes). Unless the cat made a kill, this pattern was repeated many times a night.[59]

While learning to hunt, kittens walk slowly, scanning from one side of the trail to the other. If anything moves, they immediately focus on that area. Movement is clearly important in locating prey, as young hand-reared captive pumas were seen to pass within inches of rabbits that moved only once and managed to remain downwind. Surprisingly, these young kittens were able to follow even meager scent trails, and they also used sound cues to locate prey. Observations of these pumas "in training" suggested that experience plays a major part in prey selection, as they needed to have eaten a prey animal before they came to regard it as potential prey. An opossum encountered on a walk by one kitten was sniffed and batted around, but ignored as a potential meal. After having been fed several road-killed opossums, however, the kitten attacked and killed the next opossum he encountered.[60]

Feeding Ecology

Pumas kill and eat prey ranging in size from mice to moose, but prey size varies with latitude.[19,23] In temperate areas this cat regularly preys on animals as large as or larger than itself, whereas in tropical regions the puma preys mostly on animals that weigh less than half its own weight. This difference reflects the relative availability of different-sized prey and possibly competition from jaguars in the tropics.

Across most of North America. deer make up 60 to 80 percent of the puma's diet,[23] and the mean weight of prey taken is 39 to 48 kilograms.[19] However, in southwestern Florida, where deer numbers are low, pumas feed extensively on feral pigs, raccoons, and armadillos, and the mean weight of prey drops to 17 kilograms. Deer account for about a third of the cat's diet in this area.[19,61] Only 75 kilometers to the southeast, in Everglades National Park, where deer are more abundant, they are again the major prey of pumas, contributing 78 percent of the biomass consumed.[62]

In Central and South America pumas feed on a variety of small and medium-sized (1–15 kilograms) mammals such as brocket deer, pudu, paca, agoutis, hares, armadillos, viscachas, and several species of marsupials. Pumas also kill larger prey such as guanacos, marsh deer, pampas deer, peccaries, capybaras, rheas, and horses and cattle.[19,23,63,64,65] White-tailed deer were the dominant prey of pumas in Jalisco, Mexico.[66] In the Venezuelan llanos, juvenile collared peccary, white-tailed, deer, capybara, and caiman were the four most important prey of pumas. The mean weight of vertebrate prey consumed was 8.4 kilograms, but this decreased to 4.7 kilograms when livestock were excluded.[67]

The only long-term study of pumas in South America is from Torres del Paine National Park, Chile, near the extreme southern limit of the puma's range.[68,69] In this area guanacos and hares are the major prey, and when the guanaco population increased, pumas ate more guanacos. The mean weight of prey consumed increased from 16 to 33 kilograms as the puma's diet tracked changes in guanaco abundance.

Pumas can also be quite individualistic or idiosyncratic when it comes to prey selection. In Nevada some have learned how to kill wild horses,[70] and in Mexico a female puma killed 72 horses, mule yearlings, and colts over a nine-and-a-half-month period.[71] Pumas will also indulge in surplus killing sprees, particularly with domestic sheep.[23,72,73] In one incident, 192 sheep were killed in a single night.[4]

Cats are opportunistic predators, and thus it is not surprising that in many parts of North America puma diets change with the seasons. In Idaho the pumas' spring and summer diet reflects seasonal increases in the numbers of ground squirrels and small mammals as the cats switch to feeding on these smaller, more abundant prey.[47] In California the cats feed on pigs more often in the wet season, when they are most abundant.[74] Declines in their major prey may also force the cats to switch to alternative prey.[75]

Pumas will kill almost any animal that puts itself in a vulnerable position. With few exceptions, studies in North America show that older deer of both sexes and fawns or calves appear to be most vulnerable to puma predation, and there is some suggestion that bucks may be easier to catch in winter than at other times of the year.[76,77,78,79,80] In the Junction Wildlife Management Area of British Columbia, pumas specialize on bighorn sheep rams, taking advantage of the ram's restricted rear and peripheral vision.[81] In the Sheep River area of Alberta, Canada, male pumas specialize on moose calves, which make up 89 percent of their diet. Females in the same area feed mainly (80 percent) on elk and deer; only 16 percent of their diet is moose.[82] In southern Chile pumas prey intensively on young, yearling, and female guanacos in winter and spring. At this time of year most male guanacos are in large bachelor groups, which probably makes them more difficult to stalk.[69,83] In many areas prey are simply taken in proportion to their availability, and prime-aged, healthy animals and those in poor condition are equally likely to be killed.

Pumas take full advantage of grass, bushes, rocks, cliffs, or any feature of the terrain to stalk as close to their prey as possible before making the final rush. Successful attacks are usually launched from distances of 2.5 to 10 meters.[64,79,83] When stalking, pumas often try to maneuver themselves into a position where they can attack the prey from above.[69,83] In Alberta, radio-collared pumas commonly used ridges and tops of steep slopes and attacked downhill. Most kills were on hillsides averaging 15° to 20° slope. Interestingly, successful attack distances were different for moose and deer. Moose, most of which were calves, were killed 19 meters from the point where the cat launched the attack, whereas for deer the average distance was 52 meters, suggesting that deer are quicker.[82]

The likelihood of a successful kill obviously depends on the cat's ability to get close enough to the prey, which in turn depends on stalking cover. Few studies have examined cover as a critical variable in prey capture, but there are several general accounts that indicate its importance. Chilean pumas hunted in areas with greater than average shrub or tree cover; vegetative cover at forty-five kill sites was 22 percent, compared with 7 percent for the general area. The vast majority of kills in Chile were made on vegetated slopes or in gullies.[69] Similarly, in Idaho most kills were made in rough, broken terrain on bluffs, on densely forested slopes, or in brush-covered ravine and creek bottoms.[47,77] In the Diablo Mountains, California, three-quarters of all puma kills were found in creek bottoms.[74] Clearly, deer and elk are more vulnerable to puma predation when they spend time in these types of terrain. Puma predation on pronghorn was negligible on the open plains, the pronghorn's typical habitat, but a population living in an area with rugged, brushy terrain was vulnerable. In this area, puma predation on pronghorn females was high enough to decrease the population.[31]

Once in position, the cat launches itself at the prey, often catching it on the side or rump with its front claws. The impact knocks the animal off balance, and while holding on with its claws, the puma delivers a killing bite to the neck or throat. Reconstruction of events based on signs in snow indicates that many kills are made cleanly, whereas at other times there is evidence of a struggle. Death is not always instantaneous, even with a neck bite. Hunters in California watched a puma chase a female mule deer into a creek bottom. When the cat emerged into a small clearing it was carrying the deer, its jaws clamped firmly on the back of the deer's neck. When one hunter fired a warning shot to his partner, the cat dropped the deer, which then raised its head. The cat quickly seized the deer by the neck and carried it off.[84] Pumas kill animals such as rodents, ground squirrels, hares, piglets, and small deer with a bite to the back of the neck; larger prey are usually killed with a throat bite, and death results from suffocation. Adult elk, which may be as much as seven times the body weight of the puma, are killed with a throat bite or, less commonly, by leaping onto the elk's back and breaking the neck with a bite just below the base of the skull.[77,85] Researchers in Canada observed that some adult elk and moose calves killed by puma bore no canine marks on the neck or throat; they suspect that the animals' necks were broken by the impact of the attack.[82]

The attack can be a dangerous moment for the cat, especially if the prey is large. Deer and elk have sharp antlers and hooves, and pumas have been injured and even killed in struggles on steep and unstable terrain. There are records of pumas being killed during attacks on burros, elk, and mule deer, while others have died from injuries inflicted by their prey.[59,70,86] On one occasion the carcasses of a puma and mule deer were found lying together; the puma had evidently died of a broken neck sustained in the struggle. One puma was found at the base of a cliff with a broken skull, and another puma skull was found with a piece of mountain mahogany wood piercing the braincase, an injury that may have happened during a struggle with a prey animal. Other accounts record pumas dying from massive chest injuries, impalement on branches, and toxemia.[87,88,89] Such fatalities are more likely to happen to inexperienced cats or old and infirm ones. In one puma study, 27 percent of natural mortality was related to injuries sustained while trying to capture prey.[89]

Any incapacitating injury to a solitary hunter is likely to result in death. Hornocker recalls an adult female who was seriously injured during an attempt to capture an elk. Tracks in the snow showed that the cat and deer had slid down a steep slope and struck a tree. When the puma was captured three weeks later, she was found to have a broken jaw; her two lower canines had been torn out, and she had puncture wounds on her shoulder and hip. She was in very poor condition and had lost 30 pounds in three weeks.[77] Serious injuries are not always sustained in battles with large prey; puma have been found with numerous porcupine quills embedded in the face and lips. But some puma feces consist almost entirely of porcupine quills,

suggesting that the cat can swallow them without much harm.[4]

Though the puma is lightly built, it appears to be a match for the leopard when it comes to feats of strength. Pumas can drag and carry their kills for considerable distances, and on very rare occasions may take their prey into trees. In Arizona, M. E. Musgrave of the former U.S. Biological Survey reported seeing "a horse weighing eight or nine hundred pounds which a mountain lion has dragged twenty-five or thirty feet, as proven by tracks in the snow."[18]

Prey killed in the open are almost always dragged into some brush or dense thicket before the puma begins eating. The cat remains near the kill—in one case for as long as nineteen days—with only occasional short trips away until the carcass is completely consumed.[47] In 1928 Gilbert Wade spent the summer in the Sequoia National Park working as a fire lookout. From his tower he was able to watch a female puma and her two kittens for more than two months, and was even lucky enough to see her make a kill. Wade describes how the puma carried the doe to a level place and then began to eat.

> The lion then walked back, and placing her left foot on the flank of the deer ripped the stomach open with the right. She then tore away the flank of the deer, eating some of it and the short ribs. She cleaned the small intestines by pulling them from under her foot and ate a considerable amount of them. She ate well into the loin before she seemed satisfied. All during this time she would stop and look around at very short intervals. Apparently at some given signal, the two cubs now came down out of the near-by brush. The lioness stood guard while the youngsters ate from the hams and insides.[4]

After the kill, the cat may begin to eat immediately or may spend time preparing the carcass. Pumas usually pluck birds before eating them,[90] and they sometimes pluck hair and quills from mammalian prey.[4] Regardless of where they start eating, pumas feed in a crouched position, with the head on one side, slicing off large chunks of meat with the carnassial teeth.

Some older anecdotal accounts suggest that pumas can eat half a large male deer in a night, but these are obviously exaggerations. Jay Bruce, a California mountain lion hunter, weighed the full stomachs of the many pumas he shot and found that they had typically eaten 2.2 to 3.6 kilograms of meat. He thought that this represented a large meal for a puma.[91] More recently, captive feeding trials showed that pumas can eat as much as 10 kilograms in a twenty-four-hour period,[92] although in most zoos pumas are fed 1.6 to 5.5 kilograms of fresh meat per day and fasted one day a week.

An energetics model predicted that rates of consumption for single adults should vary from 2.2 to 2.7 kilograms for females and 3.4 to 4.3 kilograms for males.[56] In California an adult female and her two five-month-old young made six kills in twenty-nine days; together the family consumed an estimated 149 kilograms of meat, or 5.1 kilograms per cat per day.[74] One puma, or possibly two, fed on an adult female elk kill for twenty-seven days, consuming an estimated 165 kilograms, or 6.1 kilograms per day.[93] An adult male puma in Alberta ate substantially more than females in the same area, consuming an average of 7.2 kilograms per day between the beginning of December and early April. The average daily intake for a female without kittens was 4.6 kilograms.[82] Pumas typically consume all edible parts of a carcass, leaving little other than bones, hooves, and stomach contents. However, in areas with abundant prey, pumas sometimes feed lightly and then depart.

Pumas that intend to return to a carcass sometimes cover the remains with leaves, grass, sand, snow, or whatever is available. One puma larder discovered in Montana contained the relatively fresh remains of a mountain sheep and two deer.[94] The puma's habit of covering the remains of a carcass with leaves and debris has proved fertile ground for apocryphal hunting stories, and a scan of the old literature might easily convince one that the cat regularly takes advantage of any and all opportunities to cover exhausted travelers with leaves. Many hunters and woodsmen have written of spending the night out in the forest wrapped in a blanket, only to awaken the next morning covered with a pile of leaves. Most of the stories conclude with the hunter awakening just as the female puma returns with her kittens, and almost all of the hunters manage to shoot the puma just before it attacks. In his thorough review of the topic, Jim Bob Tinsley relates the story of a Pennsylvania wilderness hunter named Jonathan Wheaton who lay down to rest on Capouse Mountain and dropped off to sleep. According to Tinsley, "He awakened to find himself covered with sticks and leaves. Knowing the habits of the puma, Wheaton decided that a female had reserved him for her offspring and would soon return. He climbed a nearby tree and

shot the mother when she came back with her two young."[3]

Puma kills are often scavenged by other mammals, including coyotes, foxes, bobcats, wolves, pigs, and bears, despite the fact that the vicinity of these kills would seem to be a very dangerous place for the smaller carnivores as the cat sometimes rests nearby and guards the remains. Studies in Idaho and Montana indicate that bobcats and coyotes scavenging at puma caches are sometimes killed by the puma.[95,96] It is difficult to assess the quantity of meat lost to these scavengers, but in Idaho seventy-nine of a hundred puma kills were scavenged by coyotes, and groups of coyotes often consumed or cached the remains of deer or elk carcasses in less than twenty-four hours.[95] Losses of this magnitude can affect the number of kills a puma makes. In the Junction Wildlife Management Area of central British Columbia, coyotes harassed pumas at kills, sometimes causing the puma to abandon the carcass. In one area where coyote populations were not controlled, the predation rate of a female puma with kittens was 2.6 kills per week, whereas the predation rate of a female with kittens was only 1.1 per week in an area with coyote control.[81]

Consorting males and females occasionally share kills, but most puma groups consist of a female and her kittens. Females with large kittens may associate with a male at kills, but they do so rarely when their kittens are small, presumably because of the possibility of infanticide.[47,76,79,97,98]

Several attempts have been made to estimate kill rates and the number of deer a puma consumes per year. In Utah biologists estimate that a puma would have to kill an adult-sized deer every eight to sixteen days, and that a female with three large kittens would require one deer every three days. Overall, this equals one deer a week for each adult puma.[56] Hornocker followed an adult female and her three 70-pound kittens for eighteen days, during which the family killed and ate four mule deer. Another female with three 70-pound kittens killed one elk in twelve days. He concluded that a mature cat kills a deer every ten to fourteen days in the winter.[77] Estimates from Arizona are very similar, and suggest that a single female kills a deer or calf every ten days, but a female with kittens must kill more often, about once every seven days.[78] In the Sheep River area of Alberta, an adult female without young killed mule deer, principally fawns, once every thirteen days, consuming about 2.5 kilograms of meat per day. A female with small kittens killed a deer every ten days, and killed one every seven days when her young were a year old. An adult male puma in the same area killed four moose calves in fifty-two days, or one calf every thirteen days.[82] Pumas in California killed an estimated forty-eight large and fifty-eight small prey annually, and spent an average of 2.9 days with each large kill.[59]

Hunting success rates are difficult to determine, but when only the final attack is considered as an attempt, the rate can be high. Hornocker found that thirty-seven out of forty five, or 82 percent, of attacks on deer resulted in a kill.[77] In Argentina, only one of ten attacks on viscachas was successful.[64]

For years human hunters considered pumas vermin and pests, believing that they had a significant negative impact on deer herds. Pumas were shot, trapped, and poisoned in the belief that control of the cats would result in more deer. Because of this perceived threat to deer herds, numerous attempts have been made to assess the impact of pumas on prey populations. Results from studies in many areas suggest that puma predation is inconsequential in regulating prey populations; prey numbers increased in several of the areas while puma populations remained stable.[28,69,71,74,77,88,99] In other studies, puma predation appeared to be an important factor depressing deer numbers.[78,100,101] However, few if any studies demonstrate conclusively the limiting nature of puma predation, although where deer populations are already low due to overhunting, severe winters, or poor recruitment, pumas can temporarily limit those populations. Under normal circumstances, social constraints are thought to maintain puma populations below a level set by prey densities.[47]

A notable exception to this pattern may occur where the cat has expanded its range into previously unoccupied areas. Berger and Wehausen argue that pumas were historically absent from the Great Basin Desert of Nevada, but following human introduction of livestock into the region, the natural vegetation was modified to favor mule deer, which thus supported the expansion of pumas into the area. Native bighorn sheep, which had experienced little effective predation prior to the arrival of pumas, were decimated in some localities, and attempts to reestablish bighorn sheep in a few areas were accomplished only by controlling puma numbers.[102] However, translocations of bighorn sheep into areas with higher mule deer densities appear to be successful even in the presence of pumas. Bighorn sheep from Nevada and Arizona were translocated to Colorado between 1983 and 1985, and

no losses to pumas were noted there as recently as 1991.[73] In the Sheep River area of Alberta, where a variety of other ungulate prey are available, bighorn sheep are seldom killed by pumas.[82] Results from a study in New Mexico, where pumas were removed as part of an experiment, showed that puma control efforts were largely ineffective in increasing bighorn sheep populations.[99] However, removal of pumas was apparently responsible for reversing a population decline among Sierra Nevada bighorn sheep,[103] and removal has been proposed as a management option to enhance the recovery of an endangered population of bighorn sheep in the Peninsular Ranges, California.[104]

Social Organization

Like most felids, pumas live alone, and apart from associations for mating purposes, the only prolonged contact is between females and their kittens. Pumas do, however, maintain contact with conspecifics through occasional direct encounters and more frequently by various visual, auditory, and olfactory forms of indirect communication. Because the cats are adaptable to such a wide range of environmental circumstances, their spatial arrangements and social dynamics vary from place to place. In general, breeding adult females show a high degree of site fidelity, living out their lives in areas that are variously called territories, home ranges, or home areas. Male ranges are not as fixed spatially and tend to shift as vacancies occur. The home ranges of resident males typically overlap the ranges of one or more females, and the ranges of resident males may overlap one another extensively, slightly, or not at all. Similarly, the ranges of resident females may show little overlap or overlap extensively. For both sexes, even where ranges overlap, there are likely to be core areas within those ranges that are not used by other cats of the same sex. Within the breeding population, sex ratios typically favor females. Once established, a resident usually holds an area until it dies or, in the case of males, is ousted by another male. Males replace males and females replace females. This system of breeding ranges is overlain by another segment of the population that includes nonbreeding young adults, which are dispersers, transients, or immigrants, and older nonreproductive animals. These animals often travel widely, crossing and recrossing occupied areas in search of a vacancy and making probes into uninhabited terrain looking for suitable places to settle. In some areas daughters have established a home range next to or partially overlapping their mother's range or have acquired their mother's range following her death.[23,47,49,58,70,73,88,97,99,105,106,107,108]

Females do not usually breed until they have secured a range and established themselves as residents.[47,108,109] The number of female residents in an area usually remains fairly stable, since female ranges are closely linked to resources needed to rear young. The number of resident females can increase if prey populations increase substantially or if daughters carve out ranges next to their mothers.[99,109,110] Long-term residents are undoubtedly thoroughly familiar with their home ranges, which is important for hunting success and consequently for rearing offspring.[111] Females generally retain their ranges for several years. Male tenure is shorter, and male ranges are more likely to fluctuate in size as neighboring males compete for access to more females.

This relatively stable situation can be altered by sport hunting.[112,113] Hunting keeps the social system in a state of flux, as it removes residents who normally would have remained in their areas for several years. The social dynamics between individuals that know each other well versus those between animals that are still jockeying for space are likely to be quite different.[114] Logan and his colleagues speculate that "frequent removal of established resident males and the consequent vacancy of home areas may increase the activity of transient males and the amount of competition for available areas. Unaware of the social status of other lions and without the regular communication systems maintained by residents through scrapes, males may encounter other males more frequently and compete for tenure (dominance) directly through fighting."[115] In the Sheep River area of Alberta, a single male was dominant over six to eight females for seven years. Following his removal by hunters, ownership of his former range was contested by three males, including the previous resident's neighbor. Interestingly, the dominant male himself had expanded his range when his neighbor was shot by a hunter years earlier. Harvest strategies that remove a large segment of the male population are also potentially disruptive because of the increase in kitten mortality that could result.[107] New males may kill kittens, since loss of a litter induces estrus in females. Hunted populations are characterized by rapid home range turnover and few or no transients, as this segment of the population rapidly fills the vacancies created by the shooting of residents.[58,107,116]

Sport hunting is a major source of puma mortality in many parts of the western United States, account-ing for 20 to 50 percent of the annual mortality in such states as Arizona, Colorado, Nevada, Montana, and Texas.[23,70,73,116,117] In Alberta, harvest levels are set so that only about 10 percent of the population is taken annually.[21] What effect hunting has on puma population dynamics is not well known, but two studies offer some insights into the process. A field experiment in southern Utah simulated a sport harvest with a one-time removal of 27 percent of resident pumas. The natural deaths of five resident adults raised the level to 42 percent. The adult segment of the population recovered in nine months, but it took two years for the population to recover to its preharvest level, suggesting that an annual harvest would further slow population recovery. The Utah experiment shows that both the level of harvest and the sex and age of the cats removed affects the recovery of a population; loss of resident adult females has the greatest impact.[118] In a classic piece of work in New Mexico, the effects of an extreme harvest were examined in an experimental removal of thirteen pumas (53 percent of resident adults and 58 percent of independents) from a portion of the study area. It took thirty-one months for the adult segment of the population to recover to pretreatment levels; at recovery, the new adult sex ratio was the same as before the removal.[99] In both experiments, immigrants and young born in the area formed the new populations.

Calculations of the impact of sport hunting on puma populations must include natural mortality. The question is, can hunted populations sustain harvest levels of 20 to 50 percent in addition to deaths from other causes, or does hunting mortality compensate for losses due to natural mortality? In a nonhunted population in southern Florida, the average annual mortality rate was 17 percent,[119] and in another unhunted population in southern Utah it was 28 percent.[118] Some mortality, such as that related to accidents and prey capture, will occur regardless of puma density and would be additive to other mortality. If harvest mortality in hunted populations is additive to natural mortality, then these populations could conceivably suffer annual losses of 40 to 60 percent, a rate that could soon lead to local extinction.

Home range sizes of pumas vary considerably across their geographic distribution, and the smallest ranges tend to occur in areas where prey densities are high and prey are not migratory.[23,88] In southeastern British Columbia, annual female ranges measured 55 square kilometers and those of males 151 square kilometers.[97]

By contrast, in southern Utah the annual ranges of resident females and males averaged 685 and 826 square kilometers respectively.[109] In general, home range sizes of females are smaller than those of males in the same area. For females, range size is set by a number of ecological variables, the most important of which is prey availability. Female range sizes also tend to decline with increasing puma density, whereas those of males tend to increase. Male ranges are keyed more to female distribution than to prey density, and thus larger ranges are thought to be correlated with increased mating opportunities.[47,88,99,108,109,110]

Like home range sizes, puma densities vary by several orders of magnitude. The lowest reported adult densities (0.37 to 0.5 per 100 square kilometers) are from southern Utah, which is also an area with extremely large puma home ranges.[105] Densities exceeding 4 adults per 100 square kilometers do not appear to be common in North America, although estimates of 7–8 per 100 square kilometers are reported for concentrations in winter, but these densities include all age classes.[23,97,98,99,116,117]

Most felids maintain their land tenure system and social interaction patterns through the deposition of scent and visual marks,[120] and the puma is no exception. However, surprisingly little is known about the puma's patterns of scent marking and communication, given that the cat has been studied at many sites and that research has been ongoing for ten to twenty years at several of those sites. Most of the available information on scent marking and home range maintenance was gathered in the 1970s by Seidensticker and others involved in the landmark study of pumas in Idaho.[47]

The principal mode of communication appears to be via scrapes and fecal mounds; males make nearly all of the scrapes, and females create most of the mounds.[47,58,72] Scrapes are usually made by pressing both hind feet to the ground and pushing backward in a stroking motion. The scratches or marks left in the soil, leaf litter, or snow vary in size from 15 to 30 centimeters wide and 15 to 46 centimeters long. Feces and urine are sometimes deposited on the scrape, thus drawing both visual and olfactory attention to the mark. Both males and females sometimes bury their feces, and the resulting piles of earth and debris form characteristic mounds about a meter in diameter. These scat mounds are often associated with kills and are frequently made near prominent trees, so it is likely that these piles also serve a communication function.

Neither sex sprays urine in the manner of other large felids, which is very unusual, considering that this behavior is common in all other felid species studied to date.[121,122]

Like snow leopards, pumas living in mountainous terrain tend to scrape in predictable places, such as along ridges, under rimrocks, in narrow gaps or mountain passes, and by water sources and kills. Topographic features probably restrict or channel the cats' movements through certain routes, and from a communication standpoint these pathways are efficient sites for marking. Seidensticker found that resident males scraped more frequently in areas where their ranges abutted or overlapped those of neighboring males, suggesting that scrapes function as boundary markers.[47] In another study scrapes were scattered throughout each male's home range and not concentrated at boundaries, but at this site male ranges overlapped extensively. In this case, the scrapes were viewed as "bulletin boards" that males and females visited to ascertain the presence of other pumas in the area.[58]

Pumas also communicate with a variety of vocalizations, including a purr, mew, hiss, growl, and spit.[8,123,124] Another close-range vocalization is a muffled, short, atonal call of low amplitude, which sounds like "wah-wah"; this call is peculiar in that it is found only in the puma, Eurasian lynx, bobcat, jaguarundi, caracal, both species of golden cats, and probably the serval.[125] Pumas do not roar, and their only long-range call is the well-known "scream," which has received a great deal of attention, but it is not often heard.[47] Writers have described the call as being "terror striking," "like the shriek of a vampire woman," and "unearthly." McCabe described the sound as "much like the roar of an African lion in a zoo, although of a higher pitch and shorter duration."[126] Vernon Bailey, chief field naturalist of the U.S. Biological Survey, described the scream as "heavy and prolonged, slightly rising and falling and fairly well indicated by the letters o-o-W-O-U-H-u-u."[4]

The most frequently heard vocalization seems to be a shrill, whistle-like call. Stanley Brock described the development of this call in his tame young female puma named Leemo: "Every time I approached her, or passed close by, I would call her by name, and very often give her a tidbit as well. She invariably responded with a high pitched, cheeping, whistle. It is a very difficult sound to imitate, but if you spell the meeow of a cat with a *wh* instead of a *m*, and try to whistle the sound instead of speaking it . . ." He added, "Later when Leemo grew up, the call became loud enough to be audible on a still day at 300 yards."[127]

Researchers studying pumas in the San Andres Mountains of New Mexico also heard high-pitched whistles from a family group as far away as 300 meters, but it was not clear how many cats called or how far apart they were from each other. An orphaned female also whistled, but the "vocalization consisted of an upward scaling, piercing whistle followed by a downward scaling whistle and 3 short monotonal whistles."[58] Researchers heard a variety of other vocalizations during five male-female associations, including "low gargling growls, throaty yowls, squeaks and whistles." The yowls and whistles were heard up to 200 meters away, and whistles, squeaks, and growls were heard when an observer was within 50 to 100 meters of the pair. Solitary pumas of both sexes also gave "ouch" calls; most of these calls were made during crepuscular hours and were thought to signify frustration or serve as a form of advertisement.[99]

Vocalizations are also used to indicate sexual receptivity, although urine marks are probably a more frequently used form of advertisement. George Rabb, director of the Brookfield Zoo, describes a female's estrous behavior as being "marked by persistent yowling or caterwauling much like that of a domestic cat but amplified and harsher," and added that "the male replied to her cries with less loud yowls of his own."[128] Besides this "screaming," rubbing, rolling, clawing, and other behavioral changes are also reported for captive females during the early stages of sexual receptivity.[129,130] There are few observations of sexual activity among free-ranging pumas, although what was thought to be the onset of estrus in a puma in Big Bend National Park, Texas, was marked by a series of loud, snarling yowls and an increase in the frequency of scent marking.[28] Caterwauling by a female puma in Carlsbad Caverns National Park, New Mexico, occurred during a suspected estrus. Ten bouts of calling, totaling at least five hundred vocalizations, were heard over a six-hour period, and during this time the female walked 5 kilometers. About three months later the female gave birth.[117]

Reproduction and Development

Most of what is known about the puma's estrous cycle comes from observations of captive animals. Data from captive pumas suggest that estrus, or the period of receptivity, lasts about seven to eight days, but ranges from four to twelve days.[128,129,130,131] In the wild, breeding pairs have stayed together for one to sixteen days, but one to four days is typical.[47,58,99,108,132] Behavioral observations of captive females suggest that the length of the estrous cycle varies from twenty-three to sixty days, but information from radio-tagged pumas indicates that the estrous cycle is three to four weeks long.[99,133]

Pumas in southern Florida cycle again and mate soon after a litter is lost, regardless of the time of year or how long the litter was reared.[133] However, females from northern latitudes often do not resume mating activities for several months.[88] A female in northern Idaho, for example, may not cycle again if her next litter would be born in the winter or at a time when survival of young is likely to be low. Females in New Mexico mated again, on average, 101 days after losing a litter.[99]

There is wide variation in the age of first reproduction for female pumas, the youngest recorded being 18 months and the oldest 43 months of age.[23,70,134] In a large sample of known-age females in New Mexico, the average age of first reproduction was 29.1 months (range 19–37 months).[99] Variation in the age of first reproduction is thought to reflect the age at which a female acquires a home range, with residency being a prerequisite for breeding. Among captive pumas, the age of first breeding ranges from 21.8 months to 33 months.[129,130] The age of male reproductive maturity is largely unknown. Of six known-age males in New Mexico, the average age of first reproductive activity was 24.3 months (range 21–27 months), with successful matings occurring in two associations.[99] A captive-raised male sired a kitten when he was two years old.[135] When their cubs survive to independence, females give birth every twelve to thirty-four months, but on average, interbirth intervals vary from seventeen to twenty months.[70,73,97,99,105,107,115] However, not all females in a population may reproduce successfully. In New Mexico, of fifty-two adult females, only thirty-nine (75 percent) produced live young.[99]

The mating behavior of pumas is similar to that of other large cats. Initially, the female undergoes a period of mixed aggression and solicitation. As her receptivity increases, courtship becomes more active, with calling, body rubbing, and close following by the male. In New Mexico, three females associated with two different males during a single heat period. One female was with a male for two days, and over the next three days she was with a different male, suggesting that the estrous period was five days long.[99] During copulation the male often grips the neck fur of the female with his teeth, and mating may be accompanied by screams and yowls from both male and female.

Pumas are thought to be induced ovulators, in which repeated copulation is necessary to stimulate ovulation.[136] One study reported copulation rates of two to twenty per day over a six- to eleven-day period.[129] Another study noted that one female mated eleven times in eighty minutes; another engaged in nine copulations in sixty minutes, while another pair mated twenty-three times in ten hours.[130,137] Copulations lasted less than one minute, as is typical of large felids.[138] Conception rates in pumas, as in other felids, do not appear to be high.[23] In New Mexico, of 147 breeding associations, only 33 (22 percent) resulted in kittens.[99]

After a gestation period of about ninety-two to ninety-three days, the female gives birth to a litter of one to six kittens (mean litter size = 2.67).[23] Large litters are not uncommon, and an analysis of 258 litters showed that nearly half (43.4 percent) consisted of three kittens, almost a third (29.8 percent) of two kittens, and about a fifth (18.2 percent) of four kittens. These numbers were generally obtained at one or more months post-birth, however, so litter size at birth may be slightly higher.[139] In New Mexico, the average size of 53 litters within a month post-birth was 3.02, and the mean size of first litters was 3.38.[99]

Birth dens are secluded and protected, and can be in a variety of concealed places such as in shallow caves or rock piles, in thickets, under overhanging foliage, or among the roots of a fallen tree. Two birth dens in southern Florida were in thickets surrounded by nearly impenetrable vegetation, and both were oval depressions measuring 1 to 2 meters long by 0.5 to 1 meters wide.[51] A birth den in California was described as a lair "about 6 feet long and 2 feet wide. The nest was bedded with pine needles, probably carried in the den by wood rats for their nests at some time. . . . There was also a small opening, perhaps 8 inches in diameter, through which the sun would shine on the kittens in the nest."[4]

Surprisingly, even in temperate North America, births have been recorded in all months of the year. However, in areas where winters are severe, the majority of births occur between April and September.[23,88,107,139] The seasonal availability of food may be as important as weather in influencing when young are born, and it may be that early fall births, as have been reported in Utah, represent a compromise between

the two constraints of cold weather and food availability.[140] In southern Utah, females have extremely large ranges, measuring 500 square kilometers or more, and concentrations of mule deer, the cat's primary prey, occur only in the winter. Females with young kittens are confined to a small subset of their usual home range, and they must be able to secure food regularly and predictably. The only way a female can meet these increased nutritional demands within a small area is to exploit a localized and concentrated source of food. Winter concentrations of mule deer may provide such a resource. In New Mexico, of seventy-eight litters, thirty-two (41 percent) were born in July–September, which coincides with the peak of mule deer fawn births.[99]

Newborn puma kittens have densely spotted, brownish buff fur and weigh about 400 to 500 grams.[23,141,142] The markings remain obvious until the kittens are four months old, become somewhat faded by eight months, and are difficult to see except on the hindquarters by ten months. The kittens' eyes are light blue when they first open between days five and fourteen. When the young are about eight months old their eyes start to change color, and by sixteen months their eyes are the same yellow-brown as those of adults.[88,130,143]

The mother is with her kittens almost constantly during the first few days after birth. A four-day-old kitten nursed eight to twelve times per twenty-four hours.[143] By the time the young are a week old they are able to go for longer periods without nursing, and the mother spends more time hunting. A radio-tagged female in southern Florida spent more than half her time (57 percent) at the den when her kittens were six to seventeen days old, but this decreased to 31 percent when the young were twenty-four to thirty-four days old.[132] Even in the first weeks, females are sometimes away from the den for more than twenty-four hours, and in Idaho some females left their small kittens unattended for as long as two days.[47,77]

During the first month of the kittens' life the den is the female's center of activity. The home ranges of two radio-tagged females in southern Florida decreased by more than 80 percent immediately after the birth of their young; similarly, the ranges of females in Alberta decreased by 50 percent or more when they had kittens.[107,132] This sudden home range contraction after the birth of young is common to all the large cats, so much so that field biologists now use it as a reliable way to determine when a radio-collared cat gives birth.

By the time they are two weeks old, puma kittens usually have their eyes open and are beginning to play and move around. Some kittens attempt to walk as early as a week after birth, but most remain wobbly until they are two weeks old. By three weeks of age the kittens are grooming themselves, and seven- to eight-week-old kittens are quite agile. Kittens continue to nurse until two months of age.[99,130,143] There are vague references to puma mothers taking meat back to their kittens at a den, but evidence of this behavior is difficult to find. During fifteen years of tracking pumas with hounds, Roy McBride recorded three instances of females carrying meat back to their young. He described one instance: "By one o'clock we had trailed the lion to a large cliff near the river where the dogs found her, three kittens, and a piece of deer shoulder. The kittens didn't look old enough to be weaned or to be eating meat, but nevertheless, the meat was there, whether to accustom the kittens to it or to be of future use to the female."[71]

At about six months of age the young begin to travel and hunt with their mother, but they do not accompany her all the time. In Utah, the tracks of kittens less than seven months old were observed with their mother's only 19 percent of the time the adult's tracks were located.[144] The time when the young begin to accompany their mother on hunts is the start of a period of great nutritional stress for the mother. Not only must she contend with their potential interference during the hunt, but she must also increase the number of kills she makes, and as the young get larger their needs increase. Calculations based on energy requirements and kill frequencies suggest that a female without young has to kill a mule deer about every sixteen days to sustain herself. However, for a female with three three-month-old young, the rate increases to one deer every nine days, and by the time the young are fifteen months old, it is one deer every three days.[56] These nutritional demands could be filled by jackrabbits or ground squirrels, but only when these smaller prey are superabundant—a female and three fifteen-month-old young would need seven or eight jackrabbits a day to survive. The high energy requirements of females with young have led to the speculation that breeding populations of pumas may exist only where deer-sized prey are abundant.[56] In areas where large prey are not abundant, kitten survival is probably reduced, as females have to travel widely or exist on small prey.

Young pumas acquire their permanent canines by eight months of age, and the eruption of these teeth coincides roughly with the youngest age at which orphaned young have survived. Three six-month-old kittens orphaned when their mother was accidentally killed by dogs during a capture attempt remained together for about three months. The male managed to kill a deer when he was nine months old, but the two females died before they were a year old.[140] McBride recounts two instances of six- to seven-month-old kittens surviving without their mother, in one case by preying on goats and sheep.[71] In New Mexico, two female kittens orphaned at 7.5 and 9.8 months of age survived; one stayed on her natal range and produced a litter, and the other was killed by a subadult male puma.[99]

There are two records of successful reintroductions involving orphaned female pumas. Both females were released into the wild at about seven months of age, and both established home ranges. One of the females bred and raised a litter four years after being released.[145] Hornocker and his colleagues believe that young pumas should not be released until they are at least six or seven months old, and preferably at a time when ground squirrels and small mammals are abundant. They also suggest that the kittens be raised in seclusion and fed in a manner that prevents attachment to people or the association of humans with food. One of three siblings released by Hornocker and his colleagues had obviously learned to associate food with humans and the field station where it was raised. This cat eventually had to be destroyed as it was believed to pose a potential threat to people.

Attempts to train captive-raised puma kittens for a life in the wild have met with mixed success. A young male puma whose training was started at one month of age was, by ten months of age, able to hunt and stalk natural prey, but retraining of three six- to fifteen-month-old pumas was less successful.[60] A major problem is, of course, concern over the release of a human-socialized puma in the proximity of people. Three captive-raised animals were included in a group of ten pumas released in northern Florida as part of an experiment to evaluate the feasibility of reintroduction. The male and two females adapted quickly to the area, all three established home ranges, and the male mated successfully with another experimental cat. However, this same male was later removed from a hunt club after members complained that it was not wary of humans. The females were removed from the wild at the end of the one-year study.[146]

Young pumas are typically not independent until they are at least a year old. In one sample of thirty kittens from eighteen litters, the average age of independence was 15.2 months (range 10 to 21 months).[107] In New Mexico, the average age of independence was 14 months for six males and 13 months for nine females.[99] In southern Florida, young male pumas become independent at 12 to 18 months of age.[147]

When the young are about a year old, the close association of family members starts to break down, and individuals begin spending more time alone, although littermates occasionally remain together for a few months while continuing to use their mother's range.[99,107,108] Sometimes a female will leave her young at a kill or rest site within her range and not return, thereby initiating the process of independence.[47,148] Independence is followed shortly by dispersal, or movement away from the natal area, although there are observations of some animals staying on in their natal ranges until they were twenty-six months old.[74]

Information compiled for 148 young pumas (70 females, 78 males) from thirteen different studies shows that young usually disperse between the ages of fourteen to twenty-one months, or in most cases prior to reproductive maturity.[23,73,97,99,105,108,148] However, not all young disperse. Two male pumas remained in their natal ranges and at least twenty-one females were philopatric, staying in or near their natal ranges. Some of these females acquired the vacant range of their mother, whereas others settled in a vacant range adjoining their mother's range.

The degree of female philopatry varies among and within areas. The majority of subadult females in the New Mexico, Utah, and Alberta populations stayed on or near their natal ranges; others dispersed short distances.[99,105,107] In other areas only a few females stayed, and the majority dispersed. Why some females stay and others leave, even in the same area, is not known. The answer probably lies in a combination of factors, including the frequency of vacant ranges, population density on and off the study area, habitat quality, kitten mortality, and hunting pressure.

Dispersing subadult male pumas travel extensively, often spending several months in the process, and travel distances of 85 to 100 kilometers are common. Indeed, the average dispersal distance for eight males in New Mexico was 101 kilometers.[99] Several males have been found 150 to 275 kilometers from their birthplaces, and one young male marked in Wyoming was later killed in Colorado, about 480 kilometers from his natal area.[16] In contrast, the average dispersal distance for females who left their natal area was about 40 kilometers, although there are a few accounts of females traveling more than 100 kilometers.

The greater dispersal distances of males partly reflect the fact that ranges of resident males are several times larger than those of females; thus, a subadult male has to travel significantly farther to locate areas where there are no or few dominant males, but where mature females and an adequate prey base exist. Females, on the other hand, appear to stay as close to their natal area as they can, a pattern that results in small enclaves of related females.[99] Such an arrangement has also been documented for tigers.[149]

Dispersal appears to be a hazardous time in a puma's life, but it is very difficult to collect mortality or survival data on this phase of life. In many cases young pumas simply disappear, their fates unknown. Resident male pumas are responsible for most of the mortality among dispersers. In Florida, two dispersing males and one transient male were killed by a resident male.[51,108] Four females and at least seven males trying to establish residency in New Mexico were killed by adult males,[58,99] and in six other studies there are records of adult males killing subadult or yearling animals.[71,73,97,107,148,150] Intraspecific strife is thus a major source of mortality. The other major sources of known mortality among dispersers are sport hunting or collisions with vehicles.[99,107,108,115,117] In California two of nine dispersers survived to establish a range,[148] and in western Colorado two of twelve survived to establish a range.[73] Once an animal has established a breeding range, its risk of death is greatly reduced, and females in particular have been known to live in the same area for as long as ten years.[74]

A study in the Santa Ana Mountains of southern California showed that dispersing male pumas occupied a series of small, temporary ranges during the several months it took them to find a permanent place to live.[148] The only female disperser in the study covered at least 342 kilometers during her four months of wandering, and, finding nowhere suitable to settle, she returned to her natal area, where she died shortly thereafter. In this highly urbanized landscape the cats often moved along the urban-wildland interface, probing habitat peninsulas and occasionally venturing into urban areas. Corridors, one of which was 6 kilometers long, were traversed only at night, but even narrow (100-meter-wide) forested habitats were suitable as corridors. Areas with artificial lighting were avoided by dispersers. The cats crossed under freeways and highways via drainages, bridges, or culverts.[148,151] Pumas in southern Florida are also known to use underpasses along Interstate 75.[152]

Pumas can be long-lived animals in captivity, reaching nineteen to twenty years of age,[153] but like other cats, they do not fare nearly so well in the wild. There are records of two wild-caught 17-year-old pumas from the state of Washington,[154] although in a long-term study in California females lived an average of 7.5 years, while males lived just over 6.5 years. One female was at least 13 years old.[74]

STATUS IN THE WILD
Outside the United States
The puma is not legally protected in Ecuador, El Salvador, or Guyana. Hunting is regulated in Canada, Mexico, and Peru and prohibited in Argentina, Brazil, Bolivia, Chile, Colombia, Costa Rica, French Guiana, Guatemala, Honduras, Nicaragua, Panama, Paraguay, Suriname, Venezuela, and Uruguay. The puma is listed on CITES appendix II except for three subspecies, which are listed on appendix I.[155]

In South and Central America, loss of habitat and prey has undoubtedly reduced puma numbers, although the cat's status remains unknown over most of the southern portions of its range. Although hunting of pumas is prohibited in most South and Central American countries, cats that prey on livestock are often shot.

Inside the United States
Today, pumas are one of the few large predators in North America that people can legally chase with dogs and hunt for sport. In some states, the taking of pumas is restricted to nuisance cats or those preying on domestic stock.

Puma hunters in North America typically use trained hounds to track the cat's scent, chasing the cat until it climbs a tree or takes refuge on some other prominence. Some authorities call the puma the greatest game animal in North America, citing the need to use dogs, the inaccessibility of its habitat, and the speed and cunning of the quarry. A hunt can also be dangerous. Cornered or wounded mountain lions occasionally attack dogs or people, but most injuries occur in accidents that happen when riders try to follow hounds over steep, rocky terrain.

In a few areas hunters remove large numbers of pumas each year, apparently without depleting the adult population. In Montana, for instance, in an area where winter densities may reach seven pumas per 100 square kilometers, annual harvest removed 22 percent of the females and 48 percent of the males present, but the adult population was not depleted for long, as pumas from both on and off the area quickly filled vacant ranges.[116] Sustained harvest of pumas at the level reported in Montana is nevertheless dependent on a source of immigrants to aid in population recovery, and this level of harvest probably cannot be maintained for more than two years in succession.

Based on population growth data collected after the experimental reduction of a puma population in New Mexico, the recommendation for a sustained harvest was to restrict annual offtake to 8 percent of the adult males and to strictly limit the killing of females, as most are likely to have dependent young during the normal hunting season.[100]

The Montana study also found that snow conditions and road access largely determined the amount, timing, and distribution of puma harvest. The cats were most vulnerable after a fresh snowfall, when it took hunters an average of 1.7 hours to tree a puma. Eighty-seven percent of hunts were successful when dogs were released on puma tracks.[116]

Puma hunting is big business, and in 1990 the sporting kill in eleven western states was 1,875 cats, with more than 200 apiece being taken in Arizona, Colorado, Utah, Idaho, and Montana.[2] Despite being hunted throughout most of their range, puma numbers appear to be stable or increasing in North America as states have implemented greater restrictions on the number of pumas that can be harvested. Along with tighter control of hunting has come improved habitat conditions and better management of ungulate populations.[2,16,113]

In the 1960s, many Western states changed the status of the puma from predator to game animal; however, the results of a 1990 referendum in California gave the puma complete protection from hunting in that state.[2]

Conflict with Humans
When people introduced sheep and cattle to North America, the puma began to include livestock in its diet. Public sentiment was on the side of the rancher, and in 1915 stockmen lobbied Congress to set up a program to eliminate predators. In 1931 the Animal Damage Control Act was passed, and between 1937 and 1970 government trappers killed 7,255 pumas, 477,104

bobcats, and equally huge numbers of bears, wolves, and coyotes. Bounties were offered for pumas in Arizona, California, and British Columbia. According to U.S. Fish and Wildlife Service statistics, a minimum of 66,665 pumas were killed between 1907 and 1978.[2,36]

The Animal Damage Control program continues to operate today, but at a reduced level. In 1990 the ADC program spent $29.4 million in federal dollars and about $15 million in state funds to destroy animal and bird pests, including forty-one pumas. The amount of damage caused by these pests was estimated at $1.4 million, considerably less than the cost of eradicating them.[2]

Pumas will kill all types of domestic livestock, but they prey mainly on sheep and calves, sometimes killing and disabling many more animals than they can possibly eat. In Arizona, records show that 60 percent of the cattle kills were calves under three months of age and 80 percent were under six months of age.[72,78] Most cattle killing occurs in southern states such as Arizona and New Mexico because in their mild climate calves are born on the range.

An enormous amount of time and money has been directed toward eradicating livestock-killing pumas, but when the total number of livestock killed each year is compared with the total number of livestock grazed, the numbers are insignificant. In Nevada, sheep losses to pumas average 0.29 percent.[156] Slightly more cattle are lost in Arizona, but the numbers are not large compared with losses to disease and other causes of mortality. For example, in 1983, about 900 cattle from 119 ranches were believed killed by pumas in Arizona.[157] The usual pattern is for one or two ranches to suffer heavy losses while others are barely impacted, although economic losses may be high for certain ranchers. Most of the variation in predation on cattle appears to be due to differences in management and native prey densities; losses of livestock are often heaviest in areas where mild climates allow year-long cow-calf operations. Puma depredation was reduced in these areas when the ranchers switched to steer operations, and in other places a change from sheep to cattle significantly reduced losses.[158] Sheep are vulnerable to attack wherever they are grazed in puma habitat, and they seem to be particularly vulnerable to predation in summer when they are pastured at high elevations. Pumas typically kill several sheep at a time, often twenty in a single night, probably because the sheep's habit of milling around in a panic triggers the cat's pursue-and-kill reflex.[88,90,159]

Traditionally, the solution to puma depredation of domestic stock has been either to try to reduce the puma population in general or to target the particular puma doing the killing. The general population reduction approach has not been terribly successful, as it is very costly and generally ineffective.[2,157] Because such broad-brush eradication programs are usually conducted at public expense, they provoke many legitimate complaints that such removals constitute excessive public subsidy of sheep and cattle ranchers.

Of the alternative approaches to dealing with puma depredation, most have met with mixed success, and many appear to be site-specific. In California ranchers have reduced losses to pumas by not dehorning their cattle, and they have also used fire to create openings in brushy areas; open sites have less stalking cover and fewer cattle kills.[158]

Sheep present a special problem when it comes to minimizing the number killed by predators. The traditional advantage of sheep over cattle is that they can be herded and thus protected against predators; indeed, many federal ranges mandate that sheep be accompanied by herders. Unfortunately, there is a trend away from herding because of the shortage of good shepherds and the high costs of hiring workers. Guard dogs, as used in Europe, have not been as successful in states like New Mexico and Arizona because of the low carrying capacity of the range. Sheep must spread out widely to find enough forage, and guard dogs cannot operate effectively under these conditions.[160]

Compensation programs that reimburse farmers and ranchers for losses to predation are operating in Colorado and Wyoming. Current management programs in most states involve a mixture of sport hunting and "removal" of the individual puma that is causing the livestock losses. However, there is little evidence to support or refute the notion that sport hunting reduces livestock losses. Many wildlife managers believe that the conflict between ranchers and predators will intensify in the future. While authorities will continue to remove problem pumas, public opinion will increasingly call on ranchers to improve husbandry techniques.

Pumas rarely pose a direct threat to humans. Compared with the similar-sized leopard, this cat is a gentle, retiring animal that almost never attacks people. Records of mountain lion attacks on humans in the United States and Canada between 1890 and 1989 show a total of thirty-six attacks; eleven resulted in human deaths. Most of the victims were children (79 percent). In fifteen cases the cat was killed, and of these cats, twelve (80 percent) were underweight or sick, but three were healthy adults.[161]

However, as more people settle in remote areas and use of national and state parks rises, the potential for conflict between humans and wildlife increases. A major concern is that pumas will habituate, or lose their fear of being in close proximity to humans. In a one-year study of puma behavior and visitor use in Big Bend National Park, Texas, radio-tagged pumas often passed close to campsites at night or rested near heavily used trails in the daytime. The only negative incident involved a young male puma that showed no fear of humans, which necessitated his removal from the park.[162,163]

The fatal attacks in 1994 on two women in California by pumas have prompted hunters in that state to call for a repeal of the hunting ban protecting the cats.[161,164] Despite the danger, in many parts of the western United States there appears to be strong public support for the cat.[165] Participants at a 1991 symposium on mountain lion–human interaction called for increased understanding of the conflicts, and showed great interest in searching for ways to facilitate coexistence.[166,167,168,169]

Other Threats

Outright loss and fragmentation of habitat are major threats to the long-term survival of puma populations across their geographic range. In California and Florida many pumas are hit and killed by vehicles as heavily traveled roads divide populations and even the home ranges of individual pumas.[119,148,151,170]

Elevated concentrations of mercury were thought to be responsible for the death of one puma in Everglades National Park, Florida, and were strongly implicated in the deaths of two others. Females with high mercury levels had poor reproductive success.[171,172]

CONSERVATION EFFORTS

The puma has only recently been given protection in the southeastern United States. The subspecies *Puma concolor coryi*, known as the Florida panther, was fully protected in Florida in 1958, but was believed to be extinct until an individual was discovered in 1973. Today, an estimated seventy to eighty individuals form the total population of the subspecies, which is restricted to southern Florida.[34]

The 1973 discovery of a surviving puma sparked new interest in the cat, and in 1976 the U.S. Fish and Wildlife Service appointed a Florida Panther Recov-

ery Team and charged them with the task of preparing and coordinating a recovery plan for the Florida panther. A "revised recovery plan" was approved in December 1981, and in 1987 a "completed revision of the Florida Panther Recovery Plan" was published. The objective of the plan is to establish three viable, self-sustaining populations within the historic range of the subspecies.[173]

Despite the vast acreage (795,000 hectares) of the Big Cypress National Preserve and the adjoining Everglades National Park, many Florida panthers are killed while attempting to cross the state's busy highways. Between December 1979 and May 1991, thirty-two panther deaths were documented, and collisions with vehicles caused fifteen (46.9 percent) of these deaths. Twelve of these fifteen road kills occurred on two busy highways that bisect major swamp forests.[119] When Alligator Alley, the major east-west highway across southern Florida, was upgraded to a four-lane interstate highway, a 64-kilometer portion of the road was fenced and equipped with wildlife underpasses. Wildlife attempting to cross the road are funneled into the underpasses by a 3-meter-high chain-link fence installed along both sides of the highway. Animals using the underpasses photograph themselves by breaking an infrared beam that triggers a camera. The camera study showed that panthers used the underpasses at night, and concluded that the underpasses provided a "safe and acceptable means of travel under highways," reduced panther mortality, and prevented further fragmentation of the panther's habitat.[152]

To address the problems of small population size and the need to eventually establish populations in other areas, the state wildlife agency brought several wild Florida panthers into captivity for a captive breeding program. Subsequently, both captive-bred and wild-caught pumas from Texas were released into northern Florida as part of an experiment to evaluate the feasibility of reintroduction.

In the first reintroduction effort in northern Florida, seven wild-caught Texas pumas were released in an area of good panther habitat. Some of the cats showed signs of settling in and had begun to establish ranges, but the onset of the hunting season caused them to abandon their ranges and begin wandering. Three animals were shot or poached within the first six months, and the remaining four had to be recaptured within ten months. Two of the four that were recaptured had been killing domestic livestock or exotic hoofed stock.[174]

In the second reintroduction experiment, three captive-born and seven wild-caught Texas pumas were released in northern Florida in February 1993. Six months into the study it was evident that early losses would again be high; one cat had been killed by a car, another by a poacher, and a third removed because of landowner complaints. However, this time around, the introduced population persisted for much longer. A year to fourteen months into the study, two more animals had died due to poaching and another had to be removed for overfamiliarity with people. Approximately two years after release two more had to be removed, one because it was roaming too far and the other because it was killing calves. Another was hit and killed by a car after it had been in the wild for twenty-five months.[146] These two studies have been extremely valuable in illustrating potential problems and establishing reasonable expectations for future reintroductions.

A third reintroduction experiment was initiated in March 1995. Eight wild-caught Texas female pumas were released in southern Florida with the intent that they would become part of the breeding population and restore the genetic variability that has been lost from the Florida cats due to inbreeding. Restoring the genetic integrity of the Florida panther should ameliorate the negative effects of inbreeding,[175] although whether such measures are actually necessary is a subject of debate.[32,34,176]

Another management concern is that roughly half of the panthers currently living in southern Florida are on private lands, many of which are suitable for a variety of agricultural and urban uses.[170,177,178] The Florida Fish and Wildlife Conservation Commission is working with the American Farmland Trust on a joint project to improve cooperation with private landowners, and numerous state and federal agencies are working with private landowners to either preserve key corridors and essential pieces of habitat or to purchase habitat. In 1989 the Florida Panther National Wildlife Refuge was established, and the U.S. Fish and Wildlife Service has begun the process of acquiring additional habitat.

TABLE 49 MEASUREMENTS AND WEIGHTS OF ADULT PUMAS

HB	n	T	n	WT	n	Location	Source
1,380 (1,200–1,500)	12m	790 (730–830)	12m	71.0 (57–76)	11m	Canada	179
1,240 (1,080–1,310)	36f	710 (610–820)	36f	44.0 (34–50)	34f	Canada	173
1,332 (1,220–1,420)	9m	832 (720–920)	9m	61.6 (51.8–70.8)	8m	Colorado	73
1,244 (1,060–1,370)	13f	778 (720–840)	13f	44.5 (38.5–49.9)	14f	Colorado	73
1,347 (1,260–1,440)	10m	769 (700–830)	10m	58.9 (56.2–64.4)	10m	New Mexico	58
1,179 (1,110–1,260)	11f	711 (630–770)	11f	30.7 (27.2–36.3)	11f	New Mexico	58
1,386 (1,200–1,680)	34m	690 (605–804)	34m	53.6 (39.0–69.9)	43m	Florida	180
1,261 (1,031–1,410)	25f	658 (570–880)	25f	36.1 (22.7–49.0)	37f	Florida	180
1,198 (1,070–1,360)	7m	679 (640–780)	7m	53.1 (41.5–68.0)	7m	Brazil	54
1,076 (950–1,170)	10f	639 (580–700)	10f	36.9 (25.0–45.0)	10f	Brazil	54
1,220 (1,000–1,380)	4f	722 (670–810)	4f	45.1 (36.5–57.0)	4f	Chile	22
1,315 (1,220–1,450)	6m	745 (680–800)	6m	68.8 (55–80)	6m	Chile	22

Note: HB = head and body length (mm), T = tail length (mm), WT = weight (kg). n = sample size. Sex: m = male, f = female, ? = unknown. Mean values are presented only for sample sizes of three or more. Range of values is in parentheses.

TABLE 50 FREQUENCY OF OCCURRENCE OF PREY ITEMS IN THE DIETS OF NORTH AMERICAN PUMAS (PERCENTAGE OF SAMPLES)

Prey items	Florida[61] Scats (n = 257)	California[74] Scats (n = 46)	Utah[76] Scats (n = 239)	Alberta, Canada[21] Scats (n = 58)
Odocoileus hemionus Mule deer		74.0	80.3	14.1
Odocoileus virginianus White-tailed deer	28.0			1.6
Alces alces Moose				20.3
Cervus elaphus Elk			0.4	18.8
Unclassified deer and elk				12.5
Sus scrofa Wild pig	42.0	20.0		
Procyon lotor Raccoon	12.0			
Dasypus novemcinctus Armadillo	8.0			
Lagomorphs (Rabbits and hares)	4.0	2.0	17.2	3.1
Other carnivores	0.4	4.0	4.6	
Marmota flaviventris Marmot			1.7	
Erethizon dorsatum Porcupine			0.8	4.7
Castor canadensis Beaver			1.7	7.8
Rodents	2.5	8.0	12.1	3.1
Reptiles	0.7			
Birds	0.4	2.0	1.3	
Livestock	2.0	4.0	0.4	
Unknown animals			3.8	
Plant material	2.5	13.0	5.9	
Minimum number of vertebrate prey items	281	53	316	64

TABLE 51 FREQUENCY OF OCCURRENCE OF PREY ITEMS IN THE DIETS OF CENTRAL AND SOUTH AMERICAN PUMAS (PERCENTAGE OF SAMPLES)

Prey items	Torres del Paine NP, Chile[69] Scats (n = 405)	Paraguayan Chaco[63] Scats (n = 95)	Hato Piñero, Venezuela[67] Scats (n = 42)	Mexico-Texas border[71] Scats (n = 780)
Marsupials		15.0		
Armadillos		10.8		
Anteaters		4.2		
Carnivores	3.5			1.5
Lama guanicoe Guanaco	32.8			
Mazama and *Odocoileus* Brocket and white-tailed deer		10.8	9.8	51.0

(continued)

TABLE 51 (continued)

Prey items	Torres del Paine NP, Chile[69] Scats ($n = 405$)	Paraguayan Chaco[63] Scats ($n = 95$)	Hato Piñero, Venezuela[67] Scats ($n = 42$)	Mexico-Texas border[71] Scats ($n = 780$)
Hydrochaeris hydrochaeris Capybara			9.8	
Catagonus wagneri Chacoan peccary		3.3		
Tayassu pecari White-lipped peccary			2.4	
Tayassu tajacu Collared peccary		5.0	17.1	5.6
Lepus capensis Hare	70.9			
Sylvilagus brasiliensis Cottontail rabbit		8.3	7.3	0.1
Dolichotis salinicola Mara		4.2		
Galea musteloides Yellow-toothed cavy		9.2		
Rodents	3.2		19.5	11.2
Unidentified rodents and rabbits		15.0		
Birds	10.0	6.6		0.8
Reptiles		2.5	9.8	
Livestock	6.2		24.4	15.0
Horse/burro				3.8
Unidentified mammals	10.3			
Plant material		14.0		
Minimum number of vertebrate prey items	590	120	41	780

TABLE 52 LEGAL STATUS OF PUMAS IN THE UNITED STATES

State	Status	Present/ Absent	State	Status	Present/ Absent
Alabama	Protected	A	Maine	Extirpated	A
Alaska	Unprotected	A	Maryland	Endangered	A
Arizona	Game	P	Massachusetts	Protected	A
Arkansas	Protected	A	Michigan	Unprotected	A
California	Protected	P	Minnesota	Unprotected	A
Colorado	Game	P	Mississippi	Endangered	A
Connecticut	Protected	A	Missouri	Endangered	A
Delaware	Endangered	A	Montana	Game	P
Florida	Endangered	P	Nebraska	Unprotected	A
Georgia	Protected	A	Nevada	Game	P
Idaho	Game	P	New Hampshire	Endangered	A
Illinois	Endangered	A	New Jersey	Endangered	A
Indiana	Extirpated	A	New Mexico	Game	P
Iowa	Unprotected	A	New York	Endangered	A
Kansas	Protected	A	North Carolina	Protected	A
Kentucky	Protected	A	North Dakota	Unprotected	A
Louisiana	Protected	A	Ohio	Extirpated	A

TABLE 52 *(continued)*

State	Status	Present/Absent	State	Status	Present/Absent
Oklahoma	Protected	A	Utah	Game	P
Oregon	Game	P	Vermont	Endangered	A
Pennsylvania	Unprotected	A	Virginia	Protected	A
Rhode Island	Extirpated	A	Washington	Game	P
South Carolina	Protected	A	West Virginia	Unprotected	A
South Dakota	Protected	A	Wisconsin	Unprotected	A
Tennessee	Endangered	A	Wyoming	Game	P
Texas	Unprotected	P			

Sources: 2,24,26,39

REFERENCES

1. Barnes, C. T. 1960. *The cougar or mountain lion.* Salt Lake City, UT: Ralton Company.

2. Hansen, K. 1992. *Cougar: The American lion.* Flagstaff, AZ: Northland Publishing Company.

3. Tinsley, J. B. 1987. *The puma: Legendary lion of the Americas.* El Paso, TX: Texas Western Press.

4. Young, S. P. 1946. History, life habits, economic status, and control, part I. In S. P. Young and E. A. Goldman, *The puma, mysterious American cat,* 1–173. Washington, DC: American Wildlife Institute.

5. Werdelin, L. 1983. Morphological patterns in the skulls of cats. *Biol. J. Linn. Soc.* 19: 375–391.

6. Pocock, R. I. 1917. The classification of existing Felidae. *Ann. Mag. Nat. Hist.,* ser. 8, 20: 329–350.

7. Hast, M. H. 1989. The larynx of roaring and non-roaring cats. *J. Anat.* 163: 117–121.

8. Peters, G., and M. H. Hast. 1994. Hyoid structure, laryngeal anatomy, and vocalizations in felids (Mammalia: Carnivora: Felidae). *Z. Säugetierk.* 59: 87–104.

9. Morgan, G. S., and K. L. Seymour. 1997. Fossil history of the panther (*Puma concolor*) and the cheetah-like cat (*Miracinonyx inexpectatus*) in Florida. *Bull. Fla. Mus. Nat. Hist.* 40(2): 177–219.

10. Van Valkenburgh, B., F. V. Grady, and B. Kurtén. 1990. The Plio-Pleistocene cheetah-like cat *Miracinonyx inexpectatus* of North America. *J. Vert. Paleontol.* 10: 434–454.

11. Kurtén, B. 1976. Fossil puma (Mammalia: Felidae) in North America. *Neth. J. Zool.* 26(4): 502–534.

12. Adams, D. B. 1979. The cheetah: Native American. *Science* 205: 1155–1158.

13. Culver, M., W. E. Johnson, J. Pecon-Slattery, and S. J. O'Brien. 2000. Genomic ancestry of the American puma (*Puma concolor*). *J. Hered.* 91: 186–197.

14. Wozencraft, W. C. 1993. Order Carnivora. In *Mammal species of the world,* ed. D. E. Wilson and D. M. Reeder, 279–348. Washington, DC: Smithsonian Institution Press.

15. Hemmer, H. 1978. The evolutionary systematics of living Felidae: Present status and current problems. *Carnivore* 1: 71–79.

16. Hornocker, M. G., and H. Quigley. 1987. Mountain lion: Pacific coast predator. In *Restoring America's wildlife, 1937–1987,* ed. H. Kallman, 177–189. Washington, DC: United States Fish & Wildlife Service.

17. Seidensticker, J. C. 1991. Pumas. In *Great cats,* ed. J. C. Seidensticker and S. Lumpkin, 130–137. Emmaus, PA: Rodale Press.

18. Musgrave, M. E. 1926. Some habits of mountain lions in Arizona. *J. Mammal.* 7: 282–285.

19. Iriarte, J. A., W. L. Franklin, W. E. Johnson, and K. H. Redford. 1990. Biogeographic variation of food habits and body size of the American puma. *Oecologia* 85: 185–190.

20. Emmons, L. H. 1987. Comparative feeding ecology of felids in a Neotropical rainforest. *Behav. Ecol. Sociobiol.* 20: 271–283.

21. Pall, O., M. Jalkotzy, and I. Ross. 1988. The cougar in Alberta. Report to the Fish and Wildlife Division, Alberta Forestry, Lands and Wildlife. 145 pp.

22. Johnson, W. E., Laboratory of Genomic Diversity, National Cancer Institute, FCRDC, Frederick, Maryland. Personal communication.

23. Anderson, A. E. 1983. A critical review of literature on puma (*Felis concolor*). Colorado Division of Wildlife, Special Report 54. 91 pp.

24. Maehr, D. S., and C. T. Moore. 1992. Models of mass growth for 3 North American cougar populations. *J. Wildl. Mgmt.* 56: 700–707.

25. Gay, S. W., and T. L. Best. 1995. Geographic variation in sexual dimorphism of the puma (*Puma concolor*) in North and South America. *Southwest. Nat.* 40: 148–159.

26. Gay, S. W., and T. L. Best. 1996. Age-related variation in skulls of the puma (*Puma concolor*). *J. Mammal.* 77: 191–198.

27. Gonyea, W. J. 1976. Adaptive differences in the body proportions of large felids. *Acta Anat.* 96: 81–96.

28. Pence, D. B., R. J. Warren, D. Waid, and M. J. Davin. 1987. Aspects of the ecology of mountain lions (*Felis concolor*) in Big Bend National Park. Final Report. U.S. Department of the Interior, National Park Service, Santa Fe, NM.

29. Van Pelt, A. F. 1977. A mountain lion kill in southwest Texas. *Southwest. Nat.* 22: 271.

30. Engstrom, M. D., and T. C. Maxwell. 1988. Records of mountain lion (*Felis concolor*) from the western Edwards Plateau of Texas. *Texas J. Sci.* 40: 450–452.

31. Ockenfels, R. A. 1994. Mountain lion predation on pronghorn in central Arizona. *Southwest. Nat.* 39: 305–306.

32. Wilkins, L., J. M. Arias-Reveron, B. Stith, M. E. Roelke, and R. C. Belden. 1997. The Florida panther *Felis concolor coryi:* A morphological investigation of the subspecies with a comparison to other North and South American cougars. *Bull. Fla. Mus. Nat. Hist.* 40(3): 221–269.

33. Belden, R. C. 1989. The Florida panther. In *Audubon Wild-*

life Report 1988/1989, ed. W. J. Chandler, 515–532. New York: The National Audubon Society.

34. Maehr, D. S. 1997. *The Florida panther*. Covelo, CA: Island Press.

35. Young, S. P., and E. A. Goldman. 1946. *The puma, mysterious American cat*. Washington, DC: American Wildlife Institute.

36. Nowak, R. M. 1976. *The cougar in the United States and Canada*. Unpublished report to the New York Zoological Society and U.S. Fish and Wildlife Service Office of Endangered Species, Washington, DC. 190 pp.

37. Wright, B. S. 1972. *The eastern panther: A question of survival*. Toronto: Clark Irwin.

38. Nero R. W., and R. E. Wrigley. 1977. Status and habits of the cougar in Manitoba. *Can. Field Nat.* 91: 28–40.

39. Downing, R. L. 1984. The search for cougars in the eastern United States. *Crptozoology* 3: 31–49.

40. Cumberland, R. E., and J. A. Dempsey. 1994. Recent confirmation of a cougar, *Felis concolor*, in New Brunswick. *Can. Field Nat.* 108: 224–226.

41. Stocek, R. F. 1995. The cougar, *Felis concolor*, in the Maritime Provinces. *Can. Field Nat.* 109: 19–22.

42. Eisenberg, J. F. 1989. *Mammals of the Neotropics*. Vol. 1, *The northern Neotropics*. Chicago: University of Chicago Press.

43. Emmons, L. H., and F. Feer. 1990. *Neotropical rainforest mammals*. Chicago: University of Chicago Press.

44. Redford, K. H., and J. F. Eisenberg. 1992. *Mammals of the Neotropics*. Vol. 2, *The southern cone*. Chicago: University of Chicago Press.

45. Ceballos, G., and D. Navarro. 1991. Diversity and conservation of Mexican mammals. In *Latin American mammalogy*, ed. M. A. Mares and D. J. Schmidly, 167–198. Norman: University of Oklahoma Press.

46. Oliveira, T. G. de. 1993. *Neotropical cats: Ecology and conservation*. São Luís, Maranhão: EDUFMA.

47. Seidensticker, J. C., M. G. Hornocker, W. V. Wiles, and J. P. Messick. 1973. Mountain lion social organization in the Idaho Primitive Area. *Wildl. Monogr.* 35: 1–60.

48. Logan, K. A., and L. L. Irwin. 1985. Mountain lion habitats in the Big Horn Mountains, Wyoming. *Wildl. Soc. Bull.* 13: 257–262.

49. Laing, S. P., and F. G. Lindzey. 1991. Cougar habitat selection in south-central Utah. In *Mountain lion-human interaction*, ed. C. E. Braun, 27–37. Denver: Colorado Division of Wildlife.

50. Belden, R. C., W. B. Frankenberger, R. T. McBride, and S. T. Schwikert. 1988. Panther habitat use in southern Florida. *J. Wildl. Mgmt.* 52: 660–663.

51. Maehr, D. S., E. D. Land, J. C. Roof, and J. W. McCown. 1990. Day beds, natal dens, and activity of Florida panthers. *Proceedings of the annual conference of the Southeastern Association of Fish and Wildlife Agencies* 44: 310–318.

52. Schaller, G. B., and P. G. Crawshaw. 1980. Movement patterns of jaguar. *Biotropica* 12: 161–168.

53. Crawshaw, P. G. Jr., and H. B. Quigley. 1991. Jaguar spacing, activity, and habitat use in a seasonally flooded environment in Brazil. *J. Zool.* (Lond.) 223: 357–370.

54. Crawshaw, P. G. Jr. 1995. Comparative ecology of ocelot (*Felis pardalis*) and jaguar (*Panthera onca*) in a protected subtropical forest in Brazil and Argentina. Ph.D. dissertation, University of Florida, Gainesville.

55. Scognamillo, D. G. 2001. Ecological separation between jaguar and puma in a mosaic landscape in the Venezuelan llanos. Master's thesis, University of Florida, Gainesville.

56. Ackerman, B. B., F. G. Lindzey, and T. P. Hemker. 1986. Predictive energetics model for cougars. In *Cats of the world: Biology, conservation, and management*, ed. S. D. Miller and D. D. Everett, 333–352. Washington, DC: National Wildlife Federation.

57. Van Dyke, F. G., R. H. Brocke, H. G. Shaw, B. B. Ackerman, T. P. Hemker, and F. G. Lindzey. 1986. Reactions of mountain lions to logging and human activity. *J. Wildl. Mgmt.* 50: 95–102.

58. Sweanor, L. L. 1990. Mountain lion social organization in a desert environment. Master's thesis, University of Idaho, Moscow.

59. Beier, P., D. Choate, and R. H. Barrett. 1995. Movement patterns of mountain lions during different behaviors. *J. Mammal.* 76: 1056–1070.

60. Bogue, G., and M. Ferrari. 1976. The predatory "training" of captive reared puma. In *The world's cats*, vol. 3, no. 1, ed. R. L. Eaton, 36–45. Seattle: Carnivore Research Institute, Burke Museum, University of Washington.

61. Maehr, D. S., R. C. Belden, E. D. Land, and L. Wilkins. 1990. Food habits of panthers in southwest Florida. *J. Wildl. Mgmt.* 54: 420–423.

62. Dalrymple, G. H., and O. L. Bass Jr. 1996. The diet of the Florida panther in Everglades National Park, Florida. *Bull. Fla. Mus. Nat. Hist.* 39(5): 173–193.

63. Taber, A. B., A. J. Novaro, N. Neris, and F. H. Colman. 1997. The food habits of sympatric jaguar and puma in the Paraguayan Chaco. *Biotropica* 29: 204–213.

64. Branch, L. C. 1995. Observations of predation by puma and Geoffroy's cats on the plains vizcazcha in semi-arid scrub of central Argentina. *Mammalia* 59: 152–156.

65. Rau, J. R., D. R. Martinez, and A. Munoz-Pedreros. 1995. Trophic ecology of pumas in southern South America. In *Integrating people and wildlife for a sustainable future*, ed. J. A. Bissonette and P. R. Krausman, 602–604. Bethesda, MD: The Wildlife Society.

66. Nuñez, R., B. Miller, and F. Lindzey. 2000. Food habits of jaguars and pumas in Jalisco, Mexico. *J. Zool.* (Lond.) 252: 373–379.

67. Maxit, I. 2000. Prey use by sympatric puma and jaguar in the Venezuelan llanos. Master's thesis, University of Florida, Gainesville.

68. Johnson, K. A., and W. L. Franklin. 1984. Ecology and management of the Patagonia puma (*Felis concolor patagonica*) in southern Chile. In *Proceedings of the second mountain lion workshop*, ed. J. Roberson and F. Lindzey, 141–146. Salt Lake City, UT: Utah Division of Wildlife Resources.

69. Iriarte, J. A., W. E. Johnson, and W. L. Franklin. 1991. Feeding ecology of the Patagonia puma in southernmost Chile. *Revista Chilena Historia Nat.* 64: 145–156.

70. Ashman, D. L., G. C. Christensen, M. C. Hess, G. K. Tuskamotoa, and M. S. Wickersham. 1983. *The mountain lion in Nevada*. Nevada Department of Wildlife Report 4–48–15, Reno. 75 pp.

71. McBride, R. T. 1976. Status and ecology of the mountain lion (*Felis concolor stanleyana*) of the Texas-Mexico border. Master's thesis, Sul Ros State University, Alpine, Texas.

72. Shaw, H. G. 1990. *A mountain lion field guide*, 4th ed., Special Report 9. Arizona Game and Fish Department.

73. Anderson, A. E., D. C. Bowden, and D. M. Kattner. 1992. *The puma on Uncompahgre Plateau, Colorado*. Colorado Division of Wildlife, Technical Publication no. 40. 116 pp.

74. Hopkins, R. A. 1989. Ecology of the puma in the Diablo

Range, California. Ph.D. dissertation, University of California, Berkeley.

75. Leopold, B. D., and P. R. Krausman. 1991. Factors influencing desert mule deer distribution and productivity in southwestern Texas. *Southwest. Nat.* 36: 67–74.

76. Ackerman, B. B., F. G. Lindzey, and T. P. Hemker. 1984. Cougar food habits in southern Utah. *J. Wildl. Mgmt.* 48: 147–155.

77. Hornocker, M. G. 1970. An analysis of mountain lion predation upon mule deer and elk in the Idaho Primitive Area. *Wildl. Monogr.* 21: 1–39.

78. Shaw, H. G. 1977. Impact of mountain lions on mule deer and cattle. In *Proceedings of the 1975 predator symposium*, ed. R. L. Phillips and C. J. Jonkel, 17–32. Missoula: Montana Forestry and Conservation Experimental Station, School of Forestry, University of Montana.

79. Robinette, W. L., J. S. Gashwiler, and O. W. Morris. 1959. Food habits of the cougar in Utah and Nevada. *J. Wildl. Mgmt.* 23: 261–273.

80. Spalding, D. J., and J. Lesowski. 1971. Winter food habits of the cougar in south central British Columbia. *J. Wildl. Mgmt.* 35: 378–381.

81. Harrison, S. 1990. Cougar predation on bighorn sheep in the Junction Wildlife Management Area, British Columbia. Master's thesis, University of British Columbia, Vancouver.

82. Ross, P. I., and M. G. Jalkotzy. 1996. Cougar predation on moose in southwestern Alberta. *Alces* 32: 1–8.

83. Wilson, P. 1984. Puma predation on guanacos in Torres del Paine National Park, Chile. *Mammalia* 48: 515–522.

84. Smallwood, K. S. 1993. Mountain lion vocalizations and hunting behavior. *Southwest. Nat.* 38: 65–67.

85. Cunningham, E. B. 1971. A cougar kills an elk. *Can. Field Nat.* 85: 253–254.

86. Gashwiler, J. S., and W. L. Robinette. 1957. Accidental fatalities of the Utah cougar. *J. Mammal.* 38: 123–126.

87. Lindzey, F. G., B. B. Ackerman, D. Barnhurst, and T. P. Hemker. 1988. Survival rates of mountain lions in southern Utah. *J. Wildl. Mgmt.* 52: 664–667.

88. Lindzey, T. 1987. Mountain lion. In *Wild furbearer management and conservation in North America*, ed. M. Novak, J. A. Baker, M. E. Obbard, and B. Malloch, 657–668. North Bay, Ontario: Ontario Trappers Association.

89. Ross, P. I., M. G. Jalkotzy, and P.-Y. Daoust. 1995. Fatal trauma sustained by cougars, *Felis concolor*, while attacking prey in southern Alberta. *Can. Field Nat.* 109: 261–263.

90. Leyhausen, P. 1979. *Cat behavior: The predatory and social behavior of domestic and wild cats*. New York: Garland STPM Press.

91. Grinnell, J., J. S. Dixon, and J. M. Linsdale. 1937. *Furbearing mammals of California: Their natural history, systematic status and relations to man*. Vol. 2. Berkeley: University of California Press.

92. Danvir, R. E., and F. G. Lindzey. 1981. Feeding behavior of a captive cougar on mule deer. *Encyclia* 58: 50–56.

93. Thompson, M. J., and W. C. Stewart. 1994. Cougar(s), *Felis concolor*, with a kill for 27 days. *Can. Field Nat.* 108: 497–498.

94. Holt, D. W. 1994. Larder hoarding in the cougar, *Felis concolor*. *Can. Field Nat.* 108: 240–241.

95. Koehler, G. M., and M. G. Hornocker. 1991. Seasonal resource use among mountain lions, bobcats, and coyotes. *J. Mammal.* 72: 391–396.

96. Boyd, D., and B. O'Gara. 1985. Cougar predation on coyotes. *Murrelet* 66: 17.

97. Spreadbury, B. R., K. Musil, J. Musil, C. Kaisner, and J. Kovak. 1996. Cougar population characteristics in southeastern British Columbia. *J. Wildl. Mgmt.* 60: 962–969.

98. Jalkotzy, M., and I. Ross. 1991. The Sheep River cougar project, Phase III, Cougar/prey relationships. Unpublished report. Associated Resource Consultants, Ltd., Calgary, Alberta, Canada. 27 pp.

99. Logan, K. A., L. L. Sweanor, T. K. Ruth, and M. G. Hornocker. 1996. Cougars of the San Andres Mountains, New Mexico. Final report, Federal Aid in Wildlife Restoration Project W-128-R. Santa Fe: New Mexico Department of Game and Fish.

100. Neal, D. L. 1989. Mountain lion density and movement in the Central Sierra Nevada. In *Proceedings of the third mountain lion workshop*, ed. R. H. Smith, 72. Prescott: Arizona Chapter, The Wildlife Society and Arizona Game and Fish Department.

101. Waid, D. D. 1990. Movements, food habits, and helminth parasites of mountain lions in southwestern Texas. Ph.D. dissertation, Texas Tech University, Lubbock.

102. Berger, J., and J. D. Wehausen. 1991. Consequences of a mammalian predator-prey disequilibrium in the Great Basin Desert. *Conserv. Biol.* 5: 244–248.

103. Bleich, V. C., C. D. Hargis, J. A. Keay, and J. D. Wehausen. 1991. Interagency coordination and the restoration of wildlife populations. In *Natural areas and Yosemite: Prospects for the future*, ed. J. Edelbrock and S. Carpenter, 277–284. Denver, CO: U.S. National Park Service, Denver Service Center.

104. Hayes, C. L., E. S. Rubin, M. C. Jorgenson, R. A. Botta, and W. M. Boyce. 2000. Mountain lion predation on bighorn sheep in the Peninsular Ranges, California. *J. Wildl. Mgmt.* 64: 954–959.

105. Lindzey, F. G., W. D. van Sickle, B. B. Ackerman, D. Barnhurst, T. P. Hemker, and S. P. Laing. 1994. Cougar population dynamics in southern Utah. *J. Wildl. Mgmt.* 58: 619–624.

106. Hopkins, R. A., M. J. Kutilek, and J. Shreve. 1986. Density and home range characteristics of mountain lions in the Diablo Range of California. In *Cats of the world: Biology, conservation, and management*, ed. S. D. Miller and D. D. Everett, 223–235. Washington, DC: National Wildlife Federation.

107. Ross, P. I., and M. G. Jalkotzy. 1992. Characteristics of a hunted population of cougars in southwestern Alberta. *J. Wildl. Mgmt.* 56: 417–426.

108. Maehr, D. S., E. D. Land, and J. C. Roof. 1991. Social ecology of Florida panthers. *Natl. Geogr. Res.* 7: 414–431.

109. Hemker, T. P., F. G. Lindzey, and B. B. Ackerman. 1984. Population characteristics and movement patterns of cougars in southern Utah. *J. Wildl. Mgmt.* 48: 1275–1284.

110. Quigley, H. B., G. M. Koehler, and M. G. Hornocker. 1989. Dynamics of a mountain lion population in central Idaho over a 20-year period. In *Proceedings of the third mountain lion workshop*, ed. R. H. Smith, 54. Prescott: Arizona Chapter, The Wildlife Society, Arizona Game and Fish Department.

111. Stamps, J. 1995. Motor learning and the value of familiar space. *Am. Nat.* 146: 41–58.

112. Hornocker, M. G., and T. Bailey. 1986. Natural regulation in three species of felids. In *Cats of the world: Biology, conservation, and management*, ed. S. D. Miller and D. D. Everett, 211–220. Washington, DC: National Wildlife Federation.

113. Hornocker, M. G. 1992. Learning to live with mountain lions. *Natl. Geogr.* 182: 52–65.

114. Zajonc, R. B. 1971. Attraction, affiliation and attachment. In *Man and beast: Comparative social behavior*, ed. J. F. Eisenberg and

W. S. Dillon, 141–179. Washington, DC: Smithsonian Institution Press.

115. Logan, K. A., L. L. Irwin, and R. L. Skinner. 1986. Characteristics of a hunted mountain lion population. *J. Wildl. Mgmt.* 50: 648–654.

116. Murphy, K. M. 1983. Relationships between a mountain lion population and hunting pressure in western Montana. Master's thesis, University of Montana, Missoula.

117. Smith, T. E., R. R. Duke, M. J. Kutilek, and H. T. Harvey. 1986. Mountain lions (*Felis concolor*) in the vicinity of Carlsbad Caverns National Park, NM and Guadalupe Mountain National Park, TX. Final report. Santa Fe, NM: U.S. Department of the Interior, National Park Service.

118. Lindzey, F. G., W. D. van Sickle, S. P. Laing, and C. S. Mecham. 1992. Cougar population response to manipulation in southern Utah. *Wildl. Soc. Bull.* 20: 224–227.

119. Maehr, D. S., E. D. Land, and M. E. Roelke. 1991. Mortality patterns of panthers in southwest Florida. *Proceedings of the annual conference of the Southeastern Association of Fish and Wildlife Agencies* 45: 201–207.

120. Gorman, M. L., and B. J. Trowbridge. 1989. The role of odor in the social lives of carnivores. In *Carnivore behavior, ecology and evolution*, ed. J. L. Gittleman, 57–88. Ithaca, NY: Cornell University Press.

121. Wemmer, C., and K. Scow. 1977. Communication in the Felidae with emphasis on scent marking and contact patterns. In *How animals communicate*, ed. T. A. Sebeok, 749–766. Bloomington: Indiana University Press.

122. Mellen, J. D. 1993. A comparative analysis of scent-marking, social and reproductive behavior in 20 species of small cats (*Felis*). *Am. Zool.* 33: 151–166.

123. Peters, G. 1978. Vergleichende Untersuchung zur Lautgebung einiger Feliden (Mammalia, Felidae). *Spixiana*, suppl. 1: 1–206.

124. Peters, G. 1984. On the structure of friendly close range vocalizations in terrestrial carnivores (Mammalia: Carnivora: Fissipedia). *Z. Säugetierk.* 49: 157–182.

125. Peters, G. 1987. Acoustic communication in the genus *Lynx* (Mammalia: Felidae)—comparative survey and phylogenetic interpretation. *Bonn. Zool. Beitr.* 38: 315–330.

126. McCabe, R. A. 1949. The scream of the mountain lion. *J. Mammal.* 30: 305–306.

127. Brock. S. E. 1966. *Leemo: A true story of a man's friendship with a mountain lion.* New York: Taplinger.

128. Rabb, G. B. 1959. Reproductive and vocal behavior in captive pumas. *J. Mammal.* 40: 616–617.

129. Mehrer, C. F. 1975. Some aspects of reproduction in captive mountain lions *Felis concolor*, bobcats *Lynx rufus* and lynx *Lynx canadensis*. Ph.D. dissertation, University of North Dakota, Grand Forks.

130. Eaton, R. L., and K. A. Velander. 1977. Reproduction in the puma: Biology, behavior and ontogeny. In *The world's cats*, vol. 3, no. 3, ed. R. L. Eaton, 45–70. Seattle: Carnivore Research Institute, Burke Museum, University of Washington.

131. Sadleir, R. M. F. S. 1966. Notes on reproduction in the larger Felidae. *Int. Zoo Yrbk.* 6: 184–187.

132. Maehr, D. S., E. D. Land, J. C. Roof, and J. W. McCown. 1989. Early maternal behavior in the Florida panther (*Felis concolor coryi*). *Am. Midland Nat.* 122: 34–43.

133. Maehr, D. S. 1991. Response of the wild Florida panther population to removals for captive breeding. Annual Performance Report. Florida Game and Fresh Water Fish Commission, Tallahassee.

134. Maehr, D. S., J. C. Roof, E. D. Land, and J. W. McCown. 1989. First reproduction of a panther (*Felis concolor coryi*) in southwestern Florida, U.S.A. *Mammalia* 53: 129–131.

135. Belden, R. C., and J. W. McCown. 1993. Florida panther captive breeding/reintroduction feasibility. Annual performance report. Florida Game and Fresh Water Fish Commission, Tallahassee.

136. Bonney, R. C., H. D. M. Moore, and D. M. Jones. 1981. Plasma concentrations of oestradiol-17ß and progesterone, and laparoscopic observations of the ovary in the puma (*Felis concolor*) during oestrus, pseudopregnancy and pregnancy. *J. Reprod. Fert.* 63: 523–531.

137. Eaton, R. L. 1976. Why some felids copulate so much. In *The world's cats*, vol. 3, no. 2, ed. R. L. Eaton, 73–94. Seattle: Carnivore Research Institute, Burke Museum, University of Washington.

138. Lanier, D. L., and D. A. Dewsbury. 1976. A quantitative study of copulatory behaviour of large Felidae. *Behav. Proc.* 1: 327–333.

139. Robinette, W. L., J. S. Gashwiler, and O. W. Morris. 1961. Notes on cougar productivity and life history. *J. Mammal.* 42: 204–217.

140. Hemker, T. P., F. G. Lindzey, B. B. Ackerman, and A. J. Button. 1986. Survival of cougar cubs in a non-hunted population. In *Cats of the world: Biology, conservation, and management*, ed. S. D. Miller and D. D. Everett, 327–332. Washington, DC: National Wildlife Federation.

141. Volf, J. 1972. Exigences alimentaires et dentition des jeunes de trois espèces de félides. *Mammalia* 36: 683–686.

142. Blonk, H. L. 1965. Einige bemerkungen über das fellmuster bei einem Surinam-puma, *Puma concolor discolor* (Schreber 1775). *Säugetierk. Mitt.* 13: 39–40.

143. Toweill, D. E. 1986. Notes on the development of a cougar kitten. *Murrelet* 67: 20–23.

144. Barnhurst, D., and F. G. Lindzey. 1989. Detecting female mountain lions with kittens. *Northwest Science* 63: 35–37.

145. Hornocker, M. G., and G. M. Koehler. 1984. Reintroducing orphaned mountain lion kittens into the wild. In *Proceedings of the second mountain lion workshop*, ed. J. Roberson and F. Lindzey, 167–169. Salt Lake City: Utah Division of Wildlife Resources.

146. Belden, R. C. 1994. Florida panther reintroduction feasibility study. In *Proceedings of the Florida Panther Conference*, ed. D. B. Jordan, 154–190. Atlanta, GA: U.S. Fish and Wildlife Service.

147. Maehr, D. S. 1990. Tracking Florida's panthers. *Defenders* 65: 10–15.

148. Beier, P. 1995. Dispersal of juvenile cougars in fragmented habitat. *J. Wildl. Mgmt.* 59: 228–237.

149. Smith, J. L. D., C. W. McDougal, and M. E. Sunquist. 1987. Female land tenure system in tigers. In *Tigers of the world: The biology, biopolitics, management, and conservation of an endangered species*, ed. R. L. Tilson and U. S. Seal, 97–109. Park Ridge, NJ: Noyes Publications.

150. Lesowski, J. 1963. Two observations of cougar cannibalism. *J. Mammal.* 44: 586.

151. Beier, P. 1993. Determining minimum habitat areas and habitat corridors for cougars. *Conserv. Biol.* 7: 94–108.

152. Foster, M. L., and S. R. Humphrey. 1995. Use of highway underpasses by Florida panthers and other wildlife. *Wildl. Soc. Bull.* 23: 92–94.

153. Jones, M. L. 1977. Record keeping and longevity of felids

in captivity. In *The world's cats*, vol. 3, no. 3, ed. R. L. Eaton, 132–138. Seattle: Carnivore Research Institute, Burke Museum, University of Washington.

154. Matson, G., and J. Matson. 1993. Matson's Laboratory. Progress Report 13: 1–12.

155. Nowell, K., and P. Jackson. 1996. *Wild cats: A status survey and conservation action plan*. Gland, Switzerland: International Union for Conservation of Nature and Natural Resources (IUCN).

156. Suminski, H. R. 1982. Mountain lion predation on domestic livestock in Nevada. *Proc. Vert. Pest Conf.* 10: 62–66.

157. Shaw, H. G. 1984. Cattle growers and lions. In *Proceedings of the second mountain lion workshop*, ed. J. Roberson and F. Lindzey, 119–129. Salt Lake City: Utah Division of Wildlife Resources.

158. Bowns, J. E. 1984. Predation-depredation. In *Proceedings of the second mountain lion workshop*, ed. J. Roberson and F. Lindzey, 204–215. Salt Lake City: Utah Division of Wildlife Resources.

159. Guggisberg, C. A. W. 1975. *Wild cats of the world*. New York: Taplinger.

160. Green, J. S., and R. A. Woodruff. 1990. Livestock guarding dogs: Protecting sheep from predators. Agricultural Information Bulletin 588, U.S. Department of Agriculture, Washington, DC.

161. Beier, P. 1991. Cougar attacks on humans in the United States and Canada. *Wild. Soc. Bull.* 19: 403–412.

162. McBride, R. T., and T. K. Ruth. 1988. Mountain lion behavior in response to visitor use in the Chisos Mountains of Big Bend National Park, Texas. Final Report, U.S. Department of the Interior, National Park Service, Santa Fe, NM.

163. Ruth, T. K., J. M. Packard, D. S. Neighbor, and J. R. Skiles. 1991. Mountain lion use of an area of high recreational development in Big Bend National Park, Texas. In *Mountain lion-human interaction*, ed. C. E. Braun, 20. Denver: Colorado Division of Wildlife.

164. Cat News. 1995. California mountain lion "Hot Spot" closed. *Cat News* 22: 13.

165. Seidensticker, J., and S. Lumpkin. 1992. Mountain lions don't stalk people. True or false? *Smithsonian* 22: 113–122.

166. Lindzey, F. G. 1991. Needs for mountain lion research and special management studies. In *Mountain lion-human interaction*, ed. C. E. Braun, 52–53. Denver: Colorado Division of Wildlife.

167. Lindzey, F. G. 1991. Managing lions in a changing social environment. In *Mountain lion-human interaction*, ed. C. E. Braun, 81–82. Denver: Colorado Division of Wildlife.

168. Benson, D. E. 1991. Bridging philosophy and management for lions and people. In *Mountain lion-human interaction*, ed. C. E. Braun, 83–85. Denver: Colorado Division of Wildlife.

169. Hornocker, M. G. 1991. A synopsis of the symposium and challenges for the future. In *Mountain lion-human interaction*, ed. C. E. Braun, 54–55. Denver: Colorado Division of Wildlife.

170. Maehr, D. S., and J. A. Cox. 1995. Landscape features and panthers in Florida. *Conserv. Biol.* 9: 1008–1019.

171. Roelke, M. E., D. P. Schultz, C. F. Facemire, S. F. Sundlof, and H. E. Royals. 1991. Mercury contamination in Florida panthers. A report of the Florida Panther Technical Subcommittee to the Florida Panther Interagency Committee, December 1991.

172. Facemire, C. F. 1994. Reproductive impairment in the Florida panther: Are environmental contaminants a factor? In *Proceedings of the Florida Panther Conference*, ed. D. B. Jordan, 413–421. Atlanta, GA: U.S. Fish and Wildlife Service.

173. U.S. Fish and Wildlife Service. 1987. Florida Panther (*Felis concolor coryi*) Recovery Plan. Florida Panther Interagency Committee, U.S. Fish and Wildlife Service, Atlanta, GA. 75 pp.

174. Belden, R. C., and B. W. Hagedorn. 1993. Feasibility of translocating panthers into northern Florida. *J. Wildl. Mgmt.* 57: 388–397.

175. U.S. Fish and Wildlife Service. 1994. Florida panther recovery plan. Genetic restoration of the Florida panther. Gainesville, FL.

176. Maehr, D. S., and G. B. Caddick. 1995. Demographics and genetic introgression in the Florida panther. *Conserv. Biol.* 9: 1295–1298.

177. Maehr, D. S. 1990. The Florida panther and private lands. *Conserv. Biol.* 4: 167–170.

178. Alvarez, K. 1993. *Twilight of the panther: Biology, bureaucracy and failure in an endangered species program*. Sarasota, FL: Myakka River Publishing.

179. Ross, P. I., and M. G. Jalkotzy. 1989. The Sheep River cougar project, Phase II. Final report. Arc Associated Resource Consultants Ltd., Calgary, Alberta.

180. Belden, R. C., biological scientist, Florida Game and Freshwater Fish Commission, Gainesville, FL. Personal communication.

Clouded leopard

Neofelis nebulosa (Griffiths, 1821)

Looking like a big cat in miniature, the clouded leopard has the powerful, robust build of a large cat and, for its size, the longest canines of any living felid. Though a large clouded leopard can weigh almost as much as a common leopard, taxonomists have traditionally not included clouded leopards with the *Panthera*, or "big" cats. Indeed, the clouded leopard is a good example of a major stumbling block in the long and continuing effort to understand the systematics of the Felidae. Based on their morphological characteristics and vocalizations, the lion, leopard, tiger, jaguar, snow leopard, and clouded leopard form a monophyletic group.[1,2,3] However, molecular studies suggest that the clouded leopard appeared much earlier than the *Panthera* cats, having diverged from the line leading to the modern *Panthera* in the early Pliocene epoch, possibly as early as the Miocene, about 5 to 6 million years ago. These studies suggest that clouded leopards are not closely allied to the *Panthera*,[4,5,6] but there is still no consensus among morphological, behavioral, and molecular taxonomists.[2,3,6]

DESCRIPTION

The clouded leopard is about the size of a small leopard. The tail is long, nearly as long as the head and body, and the legs are short and stout, ending in broad paws. The ears are relatively short and rounded, and the backs of the ears are black with a central grayish spot. The cat's skull is long and low, with well-developed crests for the attachment of jaw muscles. This feature is probably related to the cat's exceptionally long canine teeth; the upper pair of canines may measure 4.0 centimeters or longer.[7] These teeth are so long that some people have compared them to those of the extinct saber-toothed cats. However, unlike the bladelike teeth of the saber-toothed cats, the canines of clouded leopards are more rounded in cross section, and their lower canines are also quite large, not reduced like those of the extinct cat.[8] There is a very broad gap between the canines and the premolars, and the first upper premolar is often missing.[9,10]

Clouded leopard fur is instantly recognizable by its distinctive cloud-shaped markings. On the cat's back and sides the background color varies from earthy brown or dark gray to pale or rich yellowish brown, shading to white or pale tawny on the undersides. The fur is marked with large, elongate or squarish dark blotches on the sides, separated by areas of the paler ground color. Each blotch is often partially outlined in black on the posterior edge, shading to a lighter color

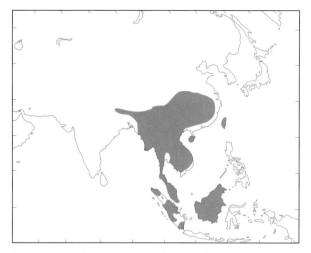

Figure 40. Distribution of the clouded leopard.

at the anterior edge. In some forms the pattern on the flanks is more rosettelike, the blotches being smaller and less elongated. Small black spots mark the crown, and a black patch occurs above each eye. The muzzle is white, and there are black stripes on the cheeks, some of which extend onto the neck. A black line runs from behind each ear onto the nape. Large black spots mark the undersides and the limbs. The tail is well furred and thick and is marked with black rings, some of which may be broken.[7,9] Black or melanistic clouded leopards have been reported only from Borneo.[11]

The marking patterns on the coat resemble those of the marbled cat, a species that also has a very long tail, but the clouded leopard is a much larger cat. This cat's extraordinarily beautiful coat has made it a popular animal in the fur trade. The coat markings have given rise to its English common name as well as other names, such as "mint leopard" in China, where the cat's blotches are thought to look like mint leaves.[12]

DISTRIBUTION

Clouded leopards are found south of the Himalaya in Nepal, Sikkim, Bhutan, and Assam and south to Myanmar, southern China, Taiwan, Vietnam, Laos, Cambodia, Thailand, peninsular Malaysia, Sumatra, and Borneo (fig. 40).[7,13,14,15,16,17,18,19,20,21]

ECOLOGY AND BEHAVIOR

What little is known of the natural history of clouded leopards stems largely from brief glimpses of the animal in the wild and from observations of captives. Many early accounts depict the clouded leopard as a rare, secretive, arboreal, and nocturnal denizen of dense primary forest.[9,22,23,24,25,26,27] This description still appears to be fairly accurate, although more recent observations suggest that clouded leopards may not be as arboreal or nocturnal as previously thought.

Physically, the clouded leopard is well suited to an arboreal lifestyle. This cat's long, thick tail, short legs, and large feet allow it to move easily through the trees. Hemmer's observations of captive animals show that they are able to climb slowly down a vertical trunk headfirst, move along horizontal branches while hanging beneath them like a sloth, and hang from branches by their hind feet.[28] The clouded leopard's arboreal abilities are thought to rival those of the highly arboreal margay of South America, and statements such as Weigel's observation that "the clouded leopard can move so skillfully it can seize monkeys, squirrels, and birds in the treetops"[29] have strengthened the notion that it is a strictly arboreal hunter. The arboreal habits of the cat are also suggested by its Malaysian name, *harimau-dahan*, meaning "branch-tiger."[16] However, Guggisberg pointed out that many of the specimens bagged by European sportsmen were taken on the ground.[7] They were usually animals that had moved out of cover while a stretch of forest was being beaten for other game. According to the early hunting literature, clouded leopards were also occasionally brought to bay on the ground by hunting dogs.[25]

A 1986 survey of villagers, timber workers, and forestry officials in Sabah and Sarawak resulted in 161 first-hand reports of clouded leopard sightings, about one-third of which had occurred in the year prior to the survey.[16] Of all the sightings, 82 percent were of clouded leopards traveling on the ground, usually on roads and trails in either primary or selectively logged secondary forest. Almost all the sightings of clouded leopards in trees were in primary forest, and 75 percent of these were during the daytime. The survey team concluded that clouded leopards were not truly arboreal, but used trees in primary forest as daytime rest sites. Elevated sites were thought to be important as refuges from the terrestrial leeches found in many Asian forests. The team further concluded that, while the clouded leopard may prefer tall trees, the absence of such trees does not appear to restrict the cat's activities. Other reports suggest that clouded leopards use mangrove forests, a habitat typically lacking in tall trees. Clouded leopards have been found in coastal hardwood forests at sea level and in coniferous forests at elevations of 3,000 meters in Taiwan.[15]

In southern Nepal in 1987, the capture of two clouded leopard cubs and a subadult male in marginal dry woodlands suggested that the species may be more flexible in its habitat needs than previously thought.[19] The subadult male was radio-collared and released into Royal Chitwan National Park, about 100 kilometers east of where it was captured. The cat was followed for ten days, after which it was lost. In the first week after release the cat frequently rested during the daytime in tall, dense grasslands on the floodplain in the park. It later moved into the sal forest of the Siwalik hills and was last located about 8 kilometers west of the release site. All the monitoring indicated that this cat was terrestrial.

Though solid conclusions about the clouded leopard's lifestyle await an in-depth study, it is possible to make a few preliminary observations. The margay's arboreal capabilities are well known, but the single margay that has been radio-collared to date was found to travel mostly on the ground.[30] The same is likely to be true of the much larger clouded leopard, as movement on the ground is faster and more efficient. Clouded leopards are clearly able to hunt on the ground, and the extent to which they either hunt arboreal prey or spend time in trees may differ by habitat and be influenced by the presence of larger predators such as the common leopard and tiger.

Some daytime movement has been observed in the wild and in captive animals, suggesting that clouded leopards are not strictly nocturnal. Other observers have suggested that clouded leopards are crepuscular. However, the time of day when these cats are active probably depends on the activity of their prey and levels of human disturbance.

Feeding Ecology

What little is known of the feeding ecology of the clouded leopard suggests that it preys on a variety of arboreal and terrestrial vertebrates. In India the cat feeds on small deer and other animals of similar size, including domestic stock such as goats and pigs.[9] Birds and poultry are sometimes taken; the subadult male captured in Nepal was caught inside a chicken coop.[19] In Borneo the cat is reported to prey on pigs, deer, monkeys, orangutans, and smaller mammals.[31] A recent survey from Malaysian Borneo includes reports of clouded leopards with kills of young sambar deer, barking deer, mouse deer, bearded pig, palm civet, gray leaf monkey, fish, and porcupine. A barking deer and a bearded pig appeared to have been killed by a bite to the back of the neck.[16]

Selous and Banks, who kept a young male clouded leopard in captivity in Sarawak, observed that it refused dead meat, but consumed two chickens a day. The cat carefully plucked the chickens and also licked the fur off a monkey before starting to feed.[25] Weigel reports that the clouded leopard often tears meat off its prey by grabbing the meat with its incisors and canines and then jerking its head up, a behavior typically seen only in big cats.[32]

Social Organization

Nothing is known of the social organization of clouded leopards. There is some speculation that they may live in pairs, based on observations of two cats emerging from cover together and of a male and female clouded leopard extracting an adult male proboscis monkey from a tree and killing it.[11] It is most likely that these observations involve courting pairs, however, or a female and her large offspring.

Presumably clouded leopards demarcate their home ranges with the usual system of scent marks and scrapes. In captivity, the scent-marking behavior of clouded leopards includes urine spraying, scraping, rubbing the head on objects, and clawing logs.[28,33,34]

Clouded leopards have the typical repertoire of felid vocalizations, including the mew, hiss, spit, and growl, but they probably do not purr.[3,28,35,36,37] In friendly close-contact situations they make a short, low-intensity, snorting call—an activity that has been dubbed "prusten."[38] Prusten is not common in felids; only tigers, snow leopards, and jaguars also vocalize in this manner.[35] Indeed, the clouded leopard shows such a close relationship with the tiger in its vocalizations that some taxonomists have placed the tiger in the genus *Neofelis* with the clouded leopard.[39] The clouded leopard also has a long (one to five seconds) moaning call that is reported to travel quite some distance. In Thailand clouded leopards are rumored to use elevated areas known as "tiger hills" to deliver these calls.[13] It is uncertain whether the call serves a mating function, keeps animals apart, or both.

Reproduction and Development

Nothing is known of the clouded leopard's mating behavior in the wild. This is a serious shortcoming, because breeding this cat in captivity has proved to be difficult. Institutions such as Howlett's Zoo in England

and the Rare Feline Breeding Center in Florida have had excellent breeding success, but they are exceptions. Mating encounters between captive clouded leopards often result in aggressive behavior, and males are known to kill females with a neck bite that breaks the spine or neck.[40,41] Many breeders believe that compatible pairs are essential for successful breeding. Although these cats do not appear to be monogamous in the wild, the most successful way of breeding them in captivity seems to be to raise a male and a female together from the time they are a few weeks old, thereby establishing a pair when the cats are young.[42,43]

Two hand-reared clouded leopards at the San Diego Zoo first mated when the female was twenty-one months old and the male twenty-two months old. Numerous copulations were observed over a period of four days; twelve copulations were observed in one eight-hour period. The average length of a copulation was twenty-five seconds (range fifteen to sixty-three seconds). The male applied the stereotypic neck bite before intromission, at which time the female vocalized. These matings resulted in the birth of two young 89 days later.[34]

The gestation period ranges from 85 to 109 days, but 88 to 95 days seems more typical.[43,44,45,46] Litters of one to five young have been reported, but twins appear frequently. Newborns weigh from 140 to 280 grams.[37,46,47,48] At birth the kitten's coat has the large lateral spots of the adult's, but the spots are all black; the young do not obtain their adult coloration until they are six months old. Kittens open their eyes at 2 to 11 days of age; they are walking by 19 to 20 days, able to climb at six weeks, and beginning to eat solid food sometime between seven and ten weeks, although suckling continues until they are 80 to 100 days old.[43,44,45] Fellner reports that young clouded leopards were able to kill a chicken when they were 80 days old.[44]

Clouded leopards reach sexual maturity by twenty to thirty months of age.[34,37,46,47] There is little information on the interbirth interval of clouded leopards because in captivity it is sometimes necessary to remove kittens from the den shortly after birth for hand rearing.[48] A female clouded leopard at the Frankfurt Zoo had two litters about one year apart,[44] and a female at the Dresden Zoo also produced successive litters about one year apart.[43] At the Dublin Zoo one female gave birth to a new litter about sixteen months after she had the first, and successfully reared these kittens herself; for another female the interbirth interval was ten months.[46]

There are two zoo records of clouded leopards living to the age of fifteen years, and another in the Philadelphia Zoo lived to be almost seventeen years old.[49]

STATUS IN THE WILD

Little is known of the clouded leopard's status in any part of its geographic range. In Sumatra the conversion of primary forest to agriculture has increased dramatically in recent decades. Estimates vary, but 65 to 80 percent of lowland forests have disappeared, and possibly 15 percent of mountain forests are gone. The consequences of this change cannot favor the clouded leopard. Another threat to the species is the use of poisons by villagers to eliminate predators that attack cattle and poultry. The cat may also be poisoned simply for its skin, which may fetch U.S.$2,000 on the black market. The clouded leopard is still reported to occur in Sumatra, but only in a few discontinuous areas, and its general status is unknown.[17,18]

In 1974 McCullough reported that clouded leopards were still likely to be present in the Central Mountain Range of Taiwan, although no direct evidence was found.[50] A 1986 status survey in Taiwan by Rabinowitz reported no sightings of clouded leopards since 1983 and a general decline in observations of the cat from the mid-1970s. While the decrease in sightings may be related to fewer people hunting, the long-term survival of the cat in Taiwan is threatened by deforestation and poaching of the cat's prey. Large game species located within two days' walking distance of human habitation are dwindling rapidly, as the market for meat and animal products is a thriving business.[15]

A new market for imported clouded leopard skins has appeared in Taiwan, with skins being smuggled in from mainland China.[51] Clouded leopard skins were used as ceremonial jackets by tribal people in Taiwan before their conversion to Christianity; great symbolic significance attached to the killing of a clouded leopard, and the hunter was afforded heroic status. With the influx of imported hides the symbolic importance has been lost; many men are apparently now willing to pay U.S.$1,500 for a pelt, whose ownership has simply become a status symbol.[52]

In China, Wang Zong-Yi and Wang Sung report that the clouded leopard is threatened by overhunting for its fur and body parts.[53] Clouded leopard pelts and bones are sold openly, even though it is illegal, and skins can be bought in markets for U.S.$50–$75.[14] In 1987 a restaurant owner in Huizhou was fined for trading two clouded leopards, one of which he had bought from a farmer for U.S.$270.[54] A recent survey in Jiangxi Province indicated that clouded leopard populations has declined to 30 percent of their mid-1950 levels.[55] An estimated thirty to forty clouded leopards are trapped each year in Jiangxi, many of them caught in traps set for wild pigs and deer. While the cat appears to be widespread and common in Jiangxi, incidental trapping poses a serious threat.[56]

In Malaysian Borneo the clouded leopard is not abundant, but it still inhabits many areas and, according to Rabinowitz and co-workers, "seems to be in no imminent danger of extinction." They caution, however, that current deforestation and logging operations may alter the status of this cat in the near future.[16]

Loss of forest cover and hunting for skins has also contributed to the decline of the clouded leopard in Bangladesh. The cat now occurs in small numbers in the undisturbed evergreen forests of Chittagong and Chittagong Hill Tracts. Skins are openly sold in the Chittagong market, where in 1983 a pelt brought U.S.$100. Khan believes that many of the skins sold in Chittagong represent animals caught in the neighboring forests of Myanmar and India.[57]

Clouded leopards were thought to be extinct in Nepal until 1987, when four animals were found. Prior to this, the last record of the animal in Nepal dates from 1863.[19] Despite the fact that the animal is listed on appendix I of CITES, of which Nepal is a member, clouded leopard pelts are still available in the fur markets of Kathmandu.[58]

Clouded leopards are reported to occur in several parks and wildlife sanctuaries in Thailand, although their status is uncertain. The cat's continued existence in Thailand is threatened by deforestation, hunting for pelts, and capture for the live animal trade. As recently as 1979, clouded leopards were being offered for sale in Bangkok for U.S.$2,000 to $3,000.[13,59] A recent threat to the species in Thung Yai Wildlife Sanctuary, Thailand's largest and richest virgin rainforest, has been removed by the Thai government's 1987 decision to suspend plans to build a hydroelectric dam on the River Kwai.[60]

STATUS IN CAPTIVITY
The clouded leopard is reasonably well represented in zoos. In 1986 the Species Survival Plan summary reported that 224 clouded leopards were held in seventy-

nine institutions throughout the world, 86 of them in North American zoos. However, the species is difficult to breed in zoos, and less than 20 percent of adult fe-males listed in the *International Clouded Leopard Studbook* have bred successfully in captivity.[34]

TABLE 53 MEASUREMENTS AND WEIGHTS OF ADULT CLOUDED LEOPARDS

HB	n	T	n	WT	n	Location	Source
1,020	3m	842	3m	19.1	3m	Nepal/Sikkim	9
(953–1,067)		(737–914)		(17.7–20.2)			
686, 813	2f	610, 635	2f			Nepal/Sikkim	9
813	1m	775	1m			Thailand	9
750–950	?	550–800	?	16–23	?	Thailand	13
825	1f	716	1f	11.4	1f	Malaysia	61
952, 1,066	2?	736, 917	2?	16.6	1?	China	62
940	1f	820	1f	11.5	1f	Thailand	63
1,080	1m	870	1m	18	1m	Thailand	63

Note: HB = head and body length (mm), T = tail length (mm), WT = weight (kg). n = sample size. Sex: m = male, f = female, ? = unknown. Mean values are presented only for sample sizes of three or more. Range of values is in parentheses.

REFERENCES

1. Hemmer, H. 1981. Die evolution der Pantherkatzen—Modell zur Überprüfung der Brauchbarkeit der hennigschen Prinzipien der phylogenetischen Systematik für wirbeltierpaläontologische Studien. *Paläontol. Z.* 55: 109–116.

2. Salles, L. O. 1992. Felid phylogenetics: Extant taxa and skull morphology (Felidae, Aeluroidea). *Am. Mus. Novitates* 3047: 1–67.

3. Peters, G., and M. H. Hast. 1994. Hyoid structure, laryngeal anatomy, and vocalization in felids (Mammalia: Carnivora: Felidae). *Z. Säugetierk.* 59: 87–104.

4. Collier, G. E., and S. J. O'Brien. 1985. A molecular phylogeny of the Felidae: Immunological distance. *Evolution* 39: 473–487.

5. O'Brien, S. J., G. E. Collier, R. E. Benveniste, W. G. Nash, A. K. Newman, J. M. Simonson, M. A. Eichelberger, U. S. Seal, D. Janssen, M. Bush, and D. E. Wildt. 1987. Setting the molecular clock in Felidae: The great cats, *Panthera*. In *Tigers of the world: The biology, biopolitics, management, and conservation of an endangered species*, ed. R. L. Tilson and U. S. Seal, 10–27. Park Ridge, NJ: Noyes Publications.

6. Wayne, R. K., R. E. Benveniste, D. N. Janczewski, and S. J. O'Brien. 1989. Molecular and biochemical evolution of the Carnivora. In *Carnivore behavior, ecology, and evolution*, ed. J. L. Gittleman, 465–494. Ithaca, NY: Cornell University Press.

7. Guggisberg, C. A. W. 1975. *Wild cats of the world*. New York: Taplinger.

8. Van Valkenburgh, B., and C. B. Ruff. 1987. Canine tooth strength and killing behaviour in large carnivores. *J. Zool.* 212: 379–397.

9. Pocock, R. I. 1939. *The fauna of British India including Ceylon and Burma.* Vol. 1, *Mammalia.* London: Taylor and Francis.

10. Werdelin, L. 1983. Morphological patterns in the skulls of cats. *Biol. J. Linn. Soc.* 19: 375–391.

11. Gibson-Hill, C. A. 1950. Notes on the clouded leopard [*Neofelis nebulosa* (Griffith)]. *J. Bombay Nat. Hist. Soc.* 49: 543–546.

12. Allen, G. M. 1938. *The mammals of China and Mongolia.* American Museum of Natural History.

13. Lekagul, B., and J. A. McNeely. 1977. *Mammals of Thailand.* Bangkok: Association for the Conservation of Wildlife.

14. Tan, B. 1984. The status of felids in China. In The plight of the cats: Proceedings of the meeting and workshop of the IUCN/SSC Cat Specialist Group at Kanha National Park, Madhya Pradesh, India, 33–47. Unpublished report, IUCN/SSC Cat Specialist Group, Bougy-Villars, Switzerland.

15. Rabinowitz, A. 1988. The clouded leopard in Taiwan. *Oryx* 22: 46–47.

16. Rabinowitz, A., P. Andau, and P. P. K. Chai. 1987. The clouded leopard in Malaysian Borneo. *Oryx* 21: 107–111.

17. Santiapillai, C., and K. R. Ashby. 1988. The clouded leopard in Sumatra. *Oryx* 22: 44–45.

18. Santiapillai, C. 1989. The status and conservation of the clouded leopard (*Neofelis nebulosa diardi*) in Sumatra. *Tigerpaper* 16(1): 1–7.

19. Dinerstein, E., and J. N. Mehta. 1989. The clouded leopard in Nepal. *Oryx* 23: 199–201.

20. Corbet, G. B., and J. E. Hill. 1992. *The mammals of the Indomalayan region.* Oxford: Oxford University Press.

21. Choudhury, A. 1993. The clouded leopard in Assam. *Oryx* 27: 51–53.

22. Raffles, S. 1821. Descriptive catalogue of a zoological collection made in Sumatra. *Trans. Linn. Soc. Lond.* 13: 239–274.

23. Sterndale, R. A. 1884. *Natural history of the Mammalia of India and Ceylon.* Calcutta: Thacker, Spink.

24. Swinhoe, R. 1862. On the mammals of the island of Formosa (China). *Proc. Zool. Soc. Lond.* 23: 347–365.

25. Selous, E. M., and E. Banks. 1935. The clouded leopard in Sarawak. *Sarawak Mus. J.* 4: 263–266.

26. Wood, H. S. 1949. The clouded leopard. *J. Bengal Nat. Hist. Soc.* 23: 77–79.

27. Prater, S. H. 1971. *The book of Indian animals*, 3rd (revised) ed. Bombay: Bombay Natural History Society.

28. Hemmer, H. 1968. Untersuchungen zur Stammesgeschichte der Pantherkatzen (Pantherinae). Tiel II. Studien zur Ethologie des *Neofelis nebulosa* (Griffith 1821) und des Irbis *Uncia uncia*

(Schreber 1775). *Veröff. Zool. Staatssamml. München* 12: 155–247.

29. Weigel, I. 1961. Das Fellmuster der wildlebenden Katzenarten und der Hauskatze in vergeleichender und stammesgeschichtlicher Hinsicht. *Säugetierk. Mitt.* 9: 1–120.

30. Konecny, M. J. 1989. Movement patterns and food habits of four sympatric carnivore species in Belize, Central America. In *Advances in Neotropical mammalogy*, ed. K. H. Redford and J. F. Eisenberg, 243–264. Gainesville, FL: Sandhill Crane Press.

31. Payne, J., C. Francis, and K. Phillips. 1985. *A field guide to the mammals of Borneo*. Malaysia: The Sabah Society.

32. Weigel, I. 1972. Small felids and clouded leopards. In *Grzimek's animal life encyclopedia*, vol. 12, *Mammals* III, ed. H. C. B. Grzimek, 281–332. New York: Van Nostrand Reinhold.

33. Wemmer, C., and K. Scow. 1977. Communication in the Felidae with emphasis on scent marking and contact patterns. In *How animals communicate*, ed. T. A. Sebeok, 749–766. Bloomington: Indiana University Press.

34. Yamada, J. K., and B. S. Durrant. 1988. Vaginal cytology and behavior in the clouded leopard. *Felid* 2: 1–3.

35. Peters, G. 1984. A special type of vocalization in the Felidae. *Acta Zool. Fennica* 171: 89–92.

36. Peters, G. 1978. Vergleichende Untersuchung zur Lautgebung einiger Feliden (Mammalia, Felidae). *Spixiana*, suppl. 1: 1–206.

37. Andrews, P., Hexagon Farm Wild Feline Breeding Facility, 1187 Merrill Road, San Juan Bautista, CA. Personal communication.

38. Peters, G. 1984. On the structure of friendly close range vocalizations in terrestrial carnivores (Mammalia: Carnivora: Fissipedia). *Z. Säugetierk.* 49: 157–182.

39. Leyhausen, P., B. Grzimek, and V. Zhiwotschenko. 1990. Panther-like cats and their relatives. In *Grzimek's encyclopedia*, vol. 4, *Mammals*, 1–49. New York: McGraw-Hill.

40. Collins, L. 1987. Clouded leopard. *Zoogoer* 16: 13.

41. Seager, S. W. J., and C. N. Demorest. 1978. Reproduction of captive wild carnivores. In *Zoo and wild animal medicine*, ed. M. E. Fowler, 667–706. Philadelphia: W. B. Saunders.

42. Baudy, R. E. 1971. Notes on breeding felids at the Rare Feline Breeding Center. *Int. Zoo Yrbk.* 11: 121–123.

43. Geidel, B., and W. Gensch. 1976. The rearing of clouded leopards in the presence of the male. *Int. Zoo Yrbk.* 16: 124–126.

44. Fellner, K. 1965. Natural rearing of clouded leopards *Neofelis nebulosa* at Frankfurt Zoo. *Int. Zoo Yrbk.* 5: 111–113.

45. Fellner, K. 1968. Erste naturliche Aufzucht von Nebelpardern (*Neofelis nebulosa*) in einem zoo. *Zool. Garten* (n.f.) 33: 105–137.

46. Murphy, E. T. 1976. Breeding the clouded leopard at Dublin Zoo. *Int. Zoo Yrbk.* 16: 122–124.

47. Fontaine, P. A. 1965. Breeding clouded leopards (*Neofelis nebulosa*) at Dallas Zoo. *Int. Zoo Yrbk.* 5: 113–114.

48. Eaton, R. L. 1984. Survey of smaller felid breeding. *Zool. Garten* (n.f.) 54: 101–120.

49. Acharjyo, L. N., and Ch. G. Mishra. 1981. Some notes on the longevity of two species of Indian wild cats in captivity. *J. Bombay Nat. Hist. Soc.* 78: 155.

50. McCullough, D. R. 1974. Status of larger mammals in Taiwan. World Wildlife Fund Report. Taipei, Taiwan: Tourism Bureau.

51. Nowell, K. 1990. Formosa and the clouded leopard. *Cat News* 13: 14–15.

52. Nowell, K. 1990. The clouded leopard (*Neofelis nebulosa*) and wildlife trade in Taiwan. *Felid* 4(1): 16.

53. Wang, Z.-Y., and S. Wang. 1986. Distribution and recent status of the Felidae in China. In *Cats of the world: Biology, conservation, and management*, ed. S. D. Miller and D. D. Everett, 201–209. Washington, DC: National Wildlife Federation.

54. Cat News. 1987. Chinese restaurant fined for trading in clouded leopards. *Cat News* 7: 25.

55. Lu, H., and H. Sheng. 1986. The status and population fluctuation of the leopard cat in China. In *Cats of the world: Biology, conservation, and management*, ed. S. D. Miller and D. D. Everett, 59–62. Washington, DC: National Wildlife Federation.

56. Koehler, G. M. 1991. Survey of remaining wild population of south China tigers. Final project report, WWF Project 4512/China.

57. Khan, M. A. R. 1986. The status and distribution of the cats in Bangladesh. In *Cats of the world: Biology, conservation, and management*, ed. S. D. Miller and D. D. Everett, 43–49. Washington, DC: National Wildlife Federation.

58. Barnes, L. 1989. Illegal furs on Durbar Marg. *Himal* 2: 25–26.

59. Humphrey, S. R., and J. R. Bain. 1990. *Endangered animals of Thailand*. Gainesville, FL: Sandhill Crane Press.

60. Thai dam plans suspended. 1988. *Felid* 2(3): 15.

61. Medway, L. 1978. *The wild mammals of Malaya (peninsular Malaysia) and Singapore*, 2nd ed. Oxford: Oxford University Press.

62. Shaw, T. H. 1962. *Economic fauna of China: Mammals*. Beijing: Scientific Press.

63. Austin, S. C., and M. E. Tewes. 1999. Ecology of the clouded leopard in Khao Yai National Park, Thailand. *Cat News* 31: 17–18.

Lion

Panthera leo (Linnaeus, 1758)

The earliest true lions appeared in Europe 600,000 years ago. Believed to be the largest cats that ever lived, these early cave lions were some 25 percent larger than today's largest lions. The European cave lion (*Panthera leo spelaea*) spread from Europe to eastern Asia, and fossil material about 400,000 years old has been found at China's Peking Man site in Choukoutien, where fossil tigers have also been found.[1] Cave paintings and fossil evidence from 200,000 years ago show that cave lions later coexisted with early humans—lion bones have been found alongside artifacts from Neanderthal people.

The North American lion (*Panthera atrox*) closely resembles the European cave lion. Fossils of *P. atrox* have been found in eastern Siberia, Alaska, and at other sites in North America.[2] At one time the lion was probably the world's most wide-ranging land mammal, found from Africa through Eurasia and North America into South America.[3] *P. atrox* survived in North America until about 11,500 years ago, living alongside humans, dire wolves, horses, and bison.[4,5] Several authorities believe that *P. atrox* may have been social, living in prides or groups like the lions of today.[3]

During the Pleistocene epoch lions lived as far north as England and ranged east to Palestine, Persia, Arabia, and India. Around 5,000 years ago, the Pharaohs of the Nile civilization used the lion prominently in their art, and many tombs were decorated with elaborate carvings and friezes depicting lions. The Great Sphinx of Egypt has a human head and the body of a lion. The Egyptians worshiped the Sphinx as the guardian of the Nile and of the pyramids where their kings were entombed.

Surprisingly, lions also dominate the folklore and art of Sri Lanka, an island that has neither lions nor tigers today. There is no fossil evidence that tigers ever reached Sri Lanka, but a single fossil lion tooth and the frequent appearance of the lion in Sri Lankan art, legend, and folklore suggest that the animal may have survived on the island until historic times. The Sinhalese are the majority ethnic group in Sri Lanka; literally translated, *sinhalese* means "lion race." Early Sri Lankan sculptures of lions bear a strong resemblance to the living animal, but later images, which might have been carved after the lion became extinct on the island, are much more stylized. There is also a great deal of similarity between the African name for lion, *simba,* and the Indian *singa,* suggesting that one may have been derived from the other.[6] Most people believe that the lion was confined to northwestern India

and, like the tiger, did not reach Sri Lanka before the island separated from the mainland. However, P. Deraniyagala, former curator of the Colombo Museum, believes that the fossil tooth and frequent reference to the lion in Sri Lankan culture suggests that the lion did inhabit Sri Lanka at one time.

China is even further outside the lion's known geographic range than Sri Lanka, but lions appear frequently in Chinese ornaments, temple statues, and stone carvings. Though live lions were probably imported from India from time to time as gifts to emperors, the lion image probably came to China from Nepal and northern India along with the pagoda style of architecture.[7]

Superficially similar to the South American "jaguar transformations" that occur when a shaman "becomes" a jaguar are the practices of the "lion men" of Africa. Guggisberg records how witch doctors in the Singida area, in what was at that time Tanganyika, ran a lucrative extortion business in the early twentieth century by threatening to turn themselves into lions and kill people who did not pay them. Many people were murdered by young men dressed as lions, wearing lion paws as gloves on their hands and feet. These *mbojo,* or "lion men," reappeared in the same area in 1946, some twenty-five years later, and 103 deaths were attributed to their activities. Murders were made to look like the work of man-killing lions, and the common belief in were-lions was exploited by secret societies.[8]

In biblical times lions were common in Palestine, so it is not surprising that the Bible contains many references to lions and parables about their behavior. When the king cast Daniel into the lions' den as a test of faith, Daniel survived the night, and the test. Later the lion's reputation for kindness and magnanimity was extended by Pliny and Aristotle. According to Pliny, the lion was reputed to be the only wild creature to be "gentle to those who humble themselves to him and will not touch any such upon their submission, but spares whatever creature lieth prostrate before him." Pliny also reported that "lions are not at all crafty and fraudulent, neither are they suspicious. They never look askew but always cast their eyes directly forward, and they do not like any man to look sidelong upon them."[7]

In Europe, lions symbolized courage in battle, represented royalty and power in heraldry, and were the protectors and companions of saints. Richard the Lion-Heart of England is the best known of many rulers who took the lion's name to illustrate and enhance their courage and majesty. Kings and noblemen began displaying images of lions on their shields, but the image became so popular that a whole slew of different positions had to be invented for the heraldic lion—one foot in the air (rampant), two feet in the air (salient), seated (sejant), and many others.[7]

The ancient Romans imported thousands of lions from North Africa for personal pets, menageries, and public spectacles. Fights that pitted lions against gladiators and mounted guards were popular entertainment. Though some of the more humane Romans were indignant at the poor treatment of the king of beasts, others, such as Julius Caesar and Germanicus, slaughtered hundreds of lions for public spectacle.

In the Middle Ages a few lions were kept in European menageries in Germany, England, France, and Italy. The best known of these early zoological collections was the one belonging to Henry I of England that was eventually moved to the Tower of London, where it remained until 1840.

Occasionally lions were forced to fight tigers, but apparently the tigers always won. This observation was confirmed more recently in the 1950s by a keeper at the Bronx Zoo, where a lion cub named Zambezi and a young tiger named Ranee were raised together. Their occasional fights always resulted in victory for the tiger. Alfred Martini, the keeper, described the tiger as being a better fighter, "like a clever boxer against a heavy hitter, shrewder and trickier."[9]

DESCRIPTION

Describing the lion in his 1607 volume, *History of four-footed beasts*, Edward Topsell wrote, "The color of lions is generally yellow. The hair of some of them is curled, and some of them have long, shaggy, thin hair, not standing upright but falling flat, longer before and shorter behind; and although the curling of the hair is a token of sluggish timidity, yet if the hair is long and curled on the top only, this portends sluggish animosity."[10]

Temperament aside, lions are well known for their unpatterned coats, which can be anywhere from light buff or silvery gray to yellowish red or dark brown. The underparts are generally a paler version of the overall coat color. Both males and females have a black tuft or tassel on the end of the tail and a horny patch of calloused skin on the last tail vertebra. There is a black patch on the back of each ear. Melanism and albinism seem to be uncommon in lions. Albino lions are occa-

sionally recorded in Kruger National Park, and three white lions were born in 1975 in the Timbavati Nature Reserve in the Transvaal.[11]

The fur of newborn lion cubs is patterned with dark rosettes that fuse to form stripes in some places. A faded version of these dark, circular, leopardlike coat markings remains on the belly skin of subadults and some adult females. This coat pattern suggests that the ancestors of modern lions lived in more densely forested habitats.[12]

There are few obvious differences between the African and Asiatic lion subspecies. The Asiatic lion has a pronounced belly fold, a flap of skin that runs the length of the belly between the front and hind legs. This fold of skin is almost always present in Asiatic lions, but is rarely seen in African lions. Asiatic lions also have a thicker coat, a longer tail tassel, and a scantier mane.[12,13]

The male lion's distinctive mane can be yellow, brown, or reddish brown in young animals but seems to darken with age. Young males begin to grow a mane as they mature, usually at around three and a half years of age, but as Schaller observes, "the growth rate of the mane varies with the individual, with some having but a short ruff at the age of 4 years and others a heavy mane."[14]

Manes come in all sizes, and they generally increase in length and thickness as the lion gets older. A mane makes an adult male look impressive and serves as a conspicuous visual signal. In open habitat a mane can be seen at some distance. With his mane, combined with a stiff-legged tail-up display posture that Jonathan Kingdon calls the "lion strut," a male lion presents an identifiable and intimidating figure even at a distance.[15] As human biologists studying lions can distinguish among individuals based on their mane colors and characteristics, it seems likely that lions themselves are also able to recognize distant individuals by their manes.

A secondary function of the mane may be protection of the head and neck region during fights. As Schaller says, "The dense mat of hair absorbs blows and harmlessly tangles claws in a part of the body toward which most social contact is directed; bites too may leave an opponent with a mouthful of hair rather than skin."[14]

Physically, lions and tigers are built along very similar lines. Well-muscled forequarters, designed to grapple with large prey, taper to slender hind legs. Topsell described the lion's physique perfectly when he wrote,

"A lion's shoulders and breasts are very strong, as also the forepart of his body, but the members of the hinderparts do degenerate."[10] Male lions stand about 123 centimeters at the shoulder and weigh 145 to 225 kilograms, while the smaller females stand about 107 centimeters and weigh 83 to 168 kilograms. On average, males are about 50 percent heavier than females.[16,17] Tail length is commonly 40 to 50 percent of head and body length.

The lion's skull differs little from that of the tiger: both are solidly built, with massive zygomatic arches and a large sagittal crest for the attachment of powerful jaw and neck muscles. The canine teeth are long, measuring about 60 millimeters. However, the lion's humeroradial index (a measure of its limb proportions), at 98.3, is closer to that of the cheetah (101.3) than to that of the tiger (89.8), suggesting that the lion has become slightly more specialized for running.[18,19] Still, the lion's massive limbs are built more for use as weapons than for running, and lions rarely do any sustained chasing. As Schaller says, "Lions have little stamina —a fast run of a hundred meters makes them pant— and they are unable to pursue an animal rapidly over long distances."[14] When they do run, lions can reach top speeds of 48 to 59 kilometers per hour.[20]

DISTRIBUTION

Today the lion is found only in sub-Saharan Africa and in the Gir Forest of northwestern India (fig. 41). However, until 200 years ago the species was quite widely distributed in North Africa, Arabia, the Middle East, and northwestern India.[21]

Around the middle of the seventeenth century there were lions along the Moroccan Mediterranean coast, but by 1911 only a few survived in Morocco. Lions were once abundant in Algeria and were recorded as inflicting great damage to domestic livestock. By 1868 General Marguerite estimated that the lion had become scarce, and the last animal was thought to have been shot in 1893 not far from Constantine.[7]

In the Middle East the lion was once found throughout the forests of Syria, Iraq, and southwest Iran, but it disappeared as forests were cut and prey declined. The last reliable sighting was in Iran in 1942.[22] In South Africa the lion is now confined to the eastern Transvaal and the Kalahari Gemsbok National Park.[23]

ECOLOGY AND BEHAVIOR

To most people, lion habitat is exemplified by the well-known Serengeti plains of East Africa, but the Seren-

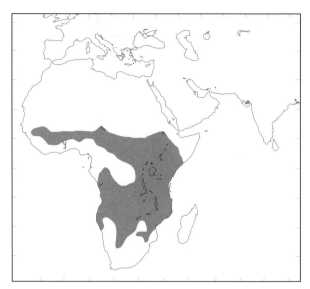

Figure 41. Distribution of the lion.

geti's wooded grasslands and rolling shortgrass plains are quite different from the lion's habitat over much of its geographic range. Elsewhere lions live in woodlands, dry forest, scrub, and even deserts. Visibility is the common factor throughout these various habitat types; compared with tigers, jaguars, and leopards, lions are at home in more open areas.

Lions are primarily terrestrial. Though they are not particularly adept climbers, lions in Africa's Lake Manyara National Park in Tanzania and Queen Elizabeth National Park in Uganda often spend the day resting in the branches of a tree. Guggisberg suggests that this may be a way of avoiding biting insects such as tsetse and *Stomoxyx* flies, which swarm around bushes and do not go into the branches, but it has also been suggested that this habit was initially a means to escape from buffalo and elephants.[7,24] Lions have also been known to jump fences 2 to 3 meters high. Young lions are quite good climbers and quite often play in a tree; cubs have also been known to take to the branches if they are chased by dogs.

Lions seem to dig more than other big cats, and there are frequent observations of lions excavating aardvark burrows to reach warthogs. Describing a lioness doing some very strenuous digging in Nairobi National Park, Guggisberg writes, "She was standing almost on her head in an aardvark hole and was throwing out the earth with her paws exactly like a dog burying a bone. . . . After about half an hour she suddenly gave up and left the hole, which had become so big that half her body was hidden in it."[7]

Though lions do not lie in water during the day to cool themselves as tigers do, they are nevertheless quite capable swimmers. There are records of them regularly swimming across the Okavango and other major rivers.[7]

Lions drink water every day if it is readily available, and observations of prides in the Serengeti and the nearby Ngorongoro Crater show that they drink after every meal.[25] However, lions also seem to be able to manage without drinking at all if water is scarce or unavailable. Lions living in desert or semidesert habitats are able to get sufficient moisture from the blood and body fluids of their prey. Indeed, most of the lion's range within the Kalahari Desert is without surface water. Fritz Eloff followed several different prides of lions in Kalahari Gemsbok National Park for up to twelve days at a time and found that some prides drank more frequently than others. On one occasion three young male lions went without water for nine days during a period of intense heat. During this time the three lions killed one bat-eared fox and three porcupines, so they were obviously not getting much water from their food. Another group of four adult females and a six-month-old cub drank on the first and third nights of the monitoring period, then did not drink for seven consecutive days, during which time they killed an ostrich, two porcupines, and two adult gemsbok. In the Kalahari and other arid environments, lions regulate their body temperature and reduce loss of water through evaporation by resting during the hottest part of the day.[26,27,28]

Lions appear to be primarily nocturnal, but, as with other felids, there are no hard and fast rules as to when they are active. The availability of stalking cover, prey abundance, and habitat type influence when lions are active. Activity patterns may also depend on the season, ambient temperatures, and whether the lions themselves are hunted or disturbed by people. Guggisberg records several instances of lions becoming nocturnal in response to sport hunting.[7] Lions in the Serengeti have two major peaks of activity, one just after dark and another between 0200 and 0400 hours.[14]

Of all the felids, lions are the least active. Two prides, one in the Serengeti and the other in Ngorongoro Crater, were both inactive for an average of about nineteen hours per day. About two to three hours a day was spent traveling, and about an hour was spent hunting and feeding.[25] Lions in Nairobi National Park keep a similar schedule: they rest for twenty hours, spend three hours moving and hunting, and spend about one hour a day feeding.[29] Lions in these parks travel only about 2 to 9 kilometers per day, with the longer distances recorded for lions on the Serengeti plains, where prey abundance is lower.[25] In the arid environments of the Kalahari and Etosha National Park in Namibia, where ungulates are few and far between, lions travel an average of 12 to 13 kilometers per night.[30,31] Stander calculates that lions in Etosha spend about seven hours a night engaged in searching, stalking, and feeding.[31]

A stalk-and-ambush predator must have some form of cover to enable it to approach its prey to within striking distance. For forest-dwelling felids this is not usually a problem, but for lions living in open terrain, cover can become a crucial constraint. The few studies that have measured the importance of stalking cover indicate that the distance covered in the final charge is strongly correlated with the likelihood of a kill. Lions in the Ngorongoro Crater had a high probability of catching Thomson's gazelles when the attack was launched at a distance of 7.6 meters or less, but the probability fell to zero at 15.2 meters.[32] In the Ishasha area of Queen Elizabeth National Park, grass height had a marked influence on hunting success. Hunting success increased with grass height up to 0.8 meters, probably because lions that were able to approach within 20 meters of prey were much more likely to make a kill. At grass heights exceeding 0.8 meters, lions were apparently less able to coordinate a close approach.[33]

Though vegetation is usually thought of as the main type of stalking cover, hunting lions also use termite mounds, gullies, riverbanks, and other features of the terrain to get closer to a potential meal. Studies of lions in the semiarid habitats of Etosha and Queen Elizabeth National Parks illustrate how, in the absence of vegetation, lions make full use of the cover of darkness to approach prey. In both areas, hunting success was greater during moonless periods.[33,34]

Weather can also provide hunting cover. Van Orsdol found that lions tended to initiate hunts more often when storms were imminent, perhaps because a storm reduced the prey's ability to detect them. On five occasions Van Orsdol saw resting lions begin hunting in mid-afternoon when an approaching storm created high winds.[33] Similarly, Etosha lions hunting springbok and zebras were more successful when it was windy.[34]

Lions usually find their prey by searching slowly through suitable habitats, but they are always alert to opportunities for a meal. Lions usually make their own kills, but they are not above scavenging from other predators. They have been observed stealing carcasses from cheetahs, leopards, and hyenas.

Feeding Ecology

Like most of the big cats, lions have been recorded as feeding on almost every imaginable land mammal and even a few aquatic species. Ungulates are their principal prey, but birds, hares, ostrich eggs, a python, fish, crocodiles, and even other lions are on the list of recorded prey.[7,14] Along Namibia's Skeleton Coast lions hunt fur seals, walking as far as 50 kilometers a day along the beach, scavenging for cormorant and seal carcasses washed up by the tide.[35] In the Moremi Wildlife Reserve in the Okavango Delta, predation by lions and leopards is the main cause of adult mortality among baboons.[36] Lions have also been known to kill and eat chimpanzees, though the two usually occupy different habitats. In the Mahale Mountains National Park in Tanzania, chimpanzee remains representing at least four different individuals were found in lion scats.[37]

The ungulate prey that lions hunt is influenced largely by relative prey abundance, with the most locally available species being the dominant item in the diet. However, local prey densities change, and thus so do lion diets. Long-term studies in the Serengeti, for example, show that seven ungulate species account for 90 percent of all kills and meat eaten.[38] When wildebeests are abundant on the plains in the wet season they are the most frequently killed prey, whereas in the dry season lions take the more common Thomson's gazelle and warthog. In the Serengeti woodlands, lion predation is greater on buffalo, which are consistently available on a year-round basis.

Such adaptability is also seen in prey size. Lions eat a variety of prey, ranging in size from hares and antelope fawns, which may weigh 2 kilograms or less, to giraffes and the occasional young elephant, which may weigh as much as 1,000 kilograms.[39] In the Kalahari Desert lions often have to make do with small prey for days on end. One pride of three males managed to kill only three porcupines and a bat-eared fox in the ten nights they were followed.[40] In the Gir Forest of India lions feed mainly on 50-kilogram chital deer, occasionally taking the larger sambar and nilgai, as well as domestic stock.[41] But though lions can and often do live on small prey, in the Serengeti and in many other parts of Africa where large grazing animals such as wildebeests, zebras, and buffalo are abundant, lions specialize in killing prey that weigh as much as or more than themselves. At the top end of the prey size range are giraffes (716 kilograms), hippos, and buffalo (500 kilograms). In Lake Manyara National Park lions routinely kill Cape buffalo; these 400–600-kilogram bovids make up more than half the lion's diet in Manyara.[42]

Lions use different hunting methods for different types of prey. They take small animals such as antelope fawns opportunistically, and will chase sick or injured animals when the situation looks ripe for an easy kill. Lions also ambush prey, concealing themselves in tall grass or bushes, often in places where animals come to drink. Lions living in shortgrass areas where there is not much stalking vegetation usually hunt under the cover of darkness.

Head lowered, ears down, and belly to the ground, a stalking lioness is the epitome of focus and concentration. To make a kill, she must get within 30 meters of her prey before she launches the final rush. When attacking a large animal such as a zebra or buffalo, a lioness often hooks her front claws into the victim's rump or throws the animal off balance by twisting its neck. When a group of lions are involved in the kill, the prey is often seized by the muzzle, nape, or throat.

Schaller observed lions employing several different hunting strategies in the Serengeti. He saw single lions stalking prey, lions hunting together but without any apparent cooperation, and groups of lions clearly coordinating their efforts to capture prey.[14] In Etosha National Park, Stander watched individually identified lions in 486 communal hunts.[43] He found that each lioness in a given pride repeatedly occupied the same position in a hunting formation. Cooperative hunts were the most successful—27 percent resulted in a meal. Single lionesses were much less successful in capturing large and fleet-footed prey; only 2.3 percent of such hunts resulted in the lioness making a kill.

Stander classified cooperatively hunting lionesses, like members of a rugby team, as "wings" or "centers" according to the position they assumed during the hunt, and found that wing lionesses initiated attacks significantly more often than center lionesses. Center lionesses captured prey from an ambush position significantly more often than wings did. Lionesses that occupied the center stalking position usually stalked very short distances and mostly lay watching the prey and the stalking activities of the wings. In other words, lionesses hunted cooperatively by division of labor, with the left and right wings circling the prey and the centers lying in a position from which they could capture prey fleeing from the wings.[43]

Lions subdue their victims in various ways, depending on the size of the prey and how vigorously it defends itself. Small animals such as Thomson's gazelles, hares, and antelope fawns are knocked over with a quick blow, grabbed with both paws, and killed with a bite to the neck or throat. Wildebeests and zebra-sized animals are knocked down with the impact of the lion's body or grabbed and dragged down, then bitten and held by the neck, nose, or throat. The animal is killed with a bite to the throat, which results in strangulation, or suffocated with a nose bite. Lions sometimes hold the nose of the victim with one paw, pulling the head down to the chest so that the animal breaks its neck when it falls. During the struggle the lion's hind legs usually remain on the ground. Buffalo, giraffes, eland, and other very large prey are killed in much the same way as wildebeests, though there are reports of lions hamstringing buffalo and giraffes.[7,14,15] In the Kalahari, lions avoid the lethal horns of the gemsbok by attacking from behind, frequently breaking the animal's back.[40]

The type of killing bite usually depends on the size of the prey, with throat bites typically being used to kill larger animals. Lions in Etosha National Park kill adult springbok and other large ungulates with a throat bite 72 percent of the time, but some also use a nose bite and nape bite occasionally. However, variation within prides suggests that there may also be some cultural transmission of particular killing bites. A nose bite was only used by some lionesses in two prides; it was not observed in two other prides in Etosha National Park.[43]

Lions may carry small prey or pieces of a carcass to the nearest thicket before starting to eat. Large animals are usually eaten where they fall, and feeding begins almost immediately. As Schaller remarks, "Wildebeest and zebra kills are seldom moved far, not only because of their weight but also because any attempt by one lion to drag a body away often may cause others to pull in the opposite direction, as if afraid of being deprived of a meal."[14] Indeed, compared with the often lengthy distances leopards and tigers have been known to drag their kills, lions seem to begin their meals almost without preliminaries. Surrounded by the ever-hungry combination of pridemates and scavengers, it may not be worth a lion's time to move a kill that will be consumed within an hour. Instead, it is in the lion's best interest to eat fast—and they do. According to Schaller, "lions bolt meat so rapidly that if many are present only the skeleton of a zebra may be left after 30 minutes."[14]

When several lions are present at a kill, the carcass is usually torn to pieces and each lion eats whatever it can reach, with the viscera, thighs, and rump being eaten first. In some places lions reportedly disembowel the prey and bury the viscera,[7,44] but this behavior is apparently rare in the Serengeti.[14]

Lions can eat enormous amounts of meat at a sitting. Schaller records one male lion eating 33 kilograms during a night, while another ate 27.4 kilograms. Four lionesses each ate 25 kilograms of zebra in five hours, and two males ate an estimated 43 kilograms of topi in twenty hours. Schaller estimated that lions fed at an average rate of twenty minutes per kilogram per lion.[14]

If a group of lions cannot finish a large kill, they occasionally try to protect the remains by lying nearby, and sometimes they even try to bury the carcass. However, over most of the lion's African range, the habitat is so open and the scavengers so numerous that the typical felid behavior of scraping earth and leaves over a carcass is ineffective. Of several hundred kills examined in the Serengeti, Schaller recorded only thirteen instances of lions covering the remains.[14] Lions usually scrape dirt over a carcass when they have eaten their fill and are abandoning the kill; it may be, as Jonathan Kingdon suggests, that this behavior is a nonfunctional vestige of an original pattern in which kills were cached and revisited.[15]

Though lions and the other big cats all hunt large prey with the same basic stalk-and-ambush techniques and live under a similar feast-or-famine regime, there is one striking difference in the lion's feeding ecology: None of the other big cats hunt and kill under such intense pressure from scavengers. In open areas such as the Serengeti, scavengers and other predators can spot a kill made during the day almost as soon as it is made. Vultures begin to descend as the prey stops kicking, and other lions, hyenas, and jackals home in on the descending birds. However, lions feeding at a kill can deter most scavengers, and several lions can defend a carcass against hyenas or fend off hundreds of vultures. A group of twenty-five hyenas had their wildebeest taken away by two male lions, and three young male lions and four lionesses appropriated an eland kill from twenty-one hyenas. However, when only one of the young males remained at the eland kill, the hyenas charged, and the male trotted off to join the other members of his pride. In a nonfeeding situation, two lionesses climbed trees to escape from a mob of eighteen hyenas.[45]

How often lions kill obviously varies, and numerous environmental and biological factors interact to influence their hunting success. The reported kill rate of individual lions varies from a low of ten to twelve prey per year to a high of forty-seven; thus there is no standard. In Etosha National Park lions averaged a kill for every 6.7 hunts, a success rate of 15 percent. However, the capture success rate for zebra was 11 percent, whereas for wildebeest it was 30 percent. Of twenty-seven hunts of springhare, fourteen (52 percent) were successful.[31,34] In other areas, success rates varied from 21 to 38.5 percent.[14,30,32]

Among other variables, hunting success rates vary with vegetation height, prey behavior, and lunar phase. All of these factors change from week to week, even for the same pride. In South Africa's Kruger National Park, Gus Mills followed lion groups continuously for fourteen days at a time. One group consisting of two adults with seven one-year-old cubs made only one significant kill, a zebra foal, during the two-week period. During another two-week period, however, the same group killed at a far greater frequency.[46]

In his elegantly designed study of lions in Uganda, Karl van Orsdol compared lion foraging behavior and hunting success in two areas with markedly different vegetation and prey.[33] Van Orsdol used these two areas to examine the effects of cover, lion group size, prey group size, and lunar phase on hunting success. In the Mweya area, where the 5-centimeter grass provided no stalking cover and prey density was low, lions watched for warthogs and other easy-to-catch prey from daytime rest sites. By remaining alert to hunting opportunities while they rested during the day, the Mweya pride was able to find food during the day without actively searching. At night these lions moved around their ranges hunting for larger game. In Ishasha, where the vegetation was taller and prey density more than four times higher, lions hunted primarily on moonless nights, when their hunting success was greatest. Despite these differences in vegetation, prey density, and lion hunting styles, the overall success rate of hunts did not vary greatly between the two sites. In Mweya 27.1 percent of hunts succeeded, whereas 30.5 percent of hunts ended in a kill at Ishasha.

In comparison with other felids, lions are generally more successful hunters, but since they commonly have to share their kills with other pride members, the critical factor is whether individuals obtain their estimated minimum daily requirement of 5 to 8.5 kilograms of meat per lioness per day.[47] The rate of daily food intake by individual lions obviously depends on the kill rate, the number of lions feeding on the kill, prey size, and prey abundance. For example, during "prey-poor" seasons on the Serengeti plains, the average daily food intake of a pride was less than 3 kilograms per lioness, but the intake increased to almost 6 kilograms per lioness during the "prey-good" seasons.[25] Small prey such as impalas (30 kilograms) provide proportionally less meat to a large lion group than would a buffalo (500 kilograms); if they have a choice, large prey are preferred even by small groups of lions.[48] However, in the Kalahari, where large ungulate densities are extremely low and small mammals and juvenile ungulates constitute more than 50 percent of kills, lions were able to obtain an estimated 4.95 kilograms per day per individual.[30] In Etosha National Park a group of nine lionesses were followed for thirteen consecutive days, during which they consumed an average of 2.01 kilograms per day per lioness. In contrast, a group of seven lionesses followed for nine consecutive days consumed an average of 14.43 kilograms per day per lioness.[31]

When prey are abundant, daily intake rates per individual are high, and the rates are not related to prey size or the size of lion groups.[47] It is during periods of prey scarcity that these factors become important. Studies in the Serengeti show that solitary females and groups of five to seven females had the highest daily per capita intake rates when prey were scarce. Groups of two to four females did not fare as well, and the differences were related to prey size. Solitary females did not often share their kills and thus obtained a larger share of meat, whereas larger groups were able to kill larger prey, which resulted in an individual consumption rate equal to that of solitary females.[47] During the dry season in Etosha National Park, when prey are scarce, pairs of lionesses had the highest daily intake rate (12 kilograms per lioness), even though their hunting success rate was low (10 percent). Groups of six or seven had the second highest intake rate (10.3 kilograms), but this was related to increased hunting success (34.2 percent), not to larger groups taking larger prey.[31]

Whether pride size is linked to foraging success and whether prey size determines lion group size are the subjects of much debate.[47,49,50,51,52,53,54,55,56,57] In the best data set to date, Packer and his colleagues have shown that many factors other than foraging success influence lion grouping patterns. They conclude that "female lions have many other problems to solve besides catching their next meal."[47]

Social Organization

The social organization of the archetypal solitary big cat consists of a single male range that overlaps the ranges of several females. Each cat hunts for itself, although individuals may meet at large kills or encounter one another occasionally as they travel about their ranges. The social system of lions is different. In the Gir Forest of India, male and female lions lead separate lives and rarely associate with each other except during mating activities and at large kills. Prides are composed of related females, their young, and subadult male offspring. The average number of adult females in a pride is 4–5 (range 1–11). Males form coalitions of two to six individuals, patrol territories, and make their own kills. One or more lionesses and their young live within the males' territories, but there appears to be a marked difference in their habitat use. Lionesses tend to favor riverine forest, while males spend their time on relatively dry, open hilltops. Ravi Chellam and his colleagues have found that Gir Forest males patrol ranges of 100 to 140 square kilometers, while lionesses have home ranges of about 50 square kilometers.[58]

At the other end of the spectrum lie the well-studied lions of the Serengeti plains. In the Serengeti a pride consists of two to eighteen adult females, their cubs, and one to seven males. All the females are related, and this group of sisters, daughters, cousins, and aunts forms the stable core of the pride. Lionesses do most of the hunting and killing, but the pride males displace females and cubs at kills. Breeding coalitions of males compete with other coalitions for access to females, and their tenure with a pride can be as short as a few months or last for several years. Lionesses and their offspring may occupy the same area for generations, but adult males either leave the pride of their own accord or, more likely, are ousted by a new group of males. Young males usually leave their natal pride along with their brothers or half-brothers, but if a young lion is the only male in his litter, he may join with males from other prides, usually choosing companions of the same age and size. Male coalitions of two or three commonly contain nonrelatives; larger coalitions are made up of relatives. These young adults lead a nomadic life, scavenging and learning to hunt and trying to avoid being attacked by resident males. Once the young males are sexually mature, they try to take over a pride

of females. Male coalitions occasionally take over two adjoining prides, but males attempting a takeover are often repelled by females with small cubs because incoming males kill young cubs.[14,59,60,61,62,63,64,65]

While the pride is the stable unit of the lion's social system, this system is not inflexible. During a prolonged drought in the central Kalahari, prey densities declined to such a low level that the normal social system collapsed. Pride males and females abandoned their territories and became nomadic, traveling well outside their former haunts. Females cooperated with unrelated females in hunts, associations changed frequently, and even when conditions improved, few lionesses returned to their original territories. The new prides that formed typically included unrelated females.[28]

In Kruger National Park, when both sexes were hunted extensively, female lions from different prides joined together to form new prides, and males accepted additional males after joining prides.[66] Similarly, in an area of Zambia where male lions were heavily hunted, male coalitions were small (0.67 to 1.5 males per pride) and their ranges did not cover the entire range of a pride. Females mated with males from different prides, and one pride male accepted additional males during his tenure.[67]

The lion social system is also fluid with respect to foraging. Pride members are frequently scattered around the territory in small groups, which coalesce or split like "fusion-fission" groups in primates. Some groups form close associations, referred to as "subprides," that may seldom interact with other pride members. Studies in the Serengeti and Ngorongoro Crater also show that some individual pride members may consistently lag behind or refrain from communal hunts or expelling intruders. Such "selfishness" in a social system based on cooperation indicates that lion society is much more complex than previously imagined.[47,68,69,70,71,72,73,74]

Home range sizes of lions are set largely by the biomass of prey available during the lean times. Similarly, pride size is also correlated with the lean-season abundance of prey.[54] Lion prides in the prey-rich Serengeti woodlands have territories of about 65 square kilometers, whereas prides living on the plains require over 184 square kilometers during the lean season. Prides in the woodlands number about 20 individuals, compared with 13 on the plains.[14,54,60] The largest pride size reported for the Serengeti is 35.[75] When prey biomass increased in the Serengeti between 1966 and 1977, so did the size of fourteen prides.[76] In Etosha National Park, where prey biomass is substantially less than in East Africa, seven prides and two adult males used areas that ranged in size from 150 square kilometers to 2,075 square kilometers. Pride size in Etosha is also smaller than in East Africa, averaging almost 7 individuals (1.8 adult males and 4.8 adult females).[77] In the Kalahari Gemsbok National Park, pride size was estimated at 4.2.[26]

Because home range size and pride size are correlated with prey biomass, lion density also reflects changes in food availability. Not surprisingly, lion densities in Etosha National Park and the Kalahari are extremely low, with estimates of 1.5 to 2.0 lions per 100 square kilometers.[77,78] In some East African parks lion densities are remarkably high, with numbers reaching 35 to 45 individuals per 100 square kilometers during the lean season.[54] The highest recorded lion density is in the confines of Ngorongoro Crater, where at one time there were 100 lions in 181 square kilometers, or 55 individuals per 100 square kilometers.[79] Lions typically live at densities that are higher than those of many other felid species. Even the Gir Forest lions, which live in conditions broadly similar to some tiger habitats and feed on the same prey tigers do, still manage to live at higher densities than do tigers.[58]

Where pride territories are large, there is some spatial overlap with neighboring territories, but where territories are small there is little overlap. At high lion densities, competition for resources can be intense, and pride males regularly patrol the boundaries of their territory to check for intruding males. Pride lionesses also defend their hunting areas, water holes, and denning sites against other females. Besides making routine visits to all parts of their territory, pride members also use indirect methods to indicate occupancy.

Like other felids, lions scent-mark by swinging their hindquarters round against a bush or tree trunk and spraying urine onto the object. Both sexes scent-mark in this way, but males spray more frequently than females. Pride males actively patrol their territory, spraying bushes and raking the ground with their hind feet. According to Schaller, when one lion scrapes or sprays, the others in a pride are often stimulated to do the same, often in the same place. Some landmarks along regularly traveled routes become scent posts and are sprayed and resprayed, thus serving to indicate that the area is occupied.[14]

Lions are also quite vocal, being best known for their roaring. Roaring is one of about a dozen vocalizations in the lion's repertoire; lions also growl, snarl, hiss, meow, grunt, and puff. Puffing, which sounds like a stifled sneeze, is used in friendly close-contact situations. Puffing has also been recorded for leopards, but not for other felids. Whether lions purr has been questioned,[80,81] although courting lions and a pet cub reportedly purred.[14,82,83]

Many authors have commented on the function of roaring, which is believed to be a territorial display,[84,85] a spacing mechanism,[7,86,87] a device to ensure group cohesion and facilitate contact,[82] or all of the above.[14] When tape recordings of aggressive roars are played within the territories of prides, lionesses respond by rushing to expel the intruders, suggesting that roars serve to advertise territorial occupancy.[72] The responses of lionesses vary, however, depending on their assessment of the number of intruders; they are more likely to approach when only a single intruder roars.[73] Both male and female lions roar, but the male's call is deeper and louder than that of the female. Lions usually roar while standing, and when one group member roars the others are often stimulated to join in. When lions roar together, the sounds are often synchronized so that they follow one another directly ("unhh-unhh"), lengthening and extending the sound and presumably increasing its effect on neighboring lions, who may also roar in response. To the human ear a lion roar is audible from five miles, but lions can probably hear another lion roaring from farther than that. Lions roar most often at dawn, dusk, and midnight, when they are most active.[7,14,87]

Reproduction and Development

Lionesses seemingly differ from other large felids in that there are no references to their advertising their impending sexual receptivity either by calling or by increasing their frequency of scent marking. Such behavior is presumably not needed, as pride males and females interact regularly. Instead, a male is apparently able to determine a lioness's state of sexual receptivity by smelling her anal area and by her willingness to mate. If she is in heat or approaching it, he will attempt to stay with her.

A lioness in estrus is as restless as the proverbial "cat on a hot tin roof." She rolls, twists and turns, jumps up and walks a few paces, then lies down in front of the male, who remains close by, moving as she moves. If the male attempts to mount, the lioness may evade his advances and swat at him or growl and snarl. When he is finally allowed to mount, the male sometimes grasps the female by the neck in the typical felid neck bite. Copulation averages twenty-one seconds, lasting from eight to seventy seconds,[14,88] and occurs frequently, about once every twenty-five minutes.[64] A pair of captive lions was observed to copulate 360 times in eight days.[15] Schaller observed one nomadic male to mate 157 times in fifty-five hours. During this time he did not eat, even though some lionesses were feeding on a wildebeest 100 meters away. Estrus lasts on average four days and recurs every two or three weeks until the female conceives.

Pride males rarely fight each other over estrous females except when ownership of the female is not clear or consorting males get too close.[64] As the females in a pride tend to come into estrus at the same time,[14,60,64] rival males within a coalition can come into close proximity. The first male to reach an estrous female takes possession of her, and he usually stays close (1 meter or less) to her, herds her, and tries to prevent other males in the coalition from getting close to her. This guarding behavior begins one or two days prior to mating and sometimes lasts for six days afterward. Toward the end of estrus the pair mate less frequently, and as the male's interest wanes, the female may seek additional partners. Other pride males can then mate with her, giving rise to the notion that males "share" females. However, studies in the Serengeti and Ngorongoro show that not every male in a coalition may get to mate, whether the males are relatives or not. Instead, differences in mating success are greatest in coalitions in which there are marked differences in the sizes or ages of males. Young, elderly, and small males achieve much lower reproductive success.[64]

Male reproductive success is also highly skewed in large coalitions. Large coalitions are better at taking over prides, hold residence for longer periods, and thereby gain access to more females over their life spans.[63,89] However, at coalition sizes of four or more, not every male may get to mate. Genetic analysis has shown that these large coalitions are composed entirely of relatives. Thus, the nonbreeders in the coalition are helping to increase the reproductive success of their kin, with whom they share a significant proportion of their genes.[90]

Another critical element in the reproductive success of males is tenure length. Following a pride takeover, the incoming males kill small cubs and evict older young, thereby inducing females to come into estrus and mate.[60,91] From an incoming male's point of view, infanticide makes a great deal of sense and prob-

ably represents his best chance to leave offspring of his own. When a lioness loses her young, she becomes sexually receptive almost immediately, and can conceive as soon as two weeks after the death of her previous litter, although the interval is usually much longer.[14,91] On average, females conceive again 134 days after the loss of their cubs, whereas females with surviving young will not mate again until their young are more than eighteen months old. Thus, killing small cubs after a takeover greatly reduces the time it takes to produce new young. Furthermore, since the average tenure length of male coalitions in the Serengeti is only twenty-six months, some males may not breed at all unless female receptivity is advanced.[89] Because lion cubs are vulnerable to adult males for about two years, an incoming male must sire his own young as quickly as possible so he can be around to protect them. Males that manage to remain with the same pride long enough to sire successive litters also gain because females will mate with them three months earlier than they would with newly arrived males.[91] In Etosha National Park, the average length of male tenure for three prides was 3.2 years (range 2.5 to 4 years).[77]

The reproductive success of pride females is more difficult to determine, since the number of females in the group can vary over time, but studies in the Serengeti show that prides of three to ten adult females have higher per capita reproductive rates than smaller or larger prides.[89] Small and large prides suffer more male takeovers, and since more than a quarter of all cubs are killed by invading males, the reproductive success of these females is reduced. Mortality rates for single females and pairs are also high, which again is probably related to higher rates of male takeovers and the results of one or two females trying to defend their small cubs from incoming males. Lionesses defend their young vigorously, and are sometimes killed in the process. Large prides appear better able to protect their cubs from new males.[74]

Pliny reported that lion cubs were unformed at birth "like small gobbets of flesh, no bigger than weasels."[7] Before much was known of their biology, there was some argument as to whether lion cubs were born alive or came to life later. As Topsell wrote, "Some are of the opinion that the whelps are brought forth without life and they remain lifeless for three days, until by the roaring of their father and by breathing in their face they are quickened. But Isidorus declares that for three days and three nights after their littering they do nothing but sleep and at last are awakened by the roaring of their father. So it seems without controversy they are senseless for a certain space after their whelping."[10]

Since that time, studies have shown that gestation lasts 102 to 115 days,[88,92,93] after which the pregnant lioness selects a secluded den among rocks or in dense grass. Births do not seem to be confined to any particular season, but because females in a pride tend to come into estrus synchronously, pride females often give birth within a few weeks of one another.

Litter size in the wild is rarely known, since newborn cubs remain hidden for several weeks. Mortality during this period probably goes undetected. In the Serengeti, Schaller found that litter size at two months varied from 1.7 to 1.9 on the plains to 2.3 in the woodlands.[14] Estimates of litter size in other areas vary from 2.3 to 3.3.[54] Litter sizes appear to vary little with the age of the female until she reaches eleven years, when her reproductive performance starts to decline.[89] In captivity, a litter of 7 cubs was born at the Arnhem Zoo in the Netherlands, all of which survived.[94] The mean size of 707 litters born at the Leipzig Zoological Garden was 3.01; litter sizes smaller than the average were recorded for females younger than five years and older than twelve years.[93]

Some cubs are born with their eyes open; others open their eyes within the first two weeks of life. Milk teeth start to appear at about three weeks of age, and permanent teeth at about a year. The lioness keeps the cubs at the birth den for six to eight weeks, leaving them for twenty-four to forty-eight hours at a time while she hunts for her next meal. Alone, the cubs are almost completely defenseless, and many are killed by leopards, hyenas, and even other lions. If food is scarce, a lioness will sometimes move her cubs when they are about a month old, but at this age they find it difficult to keep up with her. Solitary nomadic lionesses rarely succeed in raising young.[14]

When the cubs are a month to six weeks old, their mother rejoins her pride. Since other lionesses in the pride will also have given birth, the mothers form a crèche and remain together for the next eighteen months.[74] Pride lionesses without young tend to keep to themselves. Cubs will suckle from any lactating female if given the opportunity, but females try to give milk primarily to their own young.[95] Milk is the cubs' main diet for the first two months or so, at least until their mother starts leading them to kills. This may happen as early as six weeks of age; prior to that time

the cubs ignore meat. Schaller observed this behavioral change in a lion cub he raised as a pet—it showed no interest in meat until it was five weeks old. Cubs are not seen regularly with the pride until they are old enough to keep up with the group when it moves; this usually occurs when they are about two months old.

For cubs, the ability to suckle from any lactating female has both advantages and disadvantages. Cubs can nurse from other females if their own mother has little milk, and older cubs can sometimes continue to nurse far beyond their normal weaning time. Schaller noted some cubs suckling when they were twelve months old, even though their mother's milk supply had disappeared when they were seven months old.[14] However, if there is a major age difference among the cubs in a pride, the youngest cubs are often at a disadvantage in a system of communal suckling. They are too small to compete for nipples and may be squashed or shouldered out of the way unless their own mother intervenes.

Small cubs are at a similar disadvantage when it comes to feeding at a carcass. Females give their cubs access to kills, but competition at kills is fierce, and cubs may be edged out or driven away. Furthermore, in areas where food availability declines seasonally, cub survival can be affected greatly.[59,89] Starvation was the major cause of death for six- to twelve-month-old cubs in Schaller's study area—28 percent of cubs starved to death.[14]

In a comparison of two prides, one on the Serengeti plains and another in Ngorongoro Crater, mortality of mobile cubs (two months and older) was much higher on the plains. A significantly greater proportion of Crater cubs than cubs on the plains survived to one year of age.[25] Lionesses on the plains have to travel significantly farther to find food than Crater females, and during periods of prey scarcity weakened cubs that are unable to keep up with the pride may be abandoned. Cub mortality on the plains was greatest in the dry season, when prey were scarce and water sources were widely scattered.

It takes young lions a long time to become proficient hunters. Though they watch and stalk small prey when they are only a few months old, they do not usually start to join the pride in the hunt until they are eleven months old. By the time they are fifteen or sixteen months old, they weigh about 50 kilograms and they regularly participate in the hunt, sometimes even capturing prey. Cubs are fully dependent on adults for food until they are about sixteen months old; even then, they still find it difficult to subdue large prey without an adult's help.[14]

Stander watched an eighteen-month-old lioness learning to hunt and remarked that the process "revealed a very complex level of learning."[43] The young lioness did not merely imitate her mother, but occupied very different stalking roles, independent of the role of her mother and the other hunting lionesses. Stander came to the conclusion that stalking activities were partly innate behavior and partly developed through learning. By the time they are two years old, lionesses are competent hunters.[14,47]

Subadult lions, those twenty-five to forty-eight months of age, may still be using the pride's range, although most subadult males have left by forty-eight months. In contrast, most subadult females remain in their natal ranges for their entire lives.[62,65] Leaving the natal range is sometimes voluntary, but more commonly the departure is associated with a male takeover of the pride. When a group of resident males is ousted by a new male coalition, the incoming males evict all the large young and usually kill any small cubs. Thus young lions may be forced to disperse as early as sixteen months of age, or subadult females may choose to stay and mate with the incoming males.

Lionesses have a high reproductive potential. They typically have their first litter at three to four years of age, and they remain reproductively active until they are about fifteen years old. The average interval between births, when the previous litter has survived, is twenty-four months.[65] Assuming a litter size of three, a female could potentially have fifteen young in her lifetime. However, this high reproductive potential is rarely realized, even though cub survival does not change with maternal age.[89] One Serengeti lioness nicknamed "Blondie" had seven litters over a period of twelve years, and of these she raised two, a total of six cubs. Schaller calculated that 67 percent of cubs die each year from a variety of causes, including starvation, predation, infanticide, and abandonment.[14]

"Like most female mammals," Packer writes, "female lions live longer than males. Serengeti females can live as long as eighteen years and remain fertile until they are about fifteen."[79] Zoo lions live an average of thirteen years, but the record is held by a lioness in the Cologne zoo who lived to be almost thirty years old.[8] There are a few examples of wild lions reaching a comparatively old age. A sixteen-year-old male was

recorded from Kruger National Park.[96,97] A lioness in Nairobi National Park died at the estimated age of twenty-two years, and in Etosha another lioness lived to be more than sixteen years old before she disappeared.[77]

CONSERVATION EFFORTS

The story of the Asiatic lions of the Gir Forest in northwestern India is a conservation classic. A perfect example of the problems faced by an isolated population of large carnivores, the tale includes a dwindling geographic range, domestic stock raiding, man-killing, and genetic impoverishment.[41,58,98,99,100]

Lions once roamed through eastern Europe, across Syria, Mesopotamia, Persia, and eastward as far as central India.[101] Their precipitous decline in numbers came only in the nineteenth century, when the widespread use of firearms eliminated lions everywhere except India by 1884. Today the sole surviving population of wild Asiatic lions is confined to the 1,412 square kilometers of Gir Forest in the state of Gujarat. The Gir Forest was once the hunting preserve of the Nawab of Junagadh. In 1913, when lion numbers had fallen to around twenty individuals, the Nawab instituted protective measures to halt the decline. By 1950 lion numbers had increased to about 220, but heavy grazing by domestic cattle was destroying the forest undergrowth. Less and less vegetation was available for the wild ungulates, which were rapidly displaced by buffalo, cows, and goats. In 1955, when Lee Talbot of the IUCN visited the Gir Forest, he saw thousands of domestic livestock competing with a few wild ungulates. During a two-week visit he saw only three chital, two small herds of nilgai and chinkara, and one wild pig.[102,103]

In 1957 the Indian government attempted to establish a second population of Asiatic lions outside the Gir Forest, moving a lion and two lionesses to the Chandraprabha Wildlife Sanctuary in north-central India. The population increased to eleven, but the group suddenly disappeared in 1965.[58]

By the late 1960s concern for the Asiatic lion's continued survival led to three major ecological studies, which examined the lion-ungulate-domestic stock community in the Gir.[99,104] At that time, some 7,000 Maldharis (cattle grazers) and their 24,000 buffalo and cattle lived in the region. Early results found that only 4 percent of the grass was used by wild animals; about 88 percent was eaten by domestic stock.[98] Not surprisingly, the remains of domestic animals were found in 75 percent of lion scats. In 1972 the Forest Department and state government initiated a long-term management program. Nearly half of the 845 Maldhari families were resettled, and domestic livestock were banned from grazing in the forest.

Two decades of protection have resulted in a lion population of about three hundred individuals. A 1986 study by the Wildlife Institute of India shows conclusively that protection and the removal of villagers and their livestock have had a positive effect — chital, sambar, and nilgai numbers have increased dramatically, and the lions' diet now consists of 60 to 65 percent wild ungulates.[58,105] But despite these positive signs, the Gir lions are isolated and surrounded by villages and livestock. As the population grows, lions are increasingly coming into conflict with humans, and since May 1988 there has been an increase in the number of lion attacks on people. A study by Saberwal and his colleagues at the Wildlife Institute of India documented eighty-one human injuries and sixteen deaths between May 1988 and August 1990. Interviews with local people suggest that lions have become noticeably more aggressive, attempting to force their way into house compounds and cowsheds. As part of the ongoing effort to deal with lions wandering outside the Gir Forest Protected Area, the Forest Department has captured ninety-nine lions and released them back into the middle of the Gir. Unfortunately, there are few data to show whether this translocation strategy is effective or not, but one adult female was recaptured close to where she was initially captured.[106]

Most of the villagers who live within 5 kilometers of the Gir complain of losing livestock to lion predation. Though a compensation system exists, villagers maintain that its procedures are cumbersome and complicated. On one hand, villagers complain that kills must be reported and officially inspected within 24 hours before compensation is allowed, and getting an official to make the inspection is difficult. On the other hand, Forest Department personnel counter that villagers deliberately leave old or sick livestock out for the lions to kill and then try to claim compensation. Many local people feel that they should be allowed to return to the practice of grazing their domestic stock within the Gir Forest and that lions that stray beyond the boundaries of the protected area should be shot.[106]

Without doubt, the Gir lions are running out of space. The 1990 census suggests that the last five years

have seen a 20 percent increase in the lion population. In 1995 the number of lions was estimated at 304, up from 284 in 1990.[105] The few data on the sex and age of the animals captured outside the protected area suggest that they are mostly young animals dispersing from their natal areas. At this stage the options are few. A large human population surrounds the Gir Forest, and many people move through the protected area to visit four large permanent temples in the forest. By 1992 the lions had been involved in more than two hundred attacks on humans, and twenty-three people had died.[106] The potential for more attacks on humans is high, and as more lions disperse outside the protected area, the chances are great that attacks on livestock will increase. Lion density within the Gir is now one per 5 square kilometers — higher than that recorded for lions in many parts of Africa. At this stage it is unlikely that habitat management schemes can improve prey density so that more lions can be packed into the existing space, nor is there room to increase the size of the protected area.[41] Suggested options include removal of problem lions to zoos within India and overseas and translocation of lions to other protected areas. Both of these options have merit. Unfortunately, there is no ideal site to introduce translocated lions to, although three areas are being considered. However, there is a great need for a well-designed captive breeding program for Asiatic lions, and there is great demand for pure Asiatic lions by international zoos. Two of the five founder animals of the Species Survival Plan for Asiatic lions were found to be descendants of African lions.[100,107,108]

In 1993 an epidemic of canine distemper virus struck the lions in the Serengeti region of Tanzania. How the virus managed to cross the species barrier is unknown, but some prides suffered 80 percent mortality, while others were seemingly unaffected. Before running its course, the virus affected one-third of the Serengeti's three thousand lions and spread to lions in the adjoining Masai Mara Reserve. The disease is believed to have originated in the 30,000 or so domestic dogs that live around the fringes of the park. Researchers have started "Project Life Lion," a massive campaign to vaccinate as many dogs as possible.[109,110]

Compared with tigers or leopards, lions rarely seem to turn to people as prey. There are a few famous man-eaters such as "Chiengi Charlie," who in 1909 terrorized the government post of Chiengi on the border of what was then known as the Belgian Congo and Northern Rhodesia. "Chiengi Charlie" was a very large, light-colored male lion who became known as the "white lion" after he killed several villagers in the area. After being speared and chased, the "white lion" later joined forces with two other males, and together the three raided villages for several months. The "white lion" and one of the others were eventually killed in gun traps.[7]

The most famous man-eating lions were the subject of a 1907 book called *The Man-Eaters of Tsavo*, written by Colonel J. H. Patterson. These two lions had the distinction of holding up work on the Uganda Railway when they took to raiding the workers' camps at night and carrying off the Indian railway workers. At one stage construction was halted for three weeks when many of the workers deserted, some believing that the lions were devils in animal form. Patterson, the engineer in charge of the Tsavo section, happened to be a keen hunter, and he devoted himself to catching the man-eaters. After months of frustration, Patterson finally managed to shoot the lions, which were later exhibited in the Field Museum of Chicago.

More recently, in 1989, three man-eating lions were shot and killed in north-central Tanzania. One lion reportedly chased a dog into a house and grabbed a ten-year-old boy who was sleeping there. The lion ate the boy and stayed in the house until the next morning, when it was shot by the boy's father. The project director of the nearby Selous Reserve speculates that the lions may have been driven to seek out people as food because excessive hunting had wiped out most of their prey. Other officials thought that some of the deaths attributed to lions had been paid murders by "lion men."[111]

The solution to problem lions often boils down to two options, shoot them or move them. For the most part, the traditional answer has been to shoot them, sometimes in great numbers. Some of the most dramatic lion removal schemes occurred in South Africa in the eastern Transvaal, where early settlers had decimated the large ungulate populations. In 1889 the area that is now Kruger National Park was first brought under protection, and in 1902 a policy of carnivore reduction was initiated so that game populations would recover and grow. From the beginning of the century until 1933, lions, leopards, hyenas, wild dogs, and cheetahs were systematically shot, trapped, and poisoned. Between 1903 and 1927, 1,272 lions and 660 leopards were killed. The predator control policy was discontinued in 1960, but ten years later, when wildebeests and zebras began to decline in the central district of Kruger, the subject of predation by lions again became an issue.[66]

In 1974, in a cropping experiment designed to study the effects of lion removal, 129 lions were killed in the central district of Kruger. The vacant area seemed to attract subadult lions, especially males, and the cropped areas were quickly recolonized. The study concluded that cropping was of questionable value in terms of increasing the prey population.[66] However, in specific instances when lions kill people or livestock, removing the offending lions has proved effective as long as the problem individuals can be identified.

Over the last twenty years authorities have increasingly attempted to translocate offending animals as an alternative to shooting them, but it is difficult to find suitably unpopulated areas to receive problem animals. Translocations have many difficulties, not the least of which is that the animals are rarely monitored after they have been moved to the new area, so there are few records of their fate. More often than not the translocated animal either returns to its former home range, continues killing domestic stock in its new range, or simply disappears.

Lions have also been reintroduced into parts of their former range to try to reestablish populations. In South Africa lions had been absent from the Hluhluwe/Umfolozi Park since predators were eradicated in the 1920s. In 1958 a lone male lion wandered into the reserve, and in 1965 two adult females and two female cubs were introduced by the authorities. The population increased rapidly, but since the mid-1970s, authorities have had to cull to keep lion numbers at about a hundred because the area is surrounded by livestock farmers.[112] Two other lion reintroductions are currently under way in the same area.[113]

A model example of conflict resolution between lions and farmers near Etosha National Park, Namibia, was developed between 1982 and 1986 as part of a study of management options for dealing with stock-raiding lions.[114] Etosha National Park is surrounded by farmers raising cattle and goats, and each year these pastoralists suffer substantial losses to lions. Farmers retaliate, shooting an estimated 10 percent of the area's lions each year. Park authorities were faced with the difficult task of trying to reduce livestock losses while at the same time attempting to discourage farmers from shooting lions on an ad hoc basis. A detailed study of marked prides and radio-collared individuals showed that stock-raiding lions could be separated into two basic categories. The majority of lions that ventured outside the park into farmland were classified as "occasional raiders." These were usually large prides consisting of females with subadult cubs; they seemed to be inexperienced at killing domestic animals and were not difficult to shoot. These "occasional raiders" were easily lured back into the park, and when translocated, they tended not to return to their stock-raiding habits. The other category consisted of "problem animals," which were often adult or subadult males, animals that may have been ousted in takeovers or driven from their natal prides. These problem lions became habitual livestock killers and were extremely wary and difficult to destroy or immobilize. Translocation appeared to be the most successful management

option for "occasional raiders," even though lions that were moved short distances all returned to their home ranges. However, translocation is not an option for most "problem animals"; habitual stock raiders translocated into areas anywhere near farms simply resumed their cattle-killing habits. Once a lion is identified as a habitual livestock killer, the best interests of farmers, conservationists, and other lions are served by destroying the problem animal.

The Etosha study is distinguished by its intensive efforts to identify and track individual lions and their prides. Translocated animals were carefully monitored, and the authorities went to great lengths to maintain good relationships with farmers. As a result they were able to come up with a management strategy that struck a balance between the needs of farmers and the aims of conservationists.[114]

TABLE 54 MEASUREMENTS AND WEIGHTS OF ADULT LIONS

HB	n	T	n	WT	n	Location	Source
				193.3 (172.0–215.9)	26m	Rhodesia	16
				133.6 (110–165)	23f	Rhodesia	16
				188.4 (164–214)	11m	Kalahari	16
				139.8 (127–153)	8f	Kalahari	16
				174.9 (145.4–201.7)	25m	East Africa	16
				119.5 (90.0–167.8)	15f	East Africa	16
1,642 (1,369–1,830)	3m	941 (863–996)	3m	142.7, 157.3	2m	Botswana	115
1,511, 2,197	2f	825, 965	2f	106.4	1f	Botswana	115
1,947 (1,880–1,981)	3m	838 (787–889)	3m			India	13

Note: HB = head and body length (mm); T = tail length (mm); WT = weight (kg). n = sample size. Sex: m = male, f = female, ? = unknown. Mean values are presented only for sample sizes of three or more. Range of values is in parentheses.

TABLE 55 OCCURRENCE OF PREY ITEMS IN THE DIETS OF AFRICAN LIONS (PERCENTAGE OF KILLS)

Prey items	Serengeti plains[14] Kills (n = 280)	Kafue NP, Zambia[116] Kills (n = 410)	Kruger NP[117] Kills (n = 12,313)	Kalahari[118] Kills (n = 370)
Connochaetes taurinus Wildebeest	56.7	6.1	23.6	37.0
Gazella thomsoni Thomson's gazelle	7.5			

TABLE 55 *(continued)*

Prey items	Serengeti plains[14] Kills (n = 280)	Kafue NP, Zambia[116] Kills (n = 410)	Kruger NP[117] Kills (n = 12,313)	Kalahari[118] Kills (n = 370)
Aepyceros melampus Impala		2.0	19.7	
Kobus defassa Waterbuck		5.9	10.5	
Antidorcas marsupialis Springbok				13.0
Alcelaphus buselaphus Hartebeest	0.4	16.3		7.0
Equus sp. Zebra	28.9	7.3	15.8	
Oryx gazella Gemsbok				32.4
Taurotragus oryx Eland	3.2	2.9	0.5	4.3
Phacochoerus aethiopicus Warthog		9.5	1.9	
Giraffa camelopardalis Giraffe			3.9	
Syncerus caffer Buffalo		30.5	9.2	
Tragelaphus scriptus Bushbuck		0.2	0.3	
Tragelaphus sp. Kudu		1.0	10.9	
Redunca redunca Reedbuck		2.0	0.3	
Hippotragus equinus Roan antelope		5.6	0.3	
Hippotragus niger Sable		5.1	1.5	
Gazella granti Grant's gazelle	1.1			
Damaliscus lunatus Tsessebe			0.4	
Damaliscus korrigum Topi	1.4			
Cephalophus sp. Duiker		0.2	0.1	
Struthio camelus Ostrich			0.1	4.1
Hystrix sp. Porcupine		0.5	0.1	1.9
Orycteropus afer Aardvark				0.3
Potamochoerus porcus Bushpig		2.0		
Hippopotamus amphibius Hippopotamus		1.4		

(continued)

TABLE 55 *(continued)*

Prey items	Serengeti plains[14] Kills (n = 280)	Kafue NP, Zambia[116] Kills (n = 410)	Kruger NP[117] Kills (n = 12,313)	Kalahari[118] Kills (n = 370)
Kobus leche Lechwe		0.5		
Kobus vardoni Puku		1.0		
Carnivores	0.8		0.4	

TABLE 56 OCCURRENCE OF WILD AND DOMESTIC PREY ITEMS IN THE DIETS OF GIR FOREST LIONS (PERCENTAGE OF KILLS)

Prey items	Gir Forest, India[41] Kills (n = 142)
Axis axis Chital	43.0
Cervus unicolor Sambar	14.8
Other wild mammals	7.0
Domestic cattle	21.1
Domestic buffalo	12.7
Camel	1.4

REFERENCES

1. Kurtén, B. 1988. *Before the Indians.* New York: Columbia University Press.

2. Kurtén, B. 1985. The Pleistocene lion of Beringia. *Ann. Zool. Fennici* 22: 117–121.

3. Kurtén, B., and E. Anderson. 1980. *Pleistocene mammals of North America.* New York: Columbia University Press.

4. Guthrie, D. 1990. *Frozen fauna of the mammoth steppe: The story of Blue Babe.* Chicago: University of Chicago Press.

5. Morgan, G. F., and K. L. Seymour. 1997. Fossil history of the panther (*Puma concolor*) and the cheetah-like cat (*Miracinonyx inexpectatus*) in Florida. *Bull. Fla. Mus. Nat. Hist.* 40(2): 177–219.

6. Deraniyagala, P. E. P. 1958. *The Pleistocene of Ceylon.* Colombo: Ceylon National Museums Natural History Series.

7. Guggisberg, C. A. W. 1963. *Simba: The life of the lion.* New York: Chilton Books.

8. Guggisberg, C. A. W. 1975. *Wild cats of the world.* New York: Taplinger.

9. Cheer, P. 1966. *The lion in fact and fiction.* New York: Harlin Quist.

10. South, M., ed. 1981. *Topsell's histories of beasts.* Chicago: Nelson-Hall.

11. McBride, C. 1977. *The white lions of Timbavati.* London: Paddington Press.

12. Pocock, R. I. 1939. *The fauna of British India, including Ceylon and Burma.* Vol. 1, *Mammalia.* London: Taylor and Francis.

13. Pocock, R. I. 1930. The lions of Asia. *J. Bombay Nat. Hist. Soc.* 34: 638–665.

14. Schaller, G. B. 1972. *The Serengeti lion.* Chicago: University of Chicago Press.

15. Kingdon, J. 1989. *East African mammals: An atlas of evolution in Africa.* Vol. 3A, *Carnivores.* Chicago: University of Chicago Press.

16. Smuts, G. L., G. A. Robinson, and I. J. Whyte. 1980. Comparative growth of wild male and female lions (*Panthera leo*). *J. Zool.* (Lond.) 190: 365–373.

17. Silva, M., and J. A. Downing. 1995. *CRC handbook of mammalian body masses.* Boca Raton, FL: CRC Press.

18. Gonyea, W. J. 1976. Behavioral implications of sabretoothed felid morphology. *Paleobiology* 2: 333–342.

19. Hemmer, H. 1974. [Studies of the phylogenetic history of the pantherines (Pantherinae) III. On the races of the lion *Panthera leo* (Linnaeus, 1758).] *Veröff. Zool. Staatssamml. München* 17: 167–280.

20. Chassin, P. S., C. R. Taylor, N. C. Heglund, and H. J. Seerherman. 1976. Locomotion in lions: Energetic cost and aerobic capacity. *Zoology* 49(1): 1–10.

21. Nowak, R. M. 1991. *Walker's mammals of the world,* 5th ed. Vol. 2. Baltimore: Johns Hopkins University Press.

22. Harrington, F. A. 1977. *A guide to the mammals of Iran.* Teheran: Department of the Environment.

23. Stuart, C. T., and V. J. Wilson. 1988. *The cats of southern Africa.* Bulawayo, Zimbabwe: Chipangali Wildlife Trust.

24. Makacha, S., and G. B. Schaller. 1969. Observations on lions in the Lake Manyara National Park, Tanzania. *E. Afr. Wildl. J.* 7: 99–103.

25. Hanby, J. P., J. D. Bygott, and C. Packer. 1995. Ecology, demography, and behavior of lions in two contrasting habitats: Ngorongoro Crater and the Serengeti Plains. In *Serengeti II: Dynamics, management, and conservation of an ecosystem,* ed. A. R. E. Sinclair and P. Arcese, 315–331. Chicago: University of Chicago Press.

26. Eloff, F. C. 1973. Water use by the Kalahari lion *Panthera leo vernayi*. *Koedoe* 16: 149–154.

27. Clarke, B. C., and H. H. Berry. 1992. Water flux in free-living lions (*Panthera leo*) in the Etosha National Park, Namibia. *J. Mammal.* 73: 552–558.

28. Owens, M., and D. Owens. 1984. Kalahari lions break the rules. *Int. Wildl.* 14: 4–13.

29. Rudnai, J. A. 1976. Activity rhythm of a free-ranging lion population. In *The world's cats*, vol. 3, ed. R. L. Eaton, 60–72. Seattle: Carnivore Research Institute, Burke Museum, University of Washington.

30. Eloff, F. C. 1984. Food ecology of the Kalahari lion *Panthera leo*. *Koedoe* 27 (suppl.): 249–258.

31. Stander, P. E. 1992. Foraging dynamics of lions in a semi-arid environment. *Can. J. Zool.* 70: 8–21.

32. Elliott, J. P., I. McT. Cowan, and C. S. Holling. 1977. Prey capture by the African lion. *Can. J. Zool.* 55: 1811–1828.

33. Van Orsdol, K. G. 1984. Foraging behaviour and hunting success of lions in Queen Elizabeth National Park, Uganda. *Afr. J. Ecol.* 22: 79–99.

34. Stander, P. E., and S. D. Albon. 1993. Hunting success of lions in a semi-arid environment. *Symp. Zool. Soc. Lond.* 65: 127–143.

35. Berry, H. 1991. Namibia's seal-eating lions in danger. *Cat News* 14: 10–11.

36. Busse, C. 1980. Leopard and lion predation upon Chacma baboons living in the Moremi Wildlife Reserve. *Botswana Notes & Records* 12: 15–21.

37. Tsukahara, T. 1993. Lions eat chimpanzees: The first evidence of predation by lions on wild chimpanzees. *Am. J. Primatol.* 29: 1–11.

38. Scheel, D., and C. Packer. 1995. Variation in predation by lions: Tracking a movable feast. In *Serengeti II: Dynamics, management, and conservation of an ecosystem*, ed. A. R. E. Sinclair and P. Arcese, 299–314. Chicago: University of Chicago Press.

39. Ruggiero, R. G. 1991. Prey selection of the lion (*Panthera leo* L.) in the Manovo-Gounda-St. Floris National Park, Central African Republic. *Mammalia* 55: 23–33.

40. Eloff, F. C. 1973. Ecology and behavior of the Kalahari lion. In *The world's cats*, vol. 1, ed. R. L. Eaton, 90–126. Winston, OR: World Wildlife Safari.

41. Chellam, R., and A. J. T. Johnsingh. 1993. Management of Asiatic lions in Gir Forest, India. *Symp. Zool. Soc. Lond.* 65: 409–424.

42. Prins, H. H. T., and G. R. Iason. 1989. Dangerous lions and nonchalant buffalo. *Behaviour* 108: 262–296.

43. Stander, P. 1992. Cooperative hunting in lions: The role of the individual. *Behav. Ecol. Sociobiol.* 29: 445–454.

44. Stevenson-Hamilton, J. 1954. Wild life in South Africa. London: Cassell.

45. Kruuk, H. 1972. *The spotted hyaena: A study of predation and social behavior*. Chicago: University of Chicago Press.

46. Mills, G. 1990. The lion (*Panthera leo*) and cheetah (*Acinonyx jubatus*) in Kruger National Park, South Africa. *Felid* 4(1): 13.

47. Packer, C., D. Scheel, and A. E. Pusey. 1990. Why lions form groups: Food is not enough. *Am. Nat.* 136: 1–19.

48. Scheel, D. 1993. Profitability, encounter rates, and prey choice of African lions. *Behav. Ecol.* 4: 90–97.

49. Kruuk, H., and M. Turner. 1967. Comparative notes on predation by lion, leopard, cheetah and wild dog in the Serengeti area, East Africa. *Mammalia* 31: 1–27.

50. Kleiman, D. G., and J. F. Eisenberg. 1973. Comparisons of canid and felid social systems from an evolutionary perspective. *Anim. Behav.* 21: 637–659.

51. Caraco, T., and L. L. Wolf. 1975. Ecological determinants of group sizes of foraging lions. *Am. Nat.* 109: 343–352.

52. Lamprecht, J. 1981. The function of social hunting in larger terrestrial carnivores. *Mammal Rev.* 11: 169–179.

53. Rodman, P. S. 1981. Inclusive fitness and group size with a reconsideration of group sizes in lions and wolves. *Am. Nat.* 118: 275–283.

54. Van Orsdol, K. G., J. P. Hanby, and J. D. Bygott. 1985. Ecological correlates of lion social organization (*Panthera leo*). *J. Zool.* (Lond.) 206: 97–112.

55. Clark, C. W. 1987. The lazy adaptable lions: A Markovian model of group foraging. *Anim. Behav.* 35: 361–368.

56. Gittleman, J. L. 1989. Carnivore group living: Comparative trends. In *Carnivore behavior, ecology, and evolution*, ed. J. L. Gittleman, 183–207. Ithaca, NY: Cornell University Press.

57. Giraldeau, L.-A., and D. Gillis. 1988. Do lions hunt in group sizes that maximize hunters' daily food returns? *Anim. Behav.* 36: 611–613.

58. Chellam, R. 1993. Ecology of the Asiatic lion (*Panthera leo persica*). Ph.D. dissertation, Saurashtra University, Rajkot, India.

59. Bertram, B. C. R. 1973. Lion population regulation. *E. Afr. Wildl. J.* 11: 215–225.

60. Bertram, B. C. R. 1975. Social factors influencing reproduction in wild lions. *J. Zool.* (Lond.) 177: 463–482.

61. Bertram, B. C. R. 1978. *Pride of lions*. London: Dent.

62. Hanby, J. P., and J. D. Bygott. 1987. Emigration of subadult lions. *Anim. Behav.* 35: 161–169.

63. Bygott, J. D., B. C. R. Bertram, and J. P. Hanby. 1979. Male lions in large coalitions gain reproductive advantages. *Nature* 282: 839–841.

64. Packer, C., and A. E. Pusey. 1982. Cooperation and competition within coalitions of male lions: Kin selection or game theory? *Nature* 296: 740–742.

65. Pusey, A. E., and C. Packer. 1987. The evolution of sex-biased dispersal in lions. *Behaviour* 101: 275–310.

66. Smuts, G. L. 1978. Effects of population reduction on the travels and reproduction of lions in Kruger National Park. *Carnivore* 1: 61–74.

67. Yamazaki, K. 1996. Social variation of lions in a male-depopulated area in Zambia. *J. Wildl. Mgmt.* 60: 490–497.

68. Packer, C. 1986. The ecology of sociality in felids. In *Ecological aspects of social evolution*, ed. D. I. Rubenstein and R. W. Wrangham, 429–451. Princeton: Princeton University Press.

69. Packer, C., and L. Ruttan. 1988. The evolution of cooperative hunting. *Am. Nat.* 132: 159–198.

70. Cairns, S. J. 1990. Social behavior within prides of lions (*Panthera leo*). Ph.D. dissertation, Cornell University, Ithaca, New York.

71. Scheel, D., and C. Packer. 1991. Group hunting behaviour of lions: A search for cooperation. *Anim. Behav.* 41: 697–709.

72. Heinsohn, R., and C. Packer. 1995. Complex cooperative strategies in group-territorial African lions. *Science* 269: 1260–1262.

73. McComb, K., C. Packer, and A. Pusey. 1994. Roaring and numerical assessment in contests between groups of female lions, *Panthera leo*. *Anim. Behav.* 47: 379–387.

74. Packer, C., and A. E. Pusey. 1997. Divided we fall: Cooperation among lions. *Sci. Am.* 276: 52–59.

75. Schaller, G. B. 1969. Life with the king of beasts. *Natl. Geogr.* 135(4): 494–519.

76. Hanby, J. P., and J. D. Bygott. 1979. Population changes in lions and other predators. In *Serengeti: Dynamics of an ecosystem*, ed. A. R. E. Sinclair and M. Norton-Griffiths, 249–262. Chicago: University of Chicago Press.

77. Stander, P. E. 1991. Demography of lions in Etosha National Park, Namibia. *Madoqua* 18: 1–9.

78. Mills, M. G. L., P. Wolf, E. A. N. Le Riche, and I. J. Myer. 1978. Some population characteristics of the lion (*Panthera leo*) in Kalahari National Park. *Koedoe* 21: 163–171.

79. Packer, C. 1994. *Into Africa*. Chicago: University of Chicago Press.

80. Peters, G. 1984. On the structure of friendly close range vocalizations in terrestrial carnivores (Mammalia: Carnivora: Fissipedia). *Z. Säugetierk.* 49: 157–182.

81. Peters, G., and M. H. Hast. 1994. Hyoid structure, laryngeal anatomy, and vocalization in felids (Mammalia: Carnivora: Fissipedia). *Z. Säugetierk.* 59: 87–104.

82. Rudnai, J. A. 1973. *The social life of the lion*. Lancaster, England: Medical and Technical Publishing Company.

83. Leyhausen, P. 1979. *Cat behavior: The predatory and social behavior of domestic and wild cats*. New York: Garland STPM Press.

84. Schenkel, R. 1966. Play, exploration and territoriality in the wild lion. *Symp. Zool. Soc. Lond.* 18: 11–12.

85. Ulmer, F. 1966. Voices of the felidae. *Int. Zoo Yrbk.* 6: 259–262.

86. Smuts, G. L. 1982. *Lion*. Johannesburg: Macmillan.

87. Stander, P. E., and J. Stander. 1988. Characteristics of lion roars in Etosha National Park. *Madoqua* 15: 315–318.

88. Cooper, J. 1942. An exploratory study on African lions. *Comp. Psychol. Monogr.* 17(7): 1–48.

89. Packer, C., L. Herbst, A. E. Pusey, J. D. Bygott, J. P. Hanby, S. J. Cairns, and M. Borgerhoff Mulder. 1988. Reproductive success of lions. In *Reproductive success*, ed. T. H. Clutton-Brock, 363–383. Chicago: University of Chicago Press.

90. Packer, C., D. A. Gilbert, A. E. Pusey, and S. J. O'Brien. 1991. A molecular genetic analysis of kinship and cooperation in African lions. *Nature* 351: 562–565.

91. Packer, C., and A. E. Pusey. 1983. Adaptations of female lions to infanticide by incoming males. *Am. Nat.* 121: 716–728.

92. Sadleir, R. 1966. Notes on reproduction in the larger Felidae. *Int. Zoo Yrbk.* 6: 184–187.

93. Seifert, S. 1978. Untersuchungen zur Fortpflanzungsbiologie der im Zoologischen Garten Leipzig gehaltenen Großkatzen (Panthera, Oken, 1816) unter besonderer Berücksichtigung des Löwen—*Panthera leo* (Linné, 1758). Berlin: VER Verlag Volk und Gesundheit.

94. van Hooff, J. A. R. A. M. 1965. A large litter of lion cubs at Arnhem Zoo. *Int. Zoo Yrbk.* 5: 116.

95. Pusey, A. E., and C. Packer. 1994. Non-offspring nursing in social carnivores: Minimizing the costs. *Behav. Ecol.* 5(4): 362–374.

96. Smuts, G. L., J. L. Anderson, and J. C. Austin. 1978. Age determination of the African lion (*Panthera leo*). *J. Zool.* (Lond.) 185: 115–146.

97. Whyte, I. J., and G. L. Smuts. 1988. Dentition and life history of a 16-year-old known-age free-living male lion *Panthera*

98. Joslin, P. 1973. Factors associated with decline of the Asiatic lion. In *The world's cats*, ed. R. L. Eaton, 127–141. Winston, OR: World Wildlife Safari.

99. Joslin, P. 1984. The environmental limitations and future of the Asiatic lion. *J. Bombay Nat. Hist. Soc.* 81: 648–664.

100. O'Brien, S. J., J. S. Martenson, C. Packer, L. Herbst, V. de Vos, P. Joslin, J. Ott-Joslin, D. E. Wildt, and M. Bush. 1987. Biochemical genetic variation in geographic isolates of African and Asiatic lions. *Natl. Geogr. Res.* 3(1): 114–124.

101. Kinnear, N. B. 1920. The past and present distribution of the lion in south eastern Asia. *J. Bombay Nat. Hist. Soc.* 27: 33–39.

102. Jackson, P. 1982. Improved prospects for Asia's last lions. *Tigerpaper* 9(1): 11–13.

103. Saberwal, V., R. Chellam, A. J. T. Johnsingh, and W. A. Rodgers. 1990. Lion-human conflicts in Gir Forest and adjoining areas. Unpublished report. Wildlife Institute of India, New Forest, Dehra Dun. Mimeographed, 64 pp.

104. Berwick, S. 1974. The Gir Forest: An endangered ecosystem. *Am. Sci.* 64: 28–40.

105. Singh, H. S. 1997. Population dynamics, group structure and natural dispersal of the Asiatic lion *Panthera leo persica*. *J. Bombay Nat. Hist. Soc.* 94: 65–70.

106. Saberwal, V., J. P. Gibbs, R. Chellam, and A. J. T. Johnsingh. 1994. Lion-human conflict in the Gir Forest, India. *Conserv. Biol.* 8: 501–507.

107. O'Brien, S. J., P. Joslin, G. L. Smith III, R. Wolfe, N. Schaeffer, E. Heath, J. Ott-Joslin, P. P. Rawal, K. K. Bhattacharjee, and J. S. Martenson. 1987. Evidence for African origins of founders of the Asiatic Species Survival Plan. *Zoo Biol.* 6: 99–116.

108. Wildt, D. E., M. Bush, K. L. Goodrowe, C. Packer, A. E. Pusey, J. L. Brown, P. Joslin, and S. J. O'Brien. 1987. Reproductive and genetic consequences of founding isolated lion populations. *Nature* 6137: 328–331.

109. Morell, V. 1994. Serengeti's big cats going to the dogs. *Science* 264: 1664.

110. Cat News. 1995. Serengeti lions recovering from canine distemper epidemic. *Cat News* 23: 9.

111. Cat News. 1990. Maneating lions killed. *Cat News* 12: 19.

112. Anderson, J. L. 1981. The re-establishment and management of a lion *Panthera leo* population in Zululand, South Africa. *Biol. Conserv.* 19: 107–117.

113. Anderson, J. L. 1992. Re-establishing large predators. *Reintroduction News* 4: 9.

114. Stander, P. E. 1990. A suggested management strategy for stock-raiding lions in Namibia. *S. Afr. J. Wildl. Res.* 20(2): 37–43.

115. Smithers, R. H. N. 1971. *The mammals of Botswana*. National Museum of Southern Rhodesia, Museum Memoir no. 4. Salisbury: Trustees of the National Museums of Rhodesia.

116. Mitchell, B., J. Shenton, and J. Uys. 1965. Predation on large mammals in the Kafue National Park, Zambia. *Zool. Afr.* 1: 297–318.

117. Pienaar, U. de V. 1969. Predator-prey relationships amongst the larger mammals of the Kruger National Park. *Koedoe* 12: 108–176.

118. Mills, M. G. L. 1990. *Kalahari hyaenas*. London: Unwin Hyman.

Jaguar

Panthera onca (Linnaeus, 1758)

All the big cats have inspired their share of myths and legends, but only the jaguar has dominated the religion and culture of a continent. From the beginning of recorded time in Central and South America, the image of the jaguar has loomed larger than life throughout art, religion, and myth.[1,2,3] In Peru, five-thousand-year-old jaguar sculptures have been unearthed among the artifacts from the Chavin de Huantar, the earliest known civilization in South America. Some two thousand years ago the Olmec people of southern Mexico created giant pavement mosaics of a fierce jaguar god and carved elaborate twenty-ton statues of jaguar heads. The Olmec believed that a woman was once raped by a jaguar and gave birth to the "thunder-child."[4] This was the beginning of a race of were-jaguars, which had a mix of human and jaguar features. Many of the rain gods and thunder deities of later civilizations can be traced back to the Olmec were-jaguars.[5,6]

Almost everywhere in South America the jaguar is closely identified with thunder, lightning, and rain. A modern Tukano Indian myth says, "The sun created the jaguar to be his representative on earth. He gave him the yellow color of his power and he gave him the voice of thunder which is the voice of the sun."[7]

As well as being associated with natural phenomena such as sun and rain, the jaguar is universally believed to be the master of animals and thus is closely associated with hunting rituals. The shaman must obtain permission from the jaguar for hunters and fishermen to kill game. On ceremonial occasions, shamans and priests paint their faces with spots or wear jaguar skins, teeth, and claws. They growl and mimic the jaguar's movements while singing to the jaguar spirit. The shaman establishes contact with the spirit world by taking narcotic snuff and going into a trance. During this trance the shaman's soul is believed to turn into a jaguar and roam the forest.[7]

Jaguar transformation is a complex ceremonial ritual, the cornerstone of which is the moral ambivalence of the jaguar image. Once transformed, the shaman can do good or evil. He can cure someone of a disease or take vengeance on an enemy. The jaguar not only lends the shaman his form as a disguise, but he also lends him his powers.[7]

When a man turns into a jaguar, for all intents and purposes he becomes the cat. He eats raw meat, sleeps on the ground, and avoids fire.[8] He has the voice of the jaguar as well as the cat's enhanced powers of vision and hearing. He remains a man only in his attitudes to human beings; he is a man shorn of all his cultural restrictions, free of the rules and taboos of society.

To the Indians the jaguar is a symbol of power, the dominant force in the forest. It is the master of all dimensions: it can run, swim, and climb, and it hunts the same animals they do. The Indians also believe that the jaguar is a great transformer, not only because of its physical versatility but also because of the variety of its coat patterns. The Indians differentiate between four or five types of jaguars according to their coat color and hunting habits, and the black jaguar is said to be the fiercest of all.[8]

The jaguar is known as *el tigre* throughout much of South America, but the name *jaguar* was originally *ya-guará*, which is said to mean "wild beast that overcomes its prey at a bound."[9] Alternatively, *yagua* also means "dog," the puma being known as *yagua pita,* or "red dog." In Brazil the jaguar is also called *onca.*[10]

DESCRIPTION

The jaguar is the largest felid in the Americas. Morphologically, it is similar to the leopard.[11,12,13] Molecular studies also suggest that the jaguar and leopard are closely related members of the genus *Panthera.*[14,15] The jaguar, however, is heavier and looks like a much more powerful animal. The jaguar lacks the lithe grace of the leopard; instead, it is a strong, stocky-looking cat, deep-chested, with an unusually large head and short, sturdy limbs.[16] Even the jaguar's canine teeth are more robust and have a more powerful bite than those of the other big cats.[17,18,19]

According to legend, the jaguar acquired its spotted coat by daubing mud on its body with its paws, and the markings on some animals do look like paw prints. On the jaguar's back and sides, large black or dark brown clusters of spots, called rosettes, or irregularly shaped blotches mark a background color that varies from pale yellow to tawny. These large rosettes frequently have one or more black dots in the center. The rosette pattern extends onto the white belly, throat, and insides of the limbs, where it appears as solid ovals or irregular spots. In general, though, the jaguar's coat coloration and markings are extremely variable, and while the jaguar's rosettes are larger and less numerous than those of the leopard, it is sometimes difficult to tell the pelts of these two cats apart.[9,20,21,22]

The tail is marked with black spots, and there are several black rings or bands on the last half. The ears are short and rounded, and the backs of the ears are black with only a faint buff central spot. Melanism appears to be more common among jaguars than any other large cats;[23,24] on these blackish brown or black individuals the rosette pattern is often visible beneath the dark background coat color. Black jaguars were once regarded as a separate species, and some Indian tribes still believe that black jaguars are bigger and never mingle with spotted jaguars.

The Swiss naturalist Rengger was one of the first people to draw attention to the regional variation in jaguar size.[25] Certainly there is no such thing as an average-sized jaguar, for the mean body weight of this cat may vary by 100 percent, depending on where it lives. Despite legend and their overwhelming appearance of robust power, jaguars in some forested areas are not much heavier than a large retriever. The average weight for an adult male jaguar in Central America is 56 kilograms, and for adult females the average is only 41 kilograms.[26] The largest jaguars are found in the floodplains of the Pantanal region of Brazil and the Venezuelan llanos, where males average 102 kilograms and females 72 kilograms. The size difference between jaguars from forested and floodplain habitats is thought to reflect the availability of large prey.

DISTRIBUTION

Today, the jaguar ranges through Central America to eastern Colombia, Venezuela, Suriname, the Guianas, Brazil, and south into Peru, Bolivia, the Paraguayan Chaco, and northern Argentina. Jaguars have been eliminated from many parts of their former range, and within the last fifty years their range has been markedly reduced, having receded southward from the United States and Mexico about 1,000 kilometers. In South America the jaguar's range has receded northward about 1,500 km, and the cat no longer occurs in Uruguay and much of Argentina (fig. 42).[21,27,28,29]

In North America the jaguar's historical range is believed to have extended from Oregon to Pennsylvania.[30] Though it had disappeared from the Northeast before Columbus's time, the jaguar continued to survive in some of the southwestern states until quite recently.[31,32,33] The last California jaguar was killed at Palm Springs in 1860, but jaguars continued to survive in Arizona, Texas, and New Mexico until the twentieth century.[10] In 1920 one was seen crossing a highway three miles northwest of Tucson, Arizona. A jaguar was shot in Texas in 1946, and another in Arizona in 1949. A jaguar was captured in Arizona in 1971. Since then there have been a few rumors of jaguar sightings, and one was reportedly shot in Arizona in 1986.[32,34] In

Figure 42. Distribution of the jaguar.

March 1996, a mountain lion hunter in southeastern Arizona was following his dogs, which were hot on the trail of a cat, only to discover that the cat was a male jaguar. The story and photographs of the event are recounted in Warner Glenn's *Eyes of Fire*.[35]

ECOLOGY AND BEHAVIOR

Jaguars are typically found in a variety of tropical and subtropical habitats from sea level to about 1,200 meters elevation. There are, however, records of jaguars at 3,800 meters in Costa Rica and at 2,700 meters in Bolivia, and tracks were seen at 2,100 meters in northern Peru.[8] While the jaguar is commonly thought of as a denizen of dense tropical forest, it also inhabits a wide range of other habitat types, including arid scrub and swampy grasslands, and has been recorded from montane forest, lowland evergreen forest, dry deciduous forest, and mangrove swamps.[10,36,37,38,39] Throughout much of its range the jaguar is strongly associated with streams and watercourses. These cats are excellent swimmers that have been seen crossing large rivers, and, like tigers, they sometimes spend the heat of the day half-submerged in a stream.

In Mexico, Leopold observed that jaguars often followed large rivers in their travels and as a result were occasionally found in areas where watercourses penetrated drier areas. One old male jaguar killed in 1955 in Baja California is a good illustration. Leopold surmised that this animal must have traveled at least 500 miles from regularly occupied jaguar habitat, wandering across the Sonoran Desert and crossing the Colorado River.[36] The rugged Sierra Madre Occidental, Mexico, was the likely travel corridor used by the male jaguar that appeared recently in southeastern Arizona.

A study of radio-collared jaguars in the Pantanal region of Brazil showed that they seemed to favor gallery forest and forest patches. Open forest and grassland habitat types were used significantly less than expected based on their availability.[40,41] Similar observations were recorded for radio-tagged jaguars in the Venezuelan llanos.[42,43]

As the largest cat of the Americas, the jaguar is the dominant predator. It moves and hunts on the ground, but can also climb if the need arises. Radiotelemetry studies have shown that jaguars can have quite variable activity patterns. In Peru and Brazil they were active both day and night, but in Mexico, Belize, and Venezuela they were primarily nocturnal.[41,42,43,44,45,46,47] Whether jaguars hunt during daylight probably depends to a large degree on prey activity patterns and possibly on human disturbance. Jaguars preying on cattle frequently hunt during the daytime,[48] and jaguars are also diurnal in areas where turtles and crocodilians form an important part of their diet.[49]

Feeding Ecology

Jaguars are opportunistic predators and are capable of killing and consuming almost any type of prey they encounter, ranging in size from turtle eggs and two-pound armadillos to domestic cattle that may weigh a thousand pounds, or three to four times the cat's body weight. Leopold quotes a knowledgeable hunter in Mexico, who had killed some sixty jaguars, as saying that the contents of no two stomachs were the same.[36]

Jaguars usually hunt by walking slowly along trails, watching and listening for prey. They may also choose a likely spot and wait in ambush, or they may patrol river beaches, looking for basking crocodilians or waiting for turtles to come ashore to lay their eggs. Once they have detected an animal, they attempt to get as close as possible without being noticed. Rengger's observations of jaguars hunting capybaras (large, semiaquatic rodents) along the banks of the Rio Paraguay are particularly vivid. He describes how the jag-

uar, after spotting a capybara, painstakingly stalks its victim: "Serpent-like it winds its way over the ground, pausing for a minute or so to observe its quarry, often making a considerable detour to approach it from another direction where there is less risk of being detected. After it has been successful in getting close to its prey, the jaguar pounces on it in one, rarely two, bounds, presses it against the ground, tears out its throat and carries it, still struggling, into a thicket."[25] Jaguars have even been seen to jump into the water after capybaras and seize them before they can dive to safety.

The list of prey species eaten by jaguars is long, and varies with geographic location and prey availability. More than eighty-five prey species are reported,[21] and recent studies of jaguars in Belize, Venezuela, Brazil, Peru, Mexico, and Paraguay emphasize how varied and all-encompassing this cat's diet can be.

In the seasonally flooded grasslands, or llanos, of Venezuela, jaguars feed mainly on capybaras, spectacled caimans, freshwater turtles, collared peccaries, deer, and cattle.[9,37,42,43] Similarly, in the Brazilian Pantanal, a vast wetland area, jaguars feed on cattle, white-lipped peccaries, and capybaras.[40,50,51,52,53] In Iguaçu National Park, Brazil, white-lipped and collared peccaries and deer made up 93 percent of the jaguar's diet; minor prey included coatis, agoutis, lizards, opossums, and armadillos.[45] Capybaras were the major contributor (49 percent) to the diet of jaguars living on the floodplain of the San Jorge and Cauca rivers in northern Colombia; reptiles, principally caimans, river turtles, and iguanas ranked second (36 percent).[54] In the undisturbed lowland tropical forest of Manu National Park in Peru, the bulk of the jaguar's diet consists of collared peccaries, agoutis, and large turtles.[44] In contrast, armadillos were the single most important prey in the logged secondary forest of Belize, being found in one-fourth to one-half of all jaguar feces.[44,55] In the tropical forest at La Selva, Costa Rica, sloths and iguanas appeared to be prominent in the jaguar's diet.[56] Small and medium-sized (1–15 kilograms) mammals, principally brocket deer, rabbits, armadillos, and marsupials, were important prey for jaguars in the central and northern Chaco of Paraguay.[57] In the Chamela-Cuixmala Biosphere Reserve, Jalisco, Mexico, white-tailed deer alone constituted 54 percent of the biomass consumed by jaguars. Collared peccaries, coatis, and armadillos together contributed another 44 percent. The mean weight of jaguar prey was 15.6 kilograms.[58]

Basically, jaguar diets tend to reflect the relative abundance of the various prey species in the area. While the cats seem to prefer peccaries, they do not appear to select particular sex or age classes of prey.[44,45,46,50] Leopold mentions that jaguars seem to have a particular fondness for peccaries, and the Essequibo Indians believe that each herd of peccaries has a jaguar that follows the group, picking off stragglers whenever it gets hungry.[36] Results from a field study in Peru also suggest that jaguars may indeed have a predilection for peccary. In Manu National Park, jaguars killed peccaries out of proportion to their abundance, suggesting that the cats either selectively hunted peccaries or that they were more vulnerable.[44] White-lipped and collared peccaries are also the favorite prey of jaguars in Iguaçu National Park, Brazil, and jaguar predation was a major source of mortality in peccary populations there.[45] Collared peccaries were also the most important prey of jaguars in Calakmul Biosphere Reserve, Mexico.[59,60] In the Venezuelan llanos, jaguars preyed selectively on capybaras and collared peccaries, but white-tailed deer and caimans were taken less than expected based on availability.[43]

Several naturalists have described the rattling noise made by peccary tusks as sounding like "the clicking of a thousand pairs of castanets"; this sound, combined with their rustling footsteps and vocalizations, makes them easy to find in the forest. They also leave quite a powerful smell; in 1927, Up de Graff wrote, "The strong acrid odor of the herd hangs in the air and on shrubs and overhanging branches long after the animals have passed, and can be smelled a full mile away."[61] Despite the fact that their noise and odor would seem to increase the chances of a jaguar finding the herd, peccaries are formidable prey, and there are accounts of peccaries attacking and even killing jaguars.[8,43]

Lions, tigers, and leopards typically kill large prey with a throat or neck bite. The jaguar, however, also uses a third technique that is not seen in the other large felids: it bites through the animal's skull between the ears or horns. The thick skulls of horses and cattle killed by jaguars often have one or two holes punched through the temporal bone.[9] Capybaras are sometimes killed with a bite to the back of the head, with the canines piercing the braincase; a few skulls have been found that showed how the jaguar had inserted a canine neatly into each ear of the capybara and penetrated the skull.[50]

Although turtles may seem rather unlikely prey for a big cat, these reptiles form an important part of the jaguar's diet in many parts of South America.[9,49] River turtles can weigh as much as 32 kilograms, and the females are quite vulnerable when they come ashore to lay eggs. Jaguars use their powerful bite to break back the lower edge of the turtle's carapace to gain access to the body cavity. On exceptionally large turtles the space between the carapace and the plastron is large enough for the jaguar to insert its paw and scoop out the meat without breaking the carapace. Empty, overturned turtle shells with traces of jaguar hair around the orifices are often found on favorite turtle nesting beaches. Small turtles are sometimes chewed and eaten whole. Jaguars are even able to bite into and break open the domed carapace of large tortoises. Tortoises occasionally survive an encounter with a jaguar, and some individuals have been found with deep gouges in the carapace.

Louise Emmons, who studied jaguars in Peru, noticed that many jaguar skulls in museum collections had canine teeth that were badly worn or chipped. She believes that the powerful jaws and robust canines of the jaguar may be adapted for penetrating the armorlike integument of turtles and caimans. These reptiles are numerous and represent a significant caloric return; indeed, one large turtle would easily meet the daily food requirement of a jaguar.[37,49]

Jaguars also feed on fish; however, their fishing methods have been the subject of considerable debate. Indian folk tales say that "the jaguar goes a little way out into the water, and there discharges some saliva, which attracts the fish, which the jaguar flips out onto the bank with his paw."[62] Other accounts maintain that jaguars lure fish by tapping on the surface of the water with their tails.[25,63] According to the Indians, when a jaguar does this, it imitates the sound of falling fruit to attract fruit-eating fish. Fruit-eating fish do actually exist in the Amazon, and they are attracted to the sound of fruit falling into the water.[64] Jaguars probably catch fish whenever they can. For example, in the wetlands of Venezuela and Brazil, large catfish often breed in shallow pools and lagoons. As the dry season progresses the pools dry up, leaving the fish stranded and vulnerable to storks and other predators. Jaguars have been seen "fishing" in these pools. There is also an observation suggesting that a jaguar may have caught a freshwater dolphin while it rested in shallow water.[65]

Like other large cats, jaguars usually drag large kills into dense cover before beginning to eat. There are records of large kills being moved a mile or more over very rough terrain, representing feats of strength that rival those of the tiger.[9] Edgardo Mondolfi recorded an example from Venezuela in which a female jaguar weighing 41 kilograms dragged the 180-kilogram carcass of a Brahman heifer about 200 meters over a steep and rocky ravine in dense forest.[38] At another site in Venezuela a jaguar reportedly killed a cow on the edge of the Apure River, dragged the carcass into the strong current, and swam 800 meters across the river carrying the cow. These record-length drags are almost always associated with domestic livestock and open pastures. Under these circumstances jaguars are more likely to drag a carcass farther to find suitable cover and avoid human disturbance. There is not much comparative information for drag length distances for wild prey, but in the Mato Grosso, Brazil, jaguars dragged capybara kills an average of 87 meters before beginning to eat.[50] In Venezuela, a jaguar dragged a capybara 300 meters through the forest to an opening of 50 meters in diameter, where it consumed the carcass. Jaguars spent an average of 2.5 days near a kill, during which time they were never more than 200 meters from it. They never covered the carcass.[66]

Unlike the other big cats, jaguars usually start to feed at the forequarters of their victims, beginning with the head or neck and progressing to the shoulders, chest, and then the viscera. While smaller animals are consumed entirely, jaguars often abandon large prey, leaving the hindquarters untouched. Jaguars are also unusual in that they make no attempt to cover their kills with grass or other debris,[50] a behavior that is common in tigers and pumas. Almeida remarked that jaguars in Brazil do not touch putrefied meat and do not come to either live or dead bait.[67] However, a female jaguar in the Pantanal took the lungs of a cow hung in a tree as bait, and in Belize jaguars were captured in cage traps baited with live pigs.[46,50]

In zoos jaguars are fed about 1.4 kilograms of meat per day, but there is little information from the wild on how much these cats eat. Emmons estimated that a jaguar would eat 34 to 43 grams of meat per day per kilogram of body weight, which for a 34-kilogram Peruvian jaguar translates to 1.2 to 1.5 kilograms per day, an amount similar to that consumed by captive animals.[44] In the Mato Grosso, Brazil, Schaller reported three instances in which a jaguar had eaten less than 5 kilograms from a capybara kill before abandoning it.[50]

The effect of jaguar predation on prey populations has rarely been assessed. However, on one ranch in the Mato Grosso, a combination of jaguar predation and disease severely reduced a capybara population. In a two-month period the capybara population on the ranch was reduced by 20 to 30 percent.[50] Similarly, in a recent study in Iguaçu National Park, Brazil, jaguars annually removed about 50 percent of the available peccary biomass, which, when combined with losses to poachers and farmers, was not a level that could be sustained for long.[45] In Manu National Park, jaguars and pumas combined removed an estimated 8 percent of the large mammalian prey biomass.[44] In Jalisco, Mexico, jaguars and pumas together killed about 23–29 percent of the deer population annually, which is similar to estimates reported from puma studies in the United States. The percentage of the peccary population killed annually by these two cats was estimated at 9–11 percent.[59]

The impact of jaguar predation on domestic livestock depends largely on the availability of natural prey and herd management practices. On one ranch in the Venezuelan llanos, where natural prey were abundant and herd management was excellent, jaguars and pumas were responsible for 6 percent of all calf losses. On another ranch feline predation accounted for 30 percent of all calf losses, but here husbandry practices were rudimentary and poaching had severely reduced the native prey populations.[68]

Social Organization

Jaguars are solitary hunters and seldom share kills, although there are accounts of courting pairs traveling and feeding together, females and their nearly full-grown offspring sharing a kill with a male, and newly independent siblings eating together.

Jaguars have a land tenure system similar to that of other large felids. Males occupy larger ranges than females, and even where ranges overlap, same-sex individuals tend not to use the same area at the same time. Data from two radio-tracking studies in the Pantanal region of Brazil showed that females had overlapping ranges, although range sizes at the two study sites were markedly different. The year-round home ranges of four females on the Miranda Ranch in the southern Pantanal varied from 97 to 168 square kilometers and overlapped extensively. Two of the four females were known to be mother and daughter, and it is possible that the other two were also related. An adult male's range measured 152 square kilometers. The ranges of these cats varied markedly with the seasons, being four to five times smaller in the wet season than in the dry season. Travel distances for both sexes also were small-est in the wet season. Miranda experiences severe flooding, and as low-lying areas are inundated, both predators and prey become concentrated on tracts of high ground.[40,41] At the Acurizal Ranch in the west-ern Pantanal, where flooding is not as severe, female ranges were relatively small, and a mother and her pre-sumed daughter had identical ranges of approximately 38 square kilometers, which partially overlapped with that of another female whose range was 25 square kilo-meters. Based on tracks, an adult male's range covered about 90 square kilometers and overlapped the ranges of at least two females.[51] In the Venezuelan llanos, the range of an adult male jaguar partially overlapped the ranges of at least two adult females. In the dry season one of these females used an area of 80 square kilo-meters, but it decreased to 51 square kilometers in the wet season. The other female used an area of 53 square kilometers in the wet season.[43]

A recent study in the Iguaçu-Iguazu national parks on the Brazil-Argentina border also found broad over-lap in jaguar home ranges, but there was little overlap in core areas.[45] In this subtropical forest habitat, the average home range size of three adult male jaguars was 110 square kilometers (range 86.5 to 138.6 square kilometers); an adult female's range measured 70 square kilometers.

Results from a jaguar study in the Cockscomb Basin, Belize, differed from the typical felid pattern in which breeding males tend to occupy exclusive ranges. The home ranges of four radio-tagged males varied from 28 to 40 square kilometers and overlapped extensively. Two uncollared females had ranges estimated at 10 square kilometers; their ranges were overlapped by those of the males.[46]

The densities of adult jaguars vary geographically, but surprisingly, the reported densities are not as vari-able as expected based on the likely differences in prey biomass densities. Jaguar densities are estimated at 3.2 to 4 per 100 square kilometers for three sites in Bra-zil;[45,51,53] 3.5 per 100 square kilometers in Peru;[69] 2.5 per 100 square kilometers in Colombia;[54] and 1.7 and 3.3 per 100 square kilometers in Mexico.[58,59] In Belize, jaguar density was estimated at 6 to 8 adults per 100 square kilometers, the highest yet recorded.[46]

Jaguars use a variety of methods to indicate occu-pancy of their home ranges, including urine spraying, scrapes, depositing their feces in prominent locations, claw marks, and vocalizations. However, Schaller ob-served that jaguars in the Pantanal "seem to vocalize and leave visual and olfactory markings within their ranges much less often than do other *Panthera*, includ-ing snow leopard and puma."[51] In Belize, an intense period of scent marking and scraping was noted in areas of overlap between males.[46] The overlapping male ranges and the comparatively high level of scent marking and scraping may both have been the result of social flux. During the first year of the study two res-ident male jaguars died, and several other males jock-eyed for position in a struggle to acquire the vacant ranges. Much of the marking occurred in the areas be-ing contested. Studies of other large felids suggest that a period of instability may follow the death of a resi-dent male, and that range boundaries may continue to change for a year or more before the social dynamics stabilize.[70,71]

The jaguar's best-known form of communication is roaring. Early naturalists and explorers likened the call to thunder, or to the roar of the caiman. Perry describes the jaguar's roar as "five or six repetitions of a short, sharp guttural uh, accelerating and crescending."[8] Hunters imitate the jaguar's roar by grunting into gourds or shells. The sound serves to draw the jaguar within range of the hunter's gun or spear. Both males and females roar, and there are instances of two indi-viduals engaged in intense bouts of counter-calling that lasted as long as two hours. On one occasion four jaguars called back and forth.[72]

Reproduction and Development

Roaring may function to bring jaguars together for mating purposes, and Almeida reports that females in heat travel widely, calling for a mate. One female was accompanied by four males.[73] In Venezuela there are several observations of females in heat being followed by two to three males.[9]

In captivity the inter-estrous period varies from twenty-two to sixty-five days, and females may remain in estrus for six to seventeen days.[74,75,76] The onset of es-trus is characterized by increased restlessness, pacing, rubbing, and vocalizations. Copulation is rapid and fre-quent; a pair may mate a hundred times per day.[77,78,79]

One to four cubs, usually two, are born after a ges-tation period of about a hundred days.[21] In captivity, births occur throughout the year, and this may also be true for jaguars living in tropical areas. However, in temperate portions of the jaguar's range, anecdotal evidence suggests that more births occur in the sum-mer months.[36,80] The female gives birth in a secluded site, usually in dense cover. Cubs are born with coarse, woolly, spotted coats and weigh 700 to 900 grams. Over the next fifty days they gain about 48 grams per day. Cubs open their eyes at three to thirteen days of age. By the time they are a month old, the upper and lower incisors and upper canines have erupted. The lower canines appear at about five weeks of age.[75,81]

The vocal repertoire of cubs is initially limited to bleating, which is replaced by gurgling and then by mewing at three to six months of age. By the time they are a year old, jaguars have a full adult vocal repertoire, with the exception of some calls associated with reproduction.[82,83]

The cubs are totally dependent on their mother's milk until they are ten to eleven weeks old, after which they begin to eat meat, although they may continue to suckle until they are five to six months old.[75] Cubs begin to accompany their mother when they are about two months old. Male cubs grow faster than their female siblings, and by the time they are a year and a half old males may be 25 percent heavier than their sisters. By two years of age males may be 50 percent heavier than their female siblings. There is a long period of association between mother and young, during which the cubs acquire the skills necessary to catch and kill prey. There is no information on when the young first begin to hunt by themselves, but by the time they are fifteen to eighteen months old they are often traveling independently within their mother's range and making their own kills.[53] By the time they are two years old jaguars are usually independent.

Little is known of the social circumstances associated with dispersal or the age at which it occurs, but in the Pantanal region of Brazil two radio-collared littermates, a male and a female, dispersed when they were about twenty months old. The siblings showed considerable differences in dispersal behavior. The male left the natal area and did not return, whereas the female left and returned three days later. She left and returned on at least two other occasions during the next two months before she finally dispersed. There was also a difference in the dispersal distance, with the male traveling 30 kilometers, or more than three times farther from the natal range than his sister.[53]

In Iguaçu National Park, Brazil, two subadult males dispersed at sixteen and eighteen months of age.[45] One male spent eight months dispersing. He repeatedly crossed the Iguaçu River in his travels between the Brazilian and Argentine parks, one time venturing into Paraguay, and he showed no signs of having settled before being killed by poachers. The other male

suddenly disappeared from his natal range and a month later was found 64 kilometers away. Over the next two months he traveled widely, but then appeared to settle and was twice seen in the company of a female. He died a month later, killed by poachers.

Dispersal in jaguars does not appear to be initiated by the onset of sexual maturity. Sexual maturity in females occurs between two and two and a half years of age, and possibly between three to four years of age for males,[38] although in Brazil a two-year-old male was seen keeping company with a female.[45] Longevity in the wild is unknown, but Rabinowitz estimated that few jaguars in Belize live to be more than eleven years old.[48] In captivity, jaguars have lived to the advanced age of twenty to twenty-five years, and one female was thirty-two years old.[9,73]

STATUS IN THE WILD

Emmons believes that competition with humans for food and living space will prove to be a greater threat to the jaguar than hunting or the demand for its skin. Throughout the jaguar's range large areas of land are being cleared, and rates of deforestation in South and Central America, already among the highest in the world, are projected to increase.[9] Forests are felled for timber, agricultural development and settlement, and cattle ranches. Subsistence farmers and loggers often supplement their diets by hunting wild game, and as new areas are opened up, the jaguar is placed in direct competition with people for its food. Caiman populations are hunted for their skins, and turtles, monkeys, capybaras, and fish are captured for their meat and sold in markets, all of which may reduce the prey available for jaguars.[84]

Though the handsome spotted coat of the jaguar has always been highly prized, the last two decades have seen a dramatic decline in commercial hunting for skins. Reports from the early 1800s indicate that some four thousand jaguars a year were killed across the continent of South America.[10] During the 1940s and 1950s jaguar skins were in great demand for fur coats, and as recently as 1969, by which time trade had already declined greatly, 9,831 jaguar skins, worth over one and a half million dollars, were imported into the United States.[85,86] Prices paid for raw jaguar skins reached a high of U.S.$130 to $180 in the early 1970s and then declined to a low of $10.[87,88] Since the early 1970s the jaguar has been on the list of totally protected species in most South American countries, and in 1973 it was listed on appendix I of CITES.[27] While the threat from the commercial skin trade has abated, the jaguar is still losing ground to habitat destruction, and many are shot every year as cattle killers.

In 1986, Wendell Swank and James Teer conducted a survey of the status of the jaguar by interviewing government officials, biologists, hunters, and ranchers in Mexico and South and Central America.[27] They found that within Mexico and Central America the jaguar occupies an area of approximately 483,000 square kilometers, or about 33 percent of its original range. Within its current range, it is considered to be "greatly reduced" over 28 percent of the area, "reduced" over 47 percent, and "holding its own or increasing" over the remaining 25 percent. The jaguar's main stronghold in Central America appears to be northern Guatemala and adjoining areas in southern Mexico and western Belize. In South America the jaguar still occupies about 62 percent of its historical range. Within its current range it is "greatly reduced" throughout 16 percent of the area, "reduced" throughout 20 percent, and "holding its own or increasing" over the remaining 64 percent. Swank and Teer estimated that the jaguar's range has shrunk from 15 million square kilometers at the time of European settlement to 9.3 million square kilometers in 1986.

There are no reliable figures for the total number of jaguars remaining in the wild, but there is an "optimistic estimate" of 2,500 to 3,500 for Venezuela.[89] Almeida estimated there were 3,500 jaguars in the Brazilian Pantanal, but Quigley and Crawshaw estimated the number at closer to 1,000 to 1,500.[72,90] In the Peten of Guatemala the numbers are estimated at 500 to 800.[59] The jaguar is considered to be extinct in Chile, El Salvador, and Uruguay and approaching extinction in Argentina, Costa Rica, and Panama.[27]

People continue to kill jaguars to protect their livestock. When humans introduced livestock to South America, they provided the jaguar with large, easy-to-kill prey, and not surprisingly, the jaguar took to feeding on this new food source with alacrity. The Spanish, Portuguese, and Jesuits brought cattle with them when they settled the savannas; these cattle often became feral when settlements or missions were abandoned.[91] The number of feral cattle increased rapidly, and in 1619 the governor of Buenos Aires reported that 80,000 cattle per year could be harvested for their hides without decreasing the wild herds. In about 1700 Felix de Azara estimated the number of feral cattle in South America between 26° and 41° south latitude at 48 million.[92] These numbers are comparable to those of bison in the North American Great Plains at their peak. Some reports suggest that the introduction of cattle brought about a considerable increase in jaguar numbers. Most large cattle ranches employed professional jaguar hunters. Sport hunting for jaguars under the guise of depredation control is still common, and hunters use dogs to track and bay the cats. Jaguars are also shot from tree platforms or lured to an area by hunters using a gourd, altered and played to imitate the call of the cat.

Some individual jaguars can become very destructive, causing great economic loss. However, throughout major portions of the jaguar's range, livestock are left unattended for long periods of time and often become semi-wild. These feral cattle experience considerable natural mortality through disease, accidents, and malnutrition.[68,90,93] In many places cattle now graze in areas that were formerly forest or on land that adjoins forested areas, and not surprisingly, some jaguars take advantage of these easy prey.

However, the few studies that have been conducted show that not all jaguars kill cattle. Alan Rabinowitz, who spent two years studying jaguars in Belize, found that most confirmed cattle-killing jaguars showed signs of previous shotgun wounds. He suggests that ranchers may be partially responsible for the problem when they shoot at jaguars and injure them. Rabinowitz also found that ranchers who took care of their stock and did not let them wander into the forest experienced far fewer losses to jaguars.[48]

STATUS IN CAPTIVITY
Jaguars seem to thrive in captivity, and many are held in zoos and private collections.

CONSERVATION EFFORTS
The jaguar was listed on appendix I of CITES in 1973, and with the exception of Mexico, all countries in the range of the jaguar are members of CITES. Every country that has jaguar populations also has internal laws that forbid the killing of jaguars. However, the laws are not rigorously enforced and usually allow the killing of an animal for the protection of domestic stock. In 1980 George Schaller was forced to abandon his study site in Brazil when ranchers shot both of his radio-collared jaguars. The perpetrators were not prosecuted. Enforcement of protective legislation varies from lax to erratic in remote areas, and seems to operate most efficiently at central inspection areas and at international ports and airports.

The jaguar is protected in Central and South America by several reserves and national parks. In Central America forty-six conservation units, amounting to 4.3 percent of the land area, have been established, and further proposals to protect land in the Peten region of Guatemala and Campeche in Mexico are currently being considered. In 1986 a conservation area designed specifically to protect the jaguar was established in Belize.[94] The 350,000-hectare Río Plátano Biosphere Reserve in Honduras and the 597,000-hectare Darien World Heritage Site in Panama also include regional populations of the jaguar.[95]

Historically, the jaguar has had some degree of nat-ural protection because many populations live in areas that are generally inhospitable or inaccessible to humans. This protection through inaccessibility is rapidly disappearing. Some authorities maintain that controlled sport hunting of jaguars should be considered as a conservation measure, the rationale being that such hunting would discourage opportunistic killing of jaguars and encourage local people to value the animal as a resource.[27] However, most countries with jaguar populations have been unable to regulate hunting effectively, and little is known of the population dynamics of wild jaguars. Furthermore, problem jaguars are still being killed.

TABLE 57 MEASUREMENTS AND WEIGHTS OF ADULT JAGUARS

HB	n	T	n	WT	n	Location	Source
1,565 (1,260–1,700)	16m	681 (600–800)	16m	104.5 (68–121)	26m	Venezuela	26
1,304 (1,160–1,470)	12f	619 (500–670)	12f	66.9 (51–100)	31f	Venezuela	26
1,403 (1,200–1,640)	11m	621 (550–660)	11m	96 (71–119)	36m	Pantanal, southern Brazil	40,45,50,53,67
1,344 (1,270–1,420)	7f	554 (490–610)	7f	76.8 (64–93)	22f	Pantanal, southern Brazil	40,45,50,53,67
1,290, 1,370	2m	600, 630	2m	83.6 (69–96)	9m	Amazon	26,67
1,220, 1,290	2f	500, 540	2f	43, 63	2f	Amazon	67
				31, 37	1f, 1m	Peru	44
1,247 (1,190–1,350)	3m	503 (440–550)	3m			Suriname	96
1,322 (1,105–1,460)	7m	563 (500–622)	7m	56.1 (48–66)	12m	Central America	48,59,62
				42.1 (36–51)	8f	Central America	48,59

Note: HB = head and body length (mm), T = tail length (mm), WT = weight (kg). *n* = sample size. Sex: m = male, f = female, ? = unknown. Mean values are presented only for sample sizes of three or more. Range of values is in parentheses.

TABLE 58 FREQUENCY OF OCCURRENCE OF PREY ITEMS IN THE DIETS OF JAGUARS (PERCENTAGE OF SAMPLES)

Prey items	Paraguayan Chaco[57] Scats (n = 106)	Iguaçu NP, Brazil[45] Scats (n = 73)	Cockscomb Basin, Belize[46] Scats (n = 228)	Calakmul Biosphere Reserve, Mexico[60] Scats (n = 37)
Marsupials	10.4	9.4	4.2	
Armadillos	7.4	8.5	54.0	12.0
Anteaters	3.0		9.3	2.0
Carnivores	0.7	7.5	2.0	18.0
Tapirus terrestris	1.5			
Tapir				

TABLE 58 *(continued)*

Prey items	Paraguayan Chaco[57] Scats (n = 106)	Iguaçu NP, Brazil[45] Scats (n = 73)	Cockscomb Basin, Belize[46] Scats (n = 228)	Calakmul Biosphere Reserve, Mexico[60] Scats (n = 37)
Mazama and *Odoicoileus* Brocket and white-tailed deer	23.0	8.5	6.5	8.0
Catagonus wagneri Chacoan peccary	1.5			
Tayassu sp. Peccary	2.9	35.8	5.4	42.0
Sylvilagus brasiliensis Cottontail rabbit	23.0	0.9		
Dolichotis salinicola Mara	5.9			
Galea musteloides Yellow-toothed cavy	6.7			
Dasyprocta azarae Agouti		3.8	4.3	
Agouti paca Paca		0.9	9.3	4.0
Sciurus aestuans Squirrel		1.9		
Unidentified rodents and rabbits	6.7		1.0	
Birds	2.2	8.5	0.5	10.0
Reptiles	2.2	6.6	3.0	
Primates		0.9		4.0
Plant material	21.0	3.8		
Minimum number of vertebrate prey items	135	106	185	50

REFERENCES

1. Osborne, H. 1968. *South American mythology*. Feltham, Middlesex, UK: Hamlyn Publishing Group.

2. Benson, E. P., ed. 1972. *The cult of the feline*. Washington, DC: Trustees for Harvard University.

3. Meyer, K. E. 1973. *Teotihuacán*. New York: Newsweek.

4. Reichel-Dolmatoff, G. 1972. The feline motif in prehistoric San Agustín sculpture. In *The cult of the feline*, ed. E. P. Benson, 51–68. Washington, DC: Trustees for Harvard University.

5. Coe, M. D. 1972. Olmec jaguars and Olmec kings. In *The cult of the feline*, ed. E. P. Benson, 1–18. Washington, DC: Trustees for Harvard University.

6. Covarrubias, M. 1946. *Mexico south, the isthmus of Tehuantepec*. New York: A. A. Knopf.

7. Reichel-Dolmatoff, G. 1975. *The shaman and the jaguar: A study of narcotic drugs among the Indians of Colombia*. Philadelphia: Temple University Press.

8. Perry, R. 1970. *The world of the jaguar*. New York: Taplinger.

9. Hoogesteijn, R., and E. Mondolfi. 1992. *The jaguar*. Caracas, Venezuela: Armitano Publishers.

10. Guggisberg, C. A. W. 1975. *Wild cats of the world*. New York: Taplinger.

11. Pocock, R. I. 1917. The classification of existing Felidae. *Ann. Mag. Nat. Hist.*, ser. 8, 20: 329–350.

12. Hemmer, H. 1978. The evolutionary systematics of living Felidae: Present status and current problems. *Carnivore* 1(1): 71–79.

13. Salles, L. O. 1992. Felid phylogenetics: Extant taxa and skull morphology (Felidae, Aeluroidea). *Am. Mus. Novitates* 3047: 1–67.

14. Collier, G. E., and S. J. O'Brien. 1985. A molecular phylogeny of the Felidae: Immunological distance. *Evolution* 39: 473–487.

15. Janczewski, D. N., W. S. Modi, J. C. Stephens, and S. J. O'Brien. 1995. Molecular evolution of mitochondrial 12s RNA and cytochrome *b* sequences in the pantherine lineage of Felidae. *Mol. Biol. Evol.* 12: 690–707.

16. Gonyea, W. J. 1976. Adaptive differences in the body proportions of large felids. *Acta. Anat.* 96: 81–96.

17. Werdelin, L. 1983. Morphological patterns in the skulls of cats. *Biol. J. Linn. Soc.* 19: 375–391.

18. Kiltie, R. 1984. Size ratios among sympatric Neotropical cats. *Oecologia* 61: 411–416.

19. Van Valkenburgh, B., and C. B. Ruff. 1987. Canine tooth strength and killing behaviour in large carnivores. *J. Zool.* 212: 379–397.

20. Nelson, E. W., and E. A. Goldman. 1933. Revision of the jaguars. *J. Mammal.* 14: 221–240.

21. Seymour, K. L. 1989. *Panthera onca. Mammalian Species* 340: 1–9.

22. Pocock, R. I. 1939. The races of jaguar. *Novitates Zool.* 41: 406–422.

23. Deutsch, L. A. 1975. Contribuição para o conhecimento da *Panthera onca* (Linne)— onça pintada (Mammalia-Carnivora). Curzamento de exemplares pintadas con melânicos. *Ciência Biol.* Seção 5, Zoológica 5: 369–370.

24. Dittrich, L. 1979. Die Vererbung des melanismus beim jaguar (*Panthera onca*). *Zool. Garten* 49: 9–23.

25. Rengger, J. R. 1830. *Naturgeschichte der Säugetiere von Paraguay.* Basel: Schweighauserschen Buchhandlung.

26. Hoogesteijn, R., and E. Mondolfi. 1996. Body mass and skull measurements in four jaguar populations, and observations on their prey base. *Bull. Fla. Mus. Nat. Hist., Biol. Ser.* 39(6): 195–219.

27. Swank, W. G., and J. G. Teer. 1989. Status of the jaguar— 1987. *Oryx* 23(1): 14–21.

28. Medellin, R. A., C. Chetkiewicz, A. Rabinowitz, K. H. Redford, J. G. Robinson, E. Sanderson, and A. Taber. In press. Jaguars in the new millennium: A status assessment, priority detection, and recommendations for the conservation of jaguars in the Americas. Universidad Nacional Autónoma de Mexico/Wildlife Conservation Society.

29. Roig, V. G. 1991. Desertification and distribution of mammals in the southern cone of South America. In *Latin American mammalogy, history, biodiversity, and conservation,* ed. M. A. Mares and D. J. Schmidly, 239–279. Norman: University of Oklahoma Press.

30. Daggett, P. M., and D. R. Henning. 1974. The jaguar in North America. *Am. Antiquity* 39(3): 465–469.

31. Nowak, R. M. 1975. Retreat of the jaguar. *Nat. Parks Conserv. Mag.* 49(12): 10–13.

32. Brown, D. F. 1983. On the status of the jaguar in the Southwest. *Southwest. Nat.* 28: 459–460.

33. Hock, R. J. 1955. Southwestern exotic felids. *Am. Midl. Nat.* 53: 324–328.

34. Nowak, R. M. 1991. *Walker's mammals of the world,* 5th ed. Vol. 2. Baltimore: Johns Hopkins University Press.

35. Glenn, W. 1996. *Eyes of fire.* El Paso, TX: Printing Corner Press.

36. Leopold, A. S. 1959. *Wildlife of Mexico.* Berkeley: University of California Press.

37. Emmons, L. H. 1991. Jaguars. In *Great cats,* ed. J. Seidensticker and S. Lumpkin, 116–123. Emmaus, PA: Rodale Press.

38. Mondolfi, E., and R. Hoogesteijn. 1986. Notes on the biology and status of the jaguar in Venezuela. In *Cats of the world: Biology, conservation, and management,* ed. S. D. Miller and D. D. Everett, 85–123. Washington, DC: National Wildlife Federation.

39. Bisbal, F. J. 1989. Distribution and habitat association of the carnivores in Venezuela. In *Advances in Neotropical mammalogy,* ed. K. H. Redford and J. F. Eisenberg, 339–362. Gainesville, FL: Sandhill Crane Press.

40. Quigley, H. B. 1987. Ecology and conservation of the jaguar in the Pantanal region, Mato Grosso do Sul, Brazil. Ph.D. dissertation, University of Idaho, Moscow.

41. Crawshaw, P. G. Jr., and H. B. Quigley. 1991. Jaguar spacing, activity, and habitat use in a seasonally flooded environment in Brazil. *J. Zool.* 223: 357–370.

42. Farrell, L. 1998. Ecology of puma and jaguar in the Venezuelan llanos. Master's thesis, University of Florida, Gainesville.

43. Scognamillo, D. 2001. Ecological separation between jaguar and puma in a mosaic landscape in the Venezuelan llanos. Master's thesis, University of Florida, Gainesville.

44. Emmons, L. H. 1987. Comparative feeding ecology of felids in a Neotropical rain forest. *Behav. Ecol. Sociobiol.* 20: 271–283.

45. Crawshaw, P. G. Jr. 1995. Comparative ecology of ocelot (*Felis pardalis*) and jaguar (*Panthera onca*) in a protected subtropical forest in Brazil and Argentina. Ph.D. dissertation, University of Florida, Gainesville.

46. Rabinowitz, A. R., and B. G. Nottingham. 1986. Ecology and behaviour of the jaguar (*Panthera onca*) in Belize, Central America. *J. Zool.* 210: 149–159.

47. Miller, B. J., conservation biology coordinator, Denver Zoological Foundation, Denver, CO. Personal communication.

48. Rabinowitz, A. R. 1986. Jaguar predation on domestic livestock in Belize. *Wildl. Soc. Bull.* 14: 170–174.

49. Emmons, L. H. 1989. Jaguar predation on chelonians. *J. Herpetol.* 23(3): 311–314.

50. Schaller, G. B., and J. M. C. Vasconcelos. 1978. Jaguar predation on capybara. *Z. Säugetierk.* 43: 296–301.

51. Schaller, G. B., and P. G. Crawshaw. 1980. Movement patterns of jaguar. *Biotropica* 12(3): 161–168.

52. Schaller, G. B. 1983. Mammals and their biomass on a Brazilian ranch. *Arquivos de Zoologia* (São Paulo) 31: 1–36.

53. Crawshaw, P. G. Jr., and H. B. Quigley. 1984. A ecologia do jaguar ou onca pintada (*Panthera onca*) no Pantanal Matogrossense. Final report to the Instituto Brasileiro de Desenvolvimento Florestal (IBDF), Brasilia.

54. Zuloaga, J. G. 1995. Densidad de población, hábitos alimenticios y anotaciones sobre habitat natural del jaguar (*Panthera onca* L.) en la depresión inundable del bajo San Jorge, Colombia. Título de Biólogo, Universidad Nacional de Colombia, Bogotá, Colombia.

55. Watt, E. M. 1987. A scatological analysis of parasites and food habits of jaguar (*Panthera onca*) in the Cockscomb Basin of Belize. Master's thesis, University of Toronto, Ontario.

56. Braker, H. E., and H. W. Greene. 1994. Population biology: Life histories, abundance, demography, and predator-prey interactions. In *La Selva: Ecology and natural history of a Neotropical rain forest,* ed. L. A. McDade, K. S. Bawa, H. A. Hespenheide, and G. S. Hartshorn, 244–255. Chicago: University of Chicago Press.

57. Taber, A. B., A. J. Novaro, N. Neris, and F. H. Colman. 1997. The food habits of two sympatric large felids in the Paraguayan Chaco. *Biotropica* 29(2): 204–213.

58. Nuñez, R., B. Miller, and F. Lindzey. 2000. Food habits of jaguars and pumas in Jalisco, Mexico. *J. Zool.* (Lond.) 252: 373–379.

59. Aranda, J. M. 1992. El jaguar (*Panthera onca*) en la Reserva Calakmul, Mexico: Morfometria, hábitos alimentarios y densidad de población. In *Felinos de Venezuela: Biología, ecología y conservación,* 235–274. Caracas: Fundación para el Desarrollo de las Ciencias Físicas, Matemáticas y Naturales (FUDECI).

60. Aranda, M., and V. Sánchez-Cordero. 1996. Prey spectra of jaguar (*Panthera onca*) and puma (*Puma concolor*) in tropical forests of Mexico. *Stud. Neotrop. Fauna Environ.* 31: 65–67.

61. Up de Graff, F. W. 1927. *Head-hunters of the Amazon.* Garden City, NY: Garden City Publishing.

62. Seton, E. T. 1929. *Lives of game animals.* Vol. 1, part 1, *Cats, wolves, and foxes.* New York: Doubleday, Doran.

63. Gudger, E. W. 1946. Does the jaguar use his tail as a lure in fishing? *J. Mammal.* 27: 37–49.

64. Goulding, M. 1980. *The fishes and the forest.* Berkeley: University of California Press.

65. Defler, T. R. 1994. Jaguars eat dolphins, too. *Trianea* (Act. Cien. Tecn. INDERENA) 5: 415–416.

66. Maxit, I. E. 2001. Prey use by sympatric puma and jaguar in the Venezuelan llanos. Master's thesis, University of Florida, Gainesville.

67. Almeida, A. E. de. n.d. Some feeding and other habits, measurements and weights of *Panthera onca pallustris*, the jaguar of the 'Pantanal' region of Mato-Gross and Bolivia. Mimeographed. São Paulo, Brazil.

68. Hoogesteijn, R., A. Hoogesteijn, and E. Mondolfi. 1993. Jaguar predation and conservation: Cattle mortality caused by felines on three ranches in the Venezuelan llanos. *Symp. Zool. Soc. Lond.* 65: 391–407.

69. Janson, C. H., and L. H. Emmons. 1990. Ecological structure of the nonflying mammal community at Cocha Cashu Biological Station, Manu National Park, Peru. In *Four Neotropical rainforests*, ed. A. H. Gentry, 314–338. New Haven: Yale University Press.

70. Sunquist, M. E. 1981. The social organization of tigers (*Panthera tigris*) in Royal Chitawan National Park, Nepal. Smithsonian Contributions to Zoology, no. 336. 98 pp.

71. Maehr, D. S., E. D. Land, and J. C. Roof. 1991. Social ecology of Florida panthers. *Natl. Geogr. Res.* 7: 414–431.

72. Almeida, A. E. de. 1986. A survey and estimate of jaguar populations in some areas of Matto Grosso. In *Wildlife management in Neotropical moist forests: Conservation status of the jaguar*, international symposium, Manaus, Brazil, 80–89. Paris: International Council for Game and Wildlife Conservation.

73. Almeida, A. E. de. 1976. *Jaguar hunting in the Mato Grosso.* England: Stanwill Press

74. Sadleir, R. M. F. S. 1966. Notes on reproduction in the larger Felidae. *Int. Zoo Yrbk.* 6: 184–187.

75. Stehlik, J. 1971. Breeding jaguars at Ostrava Zoo. *Int. Zoo Yrbk.* 11: 116–118.

76. Wildt, D. E., C. C. Platz, P. K. Chakraborty, and S. W. J. Seager. 1979. Oestrous and ovarian activity in a female jaguar (*Panthera onca*). *J. Reprod. Fert.* 56: 555–558.

77. Lanier, D. L., and D. A. Dewsbury. 1976. A quantitative study of copulatory behaviour of large Felidae. *Behav. Proc.* 1: 327–333.

78. Eaton, R. L. 1978. Why some felids copulate so much: A model for the evolution of copulation frequency. *Carnivore* 1(1): 42–51.

79. Seager, S. W. J., and C. N. Demorest. 1986. Reproduction of captive wild carnivores. In *Zoo and wild animal medicine*, 2nd ed., ed. M. E. Fowler, 667–706. Philadelphia: W. B. Saunders.

80. Crespo, J. A. 1982. Ecología de la comunidad de mamíferos del parque nacional Iguazu, Misiones. *Revista del Museo Argentino de Ciencias Naturales "Bernardino Rivadavia," Ciencias Ecológicas* 3(2): 45–162.

81. Hemmer, H. 1979. Gestation period and postnatal development in felids. *Carnivore* 2: 90–100.

82. Peters, G. 1978. Vergleichende Untersuchung zur Lautgeburng einiger Feliden. *Spixiana* suppl. 1: 1–206.

83. Peters, G. 1984. On the structure of friendly close range vocalizations in terrestrial carnivores (Mammalia: Carnivora: Fissipedia). *Z. Säugetierk.* 49: 157–182.

84. Jorgenson, J. P., and K. H. Redford. 1993. Humans and big cats as predators in the Neotropics. *Symp. Zool. Soc. Lond.* 65: 367–390.

85. McMahan, L. 1986. The international cat trade. In *Cats of the world: Biology, conservation and management*, ed. S. D. Miller and D. D. Everett, 461–488. Washington, DC: National Wildlife Federation.

86. Broad, S. 1987. The harvest of and trade in Latin American spotted cats (Felidae) and otters (Lutrinae). Cambridge: IUCN Conservation Monitoring Center.

87. Doughty, R., and N. Myers. 1971. Notes on the Amazon wildlife trade. *Biol. Conserv.* 3: 293–297.

88. Smith, N. G. 1976. Spotted cats and the Amazon skin trade. *Oryx* 13: 362–371.

89. Hoogesteijn, R., E. Mondolfi, and A. Michelangeli. 1986. Observaciones sobre el estado de las poblaciones y las medidas legales para la conservación del jaguar in Venezuela. In *Wildlife management in Neotropical moist forests: Conservation status of the jaguar*, international symposium, Manaus, Brazil, 30–74. Paris: International Council for Game and Wildlife Conservation.

90. Quigley, H. B., and P. G. Crawshaw. 1992. A conservation plan for the jaguar (*Panthera onca*) in the Pantanal region of Brazil. *Biol. Conserv.* 61: 149–157.

91. Caraman, P. 1976. *The lost paradise.* New York: Seabury Press.

92. Crosby, A. W. 1986. *Ecological imperialism: The biological expansion of Europe, 900–1900.* Cambridge: Cambridge University Press.

93. González-Fernández, A. J., and E. L. Delago. 1995. Incidencia y factores predisponentes de la depredasión de ganado por yaguares (*Panthera onca*) y pumas (*Puma concolor*) en los llanos boscosos de Venezuela. In *Il cursillo de manejo de fauna y zoocría*, 39–60. Guanare, Venezuela: Universidad Nacional Experimental de los Llanos Occidentales Ezequiel Zamora.

94. Rabinowitz, A. 1986. *Jaguar: Struggle and triumph in the jungles of Belize.* New York: Arbor House.

95. Nowell, K., and P. Jackson. 1996. *Wild cats: A status survey and conservation action plan.* Gland, Switzerland: International Union for Conservation of Nature and Natural Resources (IUCN).

96. Husson, A. M. 1978. *The mammals of Suriname.* Leiden: E. J. Brill.

Leopard

Panthera pardus (Linnaeus, 1758)

In 1867, when T. C. Jerdon wrote his treatise *The Mammals of India*, there was still some doubt as to whether the leopard and the panther were one or two species. At that time the panther was believed by many to be smaller than the leopard and to inhabit Africa and part of Asia.[1] In 1884, Robert Sterndale wrote:

> I feel convinced in my own mind that they are sufficiently distinct to warrant their being classed, and specifically named apart. As regards the difference in appearance of the adults there can be no question. The one is a higher, longer animal, with smooth shiny hair of a light golden fulvous, the spots being clear and well defined, but . . . the strongest difference of character is in the skulls, those of the larger [leo] pard being longer and more pointed, with a ridge running along the occiput, much developed for the attachment of muscles, whereas the smaller pard has not only a rougher coat, the spots being more blurred, but it is comparatively a more squat built animal, with a rounder skull, without the decided occipital ridge.[2]

The controversy raged on for years in the sporting and scientific press, as some experts sided with Jerdon and Sterndale while others declared themselves unable to separate the cat into two species. In 1891 Blandford pointed out that the age of the leopard in question might be the source of confusion: "Young leopards have rounder heads, without any occipital ridge to the skull and rougher fur than older animals."[3] Blandford had correctly identified the source of the confusion, but a few zoologists continued to believe that while both panthers and leopards lived in India, Africa contained only panthers. The dispute continued for another thirty years before it finally waned, and the leopard and panther were accepted as the same species.

The origin of the name *leopard* is somewhat confusing, as it was also used for the cheetah, which was known as the hunting leopard. The name *Leopardus* probably originated from Pliny's belief that the leopard was a cross between the lion (leo) and the pard (panther).[4]

DESCRIPTION

Leopards are similar in appearance to jaguars. Both jaguars and leopards have relatively short legs and convey the same sense of stocky, robust power. Jaguars are generally larger than leopards and have a larger, wider head. Both jaguar and leopard coats are marked with rosettes, but leopards usually have smaller rosettes than jaguars. Leopards and jaguars are both classified as "roaring cats," but whether these two species are more closely related than other members of the *Panthera* has not been resolved.[5,6,7]

The leopard is the largest spotted cat in Africa and Asia. Leopards have a head and body length of 1 to 1.5 meters, although there are a few records of animals measuring almost 2 meters long. The long, thin tail is about 60 to 75 percent of the head and body length. However, few individuals are likely to exceed an overall length, head and body plus tail, of 2.4 meters.[8,9] Like the puma, jaguar, and tiger, the leopard shows a great deal of size variation over its broad geographic distribution; generally, leopards of more open country tend to be larger than those of the forest. Adult males are invariably larger than females, often 30 to 50 percent heavier, and the largest males may weigh three times as much as the smallest. Some of the smallest African leopards are from the mountainous areas of the Cape Province in South Africa, where adult males weigh about 31 kilograms and females about 21 kilograms.[8,10,11] Similar weights are reported for leopards in Israel's Judean Desert.[12] In the woodland-savanna of Kruger National Park, South Africa, Bailey captured two adult males that weighed 70 kilograms; the largest female captured there weighed 43.2 kilograms.[13] There are records of African male leopards weighing in at over 90 kilograms,[14] but most of these animals had full stomachs, which can add some 20 percent to the cat's normal body weight. Male leopards from the mountains of Iran and central Asia are also large, with recorded weights of 90 kilograms.[15]

This weight disparity between the sexes, combined with the fact that males and females have different-shaped skulls, contributed to the belief that the leopard and the panther were two different species. Basically, the male skull is much larger, longer, and more angular, and when viewed from above, has what Pocock terms "a long-waisted" appearance. Males have larger teeth and a well-developed sagittal crest, which is almost absent on most female skulls. The skulls of young males can be mistaken for female skulls, as the male's skull tends to flatten and the crests to develop with age.[16] The crests provide anchorage for powerful jaw and neck muscles. This striking difference in skull morphology between the sexes, combined with the overall body size differences, suggests that males and females may have very different food habits.

The coat markings of the leopard are similar to

those of the jaguar, although the pattern is highly variable from one specimen to the next—as Rosevear noted, "so much so that almost any general statement may in some measure be faulted."[17] The markings are composites of black spots commonly referred to as "rosettes." Rosettes vary in size, shape, thickness of margins, and whether the margins are broken into two, three, four, or even five spots. The jaguar's coat is also covered with rosettes, but these have a small black spot within each central area, a mark commonly, but not always, absent in the rosettes of leopards. The rosettes cover much of the leopard's body, including the back of the neck, shoulders, flanks, back, hips, and the upper parts of the limbs. Solid black spots of varying size cover the lower limbs, belly, throat, and face, and the marks along the spine may be solid and form fairly clear lines. On the throat the spots sometimes coalesce to form a necklace. The tail is typically an amalgam of rosettes, spots, blobs, and rings, and the extreme tip is black above and white below. All the underparts from the chin to the tail are white, and the backs of the ears are white on the upper half and black below.[4,8,14]

Leopards can be individually identified by their spot patterns and coat characteristics. A combination of muzzle whisker spots, forehead patterns, patterns below the eye, necklace characteristics, and colors and spot patterns on the abdomen was found to be sufficient for a 99 percent reliable identification.[18]

These disruptive coat markings make the leopard very difficult to detect, particularly when it remains still. In Kipling's story, "How the Leopard Got Its Spots," after the Ethiopian had daubed spots on the leopard, he told the leopard, "You can lie out on the bare ground and look like a heap of pebbles. You can lie out on a leafy branch and look like sunshine sifting through the leaves; and you can lie right across the centre of a path and look like nothing in particular."[19] There are many hunting tales of leopards hiding themselves in the most meager cover. The cat's dappled coat allows it to watch without being seen, and to rest without being detected by animals that might mob it.

The basic background color of the leopard's coat is highly variable, being nearly golden to ochreous or orange-tawny in some specimens to pale red, grayish yellow, and buffy gray to olivaceous in others. The tone tends to be darker along the back than on the sides. There is also a suggestion that leopards inhabiting humid forests are dark-colored, whereas those in arid areas are pale.[20,21] The coats of older animals may also be pale.

Melanistic leopards are rarely seen in Africa but are not uncommon in southern India, and they occur frequently in Java and Malaysia, where roughly half the leopards are black.[9,16,22] In Africa, black leopards have been reported from the Aberdare Mountains of Kenya, where melanistic servals also occur, the foothills of the Ruwenzoris, the Ethiopian highlands, the Democratic Republic of the Congo, and the Republic of South Africa. Melanism has been shown to be the result of an autosomal recessive gene. Zoo data show that black and spotted cubs can be born in the same litter, and also indicate that melanistic females tend to have smaller litters than spotted females. Albino leopards have been reported from India, China, Zimbabwe, and East Africa, but the incidence of albinism appears to be rare.[4,14,23,24] Pocock records having seen only one true albino skin, which he believed came from Africa, but he also records a partially white skin in the British Museum in which the ground color was cream and the markings tan.[20]

The fur of the leopard also varies geographically. In many parts of Africa it is described as short, close-lying, and rather coarse, although the hair on the underparts is silky and soft. In India the texture of the leopard's coat is soft and smooth, about 25 mm in length, and with little underwool. In northern India, Nepal, and Sikkim the fur is coarser, thicker, and more woolly, especially in the winter season. In keeping with its cold-weather haunts, the Amur or Far Eastern leopard has long, thick fur, as much as 5 cm long on the belly, and a dense, woolly undercoat, almost as thick as that of the snow leopard.[4,22,25]

The leopard combines the power and strength of the big cats with the grace and versatility of the smaller cats. Its long, well-muscled body, thick limbs, and broad, powerful paws give it an aura of enormous physical strength, and it is difficult to believe that a cat this size can, if need be, survive on a diet of domestic dogs and hares. Like many of the smaller cat species, leopards are superb climbers, agile and at ease in the trees. They are capable of scaling even the largest tree, and one was seen scampering up the sheer wall-like trunk of a tree that measured 20 feet around. The mark of a truly accomplished climber is the ability to come down a tree headfirst, and the leopard is one of only a handful of felids that are skillful enough to descend in this manner. They are also capable of jumping considerable distances; Turnbull-Kemp watched a male leap across a ravine measuring at least 6.6 meters.[14] Leopards are quite at home in the water; despite the persistent rumor that they prefer to avoid getting their feet wet, these cats enjoy playing in the water and can swim well. During the flooding that followed the construction of a dam on Africa's Zambezi River, leopards remained on small islands and were observed to swim distances of 900 meters or more.[8]

DISTRIBUTION

The leopard has the greatest geographic distribution of any felid. Its range has been reduced in recent times, although historically it was distributed throughout northern Africa and over much of sub-Saharan Africa. Beyond Africa, the leopard's range extended east through Asia Minor, India, Sri Lanka, Southeast Asia, China, Tibet, and the Russian Far East (fig. 43).[8,10,21,25,26,27,28] The leopard is found in Java, but there are no records of its occurrence on the islands of Sumatra and Borneo, which are closer to the mainland.[29] While the leopard is still widely distributed, its former distribution was even greater. Fossil remains of leopards have been found in Pleistocene deposits throughout Europe, the Middle East, India, Java, and Africa, and the fossil record shows that leopards from Java and Palestine were much larger than recent forms.[30,31,32]

ECOLOGY AND BEHAVIOR

As might be predicted from its widespread distribution, the leopard can be found in many different habitat types. This cat is so stealthy, so bold and versatile, that it can live in many areas where other cat species cannot. Given a modicum of cover for concealment and available prey, the leopard can easily exist within the sight and sound of humans. Blyth writes, "The (leo)pard is a particularly silent creature, very stealthy, and will contrive to dodge and hide itself in places where it would appear impossible that a creature of its size could find concealment."[1] Guggisberg recalled the escape of a leopard at a fair in Nairobi; when the game scouts from Nairobi National Park were brought in to search for it, they discovered the tracks of not one but several leopards in the parks and gardens of the city.[4] In 1990, three leopards were found living in an old steam engine in Kampala Station in the middle of that city.[33]

Although they are absent from true deserts, leopards can and do live in almost every type of habitat. It is revealing to consider which factors may limit this cat's distribution. Limitations in food, cover, and water are usually the major factors affecting an animal's

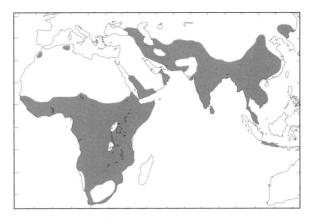

Figure 43. Distribution of the leopard.

distribution, but for a leopard the definition of these basic requisites is extremely broad. Food can be anything from beetles to ungulates the size of eland and sambar. Cover can be as rudimentary as a few scattered shrubs and trees or as dense as moist tropical evergreen forest. In the Kalahari Desert leopards have been known to drink only once in ten days,[34] and in China and Russia they survive long periods of subfreezing temperatures, although they do not appear to be well adapted to deep snow.[35]

The leopard is most commonly associated with some type of forest cover, and it is found in all forest types as well as in woodlands, acacia savannas, scrub jungles, exotic pine plantations, rocky hills, and mountainous terrain from sea level to elevations of over 5,000 meters. It lives in areas receiving almost no rainfall (50 millimeters per year) as well as in parts of West Africa and tropical Asia where the mean annual rainfall is well over 2,000 millimeters.

The two major factors that appear to limit the distribution of this tough and versatile generalist are the presence of competitors and the presence of humans. In many parts of its range the leopard coexists with other large predators. In Africa it lives alongside lions and hyenas, and in Asia it shares many habitats with tigers and wild dogs. Most of these competitors are capable of killing leopards and appropriating their kills, so in order to coexist with these predators leopards need to have access to some type of escape cover. Similarly, they can live in proximity to humans as long as they are not persecuted and have a safe retreat.

At the other end of the competitor size scale, the leopard's absence from Borneo and Sumatra may be due to an abundance of smaller felid species. John Seidensticker has suggested that the leopard was "squeezed out" of Borneo by a guild of smaller felids that effectively monopolized the arboreal and terrestrial food resources at the lower end of the prey size spectrum. In Sumatra the leopard would have been further constrained by the addition of the tiger to the suite of competitors.[29]

Despite the leopard's widespread distribution, there is surprisingly little detailed information on this elusive cat. There is an abundance of anecdotal information and a handful of studies that have relied on sightings and following tracks to discern the animal's lifestyle, but only a few studies have actually monitored the movements and activities of individual animals in the wild using telemetry.

The work of Patrick Hamilton in Tsavo National Park, Kenya, from 1972 to 1974 represented the first major study of leopards to incorporate radiotelemetry techniques.[36] At about the same time (1973), Ted Bailey initiated his study of leopards in South Africa's Kruger National Park.[13] The longest telemetry study of leopards is that of Giora Ilany in Israel; he tracked many individuals over a twelve-year period (1978–1990) and followed one female for sixteen years, starting before the study began.[12]

Small-scale radio-tracking studies have been conducted in conjunction with lion research in the Serengeti by George Schaller and Brian Bertram.[37,38] In the only study in this region to focus solely on leopards, Fumi Mizutani monitored eleven radio-tagged leopards on a ranch in Kenya.[39,40] In northeastern Namibia, Phillip Stander followed eighteen radio-tagged leopards,[41] while Peter Norton and his colleagues have radio-tracked several leopards in the Cape Province.[42,43] Radio-tracking studies of leopards have also been part of the research on tigers in southern Nepal and in southern India.[44,45,46,47] Similarly, a small number of leopards have been radio-tracked at two sites in Thailand.[48,49] Detailed studies of leopard movements, as derived from tracks and sightings, have been carried out in Sri Lanka,[50,51,52] Zimbabwe,[53] and in the Kalahari Desert.[34,54] Close observations of leopard behavior in game reserves have been made by Scott and Hes.[55,56]

There is a general belief that leopards are mostly nocturnal, and in many areas this notion appears to be true, especially in areas where they have been hunted extensively or harassed by humans.[13,25,36] Leopards are reportedly less nocturnal and more terrestrial in areas lacking tigers and lions.[49,50,57] Seidensticker found that a female leopard living within Chitwan National Park in southern Nepal, where tigers are also numer-

ous, might be active and moving at any time of the day or night.[44] In contrast, those leopards living along the park-village interface were essentially nocturnal; they were seldom found moving about during the daytime, presumably to avoid villagers.[45] When their nighttime movements were compared with those of tigers in the same area, leopards did not move as far or as continuously.[44] Instead, they seemed to spend more time just sitting and watching, a behavior that is likely to be part of their hunting strategy, but may also be a strategy for avoiding encounters with tigers. Several leopards in the park have been killed by tigers.[58] Leopards in Chitwan rarely travel far on roads, whereas tigers often do.[45]

In the Kalahari Desert leopards typically spend the daytime hours resting under vegetation or in burrows made by porcupines or aardvarks. Male leopards are too large to use most burrows and usually rest under bushes and trees. In the Kalahari leopards move mainly at night, but they frequently rest during the early part of the night and again just before dawn.[34]

In contrast, leopards living in the Judean desert of southern Israel rarely hunt at night, except when occasionally hunting porcupines or house cats in human settlements. The main food items of leopards in this area are hyraxes and ibex, both of which are diurnal, and so the leopard is also diurnal.[12]

A similar situation has been reported by Norton and Henley for leopards in the Cape Province, South Africa. They found that these leopards were mostly diurnal, showing peaks of movement in late morning and again in late afternoon or early evening, and resting from midnight until after sunrise.[43] An analysis of leopard scats from four areas in the Cape mountains showed that the leopards prey extensively on dassies (rock hyrax), which are diurnal and not available at night. Other prey in the area, mainly small antelopes, are also diurnal.[59]

In Huai Kha Khaeng Sanctuary, Thailand, a male and female leopard radio-tracked by Rabinowitz were just as likely to be found moving during the daytime as at night, and both were active about 49 to 67 percent of the time.[48] A similar activity pattern was recorded for leopards in Kaeng Krachan National Park, Thailand.[49] This pattern and degree of activity is strikingly different from most observations of leopards, although a female leopard with small cubs in Chitwan National Park was active about 75 percent of the time.[44] There are, however, few tigers in Huai Kha Khaeng and none in Kaeng Krachan, which may explain the difference in activity patterns. Alternatively, the high activity levels of these leopards may be related to a paucity of large and medium-sized prey and the need to spend more time searching for food.

Leopards do most of their hunting on the ground, but can climb extremely well when they want to. They are primarily visual hunters, often locating prey from vantage points such as trees, rock piles, and dune ridges or by visiting places where prey feed or drink. Prey are also located by sound, and leopards are quick to investigate distress calls; in the days when leopards were hunted in India, a bleating goat was commonly used as bait.

The distances traveled by leopards in their daily activities are highly variable, but at walking speeds of 3 to 6 kilometers per hour,[13,14] they can easily cover 12 kilometers in a night. Distances of 3 to 5 kilometers per day are measured in areas with abundant prey, but in less productive habitats leopards may walk 10 to 20 kilometers during a night's hunting. In the interior of the Kalahari Gemsbok National Park, both males and females moved 16 to 17 kilometers per day, and sometimes as much as 33 kilometers. Leopards in the Kalahari also moved increasingly longer distances per day as the number of days since they had last fed increased.[34,60] The longest daily movements typically are made by resident males, who not only occupy larger ranges than females, but also need to monitor the reproductive state of females in their ranges.

Occasionally, leopards will ambush prey from trees or other concealed places, but this is not a common hunting method. Kingdon cites two records of leopards making kills by leaping onto their victims from a tree.[23] In one case a leopard repeatedly climbed trees in pursuit of a herd of wildebeests and eventually was successful in leaping onto a young one. The other case involved a male leopard that managed to kill an adult eland bull, an animal about ten times its own weight. Tracks and sign indicated that the leopard had jumped onto the bull from a tree and hung onto its back while the eland dashed downhill through bushes, falling twice in its flight. When the eland fell for the third time, the leopard managed to kill it with a throat bite.

Continuous nighttime radio-tracking of leopards in Chitwan National Park suggested that these cats may employ a variant of the ambush method. The nightly travels of these leopards were punctuated by frequent stops. During these pauses the leopards appeared to select a place and wait there, immobile, for as much as half an hour. The radio signals from the transmitters on their collars indicated that the leopards were sitting perfectly still, presumably just watching. After a short period of watching and waiting, the leopards usually moved on.[45]

Leopards and tigers in Chitwan hunted in the same habitats, but there were subtle differences in the ways in which the two species used their surroundings. Leopards used the tall grasslands more often after they were cut and burned by villagers harvesting grasses; tigers hardly ever used these newly opened areas. Once the grasses grew back and reached a meter or so in height, the tigers gradually began to spend more time hunting in these areas, and the leopards increased their use of riverine forests. Both leopards and tigers used areas of dense cover such as tallgrass and riverine forest sites as resting places during the daytime.[44,45]

Leopards living outside Chitwan National Park hunted in patches of scrub as well as in sal and riverine forest. Much of this vegetation had been severely degraded and was generally more open than habitats within the park. Some of these leopards also hunted in the villages at night, and even rested during the daytime in the narrow hedges of thornbushes that bordered the villages, managing to remain undetected by passersbys and village dogs.[45]

Feeding Ecology

Leopards often catch prey opportunistically, killing vulnerable animals as they are encountered. In the Kalahari Desert, tracks revealed that leopards usually killed small prey without a deliberate stalk or chase,[54] and in the Serengeti, Bertram reported seeing leopards investigating small clumps of vegetation and pursuing any small animals flushed out.[38]

In reality, a leopard will take whatever it can catch, and while its diet in many areas consists largely of small to medium-sized mammals (5 to 45 kilograms), its ability to survive even on extremely small prey allows it to exist in places where larger game has long since been eliminated. Leopards feed on a great variety of prey of different sizes and types, and they take a much wider range of prey than most other large cats. At least 92 prey species are recorded in the diet of sub-Saharan leopards.[13] In the Serengeti, for example, a sample of 137 leopard kills included thirty-one different prey species, compared with twenty-two species in a sample of 1,180 lion kills.[37,38] In general, the leopard's diet reflects the list of prey available in the area. What is "available" depends, of course, on the size and habits of the animal being preyed upon as well as the circumstances surrounding encounters between predator and prey.

A list of mammals killed by leopards includes numerous kinds of rodents, rabbits, hares, several species of deer, duiker, antelope, pigs, zebras, jackals and foxes, porcupines, pangolins, and monkeys. Leopards also feed on birds when they can catch them, and doves, partridge, guinea fowl, peafowl, vultures, and even ostriches fall prey to this adaptable predator. Reptiles, amphibians, invertebrates, and grass are eaten as well. There is even a record of leopards in Gujarat, India, eating large numbers of watermelons.[61]

Like other felids, individual leopards may develop preferences and specialize on one particular type of prey. Such idiosyncratic behavior is probably learned. One leopard in the Ngorongoro Crater was observed to catch and eat eleven jackals in twenty-one days.[62] In the Kalahari Desert, a male leopard specialized in ambushing porcupines as they emerged from their burrows, killing four in twelve days.[54]

In areas where leopards live in proximity to humans, their diet often includes dogs, cats, and domestic stock, including sheep, goats, calves, and pigs. Instances of "surplus killing" of domestic stock sometimes occur, and while large numbers of animals may be killed in this situation (e.g., eighty animals in one night), few are actually eaten.[14]

Blyth described the leopard as "a fearful foe to the canine races, and in general to all the smaller animals."[1] Small prey do figure prominently in the diets of leopards from many areas, and their diets often include other carnivores, such as jackals, bat-eared foxes, aardwolves, mongooses, genets, lion and cheetah cubs, young spotted hyenas, and wild dog pups. The leopard's taste for dogs is well known, and there are many accounts of family pets and ranch or village dogs disappearing in the night. Why leopards should have this apparent predilection for dogs remains a mystery, but it seems to extend to the domestic dog's wild relatives, as the remains of jackals and foxes show up in many leopard feces. The hostility seems to be mutual, as packs of African wild dogs and Asiatic dholes have been seen to pursue leopards or to appropriate their kills.[14]

In some parts of its range (e.g., Sri Lanka), the leopard is the largest carnivore present and need not worry about direct attacks and competition from other large predators. However, in most areas, the leopard has to contend with an array of larger and smaller predators and scavengers. Some of these become food for the leopard; others prey on the leopard or its cubs and steal its kills. In Africa, black-backed jackals follow leopards to scavenge from their kills and are sometimes killed or eaten by leopards. Hyenas also follow leopard tracks to scavenge from kills, and lions and hyenas steal kills from leopards when the opportunity arises. Leopards have been seen killing the cubs of other carnivores, including lions, cheetahs, hyenas, and wild dogs.

Leopards become extremely cautious around larger predators such as lions and tigers, and prefer to retreat to cover or the safe haven of a tree rather than face a direct encounter. In the Serengeti lions chase leopards whenever they see them, and the leopards invariably climb a tree or retreat to a kopje. In India, Arjan Singh found that all three of the leopards he raised had "an instinctive dread of tigers" and would flee when they came across the scent of a tiger. While walking in the forest with a tame female leopard, Singh saw a tigress cross the road and observed a distinct change in the leopard's behavior, noting that "as we came within fifty yards of the point at which the tigress had disappeared, her demeanour changed entirely. Her high-spirited desire to lead the way evaporated. She went into a crouch, and her whole body lengthened as she slunk towards the big cat's trail and disappeared into the bushes. . . . At last she reappeared on the road, but crossed it fast and immediately slipped into cover on the opposite side, a picture of unobtrusive stealth."[63]

Where there are enough trees, rock piles, or other refuges, leopards are generally able to coexist with and evade larger predators. Their cautious nature and superb climbing abilities usually allow them to keep out of harm's way, but they do sometimes fall victim to the larger cats. In a small area of Chitwan National Park, five leopards were killed by tigers in less than two years.[58] Predation by lions on leopards is also known from several African parks.[37,38]

Where the leopard lives with lions and tigers, the cats feed on many of the same prey species, although competition is probably slight. In the few studies that have looked at leopard food habits in areas where they are sympatric with lions or tigers, the leopard generally feeds on a wider variety of prey, many of which are small animals or the young of the larger prey species. In the Serengeti, leopards feed on Thomson's gazelles, Grant's gazelles, reedbuck, and a variety of small prey, while lions in the same area eat mainly wildebeests, zebras, Thomson's gazelles, and buffalo.[37] In the Kalahari Desert, leopards take many juvenile animals of various species, including bat-eared foxes, porcupines, aardvarks, steenbok, duiker, and gemsbok, whereas the main food of the lion is adult gemsbok and springbok.[54] In contrast, impalas are the dominant prey of both leopards and lions in South Africa's Kruger National Park.[13]

In Chitwan National Park, leopards feed primarily on ungulates weighing less than 50 kilograms, including wild pigs, hog deer, barking deer, and fawn or yearling chital and sambar. Tigers in the same area tend to take prey weighing more than 50 kilograms and include more adult sambar, chital, and wild pigs in their diet.[45] In Nagarahole National Park in southern India, leopards prey extensively on chital, whereas tigers take the larger gaur and sambar.[47] In Huai Kha Khaeng Wildlife Sanctuary, the major prey of both leopards and tigers is barking deer, but leopards feed upon a greater diversity of small species, and they take many more primates than do tigers.[48] At another site in Thailand, the major prey of leopards were hog badgers and barking deer.[49] Leopards in Wolong Reserve, China, had a diverse diet that changed over time, with tufted deer being replaced as the dominant prey by bamboo rats following a bamboo die-off.[64] In the Russian Far East leopards prey primarily on roe deer and sika deer, while tigers take larger prey, mainly red deer and wild pigs.[35,65]

In areas where lions and tigers are absent, leopards do not appear to alter their diet to include more or much larger prey, suggesting that their selection of prey is not markedly constrained by the presence of their larger relatives. In Wilpattu National Park, Sri Lanka, for example, the suite of prey available to leopards is nearly identical to that in Chitwan, but leopards in Wilpattu have not shifted to preying extensively on the elk-sized sambar. Chital and wild pigs are the major prey of leopards in Sri Lanka, as they are in Chitwan and Nagarahole.[45,47,51,66,67]

In most areas the leopard's diet appears to track the relative densities of ungulate prey, with the most abundant species being their principal prey.[13,35,36,37,47,51,68,69,70] Leopards may, however, show preferences for various age and sex classes not only of their principal prey, but also of other species due to changes in vulnerability, the birth of young, and seasonal changes in habitat structure. In Nagarahole National Park, for example, leopards readily killed the numerically abundant chital, but took yearling male chital out of proportion to their availability in the population.[47] Similarly, in Kruger National Park, leopards

killed more young male impalas than expected, and significantly more were killed in dry seasons than in wet seasons. Leopards also preyed selectively on older female impalas in Kruger.[13] Leopards in the southern Kalahari showed a significant preference for male springbok, but in this case age was not a factor.[71] Why male ungulates, particularly young males, may be more susceptible to leopard predation is not known, although in Kruger National Park it was observed that older dominant male impalas forced subordinate males to use marginal habitats, where apparently they were more vulnerable to predation.[13]

Leopards are quite capable of killing ungulates two to three times their own weight, although they seldom do so. In Nagarahole National Park, for example, the largest prey killed weighed 93 kilograms.[47] The largest ungulate reported killed by a leopard was an adult male eland, which weigh about 900 kilograms, or about twelve times the weight of a male leopard.[23]

In some forested areas leopards take a surprisingly large number of monkeys. In the Taï National Park, Ivory Coast, two groups of mammals, including seven species of duiker and seven species of primates, constituted almost three-quarters of all prey identified in leopard feces.[72] Primates are also a common item in the diet of leopards in the Ituri Forest, Democratic Republic of the Congo, constituting 25 percent of prey items found in leopard scats. Remains of eleven of the thirteen species of diurnal primates present in the Ituri Forest were found in leopard scats. Nevertheless, the principal prey of leopards in the Ituri is medium-sized ungulates (10–22 kilograms), and large prey (>> 45 kilograms) accounted for 21 percent of items identified in scats.[73]

In Meru-Betiri Reserve, Java, where most of the ungulates have been eliminated, the predominant prey of leopards is primates. Remains of leaf monkeys and macaques were found in 65 percent of scats, followed distantly by mouse deer (5.9 percent) and a variety of other small mammals.[74]

Baboons are occasionally taken by leopards,[23,59,70,75,76] and in the Taï National Park, leopard predation was considered a significant cause of chimpanzee mortality,[77] although neither species is likely to form a significant part of the leopard's diet.

While it would seem that monkeys could easily avoid capture by climbing to the treetops, there are several eyewitness accounts of leopards "flushing" monkeys out of trees. Pocock reported that leopards caught langurs by feigning climbing the tree they were in, and when the monkeys jumped to the ground to escape, they were easily captured.[78] Similarly, Dunbar Brander described two leopards hunting langurs in a large fig tree; "one leopard was on the first branch, and another well up in the tree." Instead of climbing higher, the langurs panicked, and "some of the monkeys leaped from the top of the tree to an outer branch and thence on to the ground." Dunbar Brander recalls other occasions when monkeys behaved similarly, bailing out of trees when pursued by leopards and even dogs.[79] A redtail monkey in Africa was also seen to panic when a leopard climbed the tree it was in, and the monkey was caught on the ground.[23]

While monkeys may be frightened out of trees and small prey simply swatted, larger prey are much more difficult to catch. Leopards are amazingly proficient stalkers, and they expend considerable effort trying to get close enough to prey to launch a successful attack. Though they are typically found in dense vegetation, where stalking cover is abundant, they are masters of concealment, and in more open terrain will use bushes, rocks, grass clumps, shallow depressions, or whatever is available to get as close as possible to their target. Jonathan Kingdon remarks that leopards stalking prey in open country "have been seen to use vehicles or even dust-devils thrown up by the wind."[23]

Leopards use several different methods to catch prey. Most commonly they stalk as close as possible, belly to the ground, freezing every few seconds if the prey animal shows any signs of becoming alerted to their presence. During the stalk they may spend long periods of time motionless, waiting for the animal to settle down or move closer.

Few people have actually witnessed a leopard stalking prey, but in the Kalahari Desert, Bothma and Le Riche have reconstructed numerous hunting episodes by following tracks and sign in the soft sand. Similar methods were used by Stander in northeastern Namibia to discern the hunting methods of leopards.[41] Bothma and his colleagues have followed more than 2,065 kilometers of leopard tracks. Leopards in the Kalahari usually stalk medium-sized and large prey for about 200 meters before launching an attack, but stalking distances varied and were generally longer for larger prey. Of four exceptionally long stalks, two involved adult ostriches and measured 800 and 1,100 meters; both stalks were unsuccessful. The other two stalks involved gemsbok calves attended by a cow, measured 870 and 3,400 meters, and were both successful.

One calf was killed without a chase, whereas the other calf was killed after a chase of 7 meters.[80]

Under most circumstances the distance covered in the final charge is short, but leopards are so rarely seen making a kill that few details and measurements are available. In northeastern Namibia, leopards were, on average, able to stalk to within 4 meters of their prey, and they were much less successful when the attack was launched at distances exceeding 8 meters.[41] The only substantive data on chase distances come from the Kalahari Desert, where events surrounding kills and attempts at kills were reconstructed from tracks in the sand. In a sample of seventy-five chases, the mean chase distance for male and female leopards on all prey types was about 65 meters. Generally, the Kalahari leopards chased gemsbok, springbok, and steenbok calves for longer distances than they chased adult ungulates, suggesting that they put more effort into chasing more "catchable" prey.[34] The long-distance chases in the Kalahari are, however, probably related to its open environment.

Initial contact with the prey is often a strike with a forepaw, claws outstretched, and the force of the charge may knock the prey off its feet. Large prey are usually killed with a throat bite, while some small prey are dispatched with a bite to the back of the neck or head; others are simply swatted with a paw.[14,69] Of forty-eight leopard kills in Nagarahole National Park, 90 percent were killed with a throat bite; the remainder, consisting of sambar and chital fawns or barking deer, were killed with nape or combined nape and throat bites.[57] Some prey may demand specialized killing techniques; there are records of leopards in India killing porcupines with a head bite. A female leopard weighing 26 kilograms managed to kill a 72-kilogram ibex with a nose bite,[81] a behavior that has also been recorded for lions killing wildebeests.[37] A head-on attack on some ungulates can be risky; Eloff described a gemsbok, an ungulate that weighs about 175 kilograms, that was shot with a partially decomposed leopard impaled on its long horns.[82]

Small animals may be eaten where they are killed or carried long distances. One leopard carried a bat-eared fox for nearly 5 kilometers before eating it. Where cover is sparse, leopards either take their kills into a tree before they start to feed or drag and carry the carcass a considerable distance to find a secluded spot. In the interior of the Kalahari, where cover is minimal, female leopards commonly move their kills over 700 meters; however, cover is more abundant in the Nossob River area, and there the average distance is less than 60 meters.[54] In Nagarahole National Park the mean drag distance for seventy-six kills was 47 meters; the maximum was 400 meters for a chital kill.[57]

In parts of Africa, the presence of several competitors, such as lions, striped, brown, and spotted hyenas, and wild dogs, forces leopards to take their kills into trees. Any kill made in open habitat is likely to be detected by vultures, whose presence attracts other scavengers. In parts of the Serengeti and Masai Mara, where hyenas and lions are common, leopards frequently take their kills into trees, and this is clearly an effective strategy to avoiding losing kills to these large and dominant predators. Describing an occasion when he located a female leopard called Chui in a tree with an impala kill, Jonathan Scott wrote,

> She sat up, looking not at me but at the two hyaenas that paced around, twelve feet below her. They in turn looked upwards, trying to locate the position of what their noses were clearly telling them was meat. Lying across the same thick branch as Chui was a half-eaten impala fawn. The enticing smell of fresh meat was almost more than one of the hyaenas could endure. Momentarily the shaggy-coated hunter reared up on its hind legs, its blunt, dog-like claws pressed impotently against the rough surface of the tree trunk.[55]

Similarly, in Tsavo, leopards living in areas where hyenas were common regularly put their kills in trees, but such behavior was uncommon in areas where hyena density was low.[36] In Kruger National Park, forty-six of fifty-five (84 percent) leopard kills were cached in trees; large trees with dense foliage were preferred.[13] In Matopos National Park, Zimbabwe, where jackals and hyenas are absent, only one of thirty-eight leopard kills was found in a tree.[53] In the Kalahari, where lion and spotted hyena densities are low, only four of twenty-four leopard kills were cached in trees.[34]

The storing of kills in trees by leopards appears to be more prevalent in Africa than in Asia. In Chitwan National Park, Nepal, and Kanha and Nagarahole National Parks in India, leopards seldom take their kills into trees, even though tigers occur at high densities in these parks.[45,83] In Nagarahole, for example, only ten of seventy-seven (13 percent) kills were found in trees.[57] Leopards in these parks appear able to avoid

confrontations with tigers by hiding their kills in dense cover. The thick vegetation also reduces the possibility of disturbance and of kills being found by vultures and subsequently detected by other scavengers. Striped hyenas and Asian wild dogs are also not a threat in these parks because they are either absent or occur at very low densities.

Leopards pluck even small birds, and often pluck or lick the fur off mammals before beginning to feed. The frequency of this behavior is somewhat variable. In the Kalahari Desert hair was licked or plucked from only five of twenty-four kills before eating, but in Tsavo at least eighteen of thirty kills were plucked, and Hamilton thought that such behavior was typical.[36,54] Arjan Singh recalls being advised that his pet leopard needed roughage in the form of feathers and bones. Singh began to provide the leopard with doves, only to find that the cat "ate them with relish—but only after he has carefully plucked and discarded the feathers."[63]

The feeding sequence of leopards is also somewhat variable, especially regarding the disembowelment of prey. Early accounts reported that the first step is usually the removal of the stomach and intestines through a slit made with the teeth along the center line of the prey's belly.[14,84] This behavior was not seen with any of more than fifty leopard kills in Kruger National Park, but these were kills taken into trees.[13] Under these circumstances, as a leopard fed on the carcass, the body cavity was eventually opened and the entrails fell out or were pulled out. Bailey suggests that these differences are probably related to the difficulty of trying to disembowel a carcass lodged in a tree, whereas this could be easily done with a carcass eaten on the ground.[13]

Tigers almost always begin to feed on the hindquarters of their prey; leopards appear to be a bit more idiosyncratic about where they begin their meal. In Kruger National Park, where most leopard kills were taken into trees, the cats typically started eating in the groin and anal region; they then fed on the hindquarters, abdomen, chest, shoulders, forelegs, and lastly the neck and head.[13] Turnbull-Kemp states that "the average leopard starts to feed on the soft internal parts and the lower part of the chest, eating away the ends of the ribs, and eventually the greater portion of the muscles of the shoulders and forelegs. Attention is then turned to the hind legs and thighs."[14]

Leopards waste very little of their kills and, unlike

their larger relatives, are reported to be tidy eaters. Small animals are eaten whole, head, hooves and all, while the rumen, bones, hooves, and horns are usually all that remains of larger prey. Leopards will continue to feed on a carcass long after it has become maggot-infested, and clearly have no aversion to putrefied meat. Carrion is readily consumed as well.

Where leopards are the top predator, they need not worry about their kills being eaten by anything other than vultures and pigs. However, in parts of Africa, meat lost to scavengers and other predators can represent a significant proportion of the leopard's kills. Schaller estimates that lions in the Serengeti obtain about 5 percent of their meat by scavenging from leopards.[37] Other predators also steal leopard kills. Jonathan Scott records an occasion when the female leopard called Chui killed a topi calf within earshot of some hyenas and a troop of baboons.

> Responding instantly to the urgency of the [calf alarm] call, two of the male baboons stopped feeding and raced straight towards Chui, galloping seventy yards to confront her. The animal that led the charge was a huge male, weighing sixty or seventy pounds, not much less than Chui herself. His thick fur bristled in an impressive mantle around his neck, making him look even larger and fiercer. Chui had only one option as the hyaena and the baboons closed in on her. She dropped the calf and streaked back towards the Cub Caves as fast as her legs could carry her. She was literally running for her life.[55]

Leopards are not automatically the losers in fights with hyenas, however. On another occasion Scott's female leopard struggled with a hyena that was attempting to steal a kill from her.

> She charged, switching from defence to attack, clawing at the hyaena and sinking her dagger-like canines into his neck as he attempted to snatch the impala away. . . . The two animals continued to struggle ferociously for possession of the impala, fighting in the manner of hungry lions contesting ownership of a small kill. Neither dared release their grip on the food so as to bite the other, for fear of losing it altogether. The hyaena outweighed Chui by at least thirty pounds, and the crushing power of his jaws was second to none. But it was Chui's food and she

possessed the muscular strength which, pound for pound, rivaled that of any hyaena. The leopard wrenched the kill and the hyaena towards the euclea tree where the impala had originally hung.[55]

It is almost impossible to measure the hunting success of a secretive, solitary predator such as the leopard, but the few available estimates indicate that leopards are not highly successful. Bailey recorded that leopards were successful in only two of thirteen (16 percent) hunting attempts, and that all daytime hunting attempts were unsuccessful.[13] In the Serengeti, Bertram watched sixty-four daytime hunts, of which only three (5 percent) were successful; however, he believes that the success rate is higher at night.[38] Schaller observed nine daytime stalks by leopards, of which one (11 percent) was successful.[37] Leopards in northeastern Namibia averaged one kill for every 2.7 hunts, for a success rate of 38.1 percent.[41] In the Kalahari Desert, six of seventy-four (12 percent) known chases by male leopards ended with a kill, compared with seven of twenty-five chases (23 percent) for females with cubs. Most of these chases involved medium-sized prey; small prey are seldom chased, and the hunting success rate for this size class is not known.[54]

In captivity, leopards are fed about 1 to 1.2 kilograms of meat per day, but there is little information on the food intake of wild leopards. In the Kalahari the majority of the leopard's prey is small, not large enough to detain the cat for more than a day. In this area males consumed 3.5 kilograms per day, compared with 4.9 kilograms per day for females with cubs.[34] In Tsavo National Park males consumed 2.0 to 9.5 kilograms per night.[36] Estimates of meat consumed by two male leopards in Kruger National Park varied from 4.4 to 4.7 kilograms per day.[13] Leopards in Nagarahole National Park spent an average of 2.1 days with each kill, consuming an average of 11.2 kilograms per day per leopard.[57] In northeastern Namibia, single females had the lowest daily food intake, at 1.6 kilograms per day, followed by 2.5 kilograms per day for females with cubs and 3.1 kilograms per day for males.[41] Like other carnivores, leopards are adapted to a feast-or-famine regime, and will sometimes eat a quarter of their body weight in a day.

The feeding rates of leopards vary considerably, depending largely on prey size. Jonathan Scott, who followed a female leopard living near the Masai Mara Reserve boundary in Kenya, writes, "During one week the Mara Buffalo female and her daughter killed a dik-dik, a male Thomson's gazelle, two wildebeest calves and an impala calf. Apart from the dik-dik, which was stolen by hyenas, the edible portions of all these kills were eaten by the eighth day." Scott also records another female with two young cubs who killed and ate an adult male impala and two impala calves in four days.[55]

In Tsavo, movement data indicated that adult leopards made about eighteen "large" kills per year, and that they sometimes went for two to three weeks or more without feeding on large prey. Impalas and bushbuck accounted for 50 percent of all large kills. However, fecal analysis showed that small mammals such as dik-dik, hares, hyraxes, rodents, and ground birds formed a major part of the leopards' diet in this area.[36]

In the Kalahari Desert, male leopards killed once every 3.3 days and females with cubs once every 1.5 days, although males tended to kill larger prey. Annually, males killed 111 prey animals apiece and females with cubs 243 animals. These figures are much higher than those for leopards living in forest environments, but prey taken in the Kalahari are much smaller than elsewhere, and thus the total amount of meat consumed is probably similar.[34]

Leopards in Kruger National Park killed about one large prey per week, usually an impala, and stayed an average of 2.4 days with each kill.[13] In the Serengeti, Schaller estimated that leopards killed forty to forty-eight Thomson's gazelles in an eight-month period.[37] A habituated, free-ranging female leopard in Londo-lozi Game Reserve of South Africa was observed for 330 consecutive days, during which she was seen with twenty-eight carcasses over 10 kilograms, or about one such kill every 11.8 days.[85]

In Russia, leopards spent five to seven days with kills of adult roe or sika deer, and data from snow tracking and radio-tracking suggest that an adult leopard requires a large ungulate every twelve to fifteen days. Under poor hunting conditions or low prey density. the interval between kills of large prey can reach twenty to twenty-five days.[65]

Social Organization

Leopards are solitary, and other than a female and her young or a consorting pair, they seldom associate with one another. In 1947 Jim Corbett wrote that "male leopards are very resentful of intrusion of others of their kind in the area they consider to be their own."[86]

Fifty years later, radio-tracking studies have confirmed that animals of the same sex seldom share their home areas. The land tenure system of leopards is broadly similar to that of many other cats in that adult males typically occupy large areas that overlap the home areas of one or more adult females. Female ranges are usually smaller than those of males.

The home range sizes of female leopards in Chitwan, Tsavo, northern Serengeti, Kenya, Kruger, and Thailand are remarkably similar in size, varying from 6 to 18 square kilometers. Male ranges in these areas varied between 17 and 76 square kilometers and usually overlapped the ranges of one or more females.[13,36,38,40,44,48,49]

In arid areas or other sites of particularly low primary productivity, the home range sizes of leopards are much larger, and range overlap for same-sex animals is more common.[87] In the Israeli desert, for example, female ranges averaged 84 square kilometers, whereas those of males measured 137 square kilometers.[12] Two adult females in the Russian Far East had ranges of 33 and 62 square kilometers, whereas that of a male was at least 280 square kilometers.[65] In northeastern Namibia male ranges were even larger (mean = 451 square kilometers; range 210–1,164 square kilometers), and female ranges measured 183 to 194 square kilometers.[41]

Leopards travel widely and visit most portions of their ranges at regular intervals; sometimes an individual will crisscross its entire range in a single night. The distance a leopard travels in a night is influenced to a great extent by a combination of two major variables: how far it has to go to find food and mates, and the need to indicate that its area is occupied.

The principal means of social integration among leopards appears to be via olfactory information carried in urine, anal sac secretions, and feces. While scent may not carry as far as a call, it is more persistent, and it is not diminished by darkness, as visual signal would be. Scent also has the advantage of being able to convey information long after the animal has left the spot. Auditory, tactile, and visual signals are also used to attract mates or advertise that an area is occupied, but scent-marking appears to be an efficient method of communication among these wide-ranging, solitary predators.

Scent marks are typically deposited along commonly used travel routes, especially at road junctions or trail intersections, at conspicuous places along trails, and along home range boundaries. Some marks are renewed at intervals of a few days to a month or more, suggesting that these marks remain effective for relatively long periods. Feces and scrapes are also left at these sites, thus providing both an olfactory and a visual mark. Scrapes are made by the backward raking action of the hind feet, which removes the grass and disturbs the soil over an area about 60 centimeters long and 20 centimeters wide, creating a visual signal that is often augmented with scent.

Researchers in the Kalahari found that leopards urinate in two different ways. One is a copious urination that lacks any apparent informational significance, while the other involves squirts of small volume deposited at regular intervals. These squirts are directed at shrubs, low branches, tree trunks, or grass tufts, and are sometimes followed by raking with the hind feet. Leopards also roll in places where other animals have urinated or defecated, rake the trunks of trees with their claws, and rub their bodies against tree trunks.[54]

Similarly, leopards in Wilpattu appeared to communicate by a variety of olfactory and visual signals. Some trees were repeatedly scratched; these trees typically had a decided lean or had a large limb about 2 meters above the ground. In addition to these visual marks, the trees were often sprayed at the base with urine, and the leopards would rub themselves on the trunk, leaving traces of their body odors. Both sexes sprayed urine on vegetation and sometimes deposited urine on or near scrapes.[50,51]

A typical scent-marking sequence was described by Jonathan Scott: "Chui sat rubbing her face, forehead and throat along the underside of the fallen limb where another leopard had recently sprayed. Then she turned, arched her long tail and added her own scent message to that left by the previous leopard."[55]

What messages are being carried in these olfactory marks is uncertain, but scent almost certainly conveys information about an individual's sex, residential status, reproductive condition, and possibly individual identity. Tigers scent-mark at higher frequencies in contact zones between territories, and newly established residents also mark more frequently, suggesting that one function of scent marking is to delineate an animal's range.[88] High rates of scent marking are also associated with social dominance in territorial animals. Scent marking may also provide a means whereby animals can avoid simultaneous use of areas or, in the case of a receptive female, may serve to bring animals together.

The coughing, sawing, or rasping vocalization of the leopard may also function to bring animals together for mating or to space out individuals, depending upon their sex and their reproductive and social status. Under favorable conditions, the sawing vocalization can carry for 2 to 3 kilometers, and it is the call most often heard. Dunbar Brander described this call as a noise that "much resembles a piece of wood being sawn across with short, sharp double strokes, i.e., a thrust and a return. The leopard in making this keeps his mouth partly open and expels and inhales air back and fore across the soft palate."[79]

In Wilpattu, Tsavo, and Matopos National Parks, leopards called at any time of the day, but the frequency of calling was highest during the major movement period and at dawn and dusk. The sawing call has sometimes been associated with females in estrus, but at other times it was accompanied by active avoidance, suggesting the dual function of the call.[36,51,53] Bailey was able to correctly identify the individual leopards that he was tracking by their different-sounding calls, which suggests that leopards are also likely to recognize the calls of neighboring animals.[13]

Leopards, along with lions, have a vocalization called puffing, which is analogous to the prusten of tigers, jaguars, clouded leopards, and snow leopards. Puffing, mainly articulated through the nose, is a friendly close-range contact call associated with greeting, appeasement, courtship, or mating. The vocal repertoire of the leopard also includes the mew, grunt, snarl, spit, and hiss.[89,90]

Reproduction and Development

Arjan Singh describes the first few times his two young tame female leopards came into heat, and remarks that "as long as they remained on heat, they showed no desire to wander, staying in or around the farm, but as soon as their cycles ended . . . a powerful restlessness gripped them."[63] Their wanderlust persisted throughout the gaps between estrous periods, and at this time they traveled widely. The scent marks laid down during these travel bouts probably informed the resident male leopard that there were two females in the area and that they would soon be ready to mate. Such behavior is reminiscent of that of tigresses, who scent-mark more frequently in the intervals between heats.[45] Given the fact that male leopards travel over very large ranges, these scent marks undoubtedly advertise the presence of a female and her state of sexual receptivity, thus ensuring that the male is in the right place at the right time. However, Bailey's observations suggest that female leopards scent-mark more frequently during the peak mating period.[13]

Zoo records show that females may come into estrus at any time of the year and that they remain in heat for one to two weeks. If conception does not occur, the female will cycle again; the average length of time between estrous periods is forty-five days, with a variation from twenty to fifty days.[91] The onset of a heat is associated with an increase in head rubbing, rolling, and vocalizing. If a male and female are not familiar with each other, there are often several noisy and aggressive encounters before mating occurs. When the mating takes place between animals who know each other, the female will often roll on her back in front of the male or rub his cheeks. She will then crouch while he mounts and begins pelvic thrusting. Once the penis is inserted, copulation lasts about three seconds.[92] During copulation the male commonly bites or grips the female's nape. Copulation often ends with the female turning and snarling at the male, who leaps away. During the peak of estrus mating occurs frequently; one pair copulated sixty times during a nine-hour period.[93]

Observations in the wild suggest that mating associations are brief. In the Kalahari Desert, consort pairs have not been seen together for more than one day.[54] In Kruger National Park, the average length of association was two days, but varied from one to as long as four days.[13] Bailey also noted that most courtship associations were apparently unsuccessful; only two of thirteen (15 percent) suspected matings resulted in the birth of cubs. In a captive population of eight female leopards, Eaton estimated that the maximum probability of conception was 0.65.[94]

Leopard cubs are born after a gestation period of about 96 days, although zoo records suggest that gestation can take anywhere from 90 to 105 days.[95,96] Litter size commonly varies from one to three, and there are records of females giving birth to as many as six cubs, but most litters consist of two cubs.[52,92,94,97,98,99] There is also a suggestion that litter size may differ by phenotype, with spotted leopards having larger litters (average 2.09 cubs) than melanistic leopards (average 1.70 cubs).[100]

In the Londolozi Game Reserve, the average number of cubs in five litters for one female was 2.2.[85] In the Serengeti, Schaller saw two females with two small cubs each, but three others had one large cub each.[37] Similarly, in Chitwan National Park, the mean number of small cubs in three litters was 2.3, whereas in six litters with large cubs the average was 1.3.[46]

There are few data on births in the wild, but Dunbar Brander observed that in central India "leopards bred at all times, but I have come across more cubs in April than at any other time."[79] In Ruhuna National Park, Sri Lanka, most births were judged to have occurred during the dry seasons of July–September and February–March. During these periods prey are presumably easier to catch at water holes, which is important for females trying to nurture small cubs.[52] In Kruger National Park, five of six litters observed were born early in the wet season (November–December), which coincides with the peak in impala births and cover.[13] In neighboring Londolozi Game Reserve, a sample of five births showed no seasonality.[85] In Russia, small cubs have been seen at various times of the year, but most births occur in spring.[25]

Females use caves, thickets, hollow trees, abandoned burrows, and rock piles as birth dens. Cubs are born with their eyes closed, and open them four to nine days later. In a small sample of captive-born young, cubs measured 360 to 483 millimeters from nose to tail tip, and weighed 430 to 1,000 grams. The cubs' fur is short and faintly spotted, and they have black whiskers.[25,93,95]

The first few days after the cubs are born, the mother spends all her time at the den, resting, nursing, and looking after her young. However, she must hunt, and to do so she must leave the cubs. This is the time when her selection of a safe den becomes crucial, because while she is away the defenseless cubs are very vulnerable to other predators. Most cub mortality occurs during the first months of life, and in the wild the young fall prey to lions, tigers, and hyenas.[14,56,70,84] Cub mortality in the first year is estimated at 40 to 50 percent.[13,46,101,102] Male leopards have also been observed killing young cubs. In southern Israel at least eleven cubs were killed by three different males over a nine-year period.[81] Female leopards in this area have to travel extremely long distances to find food, and it is not uncommon for them to leave twelve-day-old cubs for up to four days. Similarly, in northeastern Namibia, females also leave their young unattended for long periods. Stander found that three-month-old cubs did not accompany their mothers on hunting trips, but were left alone for periods of one to seven days.[41]

In Nepal, a leopard with three twenty-day-old cubs was radio-tracked for 168 continuous hours (seven days and nights). At the beginning of the tracking session she spent 33 hours with the cubs, then left for 33 hours, returned for 11.5 hours, then left for another 36 hours. The session ended with her spending 29 hours at the den. She spent more time with the cubs at night, and at no time was she more than 2 kilometers from the den. One month later a four-day continuous tracking session revealed a similar pattern.[103]

While the cubs are confined to the den, the mother's movements are restricted to a small area nearby. However, she does not necessarily leave the cubs at one den, but may move them every two to five days to different dens.[56,103,104] As the young gradually become more mobile, her movements are no longer restricted by the need to return to feed and protect them at a fixed den site. The family begins to travel together when the cubs are two to three months old, and this generally marks the time when the female's range gradually expands to its former size. At this time the cubs weigh 3 to 4 kilograms and are beginning to eat meat. The cubs continue to nurse until they are about four months old, by which time they weigh about 6 kilograms.[92,104]

Cubs learn to hunt by playing and pouncing on leaves, sticks, siblings, and their mother. While she is away they hone their skills by stalking grasshoppers, lizards, and birds. There are records of cubs killing hares and other small animals when they are five months old, but more usually they begin to make kills when their permanent canines appear, at about seven to eight months of age.[56,104]

The permanent canine teeth appear in the jaw alongside the deciduous teeth, before the deciduous teeth fall out. Arjan Singh remarked that the appearance of permanent canine teeth in his pet leopard "seemed to usher in a more positive approach to his environment." The young leopard began going into the forest for long periods, and he managed to kill a chital fawn and a rhesus monkey. Singh remarks that the leopard seemed "unable or unwilling" to deal with the monkey until it had been skinned.[63] This fits with other observations that young leopards and tigers may sometimes be able to kill a small animal such as a goat or a deer, but lack the skill or equipment necessary to open the carcass so they can feed.

Singh's pet leopards illustrate an important difference between the leopard and other big cats such as the lion and tiger. Young lions and tigers must learn to catch and kill large prey in order to survive, and this requires considerable skill and practice. Leopards are able to live on small prey, which are generally easier and often less dangerous to catch. Though mother leopards are patient and thorough teachers, they do not have to put in as much time schooling their cubs as do tigresses and lionesses because the ability to hunt and kill large prey is not as central to a young leopard's survival.

By twelve to eighteen months of age young leopards are generally independent of their mother, but the time of dispersal varies with the sex of the animal, local vacancies, resource availability, and the reproductive status of the mother. Observing young leopards in Kenya, Jonathan Scott noted that "by the time the cubs were a year old the young male had abandoned Mara Buffalo Rocks as a resting place. He acted in a much more independent manner than his sister, who seemed to require a closer relationship with their mother."[55] Other observers in neighboring Serengeti have recorded young males and females remaining in their mother's range until they were two to three years old. In general, however, males seem to become independent at an earlier age than their sisters. Mother-daughter relationships may be extended by the tendency of daughters to settle near their mother, sometimes appropriating part of their mother's range as their own.[13,56] Such behavior is well documented for young female tigers.[105]

While dispersal from the natal range is a major event in the young leopard's life, little is known of its timing, distances or routes traveled, or the fates of dispersers. In the Serengeti and Tsavo National Parks in Africa and Wilpattu in Sri Lanka, male leopards dispersed at ages varying from 22 to 36 months.[36,37,51] However, these males simply disappeared, and the details of their travels or fates remain unknown. In Londolozi Game Reserve a male leopard dispersed from his natal range at 14 months of age and was not seen for five months. He returned for two days before departing again.[85] In Kruger National Park radio-collared subadult male leopards were sometimes seen up to 30 kilometers from their natal ranges, but even those who explored distant areas within the park periodically returned to their natal ranges. The mortality rate of subadults in Kruger was twice that of resident adult animals.[13] In northeastern Namibia, two 24- to 25-month-old dispersing males were followed until they died. One died within six months of injuries from porcupine quills. The other traveled 162 kilometers and returned to his natal range, where five months later he was killed while raiding domestic livestock.[41]

In Nepal, two brothers and an unrelated male leopard were radio-collared in Chitwan National Park. All three were 13 months old when captured. Subsequent tracking indicated that there was little association between siblings or between mothers and cubs. Prior to dispersing, the young males gradually expanded their ranges by exploring new areas within and adjacent to their mother's range. One of the brothers dispersed at 15 months of age, and his sibling left a month later, but in the opposite direction. The unrelated male dispersed at 18 months of age. The dispersing males traveled slowly through patches of riverine and sal forest, spending several days investigating each new area before moving on. Though all three leopards went in different directions, the paths of their travels were similar in that each tended to move in a straight-line direction. They also showed broadly similar rates of travel, as each took two to four weeks to travel the 8 to 11 kilometers from his natal range to the area where he appeared to settle. However, only one male was still alive six months later, the other two having died of unknown causes.[106]

Only one of these three Nepalese leopards survived long enough to potentially reproduce, as the earliest record of mating in males is at two years of age, and there are records of males not attaining sexual maturity until 30 or 35 months of age. Sexual maturity for females follows a similar pattern. Since first, or even subsequent, matings do not always result in conception, a female may not actually produce her first litter until she is about 30 months old. In a group of six captive females, the average age at first reproduction was 42 months, but varied from 27 to 49 months.[93] In another group of eight captive females, the average age of first reproduction was 40.5 months, but varied from 27 to 52 months.[94]

Young leopards are dependent on their mothers for a year or longer, although mothers appear to become increasingly intolerant of their offspring with the impending birth of their next litter. There are few records of interbirth intervals for wild leopards, but in Londolozi Game Reserve the average for three litters was 17.1 months.[85] In Chitwan National Park the interbirth interval was 20 and 21 months,[46] and in the Serengeti it was 24 and 25 months.[37] In Kruger National Park the interval was 28.8 months.[13] Assuming that their young survive to independence, female leopards would appear to be able to produce a new litter about every two years.

In zoos, when young are removed for hand rearing shortly after birth, females re-cycle quickly and mate again, resulting in interbirth intervals of about 8 months. The shortest recorded interval between the birth of two litters was 107 days. In captivity male leopards as old as nineteen and twenty-one have continued to mate and sire litters; however, the oldest breeding female was thirteen.[94] Not surprisingly, similar data from the wild are rare, but the positions of the sexes are likely to be reversed, with females having the longer reproductive life span. While males may remain fertile longer, under natural conditions they generally have a shorter reproductive tenure because of competition from younger males. Brian Bertram used old photographs and postcards to track the history of two females in the Serengeti and estimated that they had lived for at least ten and twelve years.[107] A female in Londolozi Game Reserve produced nine litters in twelve years of observation, rearing at least sixteen cubs.[56] In the Israeli desert study, an eleven-year-old female was still producing cubs, but appeared to be nearing the end of her reproductive life. Another female was followed for sixteen years; although she was no longer breeding at the end of that period, she was still alive.[81]

STATUS IN THE WILD

Like the caracal, the leopard is in the strange position of being critically endangered in some parts of its range and considered a pest in other areas. Between 1974 and 1982, all leopards were listed as vulnerable in the IUCN Red Data Book, and all international commerce in leopards was banned. However, since 1983, several African countries have been allowed to take a limited number of trophy leopards. Export quotas are currently allowed for populations in Botswana, the Central African Republic, Ethiopia, Kenya, Malawi, Mozambique, Namibia, South Africa, Zambia, and Zimbabwe, and hunting trophies can be imported into the United States.[108]

The greatest long-term threat to the leopard's continued survival is believed to be the expansion of livestock raising. The presence of livestock often causes wild leopard prey to be eliminated, either purposely, because people believe it competes with livestock, or accidentally, through overgrazing and habitat modification. Throughout the world leopards are shot when they kill domestic livestock, or carcasses are laced with organochlorine pesticides to poison leopards returning to feed on a kill.

Leopards clearly have the ability to survive near humans. They can feed on almost any type of prey, and do not have very specific habitat requirements. However, they are extremely vulnerable to persecution, especially poisoning. Their secretive habits make them extremely difficult to survey, so many of the current estimates of leopard numbers should be viewed with caution. Furthermore, outside of Bailey's work in Kruger National Park, little is known about the dynamics of leopard populations in any part of their range.

Despite this lack of data, several studies have attempted to estimate the number of leopards in various areas. An attempt by Rowan Martin and Tom de Meulenaer used a computer model based on rainfall and suitable habitat, on the premise that leopards are ultimately limited by food resources, which are in turn limited in Africa mainly by rainfall. Their report estimated the leopard population of sub-Saharan Africa to be 700,000, with confidence limits of 600,000 to 900,000. Needless to say, these estimates generated a great deal of controversy.[101]

Most wildlife specialists agree that there are still many leopards in Africa and that in some areas they are extremely common. However, several field biologists who have actually studied leopards in sub-Saharan Africa argue that many areas of suitable leopard habitat have been empty of leopards for years. Leopard specialists in Africa overwhelmingly rejected the estimate of 700,000 as excessive, suggesting that actual leopard numbers may be less than half that predicted by the computer model.

Professor J. du Bothma of the University of Pretoria, who has studied Kalahari leopards for many years, argues that "the data base upon which the assumptions are made . . . is often non-existent. Thus no matter how complicated or good the model the raw data simply do not allow the type of conclusions reached. In South Africa there are many areas suitable as leopard habitat which are simply not occupied by leopards any more."[109] Peter Norton, who conducted a radio-telemetry study of leopards in South Africa, concurs, stating that "the model is based on a number of assumptions that are not substantiated by the results of my research work in the Cape Province of South Africa."[110] After completing a survey of forest duiker in the Central African Republic, Vivian Wilson of Zim-

babwe stated that "there was no relationship whatsoever between leopard densities, habitat and rainfall. The rainfall in the area is at least 1,524 mm a year; there are hundreds of km^2 of ideal leopard habitat; large numbers of blue duiker; and yet leopard numbers are very low. Dozens of people in the area all agreed that that most of the leopards had been shot and killed many years previously, although they were still present in low numbers."[109]

In the final analysis, the Martin and de Meulenaer exercise in estimating leopard numbers illustrates several dangers involved in species conservation. The most important of these is the "magic numbers game." International organizations, park managers, journalists, and almost everyone else demands that biologists provide accurate numbers. Generalities such as Common, Rare, and Indeterminate are not sufficient. However, carnivores in general, and felids in particular, are notoriously difficult to count. They are nocturnal and secretive, and their population density, reproductive success, and longevity may vary wildly from place to place. The most important thing to remember from the leopard modeling experience is that it may be dangerous to publish such computations. The demand for numbers is so great that when no other estimates exist, authorities will use the only available data, which may very well be inaccurate.

Despite these caveats, the meager evidence from some regions indicates that leopard populations have declined severely.[111] In 1989 Professor H. Mendelssohn of Tel Aviv University described the leopard as "on the verge of extinction in Turkey and very rare in the Golan, and on Mt. Hermon, if it exists at all, the whole subspecies is highly endangered and the prospects for its continued survival are extremely slim." The last Israeli specimen was a very old male killed in 1965.[112]

Mendelssohn is only slightly more optimistic about the future of the leopard population in the Judean desert and the Negev. Prior to 1967 the Bedouin hunted every form of wildlife, but after that date conservation plans were implemented and wildlife began to recover. Leopards are common around the oasis of Ein Gedi, where ibex, hyraxes, and porcupines exist at high densities. The oasis is also visited by tens of thousands of tourists, and there is a kibbutz, a youth hostel, and a field study center there. Leopards at the oasis prey on kibbutz domestic dogs and cats. Some eight to ten leopards live in this 300–400-square-kilometer area of rugged habitat in the Judean desert, and several more live in the adjoining Negev, for a total population of fifteen to twenty animals. The population is strictly protected, but it has been isolated for some time and probably suffers from inbreeding. Another 100 to 200 leopards are thought to occur in the remote and rugged mountainous areas of Saudi Arabia, Yemen, Oman, and Turkmenistan.[108,111]

Named for the river that forms the boundary between China and Russia, the Amur or Far Eastern leopard has been identified as a genetically discrete subspecies.[113] The subspecies is believed to number fewer than a hundred individuals, with the largest population containing about thirty individuals.[35] A recovery plan has recently been developed for the Amur leopard, but its implementation is dependent on acceptance and support by the federal and regional governments in both countries.

CONFLICT WITH HUMANS

Leopards come into conflict with people in many different ways, but most commonly in the form of leopards killing domestic stock. Wherever they live close to humans, leopards take sheep, goats, dogs, and other livestock. They also occasionally kill people. In April 1989, a report in the newspaper *Rising Nepal* said that "local people had stoned to death a leopard which had killed a man collecting wood in the forest in western Nepal."[114]

Leopards that habitually kill humans are rare; most such incidents are, like the one described in *Rising Nepal*, accidents. There are also far fewer records of man-eating leopards than there are of man-eating tigers. Once a leopard has begun to prey on people, however, its stealth and boldness make it a formidable killer, capable of claiming an enormous number of victims. Man-eating leopards are often feared more than tigers because, unlike tigers, leopards frequently break into houses and huts to claim their victims. In India, Jim Corbett, the well-known naturalist and hunter, finally managed to put an end to the depredations of the man-eating leopard of Rudra-prayag after it had killed 125 people.[86] A few years later, in 1910, Corbett was called upon to hunt down the Panar leopard, an animal credited with having killed 400 human beings.[115] That he was successful is remarkable, since man-eating leopards are notoriously difficult to kill. Their characteristic leopard caution makes them difficult to drive toward a hunter, and

they learn to reject poisoned baits and not to return to kills.

Despite the fact that they remain capable of hunting natural prey, man-eaters clearly develop a taste for human flesh, and often selectively go after people even when there are equally vulnerable livestock around. In one incident the man-eating leopard of Rudraprayag pushed open the door of a goat hut and made his way through a tightly packed flock of goats to get to a young boy who was looking after the animals. Jim Corbett chillingly described the efforts of the Panar man-eater to catch him rather than the tethered goat he was using as bait. After having his men lash bundles of thorns to the tree he was sitting in, Corbett settled down to wait, "firmly seated on the branch with my coat collar pulled up well in front to protect my throat, and my soft hat pulled down well behind to protect the back of my neck. The goat was tied to a stake driven into the field thirty yards in front of me." The leopard arrived just as it was getting dark and ignored the goat, trying instead to dislodge Corbett from his perch. "Finding that he could not climb over the thorns, the leopard, after his initial pull, had now got the butt ends of the shoots between his teeth and was jerking them violently, pulling me hard against the trunk of the tree." Corbett went on to add that "the leopard was quite unafraid of me, as was evident from the fact that while tugging at the shoots, he was growling loud enough to be heard by the men anxiously listening in the village." The evening ended when Corbett finally managed to shoot the leopard after it had charged at his men.[115]

It is unclear why some leopards become man-eaters, and equally unclear why man-eaters are almost always males; only 9 of 152 man-eaters recorded by Turnbull-Kemp were female.[14] Most likely there are a number of reasons why some leopards change their diet, including injury from shotgun blasts, porcupine quills, and the like, as well as accident and mistaken identity when leopards have killed people who are crouched or kneeling on the ground. Other man-eaters are suspected of acquiring their taste for human flesh after epidemics or disasters made large numbers of human bodies available. In India, there have been occasions when large numbers of deaths caused the local people to abandon the usual cremation ritual. Instead, the bodies were thrown into rivers or ravines after having a hot coal placed in their mouths.

TABLE 59 MEASUREMENTS AND WEIGHTS OF ADULT LEOPARDS

HB	n	T	n	WT	n	Location	Source
1,107 (920–1,250)	21m	678 (510–800)	20m	30.9 (20–45)	27m	Cape Province	10
1,030 (950–1,050)	8f	677 (640–740)	8f	21.2 (17–26)	9f	Cape Province	10
1,365	8m	789	8m	60.6	8m	Kruger NP	13
1,219	11f	773	11f	37.4	11f	Kruger NP	13
1,240 (1,160–1,365)	9m	856 (845–880)	9m	49 (36–60)	9m	Zambia	116
1,113 (1,015–1,230)	7f	713 (640–780)	7f	34 (27–42)	9f	Zambia	116
				59.6 (51.7–71.3)	13m	Zimbabwe	8
				31.5 (28–35)	7f	Zimbabwe	8
1,265	11m	859	11m	56.3	11m	Sri Lanka	77
1,047	7f	775	7f	29	7f	Sri Lanka	77
1,302 (1,270–1,372)	4m	838 (762–914)	4m			India	77
1,108 (1,054–1,168)	4f	803 (762–876)	4f			India	77
1,070–1,360	6m	820–900	6m	32–48	6m	Russia	64
1,273 (1,190–1,320)	3m	780 (770–790)	3m	56.7 (40–70)	3m	Thailand	48,49
1,060, 1,090	2f	740, 750	2f	21, 25	2f	Thailand	48,49

Note: HB =.head and body length (mm), T = tail length (mm), WT = weight (kg). n = sample size. Sex: m = male, f = female, ? = unknown. Mean values are presented only for sample sizes of three or more. Range of values is in parentheses.

TABLE 60 OCCURRENCE OF PREY ITEMS IN THE DIETS OF AFRICAN LEOPARDS (PERCENTAGE OF KILLS)

Prey items	Serengeti NP[69] Kills (n = 55)	Serengeti NP[37] Kills (n = 164)	Kruger NP[70] Kills (n = 5,501)	Kalahari[71] Kills (n = 80)	Namibia[41] Kills (n = 131)
Aepyceros melampus Impala	16.3		77.7		
Tragelaphus scriptus Bushbuck	1.8		3.9		
Sylvicapra grimmia Duiker				2.5	32.8
Raphicerus campestris Steenbok				6.3	13.0
Antidorcas marsupialis Springbok				65.0	
Phacochoerus aethiopicus Warthog		0.6	1.4		
Redunca sp. Reedbuck	10.9	11.6	2.4		
Connochaetes taurinus Wildebeest	9.0	6.7	1.3	1.2	

Table 60 (continued)

Prey items	Serengeti NP[69] Kills (n = 55)	Serengeti NP[37] Kills (n = 164)	Kruger NP[70] Kills (n = 5,501)	Kalahari[71] Kills (n = 80)	Namibia[41] Kills (n = 131)
Gazella thomsoni Thomson's gazelle	27.3	63.4			
Gazella granti Grant's gazelle	3.6	6.1			
Damaliscus korrigum Topi	1.8	1.8			
Alcelaphus buselaphus Hartebeest		1.2		6.3	
Equus sp. Zebra	7.2	1.2	1.2		
Kobus defassa Waterbuck			3.9		
Tragelaphus sp. Kudu			2.9		
Tragelaphus sp. Nyala			0.4		
Damaliscus lunatus Tsessebe			0.2		
Oryx gazella Gemsbok				2.5	0.8
Taurotragus oryx Eland			0.2		3.1
Hippotragus niger Sable			0.1		
Syncerus caffer Buffalo			0.1		
Procavia sp. Rock hyrax	1.8				
Pedetes capensis Springhare	1.8				
Papio sp. Baboon	3.6	0.6			
Hystrix africaeaustralis Porcupine					2.3
Proteles cristatus Aardwolf				1.2	3.1
Orycteropus afer Aardvark				1.2	
Lepus capensis Cape hare					2.3
Acinonyx jubatus Cheetah				1.2	1.5
Small carnivores		3.6		7.4	2.3
Birds	9.0	2.4		2.5	5.3
Snakes					0.8
Rodents				2.4	

TABLE 61 FREQUENCY OF OCCURRENCE OF PREY ITEMS IN THE DIETS OF ASIAN LEOPARDS (PERCENTAGE OF SAMPLES)

Prey items	Nagarahole NP, India[47] Scats (n = 480)	Huai Kha Khaeng Wildlife Sanctuary, Thailand[48] Scats (n = 237)	Wolong Reserve, Sichuan, China[64] Scats (n = 334)
Axis axis Chital	43.7		
Muntiacus muntjak Barking deer	7.5	43.4	
Elaphodus cephalophus Tufted deer			41.0
Moschus berezovski Musk deer			5.6
Cervus unicolor Sambar	13.5	5.4	0.4
Bos frontalis Gaur	7.3		
Sus scrofa Wild pig	4.5	5.0	0.7
Primates	7.1	11.2	0.7
Tetracerus quadricornis Four-horned antelope	0.4		
Tragulus meminna Chevrotain	7.1		
Capricornis sumatraensis Serow			2.4
Budorcas taxicolor Takin			1.1
Nemorhedus goral Goral			0.2
Lepus nigricollis Hare	1.1		
Hystrix and Atherurus Porcupines	1.1	10.0	0.7
Cuon alpinus Dhole	2.6		
Arctonyx collaris Hog badger		4.0	0.9
Viverrids		0.8	
Manis javanica Pangolin		1.4	
Ochotona thibetana Pika			1.1
Rodents		5.4	17.3
Birds		1.4	2.5
Lizards		0.8	
Crabs		0.4	
Red and Giant pandas			0.6
Unidentified mammals	4.1	9.0	0.4
Minimum number of vertebrate prey items	535	272	340

TABLE 62 FREQUENCY OF OCCURRENCE OF PREY ITEMS IN THE DIETS OF TROPICAL AFRICAN FOREST LEOPARDS (PERCENTAGE OF SAMPLES)

Prey items	Ituri Forest, Democratic Republic of the Congo[73] Scats (n = 222)	Taï National Park, Ivory Coast[72] Scats (n = 215)
Neotragus sp. Dwarf antelope	2.1	1.9
Hyemoschus aquaticus Water chevrotain	2.4	1.5
Cephalophus and *Philantomba* Duikers	36.3	31.1
Potamochoerus porcus Bushpig	10.0	0.8
Hylochoerus meinertzhageni Giant forest hog		0.4
Okapia johnstoni Okapi	2.4	
Tragelaphus eurycerus Bongo		1.1
Perodicticus, Cercopithecus, Colobus, and *Pan* Primates	25.7	19.6
Viverrids	3.1	3.2
Rodents	7.9	10.0
Atherurus africana and *Hystrix* Porcupines	3.1	6.1
Manis sp. Pangolin	2.3	3.8
Dendrohyrax arboreus/dorsalis Hyrax	0.7	1.1
Unknown mammals	3.0	9.9
Birds	0.7	0.8
Reptiles	0.7	
Minimum number of vertebrate prey items	291	264

REFERENCES

1. Jerdon, T. C. 1867. *The mammals of India; a natural history of all the animals known to inhabit continental India.* Roorkee: Thomason College Press.

2. Sterndale, R. A. 1884. *Natural history of the Mammalia of India and Ceylon.* Calcutta: Thacker and Spink.

3. Blandford, W. T. 1881–1891. *The fauna of British India and Ceylon: Mammalia.* London: Taylor and Francis.

4. Guggisberg, C. A. W. 1975. *Wild cats of the world.* New York: Taplinger.

5. Salles, L. O. 1992. Felid phylogenetics: Extant taxa and skull morphology (Felidae, Aeluroidea). *Am. Mus. Novitates* 3047: 1–66.

6. Collier, G. E., and S. J. O'Brien. 1985. A molecular phylogeny of the Felidae: Immunological distance. *Evolution* 39: 473–487.

7. Janczewski, D. N., W. S. Modi, J. C. Stephens, and S. J. O'Brien. 1995. Molecular evolution of mitochondrial 12s RNA and cytochrome *b* sequences in pantherine lineage of Felidae. *Mol. Biol. Evol.* 12: 690–707.

8. Smithers, R. H. N. 1983. *The mammals of the southern African subregion.* Pretoria: University of Pretoria.

9. Daniel, J. C. 1996. *The leopard in India.* Dehra Dun: Natraj Publishers.

10. Stuart, C. T. 1981. Notes on the mammalian carnivores of the Cape Province, South Africa. *Bontebok* 1: 1–58.

11. Stuart, C. T., and T. Stuart. 1991. Regional size variation and sexual dimorphism of the leopard. *Cat News* 15: 9.

12. Ilany, G. 1981. The leopard of the Judean desert. *Israel Land and Nature* 6: 59–71.

13. Bailey, T. N. 1993. *The African leopard.* New York: Columbia University Press.

14. Turnbull-Kemp, P. 1967. *The leopard.* Capetown: Howard Timmins.

15. Harrington, F. A. Jr. 1977. *A guide to the mammals of Iran.* Tehran: Department of the Environment.

16. Pocock, R. I. 1930. The panthers and ounces of Asia. *J. Bombay Nat. Hist. Soc.* 34: 64–82.

17. Rosevear, D. R. 1974. *The carnivores of West Africa.* London: Trustees of the British Museum (Natural History).

18. Miththapala, S., J. Seidensticker, L. G. Phillips, S. B. U. Fernando, and J. A. Smallwood. 1989. Identification of individual leopards (*Panthera pardus kotiya*) using spot pattern variation. *J. Zool.* (Lond.) 218: 527–536.

19. Kipling, R. 1978. *Just so stories.* New York: Weathervane Books.

20. Pocock, R. I. 1932. The leopards of Africa. *Proc. Zool. Soc. Lond.* 1932: 543–591.

21. Harrison, D. L., and P. J. J. Bates. 1991. *The mammals of Arabia,* 2nd ed. Sevenoaks, England: Harrison Zoological Museum.

22. Pocock, R. I. 1930. The panthers and ounces of Asia. Part II. *J. Bombay Nat. Hist. Soc.* 34: 307–336.

23. Kingdon, J. 1977. *East African mammals.* Vol. 3A, *Carnivores.* Chicago: University of Chicago Press.

24. Divyabhanusinh. 1993. On mutant leopards *Panthera pardus* from India. *J. Bombay Nat. Hist. Soc.* 90: 88–89.

25. Heptner, V. G., and A. A. Sludskii. 1992. *Mammals of the Soviet Union.* Vol. 3, *Carnivores (Feloidea).* English translation, sci. ed. R. S. Hoffman. Washington, DC: Smithsonian Institution Libraries and the National Science Foundation.

26. Myers, N. 1976. *The leopard* Panthera pardus *in Africa.* IUCN Monographs, no. 5. Morges, Switzerland: International Union for Conservation of Nature and Natural Resources. 79 pp.

27. Gasperetti, J., D. L. Harrison, and W. Büttiker. 1985. The Carnivora of Arabia. *Fauna of Saudi Arabia* 7: 397–461.

28. Corbet, G. B., and J. E. Hill. 1992. *The mammals of the Indomalayan region.* Oxford: Oxford University Press.

29. Seidensticker, J. 1986. Large carnivores and the consequences of habitat insularization: Ecology and conservation of tigers in Indonesia and Bangladesh. In *Cats of the world: Biology, conservation, and management,* ed. S. D. Miller and D. D. Everett, 1–41. Washington, DC: National Wildlife Federation.

30. Kurtén, B. 1965. The Carnivora of the Palestine caves. *Acta Zool. Fennica* 107: 1–74.

31. Kurtén, B. 1968. *Pleistocene mammals of Europe.* Chicago: Aldine.

32. Neff, N. A. 1982. *The big cats: The paintings of Guy Coheleach.* 1982. New York: Abradale Press/Harry N. Abrams.

33. Cat News. 1990. Leopards find a cosy refuge. *Cat News* 13: 11.

34. Bothma, J. du P., and E. A. N. Le Riche. 1986. Prey preference and hunting efficiency of Kalahari Desert leopards. In *Cats of the world: Biology, conservation, and management,* ed. S. D. Miller and D. D. Everett, 389–414. Washington, DC: National Wildlife Federation.

35. Miquelle, D. G., T. D. Arzhanova, and V. A. Solkin, eds. 1996. A recovery plan for conservation of the Far Eastern leopard: Results of an international conference held in Vladivostock, Russia. Report to USAID Russian Far East Environmental Policy and Technology Project.

36. Hamilton, P. H. 1976. The movements of leopards in Tsavo National Park, Kenya, as determined by radio-tracking. Master's thesis, University of Nairobi, Nairobi.

37. Schaller, G. B. 1972. *The Serengeti lion.* Chicago: University of Chicago Press.

38. Bertram, B. C. R. 1982. Leopard ecology as studied by radio tracking. *Symp. Zool. Soc. Lond.* 49: 341–352.

39. Mizutani, F. 1993. Home range of leopards and their impact on livestock on Kenyan ranches. *Symp. Zool. Soc. Lond.* 65: 424–439.

40. Mizutani, F., and P. A. Jewell. 1998. Home-range and movements of leopards (*Panthera pardus*) on a livestock ranch in Kenya. *J. Zool.* (Lond.) 244: 269–286.

41. Stander, P. E., P. J. Haden, //. Kaqece, and //. Ghau. 1997. The ecology of asociality in Namibian leopards. *J. Zool.* (Lond.) 242: 343–364.

42. Norton, P. M., and A. B. Lawson. 1985. Radio tracking of leopards and caracals in the Stellenbosch area, Cape Province. *S. Afr. J. Wildl. Res.* 15: 17–24.

43. Norton, P. M., and S. R. Henley. 1987. Home range and movements of male leopards in the Cedarberg Wilderness Area, Cape Province. *S. Afr. J. Wildl. Res.* 17: 41–48.

44. Seidensticker, J. 1976. On the ecological separation between tigers and leopards. *Biotropica* 8: 225–234.

45. Sunquist, M. E. 1981. The social organization of tigers (*Panthera tigris*) in Royal Chitawan National Park, Nepal. Smithsonian Contributions to Zoology, no. 336. 98 pp.

46. Seidensticker, J., M. E. Sunquist, and C. McDougal. 1990. Leopards living at the edge of Royal Chitwan National Park, Nepal. In *Conservation in developing countries: Problems and prospects,* ed. J. C. Daniel and J. S. Serrao, 415–423. Bombay: Bombay Natural History Society

47. Karanth, K. U., and M. E. Sunquist. 1995. Prey selection by tiger, leopard and dhole in tropical forest. *J. Anim. Ecol.* 64: 439–450.

48. Rabinowitz, A. 1989. The density and behavior of large cats in a dry tropical forest mosaic in Huai Kha Khaeng Wildlife Sanctuary, Thailand. *Nat. Hist. Bull. Siam Soc.* 37: 235–251.

49. Grassman, L. I. Jr. 1999. Ecology and behavior of the Indochinese leopard in Kaeng Krachan National Park, Thailand. *Nat. Hist. Bull. Siam Soc.* 47: 77–93.

50. Eisenberg, J. F., and M. Lockhart. 1972. An ecological reconnaissance of Wilpattu National Park, Ceylon. Smithsonian Contributions to Zoology, no. 101. 118 pp.

51. Muckenhirn, N. A., and J. F. Eisenberg. 1973. Home ranges and predation of the Ceylon leopard. In *The world's cats,* vol. 1, ed. R. L. Eaton, 142–175. Winston, OR: World Wildlife Safari.

52. Silva, M. de, and B. V. R. Jayaratne. 1994. Aspects of population ecology of the leopard (*Panthera pardus*) in Ruhuna National Park, Sri Lanka. *J. S. Asian Nat. Hist.* 1: 3–13.

53. Smith, R. M. 1977. Movement patterns and feeding behaviour of leopard in the Rhodes Matopos National Park, Rhodesia. *Arnoldia Rhodesia* 8: 1–16.

54. Bothma, J. du P., and E. A. N. Le Riche. 1984. Aspects of the ecology and the behaviour of the leopard *Panthera pardus* in the Kalahari Desert. *Koedoe* (suppl.) 27: 259–279.

55. Scott, J. 1985. *The leopard's tale.* London: Elm Tree Books.

56. Hes, L. 1991. *The leopards of Londolozi.* London: New Holland.

57. Karanth, K. U., and M. E. Sunquist. 2000. Behavioural correlates of predation by tiger (*Panthera tigris*), leopard (*Panthera pardus*), and dhole (*Cuon alpinus*) in Nagarahole, India. *J. Zool.* (Lond.) 250: 255–265.

58. McDougal, C. 1988. Leopard and tiger interactions at Royal Chitwan National Park, Nepal. *J. Bombay Nat. Hist. Soc.* 85: 609–610.

59. Norton, P. M., A. B. Lawson, S. R. Henley, and G. Avery. 1986. Prey of leopards in four mountainous areas of the southwestern Cape Province. *S. Afr. J. Wildl. Res.* 16: 47–52.

60. Bothma, J. du P., and E. A. N. Le Riche. 1990. The influence of increasing hunger on the hunting behaviour of southern Kalahari leopards. *J. Arid Environ.* 18: 79–84.

61. Digveerendrasinh. 1995. Panthers eating water-melons. *J. Bombay Nat. Hist. Soc.* 92(3): 407.

62. Estes, R. D. 1967. Predators and scavengers. Parts 1, 2. *Nat. Hist.* 76(2): 20–29, 76(3): 38–47.

63. Singh, A. 1982. *Prince of cats.* London: Jonathan Cape.

64. Johnson, K. G., W. Wang, D. G. Reid, and J. Hu. 1993. Food habits of Asiatic leopards (*Panthera pardus fusea*) in Wolong Reserve, Sichuan, China. *J. Mammal.* 74: 646–650.

65. Miguelle, D. G., E. N. Smirnov, H. G. Hornocker, I. G. Nikolaev, and E. N. Matyushkin. 1996. Food habits of Amur tigers in Sikhote-Alin Zapovednik and the Russian Far East, and implications for conservation. *J. Wildl. Res.* 1: 138–147.

66. Amerasinghe, F. P., and U. B. Ekanayake. 1992. Prey hair remains in leopard faeces at Ruhuna National Park. *Cey. J. Sci. (Biol. Sci.)* 22: 14–16.

67. Amerasinghe, F. P., U. B. Ekanayake, and R. D. A. Burge. 1990. Food habits of the leopard (*Panthera pardus fusca*) in Sri Lanka. *Cey. J. Sci. (Biol. Sci.)* 21: 17–24.

68. Mitchell, B. L., J. B. Shenton, and J. C. M. Uys. 1965. Predation on large mammals in the Kafue National Park, Zambia. *Zool. Africana* 1: 297–318.

69. Kruuk, H., and M. Turner. 1967. Comparative notes on predation by lion, leopard, cheetah and wild dog in the Serengeti area, East Africa. *Mammalia* 31: 1–27.

70. Pienaar, U. De V. 1969. Predator-prey relationships amongst the larger mammals of the Kruger National Park. *Koedoe* 12: 108–176.

71. Mills, M. G. L. 1984. Prey selection and feeding habits of the larger carnivores in the southern Kalahari. *Koedoe* (suppl.) 27: 281–294.

72. Hoppe-Dominik, B. 1984. Etude du spectre des proies de la panthère, *Panthera pardus*, dans le Parc National de Taï en Côte d'Ivoire. *Mammalia* 48: 477–487.

73. Hart, J. A., M. Katembo, and K. Punga. 1996. Diet, prey selection and ecological relations of leopard and golden cat in the Ituri Forest, Zaire. *Afr. J. Ecol.* 34: 364–379.

74. Seidensticker, J., and I. Suyono. 1980. *The Javan tiger and the Meru-Betiri Reserve, a plan for management.* Gland, Switzerland: International Union for Conservation of Nature and Natural Resources (IUCN).

75. Grobler, J. H., and V. J. Wilson. 1972. Food of the leopard *Panthera pardus* (Linn.) in the Rhodes Matopos National Park, Rhodesia, as determined by faecal analysis. *Arnoldia Rhodesia* 5: 1–9.

76. Busse, C. 1980. Leopard and lion predation upon Chacma baboons living in the Moremi Wildlife Reserve. *Botswana Notes & Records* 12: 15–21.

77. Boesch, C. 1991. The effects of leopard predation on grouping patterns in forest chimpanzees. *Behaviour* 117: 220–242.

78. Pocock, R. I. 1939. *The fauna of British India including Ceylon and Burma.* Vol. 1, *Mammalia.* London: Taylor and Francis.

79. Dunbar Brander, A. A. 1923. *Wild animals in central India.* London: Edward Arnold.

80. Bothma, J. du P., and E. A. N. Le Riche. 1989. Evidence of a flexible hunting technique in Kalahari leopards. *S. Afr. J. Wildl. Res.* 19: 57–60.

81. Ilany, G. 1990. The leopard (*Panthera pardus*) in Israel. *Cat News* 12: 4–5.

82. Eloff, F. C. 1973. Ecology and behavior of the Kalahari lion. In *The world's cats,* vol. 1, ed. R. L. Eaton, 90–126. Winston, OR: World Wildlife Safari.

83. Schaller, G. B. 1967. *The deer and the tiger.* Chicago: University of Chicago Press.

84. Stevenson-Hamilton, J. 1947. *Wildlife in South Africa.* London: Cassell.

85. Le Roux, P. G., and J. D. Skinner. 1989. A note on the ecology of the leopard (*Panthera pardus* Linnaeus) in the Londolozi Game Reserve, South Africa. *Afr. J. Ecol.* 27: 167–171.

86. Corbett, J. 1947. *The man-eating leopard of Rudraprayag.* London: Oxford University Press.

87. Jenny, D. 1996. Spatial organization of leopards *Panthera pardus* in Taï National Park, Ivory Coast: Is rainforest habitat a "tropical haven"? *J. Zool.* (Lond.) 240: 427–440.

88. Smith, J. L. D., C. McDougal, and D. Miguelle. 1989. Scent marking in free-ranging tigers, Panthera tigris. *Anim. Behav.* 37: 1–10.

89. Peters, G. 1984. On the structure of friendly close range vocalizations in terrestrial carnivores (Mammalia: Carnivora: Fissipedia). *Z. Säugetierk.* 49: 157–182.

90. Peters, G., and M. H. Hast. 1994. Hyoid structure, laryngeal anatomy, and vocalization in felids (Mammalia: Carnivora: Felidae). *Z. Säugetierk.* 59: 87–104.

91. Sadleir, R. M. F. S. 1966. Notes on reproduction in the larger Felidae. *Int. Zoo Yrbk.* 6: 184–187.

92. Lanier, D. L., and D. A. Dewsbury. 1976. A quantitative study of copulatory behaviour of large Felidae. *Behav. Proc.* 1: 327–333.

93. Desai, J. H. 1975. Observations on the reproductive biology and early postnatal development of the panther, *Panthera pardus* L., in captivity. *J. Bombay Nat. Hist. Soc.* 72: 293–304.

94. Eaton, R. L. 1977. Reproductive biology of the leopard. *Zool. Garten* 47: 329–351.

95. Hemmer, H. 1979. Gestation period and postnatal development in felids. *Carnivore* 2: 90–100.

96. Seager, S. W. J., and C. N. Demorest. 1978. Reproduction of captive wild carnivores. In *Zoo and wild animal medicine,* ed. M. E. Fowler, 667–706. Philadelphia: W. B. Saunders.

97. Zuckerman, S. 1953. The breeding of mammals in captivity. *Proc. Zool. Soc. Lond.* 122: 827–950.

98. Dobroruka, L. J. 1968. A note on the gestation period and rearing of young in the leopard. *Int. Zoo Yrbk.* 8: 65.

99. Reuther, R. T., and Y. Doherty. 1968. Birth seasons of mammals at San Francisco Zoo. *Int. Zoo Yrbk.* 8: 97–101.

100. Robinson, R. 1969. The breeding of spotted and black leopards. *J. Bombay Nat. Hist. Soc.* 66: 423–429.

101. Martin, R. B., and T. de Meulenaer. 1988. *Survey of the status of the leopard* Panthera pardus *in sub-Saharan Africa.* Lausanne, Switzerland: Secretariat of the Convention on International Trade in Endangered Species of Wild Fauna and Flora.

102. Caro, T. M. 1994. *Cheetahs of the Serengeti plains.* Chicago: University of Chicago Press.

103. Seidensticker, J. 1977. Notes on early maternal behavior of the leopard. *Mammalia* 41: 111–113.

104. Adamson, J. 1980. *Queen of Shaba: The story of an African leopard.* London: Collins.

105. Smith, J. L. D., C. W. McDougal, and M. E. Sunquist. 1986. Female land tenure system in tigers. In *Tigers of the world: The biology, biopolitics, management, and conservation of an endangered species,* ed. R. L. Tilson and U. S. Seal, 97–109. Park Ridge, NJ: Noyes Publications.

106. Sunquist, M. E. 1983. Dispersal of three radiotagged leopards. *J. Mammal.* 64: 337–341.

107. Bertram, B. C. R. 1978. *Pride of lions.* New York: Charles Scribner's Sons.

108. Nowell, K., and P. Jackson. 1996. *Wild cats: A status survey and conservation action plan.* Gland, Switzerland: International Union for Conservation of Nature and Natural Resources (IUCN).

109. Cat News. 1989. The status of leopard in sub-Saharan Africa. *Cat News* 11: 5.

110. Norton, P. M. 1990. How many leopards? A criticism of Martin and de Meulenaer's population estimates for Africa. *S. Afr. J. Sci.* 86: 218–220.

111. Shoemaker, A. H. 1993. *The status of the leopard,* Panthera pardus, *in nature: A country by country analysis.* Columbia, SC: Riverbanks Zoological Park.

112. Mendelssohn, H. 1989. Felids in Israel. *Cat News* 10: 2–4.

113. Miththapala, S., J. Seidensticker, and S. J. O'Brien. 1996. Phylogeographic subspecies recognition in leopards (*Panthera pardus*): Molecular genetic variation. *Conserv. Biol.* 10: 1115–1132.

114. Cat News. 1989. Leopard stoned to death. *Cat News* 11: 9.

115. Hawkins, R. E. 1978. *Jim Corbett's India.* Oxford: Oxford University Press.

116. Wilson, V. J. 1976. The leopard in eastern Zambia. In *The world's cats,* vol. 3, no. 2, ed. R. L. Eaton, 29–38. Seattle: Carnivore Research Institute, Burke Museum, University of Washington.

Plate 25. About the size of a domestic cat, Geoffroy's cat is a versatile predator found throughout the subtropical and temperate regions of southern South America.

Plate 26. When frightened or nervous the Pampas cat of South America erects the long mane-like hairs on its back and flattens its ears.

Plate 27. Found only in the rocky treeless zone of the high Andes, the Andean mountain cat is the small-cat analogue of the snow leopard.

Plate 28. At about 2 kg, the diminutive kodkod is one of the world's smallest cats. An accomplished climber, it preys on birds, lizards, and rodents.

Plates 29 and 30. The manul's short blunt ears are set low on the sides of its head. The position of the ears may help the cat keep a low profile when stalking prey in open terrain. The manul has long hair, a heavy body, and short, stout legs. It is found at high altitudes in semidesert and steppe regions of central Asia.

Plate 31. The leopard cat varies greatly in size across its geographic range. The individual pictured here, from the Russian Far East, is about four times heavier than a leopard cat from Malaysia.

Plates 32 and 33. About the size of a domestic cat, the flat-headed cat has webbed feet and partially retractile claws. It is thought to be a small fishing cat as it swims well and has been seen hunting frogs and fish along streams.

Plates 34 and 35. The tiny rusty-spotted cat of India and Sri Lanka has not been studied in the wild. Captive animals are known to be excellent climbers, so these cats may spend part of their time hunting in trees.

Plates 36 and 37. The powerful, robust-looking fishing cat is usually associated with areas of thick cover near water. Their size enables them to take a wide variety of prey. Fishing cats swim well and have been seen crouching on rocks and sandbanks, using their paws and mouths to grab fish from the water.

Plate 38. The African golden cat has one of the most variable coats of any member of the cat family. The fur can be orange, gray, or black, and spotted or unspotted.

Plate 39. With a distribution that spans about 100 degrees latitude, from Canada to the southern tip of South America, the puma is the most widely distributed of the American cats.

Plates 40 and 41. Named for their unusual cloud-shaped markings, clouded leopards have short legs, large feet, and an extremely long tail. For their size, clouded leopards have the longest canine teeth of any living cat. Little is known of this cat's diet, but it probably eats birds, monkeys, and deer.

Plate 42. Lions are the only social cats. A group of related lionesses and their cubs form the core of a pride. Daughters are often recruited into the pride but young males leave as they mature.

Plate 43. Male lions are instantly recognizable by their manes. No one is entirely sure of the function of a mane, but it may indicate physical condition.

Plate 44. The jaguar's massive jaws and strong canine teeth produce the most powerful bite of any of the big cats, enabling it to kill livestock three or four times its own weight.

Plate 45. The leopard resembles the jaguar but lacks the jaguar's robust physique. Both cats have similar coat patterns; the leopard's rosettes rarely have central spots.

Plate 46. As the only cat with stripes, the tiger is probably the most easily recognizable felid. Tigers are also the largest of the cats—an exceptional male may tip the scales at 270 kg.

Plate 47. Though its thick coat and long, bushy tail make it look larger, the marbled cat of Southeast Asia is the size of a domestic cat.

Plates 48 and 49. The snow leopard's smoke-gray pelt is patterned with spots and large dark rosettes. In winter this cat's belly fur can be almost 12 centimeters long. Found only in central Asia, the snow leopard lives in steep, rugged terrain, sometimes at elevations as high as 6,000 meters.

Tiger

Panthera tigris (Linnaeus, 1758)

Through the centuries the tiger has been used as a symbol of man's deepest fears, desires, and aspirations. It is universally feared as a powerful predator and man-eater, yet admired for its beauty, courage, and strength. Hundreds of different uses are made of various parts of the tiger's body—the fat is thought to be a tonic for rheumatism and prized as an aphrodisiac, the flesh gives courage and strength to those who eat it, and the clavicle or floating collarbone is believed to be a powerful charm against evil. The heart is eaten to acquire strength, courage, and cunning, and the brain mixed with oil and rubbed on the body cures laziness and acne.

In China, Pai Hu, the white tiger, represents autumn and was believed to be a reincarnation of the tiger star, Alpha, in the Milky Way. According to I Ching, the tiger symbolized yin, or evil, while the dragon symbolized yang, or good. It is said that "the breath of the tiger creates the wind and the breath of the dragon creates the clouds; together they create the rain which fructifies the earth and brings forth food for mankind."[1]

The tiger is also a symbol of military power and strength. In China, whole armies of soldiers went into battle dressed as tigers, and troops were issued tiger charms to instill courage. Many regiments in modern armies have adopted the tiger as an emblem, and others have incorporated the tiger into crests, badges, and coats of arms. The Chinese also saw the tiger as a symbol of authority; Chinese ambassadors were given a *hu chieh*, or tiger stick, while magistrates, teachers, and other important people sat on tiger skins. In the Hindu religion Shiva, the god of destruction and reincarnation, is depicted wearing a tiger skin and riding a tiger.

Considered to be fitting gifts for and from emperors and kings, tigers have been kept in captivity in Western Europe since classical times. The earliest records of such gifts refer to tigers presented to the citizens of Athens by King Seleucus I Nicator, who was a general under Alexander the Great. Alexander, the explorer and conqueror, complained that tigers attacked his baggage trains as he marched his armies eastward toward the Indus River, in what is today Pakistan.[1]

Around 1120, King Henry I established a flourishing menagerie near Oxford, which included the first recorded captive tiger in England. A hundred or so years later the royal menagerie was moved to the Tower of London. Various other tigers were presented to the Crown by foreign rulers such as the Holy Roman Emperor, Frederick II. However, the Tower zoo remained closed to the general public until the middle of the eighteenth century. Before that time, only royalty and their guests were allowed the privilege of seeing tigers and other rare and wonderful beasts.[1]

Killing or capturing such a magnificent quarry has always brought honor and status to the huntsman, and tigers have always been hunted. But toward the middle of the eighteenth century the general attitude toward this cat began to change, as tigers were increasingly regarded as pests. J. Forsyth wrote of "the obstacle presented by the number of these animals to the advance of population and tillage."[2] The tiger had come to symbolize evil, and the species was considered to be destructive, cowardly, and treacherous. Tiger hunting was now considered to be a humanitarian pursuit, and it soon became a popular pastime with army officers.

In Rajasthan, India, Colonel William Rice accounted for 158 tigers between 1850 and 1854,[3] while Colonel Gordon-Cumming shot 73 tigers in one district in two years.[4] By the turn of the century, tiger hunters were beginning to comment on the fact that tigers were becoming harder to find, and there was a general consensus that tigers were becoming less common. In his book *Jungle Trails in Northern India*, J. Hewitt described a place where in the 1880s a dozen tigers had been shot in two weeks. When he returned twenty-five years later, he found that "the ground had been brought completely under cultivation, and no-one could have imagined that there had ever been any cover there suitable for a tiger."[5]

Although tiger numbers were greatly reduced by habitat conversion and hunting, the tiger still had some degree of protection during the early part of the twentieth century. Royalty set aside vast tracts of land for tiger hunting, and a system of forest reserves containing large areas of undisturbed land was divided into hunting blocks. There was also a closed season for hunting, and as long as there was sufficient habitat, tiger populations were able to sustain this heavy hunting pressure.

The end of World War II ushered in an era of destruction for wildlife. There was a growing demand for tiger hunting among wealthy Westerners, and a boom in the demand for tiger skins created a new market for poachers. Sophisticated weapons were available, and together with the Jeep and the spotlight, these tools spawned a new and more destructive breed of hunter. With searchlights mounted on jeeps, gangs of joyriding hunters roamed the forests, firing at anything that moved. At the same time good tiger habitat was increasingly falling under the plow.

Just when it looked as if the tiger would surely become extinct, a series of conservation measures and international agreements managed to slow the precipitous decline in tiger numbers. Today in India, an extensive wildlife tourist industry now caters to the demands of both national and foreign tourists. The image of the tiger has come full circle; in the eyes of the world, the tiger is now a symbol of wilderness and wild places, especially in India.

DESCRIPTION

Easily recognizable as the only striped cat, the tiger is the largest of the living felids. Reliable weight data are difficult to find, however, because hunters typically measured total length, tail length, and shoulder height, but rarely carried scales. The heaviest Bengal tiger on record was a male that weighed 258.2 kilograms.[5] This weight is not unlikely, as an exceptionally large male tiger captured during studies in Nepal bottomed out a scale with a capacity of 227 kilograms.[6]

Documenting the weight of the Siberian subspecies is more difficult. Tigers from this region seem to vary considerably in size, and a literature search reveals few reliable weights. Many weights are "guesstimates," such as the weight of a male tiger from Manchuria that was "certainly not less than 300 kg."[7] Some authorities believe that Siberian tigers were larger in the past, attaining weights of nearly 364 kilograms.[8] However, using more recent measurements, the average weight for four adult males was 221 kilograms, and the largest was an old male from the Prague Zoo, which weighed 260 kilograms.[7] Tigers captured during an ongoing study in the Russian Far East ought to provide some insight into the weight question. To date, no prime adult male has been captured, but a young adult male weighed 175 kilograms, and three adult females weighed 114 to 130 kilograms. These weights are similar to those of tigers captured in Nepal.[9]

Tigers on Sumatra and other Indonesian islands are smaller and darker than those of the more northern subspecies. The fur of these southern tigers is also shorter and less dense than that of subspecies living in colder regions. In tropical areas adult males average about 2.2 to 2.5 meters in length, which is about a half meter shorter than males from northern areas, and weigh only 100 to 140 kilograms. Adult females in tropical areas weigh 75 to 110 kilograms, or roughly as much as a large leopard or jaguar. Adult male tigers in India and Nepal typically weigh 180 to 258 kilograms, and adult females weigh 100 to 160 kilograms.[10,11,12,13]

The background color of the tiger's fur is reddish orange to ocherous. The insides of the limbs and the belly, chest, throat, and muzzle are white or light cream-colored. There is a white area above the eyes, which extends onto the cheeks. A white spot is present on the backs of the ears. The tail is ringed with several dark bands. The flanks and shoulders are marked with dark vertical stripes that vary in width, spacing, length, and whether they are single or double. The stripes also extend onto the belly, and stripe patterns differ from one side of the cat's body to the other. The dark lines above the eyes tend to be symmetrical, but the marks on each side of the face can be different, and no two tigers have the same markings.

The tiger's coat pattern of black stripes against a dark gold background looks very conspicuous in most cages or enclosures. In the wild, however, even in semi-open habitats, the striped coat seems to break up the body outline, and the cat almost fades from view. Similarly, its dark, golden orange coat looks as if it would stand out like a beacon against a background of tropical green, but it blends into the forest patterns of sunlight and shadow, perfect camouflage for this large stalking predator.

Black or melanistic forms occur in many members of the cat family, but while there are accounts of black tigers, no skins or museum specimens exist. Pocock lists three records of black tigers, all of which are reported from the same general area of Myanmar, northeastern India, and Bangladesh, within 600 kilometers of each other.[10] The well-known white tigers so frequently seen in zoos are not albinos (which would be pure white with pink eyes). Rather, their chalk-white coats, ice-blue eyes, and chocolate-colored stripes are the result of a pair of recessive genes, which probably resulted from a mutation that occurred about a hundred years ago.[14,15,16,17]

All the white tigers in captivity are descendants of a white male cub captured in the forests of Rewa in Madhya Pradesh, India, in 1951.[18] The cub, named Mohan, was mated with a normal-colored tigress, but the union produced three litters of normal-colored cubs. When Mohan was paired with one of his normal-colored daughters, a litter of four white cubs was born, and all captive white tigers are descended from this mating of Mohan and his daughter Radha. Father-daughter, father-granddaughter, and brother-sister matings of these animals have combined to produce high coefficients of inbreeding, which have led to reduced fertility and increased cub mortality. White tigers also suffer from many other problems, including eye weaknesses, swayback, and twisted necks.[16,17,19]

Physically, tigers are powerful, burly animals, well equipped to single-handedly capture and subdue large prey. The skull is large and foreshortened, which increases the bite strength of the formidable set of canine teeth. A short, thick neck, broad shoulders, and massive forelimbs are ideal for grappling with prey while holding onto it with the long, retractile claws of the broad forepaws. Tigers stand taller at the shoulders than at the rear, with Bengal and Siberian tigers measuring about a meter high at the shoulders. The body is long and lithe, but the hindquarters are not as well muscled and look almost puny compared with the forelimbs. The tail typically measures less than half the head and body length.[7]

DISTRIBUTION

The geographic distribution of the tiger once extended across Asia from eastern Turkey and the Caspian Sea eastward south of the Tibetan plateau to Manchuria and the Sea of Okhotsk.[7,10,11,20] However, the tiger's range has been greatly reduced in recent times. It is now extinct in Turkey, northern Iran, Afghanistan, and the Indus Valley of Pakistan.[21,22,23,24,25] Once common over most of India and across the foothills of the Himalaya through Nepal, Sikkim, Bhutan, Assam, and Myanmar, the tiger's distribution has been greatly reduced on the Indian subcontinent.[26,27,28,29] Similarly, the tiger was once widely distributed in Laos, Thailand, Vietnam, Cambodia, and Malaysia.[12,30,31,32,33] There are no records of tigers on Borneo, but they still occur on Sumatra, although they are extinct on the islands of Java and Bali.[34,35,36,37,38] The tiger used to be found in many provinces of southern and eastern China, but only a few individuals remain in these subtropical areas. Tigers were also formerly abundant throughout northeastern China, Korea, and Russia, but their numbers have been drastically reduced, and there are only a few scattered sites in these countries where tigers currently exist (fig. 44).[8,39,40,41,42]

ECOLOGY AND BEHAVIOR

Tigers live in a great variety of habitat types, from the tropical lowland evergreen forests and monsoonal forests of Indo-Malaysia to the coniferous, scrub oak, and birch woodlands of Siberia. The tiger also thrives in the mangrove swamps of the Sundarbans in Bangla-

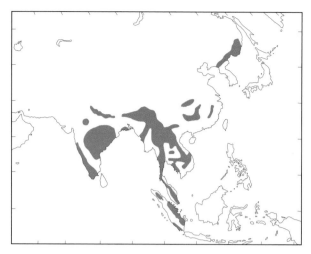

Figure 44. Distribution of the tiger.

desh and India, the dry thorn forests of north-central India, and the tallgrass jungles of the southern Himalaya. Tigers also can cope with a broad range of climates, and they have been recorded at elevations of 3,960 meters and in areas where winter snowfall is deep and temperatures fall to −30°C to −40°C. Clearly, tigers are not tied to a particular habitat type or temperature regime. Their main requirements are a supply of large prey, enough cover for stalking, and access to water. While tigers survive in a variety of habitat types, they live at higher densities in areas with high prey biomass. Tiger density and home range size are directly related to the abundance and distribution of large terrestrial prey, which, in turn, are related to habitat diversity and primary productivity. The greatest ungulate biomass in southern Asia is found in areas where grassland and forest form a mosaic; this mix of vegetation types supports a rich ungulate community.[6,11,43,44,45,46,47,48]

Tigers can swim well, and during the hot season in India and elsewhere they often spend most of the daytime lounging half-submerged in streams and ponds. There are also records of tigers periodically visiting islands in the Sunda Strait, despite a strong tidal current of more than 4 kilometers per hour. Tigers rarely climb trees, although they can and will, especially if provoked. In Chitwan National Park, Nepal, a tigress with newborn young was annoyed by the presence of a researcher in a small tree near her den site. She surged up the tree and pulled him from his perch 4.6 meters above the ground.[49] There are also observations of an adult tiger climbing a smoothed-barked tree to a height of 10 meters, and in Bangladesh during the floods of 1969 many tigers reportedly escaped the high water by climbing into trees.[50] The tiger's hind legs are slightly longer than the front legs, suggesting that its jumping ability is well developed. Jumps as long as 8 to 10 meters have been recorded, but leaps covering half that distance are more typical.[7,8,26]

Throughout most of its range the tiger coexists with leopards and Asiatic wild dogs, or dholes. While the tiger is generally the dominant predator, there are records of occasions when the large cat has been bested by a pack of wild dogs. Normally there is little interaction between the two species, as dholes are diurnal hunters while tigers are more crepuscular or nocturnal. Dholes are pack-hunting canids that weigh about 20 kilograms and live at low densities over parts of the tiger's range in India and Southeast Asia.[51,52] Dholes hunt many of the same prey as tigers, including chital, sambar, and barking deer, and on rare occasions they have been known to chase and kill tigers. On one occasion, detailed in an account written by W. Connell, two shikaris (hunting guides) watched a pack of twenty-two wild dogs drive a tiger into a dry streambed. The tiger eventually positioned himself with his back to a large tree, where he sat snarling at the dogs. During a moment when the tiger's attention wavered, the dogs attacked, swarming all over the cat in seconds. Five dogs were killed or seriously injured during this first assault, but the tiger was also badly wounded; its ears were tattered, one eye was closed, and its body was covered with gashes. Over the next hour the dogs continued to harass the tiger, then attacked again, and after this struggle the tiger could barely remain upright. On the third and final attack the dogs succeeded in disemboweling the tiger, and it succumbed. The observers "counted twelve dead dogs and could see where others had dragged themselves away."[53]

Kenneth Anderson also witnessed and described a stunning battle between a pack of wild dogs and a tigress that took place near Mysore in southern India.[54]

The dogs had spread themselves around the tigress, who was growling ferociously. Every now and again one would dash in from behind to bite her. She would then turn to attempt to rend asunder this puny aggressor, when a couple of others would rush in from another direction. In this way she was kept going continually, and I could see she was fast becoming spent. All this time the dogs were making a tremendous noise,

the reason for which I soon came to know, when, in a lull in the fray, I heard the whistling cry of the main pack. The tigress must have also heard the sound, for in sudden, renewed fury, she charged two of the dogs, one of which she caught a tremendous blow on its back with her paw, cracking its spine with the sharp report of a broken twig. The other just managed to leap out of danger. The tigress then followed up her momentary advantage by bounding away, to be immediately followed by the five remaining dogs. They were just out of sight when the main pack streamed by, in which I counted twenty-three dogs, as they galloped past me without the slightest interest in my presence.

The next day Anderson sent his trackers to investigate the outcome of the chase, and they returned with a few fragments of tiger skin. Apparently the dogs had cornered the tigress some five miles away and torn her to pieces. Five dogs had been killed in the final fight.

Leopards are socially subordinate to tigers and generally avoid encounters with the larger cats. The shikar (hunting) literature records several instances of leopards being killed while poaching from tiger kills; on at least two of these occasions the tiger ate the leopard. In February 1988 tigers killed two leopards in Sariska Tiger Preserve, India, and one of these was fed on by a tigress.[55] In Chitwan National Park, Chuck McDougal recorded five leopards killed by tigers over a period of twenty-one months; he attributed this high death rate to an increase in the number of tigers along with a simultaneous loss of habitat at the edge of the park, which forced leopards into the park.[56,57] Four of the five dead leopards were found in grasslands, where there were limited avenues of escape. Describing one of the deadly encounters, McDougal writes,

A female leopard and her two small cubs were walking along a path through grassland near the Rapti River, on the edge of the park, when they were encountered by a tigress. The latter killed the mother leopard, dragged her body 75 meters, and devoured everything except the head and front paws. The two cubs escaped but returned the next night, when the tigress found and killed them not far from where she had fed on their mother. The leopard cubs were discovered seven metres apart, where they had been dragged in opposite directions by the two small (six months old) cubs of the tigress.[56]

Leopards are found throughout most of the tiger's geographic range, and the old adage "Where tigers are numerous, leopards are few" appears to be generally true. Where both species occur, leopards coexist with tigers by avoiding situations in which encounters are likely, by specializing on smaller prey, and often by hunting when tigers are inactive.[6,58,59,60] The exceptional areas where both species are common are characterized by high prey densities, a wide variety of prey sizes, and structurally complex habitats.

Anecdotal evidence suggests that bears and wolves may also be competitors with tigers in the Russian Far East, with brown bears displacing tigers from their kills and possibly even killing tigers. A better understanding of tiger-bear interactions will undoubtedly be forthcoming from ongoing studies in Kedrovia Pad Reserve and Sikhote-Alin Reserve in the Russian Far East.[8,61]

In many parts of their range tigers have become totally nocturnal in response to human activities; however, where they are undisturbed, they can be found hunting at any time of the day or night. In general, the tiger's activity patterns tend to mirror those of its major prey. In Kanha National Park, India, Schaller reported that tigers were most active at night and rested from mid-morning to mid-afternoon, although an animal sometimes hunted throughout the day after an apparently unsuccessful night.[11] In Chitwan National Park, both male and female tigers were on the move for about ten to twelve hours per day, and most of their traveling was done at night. However, in the hot season, when daytime high temperatures averaged 36°C, tigers were much less active, and they frequently rested from early morning until late afternoon in dense cover in or near water.[6]

A change in protection levels can alter the tiger's activity patterns. India's Ranthambhore National Park was listed as a "Project Tiger" reserve in 1974, and habitat and prey numbers improved dramatically as villages were resettled and protection improved. Since 1980, tigers in Ranthambhore have become much more active during the daytime, and often hunt both during the day and at night.[62]

Tigers can survive for a short time on an assortment of smaller prey such as piglets and monkeys, but in the long term, large animals are the mainstay of the tiger's diet. Built to single-handedly overpower prey several times its own size, the tiger is more of a wrestler than a runner, and it rarely chases its prey very far. There are observations of tigers chasing sambar for 150 meters along a lakeshore in Ranthambhore National Park,

and others of Siberian tigers in the Russian Far East pursuing red deer and wild pigs through the snow for similar distances, but these are exceptions.[8,39,63] More typically, the tiger makes a stealthy approach using every available tree, rock, or bush as cover to get as close as possible to its target before it launches its attack. In the Russian Far East tigers sometimes use the dense fog that forms along the seacoast as cover to stalk deer.[8] Tigers also kill opportunistically during accidental encounters, and there are several examples of tracks showing that a tiger had literally bumped into a deer while both were walking toward each other on a trail. Under these circumstances the tiger can make a kill almost with a single pounce.

Apart from the occasional fortuitous encounter, finding food is generally a time-consuming effort, and tigers have to travel widely to find enough to eat. Not surprisingly, there are few measurements of how far tigers travel in the course of a night's hunting. George Schaller, using the tiger's average walking speed, estimated that in Kanha National Park tigers traveled 16 to 32 kilometers per night.[11] Soviet researchers, by following tiger tracks in the snow, estimated that tigers commonly travel 15 to 20 kilometers per day.[39] There are, however, accounts from eastern Siberia of tigers traveling 50 to 60 kilometers in a day, but this must be under unusual circumstances. In Chitwan National Park, where food is abundant, tigresses travel at about 0.7 kilometers per hour, or roughly 7 to 10 kilometers per night.[6] Males tend to travel farther than females, and one adult male in Chitwan regularly used the park road to traverse the length of his territory, covering the 30 kilometers in a night.[64]

Nighttime radio-tracking in Chitwan showed that tigers often hunt while moving slowly along roads and trails. These routes allow them to move quietly without having to push through dense grass and brush. Many naturalists have made similar observations, and the descriptions of hunting by Dunbar Brander are particularly apt: "The usual daily round of a tiger is to commence questing for food shortly before sunset and to continue doing so all night. In thus questing, they go at a slow walk often following the beds of nalas and jungle roads, especially so in the cold weather when cover is dense and the grass is wet and cold."[65] In the Russian Far East tigers avoid hunting in areas with deep snow cover (> 30 centimeters), partly because not many prey frequent these areas, but also because the unstable snow crust makes walking difficult. When moving through areas with deep snow, tigers often take advantage of frozen river beds, paths made by ungulates, or anywhere the snow depth is less. When the crust is thin, prey can hear the tiger's approach, and the frozen snow sometimes cuts the cat's legs. There are times during the winter in the Russian Far East when tigers cannot hunt, and there are reports of tigers starving to death during winters of unusually heavy snowfall.[8]

Some historical accounts suggest that tigers travel a beat, reappearing at places as if on a schedule, but others have not found their movements to be as predictable. Nevertheless, the movements of a hunting tiger often give the distinct impression that the animal knows its range well and knows where it is going next. A hunting tiger rarely wanders around; instead, it moves directly from one hunting area to the next as if it has a mental map of the good hunting areas within its range and knows the best routes between them. Roads and trails play an important part in these movements between hunting areas, and George Schaller observed that some routes were used several times in one week by the same tigress, sometimes on consecutive nights.[11]

The radio-collared tigers in Chitwan definitely had favorite hunting areas that they visited regularly. Some nights a tigress would choose a hiding place in one of these favored hunting areas and just wait, perhaps for a herd of deer to move closer, or for some likely prey to cross an opening, or to come for a drink. However, once a tiger had made an unsuccessful attempt at a kill, it usually gave up and moved to another hunting area, probably because the animals in the area had been alerted to its presence. Throughout most of the Indian subcontinent and Southeast Asia, many of the tiger's chief prey species have loud alarm calls. Indeed, in the old Indian shikar stories, tiger hunters often remarked that it was possible to chart a tiger's progress through the forest by listening to the alarm calls of the deer. Chital, sambar, barking deer, hog deer, and (to some extent) gaur all give loud, penetrating calls in response to tigers or leopards. When, for instance, a chital is killed or attacked, other members of the herd often mill around nearby, foot-stamping and calling in an almost deafening display of alarm. Clearly, such a noise alerts other potential prey in the vicinity of an attempted kill and probably makes it unprofitable for the tiger to continue to hunt in the area.

Feeding Ecology

Tigers will eat almost anything they can catch, from frogs to elephant calves. The menu includes birds, fish, mice, locusts, porcupines, moose, and monkeys, but these animals generally form an insignificant part of the tiger's diet. There are also records of tigers killing and eating other carnivores, such as bears, leopards, lynx, wolves, and foxes, but this is not a common occurrence either.

When it comes to large prey, a look at the kinds of animals tigers eat gives the impression that tigers from different areas specialize on different prey species. In some regions they feed primarily on sambar and rarely take chital; in other places they live chiefly on chital, while in still other areas they may kill mainly barking deer, gaur, or domestic stock. But despite these place-to-place variations, wild pigs and deer of various species are the two prey types that make up the bulk of the tiger's diet, and in general tigers require a good population of these species in order to survive and reproduce.

Almost any terrestrial vertebrate is potential tiger prey, and tigers often take those large prey that are most abundant, which in some areas include domestic buffalo and cows. Based on an analysis of feces, Schaller concluded that tigers in Kanha National Park fed primarily on the medium-sized chital, or spotted deer.[11] Over half of all the tiger feces he examined contained chital hair. The remains of larger deer, such as sambar and barasingha, and gaur (wild cattle) appeared much less frequently. Similarly, thirty-eight of a hundred tiger kills found in Kanha were chital, whereas barasingha ranked second, at twenty-six kills. Chital also occurred in over half of a small sample of tiger feces from Corbett National Park in northern India. Wild pigs were barely represented in tiger feces at Kanha and none were found in those from Corbett, suggesting that pig densities were very low at that time.[11]

Wild pigs also appeared infrequently in the tiger's diet in Chitwan National Park in the mid-1970s, probably because the pig population was decimated by a disease in 1974. For several years thereafter pigs were not commonly seen in the park, although by 1980 their numbers had rebounded substantially.[66] During the low, wild pig remains were not commonly found in tiger feces (only two out of fifty-five feces) or as kills (six out of ninety kills).[6] During declines in wild pig populations in the former Soviet Union, tigers were observed to travel widely and to prey more extensively on moose and red deer.[8,39]

The major prey of tigers in Chitwan is deer, including sambar, chital, and hog deer. Deer hair was identified in over 80 percent of all tiger feces.[6] Sambar were killed more often than expected based on their availability, suggesting that they were preferred or were more vulnerable than the smaller but more abundant chital and hog deer. More sambar were killed when stalking cover on the grasslands was temporarily eliminated by burning and both chital and hog deer subsequently congregated in large groups on the burned-over grasslands. Few chital and hog deer kills were found at this time, suggesting that these deer had become less vulnerable, increasing predation pressure on the solitary, forest-dwelling sambar.

In Nagarahole National Park in southern India, where tigers can choose from an abundant and diverse assemblage of prey species and sizes, tigers selected large prey, preferring gaur and sambar. Small prey were avoided.[60]

In the Russian Far East, wild pigs and red deer form the bulk of the tiger's diet, although which is the most important species varies annually and from one area to the next.[8,39,67] Together, wild pigs and red deer typically constitute 60 to 84 percent of tiger kills. The importance in the tiger's diet of other ungulates, such as sika deer, roe deer, musk deer, moose, and goral, varies locally and depends largely on the availability of pigs and red deer. Tiger predation on domestic stock has increased as the density of cows and horses on grazing areas adjacent to reserves has increased. During severe winters tigers will even go into remote villages to kill dogs.

Little is known of the tiger's food habits in Southeast Asia, although results from a recent study in Thailand's Huai Kha Khaeng Wildlife Sanctuary show their major prey to be the diminutive (20–28 kilogram) barking deer, or muntjac.[68] The remains of wild pigs, sambar, porcupines, and hog badgers were also found in tiger feces, but these appeared much less frequently. The predominance of barking deer in the diet is unusual and may well be related to the rarity or recent extinction of four other deer species in the study area.

Tigers kill animals from a broad range of age classes, not just the old or the very young. In Kanha, Schaller found that tigers killed adult deer of all ages, including those judged to be in their prime. Fawns were underrepresented in the kill data, but they seldom appear as kills because they are quickly consumed and their remains are not often found. Of the more than two hundred kills examined, none of the prey appeared to have been sick or suffering from a debilitating injury.[11]

The tiger kill data from Chitwan are similar to those from Kanha in that most age classes of deer are represented, including animals that appeared to be healthy, prime adults.[6,11,69] Many of the sambar kills in Chitwan, for example, were of animals judged to be between three and nine years old. There was some indication that tigers killed more male sambar and male chital than expected, and in Kanha, Schaller also found that male sambar were taken more often than females, even though males were less abundant in the population. In Nagarahole National Park, tiger predation was biased toward adult male sambar, chital, and wild pigs, and toward young gaur.[60] Male deer are often assumed to be more vulnerable than females because they tend to be solitary, travel over larger areas, are more conspicuous targets, or may be handicapped in an escape by their antlers or by injuries sustained in fights.

Tigers will kill any animal that puts itself in a vulnerable position, and few animals appear to be immune to tiger predation. Adult rhinoceroses and elephants are rarely killed, but tigers do kill animals that are considerably larger than themselves. Large prey such as water buffalo and gaur can be formidable, however, and there are records of tigers being killed by these animals, though not without a struggle. Anderson recalled a marathon battle in which "the undergrowth had been torn up and trodden down by the combatants, and to one side of this arena lay the carcass of a tiger that had been repeatedly gored and trampled by a bison [gaur]."[54] Foran witnessed an encounter between a tiger and a water buffalo cow in which "she bowled him over like a ninepin, and then rammed him against the thick trunk of a large tamarisk tree." The cow gored the tiger again and again, and then "she lifted that mangled, crushed body on her great horns, gave a sharp twist of her head, and threw the big jungle-cat, as if he were a wisp of straw, some distance away."[70] That large bovids are dangerous prey is also borne out by the fact that tigers in Nagarahole rarely attacked gaur in dense cover (two of sixty-nine kills), whereas most sambar, chital, and wild pig kills were made in dense cover.[59]

In Chitwan, most of the prey killed by tigers weighed 50 to 100 kilograms, although adult male sambar weighing more than 227 kilograms were also killed.[6] The weights of gaur, banteng, and moose killed by tigers have rarely been recorded, although adults of these species typically weigh between 500 and 1,000 kilograms, or about four to seven times the weight of the tiger. In Nagarahole National Park, the average weight of eighty-three tiger kills was 401 kilograms. This sample included several gaur weighing 1,000 kilograms, although using only kill data clearly overestimates the average weight of prey taken.[60]

Tigers use two basic techniques to kill prey. Small animals, or those weighing less than half as much as the tiger, are typically killed with a bite to the back of the neck, while larger animals are suffocated with a throat bite.[6] During the neck bite, a canine tooth is inserted between the neck vertebrae, forcing them apart and breaking the spinal cord. The probability of the cat's canines striking bone, rather than such a small space, would seem high, but cats have numerous mechano-receptors associated with the canines, and the contraction time of their jaw muscles is extremely fast, leading some researchers to suggest that cats "feel" with the ends of their canines for the gaps between the vertebrae.[71,72] In some cases an examination of prey killed by a neck bite revealed the presence of bone splinters, suggesting that not all bites do hit the gaps.[6,43]

Large animals have thick manes, large antlers, horns, and well-muscled necks, so the safest and most efficient method of killing these prey appears to be a throat bite. When it uses this method, the tiger bites the throat of its victim, often just below the junction of the jaw and neck, and crushes the animal's trachea. With its neck held to the ground, the prey cannot right itself or stand. The bite is maintained for several minutes or longer, sometimes even long after the animal has stopped struggling.[13]

Tigers take their prey into cover before beginning to eat. They often start feeding on the rump or buttocks. As the meal progresses, they open the body cavity, remove the stomach, leave it aside, and drag the carcass a short distance before continuing to feed. They typically eat in a prone position, resting on their elbows.

Tigers use their shearing molar teeth (carnassials) to open carcasses and to slice off hunks of meat. They also use the tongue, which is covered with sharp, hard papillae, to rasp flesh from bones. They sometimes grasp a bone between their front paws to steady it while they eat, or place a paw on top of a chunk of meat while they tear off pieces, but only occasionally use their forepaws to handle food. Tigers usually eat and rest intermittently, lying up close to the carcass until most of the edible parts are consumed. In Chitwan, a tigress spent three days on average with each large kill, and during this time consumed an average of 46 kilograms of meat.[6] If the tiger leaves to drink or find another rest site, it usually covers the remains by

raking leaves, dirt, grass, and even rocks over the carcass. After several days of feeding on a large prey, the carcass may be dismembered and the bones scattered over a small area. Small prey are consumed quickly, and animals weighing about 20 kilograms, the size of a barking deer or young chital, can be eaten at a single sitting.

Schaller's work indicates that an adult tiger consumes 18 to 27 kilograms of food in a night;[11] McDougal recorded that a large male ate 35 kilograms of meat in one night.[43] A tigress in Chitwan killed an adult female chital about mid-morning, and by the next morning only skin and bones remained. She had consumed about 30 kilograms of meat.[6] Larger kills, such as sambar and gaur, provide the tiger with food for more than a week, and enormous quantities of meat are eaten.[73] However, even large kills may not last long if the kill is shared among several tigers. In Chitwan, a tigress accompanied by two large young consumed 102 kilograms in two days, or about 17 kilograms per day per animal. On another occasion, a large domestic buffalo plus an adult cow were eaten in six days by four tigers. A large male fed on these kills for four days, then left, and a tigress with two large cubs then fed on the kills for two days. These tigers consumed an estimated 195 kilograms of meat and ate all the edible parts of the carcasses.[6] The maximum amount a tiger can eat in 24 hours is about one-fifth of its own body weight, which for a large male translates into 45 kilograms. While finishing a large carcass, tigers may spend more than half their time eating decomposing meat. In hot weather, meat putrefies in a couple of days, but tigers will continue to feed from a large carcass for four or five days, despite the fact that the meat is liquefying and covered with maggots.

The tiger's strength is legendary, and there are many stories about this cat's amazing ability to move a carcass that is several times heavier than itself. One account from Myanmar mentions a tiger dragging away a gaur bull weighing 770 kilograms, although thirteen men were unable to move the carcass a yard.[20] Several other records mention tigers dragging and carrying large kills for great distances; one tiger reportedly carried a full-grown horse for 500 meters, while another carried an adult heifer up a 12-foot-high embankment. While tigers prefer to take their kills to a quiet, shaded spot to feed—and this usually means dense cover—whether or not a tiger eats its kill on the spot or moves the carcass a great distance may depend on the individual. Jim Corbett gave a wonderful description of the vagaries surrounding the behavior of a tiger with a kill:

> Yesterday the tiger had covered up his kill at the spot where he had done his killing, but today it appeared to be his intention to remove his kill to as distant a place as possible from the scene of the killing. For two miles or more I followed the drag up the steep face of the densely wooded hill to where the tiger, when he had conveyed his heavy burden to within a few hundred yards of the crest, had got one of the cow's hind legs fixed between two oak saplings. With a mighty jerk uphill, the tiger tore the leg off a little below the hock, and leaving that fixed between the saplings went on with his kill. The crest of the hill at the point where the tiger arrived with his kill was flat and overgrown with oak saplings a foot or two feet in girth. Under these trees, where there were no bushes or cover of any kind, the tiger left his kill without making any attempt to cover it up.[74]

What effect predation by tigers has on prey populations is difficult to assess, although the amount of food tigers require can be estimated from individual killing rates and quantities consumed. Not surprisingly, there are few reliable estimates of how often tigers make a kill. The early hunting literature from India contains estimates that vary from 52 to 122 animals per year, but without information on prey size and the number of tigers feeding on the kills, such figures are of little value. Similarly, even when individual tigers are radio-collared and can be followed closely, estimates of the number of prey killed will be biased toward large prey, since small animals are consumed quickly. In Chitwan, radio-collared females without dependent young killed a large animal once every eight or nine days, which translates to approximately forty to forty-six kills per year.[6] Females with cubs need to kill more frequently to satisfy the energy requirements of their growing offspring.

Using the data from Chitwan, and assuming that each tigress makes 45 kills per year and eats 46 kilograms of meat from each kill, yields a figure of 2,070 kilograms of meat consumed in a year.[6] This value is probably realistic, as it is similar to the amount of meat fed to zoo tigers: 5 to 6 kilograms per day. Survey data collected from North American zoos suggest that non-reproducing females need an average of 3.7 kilograms per day, while males require an average of 4.8 kilo-

grams per day.[75] However, not all portions of a prey carcass are edible. The stomach contents, skin, and bones are not usually eaten, and these portions constitute about 30 percent of the prey animal's body weight. Thus, assuming a carcass utilization of 70 percent, for a tigress to obtain 2,070 kilograms, it is necessary for her to kill animals whose combined weight is approximately 3,000 kilograms. Males, lactating females, and tigresses providing for growing cubs would need to kill more, probably requiring some 3,400 kilograms of prey per year. These figures represent the minimum amount needed and presume that no kills are stolen or lost to humans or other predators and scavengers.

A comparison of the prey biomass available with the prey biomass removed annually gives an estimate of the cropping rate (percentage) by tigers. An overall cropping rate for an area combines the amounts removed by all predators in that area. Based on studies conducted in the Serengeti, Coche Cachu National Park, Peru, Nagarahole National Park, and Chitwan, the combined cropping rate of all predators in each of these areas is about 10 percent.[6,73,76,77] Using the minimum amount of food required per tiger, allowances for offtake by other predators, an assumed overall cropping rate of 10 percent, and some assessment of the crude biomass of prey, it is possible to approximate the minimum number of tigers a given area can support. This approximation can then be compared with the number of tigers estimated to be living in the area.

Unfortunately, biomass figures are available for only a handful of sites in Southeast Asia. In Huai Kha Khaeng National Park, where the prey biomass is estimated to be 700 kilograms per square kilometer, an area of 100 square kilometers could support one tiger and four leopards, which approximates the numbers estimated to be in the park.[68,78] At the other end of the scale, prey biomass (excluding elephants) in Nagarahole National Park is an order of magnitude greater at almost 7,658 kilograms per square kilometer.[48] Assuming that a tiger kills 3,000 kilograms of prey per year, a leopard 1,000 kilograms per year, and a dhole 300 kilograms per year, a 100-square-kilometer area in this park could support seventeen tigers, seventeen leopards, and seventeen dholes. Karanth estimated that there were ten to twelve tigers, fifteen leopards, and fourteen dholes per 100 square kilometers in the area.[73] The difference between these two estimates of the number of predators in Nagarahole is largely related to the low carcass utilization rate of tigers there; only an estimated 33 percent of gaur kills and 65 percent of sambar and chital kills were eaten by tigers. Karanth estimated that a tiger actually kills 4,221 kilograms of prey per year, a leopard 1,500 kilograms per year, and a dhole 678 kilograms per year.[73] Somewhere between the low tiger density in Huai Kha Khaeng and the high in Nagarahole National Park lies Chitwan National Park, where in the late 1970s there were an estimated eighteen tigers over two years of age living in a 245-square-kilometer area.[64] This area was considered prime tiger habitat with a prey biomass of 2,798 kilograms per square kilometer.[47,69] Assuming a 10 percent cropping rate and an energy requirement of 3,000 kilograms per tiger, the area could theoretically support twenty-three tigers.

Whether predation has a detrimental effect on individual prey species is difficult to assess because prey densities and sex and age structures are rarely known. However, in Chitwan and Kanha National Parks, where fairly reliable estimates of prey densities are available, tigers do not appear to be limiting prey populations. In Kanha during 1964 and 1965, the annual cropping rate was 20 to 25 percent. Schaller observed that tigers were having a major effect on a small localized population of barasingha, but sambar numbers remained stable, and chital and gaur numbers increased slightly.[11] Similarly, in Chitwan, the number and biomass of most prey species increased between 1974 and 1984, while the resident tiger population remained fairly stable.[44,66,69,79] These findings suggest that predation was ineffective in limiting prey numbers.

The best data available on population structure, density, and biomass of large herbivores come from Nagarahole National Park.[48] In Nagarahole the combined loss to tiger, leopard, and wild dog predation was about 14 percent of the available prey biomass.[73] Predation on chital, gaur, and wild pigs was fairly heavy, but their population densities remained steady or increased, whereas predation on sambar and barking deer appeared to hold their densities below those set by habitat conditions. Why these two species should be limited by predation is not known, although the reason is probably related to their densities and social behavior. Sambar and barking deer population densities are much lower than those of the other ungulates, and more importantly, these two species are solitary, while the others live in groups. Without the benefit of the group's shared vigilance, individual sambar and barking deer appear to be more vulnerable to predation.

The effects of predation can also vary markedly as prey species undergo short-term fluctuations in den-

sity. Wild pigs, for example, appear to be particularly prone to disease-related population crashes, and gaur have been decimated by outbreaks of rinderpest. Within a few months of the onset of an epizootic, gaur and pig numbers may be halved. During the time when pig or gaur numbers are at their nadir, predation may exert a temporary limiting influence by prolonging the recovery period. A further consequence of a reduction in the number of one prey species is that tigers may then begin to hunt a secondary prey species more intensively and, depending on the length of the recovery period, may exert considerable pressure on the secondary prey. Despite these short-term fluctuations in prey numbers and consequent shifts in predation pressure on individual species, predation does not generally appear to limit prey numbers over the long term.

Social Organization

Tiger society, like that of most felids, is characterized by individuals living and hunting by themselves. Individuals encounter one another when traveling, associate for mating, and occasionally share a kill, but the only long-term day-to-day association is between a female and her offspring. Although each tiger hunts alone, it lives its life embedded in a social system that is maintained through a combination of visual signals, scent marks, and vocalizations.

While some signals and advertisements serve to bring tigers together, others serve to maintain spatial separation and to indicate occupancy of space. The pattern of space use by tigers has not, however, been extensively studied. The general impression is that the tiger's land tenure system is flexible and varies with environmental circumstances. In Chitwan, for example, tigresses established and maintained relatively small, exclusive ranges in which they hunted and raised their young. Site fidelity was strong, with individual females occupying the same territories throughout their reproductive lives.[6,43,44,80] Except during periods of social flux, there was little overlap ($<$ 10 percent) among the ranges of neighboring females. The average home range size of tigresses residing on the prey-rich floodplain was a diminutive 20 square kilometers. Some female territories were as small as 10 square kilometers; the largest was 51 square kilometers. The variation in range sizes was attributed to differences in prey density.[6,44] Home range sizes of females in Nagarahole, where prey densities are higher than in Chitwan, are also small, about 15 to 20 square kilometers.[73]

Adult male tigers in Chitwan also maintained mutually exclusive ranges, but their territories were two to fifteen times larger than those of females.[6,43,64] Each male's range typically overlapped several female ranges, and variation in male territory sizes reflected the number of females within an individual male's domain. The largest territory was that of a male whose range overlapped the ranges of seven females.[80] The much larger ranges of males obviously contain more than enough food, water, and den sites to satisfy their needs, and emphasize that females, rather than food, are the most sought-after resources for males. Males compete for access to females, whereas females compete for access to resources vital for rearing young.

Tigers living in the Russian Far East are influenced by the same factors as tigers in Chitwan, but environmental conditions differ dramatically between the two areas, and thus land tenure patterns differ as well. On the eastern slopes of the Sikhote-Alin mountain range, for example, Siberian tigers live in areas of mixed coniferous and broad-leaved deciduous forest. The terrain is broken, hilly, and dissected by river valleys. In winter, the higher elevations are dominated by a continental climate, with bitter cold and deep snow, whereas slightly more favorable temperatures and snow depths occur along the coast, which is warmed by the Sea of Japan. A variety of prey, including wild pigs, red deer, roe deer, sika deer, and goral, reach maximum densities in this region, but prey biomass is at least an order of magnitude less than that found in Chitwan. Furthermore, in Sikhote-Alin, many prey migrate in large numbers to winter feeding areas along the coast. Thus, to meet their energy demands, tigers in this area must travel widely. Based on snow tracking data, the range sizes of female and male tigers in Sikhote-Alin were estimated at 200 to 400 square kilometers and 800 to 1,000 square kilometers, respectively.[38] These estimates appear to be close to the mark, as recent radio-tracking data show that female ranges in Sikhote-Alin are about 450 square kilometers, and male ranges are estimated to be 25 to 50 percent larger.[61] Each male's range overlaps those of one to three females, but male ranges overlap almost completely. Males do not, however, tend to use the same area at the same time. Female ranges appear to be territories, as there is little overlap between the ranges of neighboring adult females.

The ranges of tigers in Sikhote-Alin are about ten to twenty times larger than those in Chitwan, and overlap in male ranges is much more extensive. These differences are certainly due to differences in prey density and to the fact that prey are migratory; the degree of range overlap for males may be because it is energetically too expensive to try to exclude same-sex adults when ranges become so large. While the land tenure patterns of tigers in Chitwan and in Sikhote-Alin are different in some respects, they appear to illustrate the two extremes; observations of tigers from other places show variations on this common theme.[11,62,81]

Within this social system, both male and female tigers communicate via a combination of scent marks, visual signals, and vocalizations. Of these communication signals, scent marks are probably the most important. Scent is deposited as an odorous musky liquid known as "marking fluid," which cubs apparently do not produce.[82,83,84] Marking fluid, which is often mixed with urine, is sprayed backward onto upright objects from a standing position, resulting in an enhanced odor field. Scent may also be deposited on the feces from the anal glands, the secretions of which are chemically similar to marking fluid.[85] Tigers also rub the head and cheeks on objects that they have sprayed, possibly as a way to enhance their own "odor field." Visual signals include spots that have been sprayed; scrapes, which the animal makes by raking the ground with its hind feet; claw marks; and feces left in conspicuous places.

No one knows what these marks and signs convey to another animal, but there is evidence that the information includes individual identity, sex, reproductive condition, and the time the mark was made.[86,87] A tiger encountering a scent mark can tell whether the mark was made the previous day or a week ago, whether the sprayer was male or female, and, more than likely, the status of the sprayer and the likelihood of an encounter.

All this information in the form of scent is deposited along a network of commonly used travel routes to indicate that an area is occupied or being used. The marks do not necessarily exclude other tigers from an area, but the observation that transients or floaters do not remain long in occupied ranges indicates that they may be at a disadvantage. There are no direct observations as to whether these transient tigers scent-mark or not, but subadult tigers rarely scent-mark, and data from other carnivore species, such as foxes and servals, suggest that non–territory holders scent-mark infrequently or not at all.[86,87]

In Chitwan, where males and females have exclusive territories, boundaries are marked more frequently than the interiors of ranges, and the most intensive marking occurs where major trails intersect or run along a mutual boundary. Female residents mark at closer intervals and at more numerous sites than do males. On one occasion, two radio-tagged tigresses were monitored for six hours one night as they walked along their common boundary. The second tigress followed the same route as the first and visited all the same landmarks, only an hour later. Both tigresses scent-marked many trees and bushes along the boundary. Another tigress almost doubled her rate of scent marking at a boundary, from nineteen to thirty-seven trees per month, when a new female began using the adjoining area.[88]

Tigers also scent-mark intensively when they are establishing a territory. While acquiring a territory, a three-year-old tigress in Chitwan visited a 500-meter stretch of boundary eight times per month over a four-month period, and during this time she sprayed an average of forty-nine trees per month. During the same period, a long-term resident female in the adjoining range visited this same stretch about half as often and sprayed only twenty-five trees per month.[88]

Scent marks also serve to bring animals together for mating purposes. Females appear to be receptive to a male's advances for only two or three days of each estrous cycle, so it is important that the male find the female and that his visits coincide with her peak of receptivity. Studies in captivity show that tigresses scent-mark more frequently just before they are ready to mate,[89] which in the wild would function to ensure that a male is in attendance at the correct time.

Observations of free-living tigresses show a similar pattern. In the wild, a tigress's rate of scent marking increases to a peak just prior to estrus, then declines sharply during and after estrus.[80] On one occasion in Chitwan, a tigress that was presumed to be in estrus scent-marked along a road at twice her normal marking rate. A few days later, when the resident male appeared, the pair walked down the same road together, but she did not scent-mark. On another occasion, a female's estrus was precipitated by the loss of her 11-day-old cubs in a grass fire. Within two weeks of the death of her cubs, the tigress increased her rate of scent marking, and one day her tracks were followed for about 3 kilometers, over which she had scent-marked seventeen trees and one bush. The tigress had scent-marked along this same path on other occasions, but at a much lower frequency. Two weeks later the resident male arrived, and the couple spent two days together, probably mating.[6]

To convey information to others, scent marks must be placed in conspicuous, accessible places and kept up to date. Urine is usually sprayed onto elevated spots, which creates a larger odor field than if it were sprayed onto the ground. Scent marks are typically directed at tree trunks, bushes, and rocks, and the objects marked are almost invariably within a few feet of trails. Such marks have the advantage of being both visible and readily accessible. The undersides of leaning trees and rock overhangs are favorite marking sites, presumably because they are sheltered and offer protection from rain.

Because scent fades, scent marks must be regularly renewed. Evidence from the field suggests that territory holders renew their scent marks roughly every three weeks. Interestingly, this interval coincides with the observation that for wolves, the stimulus value of scent marks drops to zero after approximately twenty-three days.[90] In Chitwan, both male and female tigers visited all portions of their ranges at intervals that varied from a few days to two weeks.[6] On three occasions when a resident tigress did not renew her scent marks (presumably because she had died), about one month elapsed before another female moved into the vacant area.[88] In a similar incident, a male took one month to expand his range into an area left vacant by the death of his neighbor. Even though the male's expanded territory was now twice as large as his former area, he still visited all portions of it every two weeks—the same rate at which he had moved about the smaller range. The fact that this male revisited all parts of his range every two weeks, and presumably marked or re-marked the area, indicates that the movements of a resident male are dictated as much by the need to reinforce these "ownership" signs as by the need to find food and check on the reproductive condition of females within his range.

The general picture, then, is of a great deal of information being laid down as scent and sign, but at different rates by different individuals in a variety of social and spatial contexts. Furthermore, some odors may serve a variety of social functions. While there are few cases in which a particular function can be assigned to a scent, it is nevertheless clear that the lives of these solitary but not asocial felids are largely governed and regulated by a complicated amalgam of chemical and visual signals.

Tigers also communicate by vocalizing. Some of their vocalizations are capable of traveling long distances through dense vegetation; others are used at close quarters to exchange information during face-to-face encounters. These vocalizations may be modified by varying the intensity, duration, and rate of emission. Overall, the tiger's vocal repertoire is as varied as that of the social lion.

According to Gustav Peters, who has worked extensively on carnivore vocalizations, tigers have several types of vocalizations, including a main call, prusten, growl, snarl, grunt, moan, mew/meow, spit, and hiss.[91,92,93] They also have what is termed a coughing snarl, which is a short, harsh, loud call made with the mouth open and the teeth bared. This coughing snarl is used almost exclusively when attacking. Hunters have described the tiger making a "pooking" sound that resembles the alarm call of the sambar deer, one of the tiger's main prey species. Schaller looked at the contexts in which this call was given and came to the conclusion that the sound "serves to advertise the animal's presence and prevent sudden encounters."[11] Tigers also make a "woof" noise, which is not heard very often. They sometimes give a short, explosive woof if they are startled or surprised, as when they are hit with a tranquilizer dart.

The vocalization that most people associate with the tiger is the roar, but according to Peters, tigers are technically not one of the roaring cats. Tigers have a flexible hyoid apparatus and vocal folds with a thick fibro-elastic pad (characteristics associated with roaring cats), but a detailed analysis of the tiger's "roar" shows differences in several critical features from the roars of the lion, leopard, and jaguar.[93] It is nevertheless a well-known vocalization. Schaller describes it as "a resonant and rolling a-a-u-u-u or a-o-o-o-nh, produced by expelling the air through the open mouth while progressively closing it."[11] This call carries well and is easily heard by humans over distances of at least 3 kilometers. Roaring has been heard in a variety of contexts, including such diverse circumstances as after a tiger has killed a large animal, as a prelude to mating, during mating, and when a female is beckoning her young. The situations in which the roar is used, coupled with its propagational qualities, indicate that the call is used mainly for long-distance communication. How other tigers respond to the call obviously depends on the message, but it nevertheless advertises the caller's presence and location.

Moaning is a vocalization that is often described as a subdued roar. This call is made with the mouth partly open or closed and, like the roar, is often given as the animal walks along with its head down. Moaning does not, however, have the intensity of roaring, and is generally audible over distances of less than 400 meters.

Some, but not all, tigresses advertise sexual receptivity with bouts of roaring. In Chitwan, a female began "roaring" when she came into her first heat, continued to call during five consecutive estrous periods, and then stopped. When she first began to call, she did so only a few times each night, but after two or three days the call frequency increased until she was calling day and night. On two different occasions she roared sixty-nine times in fifteen minutes. The roaring clearly served to summon a male, for the resident male usually arrived within twenty-four hours, often announcing his appearance with his own series of roars. However, roaring during estrus appears to be idiosyncratic, as other tigresses in the same area rarely called when in heat, and even the tigress who roared during five consecutive estrous cycles did not call during subsequent heats.[6] In general, though, observers have noted that tigers roar more often during the peak mating period than at any other time.

Tigers also have several vocalizations that function in close-range situations for greeting, reassurance, appeasement, and aggression. Both the friendly and the threatening vocalizations are accompanied by body postures and facial expressions. The friendly sounds include prusten and grunts.[91,92] Prusten, a staccato puffing sound that is audible only at close range, is an integral part of the tiger's greeting behavior. It is produced by the forced exhalation of air through the nostrils and mouth, which results in a fluttering action of the lips. Tigresses use these friendly sounds most often with their young to maintain contact and give instructions, and both sexes give these vocalizations during courtship and mating.

Facial markings also play a role in close-range communication. The stripes and marks on a tiger's face and body are unique to each individual, and even a human observer can identify individuals from these markings. No one knows whether tigers themselves use these markings to recognize each other, but more than likely they make use of a combination of odor and appearance to identify neighbors and relatives.

The backs of the tiger's ears are marked with a prominent central white spot. During aggressive interactions the ears are twisted and flattened so that this conspicuous spot is facing forward, suggesting a possible intimidation function. The white ear spots may also function as signals to cubs to "follow me," as even in dim light or dense vegetation the spots are visible to cubs trailing behind their mother.

By staying on the move and regularly visiting all parts of his territory, a male can keep track of the reproductive condition of the various females living there. Males may also be alerted to a female's impending receptivity by her roaring, and these calls have been known to attract several males, who may end up fighting for the right to mate.

Hanley witnessed three males fighting over a tigress. He watched from a tree as a tigress called and was answered by three males. The first male emerged from the forest and walked toward the female, who crouched in front of him.

> But he did not get far. Quite suddenly, from a thicket near him, I saw a flash of black and red flying through the air, as a huge tiger, nearly as large as he was, almost landed on top of him. The first tiger sprang nimbly aside to avoid his attacker, and, snarling and growling with rage, he crouched low to face his adversary, which quickly sprang around. Both animals were now crouching low, their eyes narrowed to slits, the ears turned back flat on their heads, their tails lashing furiously from side to side. In a moment they came to grips, and the jungle resounded with the noise of growls and roars; and while it continued the sleek young tigress sat placidly watching the fight, cleaning her fur with her tongue.[94]

During the fight, Hanley spotted a third male sitting in the bushes nearby. When one male opened a large wound on the neck of the other, the wounded tiger broke off the fight and fled. The victor, who was also limping and injured, then approached the tigress, only to be attacked by the third male. The newcomer drove off the exhausted and injured winner of the first fight and commenced his courtship of the tigress.

While males obviously compete for mating opportunities, the frequency of serious fights probably depends on the density of tigers in an area, whether the social system is currently in a state of flux, and the age and physical condition of the resident male. Where residents have well-established ranges, the turnover rate is low, social disruption from intruders is minimal, and fights are probably rare. Fighting is likely to increase when a resident male is deposed or dies and new males struggle to take control. During times of social flux, serious fights may also occur between females.[43,44,64,80]

Intraspecific strife is likely to become more common in many parts of the tigers' geographic range as protected populations of tigers increase. Unfortunately, most of these populations are isolated and confined to small protected areas, and young tigers, who would normally leave and settle elsewhere, are unable to disperse. Any situation that results in tigers being concentrated in an area can increase social tension, competition, and consequently, the number of fights. At high tiger densities, fights between males over estrous females are also likely to become more common as more males compete for limited chances to mate.

Reproduction and Development
Mating opportunities for males are limited because in areas where food is plentiful, tigresses are usually pregnant or accompanied by dependent young.[6,43,64,95] During this time the female is in anestrus, and as a result, she may be sexually receptive only once every two years. Anestrus, the period when estrus is suspended, can also be environmentally induced. In subtropical and tropical parts of the world tigers may mate and give birth at any time of year, but Siberian tigers appear to be seasonal breeders, and there may be a seven- or eight-month anestrous period between breeding seasons. While newborn Siberian cubs have been found in the wild in all months of the year, in captivity most births occur between April and June,[8,96] which would seem to ensure that cubs are not born in the depths of winter or when food is least available.

When tigresses are reproductively active, they come into estrus about every twenty-five days.[96] Estrus is preceded by an increase in scent marking, which presumably ensures that a male will be present at the appropriate time. Radiotelemetry studies in Nepal showed that tigresses rarely spent more than a few hours with a male except when mating, and that the interval between these mating associations was commonly twenty-five days.[6] Typically, a tigress would increase her rate of scent marking, the resident male would arrive, and the couple would spend two days together, after which the male would leave. If the mating did not result in conception, the female would continue to cycle, and the male would return twenty-five days later.

In captivity, estrus in tigers is usually signaled by an increase in the frequency of calling and rolling and rubbing on objects.[89] Studies at the Minnesota Zoological Gardens on the reproductive cycle of Siberian tigers have relied on behavioral changes and hormonal assays of blood to indicate when females are in estrus. Their findings show that the average length of estrus is five days and that the interval between estrous cycles is about twenty-five days. Of the five tigresses studied intensively, one ovulated spontaneously while the other four appeared to be induced ovulators. During the study, two almost double-length (forty-two-day) cycles were recorded for one female. This interval is similar to the forty-nine-day cycles reported for captive Bengal tigers in four zoos, although those cycles were based on behavioral correlates and do not include hormonal data.[96,97]

Although the average length of estrus in the Minnesota studies was five days, there are other observations of males and females consorting for weeks and even longer, and in zoos some tigers have continued to mate for as long as twenty-one days. Individual differences may account for some of the variation in how often and for how long the pair stays together, and prolonged associations have also been noted for sexually inexperienced animals, suggesting that familiarization is an important prelude to mating. In Ranthambhore National Park, Fateh Singh and Valmik Thapar watched a courtship that went on for more than a month. "As the days passed the pair became very vocal, often filling the night air with the widest range of growls, cries and moans I have ever heard. Kublai's interest seemed to be growing day by day. More and more frequently we would observe him nuzzling Noon or, when the two were apart, sniffing the ground where she had walked or rested. Their interactions seemed to be increasing in intensity all the time." No copulations were observed during the month-long association, but the pair were seen mating after thirty-five days of regular interaction.[63]

A receptive tigress is both provocative and aggressive, alternately vocalizing and rolling on the ground in front of the male, then spitting and striking at him with her claws. The male has to be accepted by the female, so he does not retaliate, but presses on with his advances. Gradually the female's behavior changes and she permits him to approach. Kailash Sankhala, former director of the Delhi Zoo, graphically describes one such encounter:

> The tigress "kisses" the tiger—bites him gently —turns, rubs her body against his, raises her tail, and finally presents herself by sitting with forelimbs fully extended and hind-legs more than half-bent. The tiger mounts her in a half-knees-

bent position without putting any pressure on her body and she emits low, deep "Oaar oaaa" sounds. As the act comes to a climax, the tiger lowers his head and grips the skin folds of her neck firmly but carefully; this position helps both to achieve proper orientation at the time of the climax. The tiger then gives the peculiar high-pitched squeal . . . , the tigress growls, and finally gives a sudden jerk to dislodge the male. She turns round to face the tiger and starts boxing.[28]

The amount of aggressive behavior on the part of the female varies depending on the individual, her age and experience, and whether she is familiar with the male. If pairs are accustomed to each other, females usually show less aggressive behavior. There is less snarling and spitting during the preliminaries, and the tigress often does not strike at the male after copulation. When a tigress is in estrus for the first time, she may be intimidated by the male and rebuff his advances; data from zoos suggest that a period of familiarization must occur before mating is successful. One young tigress in Chitwan was found consorting with a male during her first seven estrous periods, but did not become pregnant, although it is unknown whether mating actually occurred. On the eighth occasion the pair mated successfully, and about three months later the tigress gave birth to her first litter.[6]

Tigers, like lions, copulate frequently. Despite some records of spontaneous ovulation, the general consensus is that felids are induced ovulators. This means that females require a certain number of copulations within a critical period of time to stimulate ovulation. Most of the information on copulation frequency comes from zoos. Sankhala reports, "On the first day of oestrus the frequency of copulation is low, increasing on the third day to as many as 52 times. From the fifth day on it declines."[28] Another observation of captive Bengal tigers records seventeen copulations in a day, and in the wild, eight copulations were seen in eighty-eight minutes.[63] The duration of each copulation is short, typically less than fifteen seconds.[98]

A tigress's pregnancy lasts for about 103 days. She may give birth to one to seven young, although a tigress in the wild is rarely accompanied by more than two or three cubs. In Nepal, the average size of 49 litters was 2.98.[80] In zoos, the average litter size at birth is 2.8, and equal numbers of males and females are born. In India and Southeast Asia cubs may be born at any time of the year; zoo data from India indicate that there may be a birth peak in March–June and another smaller peak in August–October.[28] Data from Nepal suggest that most births there occur from May to July, with a minor peak in December.[80] Siberian tigers have a more definite birth peak, and data on 530 litters born in zoos in the Northern Hemisphere show that most cubs are born in the spring, between April and June.[96]

Shortly before the birth, the tigress selects a secluded place to have her young. The birth den may be in a rock crevice or cave, an impenetrable thicket, or a shallow depression in dense grass. The cubs are born blind and helpless, weighing 785 to 1,610 grams, but they grow fast and often quadruple their birth weight by the time they are a month old.[99] Their eyes may open any time between six and twelve days of age, but they remain shortsighted and somewhat bleary-eyed for another month.

During the first few weeks of the cubs' lives the tigress spends most of her time at the den, leaving only for short periods to drink or hunt. Her movements are greatly curtailed by the need to attend to her small cubs, and for the first month after the cubs' birth her range shrinks dramatically to a fraction of its former size.[6]

Observations of early maternal behavior in captivity show that in the first day after giving birth a tigress spends 70 percent of the daylight hours engaged in nursing her young. By ten days after birth this proportion drops to 60 percent, and by the time the cubs are forty days old, about 30 percent of daylight hours are spent in suckling. The proportion drops to 10 percent by the time the cubs are three months old, which corresponds to the time of weaning at 90 to 100 days of age.[28]

Tigresses are extremely cautious and secretive when they have young cubs, and will often move them to a new den if disturbed or threatened. In Ranthambhore National Park a tigress had hidden her fifteen- to twenty-day-old cubs in a ravine near the main road, which would normally not have been a problem, but at this time of year the road was being used by thousands of pilgrims. After threatening the pilgrims several times, the female moved her young to a safer den.[62] In Chitwan, a tigress with six-week-old cubs repeatedly charged and threatened villagers who were cutting grass near the den site. After four days of encounters with grass cutters, the tigress moved her litter to an area well away from their activities.[6] The same tigress attacked a researcher in a tree when he got too close to her four-day-old cubs, but did not move this particular litter after that incident.[49]

Although tiger cubs have a full set of milk teeth by the time they are a month old, they do not begin to eat solid food until they are six to eight weeks old. At this age their mother brings them pieces of meat or leads them to kills near the den.[28,62] Jim Corbett watched a tigress lead her two small cubs to a dead cow and described how the cubs followed step by step in her tracks, never attempting to pass each other or her, avoiding every obstacle that she avoided, no matter how small it was, and remaining rigidly motionless when she stopped to listen every few yards.[74]

Cubs continue to suckle as long as they are allowed to, sometimes until they are five or six months old, but by the time they reach this age most of their nutritional requirements are met by solid food. Lactation imposes enormous caloric demands on a female. Zookeepers remark that it is almost impossible to overfeed growing cubs and lactating females, and in the wild this period corresponds to a time when females are under enormous nutritional stress. Even when lactation ends, meeting the energy demands of growing young requires a great deal of effort. A tigress with cubs not only has to spend more time hunting and make more kills, but also has to contend with interference from her cubs, who by this time are following her around. To satisfy the needs of two cubs, a tigress must increase her killing rate by an estimated 50 percent. In Chitwan, for example, a tigress with two eight-month-old young made a large kill every five to six days, compared with one kill every eight days when she was on her own.[6]

For young cubs, the vicinity of a kill can be a dangerous place because of the likelihood of encountering other tigers there. There are records of males killing cubs, and some of these instances of infanticide occurred at kills. Bait sites are also dangerous places. Some tourist operations have used live buffalo as baits to attract tigers to sites where they can be viewed from a hide by tourists. Chuck McDougal has found that tigresses with small cubs rarely take buffalo used as baits, but those with older, and less vulnerable, young make much more frequent use of such baits. A female with large but still dependent young may have difficulty securing enough food to feed her offspring, and a tethered buffalo must present quite an attractive meal.[100]

Cubs begin to follow their mother when they are about two months old. At this age they do not join her in the hunt, but wait quietly until she calls them. The tigress often makes a kill, feeds for a short time, then drags or carries the carcass to a safe place near the cubs. At this point she will go and fetch the cubs and lead them to the carcass. When her cubs are small, the tigress will take endless pains to avoid potential danger, and even the most habituated females, who allow tourists to view them with impunity, almost totally disappear during the first few months of their cubs' lives.

At four months of age a tiger cub is about the size of a setter dog, and spends its time play-wrestling with its siblings, jumping on its mother, and pouncing on unwary insects and sticks around the den. By six months cubs are weaned, but lack the ability or skill to kill for themselves. Though they sometimes succeed in killing small animals and birds, they lack the permanent canine teeth needed to dispatch larger prey. These long, daggerlike teeth are essential for delivering the killing bite and are also important instruments for slicing through the tough skin of a carcass.

Cubs put on weight rapidly, and males grow faster than females. At six months of age males weigh 90 to 105 pounds, whereas females are about 30 pounds lighter. The weight difference increases as they get older, and by the time they are eighteen months old a male may weigh a hundred pounds more than his sister. The appearance of permanent canine teeth between twelve and eighteen months of age heralds a period of rapid weight gain, and the young are now physically equipped to make their own kills, though they still have to refine their hunting techniques.[28,64,95]

Young tigers learn to kill for themselves by imitation and practice, and their mother provides them with opportunities to test their skills. Partly because they lack the permanent canines, but also because of inexperience, even quite large cubs are often unable to kill a tethered buffalo. They bite and claw the unfortunate beast, sometimes managing to pull it down, but they do not seem quite sure where or how the killing bite should be delivered.

George Schaller vividly describes a scene he witnessed in Kanha National Park when a tigress was teaching her three twelve-month-old cubs how to kill. As he watched at a bait site, a tethered buffalo kept the three cubs at bay for two and a half hours. When the tigress arrived, she grabbed the buffalo by the hind leg and threw it to the ground. The cubs leaped onto it, biting and clawing at random, while the tigress released her grip and stepped back. The buffalo shook the cubs off and struggled to its feet with only superficial wounds. The cubs tried again, with the same lack of success, until the tigress threw the buffalo to the ground with the same technique she had used earlier. Once again the cubs swarmed over the buffalo, biting and clawing, but as soon as the tigress released her hold, the buffalo once again rose to its feet. The buffalo was finally killed, but it was a war of attrition. Schaller observes that the cubs seemed to be "reasonably adept at pulling it down but they failed to kill efficiently, largely confining their attack to biting and clawing around the rump, back, and belly rather than grasping the throat."[11]

Male cubs learn to kill on their own and become independent sooner than females. By fifteen months of age males often leave their mother for several days at a time while they test their independence. Females seem to develop more slowly and stay with their mother for longer. In Chitwan, two eighteen-month-old siblings occasionally shared a kill with their mother, and even though they still used her range, they spent more time together than they did with their mother. At this age the male cub, who weighed 350 pounds, began to wander outside his mother's range, and within a month was covering an area of 18 square miles, ranging over almost exactly the same area as his father. His sister stayed within the boundaries of their mother's 8-square-mile range for another six months before dispersing.[6]

Dispersal is a major event in the life of a young tiger because it represents a time of exploration—of movement into unknown terrain—in search of an area where it can settle and begin its own reproductive life. Dispersal is a difficult phenomenon to study, and the movements and fates of dispersers are rarely known. Surprisingly, tigers are one of the few carnivores for which we have some dispersal data, largely due to a landmark study by Dave Smith. Despite the enormous logistic difficulties associated with trying to keep track of an animal that ranges as widely as a tiger, Smith managed to monitor the movements of fourteen radio-tagged subadults in Chitwan.[95]

Smith found that young tigers became independent of their mothers at seventeen to twenty-four months of age, but continued to hunt in their natal range. This pattern is common to many mammals and allows the young to hone their hunting skills in a familiar area. After moving independently within their mother's range for a few months, the young dispersed, usually when they were eighteen to twenty-eight months old. Dispersal seems to be keyed to the mother's reproductive state, as subadults usually leave when their mother's new litter is about six weeks old and becoming mobile. One tigress had a litter that dispersed at nineteen months of age, but in this case her new cubs were only about a month old. These new cubs stayed with her for three years, probably because she did not have another litter.

Young males dispersed farther than females; the average dispersal distance for Smith's ten males was 33 kilometers, whereas the four females moved an average of 9.7 kilometers. Males were also more likely to get into serious fights or be killed during this phase of their lives. Smith documented one occasion when a subadult male killed a buffalo bait that had been tied beside the main park road and dragged it into thick cover to feed. The following morning, the area's resident male tiger was walking down the road, encountered the scene of the kill, and followed the drag mark into the bushes. A fight ensued in which large amounts of blood were lost, and the younger tiger appeared to have been severely wounded.

Young males tended to settle temporarily in marginal habitats, such as the heavily grazed forest areas bordering the park. Males also were less successful than females at establishing breeding territories; only four of the ten males managed to breed. Of the six males that did not breed, two died from injuries sustained in fights with other tigers, two were poisoned, and another disappeared from an area near a village after a man was killed. The remaining male was injured in a fight with another male tiger and would have died from his wounds, but following treatment was returned to the wild. He was subsequently removed from the wild following his fatal attack on a villager.

All four females established breeding territories, and three of the four females settled next to their mothers. The fourth female moved back and forth along a 30-kilometer belt of prime riverine habitat that was occupied by her mother and six other breeding tigresses. She crisscrossed this floodplain thirteen times in eight months before finally settling on an island 30 kilometers from her natal area. During the time she was searching for a place to settle, the young tigress traveled a minimum of 600 kilometers, crisscrossing the floodplain roughly every two and a half weeks.[95] Interestingly, this two-and-a-half-week interval corresponds to the frequency at which residents revisit and re-mark their ranges.

Two of the four females usurped parts of their mothers' territories. This pattern of daughters settling next to their mothers resulted in a neighborhood consisting of clusters of closely related females, like a dispersed lion pride. Over a nine-year period there were thirteen cases of related females becoming neighbors. Seven of the relationships were mother-daughter, two were sisters, and four were half-sisters. The minimum degree of relatedness among these females was 0.35, or roughly the same as has been recorded for lionesses in a pride.[44,95]

Young tigers continue to grow and put on muscle until they are about five years old; this prolonged period of growth is more evident in males than in females. Males become sexually mature at three to four years of age, and they generally take longer than females to acquire breeding territories. Females, on the other hand, become sexually mature when they are about three years old, but do not generally conceive until about six months later. Thus, a young tigress might have a first litter by the time she is three and a half or four years old.[80]

Once a tiger has managed to acquire a territory, the object is to maintain it for as long as possible because the longer an animal holds a territory, the more offspring it can produce. There are accounts of tigers staying in particular areas for several years, and some individuals have reportedly resided in the same area for fourteen to twenty years. These durations may be somewhat exaggerated, but they do indicate that under some circumstances tigers may reside in one area for a long time.

In Chitwan, females spent their entire reproductive lives in one area, and most were long-term residents, holding their territories for an average of seven years. Four females lived to be over twelve years old, and three of these produced four litters each. The other female, who was at least fifteen years old, produced five litters containing a total of sixteen known cubs. Eight of those cubs survived to dispersal age.[80]

Tigresses have a high reproductive potential. They normally give birth to a new litter every two years, but are capable of having more than one litter in a year if their cubs die.[80] In zoos, where cubs are sometimes removed for hand rearing, there are records of tigresses having as many as three litters in one year. In Ranthambhore one tigress had three litters at approximately three-year intervals. Amazingly, she was able to raise ten cubs from these three litters.[62] In Chitwan the interbirth interval was about two years, and most tigresses were either pregnant or accompanied by dependent young.[6,80] Little is known of the reproductive success of tigresses living in less productive habitats, although cub survival is likely to be less than in the higher-quality areas. In Chitwan, first-year cub mortality was estimated to be 34 percent, and in most cases entire litters were lost.[80]

The reproductive tenure of males is not as well known, but appears to be shorter than that of females. Male reproductive success varies greatly. In Chitwan, one radio-collared male managed to maintain control of an area containing seven females for at least four years, fathering twenty-seven cubs. Other males never managed to establish breeding territories or did not hold a territory long enough for the female to rear a litter.[80] As observed in lions, following the takeover of a male tiger's territory, the new male is likely to kill the small cubs of any tigresses in his territory, thereby inducing the females to come into estrus and mate. Unless the female's receptivity is advanced, a male may not be able to maintain control of his territory long enough for her to rear their young to independence, about two years.

Captive tigers have lived for as long as twenty-six years, and twenty years is not uncommon.[101] The oldest female to give birth in captivity gave birth to a single cub at the Rotterdam Zoo at seventeen years of age.[102] However, the life span in the wild is certainly much shorter, and a female is undoubtedly doing well if she reaches fourteen or fifteen.

STATUS IN THE WILD

Today, three of the eight tiger subspecies are extinct. The Bali (*Panthera tigris balica*) subspecies disappeared in the 1940s, and the most recent extinction was the Javan subspecies (*P. t. sondaica*), which had disappeared by about 1980.[38] The last record of a Caspian tiger (*P. t. virgata*) was in 1968, along the lower reaches of the Amu Darya River near the Aral Sea.[46]

Of the five remaining subspecies, the South China tiger (*P. t. amoyensis*) is one of the most critically endangered. In 1949 this subspecies was believed to number 4,000 individuals, but it was declared a pest and persecuted relentlessly. By 1980 over 3,000 skins had been collected. The South China tiger was given nominal protection in 1977, but the population had already been reduced to about 100 animals. The decline continues today. There are believed to be 30 to 50 animals remaining in the wild and another 32 in zoos in China. A field survey between October 1990 and February 1991 in southeastern China by Gary Koehler indicates that this subspecies still exists in scattered locations. In his report to WWF-International, he states, "Tracks and scrapes made by tigers were observed in the mountainous regions of northern Guangdong, southern, eastern and northern Hunan, and western Fujian Provinces. Reports indicate that tigers may also occur in central Jiangxi. There is evidence that reproduction is occurring in southern and northern Hunan and western Fujian."[41]

The continued existence of the South China tiger is precarious because not only has the subspecies been reduced to a few individuals, but the habitat of the remaining tigers is fragmented and exploited. Large ungulate prey occur in scattered patches of habitat among the mountains of Guangdong, Fujian, Hunan, and Jiangxi provinces, but these islands of forest are small—less than 50,000 hectares—and isolated by agriculture and forestry monocultures. The tigers remaining in these isolated patches continue to be threatened by habitat loss, capture in traps set for ungulates, and competition with humans for prey. Though the authorities maintain that the South China tiger is no longer hunted, knowledgeable people say that the cat is still poached, especially for bones and body parts, which are in great demand for traditional medicines.[41,103]

Tiger bone has been used in traditional Chinese medicine for more than a thousand years. Bones are used to calm fright and to cure dysentery, ulcers, rat bite sores, and prolapse of the anus. Powdered bone is applied to burns and eruptions under the toenail, and a bath in bone broth protects against devil possession, boils, scabies, rheumatism, and convulsions. Twenty-five kinds of Chinese medicinal drugs contain tiger bone, and in 1985 there were over 110 pharmaceutical factories producing medicines with tiger ingredients. Because of the medicinal effect attributed to it, tiger bone is now more valuable than tiger skin. The price of tiger bone varies from place to place, but traders reportedly pay poachers U.S.$130 per kilogram in Nepal, $130–175 per kilogram in Vietnam, and as much as $300 per kilogram in Russia. In seven nations within the tiger's range, one tiger skeleton is worth more than ten years' salary.[104,105] A small tiger can yield 7 kilograms of bone.[106]

The Siberian tiger is another subspecies in jeopardy. In the early 1940s the population of Siberian tigers in the Soviet Far East was estimated at 30 individuals. The Soviets imposed an official ban on tiger hunting in 1952, and since then numbers have steadily increased. In 1971 a tiger census along the Pacific seaboard of the Soviet Union found that there were approximately 130 Siberian tigers left in the Russian Far

East, and by 1985 the numbers had increased to an estimated 430.[39,67] A 1996 survey estimated that 350 to 450 tigers remained in the wild.[42] The Siberian subspecies also occurs in northeastern China, where about 30 animals were believed to remain, but none were recorded there during a survey in 1987. Subsequently, a tigress with a cub was seen in the area in late 1990. A 1998 survey suggested that 4 to 6 tigers may have been present in Jilin Province, but prey populations were low, and tracks of red deer and wild pigs were found on only a few occasions.[107] Efforts to conserve the Siberian subspecies are now focused on creating a core network of protected areas.[108]

At the turn of the twentieth century, there were so many tigers in Sumatra that they were considered vermin and rewards were paid by the East India Company for every animal killed. Based on surveys conducted between late 1972 and 1975, Marcus Borner reported that the Sumatran tiger was present in all eight provinces of the island, and estimated that there were approximately 1,000 individuals. Since then habitat loss and poaching have reduced tiger numbers. Large areas of lowland forest were lost, and by 1989 only 3 percent of Sumatra's lowland forest remained. Today, poaching continues despite the fact that the tiger has been legally protected by the Indonesian government since 1972.[35] Despite these pressures, tigers are still found in most of the major forest types on the island, as well as in many of the country's nature reserves, although there are few reserves of sufficient size and with enough prey to support a tiger population. About half of the island's tigers are thought to reside in the provinces of Aceh, Jambi, Sumatra, Selatan, and Bengkulu. The island's tiger population is currently estimated at 400 to 500.[109] Efforts are under way to estimate the number of tigers remaining in Sumatra, and in 1995 a mark-recapture study using cameras was initiated in Way Kambas National Park.[110]

The Indo-Chinese subspecies of Myanmar, Thailand, peninsular Malaysia, Cambodia, Laos, Vietnam, and neighboring China is thought to number between 1,100 and 1,800, but this should be considered a very rough estimate.[111] In 1977, Lekagul and McNeely estimated that there were 500 to 600 tigers in Thailand, but by 1990 this number had declined by 50 percent.[112] Between 1987 and 1991 Alan Rabinowitz surveyed nineteen protected areas, thirteen national parks, and six wildlife sanctuaries, documenting the destruction of much of Thailand's lowland forest. Rabinowitz estimated that there were probably 250 tigers

remaining in the country, but that only 150 of these were members of breeding populations. The remainder were scattered in small numbers in tiny, isolated patches of forest.[113] Some tiger populations in Thailand extend into neighboring countries, suggesting a need for trans-border protection.[114]

The status of tigers in peninsular Malaysia is similar to that of tigers in other areas in Southeast Asia. Tigers were once abundant in the country, and in the 1950s Colonel A. Locke estimated there were 3,000 tigers in Malaysia.[30] At this time tigers were afforded a status equal to that of a rat or squirrel and were to be killed on sight. In twenty years tiger numbers declined dramatically, and estimates in the 1970s varied from 300 to 600. Recent estimates place the number of tigers in peninsular Malaysia around 500, with the presumed population increase being attributed to conservation efforts and legislation implemented since 1972. The tiger was given total protection in 1976. In 1987, approximately 6.54 million hectares of peninsular Malaysia was still under forest cover, and much of this area will remain forested because it is unsuitable for agriculture. Today, tigers still occur in most states, but are confined to relatively small and widely separated national parks, forest reserves, and wildlife sanctuaries.[115]

The Bengal tiger (*P. t. tigris*) of India, Nepal, Sikkim, Bhutan, and Bangladesh was the first recognized subspecies. E. P. Gee estimated that there were 20,000 to 40,000 tigers in India at the turn of the twentieth century, but the next fifty years saw a period of hunting and habitat destruction that decimated the subcontinent's wildlife. Gee estimated that by 1960 tiger numbers had plummeted to 4,000.[116] As the tiger became increasingly rare, the interest of the world's sportsmen increased in anticipation of a moratorium on hunting, and shikar companies experienced a surge in business as wealthy foreigners converged to bag a trophy before it was too late. The price of tiger furs and coats soared to record heights.

By the late 1960s it was clear that the tiger was in trouble. At a 1969 meeting of the IUCN in Delhi, the species was declared endangered. A country-wide census conducted shortly thereafter put numbers at fewer than 2,000. Following this alarming news, World Wildlife Fund International and the Indian government launched "Project Tiger," a far-sighted plan to preserve the tiger and its habitat. Nine tiger reserves were set up, and forestry operations, livestock grazing, and poaching were halted in these reserves. The next step was the relocation of hundreds of villages, and thousands of people were resettled in an effort to improve and enlarge the tiger's habitat. As villages were abandoned and fields taken out of cultivation, prey species increased rapidly. Tigers responded to the new abundance of food and were soon seen stalking through the old fields — the decline had been halted, and numbers slowly began to climb. By 1991 there were eighteen tiger reserves, and official census figures put India's tiger numbers at about 5,000, though some doubt has been cast on the reliability of these numbers. While the experts are unable to agree on tiger numbers in India, they do concur that some 60 to 75 percent of tigers live in areas outside reserves, where their continued survival is precarious.[28,45,117,118]

Though Project Tiger was confined to India, neighboring Nepal also did its part to halt the decline of the tiger. In the early 1970s Nepalese and American scientists began what was to be a fifteen-year study of tiger biology and behavior in Chitwan National Park, one of three protected areas established in southern Nepal where good tiger populations still remained. Chitwan was also the site of a long-term research and monitoring program carried out by Chuck McDougal. Approximately 200 tigers are believed to live in southern Nepal, but pressures on natural resources are increasing, and poachers have been active in several parks.[6,43,57,58,64,66,69,79,119,120]

In Bhutan, the results of a 1988 country-wide survey incorporating interviews with local people indicated the presence of at least 150 tigers, with possibly an additional 100 animals not being detected. Tigers were recorded from thirty-six localities, but at only three of these was the minimum number reported to be more than ten individuals.[29]

The Sundarbans cover an area of 5,700 square kilometers in Bangladesh, 4,100 of which is forest and the remainder water. When combined with the Sundarbans of neighboring West Bengal, the total contiguous area is about 8,000 square kilometers. Some experts believe that the Sundarbans of India and Bangladesh is the only place where tigers will survive in the long term because this forest is thought to contain several hundred tigers, the largest single population of tigers anywhere. There are, however, no estimates of tiger numbers in the Sundarbans, and a recent camera-trap survey on the West Bengal side suggests that tiger density may be low, in the range of 0.6 to 3.6 tigers per 100 square kilometers.[121] At these densities, the Sundarbans tiger population would be much smaller than

projected. Estimates of prey density and more surveys are clearly needed to refine these initial tiger estimates.

The Sundarbans forest is a major source of timber, firewood, palm products, fish, and honey, and in Bangladesh alone forty-five thousand permits are issued annually for people to enter the forest to harvest these resources. Despite almost overwhelming economic problems and periodic catastrophic cyclones, every attempt is being made to manage this forest on a sustained-yield basis. The Forest Department strictly enforces the regulations that govern the exploitation of forest products, and a system of permits, checkpoints, and patrols operates to control the offtake. The future of tigers in this ecosystem is obviously dependent on a management strategy that to date has been successful.[122]

CONFLICT WITH HUMANS

The tiger is not the only large cat to include humans in its diet, but it does seem to do so more regularly than the lion, leopard, or puma. The fact that some tigers do prey on people is probably responsible for the species' larger-than-life image, which has been inflated by hunters and sensationalized by journalists in countries where tigers exist only in zoos.

The most striking thing about man-eaters is that they do not occur with the same frequency in all parts of the tiger's range. Man-eating was almost unknown, or occurred only very occasionally, in Myanmar, Thailand, peninsular Malaysia, and Sumatra, but it was a serious and persistent problem in South China, Singapore, and Manchuria. The problem in these latter areas has since been resolved because tigers have been eliminated or drastically reduced in numbers.

On the Indian subcontinent there are large portions of the country where tigers do not kill people, and the man-eating problem there is largely confined to three areas. The best-known of these is the Sundarbans of Bangladesh. Man-eating is one of the most important issues facing the conservation of tigers in the Sundarbans. Between 1975 and 1989, 521 people were killed by tigers in the Indian portion of the Sundarbans. Some 8,000 people a year receive permits to enter the Indian reserve to collect wood, honey, and fish. Of these, fishermen were found to account for 70 percent of the total number of people entering the reserve and 82 percent of the total casualties. Several studies have tried to determine why the region has so many man-eaters, and the explanations have been numerous. The lack of fresh water, a shortage of natural prey, and the large numbers of people foraging in the reserve have all been suggested as causes, but no single factor can account for the phenomenon.[122,123] A recent survey estimated that 100 to 150 people per year were being killed by tigers in the Sundarbans of Bangladesh.[124]

The authorities have instituted a variety of creative measures to reduce the depredations by problem tigers in the area, and these approaches seem to be working. Artificial ponds have been dug to collect rainwater in order to provide the wildlife with fresh drinking water. Electrified human dummies representing woodcutters, honey gatherers, and fishermen have been placed in the forest. These dummies are dressed in old urine-soaked clothes and deliver a sharp electric shock when touched. Some of the dummies have been attacked by tigers.

The most significant reduction in human deaths followed the 1987 introduction of inexpensive rubberized face masks, which are worn on the back of the head. The authorities reasoned that as tigers normally attack prey from behind, rather than face to face, a mask worn on the back of the head should be a deterrent. In a very unusual experiment, some 2,500 masks were issued to the 8,000 or so workers entering the reserve. The results were dramatic. In 1987 no one wearing a mask was killed by a tiger, but 29 people without masks were killed. Some of those killed had been wearing a mask, but were attacked by tigers when they temporarily removed it.[118]

The fact that tigers have the ability to kill people has never been in doubt; the surprise is that they rarely do so. The use of radiotelemetry has shown that they certainly have plenty of opportunities.[49] Radio-collared tigers have been found resting 10 meters from a trail where hundreds of people walk. They have been located next to a river on which tourist boats pass within a few meters of the shore, or lying in dense streambed vegetation a few meters from a well-used village bathing spot. Tigers prefer to avoid people and generally give them a wide berth. Even when provoked or approached, they will normally give a warning growl and allow the intruder to back off. As Jim Corbett so aptly wrote, "Tigers, except when wounded or when man eaters, are on the whole very good tempered. . . . Occasionally a tiger will object to too close an approach to its cubs or to a kill that it is guarding. The objection invariably takes the form of growling,

and if this does not prove effective it is followed by short rushes accompanied by terrifying roars. If these warnings are disregarded, the blame for any injury inflicted rests with the intruder."[125]

There is no single satisfactory answer to the question of what makes a man-eater. A tiger at a kill or a tigress with cubs may sometimes attack a person who disturbs them, but even if a tiger does kill someone under these circumstances, it does not invariably go on to become a man-eater. Jim Corbett was of the opinion that "a man-eating tiger is a tiger that has been compelled, through stress of circumstances beyond its control, to adopt a diet that is alien to it. The stress of circumstances is, in nine cases out of ten, wounds and in the tenth, old age." Corbett also believed that the changeover from animal to human flesh was, in most cases, accidental.[125]

Corbett's observations have stood the test of time, and our understanding of the reasons why tigers become man-eaters has not advanced much further in the fifty or so years that have elapsed since he wrote those words. The only new information that has come to light has emerged from the long-term study of known individuals in Chitwan. There are no historical records of man-eaters in the area, but 1979 saw the beginning of an outbreak of man-eating that continues today. The only positive aspect of these killings is that many of the tigers involved are animals with well-documented life histories and their circumstances prior to their becoming man-eaters are known.

The Chitwan man-eaters illustrate the several different ways in which a tiger can shift to preying on humans. The classic example involved a young male tiger who was wounded in a fight. Born in the park, the tiger left his mother's range when he was about two years old and subsequently got into a serious fight with another male. Badly wounded, he was unable to move when the park warden discovered him a few days later. The warden tranquilized him, patched up his seriously injured foreleg, and released him. The tiger recovered, but was left with a permanent limp, and for the next year and a half he survived by killing cattle along the edge of the park. His injured leg prevented him from catching wild prey, and he lived exclusively off domestic stock. One morning the inevitable happened, and he literally bumped into a young schoolteacher who was coming down to the river for his daily bath. A man walking some fifty yards behind the schoolteacher heard a scream and saw the victim struggling with the tiger. The tiger killed the schoolteacher and fled into a nearby patch of bushes. Fortunately, the warden who had patched up the tiger after his fight had also put a radio collar on him, so researchers were able to locate and tranquilize him and move him to the zoo. If he had been left in the park he might have gone on to become a habitual man-eater.

Debilitating injuries can be caused by fights with other tigers, encounters with porcupines, or gunshot wounds. Fortunately, wounds inflicted by bullets are now a much less common occurrence, although tigers are still found with shotgun pellets lodged under their hides. In the 1940s and 1950s countless tigers were wounded in casual encounters with people. Some died, some were crippled, and others managed to recover from the most lethal-looking injuries and resume their normal lifestyle. Vanigans, the well-known taxidermists in Mysore, India, have a cabinet filled with the skulls of tigers that had recovered from gunshot wounds before becoming someone's trophy. Many of the skulls and jaws are seriously deformed where the bone was shattered by a bullet and then healed, sometimes around the slug.

An amazingly large number of man-eaters appear to have been debilitated by porcupine quills. Both tigers and leopards obviously have difficulty trying to kill these 15-kilogram rodents. Corbett described a tigress living happily on deer and wild pigs until she had the misfortune of losing an eye in an encounter with a porcupine, and "got some fifty quills, varying in length from one to nine inches, embedded in the arm and under the pad of her right foreleg. Several of these quills after striking a bone had doubled back in the form of a U, the point and the broken-off end being close together. Suppurating sores formed where she had endeavoured to extract the quills with her teeth, and while she was lying up in a thick patch of grass, starving and licking her wounds, a woman selected this particular patch of grass to cut as fodder for her cattle. At first the tigress took no notice, but when the woman had cut the grass right up to where she was lying, the tigress struck once, the blow crushing in the woman's skull." The tigress left the body without feeding on it, but two days later she killed a woodcutter who came to chip wood off a fallen tree she was resting beside. She ate a small portion of the woodcutter, and the next day killed and ate a third person. After this she became a man-eater and went on to kill twenty-four people before she was shot.[125]

Though the historical accounts suggest that many man-eaters were incapacitated in some way, or were old and unable to hunt, other man-eaters appear to be in excellent condition. Both Corbett and Anderson repeatedly remarked that some man-eating tigers are fine specimens, with no visible injuries or defects.[54,125] A variety of suggestions were made as to why these healthy animals took to killing people, but until recently there was no satisfactory explanation.

Then, in 1984, a prime male tiger that fit this description began killing people in Chitwan. In this case, however, the tiger had a known history. He had recently lost his territory to another male and subsequently became a transient, wandering well beyond his former range. In the space of a few months, he killed and ate three villagers. The fourth victim survived by fending off the tiger with a sickle, and shortly thereafter the tiger was captured and moved to a zoo. He was eight to ten years old, in good health, and had no obvious injuries.

We now know that tigers ousted from their ranges tend to wander widely, get into fights with other tigers, and may end up in marginal areas where they survive by killing domestic stock. This appears to be a situation in which man-eaters are likely to be created. What was missing in the previous explanations of man-eating was the underlying social factors that could lead to the phenomenon.

Unfortunately, if social stress can lead to man-eating, then we can only expect man-eating to become more common over the next few decades. Recent efforts to save the tiger have effectively improved habitat conditions and increased the productivity and survivorship of animals living in protected areas. However, tigers are relatively long-lived, and their social system limits the number of animals that can breed in a given area. Because females commonly maintain fairly exclusive home ranges, and males do likewise, there is a limit on the number of tigers of either sex that can be fitted into a given area.

The problems begin when the number of young tigers looking for a home range exceeds the number of vacant ranges. If reserves are linked to other protected areas, then the normal process of young animals searching for a place to live can continue. But when protected areas are surrounded by agricultural land and villages, as many are, then both tigers and people are in trouble. With nowhere to go, young tigers may end up being forced to remain in the already full reserve. The resulting overpopulation increases competition, especially among males, and more fighting and injuries are to be expected. An alternative for a young tiger born into a full reserve is to make a living along the margins of the reserve, feeding on domestic stock, but this too is a situation in which man-eating may develop. If tigers are to continue to survive in the wild, future management strategies cannot rely solely on squeezing more and more tigers into protected areas. Rather, they will have to focus on developing innovative ways to allow tigers and people to use the same space.[43,49,126,127]

CONSERVATION EFFORTS

Recent efforts to conserve tigers in the wild are multifaceted and include identifying areas that are crucial to the survival of free-ranging tigers, developing survey and monitoring methods, conducting status surveys in priority areas to estimate tiger numbers, and institutionalizing methods to control trade in tiger parts.[105,111,128,129] The prioritization of areas relative to their importance for conserving tigers has not followed a taxonomic approach, but instead has taken an ecology-based approach. This has turned out to be a fortuitous strategy because recent molecular analysis shows little genomic variation among the putative tiger subspecies.[130] Furthermore, an examination of the morphological variation (skull, coat, body size) in tigers shows that most of the variation is not strongly associated with specific subspecies; rather, there is a continuous gradation in these metrics across the tiger's geographic range (i.e., the variation is clinal).[131] The results of these molecular and morphological studies are further supported by a biogeographic study showing that only three contemporary populations have ever been sufficiently isolated for the evolution of distinct populations.[132] The results of all these studies

have important implications for the conservation of tigers in the wild and in captivity.

Survey and monitoring methods for tigers have been greatly advanced by combining camera-trap photography, to identify individuals, with theoretical capture-recapture models. Karanth and his colleagues have used this methodology in a variety of environmental settings in India, and the results of their surveys clearly show the potential for generating robust estimates at sites where densities are 3 tigers per 100 square kilometers or higher. Even at lower densities the application of this technique yields estimates that are superior to ad hoc methods.[133,134]

These camera-trap surveys also support the prediction that tiger densities are positively correlated with prey densities.[46] Kaziranga National Park in northeastern India, an alluvial floodplain grassland interspersed with patches of moist forest and high prey density (58 principal prey per square kilometer) had the highest adult density (16.8 tigers per 100 square kilometers). Adult densities of 11–12 tigers per 100 square kilometers were recorded for Kanha and Nagarahole; both of these Indian parks support high prey densities.[133] These results show that tiger densities can be high in optimal habitats, and thus even relatively small parks and reserves can potentially support large numbers of tigers. Furthermore, the demographic modeling done by Karanth and Stith suggests that small tiger populations, even those with only 6–12 breeding females, may be demographically viable in a 100-year time frame. The conservation implications of these findings are enormous, as they mean that even relatively small reserves (300 to 3,000 square kilometers) may be able to support viable populations of tigers.[135]

TABLE 63 MEASUREMENTS AND WEIGHTS OF ADULT TIGERS

HB	n	T	n	WT	n	Location	Source
1,950 (1,890–2,040)	3m	1,027 (1,000–1,070)	3m	217 (209–227)	3m	Nagarahole NP, India	73
1,610	1f	870	1f	177	1f	Nagarahole NP, India	73
				235 (200–261)	7m	Chitwan NP, Nepal	9
				140 (116–164)	19f	Chitwan NP, Nepal	9
				75–110	f	Sumatra	13
				100–140	m	Sumatra	13
				115 (102–130)	3f	Sikhote-Alin, Russia	61

(continued)

Table 63 (continued)

HB	n	T	n	WT	n	Location	Source
2,300 (1,900–2,900)	5m	994 (900–1,000)	5m	225 (195–325)	9m	Russia	8
1,663 (1,460–1,770)	5f	934 (880–1,090)	4f	127 (96–160)	5f	Russia	8

Note: HB = head and body length (mm); T = tail length (mm); WT = weight (kg). n = sample size. Sex: m = male, f = female, ? = unknown. Mean values are presented only for sample sizes of three or more. Range of values is in parentheses.

TABLE 64 FREQUENCY OF OCCURRENCE OF PREY ITEMS IN THE DIETS OF TIGERS (PERCENTAGE OF SAMPLES)

Prey items	Nagarahole NP, India[60] Scats (n = 472)	Royal Bardia NP, Nepal[130] Scats (n = 215)	Huai Kha Khaeng Wildlife Sanctuary, Thailand[68] Scats (n = 38)
Axis axis Chital	31.2	74.9	
Axis porcinus Hog deer		6.7	
Cervus unicolor Sambar	24.9		7.0
Muntiacus muntjak Barking deer			42.0
Bos frontalis Gaur	17.4		
Cervus duvauceli Barasingha		1.3	
Sus scrofa Wild pig	9.4	8.5	9.0
Boselaphus tragocamelus Nilgai		1.8	
Tragulus meminna Chevrotain	3.1		
Lepus nigricollis Hare	0.2		
Hystrix sp. Porcupine	0.2	1.3	12.0
Arctonyx collaris Hog badger			9.0
Cuon alpinus Dhole	0.6		
Primates	3.9	2.2	5.0
Other mammals		3.1	2.0
Lizards			2.0
Unknown mammals			12.0
Minimum number of vertebrate prey items	490	223	43

TABLE 65 OCCURRENCE OF PREY ITEMS IN THE DIETS OF SIBERIAN TIGERS
(PERCENTAGE OF KILLS)

Prey items	Sikhote-Alin Zapoveknik, Russia[67] Kills ($n = 522$)
Cervus elaphus Red deer	54.3
Sus scrofa Wild pig	29.5
Capreolus pygargus Roe deer	6.3
Moschus moschiferus Musk deer	2.5
Alces alces Moose	1.8
Naemorhedus caudatus Goral	0.9
Cervus nippon Sika deer	0.5
Small to large carnivores	3.4
Birds	0.5

REFERENCES

1. Courtney, N. 1980. *The tiger: Symbol of freedom*. London: Quartet Books.

2. Forsyth, J. 1872. *The highlands of central India*. New Delhi: Asian Publ. Serv.

3. Rice, W. 1857. *Tiger-shooting in India; being an account of hunting experiences on foot in Rajpootana, during the hot seasons, from 1850 to 1854*. London: Smith, Elder and Co.

4. Gordon-Cumming, R. G. 1872. *Wild men and wild beasts*. London: Hamilton, Adams and Co.

5. Hewitt, J. 1938. *Jungle trails in northern India*. London: Methuen.

6. Sunquist, M. E. 1981. The social organization of tigers (*Panthera tigris*) in Royal Chitawan National Park, Nepal. Smithsonian Contributions to Zoology, no. 336. 98 pp.

7. Mazák, V. 1981. *Panthera tigris*. Mammalian Species 152: 1–8.

8. Heptner, V. G., and A. A. Sludskii. 1992. *Mammals of the Soviet Union*. Vol. 2, part 2, *Carnivora (Hyaenas and cats)*. English translation, sci. ed. R. S. Hoffmann. Washington, DC: Smithsonian Institution Libraries and the National Science Foundation.

9. Smith, J. L. D., M. E. Sunquist, K. M. Tamang, and P. B. Rai. 1983. A technique for capturing and immobilizing tigers. *J. Wildl. Mgmt.* 47: 255–259.

10. Pocock, R. I. 1929. Tigers. *J. Bombay Nat. Hist. Soc.* 33: 505–541.

11. Schaller, G. B. 1967. *The deer and the tiger*. Chicago: University of Chicago Press.

12. Khan, M. 1987. Tigers in Malaysia: Prospects for the future. In *Tigers of the world: The biology, biopolitics, management and conservation of an endangered species*, ed. R. L. Tilson and U. S. Seal, 75–84. Park Ridge, NJ: Noyes Publications.

13. Seidensticker, J., and C. McDougal. 1993. Tiger predatory behaviour, ecology and conservation. *Symp. Zool. Soc. Lond.* 65: 105–125.

14. Thorton, I. W. B., K. K. Yeung, and K. S. Sankhala. 1967. The genetics of white tigers in Rewa. *J. Zool. (Lond.)* 152: 127–135.

15. Thorton, I. W. B. 1978. White tiger genetics—further evidence. *J. Zool. (Lond.)* 185: 389–394.

16. Roychoudhury, A. K. 1978. A study of inbreeding in white tigers. *Sci. Cul.* 44: 371–372.

17. Roychoudhury, A. K., and K. S. Sankhala. 1979. Inbreeding in white tigers. *Proc. Indian Acad. Sci.* 88: 311–323.

18. Roychoudhury, A. K. 1987. White tigers and their conservation. In *Tigers of the world: The biology, biopolitics, management and conservation of an endangered species*, ed. R. L. Tilson and U. S. Seal, 380–388. Park Ridge, NJ: Noyes Publications.

19. Maruska, E. J. 1987. White tiger: Phantom or freak? In *Tigers of the world: The biology, biopolitics, management and conservation of an endangered species*, ed. R. L. Tilson and U. S. Seal, 372–379. Park Ridge, NJ: Noyes Publications.

20. Perry, R. 1965. *The world of the tiger*. New York: Athenaeum.

21. Roberts, T. J. 1977. *The mammals of Pakistan*. London: Ernest Benn.

22. Harrington, F. A. Jr. 1977. *A guide to the mammals of Iran*. Tehran: Department of the Environment.

23. Marchessaux, D. 1978. Note sur la présence ancienne du tigre, *Panthera tigris virgata* (Illiger, 1815), en Turquie. *Mammalia* 41: 541–542.

24. Joslin, P. 1986. Status of the Caspian tiger in Iran. In *Cats of the world: Biology, conservation, and management*, ed. S. D. Miller and D. D. Everett, 63. Washington, DC: National Wildlife Federation.

25. Kock, D. 1990. Historical record of a tiger, *Panthera tigris* (Linnaeus, 1758), in Iraq. *Zool. Middle East* 4: 11–15.

26. Guggisberg, C. A. W. 1975. *Wild cats of the world*. New York: Taplinger.

27. Prater, S. H. 1971. *The book of Indian animals*. Bombay: Bombay Natural History Society.

28. Sankhala, K. S. 1977. *Tiger: The story of the Indian tiger*. New York: Simon and Schuster.

29. Dorji, D. P., and C. Santiapillai. 1989. The status, distribution and conservation of the tiger *Panthera tigris* in Bhutan. *Biol. Conserv.* 48: 311–319.

30. Locke, A. 1954. *The tigers of Terengganu*. London: Museum Press.

31. Lekagul, B., and J. A. McNeely. 1977. *Mammals of Thailand*. Bangkok: Association for the Conservation of Wildlife.

32. McNeely, J. 1979. Status of tiger in Indonesia. *Tigerpaper* 6: 21–22.

33. Corbet, G. B., and J. E. Hill. 1992. *The mammals of the Indomalayan region*. Oxford: Oxford University Press.

34. Hoogerwerf, A. 1970. *Udjung Kulon: The land of the last Javan rhinoceros*. Leiden: E. J. Brill.

35. Borner, M. 1978. Status and conservation of the Sumatran tiger. *Carnivore* 1: 97–102.

36. Santiapillai, C., and S. R. Widodo. 1985. On the status of the tiger (*Panthera tigris sumatrae* Pocock, 1829) in Sumatra. *Tigerpaper* 12: 23–29.

37. Santiapillai, C., and S. R. Widodo. 1987. Tiger numbers and habitat evaluation in Indonesia. In *Tigers of the world: The biology, biopolitics, management and conservation of an endangered species*, ed. R. L. Tilson and U. S. Seal, 85–91. Park Ridge, NJ: Noyes Publications.

38. Seidensticker, J. 1987. Bearing witness: Observations of the extinction of *Panthera tigris balica* and *Panthera tigris sondaica*. In *Tigers of the world: The biology, biopolitics, management and conservation of an endangered species*, ed. R. L. Tilson and U. S. Seal, 1–8. Park Ridge, NJ: Noyes Publications.

39. Matyushkin, E. N., V. I. Zhivotchenko, and E. N. Smirnov. 1980. *The Amur tiger in the USSR*. Gland, Switzerland: International Union for Conservation of Nature and Natural Resources (IUCN).

40. Houji, L. 1987. Habitat availability and prospects for tigers in China. In *Tigers of the world: The biology, biopolitics, management, and conservation of an endangered species*, ed. R. L. Tilson and U. S. Seal, 71–74. Park Ridge, NJ: Noyes Publications.

41. Koehler, G. M. 1991. Survey of remaining wild population of South China tigers. Final project report, WWF Project 4512/China. Wildlife Research Institute, Inc., Moscow, Idaho.

42. Miquelle, D. G., H. Quigley, M. Hornocker, E. N. Smirnov, I. Nikalaev, D. Pikunov, and K. Quigley. 1993. Present status of the Siberian tiger and some threats to its conservation. In Proceedings of the International Union of Game Biologists XXI Congress, ed. I. D. Thompson, 274–278. Halifax, Nova Scotia.

43. McDougal, C. 1977. *The face of the tiger*. London: Rivington Books and André Deutsch.

44. Smith, J. L. D., C. W. McDougal, and M. E. Sunquist. 1987. Female land tenure system in tigers. In *Tigers of the world: The biology, biopolitics, management, and conservation of an endangered species*, ed. R. L. Tilson and U. S. Seal, 97–109. Park Ridge, NJ: Noyes Publications.

45. Karanth, K. U. 1987. Tigers in India: A critical review of field censuses. In *Tigers of the world: The biology, biopolitics, management, and conservation of an endangered species*, ed. R. L. Tilson and U. S. Seal, 118–132. Park Ridge, NJ: Noyes Publications.

46. Sunquist, M. E., K. U. Karanth, and F. C. Sunquist. 1999. Ecology, behaviour and resilience of the tiger and its conservation needs. In *Riding the tiger: Tiger conservation in human-dominated landscapes*, ed. J. Seidensticker, S. Christie, and P. Jackson, 5–18. Cambridge: Cambridge University Press.

47. Eisenberg, J. F., and J. Seidensticker. 1976. Ungulates in southern Asia: A consideration of biomass estimates for selected habitats. *Biol. Conserv.* 10: 293–308.

48. Karanth, K. U., and M. E. Sunquist. 1992. Population structure, density and biomass of large herbivores in the tropical forests of Nagarahole, India. *J. Trop. Ecol.* 8: 21–35.

49. Sunquist, F. C., and M. E. Sunquist. 1988. *Tiger moon*. Chicago: University of Chicago Press.

50. Mountfort, G. 1973. *Tigers*. New York: Crescent Books.

51. Fox, M. W. 1984. *The whistling hunters*. Albany: State University of New York Press.

52. Johnsingh, A. J. T. 1985. Distribution and status of the dhole *Cuon alpinus* Pallas, 1811 in South Asia. *Mammalia* 49: 203–208.

53. Connell, W. 1944. Wild dogs attacking a tiger. *J. Bombay Nat. Hist. Soc.* 44: 468–470.

54. Anderson, K. 1955. *Nine man-eaters and one rogue*. New York: E. P. Dutton and Company.

55. Rathore, F. S., and K. Sankar. 1992. Tiger kills. *Tigerpaper* 19: 6.

56. McDougal, C. 1988. Leopard and tiger interactions at Royal Chitwan National Park, Nepal. *J. Bombay Nat. Hist. Soc.* 85: 609–611.

57. Seidensticker, J., M. E. Sunquist, and C. McDougal. 1990. Leopards living at the edge of the Royal Chitwan National Park, Nepal. In *Conservation in developing countries: Problems and prospects*, ed. J. C. Daniel and J. S. Serrao, 415–423. Bombay: Oxford University Press.

58. Seidensticker, J. 1976. On the ecological separation between tigers and leopards. *Biotropica* 8: 225–234.

59. Karanth, K. U., and M. E. Sunquist. 2000. Behavioural correlates of predation by tiger (*Panthera tigris*), leopard (*Panthera pardus*), and dhole (*Cuon alpinus*) in Nagarahole, India. *J. Zool.* (Lond.) 250: 255–265.

60. Karanth, K. U., and M. E. Sunquist. 1995. Prey selection by tiger, leopard and dhole in tropical forests. *J. Anim. Ecol.* 64: 439–450.

61. Hornocker, M. G., H. B. Quigley, D. G. Miquelle, and K. S. Quigley. 1995. Siberian tiger project: Progress report. Hornocker Wildlife Research Institute, Moscow, Idaho.

62. Thapar, V. 1989. *Tigers: The secret life*. London: Elm Tree Books.

63. Thapar, V. 1986. *Tiger: Portrait of a predator*. London: William Collins.

64. Smith, J. L. D. 1984. Dispersal, communication, and conservation strategies for the tiger (*Panthera tigris*) in Royal Chitwan National Park, Nepal. Ph.D. dissertation, University of Minnesota, St. Paul, Minnesota.

65. Dunbar Brander, A. A. 1931. *Wild animals in central India*. London: Edward Arnold and Company.

66. Mishra, H. R. 1982. The ecology and behaviour of chital (*Axis axis*) in the Royal Chitwan National Park, Nepal. Ph.D. dissertation, University of Edinburgh, Aberdeen, Scotland.

67. Miquelle, D. G., E. N. Smirnov, H. G. Quigley, M. G. Hornocker, I. G. Nikolaev, and E. N. Matyushkin. 1996. Food habits of Amur tigers in Sikhote-Alin Zapovednik and the Russian Far East, and implications for conservation. *J. Wildl. Res.* 1: 138–147.

68. Rabinowitz, A. 1989. The density and behavior of large cats

in a dry tropical forest mosaic in Huai Kha Khaeng Wildlife Sanctuary, Thailand. *Nat. Hist. Bull. Siam Soc.* 37: 235–251.

69. Tamang, K. M. 1982. The status of the tiger (*Panthera tigris*) and its impact on principal prey populations in the Royal Chitawan National Park, Nepal. Ph.D. dissertation, Michigan State University, East Lansing, Michigan.

70. Foran, W. R. 1933. *Kill or be killed.* London: Hutchinson

71. Ewer, R. F. 1973. *The carnivores.* Ithaca, NY: Cornell University Press.

72. Leyhausen, P. 1979. *Cat behavior: The predatory and social behavior of domestic and wild cats.* New York: Garland STPM Press.

73. Karanth, K. U. 1993. Predator-prey relationships among the large mammals of Nagarahole National Park (India). Ph.D. dissertation, Mangalore University, Mangalore, India.

74. Corbett, J. 1954. *The temple tiger and more man-eaters of Kumaon.* Bombay: Oxford University Press.

75. Dierenfeld, E. S. 1987. Nutritional considerations in captive tiger management. In *Tigers of the world: The biology, biopolitics, management, and conservation of an endangered species,* ed. R. L. Tilson and U. S. Seal, 149–160. Park Ridge, NJ: Noyes Publications.

76. Emmons, L. H. 1987. Comparative feeding ecology of felids in a Neotropical rain forest. *Behav. Ecol. Sociobiol.* 20: 271–283.

77. Schaller, G. B. 1972. *The Serengeti lion.* Chicago: University of Chicago Press.

78. Srikosomatara, S. 1993. Density and biomass of large herbivores and other mammals in a dry tropical forest, western Thailand. *J. Trop. Ecol.* 9: 33–43.

79. Seidensticker, J. 1976. Ungulate populations in Chitawan Valley, Nepal. *Biol. Conserv.* 10: 183–210.

80. Smith, J. L. D., and C. McDougal. 1991. The contribution of variance in lifetime reproduction to effective population size in tigers. *Conserv. Biol.* 5: 484–490.

81. Panwar, H. S. 1987. Project Tiger: The reserves, the tigers and their future. In *Tigers of the world: The biology, biopolitics, management, and conservation of an endangered species,* ed. R. L. Tilson and U. S. Seal, 110–117. Park Ridge, NJ: Noyes Publications.

82. Brahmachary, R. L., and J. Dutta. 1981. On the pheromones of tigers: Experiments and theory. *Am. Nat.* 118: 561–567.

83. Brahmachary, R. L., and J. Dutta. 1987. Chemical communication in the tiger and leopard. In *Tigers of the world: The biology, biopolitics, management, and conservation of an endangered species,* ed. R. L. Tilson and U. S. Seal, 296–302. Park Ridge, NJ: Noyes Publications.

84. Brahmachary, R. L., J. Dutta, and M. Poddar-Sarkar. 1991. The marking fluid of the tiger. *Mammalia* 55: 150–152.

85. Banks, G. R., A. J. Buglass, and J. S. Waterhouse. 1992. Amines in the marking fluid and anal sac secretions of the tiger, *Panthera tigris.* Z. *Naturforsch.* 47: 618–620.

86. Macdonald, D. W. 1985. The carnivores: Order Carnivora. In *Social odours in mammals,* ed. R. E. Brown and D. W. Macdonald, 619–722. Oxford: Clarendon Press.

87. Gorman, M. L., and B. J. Trowbridge. 1989. The role of odor in the social lives of carnivores. In *Carnivore behavior, ecology, and evolution,* ed. J. L. Gittleman, 57–88. Ithaca, NY: Cornell University Press.

88. Smith, J. L. D., C. McDougal, and D. Miquelle. 1989. Scent marking in free-ranging tigers, *Panthera tigris. Anim. Behav.* 37: 1–10.

89. Kleiman, D. G. 1974. The estrous cycle of the tiger (*Panthera tigris*). In *The world's cats,* vol. 2, ed. R. L. Eaton, 60–75. Winston, OR: World Wildlife Safari.

90. Peters, R. P., and L. D. Mech. 1975. Scent-marking in wolves. *Am. Sci.* 63: 628–637.

91. Peters, G. 1984. A special type of vocalization in the Felidae. *Acta Zool. Fennica* 171: 89–92.

92. Peters, G. 1984. On the structure of friendly close range vocalizations in terrestrial carnivores (Mammalia: Carnivora: Fissipedia). *Z. Säugetierk.* 49: 157–182.

93. Peters, G., and M. H. Hast. 1994. Hyoid structure, laryngeal anatomy, and vocalizations in felids (Mammalia: Carnivora: Felidae). *Z. Säugetierk.* 59: 87–104.

94. Hanley, P. 1961. *Tiger trails in Assam.* London: Robert Hale.

95. Smith, J. L. D. 1993. The role of dispersal in structuring the Chitwan tiger population. *Behaviour* 124: 165–195.

96. Seal, U. S., R. L. Tilson, E. D. Plotka, N. J. Reindl, and M. F. Seal. 1987. Behavioral indicators and endocrine correlates of estrus and anestrus in Siberian tigers. In *Tigers of the world: The biology, biopolitics, management, and conservation of an endangered species,* ed. R. L. Tilson and U. S. Seal, 244–254. Park Ridge, NJ: Noyes Publications.

97. Seal, U. S., E. D. Plotka, J. D. Smith, F. H. Wright, N. J. Reindl, R. S. Taylor, and M. F. Seal. 1985. Immunoreactive luteinizing hormone, estradiol, progesterone, testosterone, and androstenedione levels during the breeding season and anestrus in Siberian tigers. *Biol. Reprod.* 32: 361–368.

98. Lanier, D. L., and D. A. Dewsbury. 1976. A quantitative study of copulatory behaviour of large Felidae. *Behav. Proc.* 1: 327–333.

99. Veselovsky, Z. 1967. The Amur tiger *Panthera tigris altaica* in the wild and in captivity. *Int. Zoo Yrbk.* 7: 210–215.

100. McDougal, C. 1981. Some observations on tiger behaviour in the context of baiting. *J. Bombay Nat. Hist. Soc.* 77: 476–485.

101. Jones, M. L. 1977. Record keeping and longevity of felids in captivity. In *The world's cats,* vol. 3, ed. R. L. Eaton, 132–138. Seattle: Carnivore Research Institute, Burke Museum, University of Washington.

102. Van Bemmel, A. C. V. 1968. Breeding tigers at Rotterdam Zoo. *Int. Zoo Yrbk.* 8: 60–63.

103. Tilson, R., K. Traylor-Holzer, and M. J. Qiu. 1997. The decline and impending extinction of the South China tiger. *Oryx* 31: 243–252.

104. Mills, J. A., and P. Jackson. 1994. *Killed for a cure: A review of the world wide trade in tiger bone.* Cambridge: TRAFFIC International.

105. Nowell, K., and P. Jackson. 1996. *Wild cats: A status survey and conservation action plan.* Gland, Switzerland: International Union for Conservation of Nature and Natural Resources (IUCN).

106. Cat News. 1992. Poaching for bones threatens world's last tigers. *Cat News* 17: 2–3.

107. Miquelle, D. 1998. Tigers and leopards in Jilin Province, China. *Cat News* 28: 5–6.

108. Miquelle, D., T. W. Merrill, Y. Dunishenko, E. N. Smirnov, H. B. Quigley, D. G. Pikunov, and M. Hornocker. 1999. A habitat protection plan for the Amur tiger: Developing political and ecological criteria for a viable land-use plan. In *Riding the tiger: Tiger conservation in human-dominated landscapes,* ed. J. Seidensticker, S. Christie, and P. Jackson, 273–295. Cambridge: Cambridge University Press.

109. Wartaputra, S., K. Soemarna, W. Ramono, J. Manangsang, and R. Tilson. 1994. *Indonesian Sumatran tiger conservation strategy*. Djakarta, Indonesia: Directorate-General of Forest Protection and Nature Conservation.

110. Franklin, N., S. Bastoni, D. Siswomartono, J. Manansang, and R. Tilson. 1999. Last of the Indonesian tigers: A cause for optimism. In *Riding the tiger: Tiger conservation in human-dominated landscapes*, ed. J. Seidensticker, S. Christie, and P. Jackson, 130–147. Cambridge: Cambridge University Press.

111. Toyne, P., and D. Hoyle. 1998. *Tiger status report*. Godalming, England: WWF-UK.

112. Humphrey, S. R., and J. R. Bain. 1990. *Endangered animals of Thailand*. Gainesville, FL: Sandhill Crane Press.

113. Rabinowitz, A. 1993. Estimating the Indochinese tiger *Panthera tigris corbetti* population in Thailand. *Biol. Conserv.* 65: 213–217.

114. Smith, J. L. D., S. Tunhikorn, S. Tanhan, S. Simcharoen, and B. Kanchanasaka 1999. Metapopulation structure of tigers in Thailand. In *Riding the tiger: Tiger conservation in human-dominated landscapes*, ed. J. Seidensticker, S. Christie, and P. Jackson, 166–175. Cambridge: Cambridge University Press.

115. Jasmi, A. 1998. The distribution and management of the Malayan tiger *Panthera tigris corbetti* in Peninsular Malaysia. Abstract. Year of the Tiger conference, Dallas, TX, February 10–12, 1998.

116. Gee, E. P. 1964. *Wildlife of India*. New York: Dutton.

117. Mountfort, G. 1981. *Saving the tiger*. London: Michael Joseph.

118. Jackson, P. 1990. *Endangered species: Tigers*. London: Apple Press.

119. McDougal, C. 1995. Tiger count in Nepal's Chitwan National Park. *Cat News* 23: 3–5.

120. Smith, J. L. D., C. McDougal, S. C. Ahearn, A. Joshi, and K. Conforti. 1999. Metapopulation structure of tigers in Nepal. In *Riding the tiger: Tiger conservation in human-dominated landscapes*, ed. J. Seidensticker, S. Christie, and P. Jackson, 176–191. Cambridge: Cambridge University Press.

121. Karanth, K. U., and J. D. Nichols. 2000. Ecological status and conservation of tigers in India. Final technical report to Division of International Conservation, U.S. Fish and Wildlife Service, Washington, DC and Wildlife Conservation Society, New York. Bangalore, India: Centre for Wildlife Studies. 124 pp.

122. Seidensticker, J., and A. Hai. 1983. *The Sundarbans wildlife management plan: Conservation in the Bangladesh coastal zone*. Gland, Switzerland: International Union for Conservation of Nature and Natural Resources (IUCN).

123. Hendrichs, H. 1975. The status of the tiger in the Sundarbans mangrove forest (Bay of Bengal). *Säugetierk. Mitt.* 3: 161–199.

124. Helalsiddiqui, A. S. M. 1998. Present status of wildlife, human casualties by tiger, and wildlife conservation in the Sundarbans of Bangladesh. *Tigerpaper* 25: 28–32.

125. Corbett, J. 1957. *Man-eaters of India*. London: Oxford University Press.

126. McDougal, C. 1987. The man-eating tiger in geographical and historical perspective. In *Tigers of the world: The biology, biopolitics, management, and conservation of an endangered species*, ed. R. L. Tilson and U. S. Seal, 435–448. Park Ridge, NJ: Noyes Publications.

127. McDougal, C. 1991. Man-eaters. In *Great cats*, ed. J. Seidensticker and S. Lumpkin, 204–211. Emmaus, PA: Rodale Press.

128. Dinerstein, E., E. Wikramanayake, J. Robinson, K. U. Karanth, A. Rabinowitz, D. Olson, T. Mathew, P. Hedao, and M. Connor. 1997. *A framework for identifying high priority areas and actions for the conservation of tigers in the wild*. Part I. Washington, DC: World Wildlife Fund-US and Wildlife Conservation Society.

129. Hemley, G., and D. Bolze. 1997. *A framework for identifying high priority areas and actions for the conservation of tigers in the wild*. Part II. *Controlling trade in and reducing demand for tiger products: A preliminary assessment of priority needs*. Washington, DC: World Wildlife Fund-US and Wildlife Conservation Society.

130. Wentzel, J., J. C. Stephens, W. Johnson, M. Menotti-Raymond, J. Pecon-Slattery, N. Yuhki, M. Carrington, H. B. Quigley, D. G. Miquelle, R. Tilson, J. Manansang, G. Brady, L. Zhi, P. Wenshi, H. Shi-Qiang, L. Johnston, M. Sunquist, K. U. Karanth, and S. J. O'Brien. 1999. Subspecies of tigers: Molecular assessment using "voucher specimens" of geographically traceable individuals. In *Riding the tiger: Tiger conservation in human-dominated landscapes*, ed. J. Seidensticker, S. Christie, and P. Jackson, 40–49. Cambridge: Cambridge University Press.

131. Kitchener, A. C. 1999. Tiger distribution, phenotypic variation and conservation issues. In *Riding the tiger: Tiger conservation in human-dominated landscapes*, ed. J. Seidensticker, S. Christie, and P. Jackson, 19–39. Cambridge: Cambridge University Press.

132. Kitchener, A. C., and A. J. Dugmore. 2000. Biogeographical change in the tiger, *Panthera tigris*. *Anim. Conserv.* 2: 113–124.

133. Karanth, K. U., and J. D. Nichols. 1998. Estimation of tiger densities in India using photographic captures and recaptures. *Ecology* 79: 2852–2862.

134. Carbone, C., S. Christie, K. Conforti, T. Coulson, N. Franklin, J. R. Ginsberg, M. Griffiths, J. Holden, K. Kawanishi, M. Kinnaird, R. Laidlaw, A. Lynam, D. W. Macdonald, D. Martyr, C. McDougal, L. Nath, T. O'Brien, J. Seidensticker, J. L. D. Smith, M. Sunquist, R. Tilson, and W. N. WanShahruddin. 2001. The use of photographic rates to estimate densities of tigers and other cryptic mammals. *Anim. Conserv.* 4: 75–79.

135. Karanth, K. U., and B. M. Stith. 1999. Prey depletion as a critical determinant of tiger population viability. In *Riding the tiger: Tiger conservation in human-dominated landscapes*, ed. J. Seidensticker, S. Christie, and P. Jackson, 100–113. Cambridge: Cambridge University Press.

Marbled cat

Pardofelis marmorata (Martin, 1837)

Superficially, the marbled cat, weighing just 3 kilograms, looks like a little cat, but it possesses an odd mixture of small cat and big cat characteristics. With its enlarged canines, blotched coat pattern, and broad feet, it resembles the larger clouded leopard,[1] and taxonomists have concluded that it is on the stem of the pantherine line, which includes the lynx, lion, tiger, leopard, jaguar, and snow leopard.[2,3] These five big cats, the lynx, and the marbled cat are virtually indistinguishable by either karyotype or immunological characteristics.[4,5] Indeed, the banding pattern of the marbled cat's chromosomes is identical to that of the tiger.[6]

DESCRIPTION

While it is about the size of a domestic cat, the marbled cat gives the impression of being more slender and elongated. This is mainly due to its extremely long and bushy tail, which is as long as the cat's body, if not longer. When standing or resting, the marbled cat assumes a characteristic position with its head slightly retracted and its back arched. This cat superficially resembles a clouded leopard in coat color and pattern, but the clouded leopard is a much bigger and more robust-looking cat with larger, more distinct oval markings on its coat.

The marbled cat's coat is thick and soft, with well-developed woolly underfur. The background color may vary from dark gray-brown through yellowish gray to red-brown. The flanks and back are strikingly marked with large, irregular, dark-edged blotches. The legs and underparts are patterned with black dots, and the tail is marked with black spots proximally and rings distally. There are spots on the forehead and crown, which merge into narrow longitudinal stripes on the neck and irregular stripes on the back.[1,7]

Although the marbled cat and leopard cat are similar in size and weight, the marbled cat has much bigger feet—the heel pads are about twice as large as those of the leopard cat. Morphologically, the marbled cat's feet resemble those of the clouded leopard.[1] The cat has a short, broad face, and its rounded ears are marked with white bars on the back. Its teeth, especially the canines, are more robust than those of the leopard cat.[1]

DISTRIBUTION

The marbled cat is found in northern India, Nepal, Sikkim, Assam, and south through Myanmar, Laos,

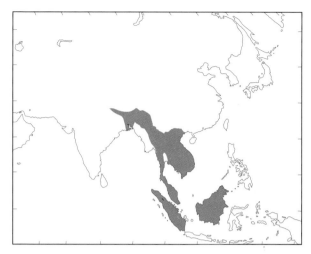

Figure 45. Distribution of the marbled cat.

Thailand, Vietnam, Cambodia, peninsular Malaysia, Sumatra, and Borneo (fig. 45). It has been recorded from sea level to elevations of 3,000 meters in northern Sikkim.[8,9,10,11,12,13,14,15]

ECOLOGY AND BEHAVIOR

"Very little is known as yet of the habits of this cat," Robert Sterndale said, writing about the marbled cat in 1884.[16] Unfortunately, the same is still true today, more than a hundred years later. The few specimens that have been collected have all come from lowland tropical forest, and the species is believed to be nocturnal and more arboreal in its habits than most other cats. This belief is supported by two separate lines of evidence. First, the marbled cat's long, slender body, extremely long tail, and broad feet suggest that it is specialized for an arboreal way of life.[1] Second, in one of the very few accounts of the marbled cat's activities in the wild, E. P. Stebbing notes that he saw this cat only twice, and on both occasions the animal was in a tree; on one occasion it was seen to be stalking birds.[7]

Birds are thought to form a major part of the marbled cat's diet, along with squirrels, rats, and possibly lizards and frogs.[1,10] A rat was found in the stomach of a marbled cat that was shot at night in a cut-over forest.[7] A specimen in captivity readily ate squirrels, birds, and frogs, but refused carrion.

Our first glimpse into the ecology and behavior of the marbled cat comes from an adult female that was trapped and radio-tagged in Phu Khieo Wildlife Sanctuary in northeastern Thailand in May 2000.[17] In the first month after capture the tagged cat was located in mountainous evergreen forest at elevations of 1,000 to 1,200 meters. It was primarily active at dusk and dawn and at night. Based on a small number of radio locations, the cat was using an area of 5.8 square kilometers.

The vocal repertoire of marbled cats is not well known, although it is reportedly similar to that of domestic cats.[18,19,20]

What is known of reproduction in marbled cats is derived from observations of only a few captive individuals. Two litters of two kittens each were born in January and February; another litter of unknown size was born in September. Gestation is estimated to vary from 66 to 82 days. Kittens weigh 61 to 85 grams at birth.[21] A hand-reared kitten opened its eyes at 12 days of age, attempted to walk at 15 days, accepted solid food when 59 days old, and by 121 days was eating meat. At 65 days the cat's behavior changed suddenly; while it retained a calm and docile nature, it became much more active and showed a great facility for jumping and climbing.[18] Sexual maturity is attained by twenty-one to twenty-two months.[21] In captivity, one marbled cat lived to the age of twelve years and three months.[22]

STATUS IN THE WILD

Throughout its range the marbled cat is thought to be rare, although it has also been suggested that its rarity simply reflects the cat's reclusive nature and penchant for remote forest areas.[23] Not surprisingly, there is little information available to indicate its current status. One marbled cat was sighted in northern Sikkim during a two-month survey for small cats.[14] Because of its dependence on forest, the major threat to this cat is habitat destruction.[13,14,24] It is also thought to be intolerant of human disturbance, abandoning a forest that is even moderately disturbed.[25]

STATUS IN CAPTIVITY

There are few marbled cats in captivity. In 1989 the International Species Inventory System (ISIS) listed four marbled cats being held in three zoos; three were captive-born and one was wild-born.[26]

TABLE 66 MEASUREMENTS AND WEIGHTS OF ADULT MARBLED CATS

HB	n	T	n	WT	n	Location	Source
460	1?	480	1?	2.4	1?	Borneo	12
490	1f	495	1f	2.5	1f	Borneo	27
470	1?	356	1?			Sikkim	1
525	1m	535	1m			Thailand	11
450–530	?	475–550	?	2–5	?	Thailand	10
620	1f	530	1f	3.7	1f	Thailand	17

Note: HB = head and body length (mm); T = tail length (mm); WT = weight (kg). n = sample size. Sex: m = male, f = female, ? = unknown. Mean values are presented only for sample sizes of three or more. Range of values is in parentheses.

REFERENCES

1. Pocock, R. I. 1932. The marbled cat (*Pardofelis marmorata*) and some other Oriental species, with the definition of a new genus of Felidae. *Proc. Zool. Soc. Lond.* 1932: 741–766.

2. Hemmer, H. 1978. The evolutionary systematics of living Felidae: Present status and current problems. *Carnivore* 1: 71–79.

3. Groves, C. 1982. Cranial and dental characteristics in the systematics of Old World Felidae. *Carnivore* 5: 28–39.

4. Wurster-Hill, D. H., and W. R. Centerwall. 1982. The interrelationships of chromosome banding patterns in canids, mustelids, hyena, and felids. *Cytogenet. Cell Genet.* 34: 178–192.

5. Collier, G. E., and S. J. O'Brien. 1985. A molecular phylogeny of the Felidae: Immunological distance. *Evolution* 39: 473–487.

6. Wurster-Hill, D. H., and D. A. Meritt. 1974. The G banded chromosomes of the marbled cat, *Felis marmorata. Mammalian Chromosomes Newsletter* 15: 14.

7. Guggisberg, C. A. W. 1975. *Wild cats of the world.* New York: Taplinger.

8. Ellerman, J. R., and T. C. S. Morrison-Scott. 1951. *Checklist of Palearctic and Indian mammals.* British Museum (Natural History), London.

9. Medway, L. 1969. *The wild mammals of Malaya (peninsular Malaysia) and Singapore*, 2nd ed. London: Oxford University Press.

10. Lekagul, B., and J. A. McNeely. 1977. *Mammals of Thailand.* Bangkok: Association for the Conservation of Wildlife.

11. Cheke, A. S. 1973. Marbled cat in Chiang Mai. *J. Siam Soc. (Nat. Hist.)* 24: 468.

12. Payne, J., C. M. Francis, and K. Phillips. 1985. *A field guide to the mammals of Borneo.* Kuala Lumpur: The Sabah Society.

13. Khan, M. A. R. 1986. The status and distribution of the cats in Bangladesh. In *Cats of the world: Biology, conservation, and management*, ed. S. D. Miller and D. D. Everett, 43–49. Washington, DC: National Wildlife Federation.

14. Biswas, B., and R. K. Ghose. 1982. Progress report of pilot survey of the World Wildlife Fund-India/Zoological Survey of India Collaborative Project on the Status Survey of the Lesser Cats in Eastern India. Project No. IUCN 1357-India.

15. Corbet, G. B., and J. E. Hill. 1992. *The mammals of the Indomalayan region*. Oxford: Oxford University Press.

16. Sterndale, R. A. 1884. *Natural history of the Mammalia of India and Ceylon*. Calcutta: Thacker, Spink.

17. Grassman, L. I. Jr., and M. E. Tewes. 2000. Marbled cat in northeastern Thailand. *Cat News* 33: 24.

18. Barnes, R. G. 1976. Breeding and hand-rearing of the marbled cat *Felis marmorata* at the Los Angeles Zoo. *Int. Zoo Yrbk.* 16: 205–208.

19. Peters, G. 1981. Das schnurren der katzen (Felidae). *Säugetierk. Mitt.* 29: 30–37.

20. Peters, G. 1984. On the structure of friendly close range vocalizations in terrestrial carnivores (Mammalia: Carnivora: Fissipedia). *Z. Säugetierk.* 49: 157–182.

21. Fagen, R. M., and K. S. Wiley. 1978. Felid paedomorphosis, with special reference to *Leopardus*. *Carnivore* 1: 72–81.

22. Jones, M. L. 1977. Record keeping and longevity of felids in captivity. In *The world's cats*, vol. 3, no. 3, ed. R. L. Eaton, 132–138. Seattle: Carnivore Research Institute, Burke Museum, University of Washington.

23. Humphrey, S. R., and J. R. Bain. 1990. *Endangered animals of Thailand*. Gainesville, FL: Sandhill Crane Press.

24. Sarker, S. U., and N. J. Sarker. 1984. Mammals of Bangladesh—their status, distribution and habitat. *Tigerpaper* 11: 8–13.

25. IUCN. 1978. International Union for Conservation of Nature and Natural Resources *Red Data Book*, Vol. 1, *Mammalia*. Gland, Switzerland: IUCN.

26. International Species Inventory System. 1989. *Species Distribution Report: Mammals*. Apple Valley: Minnesota Zoological Garden.

27. Davis, D. D. 1962. Mammals of the lowland rain-forest of north Borneo. *Bull. Nat. Mus. Singapore* 31: 1–129.

Snow leopard

Uncia uncia (Schreber, 1775)

The first description and drawing of the snow leopard appeared in 1761, in Baron Georges Louis Leclerc de Buffon's *Histoire Naturelle*. Buffon called the snow leopard an "once" and, apparently confusing it with the cheetah, described it as being easily tamed and trained for hunting and found in Persia. A few years later, in 1775, the zoologist Johann Schreber wrote the official description of the species, giving the snow leopard its scientific name *uncia*. Schreber assumed that the snow leopard inhabited "Persia, East India and China," but this was hardly surprising, as *uncia* skins that showed up in Europe at this time were few and far between, of obscure origin, and frequently misidentified as leopard or cheetah.[1,2,3,4]

Because the elusive snow leopard's haunts are so remote, early drawings of the cat and descriptions of its habits and distribution were made from skins and word of mouth. It was not until 1779 that Western naturalists began to explore and describe the little-known fauna of Russia and Siberia. Peter Pallas, the explorer and naturalist for whom Pallas's cat (the manul) is named, wrote that when he was in Siberia a snow leopard of "a very whiteish hue" had been killed on the west side of Lake Baikal, adding, "In general this [the snow leopard] is well known to the Tungusian hunters that live about that lake." Pallas added that skins of both the snow leopard and the common leopard were frequently brought to him by hunters.[5]

Though there are descriptions and drawings of a snow leopard that was said to have been kept in the menagerie at the Tower of London in 1823, the animal in question was more likely to have been a common leopard.[4] In 1851 the Antwerp zoo exhibited the first snow leopard in the West.[6] Later in the century, Moscow and London zoos also acquired snow leopards for exhibit, and the species became a little better known. In the 1890s sportsmen in search of markhor, ibex, and blue sheep began to encounter the snow leopard in the wild, and occasional observations on the cat's natural history started to appear in published accounts. However, it was not until the 1970s and 1980s that biologists began to study the snow leopard's life in the wild.[4,7,8,9,10,11,12]

The snow leopard is often called "ounce" or "once." The term is believed to have its origins with the Greeks, who used "lynx" for every medium-sized cat species. According to Ingo Rieger of the Zürich zoo, "In Roman culture, the Greek term 'lynx' was Latinized to 'lonza,' which was later transformed to the French 'lonce.' Over the centuries the 'l' of 'lonce' was mis-

taken for an article (l'once) and thus the noun was reduced to 'once.'" From there the name was Latinized to "uncia," and the snow leopard became *Felis uncia*.[4] The snow leopard has also been included in the genus *Panthera*, but it is currently placed in its own genus, *Uncia*.[13,14]

DESCRIPTION

With its pale eyes and exotically marked fur, the snow leopard is one of the most beautiful of the big cats. About the same size as or slightly smaller than a common leopard, the snow leopard has a bushy tail that is "thicker than a man's forearm" and as long as 75 to 90 percent of the cat's head and body length. This stocky cat has a well-developed chest, a relatively long body, and moderately long legs. It is a strong and muscular animal built low to the ground; indeed, it stands only 56 centimeters at the shoulder. The massive front paws are larger than the hind paws.[13,15]

A snow leopard skull can be easily distinguished from that of a common leopard. In profile the snow leopard skull has a marked step in front of the eyes, a short muzzle, and a high, domed forehead caused by an enlargement of the nasal cavities. The large nasal cavities are thought to allow the snow leopard to breathe more easily at high altitudes, where temperatures are low and oxygen is in short supply. The short, rounded ears are set wide apart, and the backs of the ears have pale centers rimmed with black. In winter the cat's ears become almost invisible, hidden by its long, dense fur. One of the snow leopard's most striking features is its hooded, hauntingly pale eyes, which always appear to be gazing into the distance. The eyes are unusual among felids in that the iris appears pale green or gray.[13,16]

The background color of the fur is smoky gray, varying to grayish buff, and the underparts of the body are whitish. Black spots mark the head, neck, and lower limbs, while the flanks, back, and tail are covered with large, dark rosettes or irregular circles. The centers of the rosettes tend to be darker than the background coat color. The markings coalesce along the back to form two dark lines that extend from the neck to the beginning of the tail. The fur is strikingly long and luxuriant; in the winter it can be over 5 centimeters long on the back, sides, and tail and almost 12 centimeters long on the belly. Such insulation is obviously important for survival in subzero temperatures.[13,15]

Like jaguars, tigers, and leopards, individual snow leopards can be identified by their markings. Spot patterns are unique for each individual.[17] Leif Blomqvist of the Helsinki Zoo devised a method of identifying snow leopards by the pattern of spots on the forehead. The number and shape of the spots in this area vary markedly between individuals, and no two captive animals have been found to have identical spots.[18]

The snow leopard's massive paws are well suited both for gripping rocky inclines and for "snowshoeing" through deep, soft snow. As zookeepers will testify, the snow leopard is also a legendary leaper. Ognev recalls seeing one leaping "not less than 15 meters uphill over a ditch."[19] While this is obviously exaggerated, there are reliable reports of snow leopards jumping 6 meters. In 1903 the first snow leopard to arrive in the United States had to be shot when it escaped from its enclosure at the Bronx Zoo by climbing through a skylight.[20] The snow leopard's long, thick tail is used as a balancing organ during climbing and leaping, and also assists the cat in keeping its balance during the swift twists and turns that accompany chases of prey.[13,21]

Snow leopards are known to become exceptionally tame and gentle in captivity, and they often form close bonds with their caretakers. Helen Freeman, of the International Snow Leopard Trust, quotes an anonymous writer as saying, "In captivity, it is far the tamest and gentlest of the large carnivora, not excepting the puma. Unlike the latter it is a sleepy, quiet animal, like a domestic cat."[20] In the wild it also seems to be one of the least aggressive of the large cats. There are few records of snow leopards attacking people, and they readily relinquish kills of domestic livestock, even to a child brandishing a stick. They rarely defend themselves, and there are many records of snow leopards being beaten or stoned to death by otherwise unarmed villagers. A Soviet report describes how a snow leopard entered a sheep pen in a high mountain pasture. "On hearing the commotion in the pen, the shepherdess rushed in and, catching the animal by its tail, with shouts began to drag it away from the wounded sheep. The ounce did not attempt to protect itself and was killed by shepherds who had arrived at the scene."[15] Helen Freeman believes that because the snow leopard's contact with humans has been quite limited until recently, it may not have had time to realize that man is a lethal adversary.

DISTRIBUTION

The snow leopard is found only in the high mountain regions of central Asia. Its range extends from the eastern edge of the Tibetan Plateau westward along the

Figure 46. Distribution of the snow leopard.

Himalaya of Sikkim, Bhutan, Nepal, and India to the Karakoram and Hindu Kush ranges of Pakistan and Afghanistan. From there its range extends northeastward over the Pamir and Tien Shan ranges in the former Soviet Union and China and through the Altai and Khangai ranges of Mongolia to the Sayan Mountains near Lake Baikal (fig. 46). The snow leopard's total historic range was in excess of 2.5 million square kilometers, but it was not found throughout this expanse. Core areas of its habitat follow long, narrow mountain ranges, and thus populations are separated into small pockets and islands, embedded in a vast high desert plateau. Current estimates put the area of snow leopard habitat at 1.2 to 1.6 million square kilometers.[22,23]

ECOLOGY AND BEHAVIOR

Besides being high-altitude animals, snow leopards are really rock specialists, and they are usually found in rugged areas where the terrain is broken by cliffs, ridges, and ravines. In the Himalaya, typical snow leopard habitat is broken, sparsely vegetated, dry alpine steppe above the treeline. Radio-collared snow leopards in the Langu Gorge, Nepal, preferred to rest on cliffs and in broken terrain, spending most of their time in areas where the slope exceeded 40°.[24,25,26] In Hemis National Park in Ladakh, a radio-collared snow leopard showed a similar preference for broken rocky areas on steep slopes and avoided smooth terrain.[27] At lower elevations in the eastern Kulun Shan in the Qinghai and Gansu provinces of China, snow leopards use the floors of the wide, flat valleys that break the mountain ranges.[28]

During the summer snow leopards range from elevations of about 2,743 meters to the snowline at 5,488 to 6,097 meters. Mountain climbers have seen snow leopard tracks at over 5,792 meters. However, these cats are also found at lower elevations; in some regions they live at 600 to 1,500 meters.[15] In northwestern Pakistan and other parts of the snow leopard's range, deep winter snow forces wild ungulates to seek food and shelter at lower elevations, and at this time of year the snow leopard follows its prey to elevations of 1,219 meters or lower.[7,16,29]

Apart from humans, the snow leopard's only competitors are wolves. At lower elevations in the Himalaya the snow leopard overlaps occasionally with the common leopard and sometimes the Asiatic wild dog (dhole). On one occasion filmmakers working on a wildlife documentary in Hemis National Park saw a snow leopard appropriate a kill from a group of four dholes. The dholes had killed a domestic goat at dusk during a snowstorm, and they had just begun to feed when a thin snow leopard appeared. The dogs moved away and watched while the leopard picked up the carcass and carried it across the valley and up onto the rocks. The dogs followed at a distance, watching and calling, but did not attempt to recover the kill.[30] Wolves use high-altitude habitats more than wild dogs or common leopards and so compete more directly with snow leopards. In Hemis National Park, Joe Fox and Chering Nurbu were crossing a 4,878-meter pass when they saw a pair of wolves moving through the high open meadows used to pasture domestic yaks in summer. "Two wolves came over the 17,000 foot ridgeline and trotted easily down the wide expanse of open meadow high above the Zanscar river gorge. As if by magic the meadows suddenly came alive for hundreds of yards all around the wolves as marmots scrambled out of their burrows, stood high on their hind legs and sent out high-pitched whistles warning each other of the wolves' presence." According to Fox, wolves are considered a greater menace to domestic animals than snow leopards in many parts of Ladakh.[31]

The snow leopard is a terrestrial hunter, most active at dawn and dusk (crepuscular), although it may hunt at any time of the day or night. In areas where this cat is not disturbed by humans it often hunts during the daytime; where it feeds extensively on domestic livestock it tends to be more nocturnal because of the need to avoid encountering humans. A hunting snow leopard uses ledges, cliffs, and whatever cover is available in the broken terrain to get close enough

to make an attack. It often makes its approach from above, and most eyewitness accounts of kills or attempted kills illustrate this hunting strategy.[10,25,32,33,34] While watching bharal, or blue sheep, in the Langu Gorge in Nepal, Gary Ahlborn saw a spectacular chase in which a snow leopard pursued a male blue sheep over a steep, rocky slope:

> After a chase of about a hundred yards, the leopard made a quick lunge forward, catching the male on the left side of its rump with its left forepaw and jaw. This sent a cloud of pelage into the air. The bharal's rear dropped nearly to the ground and its knees buckled as it turned into the slope and absorbed the leopard's blow. The leopard's momentum forced it straight down-slope, all its limbs off the ground and outstretched. Its long tail flung into the air and around to the left side, causing it to twist sidewinder-fashion in the direction of the bharal and regain its control.[35]

Not much is known about the influence of weather on the snow leopard's hunting, but there is some conjecture that the cat is a more successful hunter in rain and snow. E. P. Koshkarev, who followed snow leopard tracks in the Tien Shan mountains, was of the opinion that "a deterioration of visibility in foul weather allows the predator to approach prey more closely."[10] Naturalists and trappers have often remarked on the snow leopard's tendency to hunt soon after a heavy snowfall. No one has yet quantified these observations, but fresh snow would help a cat move silently and so might make it easier to stalk prey on steep, rocky slopes.

Deep snow does not seem to prevent snow leopards from traveling, but they use goat and horse trails, and even the tracks of wild pigs and rabbits, to avoid breaking through new snow. When no trail is available, snow leopards will walk long distances through snow that may be as much as 85 centimeters deep. In the Tien Shan, scientists followed the tracks of one snow leopard that had walked through snow for 10 kilometers without stopping to rest. The snow was so deep that in places the animal's paws had penetrated to a depth of 43 centimeters, and its belly had created a furrow in the snow.[10]

Snow leopards find their prey by walking routes that tend to follow animal trails and other natural relief features. They use trails made by livestock, wild ungulates, and humans; on one occasion a snow leopard even made use of the ski track of a scientist who was studying it. They also follow river terraces, ridge-lines, valley floors, and the beds of deep gorges, and they avoid crossing large open spaces. These cats will take a longer, more circuitous route rather than walk through open, unbroken terrain.[10]

Though hunting snow leopards seem generally averse to crossing open terrain, recent information from the Altai Mountains near the Great Gobi National Park in Mongolia shows that these cats do indeed cross very large expanses of desert and steppe. A dispersing radio-collared male was tracked to an isolated mountain massif. To get there he had to cross some 30–40 kilometers of open steppe. The researchers suspected he had made the move in a single night. The unexpected discovery that a snow leopard had managed to travel across such a vast open expanse precipitated a survey of several neighboring isolated massifs. These sites were found to contain high densities of snow leopard sign in the form of scrapes and feces. To get to these distant outcrops the cats had to cross 20–65 kilometers of open steppe or desert. Researchers speculated that these massifs and buttes formed "corridors" through the desert, and that snow leopards used these rocky islands to travel between distant mountain ranges.[36]

Feeding Ecology

In some parts of India the snow leopard is known as *bharal-mar* or *bharal-hai*, meaning "bharal killer," and bharal (blue sheep) and ibex are the cat's major prey throughout much of its range. Snow leopards also eat urial and argali sheep, wild ass, musk deer, wild pigs, gazelles, and markhor, as well as smaller prey such as marmots, pikas, hares, rabbits, pheasant, partridge, and snowcock. They are not averse to carrion, and will also kill domestic sheep, goats, cows, horses, yaks, and dogs. Snow leopards also eat grass and twigs, and several authors mention finding droppings composed entirely of willow twigs or other vegetation.[7,13,15,26,28,34,37,38,39]

This habit of eating vegetation seems to hold true across the snow leopard's range. In Pakistan more than 22 percent of the scats examined contained plant matter, and in Ladakh more than half the 50 scats examined contained vegetation, including twigs of willow and *Myricaria* bushes.[7,40] Another study in Hemis National Park in Ladakh found plant remains in 41 percent of snow leopard scats. Twenty-five of 173 scats were composed entirely of *Myricaria germanica*, a 60–250-centimeter-high shrub belonging to the Tamaricaceae.[38] George Schaller also noted an unusual

amount of *Tamarix* twigs in snow leopard scats from a reserve in the western Tien Shan.[41] Though all felids eat small amounts of vegetation, there are no reports of other cat species consuming such large quantities of greenery. It is generally believed that cats use grass and other plant material as a digestive aid or a laxative. The snow leopard's habit of eating such large quantities of vegetation may be related to eliminating parasites or, odd as it may sound, supplementing its diet. Interestingly, several closely related *Tamarix* species are colloquially known as "manna plants" because they produce a nutritious, edible exudate.

Blue sheep are the principal prey of snow leopards in the Langu Valley in West Nepal, although tahr are also taken.[25] Of twelve kills found, seven were blue sheep and five were tahr; all kills but two were adults. In Langu, subadult snow leopards weighing 20 kilograms killed adult male bharal weighing more than 55 kilograms, about three times their own body weight. An analysis of scats showed that snow leopards also ate small rodents, pikas, and game birds.

Blue sheep are also the principal food of snow leopards in northwestern India,[38] Nepal,[7,37,42] and parts of Tibet.[39] In the Chitral district of Pakistan's North-West Frontier Province, where there are no blue sheep, the winter diet of snow leopards is divided about equally between markhor and domestic stock.[7] Ibex constitute the majority (60–70 percent) of snow leopard diets in Mongolia, with marmots making up 15–20 percent and domestic stock less than 5 percent.[36]

In the western half of China's Taxkorgan Reserve in spring, 60 percent of snow leopard scats contained blue sheep remains and 29 percent contained marmot fur and bones. Feces also contained the remains of ibex, hares, snowcock, grass, and livestock. At this time of year livestock do not figure prominently in the snow leopard's diet; predation on livestock occurs more often in late winter, although the major predator of domestic stock in the reserve is wolves. In the Qinghai and Gansu Provinces of China, the snow leopard's summer diet consisted of 30 to 45 percent wild ungulates, principally blue sheep. In some areas marmots were more important than ungulates, making up 36 to 65 percent of the summer diet. Droppings also revealed that snow leopards occasionally ate hares, birds, pikas, and grass.[28]

There is a suggestion that snow leopards prey most heavily on adult male ungulates, although this hypothesis is hard to evaluate because the proportion of each sex and age class in the prey population is not often known. In a small sample of blue sheep and tahr from western Nepal, six of ten adults killed were males.[25] Similarly, Dang reported that six of seven blue sheep kills were males; two ibex kills were also males.[32] In Russia, thirty-nine of forty-eight ibex kills were males, and the majority were animals more than five years old.[15,34] In the North-West Frontier Province of Pakistan, nine of eleven markhor killed were males.[7]

Snow leopards also prey on domestic livestock, but their impact varies from place to place. Predation on livestock is usually confined to attacks on solitary grazing animals, except when the cat manages to get inside a goat or sheep shed. Under these conditions it often kills several animals. Mallon reports one instance in which a snow leopard entered a livestock shed via a ventilation hole and killed thirty-four sheep and goats.[12] Some snow leopards are killed by villagers following attacks on livestock, and these killings can be an important source of mortality for the cat.

Mallon's observations in Ladakh provide an example of snow leopard interactions with livestock and people. "During the winter of 1983–84," he reports, "there were 20 attacks by snow leopards on 15 out of 40 villages in the central Indus Valley area, rather more than usual." The attacks resulted in the deaths of a yak and at least ninety-five sheep and goats. A female snow leopard with two young was responsible for at least eight of the raids. In response to these livestock losses, villagers killed at least five snow leopards, including a female and two cubs.[12]

The proportion of domestic animals in the snow leopard's diet varies seasonally. In places such as the Langu Valley in Nepal, where there are no villages and no domestic stock, snow leopards prey on wild ungulates throughout the year.[25] In other areas, livestock form an important part of the cat's diet, but usually only during the three to four winter months.[28,33,37,38,39,41] However, winter stock losses to snow leopards can be significant. In Mongolia, the eight resident families in Schaller's 200-square-kilometer study area lost thirteen sheep and goats, sixteen horses, and seven yaks to snow leopards in 1990. Though these losses may not seem great, they amounted to 17 percent of the residents' horses and 11.9 percent of their yaks. Snow leopards in Mongolia do not prey on domestic stock in proportion to its abundance, but seem to take a disproportionate toll on horses, perhaps because horses and yaks are allowed to roam in the mountains, whereas sheep and goats are guarded by their owners. One herdsman with about 300 horses lost twenty-one of

them to snow leopards in eight months; nineteen of the victims were foals.[43]

In the Manang district (Annapurna Conservation Area) of Nepal, 95 percent of respondents to a survey on the snow leopard had a negative attitude toward the cat because of its history of predation on domestic stock.[44] People considered the snow leopard to be vermin, and more than half of the respondents suggested that the best way to reduce losses would be to exterminate the cat. In Manang most villagers live below the poverty line, earning less than the national average of U.S.$160 per year. People in the area make their living by subsistence crop and livestock farming, and each household owns an average of 26.6 animals, two-thirds of which are goats. Over a third of the households surveyed reported losing livestock to snow leopards; the average household loss was about a quarter of the national average income. Some families suffered devastating losses. One lost two horses worth about five times the national average income, and another lost eleven goats in a single attack. A further in-depth assessment of snow leopard predation on livestock in the Annapurna Conservation Area revealed the existence of depredation "hotspots." Losses in these spots sometimes exceeded 14 to 20 percent of the livestock population over a short period. Goats and sheep were more vulnerable than the larger yaks, although horses were especially vulnerable.[45]

Like other felids, snow leopards approach their prey as closely as possible before launching the final attack. They make full use of the rugged terrain to hide their approach, then rely on surprise and their own athletic abilities to catch the prey. There are few eyewitness accounts of snow leopards hunting or moving through precipitous terrain, but Gary Ahlborn vividly described a brief glimpse he had of the cat moving through an extremely rugged area in Nepal:

> The leopard moves slowly west, crossing Tillisha Stream. It doesn't use the main trail; instead it remains within a foot of the sheer escarpment edge. After walking a hundred feet it stops and with its ears cocked forward peers intently to the river below, as though it were stalking prey. Then the cat jumps and somehow clings to the steep slab rock and easily traverses down the hundred-foot cliff and onto the rockfall below.[35]

Snow leopards use this agility when pursuing prey across slopes or down mountainsides. They seem more inclined to chase prey than most of the other big cats;

several observers have noted chases of 200 to 300 meters. It may be that in steep, rocky areas a predator attacking from above gains an advantage from its initial downhill momentum. Even the most sure-footed prey may stumble when running for its life through such precipitous terrain, and by continuing the chase, the snow leopard remains in a position to profit from any such mistake.[46]

The snow leopard kills its prey with a bite to the throat or nape. Its feeding behavior varies: the prey may or may not be eviscerated, and the cat may begin to eat almost anywhere on the carcass. It may move its kill to a more secure place and may protect the carcass from scavengers such as vultures and crows.[7,15,33,34] In Nepal, radio-tagged cats consumed all edible parts of a carcass, and they did not cover the remains of their kills.[25]

Captive snow leopards are fed between 6 and 27 kilograms of food per week,[47] most commonly 1.5 kilograms a day.[48] In the wild, an adult blue sheep provides a snow leopard with food for three to five days, and radio-tagged cats in Nepal sometimes stayed with a kill for as long as a week. However, a female and her two cubs consumed an adult bharal in less than forty-eight hours.[25] Based on the movement patterns of radio-collared snow leopards in Nepal, Jackson and Ahlborn estimated that the cats killed a blue-sheep-sized prey about once every ten to fifteen days, or twenty-four to thirty-six such animals per year.[24] In areas where large prey are less abundant, snow leopards survive by killing more small animals such as marmots. Schaller estimated that 45 percent of the meat in a snow leopard's summer diet in the Anyemaqen Shan (southeastern Qinghai Province) came from marmots (average weight: 5–6 kilograms). During the winter, when marmots were hibernating, their contribution to the diet was replaced by increased predation on blue sheep or domestic livestock.[28]

Social Organization

In the past, several authors have suggested that snow leopards travel and hunt in pairs, although the sex, age, and reproductive status of the individuals involved are rarely mentioned. Recent studies of radio-tagged individuals indicate that such associations are rare. In Nepal, Jackson's radio-tracking study showed that except for females with young and mating pairs, snow leopards are solitary. Radio locations also revealed that even when all five radio-collared cats were using a relatively small area, they usually rested at least 2 kilometers apart.[26] Similarly, in Mongolia the mean distance between radio-tagged snow leopards located on the same day varied from 1.3 kilometers (between males) to 4.8 kilometers (between males and females) to 7.8 kilometers (between females).[36]

There is little information on the home range sizes of snow leopards, although where prey are scarce the ranges of the cats are likely to be large. Among felids in general, adults regularly visit and renew scent marks throughout their ranges, usually every two to four weeks. In many areas where snow leopards occur, the intervals between the appearance of tracks are much longer, suggesting that the cats are moving over extremely large ranges. In places where prey are locally abundant, home ranges are surprisingly small. An adult female in the Langu Gorge in Nepal sustained herself and one to two cubs in an area of 38.9 square kilometers. Her independent subadult daughter used an area of 19.7 square kilometers, which was a subset of her mother's range. A subadult male in the same area used a range of 22.7 square kilometers.[25] In Hemis National Park, Ladakh, one snow leopard used a 19-square-kilometer area over a period of two and a half months during the winter.[27] Similarly, based on a small number of radio locations, two adult females in the Annapurna Conservation Area used ranges of 21 and 22 square kilometers during the winter. An adult male in the same area used 13.9 square kilometers, which is obviously an underestimate of his range.[49]

Home range sizes of radio-tagged snow leopards in Mongolia, when measured using conventional ground-based telemetry locations, varied from 14 to 142 square kilometers. However, when satellite locations were included, one female's range increased in size from 58 square kilometers to a minimum of 1,590 square kilometers, which is an order of magnitude larger than any previously reported home range. The satellite-tracking data also show that snow leopards in Mongolia were commonly moving more than 12 kilometers per day; one female traveled 27.9 kilometers in a day.[36] These distances are much greater than those reported in other studies, but it is apparent that without satellite tracking the potential to underestimate home range size is enormous. The few studies that have monitored radio-tagged snow leopards have all reported significant periods of time when the cats could not be located using conventional methods, indicating that they were using larger areas. How much larger is unknown, but if the satellite data from Mongolia are any indication, snow leopards are ranging over extremely large areas to find prey and mates.

Given the remote and rugged places where the snow leopard lives, it is not too surprising that only a few density estimates exist for the species. Most estimates are based on interpretations of sign—tracks, scrapes, feces, or other spoor—and thus vary in reliability. Nevertheless, surveys in many areas indicate that snow leopards exist at low densities but can be locally abundant. One such density "hot spot" is the Langu Valley, where there was an estimated adult and subadult density of five to ten animals per 100 square kilometers.[25] Likewise, in the Manang district of the Annapurna Conservation Area, densities reached five to seven adults per 100 square kilometers.[44] A "hot spot" for snow leopards in China was in northwestern Qinghai Province, where five peasants poached fourteen snow leopards from one area in just sixty days.[50] However, snow leopard densities over vast areas of Russia, China, and Ladakh are much lower, ranging from approximately 0.5 to 1 animal per 100 square kilometers.[7,11,12,51,52]

Snow leopards use a variety of indirect and direct means of communication. Their vocal repertoire is similar to that of other felids, except that they do not purr. Furthermore, snow leopards do not roar like lions, tigers, jaguars, and leopards, but they do spit, hiss, growl, and cough-roar. They make the soft "prusten" greeting and appeasement call, and have a rich repertoire of mewlike calls. Both sexes have a "main" call, which has been described as a "piercing yowl." The call is used by females in estrus and probably helps animals locate each other.[53,54,55] In the Langu Gorge, biologists heard snow leopards yowling during the winter mating season. The calls carried long distances and were loud enough to be heard over the roar of the river. Most yowling seemed to occur in the evening, between 1900 and 2200 hours.[56]

Snow leopards communicate mainly by scent marks, which include feces, urine, and scrapes. Scrapes, the most commonly seen marks, are made by a backward raking motion of the hind feet, resulting in a conspicuous mark about 20 centimeters long. Scrapes may also be marked with feces or urine. Scrape marks occur singly or in clusters, the latter being associated with remarking or overmarking by one or several individuals. Some sites, particularly those that are highly visible, are re-marked more frequently than others.[56] In Ladakh, the heaviest concentrations of scrapes occurred around stream confluences.[40] Snow leopards make scrape marks along commonly traveled routes, which include the bases of cliffs, ridgelines, and river terraces. Their movements tend to follow the path of least resistance, and as Mallon noted, "scrapes were generally associated with some obvious topographic feature or placed where paths were forced by the relief into narrow situations."[40]

In the wild, adult males and females, and animals over a year and a half old, mark and re-mark intensively.[56] In addition to scraping, snow leopards also scent-mark by backing up to objects such as rocks or boulders, raising the tail, and squirting urine. They often spray sites that are protected from the elements, such as the undersides of overhanging rocks and boulders. Snow leopards may also cheek-rub and scrape on these urine-marked sites. In captivity, male snow leopards spray more frequently than females, although this pattern has not been confirmed in the wild.[25,29,56,57,58,59,60] The snow leopard's system of scent marking helps individuals avoid, identify, or locate one another. Scent marks are thought to convey information on individual identity, reproductive status, sex, and the time the mark was made. The marks are also likely to indicate that an area is occupied, and studies in Nepal and Ladakh found that marks were concentrated in areas of high mutual use.[40,56] Among the Langu snow leopards, the intensity of scent marking appeared to be strongly correlated with sexual activity, possibly due to the increased frequency of spraying by females. Males are likely to locate females in heat via their scent marks, as scent is the best form of advertisement in terrain where individuals are widely scattered and are otherwise unlikely to encounter each other.[56]

Reproduction and Development

Snow leopards live in habitats with extremely harsh winters, and one would predict that they would have a highly restricted mating season because of the limited months of optimal weather and prey availability. Matings in captivity have been noted from January through June, although most occur in January and February. Birth records of 427 captive snow leopards show that 89 percent of the births occurred in April, May, and June, with over half of the total (54.3 percent) in May.[61] The snow leopard is unusual among the large cats in having a well-defined birth peak (fig. 47). Few other felid species show markedly seasonal birth peaks, and in tropical and subtropical areas young may be born at any time of the year, although births often coincide with periods of prey abundance.

In the Langu Valley, observations of scent marking

and calling indicated that estrus occurs between January and March, peaking in late February.[25] In Ladakh the mating season is thought to be late March and April, as shepherds report hearing snow leopards calling at night during these months.[12] Similarly, in Nepal, George Schaller was told that the loud meows he heard in March were made by the snow leopard searching for a mate.[7] Unlike common leopards and many other cats, captive snow leopards rarely re-cycle and re-mate if a litter of cubs dies.[62]

Some data from captivity suggest that the estrous cycle is dependent on day length (photoperiod), and that snow leopards in a given location tend toward a synchrony of estrus.[63,64,65] This pattern, and the fact that females are receptive for only a few days each year, is likely to influence the level of male competition for females and probably has a profound influence on the social system.[66] In most felids (e.g., tigers, pumas, and ocelots), females live alone in separate or partially overlapping home ranges and may come into estrus at any time of the year. In this situation, one male is able to monopolize matings with several females by permanently defending a large enough piece of ground to include all their ranges and making sure that he regularly visits each female to monitor her reproductive status. Snow leopards, however, live at surprisingly high densities (five to ten per 100 square kilometers) where prey are abundant.[25,26,44] When all the females in an area become sexually receptive at the same time, it is unlikely that any one male can monopolize matings with several females. By the time the two sexes have found each other and gone through courtship and mating, there is probably not enough time for the male to find and mate with another female, because in all likelihood she will have already been inseminated by another male. Under these circumstances it is not cost-effective for males to maintain exclusive home ranges or to try to monopolize access to several females. Thus, there is likely to be considerable home range overlap among males.

The duration of estrus is reported to vary from two to twelve days, but observations of repeated copulations over a two- to three-day period suggest that the peak of estrus is shorter. Captive observations indicate that estrus usually lasts five to eight days.[65] A good indicator of estrus is an increase in rolling behavior; estrous females show significant increases in the time spent rolling. In zoos where some individuals breed and others do not, it is sometimes possible to distinguish between successful and unsuccessful breeders by

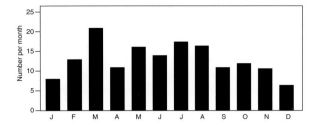

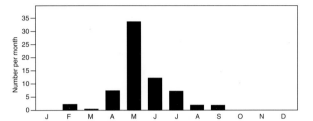

Figure 47. Distribution of birth months in (*top*) captive common leopards (*Panthera pardus*) (n = 146 litters) and (*bottom*) captive snow leopards (*Uncia uncia*) (n = 60 litters).

subtle differences in behavior. Successful males and females are more active and spend more time grooming, interacting with each other, and investigating their enclosure.[60,67,68] Copulation takes place over a period of three to six days. Pairs mate often, possibly twelve to thirty-six times a day, and coitus lasts fifteen to forty-five seconds. During mating, the female usually lies on her belly in the typical felid lordosis position with her tail arched and turned to the side. At intromission, the male grasps the female by the skin on the nape of the neck, and toward the end of copulation he gives a loud, piercing yowl.[60,69,70]

In the wild and in captivity, most young are born in May and June, following a gestation period of 94 to 103 days. Using data from sixty-seven captive gestation periods reported in the international snow leopard studbook, Blomqvist and Sten calculated that 58 percent of gestations lasted 94 to 98 days, and of these, 19 percent were 97 days.[71] Litter size varies from one to five cubs. In an examination of 203 litters born in captivity, the average litter size was 2.2. There were 97 litters of two cubs, 60 litters of three, 40 litters of one, and 6 litters of four.

The cubs are born in a secluded, sheltered den, often a cave or rock crevice. The mother reportedly lines the den with her soft belly fur, and there is a record of a den found in Szechwan that was carpeted with molted fur to a depth of 1.27 centimeters.[15] Newborn snow leopards weigh 320 to 567 grams.[13,72] Blind and helpless at birth, they are born with a thick, woolly coat to insulate them from the cold. They open their eyes when they are about seven days old. In captivity, the mother spends almost all her time at the den grooming, nursing, or resting during the cubs' first week of life.[73] This behavior is also seen in the wild; a radio-tagged female in the Langu Valley greatly reduced her movements, staying at or near the den following the birth of her cubs.[35] The young gain weight rapidly, putting on 300 to 500 grams a week for the first few weeks. When they are about four and a half weeks old, they begin to huddle together when their mother leaves the den. This is also the time when cubs begin to show the first signs of social and solitary play, rolling alone or together and waving their paws in the air or cuffing each other. At five weeks snow leopard cubs weigh 2.5 to 3 kilograms and are able to walk upright. At this age in captivity they are just beginning to eat solid foods, and the mother now starts to spend more time away from the den. At two months zoo-bred snow leopard cubs weigh about 4 kilograms. By ten weeks they are weaned and weigh 6 to 6.5 kilograms.[73,74]

There is no information from the wild as to when snow leopard cubs begin to follow their mother. The cubs are probably confined to the den for the first two months of their lives, and may begin to follow their mother sometime between the ages of two and four months. George Schaller saw what he estimated was a four-month-old cub with its mother at a goat carcass in Chitral.[7]

Like all the large cats, young snow leopards are dependent on their mothers for a relatively long time. The literature contains several references to the fact that litters born in the summer continue to travel together throughout the winter. In Langu Valley a radio-tagged female and her eighteen-month-old daughter were located together on three consecutive days; a month later the mother gave birth to a new litter. The daughter continued to use parts of her mother's range until the new cubs were a year old. Whether she stayed on after that is unknown, as the study ended.[26,75]

The nutritional demands of rearing young increase as the young grow, and a female with two six- to eight-month-old cubs needs to kill twice as much prey as a female without young. By this time the cubs are beginning to learn to hunt, but they may be more of a hindrance than a help to their mother. Jackson and Ahlborn were able to catch a glimpse of a female and her two one-year-old cubs moving through a remote mountain area. The female was "sauntering along, with the cubs doing everything but saunter beside her.

They romped. They chased one another, rolling and tumbling down the steep hillside. They stalked imaginary sheep. They leaped and charged, playing as if they were baby kittens while their mother padded along, well aware of the small herd of bharal on the slopes above."[35]

Clearly, females must go to considerable lengths to feed their growing young. When her cubs are small, the mother needs an abundant, localized food supply, as she cannot leave them unattended for long. When the cubs are older, they can travel with their mother, but she must catch twice the normal amount of prey to feed them. Considering the cubs' potentially disruptive influence on their mother's hunting efforts, a female with large dependent cubs must spend a great deal of time hunting, and it is not surprising that reports of snow leopards repeatedly killing domestic stock often refer to a female and her half-grown young.

In captivity, snow leopards become sexually mature when they are about two to three years old,[74,76,77,78] but females are often four years old before they give birth to their first litter.[73] The average life span of females in captivity is 9.6 years, but a female in the Cheyenne Mountain Zoo, Colorado, was at least eighteen years old when she gave birth to a litter. Males reach sexual maturity at about the same age as females, but similarly do not begin to successfully father litters until they are about four. Few males older than eleven years successfully sire young.[73] In captivity snow leopards have lived to be twenty-one years old.[79]

There is no information on snow leopard dispersal, and many biologists are concerned about the potential for inbreeding because these cats are confined to mountain massifs and high mountain ranges. Small populations of snow leopards live on islandlike mountains of habitat in an ocean of desolate plains, some of them hundreds of kilometers or miles from the next mountain area. There is, however, some anecdotal information suggesting that snow leopards are capable of crossing large areas of unsuitable habitat. In one case, recorded in eastern Kazakhstan in 1958, a snow leopard was seen in the hills on the northern shore of Lake Balkhash. The nearest snow leopard habitat was over 600 kilometers away, so the cat must have traveled at least that distance, possibly more. Another snow leopard was seen in the same area in the 1960s. There are several other records of snow leopards being found 150 to 200 kilometers from their regular haunts,[80] and given that documentation of these movements must be much rarer than their actual occurrence, it seems reasonable to assume that snow leopards can in fact travel long distances through habitats not suitable for their long-term residence. Recent work in the sparsely populated Gobi Desert, Mongolia, has shown that snow leopards will cross flat, open valleys as wide as 65 kilometers.[36] It takes only a few successful dispersers per decade to markedly increase the probability of population persistence and relieve the deleterious genetic effects of isolation.[81]

STATUS IN THE WILD

All indications suggest that the snow leopard has never been very common. Historically, it may have lived at high densities in small pockets of ideal habitat, but it has probably always been rare. The worldwide population of snow leopards is currently estimated at 4,500 to 7,500 animals, but it is fragmented into many smaller subpopulations that are scattered over approximately 2,300,000 square kilometers.[23]

Today, much of the snow leopard's range lies in China, and previous distribution maps for the species have tended to include the entire Tibetan Plateau. However, recent information from George Schaller's survey of Qinghai and Gansu suggests that snow leopards occupy only about 10 percent of the 2.3 million square kilometers that make up the two provinces.[28,41] Schaller adds that "hunting, often in defense of livestock, has depressed snow leopard numbers in most areas and eliminated local populations."[82] He believes that it is not possible to estimate total snow leopard numbers in China, although in his opinion, "I would guess that at least 2,000 survive in the country."

Recent status surveys in other parts of the snow leopard's range indicate that numbers are low everywhere. A 1987 expedition into northern Hunza, Pakistan, found little sign of the snow leopard's presence outside of protected areas, and even within Khunjerab National Park (2,600 square kilometers) only five scrapes were found.[83] However, in a 1988 assessment of Khunjerab National Park, Per Wegge, a Norwegian biologist, reported that snow leopards, blue sheep, and ibex were common in the park. Wegge suggests that "with a good prey base in the relatively dense populations of ibex and blue sheep—added to by the high numbers of domestic stock and optimum habitat conditions—it would not be surprising if the park contains some of the densest populations of snow leopard in Asia." According to Wegge, none of the species are threatened by hunting or habitat deterioration inside the park. Wegge estimated that snow leopards kill ap-

proximately 10 percent of the area's domestic stock, but he did not find any evidence of intensive persecution by local people.[84]

Between 1980 and 1986 David Mallon conducted six surveys of snow leopards in Ladakh, and in the best habitat he figured there were two to four snow leopards per 100 square kilometers. For all of Ladakh, an area covering more than 58,000 square kilometers, he estimates there are at least a hundred, but probably fewer than two hundred, snow leopards. Mallon's general impression formed during these six trips is that snow leopard numbers changed little in Ladakh over the period of the surveys, and he saw no evidence of the declines or sharp increases reported in other areas.[12,40]

In Nepal snow leopards are largely restricted to areas north of the main Himalayan range, with the greatest numbers occurring in the west. About 25 percent of the country is considered potential snow leopard range, but only a small proportion is protected, and 65 percent of the snow leopard population lives outside the boundaries of existing parks and reserves. The largest areas of good snow leopard habitat are in the Dolpo, Mugu, and Humla districts, especially along the Tibetan border. The range is broken into smaller subsections by deep river valleys containing temperate or subtropical forest, which probably reduce the east-west movements of snow leopards and their prey. Unprotected habitat is crucial to the survival of Nepal's snow leopard population, which numbers 350 to 500 animals.[85]

The snow leopard is rare in Siberia, but has become more common in the last twenty-five to thirty years. About eighty individuals are thought to live in the mountains of Altai, western Sayan, and eastern Sayan.[52] One of the largest populations of snow leopards is thought to be in Russia, where some estimates place numbers as high as two thousand animals. Extrapolating from field data collected in northern and central Tien Shan, Spitsin and Koshkarev estimated that in 1988 there were six hundred snow leopards in 105,200 square kilometers of habitat in Kyrgyzstan. Reserves offer some protection, but new plans for economic development are likely to affect the status of wild sheep and consequently snow leopards.[86]

During four trips to Mongolia in 1989–1990, George Schaller and his co-workers found that most snow leopards were concentrated in the rugged low desert ranges of the Transaltai Gobi and the Altai. Their general impression was that roughly a thousand snow leopards may still survive in Mongolia.[43] Mongolia is a popular destination for wealthy Western trophy hunters who want to shoot ibex and argali sheep. The money earned from these hunts has proved to be a significant source of foreign currency for the country; in 1985 the government of Mongolia earned more than a million U.S. dollars through hunting. With the success of the sheep and goat hunts, the Mongolians began to look for other species that might be hunted on a limited basis, and in 1986 proposed a program of safari hunting of snow leopards in the South Gobi, with an annual quota of five snow leopards. The fee was set at U.S.$11,200 for each snow leopard killed, and U.S.$7,840 if the animal was wounded.[87] Other animals were also listed as available during the same hunt, but their trophy fees were much lower: wild ass, $1,970; black-tailed gazelle, $750; lynx, $660; and wolf, $200.[88] Though the snow leopard is listed on appendix I of CITES, the Mongolian People's Republic is not a signatory to the CITES agreement. Thus Mongolia was able to issue hunting and export permits for snow leopards; however, any trophy snow leopards (or wild ass) acquired during a hunt could not be imported into the United States, Europe, or other CITES signatory countries. While these hunts caused a great deal of controversy, it appears that not many hunters were successful at bagging a snow leopard. None were shot in 1988 or 1989, and only one was taken in 1990.[43,89] Trophy hunting of snow leopards is no longer permitted.[90]

The major threat to the snow leopard's existence seems to be the loss of its natural prey and conflict with humans over domestic stock. Weapons are common throughout much of the cat's range, and all the snow leopard's prey, even those the size of marmots, are subject to fairly intense hunting pressure. Furthermore, compared with the other big cats, the snow leopard seems to be unusually passive when threatened by people and is easily chased off kills. Where villagers keep livestock, domestic goats and sheep often form an important part of the snow leopard's winter diet. This brings the cat into conflict with villagers, and many snow leopards are killed each year in retaliation for stock raiding.

The snow leopard has had full legal protection in all countries that are parties to CITES since 1983, but that protection exists largely on paper. Countries such as China, India, and Pakistan have neither funds nor staff to enforce regulations, and snow leopards and their prey are often shot as they are encountered.

Not surprisingly, the snow leopard's deep, luxuriant fur has always been highly prized. However, because of this cat's natural rarity, there have never been as many snow leopard skins on the market as those of the common leopard or the jaguar. Though most countries with snow leopard populations are signatories to the CITES agreement (which prohibits commercial trade in endangered species), skins and coats continue to be sold in fur markets. A full-length coat made from six to ten skins still sells for more than U.S.$60,000.[91] In 1988 and 1989 snow leopard skins and full-length coats were on sale in Kathmandu in hotel fur shops and stores that cater to tourists. The coats were far beyond the means of most local people and were designed principally for the foreign tourist market. Store owners were confident that a snow leopard coat could easily be smuggled out of the country, and offered to sew artificial fur over the illegal coats, pack the fur into an ornate pillowcase, or falsify documents stating that the coat was old and predated the CITES agreement.[92,93]

Poaching of snow leopards and their prey became a major problem after the breakup of the Soviet Union. In 1992–1993 demand for the skins, horns, and bones of snow leopards, lynx, sheep, and goats sharply increased, and prices leaped to 30 to 150 times their former level. In the winter of 1993–1994 snow leopard skins were selling for U.S.$500–$2,000, more than sixty times the minimum yearly wage in Kyrgyzstan. Even skins of the gray marmot, an important prey item for the snow leopard, were selling for U.S.$3.00 each. According to Eugene Koshkarev of the Tien Shan High Mountain Physical Geography Station in Kyrgyzstan, the current level of poaching is probably three to four times greater than it was before the breakup of the Soviet Union. The main markets for wildlife are located in Russia, among foreign tourists; however, dealers also trade in wildlife skins and animal body parts, and there is a continued demand for traps and guns.[94]

According to Professor Tan Bangjie of the Chinese Association of Zoological Gardens, snow leopard fur is not especially valued in China, but the bones are in demand for medicine as a substitute for tiger and leopard bones.[95] In the Tibet Autonomous Region the bones of a snow leopard can bring a villager as much as U.S.$190, as opposed to a pelt, which brings only $9–18. Biologist Rod Jackson believes that "unless alternatives are found to the use of snow leopard or tiger bones in Chinese medicine, these species face a bleak future."[39]

STATUS IN CAPTIVITY

The captive population of snow leopards is a textbook example of good captive management of a rare species. This has largely been made possible by an outstanding record of cooperation and information sharing between institutions and a history of careful recordkeeping by Leif Blomqvist of the Helsinki Zoo. In less than thirty years the species has moved from being poorly understood and difficult to breed in captivity to being one of the few felids for which captive populations are now secure numerically and genetically for the foreseeable future. Snow leopards now breed very successfully in captivity, and since 1980 the captive population has undergone a population explosion. Blomqvist started a studbook in 1976, and a Species Survival Plan (SSP) was implemented in 1984 when the population was still expanding and while the thirty wild-caught founders were still well represented in the population. The studbook, which is published biannually, provides information on the breeding history and genealogy of each animal and on changes in the captive population. It has been estimated that a well-managed captive population of about 230 animals will maintain nearly 90 percent of its original genetic variation for 200 years. More than 500 snow leopards are held in captivity worldwide, and the captive population is spread among many zoos, providing a safeguard against disease or natural disasters. Most snow leopard pairs are allowed to produce no more than two or three litters in their lifetimes, and currently only twenty-five to thirty cubs per year are needed to maintain a stable population in North American zoos.[48,79,96,97]

CONSERVATION EFFORTS

A network of conservation areas is being established in the mountains of central Asia. Bhutan and Sikkim have designated more than 20 percent of their geographic area as protected lands, and more than 9 percent of India, Nepal, and Pakistan is covered by conservation areas. China, Afghanistan, and the former Soviet states are not as well represented; in the latter two countries less than 1 percent of the land area is designated as conservation land.[98]

Michael Green, of the World Conservation Monitoring Center, believes that "considerable progress has been achieved in the establishment of conservation area networks in the mountains of Central Asia." Between 1987 and 1991 twenty-seven conservation areas were established, and a further seventy-six are proposed. Though many of these reserves are small, some are extensive and cross international boundaries. Qomolangma and Taxkorgan in China, together with adjacent reserves in Nepal and Pakistan, measure 40,088 square kilometers and 16,269 square kilometers, respectively.[98]

Despite this great progress in designating more conservation areas, it is clear that countries with snow leopard populations need more resources for management of these areas. Only a few receive as much as U.S.$100 per square kilometer per year; by comparison, financial support for the still underfunded tiger reserves in India is an order of magnitude higher.[98]

In 1992 the International Snow Leopard Trust (ISLT) announced Project Snow Leopard, a collaborative program in conservation.[91,99] The project has several aims:

- Promote regional cooperation in conservation in six countries.
- Improve management of mountain reserves in these six countries.
- Strengthen local conservation institutions through training and program support.
- Involve the local people in all stages of the project.
- Reduce poaching of snow leopards by providing technical support to a minimum of twelve reserves.
- Identify and begin establishment of one new major transboundary park.

The project places a high priority on the human aspects of conservation, including education, livestock depredation, poaching, and the bone trade, but it also aims to improve reserve management, identify dispersal corridors, and promote the establishment of transboundary parks.[91]

Most biologists familiar with the snow leopard and its conservation problems consider the support and cooperation of local people to be the vital ingredient in successful protection. Where natural prey has declined, domestic livestock has become a key element in the snow leopard's winter diet. Local grazers are rarely compensated for livestock losses, and as they live and graze their animals far from the eyes of the wildlife department, it is not too surprising that they usually deal with the predator in their own way. To break through local hostility to parks and conservation areas, WWF-Pakistan initiated two projects designed to give local people a role in the decision-making process. In the Khunjerab National Park, years of hostility and conflict were resolved by negotiation and compromise. The authorities agreed to allow a hundred yaks to graze in the core zone of the park in exchange for an agreement that grazers would be responsible for the protection of every wild animal in the park. Under the agreement the people could not kill snow leopards or claim compensation for livestock losses. Under the circumstances, this was the most workable option.[100]

In the Bar Valley near Gilgit, local people, who kill some three hundred ibex each year, were persuaded to protect the animals instead. The incentive that made them willing to abandon this traditional source of winter food was the option of future trophy hunting by foreign tourists. Donor agencies agreed to provide compensation for the villagers until the ibex population expands to a point at which a few trophy animals can be hunted, and in exchange local people agreed not to kill any wild animal in the area. Organizers believe that it will soon be possible to sell the rights to hunt ten trophy ibex each year, and the money earned will compensate the local people for the loss of ibex meat and livestock killed by snow leopards.[100]

In other areas people are looking into a variety of different ways to solve the problem of snow leopard predation on domestic livestock. Guard dogs have effectively reduced predator attacks on livestock in some North American rangelands, and could possibly be used in some snow leopard habitat. In Tibet, more sheep and goats are killed while feeding on the open range during the daytime than are taken from enclosures at night. Local mastiff breeds guard livestock enclosures at night, but are not as useful during the daytime.[101]

In some places it might be possible to alter people's attitudes toward wildlife by providing assistance to herders and livestock owners. Veterinary services would reduce livestock losses to a variety of diseases, infections, and predators; many domestic animals survive wolf and snow leopard attacks with only minor injuries, but die later from infected wounds.[43] Compensation schemes are notoriously difficult to administer, but they have proved effective in some areas. One of the advantages to such schemes in snow leopard habitats is that the amount of money required is quite small by Western standards. Madan Oli, a biologist studying snow leopards in Nepal, calculated that an endowment fund of U.S.$135,000 earning 12 percent interest would be sufficient to compensate local people for livestock losses in the Manang district of Nepal.[44] Such sums are within the reach of individuals, Western zoological parks, and conservation organizations, and if administrative problems can be resolved, compensation schemes could prove effective.

A pilot project of the Mongolian Association for the Conservation of Nature and the Environment is using low-cost incentives to persuade people to protect local wildlife and to find better ways of looking after their livestock. Each herding community designs its own project and determines a commodity to accept in exchange for not killing snow leopards. Surprisingly, one community chose children's clothes and good-quality flour as an incentive. Community participation in the program has been growing, and as news of the conservation initiatives has spread, other pastoral communities in northwestern Pakistan and Nepal have begun contacting local organizations about initiating their own programs.[102]

Despite the problems that must still be resolved to ensure its continued survival, the snow leopard stands out as a model of how captive breeding and a well-designed and coordinated approach to conservation in the wild can work together to aid the survival of a species.

TABLE 67 MEASUREMENTS AND WEIGHTS OF ADULT SNOW LEOPARDS

HB	n	T	n	WT	n	Location	Source
1,120 (1,030–1,250)	10?	918 (800–1,050)	8?	33 (22–39)	5?	Russia	15
1,000	1m	1,000	1m			China	103
860, 1,125	2f	870, 910	2f	52.5	1f	China	103
1,195	1f	852	1f			China	104
1,130	1f	960	1f	39	1f	Nepal	25

TABLE 67 (continued)

HB	n	T	n	WT	n	Location	Source
1,150	1m	930	1m	47	1m	Nepal	49
1,110, 1,130	2f	780, 890	2f	39, 42	2f	Nepal	49
1,066	1m	914	1m	50	1m	India/Nepal?	32
1,041, 1,117	2m	914, 914	2m			Kashmir	105
991	1f	838	1f			Baltistan	105
1,200, 1,220	2m	920, 990	2m	41.3, 40.0	2m	Mongolia	36
1,175, 1,170	2f	890, 920	2f	30.0, 38.6	2f	Mongolia	36

Note: HB = head and body length (mm), T = tail length (mm), WT = weight (kg). n = sample size. Sex: m = male, f = female, ? = unknown. Mean values are presented only for sample sizes of three or more. Range of values is in parentheses.

TABLE 68 FREQUENCY OF OCCURRENCE OF PREY ITEMS IN THE DIETS OF SNOW LEOPARDS (PERCENTAGE OF SAMPLES)

Prey items	Annapurna Conservation Area, Nepal[37] Scats (n = 213)	Hemis NP, Ladakh[38] Scats (n = 173)	Langu Valley, Mugu District, Nepal[26] Scats (n = 78)
Pseudois nayaur Blue sheep	51.6	23.4	44.9
Hemitragus jelambicus Himalayan tahr			14.1
Ovis vignei Ladakh urial		0.4	
Unidentified large mammals			15.4
Marmota himalayana	20.7	9.8	
Ochotona sp. Pika	15.9	4.3	1.3
Bos grunniens Yak	13.6	1.2	
Alticola roylei Vole	7.5		
Cricetids			11.5
Murids			11.5
Unidentified small mammals	5.6		8.9
Mustela nivalis Least weasel	4.7		
Martes foina Marten	3.8		
Horse	2.8	0.8	
Birds	1.4	3.1	2.6
Vulpes vulpes Red fox	0.9		
Lepus oiostolus Tibetan woolly hare		3.1	
Ox	0.5		
Domestic goat	0.5	10.2	
Domestic sheep	0.5	2.3	
Plant material	19.3	41.0	21.8
Minimum number of vertebrate prey items	277	151	86

REFERENCES

1. Buffon, G. L. de. 1761. *Histoire naturelle générale et particulière, avec la description du cabinet du roi.* Tome neuvième. Paris: L'Imprimerie royale. 375 pp.

2. Schreber, J. C. D. 1774–1785. *Die säugthiere in Abbindugen nach der natur mit Beschreibungen.* Erlangen, Germany: W. Walther.

3. Guggisberg, C. A. W. 1975. *Wild cats of the world.* New York: Taplinger.

4. Rieger, I. 1980. Some aspects of the history of ounce knowledge. *International pedigree book of snow leopards* 2: 1–36.

5. Pallas, P. S. 1967. *A naturalist in Russia: Letters from Peter Simon Pallas to Thomas Pennant,* ed. C. Urness. Minneapolis: University of Minnesota Press.

6. Jones, M. 1973. The snow leopard in captivity. In *The world's cats,* vol. 1, ed. R. L. Eaton, 264–272. Winston, OR: World Wildlife Safari.

7. Schaller, G. B. 1977. *Mountain monarchs.* Chicago: University of Chicago Press.

8. Jackson, R. 1979. Aboriginal hunting in West Nepal with reference to musk deer *Moschus moschiferus moschiferus* and snow leopard *Panthera uncia. Biol. Conserv.* 16: 63–72.

9. Jackson, R. 1979. Snow leopards in Nepal. *Oryx* 15: 191–195.

10. Koshkarev, E. P. 1984. Characteristics of snow leopard (*Unica uncia*) movements in the Tien Shan. *International pedigree book of snow leopards* 4: 15–21.

11. Mallon, D. P. 1984. The snow leopard in Ladakh. *International pedigree book of snow leopards* 4: 23–37.

12. Mallon, D. P. 1984. The snow leopard, *Panthera uncia,* in Mongolia. *International pedigree book of snow leopards* 4: 3–9.

13. Hemmer, H. 1972. *Uncia uncia. Mammalian Species* 20: 1–5.

14. Wozencraft, W. C. 1993. Order Carnivora. In *Mammal species of the world,* 2nd ed., ed. D. E. Wilson and D. M. Reeder, 279–348. Washington, DC: Smithsonian Institution Press.

15. Heptner, V. G., and A. A. Sludskii. 1992. *Mammals of the Soviet Union.* Vol. 2, part 2, *Carnivora (Hyaenas and cats).* English translation, sci. ed. R. S. Hoffmann. Washington, DC: Smithsonian Institution Libraries and the National Science Foundation.

16. Roberts, T. J. 1977. *The mammals of Pakistan.* London: Ernest Benn.

17. Jackson, R. 1987. Snow cats of Langu gorge. *Animal Kingdom* 90 (4): 45–53.

18. Blomqvist, L., and V. Nystrom. 1980. On identifying snow leopards, *Panthera uncia,* by their facial markings. *International pedigree book of snow leopards* 2: 159–167.

19. Ognev, S. I. 1935. Mammals of U.S.S.R. and adjacent countries. Vol. 3, *Carnivora.* English translation 1962. Washington, DC: Israel Program for Scientific Translations and Smithsonian Institution.

20. Freeman, H. 1980. The snow leopard, today and yesterday. *International pedigree book of snow leopards* 2: 37–43.

21. Rieger, I. 1984. Tail functions in ounces, *Uncia uncia. International Pedigree Book of Snow Leopards* 4: 85–97.

22. Fox, J. L. 1989. *A review of the status and ecology of the snow leopard* (Panthera uncia). Seattle: International Snow Leopard Trust.

23. Fox, J. L. 1994. Snow leopard conservation in the wild—a comprehensive perspective on a low density and highly fragmented population. In *Proceedings of the seventh international snow leopard symposium,* ed. J. L. Fox and J. Du, 3–15. Seattle: International Snow Leopard Trust and Chicago Zoological Society.

24. Jackson, R. M., and G. G. Ahlborn. 1984. A preliminary habitat suitability model for the snow leopard, *Panthera uncia,* in West Nepal. *International pedigree book of snow leopards* 4: 43–52.

25. Jackson, R. M., and G. G. Ahlborn. 1988. Observations on the ecology of snow leopard in West Nepal. In *Proceedings of the fifth international snow leopard symposium,* ed. H. Freeman, 65–87. Bombay: International Snow Leopard Trust and Wildlife Institute of India.

26. Jackson, R. M. 1996. Home range, movements and habitat use of snow leopard (*Uncia uncia*) in Nepal. Ph.D. dissertation, University of London, England.

27. Chundawat, R. S. 1990. Habitat selection by a snow leopard in Hemis National Park, India. *International pedigree book of snow leopards* 6: 85–92.

28. Schaller, G. B., J. Ren, and M. Qiu. 1988. Status of the snow leopard *Panthera uncia* in Qinghai and Gansu Provinces, China. *Biol. Conserv.* 45: 179–194.

29. Fox, J. L., S. P. Sinha, R. S. Chundawat, and P. K. Das. 1988. A field survey of snow leopard presence and habitat use in northwestern India. In *Proceedings of the fifth international snow leopard symposium,* ed. H. Freeman, 99–111. Bombay: International Snow Leopard Trust and Wildlife Institute of India.

30. Gruisen, J. van. 1993. Interactions between wild dogs and snow leopards in Ladakh. *Snow Line* 11(2): 8.

31. Fox, J. L. 1992. Conservation in Ladakh's Hemis National Park: Predator and prey. *Snow Line* 10(1): 3–6.

32. Dang, H. 1967. The snow leopard and its prey. *Cheetal* 10: 72–84.

33. Fox, J. L., and R. S. Chundawat. 1988. Observations of snow leopard stalking, killing, and feeding behavior. *Mammalia* 52: 137–140.

34. Zhirjakov, V. A. 1990. On the ecology of the snow leopard in the Zailiskky-Alatau (Northern Tien Shan). *International pedigree book of snow leopards* 6: 25–30.

35. Hillard, D. 1989. *Vanishing tracks.* New York: Arbor House.

36. McCarthy, T. M. 2000. Ecology and conservation of snow leopards, Gobi brown bears, and wild Bactrian camels in Mongolia. Ph.D. dissertation, University of Massachusetts, Amherst.

37. Oli, M. K., I. R. Taylor, and M. E. Rogers. 1993. Diet of the snow leopard (*Panthera uncia*) in the Annapurna Conservation Area, Nepal. *J. Zool.* 231: 365–370.

38. Chundawat, R. S., and G. S. Rawat. 1994. Food habits of snow leopard in Ladakh, India. In *Proceedings of the seventh international snow leopard symposium,* ed. J. L. Fox and J. Du, 127–132. Seattle: International Snow Leopard Trust and Chicago Zoological Society.

39. Jackson, R., Z. Wang, X. Lu, and Y. Chen. 1994. Snow leopards in the Qomolangma Nature Reserve of the Tibet Autonomous Region. In *Proceedings of the seventh international snow leopard symposium,* ed. J. L. Fox and J. Du, 85–95. Seattle: International Snow Leopard Trust and Chicago Zoological Society.

40. Mallon, D. P. 1988. A further report on the snow leopard in Ladakh. In *Proceedings of the fifth international snow leopard symposium,* ed. H. Freeman, 89–97. Bombay: International Snow Leopard Trust and Wildlife Institute of India.

41. Schaller, G. B., H, T. Li, J. Ren, and M. Qiu. 1988. Distribution of snow leopard in Xinjiang, China. *Oryx* 22: 197–204.

42. Oli, M. K. 1994. Snow leopards and blue sheep in Nepal: Densities and predator:prey ratio. *J. Mammal.* 75: 998–1004.

43. Schaller, G. B., J. Tserendeleg, and G. Amarsanaa. 1994. Observations on snow leopards in Mongolia. In *Proceedings of the*

seventh international snow leopard symposium, ed. J. L. Fox and J. Du, 33–42. Seattle: International Snow Leopard Trust and Chicago Zoological Society.

44. Oli, M. K. 1994. Snow leopards and local human population in a protected area: A case study from the Nepalese Himalaya. In *Proceedings of the seventh international snow leopard symposium*, ed. J. L. Fox and J. Du, 51–64. Seattle: International Snow Leopard Trust and Chicago Zoological Society.

45. Jackson, R. M., G. G. Ahlborn, M. Gurung, and S. Ale. 1996. Reducing livestock depredation losses in the Nepalese Himalaya. In *Proceedings of the 17th vertebrate pest conference*, ed. R. M. Timm and A. C. Crabb, 241–247. Davis: University of California Press.

46. Koshkarev, E. P. 1988. An unusual hunt. *International pedigree book of snow leopards* 5: 9–12.

47. Rieger, I. 1978. Management techniques of captive ounces, *Uncia uncia. International pedigree book of snow leopards* 1: 50–70.

48. Wharton, D., and S. A. Mainka. 1994. Captive management of the snow leopard. In *Proceedings of the seventh international snow leopard symposium*, ed. J. L. Fox and J. Du, 135–147. Seattle: International Snow Leopard Trust and Chicago Zoological Society.

49. Oli, M. K. 1997. Winter home ranges of snow leopards in Népal. *Mammalia* 61: 355–360.

50. Yang, Q. 1994. Further study on the geographical distribution and conservation of snow leopard in Qinghai, China. In *Proceedings of the seventh international snow leopard symposium*, ed. J. L. Fox and J. Du, 73–77. Seattle: International Snow Leopard Trust and Chicago Zoological Society.

51. Annenkov, B. P. 1990. The snow leopard (*Uncia uncia*) in the Dzungarsky Ala Tau. *International pedigree book of snow leopards* 6: 21–24.

52. Smirnov, M. N., G. A. Sokolov, and A. N. Zyryanov. 1990. The snow leopard (*Unica uncia*, Schreber 1776) in Siberia. *International pedigree book of snow leopards* 6: 9–15.

53. Peters, G. 1980. The vocal repertoire of the snow leopard (*Unica uncia*, Schreber 1775). *International pedigree book of snow leopards* 11: 137–158.

54. Peters, G. 1984. A special type of vocalization in the Felidae. *Acta. Zool. Fennica* 171: 89–92.

55. Peters, G., and M. H. Hast. 1994. Hyoid structure, laryngeal anatomy, and vocalization in felids (Mammalia: Carnivora: Felidae). *Z. Säugetierk.* 59: 87–104.

56. Ahlborn, G., and R. M. Jackson. 1988. Marking in free-ranging snow leopards in west Nepal: A preliminary assessment. In *Proceedings of the fifth international snow leopard symposium*, ed. H. Freeman, 25–49. Bombay: International Snow Leopard Trust and Wildlife Institute of India.

57. Wemmer, C., and K. Scow. 1977. Communication in the Felidae with emphasis on scent marking and contact patterns. In *How animals communicate*, ed. T. Sebeok, 749–766. Bloomington: Indiana University Press.

58. Freeman, H. 1980. Snow leopard: A co-operative study between zoos. *International pedigree book of snow leopards* 2: 127–136.

59. Freeman, H. 1982. Characteristics of social behaviour in the snow leopard. *International pedigree book of snow leopards* 3: 117–120.

60. Freeman, H. 1983. Behaviour in adult pairs of captive snow leopards (*Panthera uncia*). *Zoo Biol.* 2: 1–22.

61. Khalaf, N. A. B. 1988. Activity patterns and reproductive behaviour of snow leopards, *Panthera unica* (Schreber, 1775) at Jersey Wildlife Preservation Trust, Channel Islands. *International pedigree book of snow leopards* 5: 61–71.

62. Freeman, H. 1977. Breeding and behavior of the snow leopard. In *The world's cats*, vol. 3, ed. R. L. Eaton, 36–44. Seattle: Carnivore Research Institute, Burke Museum, University of Washington.

63. Freeman, H. 1978. Social behavior in the snow leopard and its implications for captive management. *International pedigree book of snow leopards* 1: 71–77.

64. Freeman, H., and K. Braden. 1977. Zoo location as a factor in the reproductive behavior of captive snow leopards, *Uncia unica. Zool. Garten* (n.f.) 47: 280–288.

65. Doherty, J., and D. Wharton. 1988. Breeding management of the snow leopard at New York Zoological Park. In *Proceedings of the fifth international snow leopard symposium*, ed. H. Freeman, 173–179. Bombay: International Snow Leopard Trust and Wildlife Institute of India.

66. Emlen, S. T., and L. W. Oring. 1977. Ecology, sexual selection, and the evolution of mating systems. *Science* 197: 215–223.

67. Rieger, I. 1984. Oestrous timing in ounces, *Uncia uncia*, Schreber (1775). *International pedigree book of snow leopards* 4: 99–103.

68. Zang, Z.-Y. 1988. The first success in breeding snow leopards, *Panthera uncia* in China. *International pedigree book of snow leopards* 5: 57–60.

69. Shilo, R. A., and O. V. Leonova. 1990. Management, breeding and 24-hour activities of snow leopards (*Panthera uncia*) in Novosibirsk Zoo. *International pedigree book of snow leopards* 6: 121–128.

70. Lanier, D. L., and D. A. Dewsbury. 1976. A quantitative study of copulatory behaviour of large Felidae. *Behav. Proc.* 1: 327–333.

71. Blomqvist, L., and I. Sten. 1982. Reproductive biology of the snow leopard *Panthera uncia. International pedigree book of snow leopards* 3: 71–79.

72. Andrews, P., Hexagon Farm Wild Feline Breeding Facility, 1187 Merrill Road, San Juan Bautista, CA. Personal communication.

73. O'Connor, T., and H. Freeman. 1982. Maternal behavior and behavioral development in the captive snow leopard (*Panthera uncia*). *International pedigree book of snow leopards* 3: 103–110.

74. Marma, B. B., and U. U. Yunchis. 1968. Observations on the breeding management and physiology of snow leopards *Panthera u. uncia* at Kaunas Zoo from 1962 to 1967. *Int. Zoo Yrbk.* 8: 66–73.

75. Jackson, R. M., and G. G. Ahlborn. 1989. Snow leopards (*Panthera uncia*) in Nepal-Home range and movements. *Natl. Geogr. Res.* 5: 161–175.

76. Petzsch, H. 1968. *Die katzen*. Leipzig: Urania-Verlag.

77. Koivisto, I., C. Wahlberg, and P. Muuronen. 1977. Breeding the snow leopard, *Panthera unica*, at Helsinki Zoo 1967–1976. *Int. Zoo Yrbk.* 17: 39–44.

78. Rieger, I. 1980. Some difficulties in breeding ounces *Uncia uncia*, at zoological gardens. *International pedigree book of snow leopards* 2: 76–95.

79. Wharton, D., and H. Freeman. 1988. The snow leopard in North America: Captive breeding under the Species Survival Plan. In *Proceedings of the fifth international snow leopard symposium*, ed. H. Freeman, 131–136. Bombay: International Snow Leopard Trust and Wildlife Institute of India.

80. Koshkarev, E. P. 1990. On the environment-related stability of snow leopard (*Uncia uncia*) populations in connection with their

distribution in the natural habitats and chances for spread within the USSR. *International pedigree book of snow leopards* 6: 37–50.

81. Beier, P. 1993. Determining minimum habitat areas and habitat corridors for cougars. *Conserv. Biol.* 7: 94–108.

82. Schaller, G. B. 1988. Snow leopard in China. *Snow Line* 14: 3.

83. Mallon, D. P. 1988. Snow leopards in northern Hunza. *Snow Line* 14: 8.

84. Wegge, P. 1988. Assessment of Khunjerab National Park and environs, Pakistan Survey. World Conservation Union (IUCN). Gland, Switzerland. 24 pp.

85. Jackson, R., and G. Ahlborn. 1990. The role of protected areas in Nepal in maintaining viable populations of snow leopards. *International pedigree book of snow leopards* 6: 51–69.

86. Spitsin, V., and E. Koshkarev. 1988. Status and distribution of snow leopard in Kirgizia (U.S.S.R.). In *Proceedings of the fifth international snow leopard symposium*, ed. H. Freeman, 21–23. Bombay: International Snow Leopard Trust and Wildlife Institute of India.

87. O'Gara, B. W. 1988. Snow leopards and sport hunting in the Mongolian People's Republic. In *Proceedings of the fifth international snow leopard symposium*, ed. H. Freeman, 215–225. Bombay: International Snow Leopard Trust and Wildlife Institute of India.

88. Klineburger, C., Klineburger Worldwide Travel, Gamemasters of the World, 3627 1st Ave. South, Seattle, Washington. Personal communication.

89. Cat News. 1989. Snow leopards outwit hunters. *Cat News* 10: 8.

90. Nowell, K., and P. Jackson. 1996. *Wild cats: A status survey and conservation action plan.* Gland, Switzerland: International Union for Conservation of Nature and Natural Resources (IUCN).

91. Freeman, H., R. Jackson, D. Hillard, and D. O. Hunter. 1994. Project snow leopard: A multinational program spearheaded by the International Snow Leopard Trust. In *Proceedings of the seventh international snow leopard symposium*, ed. J. L. Fox and J. Du, 241–252. Seattle: International Snow Leopard Trust and Chicago Zoological Society.

92. Barnes, L. 1989. The overt illegal fur trade in Kathmandu, Nepal. Unpublished report, Inverness Research Associates, Inverness, CA.

93. Freeman, H. 1989. The view from here. *Snow Line* 17: 2–3.

94. Koshkarev, E. P. 1994. Poaching in the former USSR. *Snow Line* 12: 6–7.

95. Liao, Y., and B. Tan. 1988. A preliminary study of the geographical distribution of snow leopards in China. In *Proceedings of the fifth international snow leopard symposium*, ed. H. Freeman, 51–63. Bombay: International Snow Leopard Trust and Wildlife Institute of India.

96. Blomqvist, L. 1984. Conservation measurements taken for the captive snow leopard (*Panthera uncia*) population and a report of the fluctuations in the stock in 1983. *International pedigree book of snow leopards* 4: 55–71.

97. Blomqvist, L. 1992. Captive snow leopard report for 1989. *Int. Zoo News* 236: 5–14.

98. Green, M. J. B. 1994. Protecting the mountains of central Asia and their snow leopard populations. In *Proceedings of the seventh international snow leopard symposium*, ed. J. L. Fox and J. Du, 223–239. Seattle: International Snow Leopard Trust and Chicago Zoological Society.

99. Hunter, D. O., R. Jackson, H. Freeman, and D. Hillard. 1994. Project snow leopard: A model for conserving Asian biodiversity. In *Proceedings of the seventh international snow leopard symposium*, ed. J. L. Fox and J. Du, 247–252. Seattle: International Snow Leopard Trust and Chicago Zoological Society.

100. Ashig Ahmad. 1994. Protection of snow leopards through grazier communities—some examples from WWF-Pakistan's projects in the northern areas. In *Proceedings of the seventh international snow leopard symposium*, ed. J. L. Fox and J. Du, 265–272. Seattle: International Snow Leopard Trust and Chicago Zoological Society.

101. Miller, D. J., and R. Jackson. 1994. Livestock and snow leopards: Making room for competing users on the Tibetan Plateau. In *Proceedings of the seventh international snow leopard symposium*, ed. J. L. Fox and J. Du, 315–333. Seattle: International Snow Leopard Trust and Chicago Zoological Society.

102. Sunquist, F. 1997. Where cats and herders mix. *Int. Wildl.* 27(1): 26–33.

103. Shaw, T. H. 1962. *Economic fauna* (Mammals). Beijing: Scientific Press.

104. Gao, Y. T., S. Wang, M. L. Zhang, Z. Y. Ye, and J. D. Zhou, ed. 1987. *Fauna Sinica, Mammalia*, vol. 8: Carnivora. Beijing: Scientific Press.

105. Ward, A. E. 1923. Game animals of Kashmir and adjacent hill provinces. *J. Bombay Nat. Hist. Soc.* 29: 23–35.

Study and Conservation

Field Research Techniques:
Recent Advances

Our previous lack of knowledge of the cat family stems from the fact that cats are notoriously difficult to observe, since they are active mainly at night and almost impossible to see in the dense vegetation where they usually live. But this situation changed in the 1970s when radiotelemetry began to give biologists their first glimpses into the dark. This technique turned a spotlight on the previously hidden lives of the secretive, solitary felids, allowing field biologists to locate an animal in dense cover or follow it across remote terrain.

RADIOTELEMETRY

Radiotelemetry involves the attachment of a miniature crystal-controlled, battery-operated VHF (very high frequency: 30–300 MHz) radio transmitter to an animal.[1] Signals emitted from the transmitter are detected with a directional antenna and a receiver. Each transmitter operates on its own frequency setting, so large numbers of individuals in an area can be monitored at the same time.

Radio transmitters are commonly attached to a collar that is fastened around the animal's neck, but they can also be implanted in the body cavity, where they can be used to monitor temperature, heart rate, and other physiological data as well as to locate the animal. A motion sensor built into the transmitter alters the pulse rate of the transmission to indicate when the animal is active or resting. The motion sensor can also be programmed to increase the pulse rate when the transmitter has remained motionless for a set length of time. This so-called "mortality switch" alerts researchers to the fact that the animal may be dead.

In the early days of radiotelemetry, transmitters and batteries were large and were used primarily on large species. Improved electronics, miniaturization of components, and longer battery life made it possible to build tiny transmitters that would operate for as long as six months on an animal as small as a 1-kilogram black-footed cat. Telemetry is now an integral part of most cat studies, and it remains one of the best ways to collect detailed data on most of the felids.

One of the major drawbacks of conventional VHF tracking is that radio signals can be reflected, deflected, or obstructed, and they diminish in strength with increasing distance from the source. The system works on line-of-sight transmission, and signal reception is greatly reduced or modified by dense forest cover and mountainous terrain. Species that move long distances and those that live in remote, inaccessible areas are difficult to find or follow on foot or in vehicles. In several studies of jaguars, snow leopards, clouded leopards, and pumas, the broken terrain and thick vegetation was so difficult to negotiate that collared animals could be located only a few times a month. Given the hours, effort, and risk that go into capturing one of these elusive cats, the cost of the telemetry gear, and the hours involved in searching for signals, two or three data points a month is an expensive, and biologically not very meaningful, return.

SATELLITE TELEMETRY

In the future, conventional transmitters coupled with GPS (Global Positioning System) telemetry will allow biologists to overcome some of the difficulties of finding animals in remote and inaccessible terrain. This technique uses a GPS receiver attached to a collar or a harness. The receiver calculates its position—and thus the position of the animal—based on data received from orbiting satellites. The GPS receiver can be programmed to calculate its own position once every twenty-four hours or more frequently, and the data can be stored in the receiver, relayed to another receiver, or recovered via low polar-orbiting relay satellites. Service Argos, Toulouse, France, operates the system that collects and processes data received by polar-orbiting Tiros-N satellites. They are part of a co-operative international project and work with NOAA and NASA to collect environmental data.

Because GPS collars and data recovery are expensive, currently about U.S.$3,500 for a collar and U.S.$3,500 for satellite time and a year of daily locations, this technology is not often incorporated into studies. However, in field trials, GPS-ARGOS units have been used on caribou, moose, polar bears, elephants, brown bears, elk, and snow leopards.[2] Fortunately, GPS technology has a large commercial market apart from the wildlife field, so the technology is developing rapidly. The next few years will see satellite tags deployed more and more frequently, especially in studies such as that of the snow leopard in Mongolia, where conventional radio tracking with hand-held receivers is ineffective and light aircraft are unavailable.

Radiotelemetry will probably continue to be the main way of obtaining detailed information on the movements and activities of cats that live in dense vegetation. However, this technique has its drawbacks: it is expensive, and the study animal must be trapped and tranquilized to attach the radio collar. Over the years we have put radio collars on hundreds of individuals of some thirty different species, but no matter how many individuals you handle, the process of trapping and tranquilizing an animal in the field is always fraught with anxiety. Even with the greatest care and expert attention, animals occasionally injure themselves in traps and snares, or die under anesthetic. Over the last twenty years improved drugs have decreased mortality rates during field anesthesia, but a risk still exists.

CAMERA TRAPPING

Today, new techniques are making it possible for scientists to collect some types of information without ever handling a cat. These new "hands-off" techniques make life easier for the animal and are often better received by landowners and wildlife departments. It is much easier to get permission to run a line of cameras in the forest than to go through the lengthy permitting process for capturing, tranquilizing, and radio-collaring animals. Several studies are now using "camera trapping" instead of trapping and radiotelemetry. In this technique, cameras equipped with an electronic triggering device are attached to trees or posts. Any animal that walks in front of a camera and breaks the electronic beam automatically takes a photograph

of itself. In some cameras a picture is taken when the unit detects motion or heat.

Camera trapping is most often used as a survey aid to find out which species are present in an area, but under the right circumstances it is also possible to use camera traps to estimate animal numbers. Ullas Karanth and Jim Nichols have developed a sampling technique for tigers using two cameras, one set on each side of a trail.[3,4,5] They use two cameras to produce matched photos of both sides of the animal because each side has a different spot or stripe pattern. The technique is analogous to the old mark-recapture method of estimating animal density, but in this case the camera does the capturing and the marks are the animals' unique coat patterns. The frequency with which known tigers turn up in the photos enables computer models to estimate what fraction of the overall population has been photographed. That estimate, in turn, leads to an estimate of the size of the population. To date the technique has been used successfully on tigers and leopards, and it should be applicable to jaguars, ocelots, and any other cat species in which individuals are uniquely marked.

MOLECULAR SCATOLOGY

Another new field technique for studying felids is the euphoniously named science of molecular scatology. The procedure is still largely experimental, but in the future biologists may be able to collect all the information they need simply by picking up scats or feces. Feces are already the best source of information on a cat's diet. Felids often consume their prey whole, but they do not digest the hair, bones, and teeth of their prey. These remains pass through the digestive tract and are deposited in the feces. Hair and teeth can usually be identified to species, allowing scientists to reconstruct the animal's diet.

Feces also contain cells shed from the lining of the intestine. Scientists can isolate and purify these cells, then amplify specific DNA sequences. Among other things, this DNA can be used to recognize individuals, determine their sex and age, and establish how they are related to one another.[6]

Though scats can provide a wealth of information, they are not always easy to find. In some studies, researchers can pick them up by the hundreds, but at other sites they are almost impossible to locate. During a study of jaguars and pumas on a ranch in Venezuela, scats were so difficult to find that the ranch cowboys were offered a significant reward for every scat they found. Despite the incentive, only a few rewards were ever claimed. Sam Wasser of the University of Washington is experimenting with the use of trained drug-sniffing dogs to search for carnivore feces.

HAIR SAMPLING

Because DNA can also be recovered from hair, a variety of hair-catching devices are being used in combination with other techniques in efforts to obtain information on population structure, genetic relationships, the number of unidentified individuals in an area, and other demographic data.[7] Developed originally to provide an inexpensive and quantifiable method for detecting lynx across large landscapes, the technique is now being tried on ocelots, bears, and other carnivores. Hair-catching devices—which can be as simple as a small square of carpet with a few small tacks protruding from the pile side—are attached to trees, logs, or other places along cat trails. To induce passing cats to cheek-rub and perhaps leave a sample of their hair, the sites are baited with a commercially available scent lure or catnip oil. Hair-catching stations can be installed over a large area at minimum cost, but the success of the technique depends on being able to get the cat to rub against the collecting device.[8]

Twenty-five years ago radiotelemetry allowed cat biologists to begin to unravel the movements and social interaction patterns of animals that were impossible to watch. Today, new and largely noninvasive techniques promise to add a level of detailed information that until recently was only dreamed of. By collecting scats, hair, and photographs, we will be able to determine individual identity, movements, genetic relatedness, reproductive status, individual food habits, mortality rates, and population density.

In the not too distant future, we will be able to collect data over huge areas, monitoring hundreds of animals. We will be able to closely monitor individuals, asking questions that we presently have no way of answering. For example, we suspect that the diets of males and females of the same species may be slightly different. If male pumas are killing different sex and age classes of prey than females, this may have important management implications. In addition, details on individual food habits, coupled with hormonal assays to measure physical condition, may tell us whether a population is stressed or thriving. On a broader level, genetic data from scats and hair will enable us to look at the effects of disturbance, fragmentation, and insularization on felid populations. We will be able to compare levels of genetic variation in fragmented and unfragmented habitats, and make robust predictions as to which species will be most vulnerable to these environmental changes.

REFERENCES

1. Kenward, R. 1987. *Wildlife radio tagging*. London: Academic Press.

2. Harris, R. B., S. G. Fancy, D. C. Douglas, G. W. Garner, S. C. Amstrup, T. R. McCabe, and L. Frank. 1990. Tracking wildlife by satellite: Current systems and performance. Fish and Wildlife Technical Report 30. Washington, DC: U.S. Department of the Interior Fish and Wildlife Service. 52 pp.

3. Karanth, K. U. 1995. Estimating tiger populations from camera-trap data using capture-recapture models. *Biol. Conserv.* 71: 333–338.

4. Karanth, K. U. and J. D. Nichols. 1998. Estimation of tiger densities in India using photographic captures and recaptures. *Ecology* 79: 2852–2862.

5. Karanth, K. U., and J. D. Nichols. 2000. Ecological status and conservation of tigers in India. Final technical report to Division of International Conservation, U.S. Fish and Wildlife Service, Washington, DC and Wildlife Conservation Society, New York. Bangalore, India: Centre for Wildlife Studies. 124 pp.

6. Kohn, M. H., and R. K. Wayne. 1997. Facts from feces revisited. *Trends Ecol. Evol.* 12: 223–227.

7. Haig, S. M. 1998. Molecular contributions to conservation. *Ecology* 79: 413–425.

8. McDaniel, G. W., K. S. McKelvey, J. R. Squires, and L. F. Ruggiero. 2000. Efficacy of lures and hair snares to detect lynx. *Wildl. Soc. Bull.* 28 (1): 119–123.

Relocating Cats:
History and Guidelines for the Future

Cats are often translocated because they come into conflict with humans and their livestock. Many of the larger cats are still shot or trapped because they kill domestic stock, but attitudes are changing, and there is increasing public pressure on authorities to take a less aggressive approach to predator problems. Today, translocation is often seen as a humane alternative to shooting a problem animal.[1,2,3,4,5] Cattle-killing jaguars, leopards, and pumas are regularly captured, relocated to a remote area, and released. But little is known of the fate of these translocated cats. Relocated animals are rarely monitored, and there is very little information on what happens to them after release. The sparse information that exists suggests that mortality is high and that the cats rarely stay in the area where they are released.

Felids also are moved in attempts to restore them to areas where they once lived. In North America and Europe, lynx are currently being reintroduced into portions of their former range. In other parts of the world, the increasing popularity of ecotourism has resulted in a new interest in translocating predators and prey into privately owned wildlife reserves. In Africa, lions, leopards, and cheetahs are now being relocated to areas from which they were extirpated decades ago. Translocation and reintroduction has also fired the imagination of restoration scientists. As habitat patches dwindle in size and biologists face the very real problem of what to do about the genetic problems of small populations, there is increasing interest in translocating cats to revitalize or augment these populations.

Compared with other taxa such as cervids and bovids, cats are generally rather poor candidates for reintroduction and translocation. They live at naturally low densities and require large areas of suitable habitat with a full complement of prey species. Because of their specialized diet, they need to have spent many months perfecting their hunting and killing behavior, preferably under the tutelage of an adult. Their land tenure system also makes reintroduction and translocation more difficult. Breeding females tend to maintain the same home ranges for their entire reproductive lives, and competition for vacant ranges is intense. Young females commonly settle next to their mother or take over their mother's home range. Female philopatry has been documented in Iberian lynx, tigers, pumas, and leopards and is expected to occur in many other species.[6,7,8,9,10,11]

Under circumstances in which site fidelity is strong, reintroduced or translocated animals competing for space with an existing population are at a tremendous social disadvantage. Not only will it be difficult for these individuals to acquire breeding territories, but as they are naïve and unfamiliar with the area, they will also be vulnerable in fights. There are numerous examples of translocated felids being killed by unknown but probably resident animals.[12,13,14,15]

LEOPARDS

The leopard has probably been the object of more translocation attempts than any other felid. Over the past forty years, hundreds of problem leopards have been captured and moved in Africa. In the mid-1950s the National Parks and Game Department of Kenya initiated a policy of translocating problem leopards to game reserves rather than killing them. Hamilton estimated that several hundred leopards were released in various parts of Kenya, but only a few were followed.[3]

Between 1969 and 1977, 108 stock-raiding leopards were released in Meru Park in Kenya. In 1977, 12 of 14 newly released leopards were fitted with radio collars, though only six of these animals could be followed reliably. All six leopards left the park, but one male returned after ten months and remained in the park. A female appeared to settle down just outside the park boundary. Another male, who had previously been unsuccessfully translocated four times for persistent livestock killing, was trapped again 80 kilometers away after killing two sheep. Contact was lost with the other three animals as they moved beyond the range of signal reception.[3] Clearly this translocation was not a great success in terms of getting leopards to stay where they were put. However, the park was small, and it obviously had its own resident population of leopards. The released animals undoubtedly had to travel widely in search of unoccupied territory.

CHEETAHS

Cheetahs are frequently trapped and shot in Namibia and Zimbabwe because they are thought to be major predators of domestic livestock. Namibia is home to 20–30 percent of the world's cheetahs, 90 percent of which live on commercial farms. Between 1980 and 1991 Namibian farmers killed 5,860 free-ranging cheetahs and exported a further 958, causing a 50 percent decline in the country's cheetah population. Recently, the Cheetah Conservation Fund has been trying to halt the killing of these endangered cats, encouraging farmers to live-trap unwanted cheetahs and send them to holding camps from which they can be relocated.[16]

Despite the fact that these slight, speedy cats seem so much less robust that the other big cats, they have fared surprisingly well during translocation and reintroduction attempts.[17] Where they have been reintroduced into protected areas that have no lions and hyenas, cheetah numbers have risen rapidly. In Pilansberg National Park in South Africa, six reintroduced cheetahs increased to a population of seventeen within a year, and in Suikerbosrand Nature Reserve, five males and three females increased to twenty-four animals within two years.[18] Three two-and-a-half-year-old males bred at the De Wildt Cheetah Breeding Station were able to capture and kill wild prey when released to the wild. However, they were unafraid of people and vehicles, and twice entered camps, where they killed and ate chickens.[19]

LIONS

In the 1920s and 1930s lions were extirpated from many parts of Africa because settlers believed they were incompatible with people and their domestic animals. Later, attempts were made to reestablish lion populations in some parks and reserves, and many lions were relocated. In South Africa in 1965 two wild females

and three cubs were moved to the Umfolozi Game Reserve from the Transvaal. In the absence of resident lions, the introduced population increased dramatically. By 1974 there were about 120 lions in Umfolozi, and over 90 lions had been destroyed because they had begun to roam outside the reserve and kill livestock. Park biologists attributed the rapid rate of increase to the facts that there were no resident lions, water and cover were plentiful, and a nonmigratory ungulate prey base provided a constant food supply.[20]

In 1992, lions and cheetahs were reintroduced to the Phinda Reserve in South Africa. Thirteen wild-caught lions and fifteen cheetahs were released after being kept in large enclosures for eight to ten weeks. All the released cats remained in the fenced reserve and established home ranges, but mortality was nearly 50 percent. Five lions and two cheetahs were killed by poachers, three lions were destroyed after they killed a tourist, and a female cheetah and her three cubs left the reserve when a gate was left open. Two male cheetahs were killed in territorial fights, and two other male cheetahs were killed by lions. Despite this high mortality, both lions and cheetahs have bred well, and many cubs have survived.[21] There are now reports of lions leaving the reserve and killing cattle and wild game.[4]

JAGUARS

In South America, jaguars that kill livestock are usually shot, but some translocation attempts have been made. In one of them, a male jaguar killing cattle on a private ranch near Iguazu National Park in Argentina was captured and moved. Within a week of being released, the animal was shot and killed by local people.[2] In Belize, a cattle-killing subadult female jaguar was captured and moved 160 kilometers to a reserve. She left the reserve, resumed cattle-killing, and was killed by a hunter about five weeks after being translocated.[22]

PUMAS

The best information on cat translocation comes from several intensive studies of pumas. A landmark study in New Mexico tracked the fates of fourteen wild mountain lions that were moved an average of 477 kilometers into an area with an existing mountain lion population.[23] The ages and social status of the translocated cats were known, as they were previously part of a study being conducted in the San Andreas Mountains of New Mexico. The cats were released within forty-eight hours of capture, and no supplemental food was provided at the point of release.

Eight of the translocated cats established home ranges, and two of the females gave birth to young. By the end of the two-year study nine of the fourteen translocated cats had died. Nearly 25 percent of the mortality occurred within the first three and a half months after release. Two males returned to their original ranges. One male took 469 days to travel the 465 kilometers back to his original area. The other traveled 490 kilometers in 166 days, regained his range, and subsequently fathered three litters of kittens.

The New Mexico study showed that translocation success varied among age classes and was most effective for animals between twelve and twenty-seven months of age. These young animals were independent from their mothers but did not yet have resident status. This age group would ordinarily be leaving their natal ranges to establish their own home ranges. Surviving cats in this age group moved the shortest distance from the release site and rapidly established home ranges.

At the other end of the age scale, translocation was least effective for two eight-year-old cats. These "old" pumas were long-established breeding residents in the original population, and they survived only 37 and 109 days after translocation.

Translocation was also rather ineffective for pumas categorized as prime adults. These cats were typically residents in the original population, and once translocated, they exhibited the greatest movement away from release sites and the most intense homing behavior.

Results from two experimental reintroductions of pumas into northern Florida are not as clear-cut. Florida is much more densely populated than New Mexico and has many more roads. In addition, the main experiment focused on comparative survival rates of wild-caught and captive-bred animals, so the effects of age and social status were partially obscured.

In 1988–1989, seven wild-caught pumas were translocated from Texas to northern Florida as surrogates in an experiment designed to test the feasibility of a planned future translocation of the endangered Florida panther.[24] This experiment differed from the New Mexico study in one important respect: in Florida the cats were moved into an area where there were no other panthers, so intraspecific strife, the main cause of mortality in the New Mexico study, was not a factor.

Within a month of release, one cat was found dead and two others had to be recaptured because they were spending too much time around humans and livestock. Two more cats were shot within six months of release. When hunting season opened, the remaining two cats left their established home ranges and began wandering. Both cats had to be removed nine to ten months after release because they were hunting domestic livestock and exotic ungulates. Though mortality was high and more than half the cats had to be removed, some of the translocated panthers established home ranges and killed large prey.

In the second Florida study, which was conducted from 1993 to 1995 in the same area as the earlier study, nineteen pumas were released.[25] Six were captive-born and raised, ten were wild-caught in Texas and translocated immediately after capture, and three were wild-caught but had been held in captivity in Florida for two to eight years. Five of the cats died: two were shot, two were killed on highways, and one died in a snare. Nine pumas had to be removed from the wild because they were interacting too closely with humans. Approximately 60 percent of the translocated animals died or had to be removed each year. The study concluded that captive-raised cats tended to establish home ranges more quickly than wild-caught cats, although the difference was not significant. Pumas born in captivity were more likely to be involved in undesirable interactions with humans and livestock.

CANADA LYNX

Over three winters, eighty-three Canada lynx were translocated from Yukon Territory in Canada to New York State in an effort to restore lynx to New York's Adirondack Park.[26] All the translocated lynx roamed over much larger areas than expected, averaging 421 square kilometers for females and 1,760 square kilometers for males. Highway mortality was high: of thirty-two known deaths, vehicles caused twelve. Despite extensive pre-release publicity and a great deal of public goodwill, the translocated lynx suffered high levels of human-caused mortality. Ultimately, scientists working on the project were not confident that the restoration would succeed.

Another effort to reintroduce Canada lynx took place in 1999 and 2000 in Colorado. Lynx were trapped in Alaska, British Columbia, and the Yukon, airlifted to Colorado, and released at eleven sites in the mountains around Vail. Forty-one radio-collared lynx were released in the winter of 1999. Twenty of these animals died within a year of release, seven of them from starvation. After reviewing the evidence, the Colorado Division of Wildlife decided that winter releases were too risky and elected to restrict further releases to the spring, when there would be more food available. Fifty-five additional lynx were released in April and May 2000.[27,28]

EURASIAN LYNX AND EUROPEAN WILDCATS

Several other felid species have been the subject of translocation and reintroduction projects. Between 1984 and 1989, 129 European wildcats were reintroduced at three sites in Germany. Although there was some evidence of reproduction, overall survival was low—about 20–30 percent.[29] Highway mortality was responsible for much of the mortality in the first few weeks after release, but habitat modification and hybridization with domestic cats were considered to be the major long-term threats.[30]

Since 1970 there have been at least eight separate reintroductions of the Eurasian lynx to seven European countries. Some of the releases were clandestine, so the exact number of animals released is unknown; however, between 1970 and 1987, approximately eighty lynx are believed to have been released into Germany, France, Switzerland, Yugoslavia, Austria, Italy, and Slovakia.[31,32,33,34,35,36,37] In Switzerland, where the population has been closely monitored, 63 percent (thirty-seven of fifty-nine) of lynx deaths were caused by humans; almost a third of these deaths were due to highway mortality.[38]

GUIDELINES FOR THE FUTURE

As we move into the new millennium, there will be more compelling reasons to move felids. In India, conservationists will need to translocate some of the few remaining Gir lions to another reserve. In the United States, wildlife biologists will want to move more Texas pumas into the Everglades to add genetic diversity to the beleaguered, dwindling population of Florida panthers. In South America, ranchers will clamor to have cattle-killing jaguars and pumas moved or legalize sport hunting schemes.[39] One organization has proposed that problem jaguars be auctioned to hunters who would pay several thousand dollars for the opportunity to dart a cat. The tranquilized jaguar would then be moved to a remote forest area and released.

Though there remains almost a clear field of study,

the data that exist do provide a few guidelines. First, we know that few cats will survive a translocation. Mortality rates are likely to be 50–70 percent, depending on the age and social status of the animals being moved. The best candidates for translocation are independent subadults in the dispersal phase of their lives. Well-established residents are not good candidates. Older cats are more likely to home; males may wander widely and may even return to their original ranges. When a cat moves over a large area, the chances are greater that it will encounter highways or humans, two of the main causes of mortality.

Unfortunately, translocation is not likely to be a solution for confirmed livestock-killing cats,[22,39,40,41] especially if natural prey populations are depleted. Moving cats may simply move the problem to another area. Unless the problem cats can be moved to sanctuaries or remote areas with adequate natural prey, their cattle-killing habits are almost certain to be resumed. Furthermore, anecdotal evidence suggests that most "problem animals" are adults—the most difficult segment of the population to translocate.

Despite the hopes of the conservation community, cats born or held in captivity for any length of time are also not likely to be good candidates for translocation. Even though captive-raised animals of both sexes establish home ranges more quickly than wild-caught transplants, captive-raised cats seem to have a decreased fear of humans and are more likely to cause problems with people and livestock. Evidence from the Florida study also indicates that captive-born kittens fail to follow their mothers on release; the following behavior that is common to all young felids seems to be less well developed in captive-raised young.

Translocation is clearly a topic that requires more research. Though most biologists would agree that felids are not good candidates for translocation, there will be occasions in the future when we will need to relocate individuals. The scant information we have at the moment suggests that we should be prepared for the fact that these efforts will involve significant mortality among the translocated cats. We also need to recognize that the success or failure of the relocation will undoubtedly hinge on how well the local human population has been prepared for the event. Ultimately, successful translocations will depend on the repeated releases of large numbers of individuals, and on an educated, receptive local human population.

TABLE 69 TRANSLOCATIONS AND REINTRODUCTIONS OF FELIDS

Species	Location	Date	Number released	Source
Puma	Florida	1988–1989	7	24
Puma	Florida	1993–1995	19	25
Puma	New Mexico	1989–1991	14	23
Puma	Alberta, Canada	1988–1989	3	5
Tiger	Malaysia	1983	6	40
Tiger	Sundarbans	1973	1	12
Lion	South Africa	1965	4	20
Lion	South Africa	1992–1993	13	21
Cheetah	South Africa	1979–1980	3	19
Cheetah	Zimbabwe	1993	15	17
Cheetah	South Africa	1995	10	42
Cheetah	South Africa	1994	2	43
Cheetah	South Africa	1984	6	18
Cheetah	South Africa	1992–1993	15	21
Lynx, Canada	New York	1988–1990	83	26
Lynx, Canada	Colorado	1999	41	27
Lynx, Eurasian	Austria	1976	9	44
Lynx, Eurasian	Switzerland	1970–1976	14+	32
Lynx, Eurasian	Slovakia	1973	6	35
Lynx, Eurasian	France	1983–1988	14	45
Serval	South Africa	1982	3	46
Wildcat	Germany	1984–1989	129	29
Leopard	Kenya	1969–1977	108	3
Leopard	India	1990	1	47

TABLE 70 EXPERIMENTAL TRANSLOCATION AND REINTRODUCTION OF PUMAS IN NORTHERN FLORIDA (1988–1989)[24]

ID. No	Sex	Origin	Age	Fate
T13	F	WC	Adult	Died 1 month post-release
T14	F	WC	Subadult	Shot 6 months post release
T15	F	WC	Adult	Removed after 9+ months in the wild
T16	M	WC	Adult	Removed after 9 months in the wild
T18	M	WC	Adult	Died (shot?) 4 months post-release
T19	F	WC	Adult	Removed after 1 month
T21	M	WC	Adult	Removed after 1 month

Note: WC = wild-caught, CB = captive-born, CR = captive-reared.

TABLE 71 EXPERIMENTAL TRANSLOCATION AND REINTRODUCTION OF PUMAS IN NORTHERN FLORIDA (1993–1995)[25]

ID No	Sex	Origin	Age	Fate
T30	F	WC/CR	4 years	Removed after 2 months
T31	F	CB	2 years	Survived in wild to end of study
T32	F	CB	2 years	Removed after 1.5 years for killing livestock
T33	M	CB	1.5 years	Removed after 1 year. Numerous interactions with humans
T35	M	WC	3 years	Shot and killed 2–3 months post-release
T36	M	WC	4 years	Recaptured and released. Shot and killed 10 months post-release
T37	F	WC	2 years	Recaptured and released. Killed by car 2 years post-release

TABLE 71 (continued)

ID No	Sex	Origin	Age	Fate
T38	F	WC	3 years	Killed by car 5 months post-release
T39	F	WC	3 years	Killed in snare 13 months post-release
T40	M	WC	1.5 years	Recaptured and released. Shot, recaptured and treated. Removed after 2 years.
T41	F	WC	3 years	Recaptured and removed, with young, 21 months post-release
T42	M	WC	10 months	Survived in wild to end of study
T43	M	WC	10 months	Survived in wild to end of study
T01	F	WC/CR	9–10 years	Survived in wild to end of study
T45	M	CB	14 months	Recaptured and removed after 6 months for killing livestock
T46	F	CB	14 months	Recaptured and removed after 9 months. Too casual around people
T02	F	WC/CR	9 years	Recaptured and removed after 5 months for feeding on livestock
T48	M	WC	3 years	Survived in wild to end of study
T47	F	WC/CR	6 months	Did not follow mother (T02) when released. Recaptured after 6 weeks

Note: WC = wild-caught, CB = captive-born, CR = captive-reared.

REFERENCES

1. Tully, R. J. 1991. Results, 1991 questionnaire on damage to livestock by mountain lion. In *Mountain lion-human interaction*, ed. C. E. Braun, 68–74. Denver: Colorado Division of Wildlife.

2. Crawshaw, P. G. 1995. Comparative ecology of ocelot (*Felis pardalis*) and jaguar (*Panthera onca*) in a protected subtropical forest in Brazil and Argentina. Ph.D. dissertation, University of Florida, Gainesville.

3. Hamilton, P. H. 1979. Translocated leopards: Where do they go? African Wildlife Leadership Foundation, Nairobi. *Wildlife News* 14: 2–6.

4. Hunter, L. 1996. Secondary reintroductions of large cats in South Africa. *Cat News* 25: 14.

5. Ross, I. P., and M. Jalkotzy. 1996. Fate of translocated cougars *Felis concolor* in Alberta. *Cat News* 25: 15.

6. Anderson, A. E., D. C. Bowden, and D. M. Kattner. 1992. *The puma on Uncompahgre Plateau, Colorado*. Colorado Division of Wildlife, Technical Publication no. 40. 116 pp.

7. Ferreras, P., J. F. Beltran, J. J. Aldama, and M. Delibes. 1997. Spatial organization and land tenure system of the endangered Iberian lynx (*Lynx pardinus*). *J. Zool.* (Lond.) 243: 163–189.

8. Smith, J. L. D., C. McDougal, and M. E. Sunquist. 1987. Female land tenure system in tigers. In *Tigers of the world*, ed. R. L. Tilson and U. S. Seal, 97–109. Park Ridge, NJ: Noyes Publications.

9. Lindzey, F. G., W. D. Van Sickle, B. B. Ackerman, D. Barnhurst, T. P. Hemker, and S. P. Laing. 1994. Cougar population dynamics in southern Utah. *J. Wildl. Mgmt.* 58: 619–624.

10. Bailey, T. N. 1993. *The African leopard*. New York: Columbia University Press.

11. Sunquist, F. 2001. Staying close to home. *Int. Wildl.* 31(3): 20–29.

12. Seidensticker, J., J. E. Lahiri, K. C. Das, and A. Wright. 1976. Problem tiger in the Sundarbans. *Oryx* 11: 267–273.

13. Singh, A. 1981. *Tara, a tigress*. London: Quartet.

14. Singh, A. 1984. *Tiger! Tiger!* London: Jonathan Cape.

15. Mills, M. G. L. 1991. Conservation management of large carnivores in Africa. *Koedoe* 34: 81–90.

16. Marker-Kraus, L., D. Kraus, D. Barnett, and S. Hurlbut. 1996. *Cheetah survival on Namibian farmlands*. Windhoek, Namibia: Cheetah Conservation Fund.

17. Atkinson, M. W., and P. Wood. 1995. The re-introduction of the cheetah into the Matusadona National Parks, Zimbabwe. *Re-introduction News* 10: 7–8.

18. Caro, T. M. 1994. *Cheetahs of the Serengeti plains*. Chicago: University of Chicago Press.

19. Pettifer, H. L. 1981. The experimental release of captive bred cheetah (*Acinonyx jubatus*) into the natural environment. In Worldwide furbearer conference proceedings: August 3–11, 1980, Frostburg, Maryland, ed. J. A. Chapman and D. Pursley, 1001–1024.

20. Anderson, J. 1992. South African carnivores. *Re-introduction News* 4: 8–9.

21. Hunter, L. 1995. The re-introduction of lions and cheetahs into northern Natal, South Africa. *Re-introduction News* 11: 15–16.

22. Rabinowitz, A. R. 1986. Jaguar predation on domestic livestock in Belize. *Wildl. Soc. Bull.* 14: 170–174.

23. Ruth, T., L. Sweanor, and M. Hornocker. 1998. Evaluating cougar translocations in New Mexico. *J. Wildl. Mgmt.* 62: 1263–1274.

24. Belden, R. C., and B. W. Hagedorn. 1993. Feasibility of translocating panthers into northern Florida. *J. Wildl. Mgmt.* 57: 388–397.

25. Belden, R. C. and J. W. McCowan. 1996. Florida panther reintroduction feasibility study. Final report. Study no. 7507. Bureau of Wildlife Research, Division of Wildlife, Florida Fish and Wildlife Conservation Commission, Tallahassee, FL 32399–1600. 70 pp.

26. Brocke, R. H., K. A. Gustafson, and L. B. Fox. 1991. Restoration of large predators: Potentials and problems. In *Challenges in the conservation of biological resources, a practitioner's guide*, ed. D. J. Decker, M. E. Krasny, G. R. Goff, C. R. Smith, and D. W. Gross, 303–315. Boulder, CO: Westview Press.

27. Byrne, G., and T. Shenk. 1999. Canadian lynx. *Re-introduction News* 18: 15–17.

28. Foster, D. 2000. Lynx thrive after 2 months in the wild. *Denver Rocky Mountain News*, June 30.

29. Büttner, K., and G. Worel. 1990. [Reintroduction of Euro-

pean wildcats in Bavaria—Project of the Bavarian League for the Protection of Nature.] (In German.) *Waldhygiene* 18: 169–176.

30. Nowell, K., and P. Jackson, 1996. *Wild cats: A status survey and conservation action plan.* Gland, Switzerland: International Union for Conservation of Nature and Natural Resources (IUCN).

31. Breitenmoser, U., and C. Breitenmoser-Würsten. 1990. Status, conservation needs and reintroduction of the lynx (*Lynx lynx*) in Europe. Strasbourg: Council of Europe.

32. Breitenmoser, U., C. Breitenmoser-Würsten, and S. Capt. 1998. Re-introduction and present status of the lynx (*Lynx lynx*) in Switzerland. *Hystrix* 10: 17–30.

33. Yalden, D. W. 1993. The problems of reintroducing carnivores. *Symp. Zool. Soc. Lond.* 65: 289–306.

34. Huber, T., and P. Kaczensky. 1998. The situation of the lynx (*Lynx lynx*) in Austria. *Hystrix* 10: 43–54.

35. Cop, J., and A. Frkovic. 1998. The re-introduction of the lynx in Slovenia and its present status in Slovenia and Croatia. *Hystrix* 10: 65–76.

36. Kaczensky, P. 1998. Status and distribution of the lynx in the German Alps. *Hystrix* 10: 39–42.

37. Stahl, P., and J.-M. Vandel. 1998. Distribution of the lynx in the French Alps. *Hystrix* 10: 3–15.

38. Breitenmoser, U., P., Kaczensky, M. Dötterer, C. Breitenmoser-Würsten, S. Capt, F. Bernhart, and M. Liberek. 1993. Spatial organization and recruitment of lynx (*Lynx lynx*) in a reintroduced population in the Swiss Jura Mountains. *J. Zool.* (Lond.) 231: 449–464.

39. Hoogesteijn, R., A. Hoogesteijn, and E. Mondolfi. 1993. Jaguar predation and conservation: Cattle mortality caused by felines on three ranches in the Venezuelan llanos. *Symp. Zool. Soc. Lond.* 65: 391–407.

40. Elagupillay, S. T. 1983. Livestock depredation problems by tigers in cattle farms. *J. Wildl. Parks* (Malaysia) 2: 136–144.

41. Norton, P. M. 1984. Leopard conservation in South Africa. *Afr. Wildl.* 38(5): 192–196.

42. Cat News. 1995. Namibian cheetahs moved to Bophuthatswana. Cat News 23: 16.

43. Cat News. 1995. A disastrous cheetah re-introduction in South Africa. *Cat News* 23: 16–17.

44. Gossow, H., and P. Honsig-Erlenburg. 1986. Management problems with reintroduced lynx in Austria. In *Cats of the world: Biology, conservation and management*, ed. S. D. Miller and D. D. Everett, 77–83. Washington, DC: National Wildlife Federation.

45. Herrenschmidt, V., and F. Léger. 1987. [The lynx *Lynx lynx* in north-eastern France: Colonization of the French Jura mountains and reintroduction of the species in the Vosges mountains.] (In French.) *Ciconia* 11: 131–151.

46. van Aarde, R. J., and R. D. Skinner. 1986. Pattern of space use by relocated servals *Felis serval*. *Afr. J. Ecol.* 24: 97–101.

47. Karanth, K. U., and M. E. Sunquist. 2000. Behavioural correlates of predation by tiger (*Panthera tigris*), leopard (*Panthera pardus*) and dhole (*Cuon alpinus*) in Nagarahole, India. *J. Zool.* 250: 255–265.

Conserving Felids in
the Twenty-First Century

All species of wild cats are threatened by habitat loss. Many of the large cats are also endangered by conflict with humans and a declining prey base. Conserving the world's felids will obviously require a multifaceted approach, with solutions tailored to individual species, specific habitats, geographic regions and cultures.

Though it is essential that we continue to create new parks and reserves, it is almost more important that we find ways to step up protection of existing protected areas. In many countries, protected area boundaries are primarily on paper, and though good wildlife laws and regulations exist, they are not enforced. Somehow we must find a way to give wildlife wardens and park guards increased status and recognition. Quality people must be recruited for the difficult and unpopular job of protection and charged with the task of implementing the existing laws. Though it sounds simple to the point of being inane, finding high-quality, dedicated personnel to control illegal hunting, grazing, and firewood collection is probably one of the most difficult challenges in wildlife conservation today. Guards and protection officers are almost always poorly paid, and people who hunt illegally or remove valuable timber, such as mahogany and sandalwood, from forest reserves often bribe officers in charge to look the other way. It is almost impossible for a forest guard of little social standing to arrest a prominent local businessman for illegal hunting. Large sums of money change hands to ensure that timber concessions are given to the right person, guards are bribed not to patrol for poachers, and restaurants and shops openly sell illegally killed wild game. Having lain awake at night in India, Nepal, Venezuela, and Malaysia and listened to gunshots echoing through legally protected forests, we are aware of how widespread the problems are and how hard they will be to solve. The key to stemming the flow of wildlife, wood, and other forest products from protected areas will be to come up with creative ways to support those whose job it is to apprehend offenders and implement the laws.

One of the most innovative approaches is being tried in India. A variety of individuals, as well as national and international nongovernmental organizations, sponsor awards ranging from US$30.00 to $250.00. The funds provide life insurance for park guards, furnish monetary awards to deserving wildlife wardens, and allow for public recognition of the generally low-paid, low-status staff of India's national parks. Though such small-fund programs are difficult to administer, they confer a great deal of status on recipients and their families. Even a US$100.00 award may represent several months' salary for a park guard.

Because only a small percentage of the world's cats live within protected areas, conservation projects outside parks and reserves will also become increasingly important. As long as they are not persecuted, many cat species can survive in multiple-use areas; some, such as the leopard, jungle cat, leopard cat, and African wildcat actually thrive alongside agriculture and humans. Multiple-use areas may serve as corridors to connect populations or as habitat for nonbreeders. However, it is important to distinguish between habitat conditions that will support dispersers and nonbreeding adults, and habitat that is rich enough in prey, water, and den sites to support a female raising young. These distinctions will be different for each species. For example, the habitat conditions that would allow a female leopard to raise young might not have enough prey or seclusion to support a tigress and her cubs.

Predation on domestic livestock continues to be one of the cat conservation world's biggest public relations problems. Large cats such as tigers, lions, jaguars, snow leopards, pumas, cheetahs, caracals, and Eurasian lynx all take domestic stock when the opportunity presents itself, and even small cats such as bobcats, jaguarundis, ocelots, and kodkods are known to kill domestic poultry. Innovative methods of reducing cat predation on livestock and better livestock husbandry and protection will become key to the conservation of many cat species. If cattle ranchers, sheep and goat herders, and even families with a few chickens can learn to manage their livestock so that it is less accessible to predators, fewer cats will be killed. In many cases, a great deal of conflict and retaliatory killing of predators could be avoided if livestock was simply placed in secure pens at night.

There is great scope for conservation organizations, zoo outreach programs, and even individuals to become involved in initiatives to reduce livestock predation. Jim Sanderson, a biologist studying the South American guiña, or kodkod, found that when landowners on Chiloé Island had access to chicken wire and were able to build pens, poultry losses were reduced and fewer cats were killed. The International Snow Leopard Trust (ISLT) and the Mountain Institute sponsor workshops in countries throughout the snow leopard's range to identify ways of reducing livestock losses to snow leopards. Participants are charged with the task of finding a set of remedial measures to reduce depredation. To receive donor support, solutions must benefit both snow leopards and villagers and involve a significant contribution of labor or materials from the community. The International Snow Leopard Trust is also providing villagers with clothes and food products in exchange for their tolerance of a low level of predation on their domestic stock.[1]

Over the last decade researchers have experimented with a variety of different approaches to reducing cat predation on livestock. One of the most promising approaches is aversive conditioning. Electric shock, which inhibits approach behavior, and conditioned taste aversion (CTA), which inhibits consumption behavior, are the two major types of aversive conditioning that have been used on felids. Electric shock treatment is usually delivered by way of electric fencing. This method is currently being used in Venezuela, where maternity or calving pastures are surrounded by solar-powered electric fences to protect valuable calves from attack by pumas.

The objective of conditioned taste aversion is to get the predator to develop an aversion to domestic livestock. Debra Forthman, director of field conservation at Zoo Atlanta, is conducting experiments to see whether CTA will work with livestock-killing big cats. Theoretically, if a nonlethal emetic salt is injected into a carcass, a predator that eats it will become sick, and will learn that eating domestic livestock has unpleasant consequences. Lithium chloride, the drug most commonly used in CTA, tastes slightly salty and has a metallic aftertaste. It must be injected into the carcass in carefully calculated doses because if the cat detects the chemical, it will not eat enough meat to become sick. CTA has been used on dozens of predator species, including bears, wolves, coyotes, and raccoons, but because cats are more selective eaters, they are difficult to dose.

In Namibia, the Cheetah Conservation Fund is working to place livestock-guarding dogs with local ranchers. The dogs, Anatolian shepherds, live with the livestock and protect them against cheetah and leopard attacks. In several cases farmers reported that the presence of a guarding dog reduced livestock losses to zero.[2] Stock-guarding dogs such as Akbash, Anatolian shepherd, Komondor, and Great Pyrenees have also been found effective at protecting sheep from predators in the western United States.[3]

Innovative approaches to cat conservation such as the ones taken by the International Snow Leopard Trust and the Cheetah Conservation Fund are not just matters of funding. They depend on individuals with vision and commitment. Such projects are difficult to duplicate because they are case- and site-specific and are usually driven by a charismatic individual. The challenge for conservation organizations around the world is to identify and nurture individuals with vision and commitment.

REFERENCES

1. Sunquist, F. 1997. Where cats and herders mix. *Int. Wildl.* 27 (1): 26–33.

2. Marker-Kraus, L., D. Kraus, D. Barnett, and S. Hurlbut. 1996. *Cheetah survival on Namibian farmlands.* Windhoek, Namibia: Cheetah Conservation Fund.

3. Green, J. S., R. A. Woodruff, and T. T. Tueller. 1984. Livestock guarding dogs for predator control: Costs, benefits, and practicality. *Wildl. Soc. Bull.* 12: 44–50.

Appendix 1
CITES Listings Governing Trade in Wild Cats

CITES is The Convention on International Trade in Endangered Species. In effect since 1975, CITES is a global treaty designed to protect plant and animal species from unregulated trade. Currently, 145 member countries have agreed to abide by the regulations established in the CITES convention.

Briefly, CITES has three appendixes, and different trade restrictions apply depending on whether a listed species is on appendix I, II, or III. All felid species are listed on either appendix I or appendix II. Each year, member countries report all transacstions that require CITES permits to the World Conservation Monitoring Centre in Cambridge, England.

APPENDIX I
Includes "all species threatened with extinction which are or may be affected by trade." Species listed on appendix I are protected from ALL international commercial trade. Appendix I species may be traded under limited noncommercial circumstances. Both import and export permits are required before a species on appendix I can be moved from one country to another.

APPENDIX II
Includes species which may not be threatened at the moment, but which may become threatened unless trade is regulated. Appendix II also includes "look-alike" species that are difficult to distinguish from species listed on appendix I. Species listed on appendix II require export permits only.

APPENDIX III
Allows countries to unilaterally list native species already protected within their own borders in order to prevent or restrict exploitation. Species listed on appendix III require export permits only.

CAT SPECIES LISTED ON APPENDIX I (AS OF MARCH 1994)
Cheetah —*Acinonyx jubatus*
Caracal—*Caracal caracal* (Asian)
Asiatic golden cat —*Catopuma temminckii*
Black-footed cat —*Felis nigripes*
Jaguarundi —*Herpailurus yaguarondi* (Central and North America)
Ocelot —*Leopardus pardalis*
Oncilla —*Leopardus tigrinus*
Margay —*Leopardus wiedii*
Iberian lynx —*Lynx pardinus*
Geoffroy's cat —*Oncifelis geoffroyi*
Andean mountain cat —*Oreailurus jacobitus*
Leopard cat —*Prionailurus bengalensis* (Bangladesh, India, and Thailand)
Flat-headed cat —*Prionailurus planiceps*
Rusty-spotted cat —*Prionailurus rubiginosus* (India)
Puma —*Puma concolor* (Florida, Central America, and eastern North America)
Clouded leopard —*Neofelis nebulosa*
Asiatic lion —*Panthera leo persica*
Jaguar —*Panthera onca*
Tiger —*Panthera tigris*
Marbled cat —*Pardofelis marmorata*
Snow leopard —*Uncia uncia*

CAT SPECIES LISTED ON APPENDIX II (AS OF MARCH 1994)
Caracal—*Caracal caracal*
Bornean bay cat —*Catopuma badia*
Chinese mountain cat —*Felis bieti*
Jungle cat —*Felis chaus*
Sand cat —*Felis margarita*
Wildcat —*Felis silvestris*
Jaguarundi —*Herpailurus yaguarondi*
Serval—*Leptailurus serval*

Canada lynx — *Lynx canadensis*
Eurasian lynx — *Lynx lynx*
Bobcat — *Lynx rufus*
Pampas cat — *Oncifelis colocolo*
Kodkod — *Oncifelis guigna*
Manul — *Otocolobus manul*

Leopard cat — *Prionailurus bengalensis*
Rusty-spotted cat — *Prionailurus rubiginosus*
Fishing cat — *Prionailurus viverrinus*
African golden cat — *Profelis aurata*
Puma — *Puma concolor*
Lion — *Panthera leo*

Appendix 2

IUCN Red List: Conservation Status of Wild Cats

The IUCN Red List is a catalogue of species known to be threatened with extinction. The list is prepared by the International Union for Conservation of Nature and Natural Resources (IUCN), based on information provided by scientists and naturalists working in the field, and each species is assigned to a category that highlights its extinction risk. Originally, species were assigned to the categories Endangered, Vulnerable, Rare, and Indeterminate. Later the categories were revised, and in 1994 the IUCN Council adopted new Red List Categories and Criteria.[1] The list is constantly under review, and updated versions are posted on the IUCN website.

The following is a summary of the 2002 IUCN Red List conservation status of the cats. The scientific names of some species on the IUCN Red List differ somewhat from the nomenclature used in this book because we have adopted the 1993 taxonomic revision as our standard of classification.

CRITICALLY ENDANGERED

Iberian lynx, *Lynx pardinus* (Temminck, 1827)

Amur leopard, *Panthera pardus orientalis* Schlegel, 1857

Amur tiger, *Panthera tigris altaica* Temminck, 1844

Anatolian leopard, *Panthera pardus tulliana* Valenciennes, 1856

Arabian leopard, *Panthera pardus nimr* Hemprich and Ehrenberg, 1833

Asiatic cheetah, *Acinonyx jubatus venaticus* Griffith, 1821

Asiatic lion, *Panthera leo persica* Meyer, 1826

Eastern cougar, *Puma concolor cougar* Kerr, 1792

Florida panther, *Puma concolor coryi* Bangs, 1899

North African leopard, *Panthera pardus panthera* Schreber, 1777

South China tiger, *Panthera tigris amoyensis* Hilzheimer, 1905

Sumatran tiger, *Panthera tigris sumatrae* Pocock, 1929

ENDANGERED

Andean mountain cat, *Oreailurus jacobitus* (Cornalia, 1865)

Bornean bay cat, *Catopuma badia* (Gray, 1874)

Snow leopard, *Uncia uncia* (Schreber, 1775)

Tiger, *Panthera tigris* (Linnaeus, 1758)

Iriomote (leopard) cat, *Prionailurus bengalensis iriomotensis* Imaizumi, 1967

Javan leopard, *Panthera pardus melas* G. Cuvier, 1809

North African serval, *Lynchailurus serval constantinus* Forster, 1780

North Chinese leopard, *Panthera pardus japonensis* Gray, 1862

Northwest African cheetah, *Acinonyx jubatus hecki* Hilzheimer, 1913

Sri Lankan leopard, *Panthera pardus kotiya* Deraniyagala, 1956

Texas jaguarundi, *Herpailurus yaguarondi cacomitli* Berlandier, 1859

Texas ocelot, *Lynchailurus pardalis albescens* Pucheran, 1855

VULNERABLE

African golden cat, *Profelis aurata* (Temminck, 1827)

Asiatic golden cat, *Catopuma temminckii* (Vigors and Horsfield, 1827)

Black-footed cat, *Felis nigripes* (Burchell, 1824)

Cheetah, *Acinonyx jubatus* (Schreber, 1775)

Chinese mountain cat, *Felis bieti* Milne-Edwards, 1892

Clouded leopard, *Neofelis nebulosa* (Griffith, 1821)

Fishing cat, *Prionailurus viverrinus* (Bennett, 1833)

Flat-headed cat, *Prionailurus planiceps* (Vigors and Horsfield, 1827)

Kodkod, *Oncifelis guigna* (Molina, 1782)

Lion, *Panthera leo* (Linnaeus, 1758)

Marbled cat, *Pardofelis marmorata* Severtzof, 1858

Rusty-spotted cat, *Prionailurus rubiginosus* (I. Geoffroy Saint-Hilaire, 1831)

Scottish wildcat, *Felis silvestris grampia* Miller, 1907

NEAR THREATENED
Geoffroy's cat, *Oncifelis geoffroyi* (d'Orbigny and Gervais, 1844)
Jaguar, *Panthera onca* (Linnaeus, 1758)
Eurasian lynx, *Lynx lynx* (Linnaeus, 1758)
Manul, *Otocolobus manul* (Pallas, 1776)
Oncilla, *Leopardus tigrinus* (Schreber, 1775)
Pampas cat, *Oncifelis colocolo* (Molina, 1782)
Puma, *Puma concolor* (Linnaeus, 1771)
Sand cat, *Felis margarita* (Loche, 1858)

LEAST CONCERN
Bobcat, *Lynx rufus* (Schreber, 1776)
Canada lynx, *Lynx canadensis* Kerr, 1792

Caracal, *Caracal caracal* (Schreber, 1776)
Jaguarundi, *Herpailurus yaguarondi* Lacépéde, 1809
Jungle cat, *Felis chaus* Schreber, 1777
Leopard, *Panthera pardus* (Linnaeus, 1758)
Leopard cat, *Prionailurus bengalensis* (Kerr, 1792)
Margay, *Leopardus wiedii* (Schinz, 1821)
Ocelot, *Leopardus pardalis* (Linnaeus, 1758)
Serval, *Leptailurus serval* (Schreber, 1776)
Wildcat, *Felis silvestris* Schreber, 1775

REFERENCE
1. IUCN. 1994. *IUCN Red List categories*. Gland Switzerland: International Union for Conservation of Nature and Natural Resources.

Appendix 3
Olfactory Communication in Felids

Although the majority of felids are solitary, their lives are nevertheless embedded in a social system, which is dependent on the existence of signaling systems to regulate the animals' interactions. In some situations, these signals serve to bring animals together; in others, they are a means of avoiding contact, or serve to separate individuals spatially. Cats use vocal, visual, and chemical signals to communicate with one another. Some vocal signals can be perceived over great distances, while others are used only in close-contact situations, where they are often combined with visual signals (see appendix 4). Vocal and visual signals, however, do not persist in the environment. In contrast, chemical signals may persist for days or weeks, and thus the message can be read for some time after the depositor has left the location. Chemical signals are well suited to the spatially and temporally dispersed lifestyles of felids, and, not surprisingly, scent-marking behaviors are widespread among the Felidae. If the scent is deposited at a prominent location or is used in combination with a visual mark, such actions increase the likelihood of the scent marks being noticed and examined by conspecifics before the scent fades. While scent marks cannot be altered or directed toward specific individuals, as vocal or visual signals can, the marks stay where they are until they fade. Their value is their persistence in all kinds of conditions and their low cost to produce.

The sources of chemical scents or odors are secretions from various glands (e.g., anal sacs, subcaudal glands, cheek glands, foot glands) as well as saliva, urine, and feces.[1,2] Cats commonly rub the head, cheeks, and other body parts on objects, substrates, and other cats, thus leaving and collecting chemical traces. Similarly, feces and urine are often deposited in a semi-ritualized manner and placed in nonrandom and conspicuous locations. At times these deposits are dispensed in token amounts, suggesting a purpose other than elimination. Furthermore, changes in the rates of

specific scent-marking behaviors are often predictably associated with reproductive activity, sexual maturation, or acquisition of a home range. Compared with dogs, cats have a poor sense of smell, but olfaction obviously plays an integral role in their social lives.

Several behaviors are associated with scent marking in cats. Rubbing of the head, cheek, and neck on objects is common in most species of felids.[3,4,5] The rubbing is deliberate, sometimes vigorous, and the cat often leans forward to bring a specific part of its body into contact with the object. These actions are done while the cat is standing, sitting, or reclining, depending on where the object is located. Rubbing is usually preceded by sniffing, licking, or biting of the object and flehmen, in which the odor is drawn over the vomeronasal organ, which is located in the roof of the mouth. In so doing, the cat characteristically gives an open-mouth grimace. A cat will typically flehm after sniffing a urine mark; the vomeronasal organ detects the presence of sex hormones in the urine.[6,7] Both sexes flehm, but males usually do so at a higher rate than females, especially during periods of mating activity. Among small felids, both sexes cheek-rub at about the same rate, but the frequency is usually higher among reproductively active pairs.[5] Cheek rubbing appears to serve several functions, including depositing scent, collecting the scent of urine marks, and as a visual display.[4,5,8] Novel and particularly odoriferous substances (e.g., carrion, vomit, feces) also appear to elicit head rubbing.[3]

Claw raking is recorded for most species of cats. It is usually performed on upright tree trunks or horizontal logs. The cat grips the trunk or log with its forearms extended and draws the claws backward, either simultaneously or alternatively in strokes. The motion may be jerky as the claws catch on bark or dense wood. The action is not thought to actually sharpen the claws but simply to remove loose pieces of the claw sheaths. For most species, claw raking does not appear to be a frequent behavior, but the marks are conspicuous and permanent. The importance of scratching in felid communication is suggested by the observation that some trees are repeatedly scratched. Cats also sniff and sometimes rub against scratch marks.

The most commonly observed form of scent marking is urine spraying. While standing, the cat points its hindquarters at an object, raises its tail to an upright position, and sprays urine backward onto the object. The urine may be a few drops emitted as a fine mist or a somewhat larger volume sprayed in a stream. Urine spraying is often accompanied by treading (scraping/scuffing) of the hind feet and vibrating of the tail. Urine spraying has been recorded for males and females of nearly all felid species. That male pumas do not spray seems unusual, especially since female pumas reportedly do so,[9] although in captivity neither sex has been seen to urinate other than in a squatting posture.[10] As residents move about their home ranges, they occasionally stop and spray urine onto trees, bushes, and other upright objects along their travel routes. In most felids, males spray at higher rates than females, but rates of scent marking are known to change. For example, in South Africa, an adult female black-footed cat regularly scent-marked throughout her range, but ceased scent-marking while she had small kittens. When the young were older, her rate of scent marking again increased. Her rate of marking increased dramatically about one and a half months prior to mating.[11,12] Resident male black-footed cats in the same area sprayed ten to twelve times per hour, but the rate increased prior to mating. On the night before he mated, one male was seen spraying 585 times.[13]

Higher rates of scent marking are also associated with territorial behavior.[14,15] Tigers mark at higher rates along boundaries with neighbors than they do in other parts of their territories. Higher rates of marking also accompany shifts in territorial boundaries, and tigers scent-mark intensively when establishing or acquiring a territory. Tigers also make more scrapes in these situations.[16] A scrape or scuff is made with the hind feet as each foot is alternately thrust backward; this repeated motion tends to remove the vegetation and scar the soil. The loosened soil and vegetation typically form a pile or mound at the end of the scrape. Among the larger cats, these scrapes may measure 30–50 centimeters long and 15–25 centimeters wide.[17] Besides being a visual mark, scrapes are sometimes anointed with urine or feces or both. The probability of the mark being encountered by other cats is further enhanced by the fact that scrapes are often made in prominent locations and along well-traveled routes; the frequency of scraping is often highest in areas where the home ranges or territories of neighbors abut or overlap. Scraping behavior is well known among the larger felids as well as cats in the ocelot lineage (e.g., ocelot, margay, oncilla, pampas cat, Geoffroy's cat, kodkod, Andean mountain cat). However, in the domestic cat lineage (e.g., European and African wildcat, sand cat, jungle cat, black-footed cat), only the manul is known to scrape.[5,18,19]

Another behavior that is often associated with urine spraying is tail twitching or quivering. It is documented for most species, but its function is not clear. It has been suggested that the tail is raised to help direct and position the spray, and that the quivering or twitching is possibly a visual signal or simply an automatic manifestation coupled to micturation.[3] Among captive small felids, tail twitching was observed only during sprays that were judged to be particularly "vigorous" in execution.[5] In free-ranging black-footed cats, tail twitching appeared to be just a part of urine-spraying behavior, as was treading with the hindfeet.[12]

While felid feces may not have the communicative significance of that reported for canids, they still appear to be important. Most felids leave their feces uncovered, which means that they are visible, and when deposited deliberately on a scrape, they become even more noticeable. Furthermore, some species commonly place their feces on prominent or elevated objects, an action that would increase both visibility and the dispersal of scent. In a few species, feces are repeatedly deposited at specific locations, which resemble latrines. The nonrandom deposition of feces along major travel routes, at road or trail junctions, and near home range boundaries strongly suggests a communication function. That some species sometimes leave their feces uncovered and at other times cover them suggests yet another motive—cats that cover their feces are trying to avoid detection. In the few circumstances in which such behavior has been documented, it is usually performed by females with small kittens.[12,20] Female farm cats have also been observed to leave their feces and urine exposed while away from the barn, but to bury them when at home.[2,21] Eliminating odors near natal dens may lessen the possibility that the kittens will be found and killed by adult males. Infanticide is a serious threat in many species of felids.

Exactly what information is being transmitted via these scents or odors is not known precisely, but it most likely includes individual identity, sex, status, reproductive state, age of the mark, and the spatial dimensions of a home range or territory. Laboratory studies show that several species of carnivores are able to identify an individual based only on the odor from specific glands.[2,22] The routine behavior of anogenital sniffing in canids is presumably an "identity check."[1,2] Wolves and dogs can discriminate between the urine of different individuals; foxes can distinguish their own urine from that of other foxes. Similarly, in encounters between strange domestic cats, the "nose check" and the circling to try to smell each other's anal regions may represent attempts to "identify" the other cat.[9] Anogenital sniffing is also likely to be used to identify an individual's sex. Behavioral tests on cats show that the sexes can be distinguished on the basis of odors from several sources.[23] In addition, the volume or frequency of marking and the pattern or height of the marks may by itself indicate sex.[24,25]

There are no specific odors or chemicals that are known to convey status or dominance, but dominant animals typically mark more frequently or deposit more scent than subordinates.[26] Higher rates of scent marking by dominant individuals are well documented in canids,[27,28,29] and it has been demonstrated that the pattern of deposition of cheek gland secretions of dwarf mongooses is associated with status.[30] In black-footed cats, individuals without home ranges rarely scent-marked.[11,12,13] Similarly, nonbreeding leopards seldom scent-marked.[31]

Scent marks also convey information on reproductive status.[1,2,22] Changes in levels of urinary estrogen are an accurate indication of changes in female receptivity, and urine marks are easily monitored by males. It has been shown that male domestic cats can detect estrus just by the smell of a female's urine or cheek glands.[23] For many species of felids, rates of scent marking are higher during periods of reproductive activity.[5] In wide-ranging species, higher rates of scent marking by females prior to estrus probably ensure not only that a male locates the female, but also that he is present during the peak of her sexual receptivity.[12,16,17,32]

The temporal importance of scent marks is inferred largely from the behavioral responses of cats to marks of different ages or to the sudden absence of marks. Cats can distinguish between new and old scent marks,[33] and it has been suggested that within neighborhoods of domestic cats, simultaneous use of zones of home range overlap is avoided by checking the "signposts." An old mark means "go ahead," while a fresh mark means "stop" or "wait." The animal who gets there first is dominant.[9] Cheetahs were observed to avoid following the route used by another group if their scent marks were less than twenty-four hours old, but older marks were sniffed and ignored.[34]

While a greater amount of urinary lipid in a scent mark can extend the functional time of the mark,[35,36,37] the scent eventually fades, and it is necessary for animals to periodically re-mark or "freshen up" old marks. How long a scent mark remains effective is not known precisely because (1) even an old scent mark may still carry a message, (2) the chemical constituents of the marks may change with social or environmental conditions, (3) dissipation rates may vary depending on where the mark was deposited, and (4) since some urine marks are deposited in association with scrape or scratch marks, the scent mark's functional life may be extended in this way. Despite all these caveats, there are several pieces of evidence suggesting that scent marks are effective for about three to four weeks. It has been shown for wolves that the stimulus value of scent drops to zero after about twenty-three days, which is the interval at which wolf packs visit most parts of their territories.[28] In dwarf mongooses, scent marks had to be renewed at intervals of three weeks or less to be effective indicators of occupancy.[30] New leopard scrapes appeared at two closely monitored sites at average intervals of 25.9 and 21.7 days.[31] Similarly, in situations in which there were cats waiting to move into unoccupied areas, the interval between the time when resident animals disappeared and when the vacancies were filled was about three to four weeks.[17,31,38,39,40]

The principal mechanism for delineating the spatial dimensions of a cat's home range or territory is probably the deposition of scent marks and scrapes along major travel routes and boundaries with neighboring animals. This is not to suggest that scent marks act like hard boundaries and that intruders are repelled at the borders. In fact, the occasional appearance of transients or probes by neighbors into occupied areas indicate that the marks do not constitute an impenetrable barrier. Intruders may, however, be intimidated or at a disadvantage, and thus are more cautious and ready to flee. They seldom stay long in occupied areas. Such behavior has been observed for leopards.[41] Whether these behavioral changes are in response to previous adverse encounters, alien scent marks, unfamiliar terrain, or to the absence of the intruder's own scent marks is not known.

How individuals respond to scent marks depends

on a variety of variables, including context, prior experience, social status, physical condition, and hormonal state, as well as psychological factors. The effect of an animal smelling its own mark may be to make it more self-assured or less anxious. In other cases the message may simply be informative, and no response is evoked or needed. However, a cat's response to the scent marks of unknown individuals may be quite different from its response to those of known individuals, which, in turn, can be influenced by the nature of its previous interactions with those individuals. In some cases the message may set in motion a suite of far-reaching physiological and emotional changes. The urine mark of a female, for example, may provoke little response from either a subadult or an adult male cat, but if she is in estrus, the adult male's behavior will change dramatically. Furthermore, if the pair already "know" each other, the subsequent courtship and copulation is likely to be much less threatening and more successful than that between unfamiliar and sexually naive partners. Physical contact between animals, especially those as well armed as cats, is a delicate situation.

TABLE 72 OLFACTORY MARKING BEHAVIOR IN FELIDS

Species	Head rubbing	Cheek rubbing	Chin rubbing	Neck rubbing	Claw raking	Urine spraying	Scraping with hind feet	Feces	Source
Lion	M	M, F		M, F	M, F	M, F	M, F	Uncovered, scattered	3,4,35,42
Tiger	M	M, F			M, F	M, F	M, F	Uncovered, conspicuous	3,4,16,17,32,35,37,43
Jaguar	M				M, F	M, F	M, F	Uncovered, scattered	3,44,45,46
Cheetah		M, F			M, F	M, F	M, F	Uncovered, conspicuous, covered	3,4,47,48
Puma	M				M, F	F	M, F	Uncovered, conspicuous, covered	3,9,49,50,51
Leopard	F	M, F		M, F	M, F	M, F	M, F	Uncovered, conspicuous	3,31,52,53,54
Snow leopard	M, F	M, F		M, F		M, F	M, F	Uncovered, conspicuous	3,4,55,56,57,58,59
Clouded leopard	M	M,F				M	M,F	Uncovered, conspicuous, covered	3,60,61
Eurasian lynx		M			M	M	M		5,40,62
Canada lynx	M,F	M, F			M, F	M, F		Uncovered, conspicuous, covered	3,5,63
Iberian lynx						M, F		Uncovered, conspicuous	64
Bobcat		M, F			M, F	M, F	M, F	Uncovered, conspicuous, covered	3,4,20,65,66,67
Caracal		M, F			M, F	M, F	M	Uncovered	5,68

(continued)

TABLE 72 (continued)

Species	Head rubbing	Cheek rubbing	Chin rubbing	Neck rubbing	Claw raking	Urine spraying	Scraping with hind feet	Feces	Source
Serval	M, F	M, F	M, F		M, F	M, F	M, F	Uncovered, conspicuous	4,5,69,70
Asiatic golden cat	M, F	M, F	M	M, F	M, F	M, F	M		3,5
African golden cat				M	F	F		Uncovered, conspicuous	5,69
Fishing cat	M, F	M, F			M, F	M, F			3,5
Jungle cat	M, F	M, F			M, F				5,71
Ocelot	M, F	M, F	M	M, F	M, F	M	M	Uncovered, conspicuous, localized	5,72
Margay		M, F	M, F			M	M	Uncovered, covered	3,4,73
Jaguarundi	M	M		M, F	M, F	M	M, F	Uncovered	3,5,74
Geoffroy's cat	F	M, F	M, F	M, F	M, F	M, F	M	Uncovered, conspicuous	5,75
Pampas cat		M	M			M	M		5
European wildcat	M, F	M, F		F	F	M, F		Uncovered, conspicuous	3,5,76
African-Asian wildcat						M, F		Uncovered, conspicuous, covered	3,4,5,77
Domestic cat	M, F	M, F	M, F	M, F	M, F	M, F		Covered	3,5,7,21,23,76,78,79
Manul	F		F		M, F	M	M	Covered	3,5
Leopard cat	M, F					M, F	M	Scattered, uncovered, covered	3,80
Sand cat	M, F	M, F		F	M, F	M, F		Covered	3,5
Rusty-spotted cat				F		M, F			5
Black-footed cat	M, F	M, F	M	M		M, F		Uncovered, scattered	5,11,12,13

Note: Behaviors reported for males (M) and females (F). Blank cell = no information.

REFERENCES

1. Ewer, R. F. 1973. *The carnivores*. Ithaca, NY: Cornell University Press.

2. Macdonald, D. W. 1985. The carnivores: order Carnivora. In *Social odours in mammals*, ed. R. E. Brown and D. W. Macdonald, 619–722. Oxford: Clarendon Press.

3. Wemmer, C., and K. Scow. 1977. Communication in the Felidae with emphasis on scent marking and contact patterns. In *How animals communicate*, ed. T. Seboek, 749–766. Bloomington: Indiana University Press.

4. Reiger, I. 1979. Scent rubbing in carnivores. *Carnivore* 11: 17–25.

5. Mellen, J. D. 1993. A comparative analysis of scent-marking, social and reproductive behavior in 20 species of small cats (*Felis*). *Am. Zool*. 33: 151–166.

6. Estes, R. D. 1972. The role of the vomeronasal organ in mammalian reproduction. *Mammalia* 36: 315–341.

7. Verberne, G. 1976. Chemocommunication among domestic cats, mediated by the olfactory and vomeronasal senses. II. The relation between the function of Jacobson's organ (vomeronasal organ) and flehmen behaviour. *Z. Tierpysychol*. 42: 113–128.

8. Reiger, I., and D. Walzthony. 1979. Markieren Katzen beim Wangenrieben? [Is felid cheek rubbing a scent marking behavior?] *Z. Säugetierk*. 44: 319–320.

9. Leyhausen, P. 1979. *Cat behavior: The predatory and social behavior of domestic and wild cats*. New York: Garland STPM Press.

10. Fiedler, W. 1957. Beobachtungen zum Markierungsverhalten einiger Säugetiere. *Z. Säugetierk*. 22: 57–76.

11. Olbricht, G., and Sliwa, A. 1997. In situ and ex situ observations and management of black-footed cats. *Int. Zoo Yrbk*. 35: 81–89.

12. Molteno, A. J., A. Sliwa, and P. R. K. Richardson. 1998. The role of scent marking in a free-ranging, female black-footed cat (*Felis nigripes*). *J. Zool*. (Lond.) 245: 35–41.

13. Sliwa, A. 1997. Black-footed cat field research. *Cat News* 27: 20–21.

14. Gosling, L. M. 1982. A reassessment of the function of scent marking in territories. *Z. Tierpsychol*. 60: 89–118.

15. Richardson, P. R. K. 1993. The function of scent marking in territories: a resurrection of the intimidation hypothesis. *Trans. R. Soc. S. Afr*. 48: 195–206.

16. Smith, J. L. D., C. McDougal, and D. Miquelle. 1989. Scent marking in free-ranging tigers, *Panthera tigris*. *Anim. Behav*. 37: 1–10.

17. Sunquist, M. E. 1981. *The social organization of tigers* (*Panthera tigris*) *in Royal Chitawan National Park, Nepal*. Smithsonian Contributions to Zoology. no. 336. 98 pp.

18. Collier, G., and S. J. O'Brien. 1985. A molecular phylogeny of the Felidae: Immunological distance. *Evolution* 39: 473–487.

19. Johnson, W. E., and S. J. O'Brien. 1997. Phylogenetic reconstruction of the Felidae using 16s rRNA and NADH-5 mitochondrial genes. *J. Mol. Evol*. 44 (suppl. 1): S98–S116.

20. Bailey, T. N. 1974. Social organization in a bobcat population. *J. Wildl. Mgmt*. 38: 435–446.

21. Panaman, R. 1981. Behaviour and ecology of free-ranging farm cats (*Felis catus* L.). *Z. Tierpsychol*. 56: 59–73.

22. Gorman, M. L., and B. J. Trowbridge. 1989. The role of odor in the social lives of carnivores. In *Carnivore behavior, ecology, and evolution*, ed. J. L. Gittleman, 57–88. Ithaca, NY: Cornell University Press.

23. Verberne, G., and J. DeBoer. 1976. Chemocommunication among domestic cats, mediated by the olfactory and vomeronasal senses. I. Chemocommunication. *Z. Tierpsychol*. 42: 86–109.

24. Kleiman, D. G. 1966. Scent marking in the Canidae. *Symp. Zool. Soc. Lond*. 18: 167–177.

25. Ewer, R. F., and C. Wemmer. 1974. The behaviour in captivity of the African civet, *Civettictis civetta* (Schreber). *Z. Tierpsychol*. 34: 359–394.

26. Ralls, K. 1971. Mammalian scent marking. *Science* 171: 443–449.

27. Macdonald, D. W. 1979. Some observations and field experiments on the urine marking behaviour of the red fox, *Vulpes vulpes*. *Z. Tierpsychol*. 51: 1–22.

28. Peters, R. P., and L. D. Mech. 1975. Scent-marking in wolves. *Am. Sci*. 63: 628–637.

29. Ryon, J., and R. E. Brown. 1990. Urine marking in female wolves (*Canis lupus*): An indicator of dominance status and reproductive state. In *Chemical signals in vertebrates*, V, ed. D. W. Macdonald, D. Müller-Swarze, and S. E. Natynczuk, 346–351. Oxford: Oxford University Press.

30. Rasa, O. A. E. 1973. Marking behaviour and its significance in the African dwarf mongoose, *Helogale undulata rufula*. *Z. Tierpsychol*. 32: 449–488.

31. Bailey, T. N. 1993. *The African leopard: A study of the ecology and behavior of a solitary felid*. New York: Columbia University Press.

32. Kleiman, D. 1974. The estrous cycle of the tiger. In *The world's cats*, vol. 2, ed. R. L. Eaton, 60–75. Seattle: Woodland Park Zoo.

33. DeBoer, J. 1977. The age of olfactory cues functioning in chemocommunication among male domestic cats. *Behav. Proc*. 2: 209–225.

34. Eaton, R. L. 1970. Group interactions, spacing and territoriality in cheetahs. *Z. Tierpsychol*. 27: 481–491.

35. Asa, C. S. 1993. Relative contributions of urine and anal-sac secretions in scent marks of large felids. *Am. Zool*. 33: 167–172.

36. Brahmachary, R. L., and J. Dutta. 1987. Chemical communication in the tiger and leopard. In *Tigers of the world*, ed. R. L. Tilson and U. S. Seal, 296–302. Park Ridge, NJ: Noyes Publications.

37. Brahmachary, R. L., J. Dutta, and M. Poddar-Sarkar. 1991. The marking fluid of the tiger. *Mammalia* 55: 150–152.

38. Laing, S. P., and F. G. Lindzey. 1993. Patterns of replacement of resident cougars in southern Utah. *J. Mammal*. 74: 1056–1058.

39. Lovallo, M. J., and E. M. Anderson. 1995. Range shift by a female bobcat (*Lynx rufus*) after removal of a neighboring female. *Am. Midland Nat*. 134: 49–412.

40. Schmidt, K., W. Jedrzejewski, and H. Okarma. 1997. Spatial organization and social relations in the Eurasian lynx population in Bialowieza Primeval Forest, Poland. *Acta Theriologica* 42: 289–312.

41. Hamilton, P. H. 1976. The movements of leopards in Tsavo National Park, Kenya, as determined by radio-tracking. Master's thesis, University of Nairobi, Kenya.

42. Schaller, G. 1972. *The Serengeti lion*. Chicago: University of Chicago Press.

43. Schaller, G. 1967. *The deer and the tiger*. Chicago: University of Chicago Press.

44. Hoogesteijn, R., and E. Mondolfi. 1992. *The jaguar*. Caracas, Venezuela: Ediciones Armitano.

45. Schaller, G., and P. G. Crawshaw. 1980. Movement patterns of jaguar. *Biotropica* 12: 161–168.

46. Rabinowitz, A., and B. G. Nottingham. 1986. Ecology and

behaviour of the jaguar (*Panthera onca*) in Belize, Central America. *J. Zool.* 210: 149–159.

47. Caro, T. M. 1994. *Cheetahs of the Serengeti plains: Group living in an asocial species.* Chicago: University of Chicago Press.

48. Burney, D. 1980. The effects of human activities on cheetahs (*Acinonyx jubatus* Schr.) in the Mara region of Kenya. Master's thesis, University of Nairobi, Kenya.

49. Seidensticker, J. C., M. G. Hornocker, W. V. Wiles, and J. P. Messick. 1973. Mountain lion social organization in the Idaho Primitive Area. *Wildl. Monogr.* 35: 1–60.

50. Sweanor, L. L. 1990. Mountain lion social organization in a desert environment. Master's thesis, University of Idaho, Moscow.

51. Shaw, H. G. 1990. *A mountain lion field guide*, 4th ed. Special Report 9, Arizona Game and Fish Department.

52. Eisenberg, J. F., and M. C. Lockhart. 1972. *An ecological reconnaissance of Wilpattu National Park, Ceylon.* Smithsonian Contributions to Zoology, no. 101. 118 pp.

53. Muckenhirn, N. A., and J. F. Eisenberg. 1973. Home ranges and predation in the Ceylon leopard. In *The world's cats*, vol. 1, ed. R. L. Eaton, 142–175. Winston, OR: World Wildlife Safari.

54. Bothma, J. du P., and E. A. N. LeRiche. 1984. Aspects of the ecology and the behaviour of the leopard *Panthera pardus* in the Kalahari Desert. *Koedoe* (suppl.) 259–279.

55. Freeman, H. 1980. Snow leopard: A co-operative study between zoos. *International Pedigree Book of Snow Leopards* 2: 127–136.

56. Freeman, H. 1982. Characteristics of social behaviour in the snow leopard. *International Pedigree Book of Snow Leopards* 3: 117–120.

57. Freeman, H. 1983. Behaviour in adult pairs of snow leopards (*Panthera uncia*). *Zoo Biol.* 2: 1–22.

58. Ahlborn, G., and R. M. Jackson. 1988. Marking in free-ranging snow leopards in west Nepal: A preliminary assessment. In *Proceedings of the Fifth International Snow Leopard Symposium*, ed. H. Freeman, 25–49. Bombay: International Snow Leopard Trust and Wildlife Institute of India.

59. Hemmer, H. 1972. *Uncia uncia. Mammalian Species* 20: 1–5.

60. Hemmer, H. 1968. Untersuchungen zur Stammesgeschichte der Pantherkatzen (Pantherinae). Tiel II. Studien zur Ethologie des *Neofelis nebulosa* (Griffith 1821) und des Irbis *Uncia uncia* (Schreber 1775). *Veröffentlichungen der Zoologischen Staatssammlung München* 12: 155–247.

61. Yamada, J. K., and B. S. Durrant. 1988. Vaginal cytology and behavior in the clouded leopard. *Felid* 2: 1–3.

62. Lindemann, W. 1955. Über die jugendentwicklung beim luchs (*Lynx l. lynx* Keer.) und bei der wildkatze (*Felis s. silvestris* Schreb.). *Behaviour* 8:1–45.

63. Saunders, J. K. 1963. Movements and activities of the lynx in Newfoundland. *J. Wildl. Mgmt.* 27: 390–400.

64. Robinson, I. H., and M. Delibes. 1988. The distribution of faeces by the Spanish lynx (*Felis pardina*). *J. Zool.* (Lond.) 216: 577–582.

65. McCord, C. M., and J. E. Cardoza. 1982. Bobcat and lynx. In *Wild mammals of North America*, ed. J. A. Chapman and G. E. Feldhamer, 728–766. Baltimore: Johns Hopkins University Press.

66. Wassmer, D. A., D. D. Guenther, and J. N. Layne. 1988. Ecology of the bobcat in south-central Florida. *Bull. Fla. State Mus., Biol. Sci.* 33(4): 159–228.

67. Marshall, A. D., and J. H. Jenkins. 1966. Movements and home ranges of bobcats as determined by radio-tracking in the upper coastal plain of west-central South Carolina. *Proceedings of the Annual Conference of the Southeastern Association of Game and Fish Commissioners* 20: 206–214.

68. Stuart, C. T. 1981. Notes on the mammalian carnivores of the Cape Province, South Africa. *Bontebok* 1: 1–58.

69. Kingdon, J. 1977. *East African mammals.* Vol. 3, part A (Carnivores). Chicago: University of Chicago Press.

70. Geertsema, A. A. 1985. Aspects of the ecology of the serval *Leptailurus serval* in the Ngorongoro Crater, Tanzania. *Neth. J. Zool.* 35: 527–610.

71. Rathore, F. S., and V. Thapar. 1984. Behavioral observations of leopard and jungle cat in Ranthambhore National Park and Tiger Reserve, Rajasthan. In The plight of the cats: Proceedings of the meeting and workshop of the IUCN/SSC Cat Specialist Group at Kanha National Park, Madhya Pradesh, India, ed. P. Jackson, 136–139. Unpublished report, IUCN/SSC Cat Specialist Group, Bougy-Villars, Switzerland.

72. Ludlow, M. E. 1986. Home range, activity patterns, and food habits of the ocelot (*Felis pardalis*) in Venezuela. Master's thesis, University of Florida, Gainesville.

73. Konecny, M. J. 1990. Movement patterns and food habits of four sympatric carnivore species in Belize, Central America. In *Advances in Neotropical mammalogy*, ed. K. H. Redford and J. F. Eisenberg, 339–362. Gainesville, FL: Sandhill Crane Press.

74. Hulley, J. T. 1976. Maintenance and breeding of captive jaguarundis at Chester Zoo and Toronto. *Int. Zoo Yrbk.* 1: 120–122.

75. Johnson, W. E., and W. L. Franklin. 1991. Feeding and spatial ecology of the *Felis geoffroyi* in southern Patagonia. *J. Mammal.* 72: 815–820.

76. Corbett, L. K. 1979. Feeding ecology and social organization of wildcats (*Felis silvestris*) and domestic cats (*Felis catus*) in Scotland. Ph.D. dissertation, University of Aberdeen, Scotland.

77. Smithers, R. H. N. 1968. Cat of the Pharaohs. *Animal Kingdom* 71: 16–23.

78. Macdonald, D. W., and P. J. Apps. 1978. The social behaviour of a group of semi-dependent farm cats, *Felis catus. Carnivore Genet Newsl.* 3: 256–268.

79. Verberne, G., and P. Leyhausen. 1976. Marking behaviour of some Viverridae and Felidae: Time-interval analysis of the marking pattern. *Behaviour* 63: 192–253.

80. Rabinowitz, A. 1990. Notes on the behavior and movements of leopard cats, *Felis bengalensis*, in a dry tropical forest mosaic in Thailand. *Biotropica* 22: 397–403.

Appendix 4
Vocal Communication in Felids

The following account is derived largely from the works of Gustav Peters and his collaborators; interested readers should refer to his publications for more details.[1,2,3,4,5,6,7,8,9,10,11,12,13] Additional material for the account was derived from a number of other references.[14,15,16,17,18,19,20,21,22,23,24,25,26,27]

Cats communicate using a variety of close-range, medium-range, and long-distance vocalizations. All felids share a basic set of acoustic signals. These signals include both sounds produced by the vocal apparatus and nonvocal sounds (such as the hiss). The acoustic signal repertoire of cats includes a few discrete vocalizations that do not grade into other vocalization types, such as the spit and hiss, and several graded systems, such as the growl-snarl, the mew-main call, and the main call with grunt element systems. Within a graded system, the discrete vocalization types are linked to each other by transitional forms. Both discrete vocalization types and those types belonging to a graded system can vary in three structural domains—amplitude (loudness or intensity), time (duration), and frequency (pitch). However, the variability of discrete vocalizations in one, two, or all three domains is usually more limited than that of vocalizations that belong to graded systems. Within a graded system, changes in motivation probably explain the transition from one vocalization type to another via intermediate or mixed forms.

The frequency range of felid vocalizations is mainly between 50 and 10,000 Hertz (Hz = 1 cycle per second), although cats can hear sounds at much higher frequencies than those of their own vocalizations. The loudest felid vocalization measured to date is 114 decibels, in a male lion during a roaring sequence. This is probably the highest amplitude a felid vocalization can have.

Defining the number of signal types used by a species depends on the criteria used for classification, but even a number does not convey the full communication potential of a species' signal repertoire. Furthermore, when the sender and the receiver are in visual contact, acoustic signals may be used in combination with facial expressions and tail and body movements or postures. With the exception of sex-specific calls associated with courtship and mating, the vocal repertoire of males and females is the same.

Most cat vocalizations are probably generated by oscillations of the vocal folds in the larynx during exhalation. Hissing apparently can be performed without involving the vocal folds. Excluding purring, the actual mechanism of sound production and modulation and the morphological structures causing the modulation are not known for any felid species. Purring is produced as air is inhaled or exhaled. The laryngeal muscles are mechanically activated, resulting in changes in pressure across the larynx, which, in turn, increases or decreases resistance to air flow. These same pressure changes also produce surface vibrations across the larynx. Thus, both the sound and the vibration of purring are the result of laryngeal interaction with air flow.[13] There is a long-standing question about which felid species can purr; for many species the data are either lacking or equivocal, and no definitive statement in this respect can be made.

A brief description of the basic sounds and calls and the context(s) in which they are used follows.

SPIT: A very short (0.01–0.02 second), relatively intense, explosive burst of noise. Rather stereotyped and not mixed with other types, but sometimes fades into a hiss. Context: Threatening behavior and fights; interspecific threats (e.g., toward humans).

HISS: An atonal sound of variable duration and low intensity, usually produced during exhalation. Rather uniform in the felids. Not usually mixed with other signal types. Context: Agonistic close-range encounters. Denotes ambivalent motivation: attack-defense.

GROWL: Variable in duration, often prolonged, low in pitch, and regularly pulsed, sounding like a deep rolling "rrrr." Produced with the mouth closed; the sound is produced in larynx. Rather uniform in the felids. Context: Like spitting and hissing, denotes an aggressive motivation. Continued growling indicates readiness to attack.

SNARL: Similar to growl, but produced with bared teeth and a variably opened mouth. Snarls are less prolonged, louder, higher in pitch, and less clearly and regularly pulsed than growls and may be uttered as a short, intense outburst. Context: Defensive sound.

GURGLE: A short (about 0.5 seconds), mixed tonal-atonal sound, fairly low in intensity and constant in pitch with pulsed amplitude modulation. The pulse repetition rate varies from 10 to 45 per second in different species, but all gurgles in cats are thought to represent the same vocalization type. Gurgles are documented in twenty-two species and are probably present in another eight. As perceived by the human observer, gurgles occur in two forms: cooing and bubbling. Cooing gurgles are characterized by rapid amplitude modulation and sound like the staccato element in the cooing of pigeons. Bubbling gurgles have a considerably slower amplitude modulation, often with fewer single pulses, and sound like water gurgling. The cheetah's stutter call is a version of the bubbling gurgle. Cooing gurgles are known or assumed for sixteen species, whereas bubbling gurgles are known or assumed for fourteen. Some species are known to produce intermediate gurgles in addition to either cooing or bubbling gurgles. Gurgles are often coupled with mews. Gurgles are functionally equivalent to prusten and puffing. Context: Close-range friendly sounds; females with kittens, during courtship and mating, and greetings.

PRUSTEN: A short (< 1 second), low-intensity, soft sound, like the snorting of a horse. The cat expels several jets of air through the nostrils, but there is also a laryngeal contribution to sound production. Prusten is recorded only in the tiger, clouded leopard, snow leopard, and jaguar. Prusten is functionally equivalent to gurgling and puffing. Context: Close-range friendly situations.

PUFF: Expulsion of short, explosive jets of air through lips and nostrils; sounds like a bout of stifled sneezing. Usually uttered in a rapid, almost rhythmic sequence of two to four sounds that lasts less than 1 second. Puffing is recorded only in the lion and leopard and is functionally equivalent to gurgling and prusten. Context: Close-range friendly situations.

PURR: Continuous, low-amplitude murmuring sound, like rolling "rrrr," produced during both inhalation and exhalation. Duration is less than 1 second to minutes on end. A domestic cat can be heard purring 3 meters away. Purrs are louder and rougher-sounding during inspiration than during expiration. Context: Females while nursing or licking kittens; hand-reared kittens snuggling up to people. Close-range sound; body contact between sender and receiver may be important.

MEW-MAIN CALL SYSTEM: The mew is the predominant low- to medium-intensity call of felids. All species perform mew-like sounds of varying intensity. Depending on the species, low-intensity forms of the mew may be remarkably similar to the familiar mew/meow sound of the domestic cat; in other species they sound considerably different. The whistle of the puma is a special derivative of the mew. Mews are variable with respect to duration, tonality, pitch, and other structural characteristics. The high-intensity forms of mews are known as main calls. All felids have low, intermediate, and high-intensity forms of this sound. The lion is the only species lacking a main call. Context: The mew is used by females with kittens and as a close-contact call. The main call is used as a long-distance signal during mating season to bring the sexes together and in other behavioral contexts.

MAIN CALL WITH GRUNT ELEMENT: This predominantly intense call belongs to the previously listed mew-main call system, but is treated separately here to reduce confusion. This call type has a higher-pitched, more tonal beginning and a deeper, louder, throaty end, the grunt element. Present only in the lion, leopard, jaguar, and tiger. These species can also give low-intensity forms of the main call with grunt element, in which the pitch change from the beginning to the end of the call is less pronounced. It is not yet known whether the clouded leopard has this call type. Context: Long-distance signal in various behavioral situations.

ROARING SEQUENCE: A high-intensity call with species-specific structure in terms of the types of calls, their sequence, their relative intensity, and their temporal pattern of emission. For each species, the number of calls in a roaring sequence usually varies within a certain range. Low-intensity forms of the roaring sequence are much more variable in some or all characters. The roaring sequence is known only in the lion, leopard, and jaguar. The roaring sequences of these animals are basically composed of the same call types: main calls with grunt element and grunts. The roaring sequences of the leopard and jaguar differ from that of the lion in that their sequences are composed mainly of grunts. Main calls with a grunt element are typical of lions. The tiger lacks the grunt and thus is not included in the "roaring" cats. Furthermore, the sequences of loud calls in tigers rarely have a regular, species-specific structure. Loud roaring was described for lions as "one or two moans, then full-throated, thundering, until it died in a series of hoarse grunts."[24] Each roaring episode lasted about forty seconds, and included an average of nine roars, followed by fifteen grunts. Context: Long-distance communication; contact or spacing call, and possibly other functions.

GRUNT: Throaty, atonal call of short duration, present only in the lion, leopard, and jaguar. In these species grunts mainly occur in the roaring sequence, most often following a single main call with grunt ele-ment. Context: Females calling cubs; adults walking alone seemingly in search of other group members.

WAH-WAH: The sound is onomatopoeic. The call is usually uttered in short bouts. A single wah is a muffled, short (0.1 second), atonal vocalization of low amplitude. Within a wah-wah bout the single sounds are relatively stereotyped and follow each other at fairly regular intervals. Context: Close approach of two animals; may be displacement activity.

OTHER VOCALIZATION TYPES: The equivalent of the grunt produced during expiration is the inhalatory "vocalized gasp," which is a regularly occurring call only in the leopard's sawing (i.e., roaring sequence). Very rarely, a few of these calls occur in the roaring sequence of the lion and jaguar.

CHATTER: Low-amplitude smacking sound caused by rhythmic clashing of the jaws. Observed only in European lynx and domestic cat. Context: When desirable prey is close but out of reach. Acoustic displacement activity, probably similar to wah-wah.

TABLE 73 VOCAL COMMUNICATION IN FELIDS

Species	Spit, hiss, growl, snarl	Gurgle	Prusten	Puff	Purr	Mew	Main call	Main call with grunt element	Roaring sequence	Grunt	Wah-wah
Lion	+,+,+,+	−	−	+	??	+	−	+	+	+	−
Tiger	+,+,+,+	−	+	−	??	+	+	+	−	−	−
Jaguar	+,+,+,+	−	+	−	??	+	+	+	+	+	−
Leopard	+,+,+,+	−	−	+	??	+	+	+	+	+	−
Cheetah	+,+,+,+	+	−	−	+	+	+	−	−	−	−
Puma	+,+,+,+	+	−	−	+	+	+	−	−	−	+
Snow leopard	+,+,+,+	−	+	−	??	+	+	−	−	−	−
Clouded leopard	+,+,+,+	−	+	−	??	+	+	??	−	−	−
Eurasian lynx	+,+,+,+	+	−	−	+	+	+	−	−	−	+
Canada lynx	+,+,+,+	+	−	−	+?	+	+	−	−	−	
Iberian lynx	+,+,+,+	+	−	−		+	+	−	−	−	
Bobcat	+,+,+,+	+	−	−	+	+	+	−	−	−	+
Caracal	+,+,+,+	+	−	−		+	+	−	−	−	+
Serval	+,+,+,+	+			+	+	+	−	−	−	+?
Asiatic golden cat	+,+,+,+	+	−	−	+	+	+	−	−	−	+
African golden cat	+,+,+,+	+	−	−		+	+	−	−	−	+
Fishing cat	+,+,+,+	+	−	−		+	+	−	−	−	
Jungle cat	+,+,+,+	+	−	−		+	+	−	−	−	−
Ocelot	+,+,+,+	+	−	−	+	+	+	−	−	−	
Margay	+,+,+,+	+	−	−	+	+	+	−	−	−	
Oncilla	+,+,+,+	+	−	−	+	+	+	−	−	−	
Jaguarundi	+,+,+,+	+	−	−	+	+	+	−	−		+

(continued)

TABLE 73 *(continued)*

Species	Spit, hiss, growl, snarl	Gurgle	Prusten	Puff	Purr	Mew	Main call	Main call with grunt element	Roaring sequence	Grunt	Wah-wah
Geoffroy's cat	+,+,+,+	+	−	−		+	+	−	−	−	
European,											
African wildcat	+,+,+,+	+	−	−	+	+	+	−	−	−	−
Manul	+,+,+,+	+	−	−		+	+	−	−	−	
Leopard cat	+,+,+,+	+	−	−	+	+	+	−	−	−	
Marbled cat	+,+,+,+	+	−	−	+	+	+	−	−	−	
Sand cat	+,+,+,+	+	−	−		+	+	−	−	−	−
Flat-headed cat	+,+,+,+	+	−	−		+	+	−	−	−	
Rusty-spotted cat	+,+,+,+	+	−	−		+	+	−	−	−	
Black-footed cat	+,+,+,+	+	−	−	+	+	+	−	−	−	−

Note: + = present, +? = probably present, ?? = equivocal, − = absent, blank cell = no data.

REFERENCES

1. Peters, G. 1978. Vergleichende Untersuchung zur Lautgebung einiger Feliden (Mammalia, Felidae). *Spixiana* (suppl.) 1: 1–283.

2. Peters, G. 1980. The vocal repertoire of the snow leopard (*Uncia uncia*, Schreber 1775). *International Pedigree Book of Snow Leopards* 2: 137–158.

3. Peters, G. 1981. Das Schnurren der Katzen (Felidae). *Säugetierk. Mitt.* 29: 30–37.

4. Peters, G. 1983. Beobachtungen zum Lautgebungsverhalten des Karakal, *Caracal caracal* (Schreber, 1776) (Mammalia, Carnivora, Felidae). *Bonn. Zool. Beitr.* 34: 107–127.

5. Peters, G. 1984a. A special type of vocalization in the Felidae. *Acta Zool. Fennici* 171: 89–92.

6. Peters, G. 1984b. On the structure of friendly close range vocalizations in terrestrial carnivores (Mammalia: Carnivora: Fissipedia). *Z. Säugetierk.* 49: 157–182.

7. Peters, G. 1987. Acoustic communication in the genus *Lynx* (Mammalia: Felidae)—Comparative survey and phylogenetic interpretation. *Bonn. Zool. Beitr.* 38: 315–330.

8. Peters, G. 1991. Vocal communication in cats. In *Great Cats: Majestic Creatures of the Wild*, ed. J. Seidensticker and S. Lumpkin, 76–77. Emmaus, PA: Rodale Press.

9. Peters, G., and M. H. Hast. 1994. Hyoid structure, laryngeal anatomy, and vocalization in felids (Mammalia: Carnivora: Felidae). *Z. Säugetierk.* 59: 87–104.

10. Peters, G., and B. A. Tonkin-Leyhausen. 1999. Evolution of acoustic communication signals of mammals: Friendly close-range vocalizations in Felidae (Carnivora). *J. Mammal. Evol.* 6: 129–159.

11. Peters, G., and W. C. Wozencraft. 1989. Acoustic communication by fissiped carnivores. In *Carnivore Behavior, Ecology, and Evolution*, ed. J. L. Gittleman, 14–56. Ithaca, NY: Cornell University Press.

12. Rieger, I., and G. Peters. 1981. Einige Beobachtungen zum Paarungs- und Lautgebungsverhalten von Irbissen (*Uncia uncia*) im Zoologischen Garten. *Z. Säugetierk.* 46: 35–48.

13. Frazer Sissom, D. E., D. A. Rice, and G. Peters. 1991. How cats purr. *J. Zool.* (Lond.) 223: 67–78.

14. Bailey, T. N. 1993. *The African leopard.* New York: Colombia University Press.

15. Caro, T. M. 1994. *Cheetahs of the Serengeti plains.* Chicago: University of Chicago Press.

16. Eisenberg, J. F., and M. Lockhart. 1972. *An ecological reconnaissance of Wilpattu National Park, Ceylon.* Smithsonian Contributions to Zoology, no. 101. 118 pp.

17. Hemmer, H. 1966. Untersuchungen zur Stammesgeschichte der Pantherkatzen (Pantherinae) Teil I. *Veröffentlichungen der Zoologischen Staatssammlung München* 11: 1–121.

18. Hoogesteijn, R., and E. Mondolfi. 1992. *The jaguar.* Caracas, Venezuela: Armitano Publishers.

19. Jackson, P., and A. Farrell Jackson. 1996. *Les félins.* Lausanne: Delachaux et Niestlé.

20. Leyhausen, P. 1979. *Cat behavior: The predatory and social behavior of domestic and wild cats.* New York: Garland STMP Press.

21. Mellen, J. D. 1993. A comparative analysis of scent marking, social and reproductive behavior in 20 species of small cats (*Felis*). *Am. Zool.* 33: 51–166.

22. Movchan, V. N., and V. R. Opahova. 1981. Acoustic signals of cats (Felidae) living in the zoo. (English summary.) *Zool. Zh.* 60: 601–608.

23. Schaller, G. B. 1967. *The deer and the tiger.* Chicago: University of Chicago Press.

24. Schaller, G. B. 1972. *The Serengeti lion: A study of predator-prey relations.* Chicago: University of Chicago Press.

25. Tembrock, G. 1970. Bioakustische Untersuchungen an Säugetieren des Berliner Tierparkes. *Milu* 3: 78–96.

26. Wemmer, C., and K. Snow. 1977. Communication in the Felidae with emphasis on scent marking and contact patterns. In *How animals communicate*, ed. T. A. Sebeok, 749–766. Bloomington: Indiana University Press.

27. Bradshaw, J., and C. Cameron-Beaumont. 2000. The signalling repertoire of the domestic cat and its undomesticated relatives. In *The domestic cat: The biology of its behaviour*, 2nd ed., ed. D. Turner and P. Bateson, 67–93. Cambridge: Cambridge University Press.

Appendix 5

Reproduction in Felids

Reproduction in felids is a rather prolonged affair involving several stages. The initial stages (courtship and mating) may take some time because individuals first have to find each other. Cats typically occupy large home ranges, and while they may recognize the scent of neighbors, face-to-face encounters between solitary-living felids appear to be an uncommon occurrence. Thus a female has to advertise her impending period of sexual receptivity, which she usually does via scent marks (see appendix 3) and calling. Scent marks are deposited around the female's range well in advance of her estrous, or heat, period, thus ensuring that a male will be present at the appropriate time. A male, having found and "read" the message in the female's scent marks, then has to locate her. However, even after he finds her, it may be some time before she permits physical contact. The individuals may be unfamiliar and even hostile to each other, which creates a potentially dangerous situation, especially since felids are so well armed. When individuals know each other, the preliminaries may be shortened, but even then events cannot be hurried. It is thus not surprising to find that in most felid species the female's estrous period is long, usually several days.

The female usually becomes attractive to the male a day or two before she is actually ready to mate, and there also are observations of pairs being together for a week or more without mating. This creates a situation in which more than one male may be in attendance, and there are several accounts of a female being followed by several males in tigers, jaguars, pumas, and European lynx, to mention just a few species. A consequence is competition among the males for mating rights. Having won the battle, the victor must still be accepted by the female. She often meets his initial advances by spitting and striking out with her claws. The male does not retaliate; he merely draws back a little, and renews his advances a moment later. Gradually, her behavior changes. She becomes the provocateur, rolling in front of him, purring, giving him playful pats, but still indignant at his attempts to make contact. Before she is ready to mate, he is put through a severe test of persistence and possibly his fighting skills as well. As Griff Ewer, the renowned carnivore ethologist, so aptly put it, a "faint heart assuredly never wins a feline fair lady."[1]

Courtship among felids typically includes fighting of a playful nature. The sex most eager to mate usually initiates the play fights, which appear to have a stimulating effect, and as the intensity of the play increases, it takes on a more sexual nature. This is a dangerous game for two such accomplished killers. However, two factors operate to prevent problems. One is the highly ritualized form of the fighting, which reduces the likelihood of bites being serious. Second, the male is inhibited from biting the female. The female may bite the male and defend herself against his unwanted advances until she is ready to mate, but the rules that govern his behavior prevent him from retaliating.[1]

The mating patterns of cats are remarkably similar, except for the timing and occurrence of the neck grip during copulation. Once a female permits contact, a typical sequence follows. As the male mounts, he may grip the loose fur of the female's neck in his teeth, which in domestic cats and many other small cats is thought to be necessary for the male to copulate safely and successfully.[2] Captive ocelot and Asiatic golden cat males differ in that while the mount is initially accompanied by a neck grip, the grip is then released, and it is not used again until intromission.[2] In larger felids the male does not usually grip the female's neck as he mounts, but may do so at ejaculation. This behavior is not invariable. There are species differences and individual differences as well, but the delayed neck grip is seen as yet another way to ensure that accidents do not happen. The mating posture itself is elegantly designed to ensure the safety of both cats. The female does not stand, but lies on her belly, and the male is positioned above her, with a front leg on either side of her shoulders and his hind legs straddling her flanks. He makes treading movements with his hind feet against her hindquarters, which stimulates her to adopt the mating posture (lordosis): tail to one side and rump slightly raised. In her prone position, the female does not look or behave like prey. Furthermore, since the male is supporting his weight on his front limbs, as necessary when treading with his hind feet, his balance is shifted forward, away from what it would be in a predatory attack. In this position the male is not able to use his front feet to grab and hold, as he would with prey.

Once mounted, the male squats on his hindquarters, which brings his genital region into close proximity to hers. The male begins pelvic thrusting, and when he finally makes a successful vaginal entry, ejaculation follows in a few seconds. There is no copulatory lock.[3] At intromission the female may give a low growl (copulatory cry), and shortly thereafter she throws the male off her back. She then twists her body around to strike at the male, who must leap back to avoid the blow. If the pair know each, other the female may not attack, but instead may go directly into a series of postcopulatory actions. She rolls on the ground, rubs her head on objects, and licks her genitalia. After a short interval, another copulation follows. After several copulations, the initiative passes from male to female. Her eagerness to mate is evident as she rubs against him, taking up a mating position in front of him, inviting mounting.

Copulations are often brief, lasting about 3 to 20 seconds in large felids,[3] but there may be repeated copulations over a short time. There is an account of lions copulating 157 times over a fifty-five-hour period,[4] and similar frequencies are documented for pumas (50–70 times per day), leopards (70–100 times per day), and tigers (50 times per day).[5] Lower copulation rates (3–15 times per day) are reported for cheetahs, ocelots, bobcats, and snow leopards,[5] but slightly higher rates are known for domestic cats (10–20 times per day).[5,6] Female black-footed cats are receptive for only a 5–10-hour period, but a dozen copulations may occur in this time span.[7]

Repeated copulations over a short time period are probably necessary to induce ovulation. Most felid species are thought to be induced ovulators, but few are actually known to be so. However, male cats have a baculum (penile bone) and penile spines, which strongly suggests a connection between sexual stimulation and ovulation. It is likely that eggs are shed from the ovary only in response to the stimuli provided by numerous copulations. A tigress, for example, failed to conceive after 30 copulations, but did so after 100.[8] Similarly, in domestic cats, ovulation occurred in only 50 percent of cases where only a single copulation was allowed; the value increased to 100 percent when four copulations were allowed.[9] These reports suggest that cats require multiple copulations, probably within a certain time interval, to induce ovulation. There also are reports from zoos in which tigers, lions, and leopards ovulated spontaneously or did so in response to some other form of physical or social stimuli.[10,11,12] In the latter cases the cats were either housed in adjacent cages, where they could see and smell each other, or in some cases several females were housed together. In these situations the cats do not appear to be classic spontaneous ovulators, but more like reflex ovulators, a label that may also apply to domestic cats.[9,13,14] There are, however, reports of spontaneous ovulation in the domestic cat.[15] Spontaneous ovulation also is reported for bobcats and Canada lynx.[16,17,18,19,20,21,22]

If the female does not become pregnant, she will in most cases enter another estrous cycle. The probability of conception per estrus appears to be low, varying from 20–40 percent in lions and tigers[8,23] to 50–67 percent in leopards, pumas, snow leopards, and ocelots.[5] These low rates of conception are probably related to inexperience, incompatibility, or an insufficient number of copulations. Most tropical felids breed at any time of the year. If a female fails to conceive, she will continue to cycle and mate until she becomes pregnant. Unlike temperate areas, which have a relatively narrow season for the optimal survival of young, in the tropics low temperatures are not a problem and food is generally available year-round. The exception to year-round breeding in the tropics occurs in areas that have prolonged dry seasons.

Females will come into heat again if a litter is lost shortly after birth. Within a few days to a week or two of the death of her litter, a female will re-cycle and begin advertising her impending sexual receptivity. However, females in areas with severe winters may not re-cycle after the death of a litter because the optimal time for mating has passed.

Gestation length in felids is largely accounted for by differences in the absolute size of the species.[24] The larger felids have longer gestation periods than the smaller species. Some differences in gestation length may be related to the birth weight of the litter. That is, for a given size class, those species having more young, by weight, will have longer gestation periods than those that produce a smaller neonatal mass. The notable exceptions are the cats in the ocelot lineage (i.e., ocelot, margay, oncilla, Geoffroy's cat, pampas cat, kodkod), which often have one young per litter, but whose gestation lengths often exceed those of similar-sized cats producing litters of two or three kittens. In general, however, larger species give birth to larger young.

Litter size within the Felidae is typically two or three young, but there is some variation. As noted above, those cats in the ocelot lineage have rather small litters, whereas those in the domestic cat lineage (i.e., jungle cat, sand cat, domestic cat, European and African wildcats) have larger litters, with three or four young being typical. Cheetahs have exceptionally large litters; four or even five young is not unusual. Litter size in Canada lynx fluctuates widely, depending on the density of snowshoe hares.

Young felids are dependent on their mother for food, protection, and training. This period of dependence can range from a few months in the domestic cat to almost two years in the tiger. During this time the female does not come into estrus, and consequently there may be prolonged intervals between matings. Large felids, such as tigers, jaguars, and leopards, typically mate every other year. The young of most small felids are dependent on their mother for a shorter time, and most small cats breed annually. The ocelot lineage is an exception to this general rule. Ocelots, margays, and oncillas typically have one young per litter, and their young mature more slowly than the offspring of other similar-sized cats. The little information that is available for these three species in the wild suggests that females may breed every eighteen to twenty-four months.

There is little information available from free-ranging cats on the age of last reproduction, although where resources are abundant adult females are likely to be pregnant or accompanied by dependent young for much (70–80 percent) of their reproductive life spans.

TABLE 74 REPRODUCTIVE DATA FOR FELIDS

Species	Female weight (kg)	Length of estrus (days)	Estrous cycle (days)	Gestation period (days)	Litter size (range in parentheses)	Birth weight (grams)	Age at sexual maturity/ first reproduction (months)	Litters per year	Sources
Lion	130	4–16	16	100–114	3 (1–7)	1,150–1,785	33–50	0.5	1,4,23,24,25,26,27,28, 29,30,31,32,33
Tiger	120	3–10	15–20 & 40–50	100–108	3 (1–7)	785–1,610	36–48	0.5	8,34,35,36,37,38,39,40, 41,42,43
Jaguar	62	6–17	37	91–110	2 (1–4)	700–900	24–36	0.5	24,29,44,45,46,47,48
Cheetah	51	2–3 & 10–14	12 (10–21)	90–95	3, 4 (1–8)	150–300	22–36	0.5	26,49,50,51,52,53,54,55, 56,57
Puma	47	4–9	23	89–98	2, 3 (1–5)	400–500	18–37	0.5	58,59,60,61,62,63,64,65, 66,67,68
Leopard	38	3–14	46	90–105	2, 3 (1–4)	300–700	24–36	0.5	4,24,29,31,42,69,70,71, 72,73,74,75,76,77,78
Snow leopard	38	2–12	15–39	94–103	2, 3 (1–7)	320–567	24–36	0.5	79,80,81,82,83,84,85
Clouded leopard	12	6	30	88–95	2, 3 (1–4)	140–280	21–30	1	84,86,87,88,89,90,91,92
Eurasian lynx	16	7–10		63–74	2, 3 (1–6)	245–430	12–24	1	24,42,84,93,94,95,96, 97,98
Canada lynx	8.6			60–70	1–5 (1–8)	175–235	10–24	1	20,22,84,99,100,101, 102,103,104,105, 106,107
Iberian lynx	9.5	1–4		63–73	2, 3 (1–4)		12–24	1	108,109,110,111
Bobcat	7.2	5–10	44	57–65	2, 3 (1–8)	280–340	9–24	1	18,101,112,113,114,115, 116,117
Caracal	10	1–3	14	70–81	2, 3 (1–6)	198–250	12–15	1	2,84,118,119,120,121, 122,123
Serval	10	1–4		70–79	2, 3 (1–4)	213–265	15–24	1	2,84,91,122,124,125,126

Species									
Asiatic golden cat	8.5	6	39	78–80	1 (1–3)	220–250	18–25	1	2,84,127,128,129,130
African golden cat	8.5			75	1, 2	180–235	11	1	131,132
Fishing cat	7.8			63–70	2, 3 (1–4)	170	15	1	2,133,134
Jungle cat	6	5		63–68	3 (1–6)	43–161	11–18	1	2,24,42,91,135,136,137,138,139
Ocelot	8.6	4–10	20–30	79–85	1, 2 (1–3)	250	20–30	0.5	2,24,140,141,142,143,144
Margay	3	4–10	32–36	76–84	1 (1–2)	85–170	12–24	0.5–1	2,91,141,145,146,147,148,149
Oncilla	1.7	3–9		62–76	1, 2 (1–4)	92–134	24–30	0.5–1	148,150,151,152
Jaguarundi	4.6	3–4	50–56	63–73	2, 3 (1–4)	?	17–26	1	2,84,153
Geoffroy's cat	3.8	2–3	20	66–76	1, 2 (1–3)	65–90	18–24	1	2,154,155,156,157,158,159
Pampas cat	2.9				1, 2 (1–3)	132	24		2,91,160
European wildcat	4	2–8		63–69	4 (1–8)	75–150	10–12	1	42,161,162,163,164,165,166,167
African-Asian wildcat	4	2–3		56–65	3 (1–5)	80–120	11–12	1	2,24,168,169
Domestic cat	2.7–4.5	1–5	15	63	4, 5 (1–10)	80–120	7–12	2–3	24,170,171,172,173,174,175
Manul	3	5	46	66–75	3, 4 (1–6)	89	13	1	2,42,91,176
Leopard cat	2.8	4–7		60–70	2, 3 (1–4)	75–130	12–14	1	24,42,91,130,177,178,179,180,181
Marbled cat	2.5			66–82	2 (1–4)	61–85	21–22	1	142,182
Sand cat	2.2	5	46	60–70	3 (1–8)	39–80	14	1–2	2,24,84,139,183
Rusty-spotted cat	1.6	5		66–70	1, 2	60–77	16	1	2,184
Black-footed cat	1.3	1–2	54	63–68	1, 2 (1–4)	60–93	8–12	1	2,7,24,185,186,187,188

Note: Blank cell = no data.

REFERENCES

1. Ewer, R. F. 1973. *The carnivores.* Ithaca, NY: Cornell University Press.

2. Mellen, J. D. 1993. A comparative analysis of scent-marking, social and reproductive behavior in 20 species of small cats (*Felis*). *Am. Zool.* 33: 151–166.

3. Lanier, D. L., and D. A. Dewsbury. 1976. A quantitative study of copulatory behaviour of large Felidae. *Behav. Proc.* 1: 327–333.

4. Schaller, G. B. 1972. *The Serengeti lion.* Chicago: University of Chicago Press.

5. Eaton, R. L. 1978. Why some felids copulate so much: A model for the evolution of copulation frequency. *Carnivore* 1: 42–51.

6. Liberg, O. 1983. Courtship behaviour and sexual selection in the domestic cat. *Appl. Anim. Ethol.* 10: 117–132.

7. Leyhausen, P., and B. Tonkin. 1966. Breeding the black-footed cat, *Felis nigripes,* in captivity. *Int. Zoo Yrbk.* 6: 178–182.

8. Kleiman, D. G. 1974. The estrous cycle in the tiger (*Panthera tigris*). In *The world's cats,* vol. 2, ed. R. L. Eaton, 60–75. Winston, OR: World Wildlife Safari.

9. Concannon, P., B. Hodgson, and D. Lein. 1980. Reflex LH release in estrous cats following single and multiple copulations. *Biol. Reprod.* 23: 111–117.

10. Seal, U. S., R. L. Tilson, E. D. Plotka, N. J. Reindl, and M. F. Seal. 1987. Behavioral indicators and endocrine correlates of estrus and anestrus in Siberian tigers. In *Tigers of the world,* ed. R. L. Tilson and U. S. Seal, 244–254. Park Ridge, NJ: Noyes Publications.

11. Schmidt, A. M., D. L. Hess, M. J. Schmidt, R. L. Smith, and C. R. Lewis. 1988. Serum concentrations of oestradiol and progesterone and sexual behavior during the normal oestrous cycle in the leopard (*Panthera pardus*). *J. Reprod. Fertil.* 82: 43–49.

12. Schramm, R. Dee, M. B. Briggs, and J. J. Reeves. 1994. Spontaneous and induced ovulation in the lion (*Panthera leo*). *Zoo Biol.* 13: 301–307.

13. Wildt, D. E., S. W. Seager, and P. F. Chakraborty. 1980. Effect of copulatory stimulation on the incidence of ovulation and serum LH in the cat. *Endocrinology* 107: 1212–1217.

14. Wildt, D. E., S. W. Seager, S. Y. W. Chan, and P. K. Chakraborty. 1981. Ovarian activity, circulating hormones and sexual behavior in the cat. I. Relationships during the coitus-induced luteal phase and the estrous period without mating. *Biol. Reprod.* 25: 15–28.

15. Scott, P. P., and M. A. Lloyd-Jacob. 1959. Reduction in the anestrous period of laboratory cats by increased illumination. *Nature* 184: 2022.

16. Duke, K. L. 1954. Reproduction in the bobcat (*Lynx rufus*). *Anat. Rec.* 120: 816–817.

17. Crowe, D. M. 1975. Aspects of ageing, growth, and reproduction of bobcats from Wyoming. *J. Mammal.* 56: 177–198.

18. Fritts, S. H., and J. A. Sealander. 1978. Diets of bobcats in Arkansas with special reference to age and sex differences. *J. Wildl. Mgmt.* 42: 533–539.

19. Van Zyll de Jong, C. G. 1963. The biology of the lynx, *Felis (Lynx) canadensis* Kerr in Alberta and the Mackenzie District, N.W.T. Master's thesis, University of Alberta, Edmonton.

20. Quinn, N. W. S., and G. Parker. 1987. Lynx. In *Wild furbearer management and conservation in North America,* ed. M. Novak, J. A. Barker, M. E. Obbard, and B. Malloch, 683–694. Ontario: Ontario Trappers Association.

21. Bronson, F. H. *Mammalian reproductive biology.* Chicago: University of Chicago Press.

22. Brand, C. J., and L. B. Keith. 1979. Lynx demography during a snowshoe hare decline in Alberta. *J. Wildl. Mgmt.* 43: 827–849.

23. Cooper, J. 1942. An exploratory study on African lions. *Comp. Psychol. Monogr.* 17: 1–48.

24. Hemmer, H. 1976. Gestation period and postnatal development in felids. In *The world's cats,* vol. 3, ed. R. L. Eaton. 143–165. Seattle, WA: Carnivore Research Institute, Burke Museum, University of Washington.

25. Asdell, S. A. 1964. Patterns of mammalian reproduction. Ithaca, NY: Cornell University Press.

26. Kingdon, J. 1977. *East African mammals: An atlas of evolution in Africa.* Vol. 3A, *Carnivores.* Chicago: University of Chicago Press.

27. Packer, C., L. Herbst, A. E. Pusey, J. D. Bygott, J. P. Hanby, S. J. Cairns, and Borgerhoff Mulder, M. 1988. Reproductive success of lions. In *Reproductive success,* ed. T. H. Clutton-Brock, 363–383. Chicago: University of Chicago Press.

28. Packer, C., and A. E. Pusey. 1982. Cooperation and competition within coalitions of male lions: Kin selection or game theory? *Nature* 296: 740–742.

29. Sadlier, R. 1966. Notes on reproduction in the larger Felidae. *Int. Zoo Yrbk.* 6: 184–187.

30. Seifert, S. 1978. Untersuchungen zur Fortpflanzungsbiologie der im Zoologischen Garten Leipzig gehaltenen Großkatzen (*Panthera,* Oken, 1816) unter besonderer Berücksichtigung des Löwen—*Panthera leo* (Linné, 1758). Berlin: VER Verlag Volk und Gesundheit.

31. Carvalho, C. T. de. 1968. Comparative growth rates of hand-reared big cats. *Int. Zoo Yrbk.* 8: 56–59.

32. Van Hooff, J. A. R. A. M. 1965. A large litter of lion cubs *Panthera leo* at Arnhem Zoo. *Int. Zoo Yrbk.* 5: 116.

33. Smuts, G. L., J. Hanks, and I. J. Whyte. 1978. Reproduction and social organization of lions from the Kruger National Park. *Carnivore* 1: 17–28.

34. Veselovsky, Z. 1967. The Amur tiger *Panthera tigris altaica* in the wild and in captivity. *Int. Zoo Yrbk.* 7: 210–215.

35. Sankhala, K. S. 1977. *Tiger: The story of the Indian tiger.* New York: Simon and Schuster.

36. Schaller, G. B. 1967. *The deer and the tiger.* Chicago: University of Chicago Press.

37. McDougal, C. 1977. *The face of the tiger.* London: Rivington Books and André Deutsch.

38. Sunquist, M. E. 1981. *The social organization of tigers* (*Panthera tigris*) *in Royal Chitawan National Park, Nepal.* Smithsonian Contributions to Zoology, no. 336. 198 pp.

39. Smith, J. L. D., and C. McDougal. 1991. The contribution of variance in lifetime reproduction to effective population size in tigers. *Conserv. Biol.* 5: 484–490.

40. Smith, J. L. D. 1993. The role of dispersal in structuring the Chitwan tiger population. *Behaviour* 124: 165–195.

41. Thapar, V. 1989. *Tigers: The secret life.* London: Elm Tree Books.

42. Heptner, V. G., and A. A. Sludskii. 1992. *Mammals of the Soviet Union.* Vol. 2, part 2, *Carnivora (Hyaenas and cats).* English translation, sci. ed., R. S. Hoffmann. Washington, DC: Smithsonian Institution Libraries and the National Science Foundation.

43. Singh, A. 1984. *Tiger! Tiger!* London: Jonathan Cape.

44. Hoogesteijn, R., and E. Mondolfi. 1992. *The jaguar.* Caracas, Venezuela: Armitano.

45. Seymour, K. L. 1989. *Panthera onca. Mammalian Species* 340: 1–9.

46. Stehlik, J. 1971. Breeding jaguars at Ostrava Zoo. *Int. Zoo Yrbk.* 11: 116–118.

47. Rabinowitz, A. R., and B. G. Nottingham. 1986. Ecology and behaviour of the jaguar (*Panthera onca*) in Belize, Central America. *J. Zool.* (Lond.) 210: 149–159.

48. Crawshaw, P. G. 1995. Comparative ecology of ocelot (*Felis pardalis*) and jaguar (*Panthera onca*) in a protected subtropical forest in Brazil and Argentina. Ph.D. dissertation, University of Florida, Gainesville.

49. Eaton, R. L. 1974. *The cheetah.* New York: Van Nostrand Reinhold.

50. Caro, T. M. 1994. *Cheetahs of the Serengeti plains.* Chicago: University of Chicago Press.

51. Wrogemann, N. 1975. *Cheetah under the sun.* Johannesburg: McGraw-Hill.

52. Laurenson, M. K., T. Caro, and M. Borner. 1992. Female cheetah reproduction. *Natl. Geogr. Res.* 8: 64–75.

53. Graham, A. D., and I. S. C. Parker. 1965. East African Wildlife Society cheetah survey; Report by Wildlife Services. East Africa Wildlife Society, Nairobi. Typescript.

54. Pienaar, U. de V. 1969. Predatory-prey relationships amongst the larger mammals of the Kruger National Park. *Koedoe* 12: 108–176.

55. Wack, R. F., L. W. Kramer, W. Cupps, and P. Currie. 1991. Growth rate of 21 captive-born, mother-raised cubs. *Zoo Biol.* 10: 273–276.

56. Kelly, M. J., M. K. Laurenson, C. D. FitzGibbon, D. A. Collins, S. M. Durant, G. W. Frame, B. C. R. Bertram, and T. M. Caro. 1998. Demography of the Serengeti cheetah (*Acinonyx jubatus*) population: The first 25 years. *J. Zool.* (Lond.) 244: 473–488.

57. Seager, S. W., and C. N. Demorest. 1986. Reproduction in captive wild carnivores. In *Zoo and wild animal medicine,* 2nd ed., ed. M. Fowler, 852–881. Philadelphia: W. B. Saunders.

58. Rabb, G. B. 1959. Reproductive and vocal behavior in captive pumas. *J. Mammal.* 40: 616–617.

59. Eaton, R. L, and K. A. Velander. 1977. Reproduction in the puma: Biology, behavior and ontogeny. In *The world's cats,* vol. 3, ed. R. L. Eaton, 45–70. Seattle, WA: Carnivore Research Institute, Burke Museum, University of Washington.

60. Ashman, D. L., G. C. Christensen, M. C. Hess, G. K. Tuskamotoa, and M. S. Wickersham. 1983. The mountain lion in Nevada. Nevada Department of Wildlife Report 4–48–15, Reno. 75 pp.

61. Seidensticker, J. C., M. G. Hornocker, W. W. Wiles, and J. P. Messick. 1973. Mountain lion social organization in the Idaho Primitive Area. *Wildl. Monogr.* 35: 1–60.

62. Logan, K. A., L. L. Sweanor, T. K. Ruth, and M. G. Hornocker. 1996. Cougars of the San Andres Mountains, New Mexico. Final Report, Federal Aid in Wildlife Restoration Project, W-128-R, New Mexico Department of Game and Fish, Santa Fe, New Mexico.

63. Maehr, D. S., J. C. Roof, E. D. Land, and J. W. McCown. 1989. First reproduction of a panther (*Felis concolor coryi*) in southwestern Florida, U.S.A. *Mammalia* 53: 129–131.

64. Anderson, A. E., D. C. Bowden, and D. M. Kattner. 1992. The puma on Uncompahgre Plateau, Colorado. Colorado Division of Wildlife, Technical Publication no. 40. 116 pp.

65. Lindzey, F. G., W. D. van Sickler, B. B. Ackerman, D. Barnkhurst, T. P. Hemker, and S. P. Laing. 1994. Cougar population dynamics in southern Utah. *J. Wildl. Mgmt.* 58: 619–624.

66. Ross, P. I., and M. G. Jalkotzy. 1992. Characteristics of a hunted population of cougars in southwestern Alberta. *J. Wildl. Mgmt.* 56: 417–426.

67. Spreadbury, B. R., K. Musil, J. Musil, C. Kaisner, and J. Kovak. 1996. Cougar population characteristics in southeastern British Columbia. *J. Wildl. Mgmt.* 60: 962–969.

68. Gay, S. W., and T. L. Best. 1996. Age-related variation in skulls of the puma (*Puma concolor*). *J. Mammal.* 77: 191–198.

69. Eaton, R. L. 1977. Reproductive biology of the leopard. *Zool. Garten* 47: 329–351.

70. Zuckerman, S. 1953. The breeding of mammals in captivity. *Proc. Zool. Soc. Lond.* 122: 827–950.

71. Dobroruka, L. J. 1968. A note on the gestation period and rearing of young in the leopard. *Int. Zoo Yrbk.* 8: 65.

72. Reuther, R. T., and Y. Doherty. 1968. Birth seasons of mammals at San Francisco Zoo. *Int. Zoo Yrbk.* 8: 97–101.

73. Desai, J. H. 1975. Observations on the reproductive biology and early postnatal development of the panther, *Panthera pardus* L., in captivity. *J. Bombay Nat. Hist. Soc.* 72: 293–304.

74. Robinson, R. 1969. The breeding of spotted and black leopards. *J. Bombay Nat. Hist. Soc.* 66: 423–429.

75. Seidensticker, J., M. E. Sunquist, and C. McDougal. 1990. Leopards living at the edge of Royal Chitwan National Park, Nepal. In *Conservation in developing countries: Problems and prospects,* ed. J. C. Daniel and J. S. Serrao, 415–423. Bombay: Bombay Natural History Society.

76. Le Roux, P. G., and J. D. Skinner. 1989. A note on the ecology of the leopard (*Panther pardus* Linnaeus) in the Londolozi Game Reserve, South Africa. *Afr. J. Ecol.* 27: 167–171.

77. Silva, M. de, and B. V. R. Jayaratne. 1994. Aspects of population ecology of the leopard (*Panthera pardus*) in Ruhuna National Park, Sri Lanka. *J. S. Asian Nat. Hist.* 1: 3–13.

78. Bailey, T. N. 1993. *The African leopard.* New York: Columbia University Press.

79. Blomqvist, L., and I. Sten. 1982. Reproductive biology of the snow leopard *Panthera uncia. International pedigree book of snow leopards* 3: 71–79.

80. Hemmer, H. 1972. *Uncia uncia. Mammalian Species* 20: 1–5.

81. Petzsch, H. 1968. *Die katzen.* Leipzig: Urania-Verlag.

82. Koivisto, I., C. Wahlberg, and P. Muuronen. 1977. Breeding the snow leopard, *Panthera uncia*, at Helsinki Zoo 1967–1976. *Int. Zoo Yrbk.* 17: 39–44.

83. Rieger, I. 1980. Some aspects of the history of ounce knowledge. *International pedigree book of snow leopards* 2: 1–36.

84. Andrews, P., Hexagon Farm Wild Feline Breeding Facility, 1187 Merrill Road, San Juan Bautista, CA. Personal communication.

85. Marma, B. B., and U. U. Yunchis. 1968. Observations on the breeding management and physiology of snow leopards *Panthera u. uncia* at Kaunas Zoo from 1962 to 1967. *Int. Zoo Yrbk.* 8: 66–73.

86. Fellner, K. 1965. Natural rearing of clouded leopards *Neofelis nebulosa* at Frankfurt Zoo. *Int. Zoo Yrbk.* 5: 111–113.

87. Fellner, K. 1968. Erste naturliche Aufzucht von Nebelpardern (*Neofelis nebulosa*) in einem zoo. *Zool. Garten* 33: 105–137.

88. Fontaine, P. 1965. Breeding clouded leopards (*Neofelis nebulosa*) at Dallas Zoo. *Int. Zoo Yrbk.* 5: 113–114.

89. Murphy, E. T. 1976. Breeding the clouded leopard at Dublin Zoo. *Int. Zoo Yrbk.* 16: 122–124.

90. Geidel, B., and W. Gensch. 1976. The rearing of clouded leopards in the presence of the male. *Int. Zoo Yrbk.* 16: 124–126.

91. Eaton, R. L. 1984. Survey of smaller felid breeding. *Zool. Garten* 54: 101–120.

92. Yamada, J. K., and B. S. Durant. 1988. Vaginal cytology and behavior in the clouded leopard. *Felid* 2: 1–3.

93. Wayre, P. 1968. Breeding the European lynx *Felis l. lynx* at the Norfolk Wildlife Park. *Int. Zoo Yrbk.* 9: 95–96.

94. Bürger, M. 1966. Breeding of the European lynx at Magdeburg Zoo. *Int. Zoo Yrbk.* 6: 182.

95. Kunc, L. 1970. Breeding and rearing the northern lynx *Felis l. lynx* at Ostrava Zoo. *Int. Zoo Yrbk.* 10: 83–84.

96. Tumlinson, R. 1987. *Felis lynx. Mammalian Species* 269: 1–8.

97. Kvam, T. 1991. Reproduction in the European lynx, *Lynx lynx. Z. Säugetierk.* 56: 146–158.

98. Schmidt, K. 1998. Maternal behavior and juvenile dispersal in the Eurasian lynx. *Acta Theriol.* 43: 391–408.

99. Saunders, J. K., Jr. 1961. The biology of the Newfoundland lynx (*Lynx canadensis subsolanus*, Bangs). Ph.D. dissertation, Cornell University, Ithaca, New York.

100. Brand, C. J., L. B. Keith, and C. A. Fischer. 1976. Lynx responses to changing snowshoe hare densities in central Alberta. *J. Wildl. Mgmt.* 40: 416–428.

101. McCord, C. M., and Cardoza, J. E. 1982. Bobcat and lynx. In *Wild mammals of North America*, ed. J. A. Chapman and G. E. Feldhamer, 728–766. Baltimore: Johns Hopkins University Press.

102. Parker, G. R., J. W. Maxwell, L. D. Morton, and G. E. J. Smith. 1983. The ecology of the lynx (*Lynx canadensis*) on Cape Breton Island. *Can. J. Zool.* 61: 770–786.

103. O'Connor, R. M. 1984. Population trends, age structure, and reproductive characteristics of female lynx in Alaska, 1961 through 1973. Master's thesis, University of Alaska, Fairbanks.

104. Koehler, G. M. 1990. Population and habitat characteristics of lynx and snowshoe hares in north central Washington. *Can. J. Zool.* 68: 845–851.

105. Poole, K. G. 1994. Characteristics of an unhunted lynx population during a snowshoe hare decline. *J. Wildl. Mgmt.* 58: 608–618.

106. Mowat, G., B. G. Slough, and S. Boutin. 1996. Lynx recruitment during a snowshoe hare population peak and decline in southwest Yukon. *J. Wildl. Mgmt.* 60: 441–452.

107. Slough, B. G., and G. Mowat. 1996. Lynx population dynamics in an untrapped refugium. *J. Wildl. Mgmt.* 60: 946–961.

108. Valverde, J. A. 1957. Notes écologiques sur le lynx d'Espagne *Felis lynx pardina* Temminck. *Terre Vie* 1957: 51–67.

109. Delibes, M., F. Palacios, J. Garzon, and Castroviejo, J. 1975. Notes sur l'alimentation et la biologie du lynx pardelle, *Lynx pardina* (Temminck, 1824), en Espagne. *Mammalia* 39: 387–393.

110. Aldama, J. J., and M. Delibes. 1991. Observations of feeding groups in the Spanish lynx (*Felis pardina*) in the Doñana National Park, SW Spain. *Mammalia* 55: 143–147.

111. Ferreras, P., J. F. Beltran, J. J. Aldama, and M. Delibes. 1997. Spatial organization and land tenure system of the endangered Iberian lynx (*Lynx pardinus*). *J. Zool.* (Lond.) 243: 163–189.

112. Young, S. P. 1978. *The bobcat of North America*. Lincoln: University of Nebraska Press.

113. Peterson, R. L. 1966. *The mammals of eastern Canada*. Toronto: Oxford University Press.

114. Gashwiler, J. S., W. L. Robinette, and O. W. Morris. 1961. Breeding habits of bobcats in Utah. *J. Mammal.* 42: 76–83.

115. Parker, G. R., and G. E. J. Smith. 1983. Sex- and age-specific reproductive and physical parameters of the bobcat (*Lynx rufus*) on Cape Breton Island, Nova Scotia. *Can. J. Zool.* 61: 1771–1782.

116. Rolley, R. E. 1987. Bobcat. In *Wild furbearer management and conservation in North America*, ed. M. Novak, J. A. Barker, M. E. Obbard, and B. Malloch, 683–694. Ontario: Ontario Trappers Association.

117. Larivière, S., and L. R. Walton. 1997. *Lynx rufus. Mammalian Species* 563: 1–8.

118. Cade, C. E. 1968. A note on the breeding of the caracal lynx, *Felis caracal,* at the Nairobi Zoo. *Int. Zoo Yrbk.* 8: 45.

119. Kralik, S. 1967. Breeding the caracal lynx at Brno Zoo. *Int. Zoo Yrbk.* 7: 132.

120. Stuart, C. T. 1981. Notes on the mammalian carnivores of the Cape Province, South Africa. *Bontebok* 1: 1–58.

121. Bernard, R. T. F., and C. T. Stuart. 1987. Reproduction of the caracal *Felis caracal* from the Cape Province of South Africa. *S. Afr. J. Zool.* 22: 177–182.

122. Stuart, C. T., and V. J. Wilson. 1988. *The cats of Southern Africa*. Zimbabwe: Chipangali Wildlife Trust.

123. Law, G., and H. Boyle. 1981. Breeding caracals at Calderpark. *Int. Zoo News* 28: 4–8.

124. Wackernagel, H. 1968. A note on breeding the serval cat, *Felis serval,* at Basle Zoo. *Int. Zoo Yrbk.* 8: 46–47.

125. Bloxam, Q. M. C. 1973. The breeding of second generation (F.2) serval cat *Felis leptailurus serval*. The Jersey Wildlife Preservation Trust, Tenth Annual Report, 41–43.

126. Geertsema, A. A. 1985. Aspects of the ecology of the serval *Leptailurus serval* in the Ngorongoro Crater, Tanzania. *Neth. J. Zool.* 35: 527–610.

127. Louwman, J. W., and W. G. van Oyen. 1968. A note on breeding Temminck's golden cat, *Felis temmincki,* at Wassenaar Zoo. *Int. Zoo Yrbk.* 8: 47–49.

128. Guggisberg, C. A. W. 1975. *Wild cats of the world*. New York: Taplinger.

129. Barnett, H. 1972. Asian golden cat born. *Int. Zoo News* 19: 93.

130. Acharjyo, L. N., and G. Mishra. 1980. Some notes on age of sexual maturity of seven species of Indian wild mammals in captivity. *J. Bombay Nat. Hist. Soc.* 77: 504–507.

131. Tonkin, B., and E. Kohler. 1978. Breeding the African golden cat in captivity. *Int. Zoo Yrbk.* 18: 147–150.

132. Leyhausen, P. 1979. *Cat behavior: The predatory and social behavior of domestic and wild cats*. New York: Garland STPM Press

133. Ulmer, R. 1968. Breeding fishing cats, *Felis viverrina,* at Philadelphia Zoo. *Int. Zoo Yrbk.* 8: 49–55.

134. Jayewardene, E. 1975. Breeding the fishing cat, *Felis viverrina,* in captivity. *Int. Zoo Yrbk.* 15: 150–152.

135. Colby, E. D. 1974. Artificially induced estrus in wild and domestic felids. In *The world's cats*, vol. 2, ed. R. L. Eaton, 126–147. Winston, OR: World Wildlife Safari.

136. Acharjyo, L. N., and R. Mishra. 1974. Weight and size at birth of two species of wild mammals in captivity. *J. Bombay Nat. Hist. Soc.* 71: 137–138.

137. Acharjyo, L. N., and S. Mohapatra. 1977. Some obser-

vations on the breeding habits and growth of the jungle cat (*Felis chaus*) in captivity. *J. Bombay Nat. Hist. Soc.* 74: 158–159.

138. Schauenberg, P. 1979. La reproduction du chat des marais *Felis chaus* (Güldenstädt, 1776). *Mammalia* 43: 215–233.

139. Roberts, T. J. 1977. *The mammals of Pakistan.* London: Ernest Benn.

140. Cisin, C. 1967. *Especially ocelots.* New York: Harry G. Cisin.

141. Eaton, R. 1977. Breeding biology and propagation of the ocelot (*Leopardus* [*Felis*] *pardalis*). *Zool. Garten* 47: 9–23.

142. Fagen, R. M., and K. S. Wiley. 1978. Felid paedomorphosis, with special reference to *Leopardus. Carnivore* 1: 72–81.

143. Emmons, L. H. 1988. A field study of ocelots (*Felis pardalis*) in Peru. *Rev. Ecol. (Terre Vie)* 43: 133–157.

144. Laack, L. L. 1991. Ecology of the ocelot (*Felis pardalis*) in south Texas. Master's thesis, Texas A & I University, Kingsville, Texas.

145. Wiley, K. S. 1978. Observations of margay behavior. *Carnivore* 1: 81.

146. Peterson, M. K., and M. K. Peterson. 1978. Growth rates and other post-natal developmental changes in margays. *Carnivore* 1: 87–92.

147. Paintiff, J., and D. Anderson. 1980. Breeding the margay at New Orleans Zoo. *Int. Zoo Yrbk.* 20: 223–224.

148. Leyhausen, P. 1990. Cats. In *Grzimek's encyclopedia of mammals*, vol. 3., 576–632. New York: McGraw-Hill.

149. Oliveira, T. G. 1998. *Leopardus wiedii. Mammalian Species* 579: 1–6.

150. Leyhausen, P., and M. Falkena. 1966. Breeding the Brazilian ocelot cat in captivity. *Int. Zoo Yrbk.* 6: 176–178.

151. Widholzer, F. L., M. Bergmann, and C. Zotz. 1981. Breeding the little spotted cat. *Int. Zoo News* 28: 17–23.

152. Quillen, P. 1981. Hand-rearing the little spotted cat or oncilla. *Int. Zoo Yrbk.* 21: 240–242.

153. Hulley, J. T. 1976. Maintenance and breeding of captive jaguarundis, *Felis jagouaroundi*, at Chester Zoo and Toronto. *Int. Zoo Yrbk.* 15: 120–122.

154. Scheffel, W., and H. Hemmer. 1975. Breeding Geoffroy's cat *Leopardus geoffroyi salinarum* in captivity. *Int. Zoo Yrbk.* 15: 152–154.

155. Kachuba, M. 1977. Sexual behavior and reproduction in captive Geoffroy's cats. *Zool. Garten* 47: 54–56.

156. Anderson, D. 1977. Gestation period of Geoffroy's cat, *Leopardus geoffroyi*, bred at Memphis Zoo. *Int. Zoo Yrbk.* 17: 164–166.

157. Law, G., and H. Boyle. 1983. Breeding the Geoffroy's cat (*Felis geoffroyi*) at Glasgow Zoo. *Int. Zoo Yrbk.* 23: 191–195.

158. Foreman, G. 1988. Behavioral and genetic analysis of Geoffroy's cat (*Felis geoffroyi*) in captivity. Ph.D. dissertation, Ohio State University, Columbus.

159. Johnson, W. E., and W. L. Franklin. 1991. Feeding and spatial ecology of the *Felis geoffroyi* in southern Patagonia. *J. Mammal.* 72: 815–820.

160. Callahan, P., curator, Cincinnati Zoo, Cincinnati, Ohio. Personal communication.

161. Meyer-Holzapfel, M. 1968. Breeding the European wild cat, *Felis s. silvestris*, at Berne Zoo. *Int. Zoo Yrbk.* 8: 31–38.

162. Volf, J. 1968. Breeding the European wild cat, *Felis s. silvestris*, at Prague Zoo. *Int. Zoo Yrbk.* 8: 38–42.

163. Haltennorth, T. 1957. *Die wildkatze.* Wittenberg-Lutherstadt: A. Ziemsen Verlag.

164. Condé, B., and P. Schauenberg. 1969. Reproduction du chat forestier d'Europe (*Felis silvestris* Schreber) en captivité. *Rev. Suisse Zool.* 76: 183–210.

165. Condé, B., and P. Schauenberg. 1978. Reproduction du chat forestier (*F. silvestris* Schr.) dans le nord-est de la France. *Rev. Suisse Zool.* 81: 45–52.

166. Corbett, L. K. 1979. Feeding ecology and social organization of wildcats (*Felis silvestris*) and domestic cats (*Felis catus*) in Scotland. Ph.D. dissertation, University of Aberdeen, Scotland.

167. Raimer, F., and E. Schneider. 1983. Vorkomen und status der wildkatze *Felis silvestris silvestris* Schreber, 1777 im Harz. *Säugetierk. Mitt.* 31: 61–68.

168. Smithers, R. H. N. 1983. *The mammals of the southern African subregion.* Pretoria: University of Pretoria.

169. Tonkin, B., and E. Kohler. 1981. Observations on the Indian desert cat, *Felis silvestris ornata*, in captivity. *Int. Zoo Yrbk.* 21: 151–154.

170. Leitch, I., F. E. Hytten, and W. Z. Billiewicz. 1959. The maternal and neonatal weights of some mammalia. *Proc. Zool. Soc. Lond.* 133: 11–28.

171. Robinson, R., and H. W. Cox. 1970. Reproductive performance in a cat colony over a ten-year period. *Lab. Anim.* 4: 99–112.

172. Beadle, M. 1977. *The cat: History, biology and behaviour.* London: Collins and Harvill Press.

173. Deag, J. M., A. Manning, and C. E. Lawrence. 1988. Factors influencing the mother-kitten relationship. In *The domestic cat: The biology of its behaviour*, ed. D. C. Turner and P. Bateson, 23–39. Cambridge: Cambridge University Press.

174. Natoli, E., and E. De Vito. 1988. The mating system of feral cats living in a group. In *The domestic cat: The biology of its behaviour*, ed. D. C. Turner and P. Bateson, 99–108. Cambridge: Cambridge University Press.

175. Bradshaw, J. S. 1992. *The behaviour of the domestic cat.* Wallingford, UK: C. A. B. International.

176. Schauenberg, P. 1978. Note sur la reproduction du manul *Otocolobus manul* (Pallas, 1776). *Mammalia* 42: 355–358.

177. Schauenberg, P. 1979. Note sur la reproduction du chat du Bengale. *Mammalia* 43: 127–128.

178. Pohle, von C. 1973. Zur zucht von Bengalkatzen (*Felis bengalensis*) im Tierpark Berlin. *Zool. Garten* 43: 110–126.

179. Dathe, H. 1968. Breeding the Indian leopard cat *F. bengalensis* at East Berlin Zoo. *Int. Zoo Yrbk.* 8: 42–44.

180. Frese, R. 1980. Some notes on breeding the leopard cat (*Felis bengalensis*) at West Berlin Zoo. *Int. Zoo Yrbk.* 20: 220–223.

181. Acharjyo, L. N., and G. Mishra. 1983. Further notes on the birth and growth of the leopard cat (*Felis bengalensis*) in captivity. *J. Bombay Nat. Hist. Soc.* 80: 207–208.

182. Barnes, R. G. 1976. Breeding and hand-rearing of the marbled cat *Felis marmorata* at the Los Angeles Zoo. *Int. Zoo Yrbk.* 16: 205–208.

183. Hemmer, H. 1977. Biology and breeding of the sand cat. In *The world's cats*, vol. 3, ed. R. L. Eaton, 13–20. Seattle, WA: Carnivore Research Institute, Burke Museum, University of Washington.

184. Callahan, P. 1991. The rusty spotted cat. *Cat Tales: Newsletter of the International Society for Endangered Cats.* Columbus, Ohio.

185. Armstrong, J. 1975. Hand-rearing black-footed cats (*Felis*

nigripes) at the National Zoological Park, Washington. *Int. Zoo Yrbk.* 15: 245–249.

186. Schürer, U. 1988. Breeding black-footed cats (*Felis nigripes*) at Wuppertal Zoo, with notes on their reproductive biology. Paper presented at 5th Conference on Breeding Endangered Species in Captivity, Cincinnati, Ohio.

187. Olbricht, G., and A. Sliwa. 1995. Comparative devel-opment of juvenile black-footed cats at Wuppertal Zoo an else-where. In *International studbook for the black-footed cat* (Felis nigripes), ed. U. Schürer and G. Olbricht, 8–20. Zoological Garden, Wuppertal.

188. Olbricht, G., and A. Sliwa. 1997. *In situ* and *ex situ* ob-servations and management of black-footed cats. *Int. Zoo Yrbk.* 35: 81–89.

Appendix 6

List of Scientific and Common Names Mentioned in the Text

MAMMALS

Order Didelphimorphia

Marmosa sp.	Mouse opossum
Didelphis marsupialis	Common opossum
Didelphis virginiana	Virginia opossum
Philander opossum	Black four-eyed opossum
Metachirus nudicaudatus	Brown four-eyed opossum

Order Xenarthra

Chaetophractus vellerosus	Hairy armadillo
Dasypus novemcinctus	Nine-banded armadillo
Tamandua mexicanus	Lesser anteater, tamandua
Choloepus hoffmani	Two-toed sloth

Order Insectivora

Hylomys suillus	Lesser gymnure
Crocidura sp.	White-toothed shrew
Crocidura cyanea	Reddish-grey musk shrew
Myosorex varius	Pygmy shrew
Amblysomus hottentotus	Golden mole
Sorex araneus	Common shrew

Order Scandentia

Tupaia glis	Tree shrew

Order Macroscelidea

Rhynchocyon sp.	Checkered elephant shrew

Order Chiroptera

Pteropus personatus	Flying fox

Order Primates

Callicebus sp.	Titi monkey
Cebus sp.	Capuchin monkey
Saguinus sp.	Tamarin monkey
Saimiri sp.	Squirrel monkey
Cercopithecus ascanius	Redtail monkey
Cercopithecus sp.	Guenon
Semnopithecus entellus	Langur
Macaca mulatta	Rhesus monkey
Colobus sp.	Black and white colobus monkey
Perodicticus sp.	Potto
Papio sp.	Baboon
Nasalis larvatus	Proboscis monkey
Presbytis hosei	Gray leaf monkey
Rhinopithecus roxellana	Golden monkey
Pongo pygmaeus	Orangutan
Pan troglodytes	Chimpanzee

Order Carnivora

Alopex lagopus	Arctic fox
Canis aureus	Golden jackal
Canis familiaris	Domestic dog
Canis latrans	Coyote
Canis lupus	Gray wolf
Canis mesomelas	Black-backed jackal
Cuon alpinus	Asiatic wild dog, dhole
Lycaon pictus	African wild dog
Otocyon megalotis	Bat-eared fox
Urocyon cinereoargenyeus	Gray fox
Vulpes corsac	Corsac fox
Vulpes rueppelli	Ruppel's fox
Vulpes vulpes	Red fox
Vulpes zerda	Fennec fox
Acinonyx jubatus	Cheetah
Caracal caracal	Caracal
Catopuma badia	Bay cat
Catopuma temminckii	Asiatic golden cat, Temminck's cat
Felis bieti	Chinese desert (mountain) cat
Felis chaus	Jungle cat, reed cat
Felis margarita	Sand cat
Felis nigripes	Black-footed cat

Felis silvestris	Wildcat	*Paradoxurus hermaphroditus*	Palm civet
Felis s. catus	Domestic cat		
Herpailurus yaguarondi	Jaguarundi	*Viverra zibetha*	Indian civet
Leopardus pardalis	Ocelot	*Putorius putorius*	Polecat
Leopardus tigrinus	Oncilla		
Leopardus wiedii	Margay	**Order Pinnipedia**	
Leptailurus serval	Serval	*Arctocephalus pusillus*	Fur seal
Lynx canadensis	Canada lynx		
Lynx lynx	Eurasian lynx	**Order Cetacea**	
Lynx pardinus	Iberian lynx	*Inia sp.*	Freshwater dolphin
Lynx rufus	Bobcat		
Oncifelis colocolo	Pampas cat	**Order Perissodactyla**	
Oncifelis geoffroyi	Geoffroy's cat	*Equus asinus*	Wild ass (African), burro (domesticated)
Oncifelis guigna	Kodkod		
Oreailurus jacobitus	Andean mountain cat	*Equus caballus*	Horse, wild horse
Otocolobus manul	Manul	*Equus hemionus*	Kulan, onager, wild ass (Asian)
Prionailurus bengalensis	Leopard cat		
Prionailurus planiceps	Flat-headed cat	*Equus burchelli*	Burchell's zebra
Prionailurus rubiginosus	Rusty-spotted cat	*Equus grevyi*	Grevy's zebra
Prionailurus viverrinus	Fishing cat	*Equus zebra*	Mountain zebra
Profelis aurata	African golden cat	*Rhinoceros unicornis*	Great one-horned rhinoceros
Puma concolor	Puma, cougar, mountain lion		
		Tapirus terrestris	Tapir
Neofelis nebulosa	Clouded leopard	**Order Hyracoidea**	
Panthera leo	Lion	*Procavia capensis*	Rock hyrax, dassie
Panthera onca	Jaguar	*Dendrohyrax sp.*	Tree hyrax
Panthera pardus	Leopard		
Panthera tigris	Tiger	**Order Tublidentata**	
Pardofelis marmorata	Marbled cat	*Orycteropus afer*	Aardvark
Uncia uncia	Snow leopard		
Herpestes ichneumon	Egyptian mongoose	**Order Artiodactyla**	
Crocutta crocutta	Spotted hyena	*Phacochoerus aethiopicus*	Warthog
Hyaena hyaena	Striped hyena	*Potamochoerus porcus*	Bushpig
Parahyaena brunnea	Brown hyena	*Sus barbatus*	Bearded pig
Proteles cristatus	Aardwolf	*Hylochoerus meinertzhageni*	Giant forest hog
Arctonyx collaris	Hog badger		
Mellivora capensis	Ratel, honey badger	*Sus scrofa*	Wild boar, wild or domestic pig
Eira barbara	Tayra		
Mephitis mephitis	Striped skunk	*Tayassu sp.*	Javelina
Gulo gulo	Wolverine	*Tayassu tajacu*	Collared peccary
Martes sp.	Marten	*Tayassu pecari*	White-lipped peccary
Mustela sp.	Weasel, ermine, stoat, mink, ferret	*Catagonus wagneri*	Chacoan peccary
		Hippopotamus amphibius	Hippopotamus
Nasua narica	Coati	*Camelus bactrianus*	Bactrian camel
Procyon lotor	Raccoon	*Camelus dromidarius*	Dromedary camel
Ailuropoda melanoleuca	Giant panda	*Lama guanicoe*	Guanaco
Ailurus fulgens	Red or lesser panda	*Tragulus sp.*	Mouse deer, chevrotain
Ursus arctos	Brown bear	*Tetracerus quadricornis*	Four-horned antelope
Genetta sp.	Genet		

Giraffa camelopardalis	Giraffe	*Bubalis bubalis*	Water buffalo
Moschus sp.	Musk deer	*Syncerus caffer*	African buffalo,
Axis axis	Chital, spotted deer		Cape buffalo
Axis porcinus	Hog deer	*Kobus* sp.	Waterbuck, lechwe, puku
Cervus duvaucelii	Barasingha	*Alcelaphus buselaphus*	Hartebeest
Cervus elaphus	Red deer, elk, wapiti	*Hippotragus* sp.	Sable, roan antelope
Cervus nippon	Sika deer	*Taurotragus* sp.	Eland
Cervus unicolor	Sambar	*Tragelaphus* sp.	Kudu, nyala, bushbuck,
Dama dama	Fallow deer		bongo
Elaphodus cephalophus	Tufted deer	*Neotragus* sp.	Dwarf antelope
Muntiacus muntjak	Muntjac, barking deer	*Hyemoschus aquaticus*	Water chevrotain
Blastocerus dichotomus	Marsh deer	*Capra hircus*	Domestic goat
Capreolus sp.	Roe deer	*Capra falconeri*	Markhor
Mazama sp.	Brocket deer	*Capra ibex*	Ibex
Odocoileus hemionus	Mule deer, black-tailed	*Capra* sp.	Tur
	deer	*Procapra gutturosa*	Black-tailed gazelle
Odocoileus virginianus	White-tailed deer	*Capricornis sumatraensis*	Serow
Ozotoceros bezoarticus	Pampas deer	*Hemitragus jelambicus*	Tahr
Pudu sp.	Pudu	*Nemorhedus* sp.	Goral
Alces alces	Moose, elk	*Budorcas taxicolor*	Takin
Rangifer tarandus	Caribou, reindeer	*Ovis ammon*	Argali sheep
Connochaetes sp.	Wildebeest, gnu	*Ovis aries*	Domestic sheep
Antilocapra americana	Pronghorn	*Ovis musimon*	Mouflon
Aepyceros melampus	Impala	*Ovis canadensis*	Bighorn sheep
Damaliscus korrigum	Topi	*Ovis dalli*	Dall sheep
Damaliscus lunatus	Tsessebe	*Ovis vignei*	Urial sheep
Antidorcas marsupialis	Springbok	*Pseudois nayaur*	Blue sheep, bharal
Antilope cervicapra	Blackbuck	*Rupicapra* sp.	Chamois
Gazella subgutturosa	Goitered gazelle	*Philantomba* sp.	Duiker
Gazella dorcas	Dorcas gazelle	*Cephalophus monticola*	Blue duiker
Gazella gazella	Chinkara, Indian gazelle	*Cephalophus dorsalis*	Bay duiker
Gazella granti	Grant's gazelle	*Cephalophus callipygus*	Peter's duiker
Gazella thomsoni	Thomson's gazelle	*Sylvicapra grimmia*	Common duiker
Oreotragus oreotragus	Klipspringer		
Madoqua sp.	Dik-dik	*Order Proboscidea*	
Raphicerus campestris	Steenbok	*Elephas maximus*	Indian elephant
Raphicerus melanotis	Cape grysbuck	*Loxodonta africana*	African elephant
Litocranius walleri	Gerenuk		
Oryx gazella	Gemsbok	*Order Philodota*	
Redunca sp.	Reedbuck	*Manis* sp.	Pangolin
Redunca fulvorufula	Mountain reedbuck		
Pelea capreolus	Rhebok	*Order Rodentia*	
Okapia johnstoni	Okapi	*Aplodontia rufa*	Mountain beaver
Bos frontalis	Gaur	*Cynomys* sp.	Prairie dog
Bos grunniens	Yak	*Marmota* sp.	Marmot
Bos javanicus	Banteng	*Sciurus* sp.	Tree squirrel
Bos taurus	Cattle	*Spermophilopsis*	Thin-toed ground squirrel
Bison bison	Bison	*leptodactylus*	
Boselaphus tragocamelus	Nilgai	*Spermophilus* sp.	Ground squirrel

Tamiasciurus sp.	Red squirrel	*Eligmondontia typus*	Highland desert mouse
Glaucomys volans	Flying squirrel	*Phyllotis darwini*	Leaf-eared mouse or
Callosciurus sp.	Tricolored squirrel		pericote
Menetes berdmorei	Berdmore's palm squirrel	*Malacothrix* sp.	Large-eared mouse
Protoxerus stangeri	Oil palm squirrel	*Saccostomus* sp.	Pouched mouse
Castor canadensis	Beaver	*Dasymys incomtus*	Shaggy swamp or water rat
Ondatra zibethicus	Muskrat	*Aethomys chrysophilus*	Red veld rat
Erethizon dorsatum	North American	*Thryonomys*	Cane rat
	porcupine	*swinderianus*	
Coendu prehensilis	Prehensile-tailed	*Reithrodon physodes*	Coney rat
	porcupine	*Hydromys chrysogaster*	Water rat
Hystrix sp.	Old World porcupine	*Otomys angoniensis*	Vlei rat
Atherurus sp.	Brush-tailed porcupine	*Tachyoryctes splendens*	African mole-rat
Dipodomys sp.	Kangaroo rat	*Cryptomys* sp.	Common mole-rat
Chaetodipus sp.	Pocket mouse	*Mastomys* sp.	Multimammate mouse
Dipus sagitta	Northern three-toed,	*Mus musculus*	House mouse
	rough-legged jerboa	*Rattus norvegicus*	Norway rat
Paradipus ctenodactylus	Comb-toed jerboa	*Rhizomys* sp.	Bamboo rat
Alticola sp.	Vole	*Baiomys* sp.	Pygmy mouse
Arvicola terrestris	Water or bank vole	*Dendromus* sp.	Climbing mouse
Clethrionomys glareolis	Red-backed vole	*Neotoma* sp.	Wood rat
Lasiopodomys brandti	Brandt's vole	*Oryzomys* sp.	Rice rat
Microtus sp.	Meadow, field vole	*Reithrodontomys gracilis*	Harvest mouse
Cricetulus migratorius	Gray hamster	*Peromyscus* sp.	Deer mouse
Cricetulus barabensis	Daurian hamster	*Sigmodon* sp.	Cotton rat
Rhombomys opimus	Great gerbil	*Pelomys fallax*	Groove-toothed rat
Gerbillurus sp.	Hairy-footed gerbil	*Ototylomys* sp.	Climbing rat
Tatera sp.	Bushveld gerbil	*Zygodontomys* sp.	Cane mouse
Ellobius tancrei	Mole-vole	*Holochilus* sp.	Marsh rat
Meriones sp.	Midday gerbil	*Heteromys anomalus*	Spiny pocket mouse
Meriones tamariscinus	Crested or tamarisk gerbil	*Echimys* sp.	Arboreal spiny rat
Apodemus sp.	Field mouse, wood mouse	*Mesomys* sp.	Spiny tree rat
Apodemus flavicollis	Yellow-necked mouse	*Proechimys* sp.	Spiny rat
Myoxus glis	Fat dormouse	*Cannomys badius*	Bay bamboo rat
Muscardinus	Common dormouse	*Cricetomys* sp.	Giant rat
avellanarius		*Rattus rattus*	Black rat
Dryomys nitedula	Forest dormouse	*Pedetes capensis*	Springhare
Eliomys sp.	Garden dormouse	*Heliophobius*	Sand rat
Steatomys sp.	Fat mouse	*argenteocinereus*	
Mus minutoides	Pygmy or grey climbing	*Thryonomys* sp.	Cane rat
	mouse	*Chinchilla* sp.	Chinchilla
Aethomys sp.	Rock mouse	*Lagidium viscacia*	Mountain viscacha
Dendromus melanotis	Pygmy climbing mouse	*Cavia* sp.	Guinea pig, cavy
Rhabdomys pumilio	Four-striped grass mouse	*Hydrochaeris*	Capybara
Arvicanthus sp.	Unstriped grass mouse	*hydrochaeris*	
Akodon sp.	Field or grass mouse	*Myoprocta* sp.	Acouchi
Auliscomys micropus	Leaf-eared mouse	*Dasyprocta* sp.	Agouti
Chelemys macronyx	Greater long-clawed	*Agouti* sp.	Paca
	mouse	*Dolichotis salinicola*	Mara

Galea musteloides	Yellow-toothed cavy	*Oenanthe* sp.	Wheatear
Myocastor coypus	Nutria or Coypu	*Crypturellus* sp.	Tinamou
		Pavo cristatus	Peafowl
Order Lagomorpha		*Penelope* sp.	Guan
Ochotona sp.	Pika	*Netta* sp.	White-eyed potchard
Lepus sp.	Jackrabbit	*Bonasa* sp.	Hazel grouse
Lepus californicus	Black-tailed jackrabbit	*Meleagris gallopavo*	Turkey
Lepus americanus	Snowshoe or varying hare	*Spheniscus magellanicus*	Magellan penguin
Lepus arcticus	Arctic hare	*Cariama cristata*	Sereima
Lepus capensis	Cape hare	*Turdus falcklandii*	Austral thrush
Lepus europaeus	European or brown hare	*Vanellus chilensis*	Southern lapwing
Lepus tolai	Tolai hare	*Ploceus* sp.	Weaver
Lepus nigricollis	Black-naped hare	*Philesturnus carunclatus*	Saddleback
Lepus saxatilis	Scrub hare	*Strigop habroptilus*	Kakapo
Sylvilagus sp.	Cottontail rabbit	*Sterna fuscata*	Sooty tern
Sylvilagus palustris	Marsh rabbit	*Pelecanoides* sp.	Diving, burrowing petrel
Oryctolagus sp.	European (Old World) rabbit	*Pachyptila vittata*	Broad-billed prion
		Phoenicoparrus sp.	Flamingo
Pronolagus sp.	Red rabbit	*Anas* sp.	Mallard duck
		Tetrogallus himalayensis	Snowcock
		Hypsipestes sp.	Bulbul
BIRDS		*Attagis* sp.	Seed snipe
Anthus novaeseelandiae	Richard's pipit	*Upucerthia dumetaria*	Earth creeper
Chersomanes albofasciata	Spike-heeled lark	*Milvago chimango*	Caracara
Cisticola aridula	Desert cisticola	*Tringa glareola*	Wood sandpiper
Eupodotis sp.	Black bustard	*Francolinus* sp.	Francolin
Mirafra apiata	Clapper lark	*Mycteria americana*	Wood stork
Mirafra sabota	Sabota lark	*Phalacrocorax* sp.	Cormorant
Mirafra africanoides	Fawn-colored lark	*Parus domesticus*	House sparrow
Oenanthe pileata	Capped wheatear	*Pezopetes capitalis*	Finch
Turnix sp.	Button quail		
Ardeotis kori	Kori bustard	**REPTILES**	
Struthio camelus	Ostrich	*Echis carinatus*	Saw-scale viper
Scelorchilus rubecula	Chucao tapaculo	*Eryx* sp.	Sand boa
Pteroptochos tarnii	Huet-huet	*Cyclura* sp.	Island iguana
Gyps rueppellii	Griffon vulture	*Amblyrhynchus cristatus*	Marine iguana
Agelastes sp.	Guinea fowl	*Caiman latirostris*	Caiman
Pterocles sp.	Sandgrouse	*Coluber* sp.	Whip snake, racer
Perdix perdix	Gray partridge	*Psammophis* sp.	Sand snake
Alectoris chukar	Chukar partridge	*Naja* sp.	Cobra
Columba sp.	Pigeon	*Python* sp.	Python
Gallus sonneratii	Grey jungle fowl	*Uromastyx* sp.	Spiny-tailed lizard
Pavo cristatus	Peafowl	*Cerastes* sp.	Horned, sand viper
Fulica atra	Coot	*Scincus* sp.	Sand skink
Tetrao sp.	Capercaillie	*Phrynocephalus* sp.	Toadhead lizard
Bubo sp.	Eagle owl	*Podocnemis expansa*	South American river turtle
Aquila chrysaetos	Golden eagle		
Upupa epops	Hoopoe	*Liolaenus pictus*	Chiloé lizard
Anthus sp.	Pipit	*Crocodilus niloticus*	Crocodile
Myrmecocichla sp.	Chat		

Photographic Credits

Photographs in the book were provided by the following photographers.

Terry Whittaker: Photos on pages 52, 60, 67, 75, 85 (photo also appears on page 83), 92 (photo also appears on page 83), 120, 135, 142, 164 (photo also appears on page 152), 205, 219, 225, 237, 241, 246, 278, 285, 305, 318, 343, 373, 377; Plates 2, 3, 5, 7, 8, 11, 12, 13, 15, 16, 18, 19, 22, 25, 29, 30, 31, 34, 35, 36, 37, 38, 40, 41, 46, 47, 48
Terry Whittaker can be reached via electronic mail to Terry.Whittaker@btopenworld.com.

Juan Beltrán: Photo on page 177 (photo also appears on page 152); Plate 23
Milo Burcham, courtesy of John Weaver: Photo on page 154 (photo also appears on page 152); Plate 20
Arturo Caso: Photo on page 113
Jeremy Holden: Plate 32 (© Jeremy Holden/FFI)
Peter Jackson: Photo on page 57; Plate 6
T. Jackson: Plates 14, 45
Gary Koehler: Photo on page 185 (photo also appears on page 152); Plate 24
A. Lawrenz: Plate 10
Jim Sanderson: Photos on pages 211, 215; Plates 27, 28
John Seidensticker: Photo on page 252; Plate 39
Alex Sliwa: Photos on pages 19, 37, 130; Plates 1, 9, 10, 17, 21, 42, 43, 44, 49
Claire Sunquist: Photo on page 99 (photo also appears on page 83)
Fiona Sunquist: Photo on page 201; Plate 26
Barbara Tonkin-Leyhausen: Photo on page 233; Plate 33
Shigeki Yasuma: Photo on page 48; Plate 4

Index

Note: Italicized numbers indicate pages with illustrations or tables. "Pl." indicates color plates.